crime and justice in America

maximus that caution
Refrain from quarrels or Arg.
ass. of inmates to to cheat fraud other inmates.
Rules that stress
maximus that forbid.

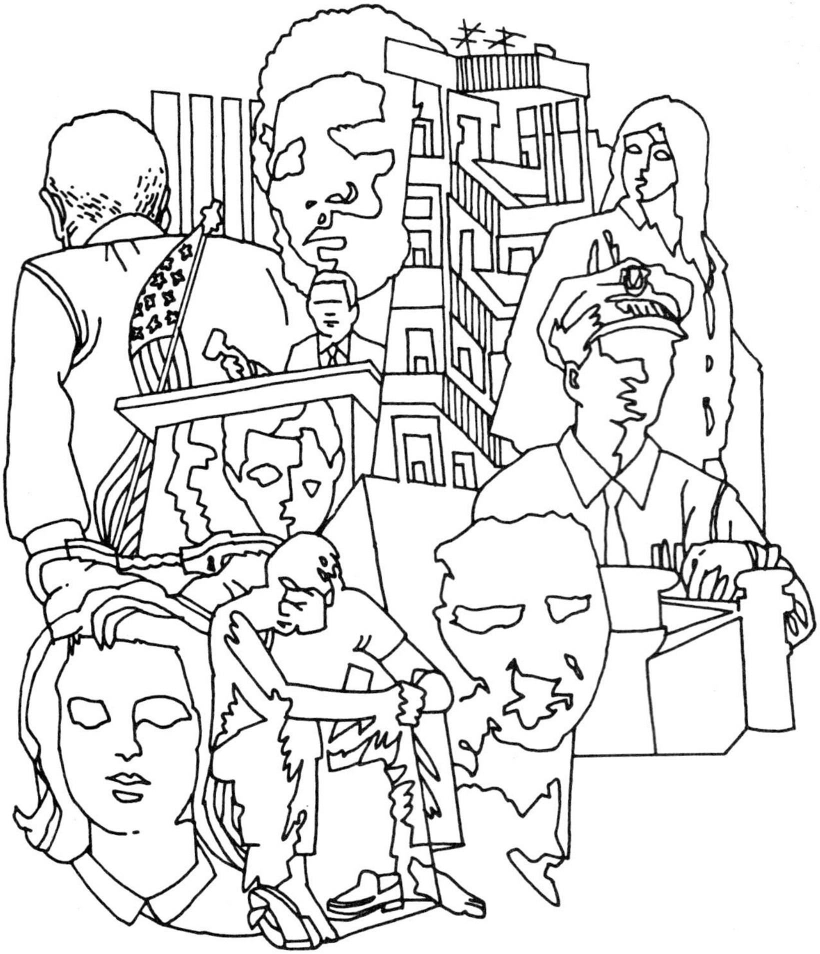

crime and justice in America:
a human perspective

Harold J. Vetter
University of South Florida

Leonard Territo
University of South Florida

WEST PUBLISHING COMPANY

St. Paul | New York | Los Angeles | San Francisco

Chapter opening photos:

1 Bettman Archive
2 Bettman Archive
3 Wide World Photos
4 David Farr
5 Robert Eckert/EKM-Nepenthe
6 Tony O'Brien/Criminal Justice Photos
7 H. Armstrong Roberts
8 Robert Eckert/EKM-Nepenthe
9 Frank Siteman/EKM-Nepenthe
10 John Maher/EKM-Nepenthe
11 United Press International
12 Wide World Photos
13 Joe Rossi/St. Paul Pioneer Press
14 Tony O'Brien/Criminal Justice Photos
15 John Maher/EKM-Nepenthe
16 Tim Jewett/EKM-Nepenthe
17 Wide World Photos
18 Dekalb County, Georgia, Police Department

Copy Editor: Barbara Bryan

COPYRIGHT © 1984   By WEST PUBLISHING CO.
50 West Kellogg Boulevard
P.O. Box 43526
St. Paul, Minnesota   55165

All rights reserved
Printed in the United States of America

Library of Congress Cataloging in Publication Data

Vetter, Harold J., 1926-
  Crime & justice in America.

  Bibliography: p.
  Includes index.
  1. Criminal justice, Administration of—United States.
2. Crime and criminals—United States. I. Territo,
Leonard. II. Title. III. Title: Crime and justice in
America.
KF9223.V47 1984   345.73'05   83-21800
ISBN 0-314-77854-3   347.3055

contents

Preface vii

1. *Crime and justice in America 1*
2. *Crime, deviance, and criminal law 41*
3. *The nature and distribution of crime 75*
4. *Factors and theories in criminality: the search for criminal man 113*
5. *Police operations and the crime laboratory 149*
6. *Trends, issues, and problems in law enforcement 195*
7. *Prosecution and defense 227*
8. *Pretrial procedures 255*
9. *The courts 281*
10. *The criminal trial 307*
11. *Sentencing and after 333*
12. *Jails and detention 363*
13. *Correctional institutions 393*
14. *Social, political, and racial forces in American prisons 423*
15. *Alternatives to confinement 453*
16. *Juvenile justice 489*
17. *The victims of crime 531*
18. *Crime control and prevention 555*

Index 585

preface

This book is intended to introduce the student to the study of crime and the administration of justice in America at a time when fear about the former and skepticism concerning the latter may have reached an all-time peak. The focus throughout this presentation is on the human dimensions of the criminal justice *system*—the police, prosecution, courts, and corrections—and the criminal justice *process*, which largely deals with the handling and disposition of people charged with the commission of crimes. We have sought to emphasize the people, rather than the institutions, as the reality behind the abstraction. Instead of concentrating on the mechanics of the criminal justice system and its often complicated operations, we have chosen to emphasize the manifold interpersonal relationships and interactions which make up the daily activities that are covered by the term "administration of justice." We have tried to describe the victim and perpetrator, the police officer and prosecutor, the judge and the defense counsel, the correctional administrator and the prison guard—and, above all, the victims of crime—in the kind of detail that will make them familiar to the reader. Consistent with this objective, the text is heavily illustrated with cases, narratives, descriptions, and visual display materials. Our hope is to be interesting as well as informative, to be entertaining as well as instructive, in our coverage of these topics.

The actions and interactions that take place in the criminal justice system are characterized by a spectrum of emotions and attributes as broad as the human condition itself—violence, pathos, humor, suspense, irritation, pettiness, greed, brutality, and occasional flashes of heroism and inspiration. We want the reader to identify with the people involved in the criminal justice system and process as individuals. Thus, when we speak of job stress among police officers, we should like the reader to be able to sense and feel the frustrations involved in irregular hours, bleak prospects for promotion, burial under a heavy load of paperwork, and the almost inevitable growth of cynicism that results from seeing one's efforts result in failure because of technicalities in the system. When we discuss the work of the correctional counselor in a community-based facility, we want the reader to share in the occasional successes as well as the frequent disappointments of the job.

In short, we believe that these are the ingredients of an interesting, informative, and potentially entertaining experience for the student and the instructor. It is better, in our judgment, to tell a story than to belabor an abstraction; and it is this consideration that has guided our selection, organization, and presentation of topics in this book.

acknowledgments

Writing a book is a solitary endeavor. However, as a process, writing is highly interactive—making the transition from an idea to a published work requires considerable goodwill and support from families, friends, colleagues, reviewers, editors, and production staff. We wish to recognize those organizations and individuals who so graciously assisted us and, in many cases, shared their works with us.

Dr. C.R. Swanson, University of Georgia, generously provided us with material that we were able to incorporate into the chapter on jails and detention. Dr. Robert Taylor, University of South Florida, wrote the Issue Paper in Chapter 5, "Terrorism—The Crime of the Future." He also developed an annotated bibliography for the instructor's manual used in conjunction with this book. Dr. David Agresti, University of South Florida, supplied several of the photos that appear in the chapter on corrections. Photos were also contributed by our long-time friend, Chief Robert L. Smith, Tampa Police Department, Tampa, Florida; Margaret C. Hambrick, Warden, Federal Correctional Institution, Butner, North Carolina; Robert J. Henderson, Superintendent, Auburn Correctional Facility, Auburn, New York; Frank W. Wood, Warden, Minnesota Correctional Facility—Oak Park Heights, Minnesota; Harold J. Miller, Warden, United States Penitentiary, Marion, Illinois; Dean J. Leech, Executive Assistant, and Michael Aun, Information Officer, U.S. Department of Justice, Federal Prison System.

Also, this book could not have had its strong human perspective if so many photographers and publishers had not been willing to share their works with us.

Typing was provided by a battery of people who collectively made innumerable contributions. Many thanks to Mike Copeland, Maggie Deutsch, Gregg Gronlund, Robin Kester, Marian Pittman, and Cecile Pulin.

Lastly, our sincerest thanks to our editor, Gary Woodruff, for his belief in this project and his support for our desire to write a different kind of book.

crime and justice in America

1
crime and justice in America

Crime in American history

The economic impact of crime
Public expenditures for criminal justice
The cost of juvenile crime

The psychological and social impacts of crime
Fear and its consequences
The impact of criminal violence
Assault on the quality of life

Defining and classifying crimes
Conventional crimes
Economic crimes
Syndicated (organized) crime
Political crimes
Consensual crimes

The administration of justice
System and process: The role of discretion and accommodation
The police
The prosecutor
The courts
Corrections

Crime control versus due process

Summary

Issue paper: High-tech crime—a glimpse at a possible future

CRIME is widely feared in American society. The exact figures are not known, but Wright and Rossi (1982) estimate that aproximately 120 million guns are held in private ownership in the United States; further, in about 15 percent of all gun-owning households, someone has used a gun in self-defense at some time. Diminishing public confidence in the ability of the criminal justice system to deal effectively with crime corresponds to a growth in sales of police whistles, deadbolt locks, intricate locks and latches, attack dogs, and karate courses. Private security has become a multibillion-dollar business that employs a larger work force than public agencies (Bilek 1977; Law Enforcement Assistance Administration 1978).

"Crime in the streets," "law and order," and "the crime problem" are phrases that capture some sense of the fear and uneasiness in all segments of American society about personal safety and property security. Not so many years ago, public concern over crime was fueled by urban rioting and campus violence. Today, public anxiety about crime has not abated—even though student protests are (at least for now) a phenomenon of the past and ghetto violence is sporadic and fitful. Quite to the contrary: a recent nationwide Gallup survey (February 1983) shows that Americans are as concerned as ever about violence and crime. A few highlights from the survey are:

1. A majority (54 percent) of Americans say that more crime occurs in their communities or neighborhoods today than one year ago; three out of four respondents believe that criminals today are more violent than they were five years ago.
2. Urban residents cited crime as the top problem facing their neighborhoods. A quarter of a century ago, crime was not named among the top ten urban problems.
3. Nearly half of all people interviewed are afraid to walk alone at night in their own neighborhoods. Fear is most pronounced in smaller communities: 32 percent of people in small towns or villages and rural areas are afraid to venture out after dark within their own communities. One person in six admits to being afraid even behind the locked doors of his or her own home.
4. One U.S. household in four has been hit by crime at least once in the past twelve months, with either property stolen or a household member victimized by physical assault. This finding confirms reports from victimization research that crime is far more frequent than indicated by official data from the Federal Bureau of Investigation (FBI).

Is the public justified in worrying so much about crime? Is present society more violent, more lawless, and more crime-ridden than in past years? To answer these questions, we must take a look at crime from a historical perspective.

Crime in American history

Apprehension about crime has been present in every period of American history. Riots and mob violence erupted in American cities during the Civil War. Rival gangster mobs battled in the streets in the Roaring Twenties. The bank-robbing exploits of Bonnie and Clyde marked the Great Depression. In fact, "crime waves" and "the crime problem," are nothing new. As noted by the President's Commission on Law Enforcement and Administration of Justice:

> A hundred years ago contemporary accounts of San Francisco told of extensive areas where "no decent man was in safety to walk the streets after dark; while at all hours, both night and day, his property was jeopardized by incendiarism and burglary." Teenage gangs gave rise to the word "hoodlum"; while in one central New York City area, near Broadway, the police entered "only in pairs, and never unarmed. . . ." "Alarming" increases in robbery and violent crimes were reported throughout the country prior to the revolution. And in 1910 one author declared that "crime, especially in its more violent forms, and among the young is increasing steadily and is threatening to bankrupt the Nation" (*Challenge of Crime in a Free Society*, 1967, p. 19).

Still, attitudes toward crime and the treatment of criminals have varied over the years.

Crime has been viewed as a sin, as an illness, as a result of individual flaws, and as a consequence of societal failure. Over the centuries criminals have been banished, beheaded, impaled, burned, flogged, mutilated, chained to oars as galley slaves, impressed into military service, exiled, and imprisoned. The intent was usually to punish the offender. However, as the ideas of sin and crime came together in Western religion, punishment took on a new dimension: penance. No longer was punishment meted out solely to get even with the offender; rather, through the punishment, the offender was to find a path to reformation and redemption.

Spiritual redemption as an approach to the reform of the criminal was a dominent theme in corrections during the Colonial period and in the first two decades of the nineteenth century. It was abandoned when it proved incapable of producing desired changes in people. Its decline was hastened by the growing urbanization and industrialization of the U.S. in the early and middle 1800s. For all practical purposes, spiritual reform for the criminal was largely discarded by the 1850s, although some of its influence endured—including its influence today within corrections. Although penitentiaries have not been very successful in reforming criminals, imprisonment has persisted as a punishment.

In the twentieth century, yet another approach to criminal reform evolved: rehabilitation was redefined as a medical, or psychiatric, problem. As a result, criminals have been operated on, given drugs, trained for jobs, counseled in groups or as individuals, conditioned, counterconditioned, and otherwise "treated" in attempts to modify mental states or behavior.

While attitudes and treatments change, crime persists. Crime may have been as frequent around the time of the Revolution as it is today. In the nineteenth century, both the cities and the frontier were dangerous; and immigrants were frequently blamed for rising crime. From 1900 to the 1930s, violent crime soared, with labor battles and racial violence contributing to the toll. Then, from about 1933 until the early 1960s, "the United States, perhaps for the first time in its history, enjoyed a period in which crime rates were either stable or declining and in which fear of crime was relatively low" (Silberman 1978, p. 30). This domestic peace contrasted with America's past and its future.

Thus, crime is not a new, and not a peculiarly American, problem; crime is timeless and universal. But it is not crime in foreign countries that Americans fear; it is crime in their own communities. The concern is not whether crime is more prevalent or less prevalent than it was in some earlier period; people are afraid of crime *right now*. Social reality is largely what a society believes about itself. If the members of a society believe they are unsafe in their homes, workplaces, and public areas, apprehension and insecurity become an important part of social reality. Has this happened in the United States, where society sees itself as beleaguered by crime?

When people perceive themselves to be threatened by crime, they take measures to protect themselves, their families, and their property. Feeling like hunted animals, people are "curfewed by their own fear" (Conklin 1975, p. 3). In daily life, fear of crime may take an even greater toll than crime itself. Individuals and communities often respond to the threat of crime by seeking refuge behind deadbolts, German Shepherds, electronic alarms, closed-circuit television cameras, and security guards; these reactions are part of the *indirect costs* of crime. *Direct costs* are measured in terms of dollars lost, injuries suffered, and lives taken.

The economic impact of crime

It is generally accepted that crime is a financial burden for everyone—as well as a source of emotional stress and physical danger. Conklin (1980) divides the economic costs of crime into five categories:

1. Direct loss of property
2. Transfer of property
3. Costs related to criminal violence
4. Illegal expenditures
5. Enforcement costs

Direct loss of property occurs in crimes such as arson and vandalism: residential and commercial buildings are destroyed or severely damaged, automobile windshields are smashed, tires are slashed, and public property is defaced and despoiled. When a television set or appliance is stolen in a burglary or cash taken in a holdup, property is transferred illegally from the victim to the criminal. Although the stolen goods are not destroyed, the victim suffers the same net loss as he or she would by actual destruction. Costs related to criminal violence include everything from the loss of productivity by an injured victim to social security and compensation payments. Expenditures for illegal goods and services such as drugs, prostitution, and gambling are a cost that can be viewed as a kind of entertainment expense—paid with income derived from a legitimate job. Enforcement costs consist of expenses incurred by agencies of the criminal justice system—police, prosecution, courts, and corrections—in enforcing criminal laws.

In 1976, the Joint Economic Committee of the U.S. Congress estimated the total economic cost of crime in the United States to be $125 billion. This cost is itemized in **figure 1.1.** White-collar, or economic, crime is by far the most expensive criminal activity in terms of financial cost to U.S. society. According to one judge, "the accountant's certificate and the lawyer's opinion can be instruments for inflicting pecuniary loss more potent than the chisel or the crowbar" (Conklin 1980, p. 45). The second largest financial cost of crime is public expenditure for criminal justice.

Public expenditures for criminal justice

Prior to 1968, the cost of enforcing laws and administering justice in the United States was chiefly borne by local and state governments. Federal expenditures for these services were largely restricted to government agencies responsible for offenses covered by federal law. For example, the Office of the Attorney General, the federal court system, and the U.S. Department of Justice were charged with investigating and prosecuting federal crimes.

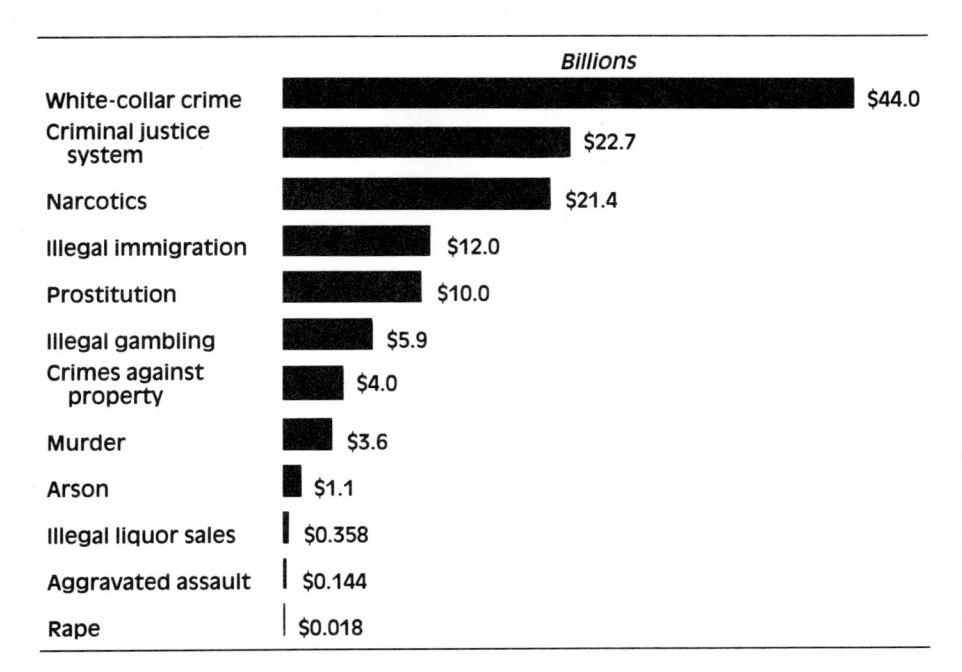

Billions

White-collar crime	$44.0
Criminal justice system	$22.7
Narcotics	$21.4
Illegal immigration	$12.0
Prostitution	$10.0
Illegal gambling	$5.9
Crimes against property	$4.0
Murder	$3.6
Arson	$1.1
Illegal liquor sales	$0.358
Aggravated assault	$0.144
Rape	$0.018

FIGURE 1.1
The financial cost of crime in the United States. Data from J. E. Conklin, Criminology (New York: Macmillan, 1981), p. 45, by permission of the author and the publisher.

This situation changed in 1968, however, with the passage of the Omnibus Crime Control and Safe Streets Act. This act made available to state and local governments substantial and steadily increasing amounts of federal dollars for activities related to law enforcement and criminal justice.

Table 1.1 breaks down expenditures for criminal justice by level of government for the years 1971–78. During this period, the total cost of operating local, state, and federal agencies of criminal justice was $24 billion. Put in perspective, this figure roughly equals the total cost of the entire Apollo space project.

The cost of juvenile crime

In 1980, the Office of Juvenile Justice and Delinquency Prevention (OJJDP) published a report assessing the economic implications of serious juvenile crime in the United States. Based on 1975 data, the OJJDP estimated the total primary direct cost of serious juvenile crime—including uncompensated costs to victims and psychic costs incurred by victims and wit-

TABLE 1.1 Direct expenditures for criminal justice (in dollars and percent change) by level of government, fiscal years 1971–78

Year	\multicolumn{4}{c}{*Millions of dollars*}
	Total	Federal	State	Local
1971	10,517	1,215	2,681	6,621
1972	11,732	1,502	2,948	7,281
1973	13,007	1,651	3,304	8,052
1974	14,842	1,859	3,900	9,092
1975	17,249	2,188	4,612	10,449
1976	19,681	2,450	5,204	12,027
1977	21,574	2,779	5,812	12,983
1978	24,087	3,090	6,689	14,308

	Percent increase			
	Total	Federal	State	Local
1971 to 1972	11.6	23.6	10.0	10.0
1972 to 1973	10.9	9.9	12.1	10.6
1973 to 1974	14.2	12.6	18.0	12.9
1974 to 1975	16.2	17.7	18.3	14.9
1975 to 1976	14.1	12.0	12.8	15.1
1976 to 1977	9.6	13.4	11.7	7.9
1977 to 1978	11.7	11.2	15.1	10.2
1971 to 1978	129.1	154.3	149.5	116.1

Note: Because of rounding, detail may not add to total.
Data from U.S. Department of Justice, *Expenditure and Employment Data for the Criminal Justice System 1978* (Washington, D.C.: U.S. Government Printing Office, 1980), p. 2, by permission of the U.S. Department of Justice.

nesses—to be $10 billion (OJJDP 1980). Indirect costs were estimated as follows:

1. The annual cost of business crime, in terms of household expenses, is approximately $400 per household.
2. Average home values in neighborhoods with high crime rates decreased between $3,500 and $5,500 in 1977 dollars.
3. Based on juvenile index crimes for 1977, processing in the juvenile justice system costs $1.4 billion annually, averaging $17 per household.
4. The average cost of a juvenile arrest is $456; of juvenile court processing for one crime, $286; and of secure detention for one night, $60.
5. Nonsecure programs cost less than secure programs; per bed construction costs for secure correctional facilities range from $40,000 to $60,000.

The psychological and social impacts of crime

Measuring the impact of crime in terms of economic factors is somewhat analogous to assessing the seriousness of an accident based on the total medical bill. Tangible possessions such as money and property can be replaced, even though their loss may impose a crushing burden. But the psychological and social costs of crime, because they involve subjective factors and intangibles, can constitute a far more serious problem.

Fear and its consequences

Fear is a basic ingredient of any psychological or social reaction to crime. It is a gut reaction that produces marked changes in individual behavior. The most intense fear is of the crimes least likely to occur: murder, assault, and forcible rape. Ironically, the perpetrator in such crimes is often a family member, close friend, or personal acquaintance. Nevertheless, what people fear most is violence at the hands of a stranger. Fear of an unknown assailant is prominent in both individual and collective responses to crime. Fear of strangers generalizes to fear of strange places, and people eventually see even public streets as unsafe. When fear of public places peaks, people avoid areas perceived as potentially hazardous. Consequently, normal activity is interrupted in various areas, removing one deterrent to criminal activity. Areas thus avoided are then increasingly frequented by persons bent upon crime.

The impact of criminal violence

Official crime reports generally distinguish between crimes against property and crimes against the person. However, this distinction ignores, or at least minimizes, the fact that property crimes inevitably affect a victim adversely beyond *observable* losses of goods or money. For example, Bard and Ellison (1974) emphasize that victims of burglary, armed robbery, assault and robbery, and rape suffer significant psychological consequences.

The psychological impact of burglary on an individual is often disregarded, because the only visible consequence to the victim may be a property loss covered by insurance. What is often not recognized, however, is that people regard their homes or apartments as extensions of themselves. A person's home is more than his or her castle: it is a physical projection of the self. Moreover, in an urban-industrial society in which privacy is at a premium, the home is the only place that offers individual security and a place to escape from the pressures of everyday life. Furthermore, every home uniquely represents the personality of its occupants. When a home is burglarized, occupants are often far more upset about the actual intrusion into the home than about the loss of property. The burglary represents a violation or intrusion into a part of the self.[1] In armed robbery, not only is personal property lost, but also the victim is deprived of self-determination while the crime is in progress. The victim's fate rests in the unpredictable hands of the robber.

In addition to loss of self-determination and personal property, assault and robbery involve an injury inflicted on the body; and the body can be regarded as the "envelope of self." The injury causes both physical and psychological pain. As Bard and Ellison suggest, "victims are left with the physical evidence reminding them that they were forced to surrender their autonomy and also the fact that they have been made to feel like less than adequate people . . . a visible reminder of their helplessness to protect or defend themselves" (1974, p. 71).

Short of homicide, forcible rape is the ultimate violation of self. Rape victims are deprived of self-determination and often suffer external physical injury. Further, the offender intrudes internally into the victim's body. As far as the victim is concerned, it makes no difference which body orifice is breached; it is the act of forceful entry into the body that causes the trauma. This forceful intrusion is one of the most trying crises a victim can sustain, particularly in view of the moral taboos surrounding the sexual function. In many cases, a rape victim is not physically injured, but suffers catastrophic psychological injury.

Assault on the quality of life

Each of us experiences the impact of economic crime whenever we make a purchase in a supermarket or department store. The costs of offenses such as shoplifting and employee pilferage are inevitably transmitted to the consumer in the form of increased prices, adding appreciably to the burden of inflation. But the harm of economic crime goes even deeper, extending to our social and economic institutions. The Chamber of Commerce of the United States assesses the damage this way: "A major long-term impact of white-collar crime is loss of public confidence in business, industry, and the professions and debasement of competition" (1974, p. 7). Edelhertz gives specific examples of how white-collar crimes affect our system of competition:

> ...every stock market fraud lessens competition in the securities market. Every commercial bribe or kickback debases the level of business competition, often forcing other suppliers to join in the practice if they are to survive. The business which accumulates capital to finance expansion by tax evasion places at a disadvantage the competitor who pays his taxes and is compelled to turn to lenders (for operating and expansion capital). The pharmaceutical company which markets a new drug based on fraudulent test results undercuts its competitors who are marketing a properly tested drug, and may cause them to adopt similar methods. Competitors who join in a conspiracy to freeze out their competition, or to fix prices, may gravely influence the course of our economy, in addition to harming their competitors and customers (1970, p. 9).

In addition to debasing competition, indifference to ethical practices can retard economic growth. For example, many companies refuse to conduct business in one particular state in which payoffs to government officials are expected (Chamber of Commerce of the United States 1974). When such abuses become flagrant, public pressure sometimes results in legislation or regulations that adversely affect the innocent as well as the guilty. The Chamber of Commerce reports that, in reaction to numerous verified abuses, a district attorney in one county has essentially banned door-to-door sales. The policy is supported by local business people who fear that the unethical practices of some door-to-door sellers will undermine the public trust in local business, thus reducing the patronage of those businesses. Unfortunately, the policy makes life nearly impossible for ethical companies that employ honest door-to-door sellers.

In a broader sense, white-collar crime affects the entire moral climate of our country. When people in positions of community leadership—corporate executives and government officials, for example—receive light penalties for offenses, our criminal justice system is undermined. And conventional offenders are provided with an opportunity to rationalize their own misconduct. The burglary in the Watergate scandal, for example, may have led many burglars to rationalize their own offenses and to question the penalties imposed on them by the courts.

Defining and classifying crimes

In colonial America, religious offenses such as blasphemy were punished as crimes. In the 1920s, it was a crime to drink Scotch. Today, it is illegal in the state of Wisconsin to sing in a bar; in Louisiana, it is illegal to appear drunk at a meeting of a literary society. Thus, crime is not synonymous with evil or deviance. A society may punish for many kinds of wrong or abnormal behavior by informal sanctions—disapproval, verbal abuse, ostracism (casting the offender out of the group). *Crimes*, however, are only those acts that violate *laws*, (i.e., formal, official, written statements of norms). No matter how reprehensible an act or the omission of an act may be, a crime has not been committed unless a specific law has been violated. Moreover, the violation must be either intentional or negligent.

Laws vary greatly with time, place, and circumstance, but they are remarkably similar in their definition of the most serious crimes, felonies. A *felony* is an offense serious enough to merit strong punishment; in the United States, felonies are punishable by one year or more in prison. Criminal homicide, forcible rape, burglary, and aggravated assault—just to name a few—are all felonies. Lesser offenses are called *misdemeanors*, generally defined in the United States as crimes for which the sentence is confinement in a county jail for less than one year; a fine may also be assessed. Drunkenness, vagrancy, disorders of the peace, and small-scale gambling are all misdemeanors.

Conventional crimes

The most serious felonies are crimes against person: criminal homicide, forcible rape, robbery, and aggravated assault. These four crimes arouse the greatest public emotion and concern. They are the "headline" crimes that create fear and incite demands for tougher and more vigorous law enforcement. However, most felonies are directed not against persons, but against property. Property crimes—burglary, larceny-theft, motor vehicle theft, arson—exclude crimes of violence.

Other offenses not commonly thought of as violent crimes or crimes against the person have the potential for violence. For example, an act of shoplifting can result in physical injury if a store employee tries to restrain the shoplifter and is attacked. Similarly, a homeowner who is wakened by a burglar may end up as a murder victim rather than a victim of breaking and entering. An arson may turn into a crime against the person if a security guard is in a building when it is torched. Thus, what starts as a crime against property may, as a consequence of circumstances, become a different crime—a crime against the person. Nevertheless, in recent years property offenses have made up the bulk of the more than 13 million crimes reported annually.

The government, for reasons long criticized by criminologists, collects data on eight offenses that make up the FBI's Crime Index: criminal homicide, forcible rape, robbery, aggravated assault, burglary, larceny-theft, motor vehicle theft, and arson. As is pointed out in chapter 3, the Crime Index provides information on "crime in the streets"; however, it fails to provide adequate coverage of "crime in the suites" (i.e., the highly profitable, large-scale property crimes perpetrated by corporations and businesses). Official statistics also fail to report accurately on "workplace crimes"—the auto mechanic who performs unneeded repairs or the microwave repairer who replaces a transistor and charges for a new mag tube; annual losses from these offenses dwarf by comparison losses from conventional crimes such as shoplifting and burglary.

Economic crimes

Criminologist Edwin Sutherland introduced the idea of white-collar crime to direct attention to crimes of the "upper world," in contrast to conventional crimes committed by the lower classes. He defined *white-collar crime* as offenses committed by "a person of respectability and high social status in the course of his occupation" (1949, p. 9). Other criminologists find Sutherland's definition too narrow. For one thing, many so-called white-collar crimes are committed by persons *outside* their occupations; for example, people file fraudulent claims for unemployment insurance, or they falsify income tax returns. For another, Sutherland's definition fails to account for businesses in which crime is the central activity—businesses such as fraudulent land-sale companies, pyramid clubs, and bogus home-improvement companies.

Today, Sutherland's white-collar crimes are often considered as part of a broader category, economic crimes. *Economic crimes* are illegal acts "committed by nonphysical means and by concealment or guile, to obtain money or property, or to obtain business or personal advantage" (Edelhertz 1970, p. 3). These crimes include:

1 *Personal Crimes.* Crimes committed by persons operating on an individual, *ad hoc* basis (credit purchases with no intention to pay; individual income tax violations; credit card frauds; bankruptcy frauds; and social security frauds).

2 *Abuses of Trust.* Crimes committed in the course of their occupations by workers operating inside business, government, or other establishments, in violation of their duty of loyalty or fidelity to employer or client (commercial bribery and kickbacks; embezzlement; securities fraud; employee theft; and padding of payroll and expense accounts).

3 *Business Crimes.* Crimes incidental to, and in furtherance of, business operations, but that are not the central purpose of the business (antitrust violations; tax violations; food and drug violations; commercial espionage; and deceptive advertising).

4 *Con Games.* White-collar crime committed as a business or as the central activity of a business (medical and health frauds; phony contests; diploma mills; charity and religious frauds; insurance frauds; and coupon redemption frauds).

By one estimate, economic crimes cost Americans about $45 billion annually (Chamber of Commerce of the United States 1974).

After many years of neglect, (since the 1940s, when Sutherland coined the phrase "white-collar crime"), economic crime is now receiving the attention due from the criminal justice system. One reason for this attention is that consumer advocacy has raised the public consciousness about economic crime. Complaints about the rudeness, stridency, and partizan zeal of groups such as "Nader's Raiders" can probably be considered testimonial to the effectiveness of their activities—and an indication that many of their barbs have hit the mark. Civil rights activism has also aroused indignation over gross disparities between sentences handed out to the poor and minorities for conventional property crimes and sentences given to middle-class or affluent whites for white-collar crimes.

THE INCREDIBLE ELECTRICAL CONSPIRACY

In what turned out to be the largest criminal proceeding in the history of antitrust violations, indictments were handed down on twenty-nine of the country's leading manufacturers of heavy electrical equipment, including Westinghouse and General Electric and their top executives. Forty-nine defendants were convicted of conspiring to fix prices, rig bids, and divide markets on electrical equipment valued at $1,750,000,000 annually. Fines totaling approximately $1,750,000 were levied against the corporations, with Westinghouse and General Electric paying the largest amounts. Jail terms of thirty days were meted out to seven of the defendants—four vice presidents, two division managers, and one sales manager.

The *modus operandi* of these business leaders would have been a credit to the operating methods of the Mafia. Fictitious names were used, illicit business was discussed on public pay phones, materials were mailed in plain manila envelopes, and wastebaskets were carefully checked at the close of meetings.

The penalties imposed by the court were viewed as excessive by the defendants and by many of their business colleagues. But the fines must be seen in perspective. A half-million-dollar fine for General Electric, for example, is no more disturbing than a parking fine of $2 for a person making $100,000 a year. As for a thirty-day jail sentence for perpetrating a multibillion-dollar fraud, the sentence is something less than the traditional city-court sanction of "ten dollars or ten days." In the words of an anonymous Pullman porter, "Steal fifty bucks and you go to jail; steal the railroad and you go to the U.S. Senate."

Watergate drew attention to the minimal sentences often received by persons convicted of nonconventional property crimes, in contrast to the more severe sentences meted out to conventional offenders. Watergate and its aftermath may have indirectly created public pressure for more effective prosecution and more stringent sentencing for economic crimes. In addition, continuing revelations about abuses of political morality (such as irregularities and illegal practices in campaign funding) may have prompted a closer scrutiny of possibly collusive relationships between political leaders and leaders of business and industry. Henceforth, we may witness a closer examination of the political-industrial connection. Concern is already growing over inappropriate appointments to federal regulatory agencies and over the propriety of high-level appointees leaving government to assume positions of responsibility in businesses and industries they once regulated.

Advocates of ecology and environmental protection have contributed greatly to increasing public awareness of economic crime. Ever since the offshore oil spill that blackened the beaches of Santa Barbara, organizations like the Sierra Club and Common Cause have pressured the government relentlessly for the passage of legislation—or for the effective enforcement of existing legislation—to prevent further despoliation of irreplaceable natural resources. These efforts have focused on the concept of corporate accountability.

In the final reckoning, our current economic difficulties may have more to do with increased national concern for white-collar crime than any other factor. Traditional American indifference to economic crime and its perpetrators may prove to be one of the luxuries of the affluent society of the 1950s and 1960s, a luxury headed for extinction along with cheap gasoline and the eight-cylinder family automobile. Now that official scrutiny has been turned to economic crime, a return to public apathy is unlikely, even if our national fortune takes a turn for the better. It may be increasingly difficult for the white-collar criminal to make a dishonest dollar.

Syndicated (organized) crime

Organization is the keynote of syndicated crime. In fact, *organized crime* is the more familiar expression for the illegal activities of syndicate criminals. Syndicated crime is a continuing and self-perpetuating conspiracy that relies heavily on fear and corruption. The roots of syndicated crime reach far back into our national history, with almost every nationality and ethnic group having been represented in the ranks at one time or another. The latter fact has given rise to the hotly disputed concept of *ethnic succession*, which maintains that immigrant arrivals used syndicated crime to attain wealth and power before finding safer and more attractive opportunities in legitimate business.

Among the principal revenue sources for syndicated crime are the illegal importation and distribution of drugs—chiefly cocaine, heroin, and marijuana—and gambling, which has an estimated annual take of billions of dollars. Another lucrative activity is loansharking, a low-risk, high-return enterprise. Syndicated crime has also infiltrated legitimate business, where it is involved in bankruptcy fraud, the manipulation of stocks and bonds, land fraud, and union racketeering (Pace and Styles 1983).

Political crimes

Traditionally, the term *political crime* refers to offenses against governments: treason, sedition, rebellion, and assassination. In the post-Watergate and Abscam era, however, the term is used increasingly to cover offenses committed by agents of the government against individuals, groups, the general public, and even foreign governments. Roebuck and Weeber (1978) have identified seven categories of political crimes:

1 Domestic intervention by government (Watergate; the FBI investigation of Dr. Martin Luther King)
2 Foreign intervention by government (the Vietnam war; CIA intervention in Chile)

3   Intervention against the government (the Weathermen faction of the Students for a Democratic Society; the Symbionese Liberation Army)
4   Domestic surveillance (FBI wiretaps and bugging; surveillance by the Internal Revenue Service)
5   Domestic confrontation (Kent State; the suppression of the Attica insurrection)
6   Evasion and collusion by the government (Kennedy's denial of the Bay of Pigs incursion; the Nixon administration's cover-up of the Watergate break-in)
7   Evasion and collusion against government (income tax evasion; draft resistance; military desertion)

Two points should be made regarding political crimes. First, ordinary crimes can be invested with political meaning and used symbolically to express dissent toward an existing political structure. Political dissent that leads to crimes against the government can be viewed as *principled deviance* (Clinard and Quinney 1973), because it often represents a deliberate violation for the purpose of demonstrating the unfairness of a law. The violation can be an isolated, individual act, but it is more often a group action.

Second, the distinctions between political crimes and more conventional crimes are easily blurred when legal codes are applied punitively for politically motivated social control. As Roebuck and Weeber observe, "There may be nothing inherently illegal in an act; but the actor is criminalized when persons in power attach the illegal label to his behavior" (1978, p. 20). Thus, political dissenters may be arrested for disorderly conduct, trespassing, parading without a permit, or violating fire ordinances.

"WHY NOT DECRIMINALIZE CORRUPTION?"

To the Editor:
Why not decriminalize corruption? Bring it into the open, into the clean, invigorating air of the free-enterprise system! Let bribery be what our distinguished corporate leaders have already testified it is: a cost of doing business, like the annual budget for paper clips.

Think of the implications! No more secret, under-the-table deals with potentates and princes. Corporations would feel free to make their offers public, like baseball tycoons bidding for pitchers in springtime. The financial sections of our newspapers will read like the sports pages:

LOCKHEED UPS ANTE TO HOLDOUT PRINCE
OFFER NOW A COOL MILLION
NEXT MOVE UP TO BOEING

The new freedom will even trickle down to shape the lives of humble citizens. Tenants looking for housing in New York will find the super's bribe routinely published in the for-rent ad: "5 rms riv view all util $495 + $175 super." Building inspectors will tack up their price lists on the peep-holed fences fronting construction projects: "To OK sand/cement ratio in concrete—$150 per fl."

Of course, attempts will be made to undermine the system. Some misguided executive may take it into his head to build a better airplane and try to peddle it on the basis of its quality alone; or some woolly-headed Congressional do-gooder, addled by anachronisms about the consent of the governed, might turn down a trip to a hunting lodge and vote his conscience. There are always a few rotten apples.

But this is an idea whose time has come.

The corrupters are coming out of the closet, and their detractors find themselves increasingly on the defensive. It's a new world, a new Utopia! From each according to his price!

KENNETH HARVEY
New Canaan, Conn., Feb. 17, 1977

From "Letters to the Editor," *New York Times,* 27 February 1977, sec. 4, p. 16.

The political crime that has received the most attention from the media, if not from criminologists, is terrorism. *Terrorism* and *terrorist* are terms of limited usefulness, at best, and are prone to causing confusion. Terrorism includes both violent acts and threats of violence. It lumps together acts committed by criminals, psychotics, self-proclaimed patriots, and others with extreme ideological convictions. It makes no distinctions between acts carried out by individuals, groups, or even governments. It encompasses the capture of an airliner and its passengers; the explosion of a bomb in a crowded shopping center; the murder of a prominent person or government official; and the seizure of a public building and its occupants. Such actions are carried out with the objective of focusing attention on a cause or grievance; in accomplishing this aim, little heed is given to the victims of the terrorist act. Victims may be carefully selected according to plan, or they may simply be caught in the path of random violence.

According to one assessment, there were nearly 700 incidents of international terrorism between 1968 and 1975, accounting for 700 dead and 1,700 injured (Anable 1976). This toll is dwarfed by deaths from fighting in Lebanon or in Northern Ireland, and is almost trivial compared with the losses in an industrial society from accidents or crime (recall that the death toll from criminal homicide in the United States topped 20,000 in 1982). The total annual dollar loss in the United States as a result of terrorism—in terms of ransom payments and blown up or burned airplanes—is less than the loss from shoplifting.

The consequences of terrorism, however, are anything but trivial. Incidents of violence and horror that directly affect only a few people can have a psychological impact on millions. Terrorist acts prompt costly, and sometimes disruptive, security precautions, and they can lead to repressive retaliation and the erosion of civil liberties. Some even challenge the accepted international order among sovereign nations.

Consensual crimes

Organized crime is profitable because many people are willing, even anxious, to buy illegal goods and services. The buyers, too, are breaking the law. Who are the victims of organized crime? Gambling, prostitution, and deviant drug use are illegal, but it is often difficult to pinpoint the victims.

Thus, these activities are often called *victimless crimes*—illegal acts in which all parties *choose* to be involved. Other victimless crimes include some types of pornography, deviant sexual acts among consenting adults, and vagrancy.

Some people argue that these crimes are *not* victimless, that they harm a broad range of people and society in general. Because social norms are violated, the offenses might instead be called *public-order* or *consensual offenses*. At any rate, many people question whether these acts—even if they are shameful, immoral, or harmful—should be defined as crimes. Two arguments are often made for decriminalizing activities such as marijuana use, pornography, and prostitution. First, critics argue that criminal sanctions against these activities constitute an unwarranted intrusion into privacy and an indefensible extension of the government's authority. In other words, is it the government's business what sexual activities consenting adults engage in? Is it the government's business if you gamble? Second, some critics claim that enforcing laws against these activities overburdens the police, the courts, and the prisons, and increases problems in the criminal justice system.

The administration of justice

As the fear of crime intensifies, so grows the debate over how crime might be decreased or prevented. The agents of the *criminal justice system*—police, prosecutors, courts, and corrections—are the main actors in the fight against crime. The police are responsible for detecting and apprehending people who violate the criminal law; prosecutors decide whether circumstances warrant prosecution; the courts decide guilt or innocence and sentence those who are convicted or plead guilty; the corrections component carries out the sentence of the court.

As described above, the administration of justice sounds neat, orderly, and systematic. Unfortunately, it is none of these things—least of all, systematic. Until recently, criminologists and practitioners of criminal justice jokingly referred to the "criminal injustice nonsystem." Now that investigative reporters and television documentaries have introduced the public to some of the idiosyncrasies of "justice American-style," such characterizations are no longer private.

The comedian Lenny Bruce once observed that "in the Halls of Justice, all of the justice is in the halls." The quip summons up a picture of lawyers and clients huddled in the drafty corridors of a mildewed county courthouse, haggling over the details of a bargained plea. Bruce was not trying to be funny: his comment was based on his own experiences within the criminal justice system (as a frequent violator of public-order statutes and drug laws). And as a rough description of how justice is administered in the United States, the remark is not without accuracy.

Some difficulty lies in the term "criminal justice system," itself. The term is a convenient fiction—an abstraction with no counterpart in reality. The American criminal justice system is not a single system but a hodgepodge of separate systems, subsystems, institutions, and procedures.

Throughout the tens of thousands of towns, cities, counties, and states in the United States, and in the federal government, there are many different types of criminal justice systems. The systems may appear similar in that they all apprehend, prosecute, convict, and try to correct lawbreakers; but no two systems are exactly alike, and very few are linked together in any comprehensive way. The popular myth that depicts the criminal justice system as a monolithic structure is described by the National Advisory Commission on Criminal Justice Standards and Goals:

> The contemporary view is to consider society's institutionalized response to crime as the criminal justice system and its activities as the criminal justice process. This model envisions interdependent and interrelated agencies and programs that will provide a coordinated and consistent response to crime. The model, however, remains a model—it does not exist in fact. Although cooperation between the various components has improved noticeably in some localities, it cannot be said that a criminal justice "system" really exists (*Corrections*, 1973, pp. 5–6).

The situation is even more complicated, however. In another report entitled *Criminal Justice System*, the commission asserts that "there are two criminal justice systems in the United States today, one of which is visible and controversial, the other of which is submerged and usually ignored" (1973, p. 1). Identifying these systems as Criminal Justice Systems 1 and 2, the report continues:

> Criminal Justice System 1 is known well. It is the traditional series of agencies that have been given the formal responsibility to control crime: police and sheriffs' departments, judges, prosecutors and their staffs, defense offices, jails and prisons, and probation and parole agencies. Criminal Justice System 1 is an overt system, the one seen each day in operation, the one customarily understood and referred to in crime and delinquency literature. Even in this report, the phrase "criminal justice system" usually refers to Criminal Justice System 1.
> But there are broader implications of the term . . . . Many public and private agencies and citizens outside of police, courts, and corrections are—or ought to be—involved in reducing and preventing crime, the primary goal of criminal justice. These agencies and persons, when dealing with issues related to crime reduction and prevention, plus the traditional triad of police, courts, and corrections, make up a larger criminal justice system, a system which this Commission calls Criminal Justice System 2.
> A State legislature, for example, becomes part of this larger criminal justice system when it considers and debates any proposed law that might affect, even remotely, any area of criminal justice activities. So also the executive agencies of the State, educational administrative units, welfare departments, youth service bureaus, recreation departments, and other public offices become a part of Criminal Justice System 2 in many of their decisions and actions. Moving outside the State and local governments, community organizations, union offices, neighborhood action groups, and employers may also be important functionaries in the second system (p. 1).

The attitude expressed by the commission has been noted less formally elsewhere, evidence that coping with crime and its consequences has become everyone's business. Unfortunately, as the commission notes in *Criminal Justice System*, "many public agencies and private citizens refuse even to acknowledge that they have a role in reducing crime" (p. 1). Moreover, the effectiveness of Criminal Justice System 1 is lessened by intramural conflicts among the police, courts, and correctional agencies.

If cooperation is poor among members of Criminal Justice System 1, it is markedly worse with respect to interactions involving members of Criminal Justice System 2. Many courts, law enforcement agencies, and correctional facilities have few (or no) working relationships with various private and public organizations that might provide valuable services to their clients. Worse, most agencies have no clear policy for obtaining such assistance, even if there is an awareness of its availability.

System and process: The role of discretion and accommodation

The word *system* connotes an orderly arrangement of parts according to some plan or design. The basic idea is that relationships among parts or components in a system are deliberate, rather than haphazard. Further, the word implies that the arrangement exists to achieve some goal or purpose. A major operating characteristic of systems is that what affects the function of one part can potentially affect other parts, as well as the entire system.

In recent years, a field has developed called *systems analysis*. Systems analysts use sophisticated mathematical and statistical procedures to study organizational structures, operations, and problems. The field draws on contributions from many other areas of inquiry—communications research, information theory, and cybernetics, to name a few. Although the methods employed by systems analysts are rather complex and rigorous, some of the key concepts—such as the *linear process model*—are easy to understand and apply. This model, shown in **figure 1.2**, schematizes a continuum, an orderly progression of events from input to output. Its developers—Coffey, Eldefonso, and Hartinger—describe systems this way: "The input is what the system deals with; the process is *how* the system deals with the input; and the output is the *results* of the process . . . ." (1974, p. 9). If this model is applied to the criminal justice system, *input* refers to selected law violations (i.e., reported crimes); *process* refers to the activities

FIGURE 1.2
Linear process model. From A. Coffey, E. Eldefonso, and W. Hartinger, An Introduction to the Criminal Justice System and Process (Englewood Cliffs, N.J.: Prentice-Hall, 1974), p. 9, by permission of the authors and the publisher.

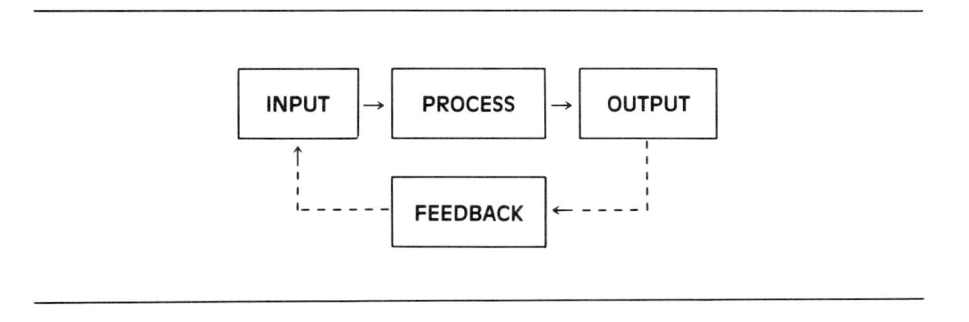

of the police, courts, and corrections; and output refers to the outcome (i.e., success or failure) of the process.

The linear process model can be applied to components of the criminal justice system, as well as to the total system. For example, as shown in **figure 1.3,** the probation subsystem receives, as input, cases selected by the courts. The goal of probation is to produce an output of individuals who will not repeat their criminal activities. This goal is to be met through presentence investigation of the offender's background and supervision within the community, without resorting to incarceration.

The linear process model reinforces the idea that whatever is done in one subsystem has direct and indirect effects upon other subsystems. For example, increased arrests by the police result in more work for prosecutors, courts, and corrections. If the corrections component of the criminal justice system is ineffective because of excessive work loads, released offenders may commit more crimes and again be apprehended by the police. This circular process is the focus of much controversy among representatives from various components of the criminal justice system. Repeat offenders are known as *recidivists.*

A major difficulty with the linear process model is that, by directing attention to the administration of justice as a system, it diverts attention from the real way justice is administered in thousands of daily transactions—namely, through discretion and accommodation. *Discretion* refers to the exercise of choice by those charged with the responsibility for and authority to carry out various tasks assigned by the laws of municipal, county, state, and federal governments. From the traffic cop who can choose between issuing a warning or a citation, to the members of the parole board who can decide whether to release an offender from prison next week, next month, or next year, practitioners in all components of the criminal justice system are armed with discretionary powers. Needless to say, although these powers are susceptible to influence and are often misused or abused, they are an indispensable requirement of the criminal justice system.

Accommodation refers to give-and-take interactions among practitioners in the crimnial justice system in the daily business of administering justice. These interactions take place within the context of a bureaucracy whose members fill a variety of work roles. The system sets objectives with regard to equity and justice, but individual practitioners within the system

INPUT
Cases Selected by Courts

PROCESS
Case Investigation
Court Recommendation
Case Supervision
Corrective treatment

OUTPUT
Nonrecidivating Offenders

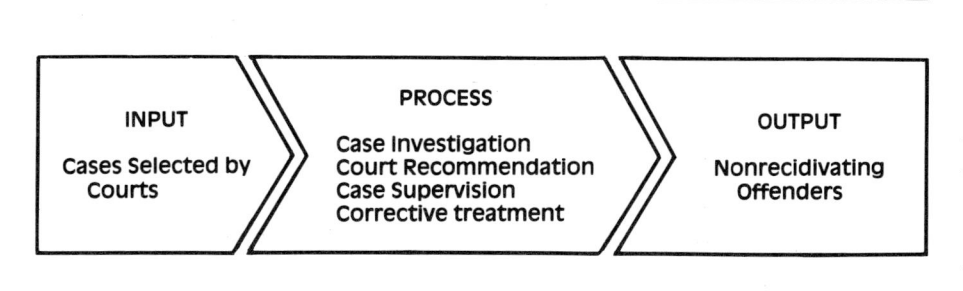

FIGURE 1.3
The probation subsystem of corrections. From A. Coffey, E. Eldefonso, and W. Hartinger, Introduction to the Criminal Justice System and Process *(Englewood Cliffs, N.J.: Prentice-Hall, 1974), p. 11, by permission of the authors and the publisher.*

have other—often competing—objectives related to job performance and efficiency. Thus, police departments are interested in "clearing" cases by arresting suspected offenders, while prosecutors are concerned about a backlog of cases. At the same time, judges complain about crowded dockets, and correctional authorities worry about overcrowding in jails and prisons. Consequently, many decisions are made through give-and-take discussions that appear to accused persons to be less than just and equitable, however conducive the decisions may be to administrative efficiency. Some of the conflicts among the objectives of the criminal justice system are discussed later in this chapter with regard to the due process and crime control models.

It is nearly impossible to overstate the importance of discretion and accommodation in the criminal justice system in the United States. Models and analogies tends to leave people with a feeling that there is some "right way" for justice to be administered, with any deviation from the prescribed path being tantamount to a miscarriage of justice. Even interactions between practitioners in the system are subject to distortion and misinterpretation. For example, when one of the authors was participating in a study of inmates on Florida's death row, he asked prisoners if they believed they had received a fair trial. With rare exceptions, the answer was no—under the circumstances, a predictable answer. But when asked why they felt their trials had been unfair, inmate after inmate replied in roughly this way: In recesses during the trial, the defense attorney (usually a public defender or court-appointed lawyer) talked in a friendly way and joked or laughed with the prosecutor's staff, leading the convicts to doubt their attorney's dedication. (Lewis, Mannle, Vetter & Allen 1979).

The administration of justice is not a series of abstract operations or processes that take place according to a blueprint or a computer program: it is a series of human interactions. Defense counsels negotiate with assistant prosecutors to reduce charges against defendants; judges confer with probation officers over presentence reports to determine if justice is better served by incarcerating offenders or letting them go. Objectives are balanced between what is needed and required for the well-being of the offender and what is needed and required for the welfare and protection of society. The tool for balance is compromise through accommodation.

The police

For both criminals and law-abiding citizens, police are the most visible part of the criminal justice system. They are the entry point for the failures of the other subsystems. More than 500,000 police officers, administrators, and civilian personnel serve in over 40,000 separate local, state, and federal agencies. Because they are the only component of the criminal justice system in direct daily contact with both criminals and the public, the police have responsibilities that make them unique among service agencies. To a considerable extent, law enforcement policies are created by police officers themselves. Kaplan observes that "a criminal code, in practice, is not a set of specific instructions to policemen but a more or less rough map of the territory in which policemen work. How an individual policeman moves around that territory depends largely on his personal discretion" (1973, p. 74). In every instance, police officers make the principal determination of whether or not to initiate the criminal process.

The highly discretionary character of police work contrasts with the widespread public view that "the police enforce the criminal laws and preserve peace mechanically, simply by arresting anyone who has deviated from legislative norms of acceptable behavior" (President's Commission on Law Enforcement and Administration of Justice, (*Task Force Report: The Police*, 1967, p. 120). In reality, the police can not enforce all criminal laws equally; even if police had such a capability, the other components of the criminal justice system would be unable to cope with the large number of violators entering the system.

Police must enforce many laws that deal with public order or moral conduct—laws that are often controversial, unpopular, ambiguous, or unenforceable, or that affect the everyday activities of law-abiding citizens, (even though they were intended to apply only to certain criminal activities). Gambling and sex are examples of just such activities regulated by law.

Finally, the police are responsible for considering the foreseeable consequences of an arrest. As the *Task Force Report* (1967) states: "In light of these inherent limitations, individual police officers, must, of necessity, be given considerable latitude in exercising their arrest power. As a result, no task committed to individual judgment is more complex or delicate. A mistake in judgment can precipitate a riot or, on the other hand, culminate in subsequent criminal activity by a person who was erroneously released by an officer" (p. 120). An unjustified arrest can have a serious and permanent effect on the course of a person's life. And with today's critical attitude toward the police, an officer's decision to act can have a long-range negative effect on his or her own future as well. The importance of the power to arrest and the need for rational exercise of this power can not be overstated.

Police are called upon to make legally correct decisions—instantly, under stress, and often without advice—that will hold up under hours of scrutiny and legal research by defense lawyers. Further, they must often settle domestic fights, deliver babies, and perform an array of other tasks not directly linked to criminal activity. At times, they are called upon to prevent crime, a task that requires, above all, an intuitive sense for suspicious conduct and an understanding of human behavior. In short, police must be "streetwise." As Dr. Ruth Levy states in the *Task Force Report*,

> reviewing the tasks we expect of our law enforcement officers, it is my impression that their complexity is perhaps greater than that of any other profession. On the other hand, we expect our law enforcement officer to possess the nurturing, caretaking, sympathetic, empathizing, gentle characteristics of a physician, nurse, social worker, etc., as he deals with school traffic, acute illness and injury, suicidal threats, missing persons, etc. On the other hand, we expect him to command respect, demonstrate courage, control hostile impulses, and meet great physical hazards . . . . He is to control crowds, prevent riots, apprehend criminals, and chase after speeding vehicles. I can think of no other profession which constantly demands such seemingly opposite characteristics (p. 121).

Traditionally, the two principal missions of the police have been maintenance of order and enforcement of the law. However, with the increasing complexity of society, numerous and varied demands have been put upon the police because of their unique authority. The National Advisory Commission on Criminal Justice Standards and Goals lists the following functions among those performed by police agencies (*Criminal Justice System*, 1973, pp. 104–5):

1. Preventing criminal activity
2. Detecting criminal activity
3. Apprehending criminal offenders
4. Participating in court proceedings
5. Protecting constitutional guarantees
6. Assisting those who cannot care for themselves or who are in danger of physical harm
7. Controlling traffic
8. Resolving day-to-day conflicts among family, friends, and neighbors
9. Creating and maintaining a feeling of security in the community
10. Promoting and preserving civil order

These functions are core elements in the contemporary role of police. As discussed in chapter 5, there is much controversy over relative importance of each function.

Law enforcement duties require only about 10 percent of a police officer's time and energy; the remaining 90 percent goes to what might be called *social-service functions*. Police officers frequently complain that there is a contest among police departments to see who can undertake the most—and most unusual—non–law enforcement projects. One police administrator (Clark 1968) recommends that police departments move from programs for delinquency prevention and family crisis intervention to various forms of offender *treatment*—such as detoxification units, week-enders, and halfway-house programs—that are currently the responsibility of the correctional subsystem. The situation is reminiscent of a statement by Raymond Chandler's fictional detective, Bernie Ohls, in *The Long Goodbye*. The novel's hero, a private investigator named Philip Marlowe, asks Ohls and his fellow detective, "You two characters been seeing any psychiatrists lately?"

> "Jesus," Ohls said, "hadn't you heard?" "We got them in our hair all the time these days. We've got two of them on the staff. This ain't police business any more. It's getting to be a branch of the medical racket. They're in and out of jail, the courts, the interrogation rooms. They write reports fifteen pages long on why some punk of a juvenile held up a liquor store or raped a schoolgirl or peddled tea to the senior class. Ten years from now guys like Hernandez and me will be doing Rorschach tests and word associations instead of chin-ups and target practice. When we go out on a case we'll carry little black bags with portable lie detectors and bottles of truth serum. Too

bad we didn't grab the four hard monkeys that poured it on Big Willie Magoon. We might have been able to unmaladjust them and make them love their mothers" (1954, p. 286).

Much of the confusion about the role of the police officer, from the viewpoints of the public and the officers themselves, stems from the terms "law enforcement" and "crime prevention." Both terms encompass designated duties of today's police officers, but despite their apparent similarity, they are not one and the same. The concept of a police force evolved from the need for an agency of government to enforce the law. As a matter of administrative convenience, the police force has since been charged with the added task of preventing crime. The presence of a police officer may, at times, serve as a deterrent to crime; what an officer does beyond that point is up to his or her discretion.

The prosecutor

After the police, the next member of the criminal justice system the accused individual has contact with is the public prosecutor. This official has the broad discretionary power to dismiss charges or to reduce them to a lesser offense to which the defendant will plead guilty. Recent studies indicate that 50–80 percent of felony cases initiated by police are dismissed by prosecutors. In a high percentage of cases in which charges are not dismissed, charges are reduced through plea bargaining, a process whereby the defendant pleads guilty to a lesser offense.[2] Although Perry Mason type trials get much play in novels and the media, more than 90 percent of criminal cases are actually resolved by guilty pleas. The usual justification for plea bargaining is that the large case load and limited resources of the courts call for the quick disposition of as many cases as possible. Heavy case loads may indeed foster frequent plea bargaining; but overburdening of some of the courts does not explain why some cases are prosecuted and others dismissed. Rather, the decision to prosecute or not to prosecute reflects the discretionary power of prosecutors.

The effectiveness of a prosecutor is usually measured by the number of convictions he or she obtains in office. Because a prosecutor's political life depends largely on success in securing convictions, it is not surprising that cases with little promise of conviction are dismissed or bargained away. Seeing no possibility of conviction, a prosecutor may negotiate for deferred prosecution—that is, for community supervision without prosecution. The public is seldom concerned about how prosecutors secure their convictions, only that they get them. As noted by Barnes and Teeters,

> when a case finally reaches the trial court, the prosecutor earnestly prepares for a real battle, not for justice, but for a conviction. His professional reputation is at stake. He must resort to all the oratory and psychological trickery he can mobilize. He is ethically no better and no worse than the defense lawyer in this judicial bout. The average trial, unfortunately, becomes more a show or contest than a struggle for justice. The judge acts as referee—to see that there is something like fair play. The jury sits in amaze-

ment, at times flattered at the compliments paid them by the lawyers, and at times incensed at the threats and insults exchanged by the lawyers in reckless fashion. During the court recess the two lawyers may often be seen slapping each other on the back in perfect amity. Here is a basic American institution in action, with tragic implications that most Americans do not grasp (1959, p. 242).

The impact of the prosecutor's discretionary power helps explain why only a small percentage of reported crimes result in imprisonment of the offender. Just what *is* the decision-making process at this critical stage?

The decision to charge an offender is made after the police have arrested the offender and presented their information to the prosecuting attorney. The prosecutor is the first *legally trained* individual to examine the facts, except in those few police departments that have legal advisors on call twenty-four hours a day. It is the prosecutor's job to decide whether to charge the suspect or dismiss ("no paper") the case. In a "no paper" action, the prosecutor decides that there is insufficient probability of conviction and thus no reason to file an information, i.e., enter a written accusation charging the suspect with having committed a specific crime or crimes.

A legal decision to proceed with prosecution requires that all elements of the alleged crime be present.[3] A narrowly defined, unlawful act must occur with the presence of criminal intent. If the intent does not apply to the specific unlawful act, the case will be on shaky legal ground. Many crimes for which offenders are arrested encompass "lesser included offenses" within their definitions. A good prosecutor can relate intent to the unlawful acts, thus building a stronger case for conviction. If the prosecutor thinks there is a possibility that the defendant will plead guilty to a lesser charge (with a lesser penalty), he or she may bargain for a reduced charge; however, if the defendant will not accept a lesser charge, the case may be dropped because of the unlikelihood of conviction. In addition to wasting state money, a trial without a conviction may hurt a prosecutor's chances for reelection or advancement.

Aside from the issue of legal sufficiency, a prosecutor also considers a complaint from an extralegal standpoint. Often, the most important extralegal considerations are matters of equity and office policy. Age, sex, race, social status, conviction record, and other factors are not related to guilt or innocence, but they are taken into account in the decision to file charges. For example, it may be office policy to divert first offenders or persons under eighteen years old to nonjudicial programs; conversely, a tough stand may be taken on certain offenses to ensure that charges are almost always filed and the cases processed through the courts.

The prosecuting attorney's initial screening of suspects is a critical stage in the criminal justice system. However, although statistics are now becoming available, there has been relatively little investigation of the screening process. As early as 1933, Baker wrote:

> How much more significant would it be to have figures on the situations arising behind closed doors in the prosecutor's office! Court statistics are enlightening to such an extent that it is now almost commonplace to designate the prosecutor as the most powerful official in local government. If

we had some means of checking the decisions of the prosecutor when the question "to prosecute or not to prosecute" arises, such figures would go much further to substantiate such a statement (p. 771).

A half century later, we are still trying to clarify this important decision-making process.

The courts

The criminal court is the core of the American judicial system. The courts are highly organized, deeply venerated, and rigidly circumscribed by law and tradition. The entire criminal justice system depends upon, and is responsible to, the court in its role as interpreter of the law. The police are guided and restricted by decisions of the court; prosecutors must weigh the legal and extralegal issues of cases in terms of the court that will try the cases; and the correctional system depends on the court for its work load. The formal processes that take place in the courtroom are not merely symbolic, but are vital for the protection of both the accused and society.

The adversary system of criminal justice pits two attorneys against each other in an effort to prove the technical guilt or innocence of suspects, while at the same time providing them with all of their constitutional rights. The judge, who may be considerably less skilled in law than either the prosecutor or the defense counsel, referees the trial on points of law. A judge's mistakes, if questioned on appeal,[4] may result in the release of an offender. However, the release of guilty individuals because of errors in the system is preferable to convicting innocent persons in haste or in the name of efficiency.

An offender may be freed or a case lost early in a trial because the court finds a mistake in the charges or a misrepresentation of the facts. The court itself may commit an error by allowing damaging or false evidence to be admitted; if this happens, the case may later be reversed by an appellate court. The court may also divert a convicted offender into treatment programs that it feels are more appropriate to the case then correctional institutions.

Although a prosecutor may have good reason to file charges against a suspect and bring a case to trial, prosecuting attorneys do make errors. These errors are usually brought to the attention of the court in the early stages of the judicial process. If a judge is convinced that charges are without foundation, he or she can dismiss a case. The judge will usually accompany the dismissal with a few unkind words to the prosecutor for wasting the court's time. It is this situation the prosecutor seeks to avoid at all costs.

On occasion, although less frequently in practice than is shown on television, a case against a suspect falls apart during the trial. Critical motions may be made in trial, such as motions to dismiss or to suppress or restrict evidence and testimony. Judges must rule on such issues, even though they know their rulings may be reversed on appeal. If a judge makes a decision that is later overturned, his or her reputation may be damaged.

On the other hand, a judge may dismiss a case and save the state the effort and expense of a trial and a long series of appeals.

In the past, judges faced relatively few choices. A suspect could be found guilty and sentenced to prison, or found innocent and released. A few persons were found "not guilty by reason of insanity," but most of those convicted were sentenced to the fortresslike prisons that predominated in the nineteenth and early twentieth centuries. Today, however, judges must choose from a much broader range of alternatives in sentencing offenders. Some of these alternatives are discussed in the following section on corrections; others are discussed in later chapters.

Corrections

Corrections refers to those agencies of social control that attempt to change, neutralize, or eliminate the deviant behavior of adult criminals and juvenile delinquents. In theory, the social and legal authority of the correctional component of the criminal justice system begins following the adjudication of guilt of an adult offender in the criminal courts, or when its services are invoked by the juvenile court in the case of a minor charged with a delinquent act. In practice, however, the correctional function may be initiated informally prior to the formal assumption of responsibility following court action. For example, most police departments have officers who specialize in work with juveniles and youthful offenders; and departments of social welfare provide protective services for children and adolescents with behavior problems. Such agencies may become involved with youngsters even before a referral is made to the juvenile court; in some cases, juveniles may be kept out of court entirely.

Corrections encompasses jails and lockups, prisons, juvenile detention centers, probation and parole programs, and various community-based treatment centers. The corrections system is plagued by an overlapping of jurisdictions, contradictory philosophies, and a welter of organizational structures that are fragmented and isolated in terms of their functions and responsibilities. Corrections has grown piecemeal, sometimes out of experience, sometimes out of sheer necessity, and sometimes out of folly.

Corrections replaces the older term *penology*, which is derived from a Latin word meaning punishment. Thus, penology—the generic term for the organized body of concepts, theories, and approaches centered on the prison and the institutional experience—signifies "science of punishment." Although the nomenclature has changed, it can reasonably be questioned whether there has been a corresponding change in the underlying mystique and ideology of prison confinement. Most prison systems in the United States reflect a punitive orientation toward criminal offenders, an approach that looks backward and deals with offenders in terms of what they did, rather than to their capacity for constructive change. This situation exists not because institutions, programs, or systems are operated by sadists, but because state prisons, until quite recently, were under no legal obligation to do more than merely keep offenders in custody for a specified period of time.

Corrections is probably the least visible part of the criminal justice system in daily operation, and correctional institutions are the least visible of all correctional facilities. Most prisons, particularly older institutions, are located in isolated, thinly populated, rural areas. Community leaders, politicians, or judges who may routinely sentence offenders to confinement in these places rarely visit them. In many instances, the remoteness and difficulty of access to prisons impose hardship on the families of prisoners and curtail chances for relatives to stay in close touch during a convict's incarceration. All too often, the public becomes aware of correctional institutions only when a prison is in the news because of a riot, prison break, guard or inmate slaying, or other dramatic event.

Prison administrators are hamstrung in most efforts at prison reform because of public outcry over escapes. To minimize escapes, wardens oversupervise, overlock, and overcount their charges. The result of such actions is institutionalization, both for the prisoners and their keepers. The prison *routine* becomes the most important aspect of prison administration, and any variation from strict and unbending custody and discipline is viewed with skepticism.

The civil rights conflicts that the "free" world tries to escape by retreating from urban ghettos to segregated suburbs are magnified in the institution, a microcosm of the outside world. Prisoners' instincts for self-preservation in this tense atmosphere are embodied in defense groups and assassination squads; bottled-up anger and frustration explode in gang rape and in intense racial conflict among inmates and between inmates and guards.

Prison overcrowding has also drawn public attention. When institutions are filled to bursting, inmates cannot escape the dangers of prison life by retreating to a safe, private cell. Prisoners exhibit high levels of anxiety and hostility in prisons too overcrowded to restrain the most dangerous and aggressive inmates. Thus, crowding leads to an increase in inmate-inmate assault and guard-inmate, inmate-guard altercations.

To the extent that public attitudes and opinions toward corrections—or, more realistically, images conveyed by the press and television—can be generalized, there is considerable agreement that (1) the corrections system is chiefly responsible for soaring crime rates in the United States; (2) that the shortcomings, inadequacies, and outright failures of corrections have burdened our society with a critical mass of hardened, dangerous criminals; (3) that the answer to dealing with violent and habitual offenders is prolonged incarceration in escape-proof prisons (with no provisions for early or conditional release); and (4) that permissiveness and leniency are foolish, reckless, and irresponsible unless reserved exclusively for certain juvenile and youthful first offenders, minor property offenders, and those convicted of white-collar or consensual crimes. In short, the public is much more likely to blame the crime problem on corrections than to recognize deeply rooted social and economic causes.

The public view, however, is susceptible to some refinement. There is a "house-that-Jack-built" quality to charges that corrections is directly responsible for any failure to deal effectively with crime. For one thing, the corrections system is unfairly taxed with problems concentrated overwhelmingly within a single component of the correctional enterprise: the prisons. Although many offenders are dealt with through facilities and programs that provide either alternatives to incarceration (such as diversion or probation) or conditional release from incarceration (such as parole or work release), discussions of correctional failures are almost always on the problems plaguing the prisons. Yet corrections inherits most of the recalcitrant, intractable, and essentially incorrigible offenders who are not handled elsewhere in the criminal justice system. And the criminal justice system eventually falls heir to nearly every unsolved social problem in our society. Many of the people who wind up in prison include individuals who are emotionally disturbed, mentally retarded, actively psychotic, ferally unsocialized, or hopelessly incompetent.

Former Georgia governor Lester Maddox, with what could be described as Pickwickian humor, once observed that the major problem facing Georgia's prisons was that they needed a better class of inmate. With a straight face—and equal justification—the same can be said for the criminal justice system in general, corrections in particular.

A growing number of criminologists and other social scientists believe that even the most treatment-oriented correctional institutions with detailed rehabilitation programs cannot live up to the goal of resocializing offenders. Efforts to maintain routines and handle everyday problems—in short, "running the show"—tend to supersede efforts at rehabilitation, especially when the efforts are in conflict. Mandated security measures are yet another obstacle to rehabilitation. Thus, the result of incarceration, more often than not, is exactly the opposite of resocialization and reformation. As Morris notes:

> "... prison may be no more than an irrelevant interlude in a career of crime.... It may well be that the true function of the prison is no more than symbolic, a statement that even if penal treatments neither reform nor deter, at least society has expressed its disapproval of crime" (1974, p. 83).

The above considerations, together with the mounting costs of incarcerating prisoners who, in many instances, do not need to be kept in prison, have renewed the urgency of the search for alternatives to confinement. As a result, some community-based correctional programs are conducted outside prison walls, are located in or near population centers, and make use of local resources and services. These programs and facilities include:

1. *Probation.* A court action that permits a convicted offender to retain freedom in the community, subject to court control and the supervision and guidance of a probation officer. Probation sustains the offender's ability to continue working and to protect his or her family's welfare, while avoiding the stigma and possible damaging effects of imprisonment.

2. *Parole.* A procedure by which prisoners are selected for release. Released prisoners are provided with the controls, assistance, and guidance they need to serve the remainder of their sentences in the free community.

3. *Halfway Houses.* Small, homelike, residential facilities located in the community for offenders who need more control than can be provided by probation or other types of community supervision. Halfway houses are also used for gradual readjustment to community life for people coming out of institutions. Halfway-house programs usually offer supervised living and counseling services, and draw upon the community for education, training, jobs, and recreation to aid in rehabilitation.

4. *Work Release.* An alternative in which offenders are confined to institutions only at night or on weekends, allowing them to pursue normal lives in their "free" time. Work-release programs provide a greater degree of community supervision and prevent a disruption of family life and employment.

5. *Prerelease Centers.* Supervised programs designed to ease the transition from total confinement to freedom. People from the community come to the prison and provide information in areas of vital interest to inmates about to be released. Subjects covered include employment, finances, family life, community services, and legal sources.

Community-based corrections has been touted as "the wave of the future" in the corrections system. However, community correctional administrators take a more sober and restrained view of the assets and limitations of the community-based approach. As Kaye Harris, formerly of the National Council on Crime and Delinquency, observes: "If community corrections can reduce the severity of sentences, reduce the harm done by imprisonment, make services available to those who are otherwise denied them or reduce the huge capital outlays for new prisons, then we can say that community corrections is a successful strategy" (Blackmore 1981, p. 17).

Crime control versus due process

The conflicts that exist among various components of the criminal justice system were mentioned earlier in this chapter. However, these conflicts involve much more than mere differences of professional opinion over procedural matters in the administration of justice. In the view of a leading authority in criminal law (Packer 1968), the real source of intramural conflicts lies in two competing systems of values. Packer suggests that these value systems give rise to quite different conceptualizations of the criminal justice process—conceptualizations he identifies as the crime control model and the due process model. The crime control model, according to Packer, is "based on the proposition that the repression of criminal conduct is by far the most important function to be performed by the criminal process" (1968, p. 158). Anything that promotes the efficient operation of this "people-processing" approach is seen to contribute to the maintenance of public order and the individual freedom of law-abiding citizens. Conversely, anything that detracts from technical efficiency is viewed as a potential threat to the security of individuals and society. For example, court decisions that restrict the use of wiretaps and other forms of electronic surveillance, that guarantee the accused a right to counsel at the beginning of the criminal process, or that curb the admissibility of evidence obtained illegally are often criticized as hindrances to law enforcement.

Implicit in (the crime control) model is the assumption that the screening performed by police and prosecutors separates a substantial majority of the innocent from those probably guilty of criminal offenses. Thus, it is the presumption of guilt that makes it possible for the system to process large numbers of people rapidly, with more than 90 percent pleading guilty. Reduced to its essentials, this model provides an administrative fact-finding process that results in either exoneration of the suspect or the entry of a guilty plea.

The goals of the crime control model are sought, for the most part, in the punishment of offenders. Two theories that provide a rationale for punishment are retribution and utilitarianism (Grupp 1971). The theory of *retribution* holds that a person who violates the law deserves to be punished. This position, as discussed in chapter 11, is also known as the doctrine of "just deserts" (i.e., punished criminals get only what is coming to them).

The theory of *utilitarianism* argues that punishment can be justified only to the extent that it accomplishes some useful and worthwhile purpose—that is, to discourage people from law-violating behavior (deterrence), to curb opportunities for repeat offenses (incapacitation), or to encourage offenders to "turn over a new leaf" and seek to change themselves in a prosocial direction (rehabilitation). Utilitarian theory poses thorny problems for the judicial process. Reliable and valid empirical support for deterrence is difficult or impossible to demonstrate for most criminal activities; and many people have strong moral, philosophical, and pragmatic objections to policies based on incapacitation. The argument that punishment and rehabilitation are compatible is taken up in chapter 11.

If the crime control model conveys as assembly-line image, then the due process model—as Packer observes—looks much like an obstacle course:

> Each of its successive stages is designed to present formidable impediments to carrying the accused any further along in the process. Its ideology is not the converse of that underlying the Crime Control Model. It does not rest on the idea that it is not socially desirable to repress crime, although critics of its application have been known to claim so. Its ideology is composed of a complex of ideas, some of them based on judgments about the efficacy of crime control devices, others having to do with quite different considerations. The ideology of due process is far more deeply impressed on the formal structure of the law than is the ideology of crime control .... (1968 p. 163).

Due process, which is deeply rooted in English common law, asserts that defendants must be formally notified of any charges placed against them. Defendants must be given an opportunity to confront their accusers and witnesses, to present evidence in their own defense, and to have this proof assessed by an impartial jury of their peers under the guidance of an impartial judge. In addition, they have a right to be represented by counsel.

The due process model rejects punishment as an appropriate goal of the criminal justice system. Instead, the model seeks rehabilitation of the offender, asserting that, in order to accomplish the tasks of rehabilitation, not only must individuals be protected against the power of the state, but they must also have access to the resources of society—resources they have been denied. Punishment and rehabilitation are seen as incompatible.

As a result of concepts in the due process model, the criminal justice system may at times seem unwieldy and inefficient in its operation. Yet it is this very lack of efficiency that expresses an abiding American value. As stated in *The Challenge of Crime in a Free Society:*

> Unquestionably adherence to due process complicates, and in many instances handicaps, the work of the courts. They could be more efficient—in the sense that the likelihood and speed of conviction would be greater—if the constitutional requirements of due process were not so demanding. But the law rightly values due process over efficient process. And by permitting the accused to challenge its fairness and legality at every stage of his prosecution, the system provides the occasion for the law to develop in accordance with changes in society and society's ideals (President's Commission on Law Enforcement and Administration of Justice 1967, p. 125).

The system may allow the guilty to go unpunished in some cases, but it safeguards other defendents in cases of questionable merit.

Summary

The problems of crime and how to cope with crime rank high as a national priority. Although earlier periods in our history may have been more lawless and violent than today, crime is still a major concern for many people. And though losses due to crimes of the "upper world" ("crimes in the suites") and syndicated crime far exceed losses due to conventional crimes such as larceny and burglary, it is "crime in the streets" that people fear most. Frustration and anger result when newspaper and television accounts imply that police waste valuable time and resources enforcing laws against consensual crimes such as gambling and prostitution.

As defined by the National Advisory Commission on Criminal Justice Standards and Goals, we have two criminal justice systems: Criminal Justice System 1, a formal, official, and highly visible system, and Criminal Justice System 2, an unofficial, less visible network of public and private agencies. The goal of System 2 is to reduce or prevent crime. The formal functions of the criminal justice system, described in this chapter, begins with the broad discretionary powers of the police and proceeds through the initiation of prosecution, the courts, and corrections. Problems faced by the correctional system have in part lead to the increasing use of alternatives to confinement, wherever possible, for nonviolent offenders. The concluding portion of the chapter was devoted to a description of the competing philosophies or value systems in American criminal law, one of the principal sources of intramural conflict in the criminal justice system.

issue paper

HIGH-TECH CRIME—
A GLIMPSE AT A POSSIBLE FUTURE

Police and criminals constantly compete with one another to exploit the fruits of science and technology. Chemistry, physics, and other branches of the natural sciences contribute to *criminalistics,* the generic term for the science and technology of criminal investigation. Laboratory applications of scientific developments in these fields have produced an array of investigative techniques ranging from ballistics and toxicology to voice print identification and handwriting analysis. The expert witness is often a medical specialist or a person with a doctorate in one of the sciences; many of the larger metropolitan police agencies retain such experts on staff.

The competition is by no means one-sided, however. Criminals are alert to new products and possibilities. When the cordless electric drill was introduced, burglars started using them to gain ready access to residential and commercial buildings. Helicopters have been used in prison breaks, and two convicts escaped from a federal maximum security prison at Marion, Illinois, by neutralizing an electronic security system with a device made in the prison workshop.

Few areas of scientific and technological development can match the impact of the computer revolution. Already the computer has begun to reshape the world. And there is every reason to believe that is will also revolutionize crime. The advent of the computer made the crime of embezzlement easier to commit and harder to detect. The theft of computer time has created new variants on the older common-law crimes of larceny and trespass. Thus computers, a valuable resource to business, industry, and government, provide matchless opportunities for criminal exploitation. Electronic data processing (EDP) crimes are wide ranging, because computer data banks generally contain information that encompasses the full scope of a business operation. Consequently, computer abuse "can take the form of embezzlement, misappropriation of computer time, theft of programs, and illegal acquisition of such proprietary information as marketing plans and forecasts, product design, secret manufacturing processes, and confidential technical data" (Chamber of Commerce of the United States 1974, p. 20). Whatever the cost of computer crime—and it has been estimated in the billions of dollars—it seems likely that such crime will increase. More than 3 percent of the total work force in the United States is now employed in computer-related jobs. And the figure continues to grow.

EDP crimes require much more sophistication and technical skill than more commonplace forms of theft. The typical "electronic criminal" is male, highly motivated, bright, energetic, and generally young (eighteen to thirty years old) (Parker and Nycum 1974). He is often the master of a technical expertise that borders on esoterica. In fact, he may find it difficult to explain the details of his crime to someone with less detailed knowledge of computer operations (Farr 1975).

The following case suggests con games:

> At Citibank cash dispensers in New York City and surrounding suburbs, an imaginative con man's scheme depleted accounts of $92,000—with the unwitting assistance of the victims. The scheme worked like this: the con man, posing as a customer, stands between two cash terminals and pretends to be talking on the service phone. A legitimate customer comes in and inserts his card into one of the terminals, only to be told by the con man that the machine isn't working. The customer withdraws his card, leaving the first machine activated, and inserts his card into the second machine. The con man

looks on surreptitiously as the customer enters his personal identification number and completes his transaction. Then, still holding the phone, the con man enters the same number and a withdrawal order on the first machine. To complete the theft, he must get the legitimate customer to insert the card once more into the first machine, and he does this by claiming that customer service thinks there is something wrong with his card. Three hundred seventy-four customers cooperated, and the courteous, well-spoken con man got away with their money (Coniff 1982, p. 62).

The persuasive power of the mere mention of the term "computer" works to the advantage of the electronic con man. Farr (1975) relates the case of a woman in Cincinnati, Ohio, who paid for purchases in several shops by check, identifying herself in each instance by presenting her bank card. While chatting with a neighbor en route to the parking lot, the woman was stopped by a man who accused her of passing a phony check: " 'We've had a negative report on your bank check card from the computer.' " The magic word "computer" implied that an infallible machine had discovered an act of wrongdoing. While the flustered woman and her friend waited in the parking lot, the man took her checkbook, bank card, and enough money to cover the last check she had written. " 'This will show your good faith,' " he told her. " 'Perhaps I can clear up the matter for you.' "

After waiting for nearly half an hour for the man to return, the two women went into the store to check on the whereabouts of the bank card and checkbook. As soon as the store manager heard their story, he advised them to contact the bank and the police. By the time the victim reported the matter to the bank, however, the con man and his accomplices had purchased goods worth $170 with her checks. The woman commented sadly, " 'My bank covered the loss because I informed them immediately. But I was so upset by being conned that I had nightmares about it for more than a month' " (p. 3).

KIDNAPPING—BY COMPUTER

R. Coniff Science Digest

At age 24 and with 6 arrests on his record, Masatoshi Tashiro was one of Tokyo's petty thieves, no more, no less. It wasn't likely that he would commit the Crime of the Century. Not of *this* century, anyway. But Tashiro did make himself a harbinger of the way criminals will work, and (to his chagrin) of the way criminals will be foiled, in the electronic world of the year 2000. He did it by computerizing the ancient crime of kidnapping, a centuries-old felony.

It started with a cash-card account, which he opened under a false name and address at a major Tokyo bank. With this magnetically coded card, depositors could make withdrawals as large as $1,000 at a time from any of 348 automatic cash dispensers located throughout Japan. Tashiro made several test withdrawals. By phoning the bank afterward, he determined that it took the computer system at least 20 minutes to tell the bank which cash dispenser station he had used. That crucial lag would be his getaway time.

Tashiro chose as his victim the four-month-old daughter of a well-known Japanese movie actor. The abduction itself was conventional—a break-in and escape while the family slept—but the ransom demand was brilliantly original. The parents were to deposit $16,500 in Tashiro's cash-card account; he gave them the account number and the false name as calmly as if he were making a real-estate deal.

His reasoning quickly became apparent to the police. They might be able to cover 348

R. Coniff, "Twenty-First Century Crime-Stoppers," *Science Digest* 90 (1982):61, by permission of the author and the publisher.

cash dispenser stations, but they would not know the one from which the kidnapper was operating until the computer told them so at least 20 minutes too late. Under the circumstances, the missing child's parents had little choice except to deposit the ransom money. First, though, the police made a countermove: they had the bank computer reprogrammed. Its new instructions were to trace any withdrawal from the ransom account instantly. When Tashiro made his first withdrawal, word flashed immediately to the central computer and from there, by radio, back to the stakeout team. The kidnapper was arrested as he strolled out of the dispenser station with the card and the cash in his hands. Shortly afterward, police recovered the missing baby from his home.

The computer criminal. Courtesy Donna Ward for Science News.

The relationship between computers and feelings of frustration or even rage has been demonstrated both in the United States and abroad. In Olympia, Washington, someone fired shots into the computer at the State Unemployment Office; in Johannesburg, South Africa, a similar incident occurred with a tax-processing computer; and antiwar demonstrators in Melbourne, Australia, "shotgunned to death" an American-made computer, leaving it a total loss (Swanson and Territo 1980).

The nature of evidence in computer offenses creates special difficulties from the standpoint of detection and investigation. For example, a single computer tape may contain more information than an entire shelf of books. This not only makes evaluation more difficult, but it also allows evidence to be destroyed easily and information to be "booby-trapped" (if an investigator tries to retrieve booby-trapped material, the material is automatically lost). For example, when the perpetrators of the famous Equity Funding swindle—which fabricated 64,000 phony insurance policies worth $1 billion—were caught, they had a computer program available that could have erased all of the evidence against them.

The problems of computer crime have prompted a search for new and increasingly sophisticated approaches to computer security. One approach is to code or encrypt information so that only people with keys can unscramble the data. Such systems are available to protect stored information, and even the owners of personal computers can buy encryption devices to keep their private affairs private. But, as Peterson (1982) points out, there is no absolute security in electronic safeguards: in the end, the human element is the ultimate weakness. Quoting a well-known expert in the field, Peterson claims that "the most effective way to break into a secure computer system is with a bribe . . . or by introducing a pretty woman or a handsome man to the right computer operator" (p. 14).

Discussion and review

1. What evidence is there to suggest that fear of crime is widespread in America?
2. Is violent crime more prevalent today than 100 years ago?
3. Which crimes are the most expensive for our society? Are these the same crimes people fear most?
4. Discuss Edelhertz's fourfold classification of white-collar and economic crimes. Do you believe it is more effective to sentence white-collar criminals to prison than to levy fines or use alternatives to imprisonment?
5. Why has political crime become an issue in recent years? What kinds of illegal activity are included by Roebuck and Weeber under this heading?
6. Why are some consensual or public-order offenses referred to as "victimless" crimes? Are they really without victims?
7. Distinguish between Criminal Justice System 1 and Criminal Justice 2, as defined by the National Advisory Commission on Criminal Justice System Standards and Goals. What are the major components of System 1?
8. Why is discretion so important in the criminal justice system?
9. Identify some of the community and transitional release programs available as alternatives to incarceration.
10. Distinguish between the crime control model and the due process model. How do these models help us understand conflicts within the criminal justice system?
11. Is crime by computer a new kind of criminal activity or merely a variation on older crimes?

Glossary

Consensual crime   Illegal acts in which the parties willingly participate in a transaction involving the sale or gift of desired goods or services (e.g., gambling or prostitution).

Criminal justice system   The complex of institutions and agencies responsible for controlling crime. The system includes the police, the prosecution, the courts, and corrections.

Economic crime   Illegal acts committed by nonphysical means and by concealment or guile to obtain money or property, to avoid the payment or loss of money or property, or to obtain business or personal advantage. *See also* White-collar crime.

Ethnic succession   A concept asserting that each group of immigrants to the United States used organized (syndicated) crime to acquire wealth and power before gaining a foothold in legitimate business.

Organized crime   A business that provides illegal, but desired, goods and services for the noncriminal public. Also known as *syndicated crime*.

Political crime   Illegal acts against the government (e.g., treason, sedition, or rebellion) or illegal acts committed by agents of government against individuals, groups, or the general public.

Public-order offense   An illegal act in which the offender engages in behavior that is not markedly different from conventional behavior (e.g., gambling or public intoxication) and which differs from many other crimes only to the extent that it usually involves only the offender. *See also* Consensual crime, Victimless crime.

Recidivist From the French *récidiver* ("to repeat"); a *recidivist* is an individual who shows commitment to criminality by repeated arrests and convictions.

Victimless crime Illegal acts between consenting adults (e.g., prostitution or homosexual behavior) that are presumed not to cause any direct harm, loss, or injury to anyone and in which there is no "victim" in the ordinary sense (as there is in robbery or burglary). *See also* Public-order offense, Consensual crime.

White-collar crime Originally used to designate offenses committed by "a person of respectability and high social status in the course of his occupation" (Sutherland 1949). The term is now being replaced by more specific terms such as *economic crime, occupational crime,* and *corporate crime.*

References

Anable, D. "World Terrorism: Tackling the International Problem." *Current Affairs* 179 (1976):51–60.

Baker, N. "The Prosecutor: Initiator of Prosecution." *Journal of Criminal Law, Criminology, and Police Science* 23 (1933):771–80.

Bard, M., and Ellison, K. "Crisis Intervention and Investigation of Forcible Rape." *Police Chief* 41 (1974):68–74.

Barnes, H. E., and Teeters, N. K. *New Horizons in Criminology.* Englewood Cliffs, N.J.: Prentice-Hall, 1959.

Bilek, A. J. *Private Security.* Cincinnati, Ohio: Anderson, 1977.

Blackmore, J. "Does Community Corrections Work? From the Experts, a Resounding 'Maybe.'" *Corrections Magazine* 7 (1981):15-18, 21-27.

Chamber of Commerce of the United States. *White Collar Crime: Everyone's Problem, Everyone's Loss.* Washington, D.C.: Chamber of Commerce of the United States, 1974.

Chandler, R. *The Long Goodbye.* Boston: Houghton Mifflin, 1954.

Clark, B. "Is Law Enforcement Headed in the Right Direction?" *Police* 12 (1968):31–34.

Clinard, M. B., and Quinney, R. *Criminal Behavior Systems: A Typology.* New York: Holt, Rinehart and Winston, 1973.

Coffey, A., Eldefonso, E., and Hartinger, W. *An Introduction to the Criminal Justice System and Process.* Englewood Cliffs, N.J.: Prentice-Hall, 1974.

Coniff, R. "Twenty-First Century Crime-Stoppers." *Science Digest* 90 (1982):60–65.

Conklin, J. E. *The Impact of Crime.* New York: Macmillan, 1975.

Conklin, J. E. *Criminology.* New York: Macmillan, 1980.

Edelhertz, H. *The Nature, Impact, and Prosecution of White Collar Crime.* Washington, D.C.: U.S. Government Printing Office, 1970.

Farr, R. *The Electronic Criminal.* New York: McGraw-Hill, 1975.

Grupp, S., ed. *Theories of Punishment.* Bloomington, Ind.: Indiana University Press, 1971.

Kaplan, J. *Criminal Justice: Introductory Cases and Materials.* Mineola, N.Y.: Foundation Press, 1973.

Law Enforcement Assistance Administration (LEAA). *Manpower Survey of the Criminal Justice System: Executive Summary.* Washington, D.C.: U.S. Government Printing Office, 1978.

Lewis, P.L., Mannle, H., Vetter, H.J., and ALlen, H.E. "A Post-Furman Profile of Florida's Condemned: A Question of Discrimination in Terms of the Race of the Victim and a Comment on *Spinkelink* v. *Wainwright.*" *Stetson Law Review* 9 (1979):1-45.

Morris, N. *The Future of Imprisonment.* Chicago: University of Chicago Press, 1974.

National Advisory Commission on Criminal Justice Standards and Goals. *Corrections.* Washington, D.C.: U.S. Government Printing Office, 1973.

National Advisory Commission on Criminal Justice Standards and Goals. *Criminal Justice System.* Washington, D.C.: U.S. Government Printing Office, 1973.

Office of Juvenile Justice and Delinquency Prevention (OJJDP). *A National Assessment of Serious Juvenile Crime and the Juvenile Justice System: The Need for a Rational Response.* Washington, D.C.: U.S. Government Printing Office, 1980.

Pace, D.F., and Styles, J.C. *Organized Crime: Concepts and Control.* Englewood Cliffs, N.J.: Prentice-Hall, 1983

Packer, H. L. *Limits of the Criminal Sanction.* Palo Alto, Calif.: Stanford University Press, 1968.
Parker, D. B. *Crime by Computer.* New York: Scribner's, 1976.
Parker, D. B., and Nycum, S. "The New Criminal." *Datamation,* January 1974, pp. 56–58.
Peterson, I. "Computer Crime: Insecurity in Numbers." *Science News* 122 (1982):12–14.
President's Commission on Law Enforcement and Administration of Justice. *The Challenge of Crime in a Free Society.* Washington, D.C.: U.S. Government Printing Office, 1967.
President's Commission on Law Enforcement and Administration of Justice. *Task Force Report: The Police.* Washington, D.C.: U.S. Government Printing Office, 1967.
Roebuck, J., and Weeber, S. C. *Political Crime in the United States: Analyzing Crime By and Against Government.* New York: Praeger, 1978.
Silberman, C. E. *Criminal Violence, Criminal Justice.* New York: Random House, 1978.
Sutherland, E.H. *White Collar Crime.* New York: Dryden Press, 1949.
Swanson, C. R., and Territo, L. "Computer Crime: Dimensions, Types, Causes, and Investigation." *Journal of Police Science and Administration* 8 (1980):304–11.
Wright, J.D., and Rossi, P.E. "Weapons and Violent Crime." Research project conducted for the National Institute of Justice, U.S. Department of Justice, Washington, D.C., as reported in *Police and Security Bulletin,* January 1982, p. 3

Notes

1. "The self is an abstract concept: sometimes called ego. It is the sum of what and who a person feels he is. A large part of the concept of self involves the body and the way in which one feels about the body, but it also includes such extensions of self as clothing, automobile, and home. For example, this may be expressed in such ways as: 'that's just the sort of home I expect him to have'" (Bard and Ellison 1974, p. 70).

2. *Plea bargaining* refers to the practice by which a prosecutor deals with a defendant to obtain information about other crimes or other offenders, or, in a situation in which the case is weak, to get the defendant to plead guilty to a lesser charge. Plea negotiation is discussed at length in chapter 8.

3. The *elements* of a crime refer to specific and precise statutory conditions of fact that must exist for a crime to have taken place. For example, it must be *dark* for "burglary in the night season" to take place.

4. *Appeal* refers to the removal of a case from an inferior court to a court of superior jurisdiction in order to obtain a review and retrial.

2
crime, deviance, and criminal law

SEVERAL

Laws and Orders

MADE AT A

GENERAL COURT

Held at Boston, February the 4th 1679/80.
EDWARD RAWSON Secretary.

Norms and socialization
Social sanctions
Normative variation

Social values and law
The value consensus and value conflict models
The value divergence model

Deviance

Law in historical perspective

Classification of crimes

Substantive criminal law
Foundations of criminal law
- Legality
- Actus reus
- Mens rea
- Concurrence of actus reus and mens rea
- Harm
- Causation
- Punishment

Characteristics of criminal law
- Politicality
- Specificity
- Uniformity
- Penal sanction

Criminal procedure
The Fourteenth Amendment
The Fourth Amendment: search and seizure
The Fifth Amendment: self-incrimination
The Sixth Amendment: right to counsel
The Rule of Law

Summary

Issue paper: Should consensual crimes be decriminalized?

LEGAL scholars may find it sufficient to define a crime as "any social harm defined and made punishable by law" (Perkins 1969, p. 9). But criminal justice authorities and criminologists are apt to find fault with such a definition. For one thing, crime is relative (i.e., behaviors covered by laws and statutes are not fixed and unchanging, but vary according to time, place, and circumstance). What the law says is illegal today may not be the same as what the law said was illegal yesterday—or what it may say is illegal tomorrow. Moreover, legal definitions of crimes would be unduly restrictive, because they would limit the study of criminal behavior to those persons who have been *officially adjudicated* (judged) "criminal" or "delinquent"; hence, much behavior that may be relevant to understanding and explaining criminal behavior might never be examined.

While recognizing the need on legal grounds to deal with crime as law-violating behavior, criminal justice professionals and criminologists find it worthwhile to consider criminal conduct as part of a much broader spectrum of *deviant behavior*. Deviance involves behavior that varies or diverges from social *norms*—the rules that regulate conduct within a group or society. Most people tend to be "socially invisible" within their communities; deviance means, among other things, that an individual or group becomes visible to the majority when the deviant behavior elicits a societal reaction.

Norms and socialization

The *norms* of a society may be simple or elaborate, but their purpose is the same: to protect the society against disruption and to safeguard its basic structure and values. Members of a society internalize the norms through a complex process of social learning known as *socialization*.

The principal agency of socialization, and the basic unit of society, is the family. Much of a culture is transmitted to children by informal learning within the family. Speech patterns, customs, and social values are acquired through communication between the generations. As an individual develops and matures, peer-group associations assume increasing importance in socialization, often becoming a source of sharp conflict with parental norms (especially during the adolescent years).

Informal learning from interactions with family and peer-group members is augmented by formal school learning. As agents of socialization, schools rank almost as high as the family and peer groups as a medium of societal perpetuation.

Social sanctions

Norms are acquired and maintained by a system of reward and punishment. When parents approve of their children's actions, they reward them with a smile, a caress, a murmur of praise, or a tangible reward of candy, cookies, or money. When children misbehave, parents mete out punishment ranging from a scolding to physical chastisement.

Rewards and punishments are incorporated into the normative structure as *social sanctions*. Sanctions may contain proscriptive or prescriptive elements. *Proscriptions* are statements of forbidden behavior (e.g., murder, rape, kidnapping, treason, and other rebellions against group authority). *Prescriptions* are statements of encouraged or reinforced behavior (e.g., getting married, raising children, holding down a steady job, paying taxes, and other forms of conduct that foster the common welfare).

Figure 2.1 illustrates how social sanctions promote "proper" behavior. Behavior toward the center of the continuum of social behavior is controlled by social norms called *folkways*. These social rules are usually enforced by *mild disapproval* (a cold stare, raised eyebrows, a reproving glance) or by *mild encouragement* (a smile, applause, an approving glance). Behavior that threatens the existence of the group or is seen as necessary to the perpetuation of the group is controlled by a set of stronger norms called *mores*. Mores are enforced by more rigorous or severe expressions of social disapproval (verbal abuse, beatings, temporary ostracism) or by greater encouragement (monetary rewards, praise, testimonials, promotions).

Normative variation

Norms do not set out a blueprint for behavior; at best, they provide a rough sketch. As Williams points out, "The institutionalized norms of social conduct never fully define concrete action. A norm is a standard (not necessarily explicit) for the course that action *should* follow, not a description of the action that actually occurs" (1970, p. 413). Norms are general; the situations within which behavior occurs, specific. Hence, behavior can vary considerably around a standard.

Note also that modern societies are composed of diverse subcultures with different norms and standards. Thus, behavior that deviates from presumably general or universal norms often involves a subcultural conflict.

Social values and law

In primitive or preliterate societies, rules governing normative behavior are perpetuated by word of mouth and passed from leader to leader. Even-

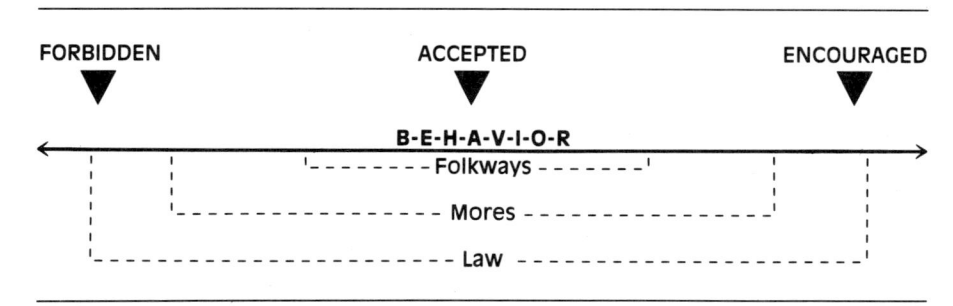

FIGURE 2.1
Continuum of social behavior.

tually, normative expectations evolve into formal statements of proper behavior that are written and codified as laws. These formal statements, which usually express the most important social values at the time, relate to objects, conditions, or states that are considered desirable and good and for which people are willing to expend time and energy to own or achieve.

The value consensus and value conflict models

The relationship between social values and laws has been interpreted in two sharply differing ways: the *value consensus model* and the *value conflict model*. The basic premise of the value consensus model is that the criminal law reflects societal values that extend beyond the interests of particular individuals or groups and can therefore be considered an expression of the social consciousness of the entire society. According to this perspective, law develops through the efforts of a unified society to preserve and protect social values. Toward this purpose, the law relies on the deliberations and rational decisions of governing bodies (such as congresses or parliaments) that incorporate the principal authority of the society (Hall, 1949).

In contrast, the value conflict model sees dissension rather than consensus, diversity rather than homogeneity—and a perennial struggle for power. As stated by Chambliss:

> Conventional myths notwithstanding, the history of criminal law is *not* a history of public opinion or public interest being reflected in criminal law legislation. On the contrary, the history of the criminal law is everywhere the history of legislation and appellate-court decisions which in effect (if not in intent) reflect the interests of the economic elites who control the production and distribution of the major resources of the society (1973 p. 430).

Economic power bestows political power, a fact reflected in this wry twist on the Golden Rule: "Them that has the gold makes the rules." According to the value conflict model, "the rules" (i.e., the law) become a tool of the dominant class to maintain and enhance its power over the weak. Law is used by the state "and its elitist government to promote and protect itself" (Quinney 1974, p. 24). One way this is done through criminal law is controlling enforcement so that certain groups are singled out and labeled as "criminals" and "members of the dangerous classes."

It is difficult to accept either the value consensus or the value conflict model as an exclusively accurate characterization of the social processes underlying the development of criminal law. Despite Quinney's assertion that the standards for what ought to be considered criminal conduct are a reflection of various group and class definitions, it appears that a consensus on crimes against the person cuts across class lines in our society. Disagreement is more likely to be found with regard to laws proscribing gambling, abortion, prostitution, and homosexual behavior between consenting adults—the offenses often designated as victimless crimes.

The value divergence model

A third position, called the *value divergence model*, recognizes the contributions of both the value conflict and value consensus models. It emphasizes that the United States is not a cultural monolith but a mosaic of diverse subcultures held together by shared beliefs and social values. It further maintains that the aggregate is stronger than the forces of divisiveness. Yet seldom in our pluralistic society can any body of statutes claim the support and allegiance of a majority of social groups.

Political scientist Stanley J. Makielski, in *Pressure Politics in America*, deals with the processes by which an *interest group*—"a collection of more than two people who interact on the basis of a commonly shared concern" (1980, p. 17)—is transformed into a *pressure group* that turns to the political system to press its demands. He defines *interests* as "the cement that binds a group together and the motivating power which impels a group into politics" (p. 21); these economic, social, or ideological interests are the base for structuring the policy concerns that characterize various groups. More importantly, the various *ways* in which pressure groups gain access through persuasion, mutual interest, established relationship, domination, or outright purchase provide the key to how such groups influence legislative activity to bring statutory changes in the law.

Deviance

Deviance is not a fundamental property of human behavior; rather, it is an attribute of certain kinds of conduct. It is a discretionary term in that it can be ascribed to almost any behavior departing from customary standards or expectations. For example, a student who attends a college commencement ceremony in the headgear of a Sorcerer's Apprentice rather than a traditional mortarboard is acting in a deviant manner. So was the woman in this example:

HOW SWEET IT IS!

SANTA CRUZ, California (AP)—A 30-year-old woman, spurned in love, disguised herself as a chocolate Easter bunny Friday and tried to hop into her neighbor's heart, but wound up under psychiatric observation instead, police said.

A city police officer, who asked not to be identified, said he was investigating a complaint of a disturbance at a man's home when he spotted what looked like a tall, chocolate rabbit coming "hippity-hoppity" out of the yard.

After a closer look, the officer discovered it was a female neighbor who had covered her nude body with chocolate glaze.

The man told the officer he had called police because of the woman's romantic advances over the last few months.

From *The Tampa Tribune*, 5 April 1980.

Schur states that human behavior is deviant "to the extent that it comes to be viewed as involving a personally discreditable departure from a group's normative expectations and elicits interpersonal or collective reactions that serve to isolate, treat, correct, or punish individuals engaged in such behavior" (1971, p. 24). This definition asserts that a deviant's behavior is regarded negatively by others and that the response to the behavior has the effect of either changing or suppressing the behavior or punishing the person who exhibits it.

Deviance is also a matter of degree: cheating on an income tax return and committing armed robbery are both viewed as deviant behavior; but the robber is much more likely to be condemned and punished than the tax violator. As emphasized in Schur's statement, normative violations do not have equally adverse effects on an individual's identity. Large sectors of society are tolerant of, or even sympathetic toward, tax violators; but robbery is universally condemned as a violent crime. People who commit such crimes are apt to be scarred for the rest of their lives.

Schur's definition also identifies possible reactions of individuals or groups to those who engage in deviant behavior. Reactions vary according to how serious a threat to basic social values the deviance is perceived, whether the deviance is viewed as voluntary or something beyond the doer's control, and whether the behavior ceases to be objectionable to a large minority, or even a majority, of people in the society. During the 1960s and 1970s, for example, alcoholism came to be viewed by both the

One aspect of deviant behavior is that it differs from the behavior expected in a particular situation. Courtesy Ellis Herwig/ Stock, Boston.

courts and the general public as a disease. Although public drunkenness continued to be subject to criminal sanctions, the movement of alcoholism from the category of criminality to the category of illness allowed people to be treated rather than punished. Other acts—such as participation in labor unions, divorce, and doing business on Sunday—have undergone a shift from condemnation, to tolerance, and finally to public approval.

In summary, the deviance of an act or an individual is relative, changeable, and a matter of degree, depending on the public's perception of, and response to, the behavior. The analysis of social definitions of, and responses to, these types of behavior has come to be known as the *labeling perspective*.

Law in historical perspective

Durant (1950) identifies four stages in the development of law: (1) personal revenge; (2) fines; (3) courts; and (4) assumption by the state of the obligation to prevent and punish wrongdoing. Revenge is embodied in the ancient principle of *lex talionis* (talion law), a phrase apparently devised by Cicero. Talion law, or "law of equivalent retaliation," was incorporated in the Babylonian Code of Hammurabi (circa 1800 B.C.), in Roman law, and in the Mosaic demand of "an eye for an eye and a tooth for a tooth." As Durant points out, talion law "lurks behind most legal punishments even in our own day" (1950, p. 27).

In operation, talion law does not *demand* retaliatory justice by depriving the perpetrator of an eye for one lost by the victim; rather, it limits the victim's legitimate claim to *no more* than an eye for the lost eye—not a tooth, an ear, or an arm, as well. Durant claims that the Abyssinians were so meticulous in this form of justice that when a boy fell from a tree, fatally injuring his companion below, judges decided that justice could only be satisfied by allowing the bereaved mother to send another of her sons to the same tree to fall upon the offender's neck.

The concept of equivalent retaliation is present today in the idea of penalties being proportionate to the gravity or severity of the offense (i.e., "letting the punishment fit the crime"). A modern version of talion law is now in effect in the Islamic republic of Iran.

THE TALION LAW, MOSLEM STYLE

In an effort to rid Iranian society of undesirable foreign influences, Islamic fundamentalists led by the Ayatollah Khomeini have returned to the kind of criminal sanctions advocated by the Koran (the holy book of Islam) and the sayings of the Prophet Mohammed. As a result, a 199-article bill known as the Law of Punishment was passed by the Iranian parliament in 1981 to establish severe penalties for murder, assault, sodomy, adultery, and drunkenness.

The bill goes to great lengths to specify fair retaliation. For example, Article 62 states: "The equality of body parts applies in the

Law of Punishment. This means that for the punishment of someone who cuts the right hand off someone else, only the right hand of the offender should be cut off. If the offender does not have a right hand, then the left hand can be cut off, and if he has neither right nor left hands, then one of his legs can be severed." For knife wounds and similar injuries, the bill specifies that punishment should be "in the same place, the same length and width and if possible the same depth." It empowers an Islamic court judge to order hair shaved to obtain "good implementation."

In Kerman, in southeastern Iran, two middle-aged women and two men—a young farmer and a worker with six children—were found guilty of prostitution, adultery, sodomy, and rape. First they were visited by Iranian clergymen, washed and clothed in white and masked with ceremonial "hoods of the dead." Then workmen buried them in earth up to their chests, and rocks, ranging in size from nuts to baseballs, were assembled not far away. The presiding judge threw the first stone; then, five onlookers bombarded each of the condemned persons with rocks. Fifteen minutes later, all four were pronounced dead.

Based on material reported in "Q'sas—The Law of Punishment," *Tampa Tribune*, November 12, 1982, p. 11A, and "Death by stoning for sex crimes," *Newsweek*, July 14, 1980, p. 40.

In the second stage of the development of law, the physical assault of talion law was replaced by fines, or the award of the appropriate damages as a means to secure equivalent retaliation. This principle is used today in some criminal cases and in cases involving civil injuries. The famous trial lawyer Melvin Belli once presented an artificial leg to a jury in a personal injury suit; he asked members of the jury how much money they would consider adequate payment for a lost limb.

Fines or settlements paid to avert personal revenge require some deliberation and adjudication of offenses and damages. Courts—a third natural development of the law—were established in response to this need. Early courts were not always judgment seats as we know them today; many were boards of voluntary conciliation. And if an offended party was dissatisfied with a court verdict, he or she was still free to seek personal revenge.

In the Middle Ages, disputes were settled through *trial by ordeal*, a practice that persisted into the twentieth century in the form of duels. Durant believes that "the primitive mind resorted to an ordeal not so much on the medieval theory that a diety would reveal the culprit as in the hope that the ordeal, however unjust, would end a feud that might otherwise embroil the tribe for generations" (1950, p. 28). Trials by ordeal were often referred to as "ordeals of God."

TRIAL BY ORDEAL

In trial by ordeal, a primitive means of determining guilt or innocence, accused persons were submitted to dangerous or painful tests believed to be under divine or supernatural control. Escape from death or injury was ordinarily taken to be a vindication of the innocence of the accused as reflected by the judgment of God (*judicium* Dei). The most common forms of ordeal were the wager of battle (or trial by combat), in which the winner was held to be innocent; the ordeal of fire, in which the accused walked barefoot over hot coals or carried a red-hot iron in his or her hand; and trial by cold water (often applied to witches), in which the accused was immersed in water and pronounced guilty if he or she floated.

Another ordeal was the corsned trial, which involved placing hallowed bread (corsned) into the mouth of the accused; if the individual swallowed the wafer, he or she was freed from punishment. In the trial of the cross, accuser and accused were placed before a cross with their arms extended; the first person to move his hands or let his arms drop was considered guilty. In the judgment of the bier, used in murder trials, the corpse of the victim was placed on a bier and the accused was required to touch the body; if blood flowed or foam appeared at the mouth of the victim, the suspect was judged guilty.

Despite attempts to curb or abolish trial by ordeal in Europe, the practice continued into the fourteenth century. In England, forms of ordeal other than trial by combat were abolished by Henry III in the year 1219, following their condemnation by Pope Innocent III in 1216. However, the "ducking stool"—used to subject suspected witches to trial by water—was still used in colonial America as late as the seventeenth century.

The fourth advance in law, according to Durant, was the assumption by the state of the obligation to punish wrongdoing and protect the citizen. Crimes came to be regarded as offenses against the state, because their commission adversely affected the community. The state enlarged its domain of authority from merely settling disputes to making an effort to prevent them.

When the Normans invaded England in the eleventh century, they found among the defeated Saxons a well-developed and workable system for maintaining public order and administering justice. The system had evolved over a lengthy period and was based on a body of *common law* derived from the customs of collective experience of Saxon society. A principal feature was its reliance on precedents to continually refine and develop suitable legal responses to meet the needs of a growing and dynamic society.

The Norman ruler, William the Conqueror, imposed his own representatives on the existing system to consolidate his power and authority. Under the royal justices appointed by William, state law became common law—called such because it originated in the customary practices of the realm and was common to all of England. Common law was firmly embedded in custom and tradition, but it continued to evolve through the process of judicial decision making.

Civil law derived from Roman antecedents and even earlier attempts by Sumerian and Babylonian societies to provide formal rules for human conduct. Nearly two millenia before the birth of Christ, a Babylonian monarch named Hammurabi formulated a code that enunciated a series of offenses and accompanying penalties. The historical significance of the Code of Hammurabi rests in its effort to standardize the relationship between crime and punishment. From such beginnings, civil law evolved as a system based on written and legislated codes.

American criminal law combines features of both civil and common law. Statutes enacted by state legislatures and the Congress are a major source of criminal law in the United States. These laws are usually compiled in codes that sort or classify statutes under separate headings. State codes are usually subject to revision at annual legislative sessions. The criminal laws of any state are found in the state penal code. Thus, to find out how Florida defines the crimes of kidnapping and indecent exposure, and the penalties imposed for them, you would look in the newest version of the Florida Penal Code, as provided in the Florida Statutes Annotated §§ 787.01 and 800.02 (West Publishing Co. 1981):

CHAPTER 787
KIDNAPPING; FALSE IMPRISONMENT; CUSTODY OFFENSES

787.01	Kidnapping
787.02	False imprisonment
787.03	Interference with custody
787.04	Felony to remove children from state or to conceal children contrary to court order

787.01 Kidnapping

(1)(a) "Kidnapping" means forcibly, secretly, or by threat confining, abducting, or imprisoning another person against his will and without lawful authority, with intent to:

1. Hold for ransom or reward or as a shield or hostage.
2. Commit or facilitate commission of any felony.
3. Inflict bodily harm upon or to terrorize the victim or another person.
4. Interfere with the performance of any governmental or political function.

(b) Confinement of a child under the age of 13 is against his will within the meaning of subsection (1) if such confinement is without the consent of his parent or legal guardian.

(2) Whoever kidnaps a person is guilty of a felony of the first degree, punishable by imprisonment for a term of years not exceeding life or as provided in § 775.082, § 775.083, or § 775.084.

CHAPTER 800
CRIME AGAINST NATURE; INDECENT EXPOSURE

800.01	Repealed
800.02	Unnatural and lascivious act
800.03	Exposure of sexual organs
800.04	Lewd, lascivious or indecent assault or act upon or in presence of child

800.01 Repealed by Laws 1974, c. 74-121, § 1, eff. Oct. 1, 1974

800.02 Unnatural and lascivious act

Whoever commits any unnatural and lascivious act with another person shall be guilty of a misdemeanor of the second degree, punishable as provided in § 775.082 or § 775.083.

800.03 Exposure of sexual organs

It shall be unlawful for any person to expose or exhibit his sexual organs in any public place or on the private premises of another, or so near thereto as to be seen from such private premises, in a vulgar or indecent manner, or so to expose or exhibit his person in such place, or to go or be naked in such place. Provided, however, this section shall not be construed to prohibit the exposure of such organs or the person in any place provided or set apart for that purpose. Any person convicted of a violation hereof shall be guilty of a misdemeanor of the first degree, punishable as provided in § 775.082 or § 775.083.

As an offshoot of statutory law, *administrative law* is comprised of rulings by government agencies at the federal, state, and local levels. The legislative or executive branch invests a body such as a board of health with the authority to establish regulations governing specific policy areas (e.g., social problems or safety and health standards). Violations of administrative laws are handled by the criminal justice system.

The meaning and intent of criminal statutes are tested and interpreted within the context of specific cases. Thus, criminal law can be "created" by judges in their rulings on statutory laws. Known as *case law*, this kind of law is heavily influenced by the principle of *stare decisis* ("let the decision stand")—the rule that requires judges to follow precedent in judicial interpretations. Without this principle, as Eldefonso and Coffey observe, "the defendant in a civil or criminal case would never know whether or not his activities were lawful" (1981, p. 36). Nevertheless, prior decisions are sometimes overruled by the higher authority of a court of appeals, thus reversing or modifying existing case law.

Classification of crimes

Crimes are legally classified as *felonies* or *misdemeanors*. In general, felonies are more serious crimes that are punishable by death or incarceration for a year or more in a state prison. Misdemeanors are less serious and are punishable by a fine or a term of up to one year in a city or county jail. There are exceptions, however, as in North Carolina where misdemeanants are confined by the Department of Corrections.

The felony-misdemeanor distinction is crucial to the criminal justice system and process. As Robin points out, the classification of a crime as a felony or a misdemeanor will affect the following (1980, p. 10):

1 The conditions under which the police can make an arrest and the degree of force that will be authorized
2 The "charges" the prosecutor will ultimately press
3 The care exercised by the trial judge in accepting a guilty plea and admitting evidence into the record
4 The availability of procedural and constitutional safeguards
5 The quality of counsel and the conduct of the court
6 The determination of which court will have trial jurisdiction

7 The sentence that can be imposed
8 The type of institution to which an offender may be eommitted
9 The conditions of release from incarceration
10 The size of the jury
11 Whether a jury verdict must be unanimous

These factors have significant consequences for the defendant; in some cases, the outcome may be a matter of life or death.

Common law originally separated crimes that were "wrong in themselves" *(mala in se)* from those that were "wrong because they were prohibited" *(mala prohibita,* i.e., any act forbidden by statute but which otherwise did not shock the conscience of the community). Today, however, these classifications find little support from contemporary legal authorities or criminologists, who regard them as simplistic and naive.

Other classifications of crime include "crimes against nature," which, in the broadest sense, include carnal knowledge of an animal, sodomy, fellatio, cunnilingus, and intercourse in any position other than face to face (even between legally married partners). The reference to these acts as "crimes against nature" does not, of course, represent an indictment from nature itself; rather it is a value judgment by a legislative body as to what is "natural." For example, if we can repose any confidence in the many investigations of sexual behavior—from Alfred Kinsey to Masters and Johnson—we must conclude that a sexual experience regarded as "unnatural" in one segment of society may actually be the norm in another group.

Another classification of crime, "crimes against humanity," was developed at the end of World War II and used by the Allies in the trials of Nazi leaders at Nuremberg. The Nazi crimes (which included genocide) were seen as being of such magnitude and severity that the offenders should be compelled to answer to all of mankind, rather than to a specific country or jurisdiction. Years later, European peace groups applied this same concept to President Lyndon B. Johnson and members of his administration, trying them *in absentia* for alleged war crimes in Vietnam.

An offense can also be classified as a *private wrong,* called a "civil injury" or *tort,* or a *public wrong,* which falls under the rubric of criminal law. A public wrong is a violation of public order for which the community may take action. The punishment imposed is for the protection of the community, not for the redress of individual injury. Private parties must seek redress through a civil court action. When an individual or organization sues another to obtain a remedy or recompense for an alleged injury, the case is a civil action. When the state prosecutes an individual or organization for violating a legislative statute, the case is usually a criminal action.

In some cases, a single offense may give rise to both civil and criminal action. Assault and battery, for example, may result in a civil action by the victim to secure damages for injuries; and the state may file criminal charges to punish the guilty party by a fine or imprisonment.

Substantive criminal law

In our brief historical sketch of the antecedents of American criminal jurisprudence, we referred rather informally to "criminal law." It is time to abandon this casual usage in favor of the more exact designation *substantive criminal law*, as distinguished from *criminal procedure*.

Substantive criminal law is concerned with acts, mental states, and accompanying circumstances or consequences that constitute the necessary features of crimes. It identifies particular kinds of behavior (acts or omissions) as wrongs against society or the state and prescribes punishments to be imposed for such conduct. Any references in this book to "criminal law" are actually references to substantive criminal law.

Criminal procedure (as discussed later in this chapter) sets forth the *rules* that direct the application and enforcement of substantive criminal law. That is, criminal procedure lays the steps that officials—police, prosecutors, judges, corrections personnel, and others—must take in the administration of justice, from arrest to conviction and beyond.

Foundations of criminal law

Anglo-American criminal law is founded upon seven basic principles traditionally observed by legislatures and the courts in formulating and interpreting the substantive criminal law: (1) legality; (2) actus reus; (3) mens rea; (4) concurrence of actus reus and mens rea; (5) harm; (6) causation; and (7) punishment. These principles are summarized by Hall as follows: "The harm forbidden in a penal law must be imputed to any normal adult who voluntarily commits it with criminal intent, and such a person must be subjected to the legally prescribed punishment" (1947, p. 18).

Legality A crime is defined legally as "an intentional act or omission in violation of a criminal law, committed without defense or justification and sanctioned by the state as a felony or misdemeanor" (Tappan 1966, p. 10). The idea that there can be no crime unless a law exists that has been violated is embodied in the ancient Latin saying *Nullum crimen sine lege*—"no crime without a law." Legality is one of the most venerated concepts in Anglo-American criminal law.

Actus reus Thoughts alone do not constitute a crime. One can legally wish an enemy dead, fantasize a rape, or harbor thoughts about income tax evasion—as long as the thoughts do not result in an action *(actus reus)* to bring about the desired result. However, it is necessary to distinguish mere thoughts from *speech*, because a crime can be committed by an act of speech under our legal system. For example, because we consider individuals acting together to be a greater threat to society than a lone offender, we regard an *agreement* by two or more persons to commit a crime as an act of *criminal conspiracy*. Nevertheless, approximately half of the states require (by statute) that an act be committed *in furtherance of the conspir-*

acy (LaFave and Scott 1972, pp. 476–78). Other crimes that can be committed by acts of speech include perjury, solicitation, and false pretense.

Mens rea A further requirement for criminal conduct is the presence of a "guilty mind" *(mens rea)* in the actor. To demonstrate mens rea, it must be proven that an individual intentionally (purposefully), knowingly, recklessly, or negligently behaved in a given manner or caused a given result. For example, a bus driver who fails to stop at an intersection and causes a collision with an automobile entering from a cross street would not be charged with a crime if it could be proven that he was unaware his brakes were defective—that he had done everything he could to avert the accident. Similarly, a person who unknowingly buys stolen goods from a local merchant is not guilty of the criminal offense of receiving stolen property, because the element of intent is missing. On the other hand, a person who drives a sports car ninety miles an hour in a residential area and kills a young child may well be convicted of manslaughter, because his behavior constitutes a reckless disregard for associated risks. In an actual case, a nightclub owner was found criminally negligent and convicted of manslaughter for failing to provide adequate fire escapes, resulting in the death of many patrons during a fire. In affirming the owner's conviction, the court held that more than mere negligence was necessary, i.e., that "a grave danger to others must have been apparent." As the court stated, "even if a particular defendant is so stupid (or) so heedless . . . that in fact he did not realize the grave danger," he is guilty of manslaughter "if an ordinary normal man under the same circumstances would have realized the gravity of the danger" (*Commonwealth* v. *Welansky* [55 N.E. 2d 902(1944)], as cited in LaFave and Scott 1972, pp. 212–13).

Offenses that involve no mental element but consist only of forbidden acts or omissions are classified as *strict-liability offenses*. Thus, a statute may simply indicate that someone who does or omits a certain act, or who brings about a certain result, is guilty of a crime. Such statutes are justified on the grounds that although there is a need to control the behavior in question, convictions would be difficult to obtain if the prosecution had to prove fault. Examples of laws imposing liability without fault include liquor and narcotics laws, pure-food laws, and traffic laws.

The law recognizes that some groups of people are unable to attain the requisite mental state for crime. Children, mental defectives, and, in some cases, those diagnosed as mentally ill, are exempt from criminal responsibility because they are unable to appreciate the nature and quality of their behavior. Mens rea is also considered lacking when people act under coercion, defending themselves or others, or act under statutory authority, (e.g., the police officer acting in the line of duty).

Concurrence of actus reus and mens rea Another basic premise of criminal law is that the act and the mental state must *concur* for a crime to have been committed. The act and the mental state are not concurrent if they are separated by a considerable gap in time. A lack of concurrence between mental state and act is a strong argument that the mental state did not activate or cause the act.

> **CASE 2.1**
>
> Angry with Carol for stealing the affections of her boyfriend, Bob, Alice plans to kill both Carol and Bob with poisoned lemonade. But when she goes to Bob's apartment to invite the couple for a picnic, she finds they have eloped. Ten years later, at an intersection in Denver, Bob (who is color blind) runs a traffic light. He and Carol are killed instantly when their Honda motorcycle is totaled in a collision with a Cherokee Chief (with ski rack) driven by—none other than—Alice.
>
> Is Alice guilty of murder? No. There was no concurrence between the intent and the harmful conduct. Fate delivered the couple into Alice's hands.

Harm An additional requirement in the criminal law is that only conduct that is harmful in some way can be considered criminal. This idea is reflected in the concept of due process, which holds that a criminal statute is unconstitutional if it bears no reasonable relationship to the matter of injury to the public. It is important to recognize, however, that criminal harm is not restricted to *physical* injury. In cases of libel, perjury, and treason, no physical injury is inflicted. Thus, the criminal law must deal with intangibles, such as harm to institutions, public safety, autonomy of women, and reputation. In essence, criminal harm signifies loss of value, because an individual who commits a crime does something contrary to community values (Hall 1947).

Causation Causation relates to crimes that require that a defendant's conduct produce a given result. Crimes such as perjury or forgery are defined so that the crime consists of both the act itself and the intent to cause the harmful result—without regard to whether that result in fact occurs. On the other hand, offenses such as intent-to-kill murder and intent-to-injure battery require a specific result. In such cases, the defendant's conduct must be the "but for" cause of the result, and the harm that actually occurs must be similar enough to the intended result that the defendant can be held responsible.

In many instances, it is difficult for the prosecution to probe a causal connection between intent and harm. For example, if A, with intent to kill, drives a knife into the heart of B, a prosecutor would have no particular difficulty demonstrating that A's action was the cause of B's death. However, the matter of intended harm varies according to person, manner, and type of harm. For example, suppose that A shoots B and—believing B is dead—leaves B's body on the interstate. B is killed when C—who doesn't see B lying on the road—runs over him. Will A be convicted of B's murder? Only if it can be demonstrated that A's conduct was a substantial factor in bringing about B's death or that what happened to B was a foreseeable consequence of A's behavior.

The rule of causation has also been applied generally in cases of *felony murder*. At issue is whether an offender can be held responsible for unintended deaths that result from the perpetration of a crime. For example, suppose A sets out to rob storeowner B. During the robbery, B, acting to protect his property, fires at A and accidentally kills a customer. The robbery foiled, A runs out of the store and a police officer shoots at him, killing a bystander. Is A responsible for either or both of these deaths? In general, the courts have ruled that if the death is a natural and foreseeable consequence of the offense, the offender is liable (LaFave and Scott, 1972, pp. 263-264). Thus, A could be prosecuted for the death of both persons in the above example.

Punishment Under the American legal system, citizens must not only be warned as to what conduct is forbidden, but they must also be made aware of the consequences of their actions. Thus, the law stipulates the sanctions for every crime.

Characteristics of criminal law

Sutherland and Cressey (1978) identify four characteristics that distinguish criminal law from other rules affecting human conduct: (1) politicality; (2) specificity; (3) uniformity; and (4) penal sanction.

Politicality Criminal laws are enacted, modified, and repealed by duly elected legislative bodies. Yet in a pluralistic society with no system of universally shared social values, what is defined as criminal behavior during a given period depends largely on what conduct politically influential and powerful groups perceive as a threat to their values. Since the turn of century, for example, Prohibition has been enacted and repealed, abortion, gambling, and pornography laws have been liberalized, and laws dealing with the possession and sale of marijuana and other drugs have been enacted and modified. This element of change and influence is known as the *politicality* of criminal law.

Specificity *Specificity* means that laws must be stated in terms that clearly indicate what conduct is expected. For example, statutes that specify punishment for commonly understood offenses such as rape or robbery are usually quite clear, but a statute that prohibits "immoral acts" in general would be difficult to interpret. Any law that requires or prohibits the commission of an act in terms so vague that people of normal intelligence must guess at the meaning violates an essential requirement of due process. A long-standing objection to some statutes for juvenile offenses is that terms such as "incorrigible" or "ungovernable" are used without definition.

Uniformity "Justice" is often portrayed as a blindfolded female who weighs evidence for the guilt or innocence of those standing before her. The ideal in American criminal jurisprudence is that *uniformity* will prevail— that all persons adjudged by the law will be treated equally, regardless of their ethnic or national origins, religious convictions or affiliations, or social standing. The theory is noble, but in practice "some people are more equal than others."

Penal sanction As we have already seen, criminal statutes must not only give people fair warning of what behavior to avoid, but they must also convey some idea of the penalties incurred when laws are violated. In the broadest terms, the goal of punishment is to protect society, for the first duty of any government is to safeguard the lives and property of its citizens. No society that tolerates unrestrained theft and violence can endure for long. Given the propensity toward aggressive and predatory behavior in many human societies, few laws without penalty would be more honored by observance.

Criminal procedure

The U.S. Constitution is the most authoritative source of criminal procedure in our country. We are introduced as school children to the first ten amendments to the Constitution, known collectively as the Bill of Rights. Most Americans know that the Bill of Rights provides certain safeguards to American citizens, safeguards covered by such phrases as "due process" and "equal protection under the law." But we are less likely to know that safeguards for the rights of the accused were not applicable to state courts until the passage of the Fourteenth Amendment in 1868. Prior to the Fourteenth Amendment, the Bill of Rights applied directly only to proceedings in federal courts.

The Fourteenth Amendment

The Fourteenth Amendment to the U.S. Constitution declares, in part, that "no State shall make or enforce any law which shall abridge the privileges or immunities of citizens of the United States, nor shall any State deprive any person of life, liberty, or property, without due process of law; nor deny any person within its jurisdiction the equal protection of the law . . . ." Together with the Thirteenth and Fifteenth amendments, which were passed just after the Civil War, the Fourteenth Amendment extended citizenship to former slaves and guaranteed them the same protections of law provided for other citizens by the Constitution. But the due process and equal protection phrases of the Fourteenth Amendment were not immediately applied to civil rights. As late as the 1940s, state courts and the U.S. Supreme Court employed these features of the Fourteenth Amendment primarily to protect business corporations from government regulation.

In 1884, in the case of *Hurtado* v. *California* (110 U.S. 516), the Supreme Court rejected the "shorthand doctrine," which sought to bind the states to a blanket application of the Bill of Rights. The subsequent judicial history of the Fourteenth Amendment involved a continuing debate within the U.S. Supreme Court between proponents of a piecemeal application of the due process and equal protection provisions and those justices who supported viewpoints that inclined toward total incorporation. **Table 2.1** highlights the major positions that have been held within the Supreme Court or by legal scholars in interpreting the meaning and significance of due process.

From 1961 to 1969—a period often referred to as the "due-process revolution"—the U.S. Supreme Court took an activist role, becoming a giver of the law rather than just an interpreter. As Swanson and Territo (1983) point out, the Warren court's activist role in extending the provisions of the Bill of Rights to criminal proceedings in the states (via the due process clause of the Fourteenth Amendment) may have been a policy decision. The Supreme Court normally writes about 115 opinions in any term. During the 1938–39 term, only five of the cases appeared under the heading of criminal law; three decades later, however, during the height of the due-process revolution, about one fourth of all decisions related to criminal law.

Among the key Supreme Court decisions in the due-process revolution were *Mapp* v. *Ohio* (367 U.S. 643[1961]), *Gideon* v. *Wainwright* (372 U.S.

TABLE 2.1 Basic interpretations of the due process clause of the Fourteenth Amendment*

Ordered Liberty (Fundamental Fairness)	The due process clause applies only those "traditional notions" of due process, such as freedom of religion, speech, and press and procedural rights, that are "implicit in the concept of ordered liberty." The Fourteenth Amendment incorporates none of the guarantees of the Bill of Rights as such.
Total Incorporation	The due process clause includes *all* rights found in the Bill of Rights, but limits the inclusion to *only* those rights enumerated therein. No unenumerated rights are recognized.
Total Incorporation Plus (Ultraincorporation)	The due process clause encompasses *all* of the specific guarantees of the Bill of Rights *plus* any additional fundamental unenumerated rights that are properly classified as essential to "fairness and individual liberty" (e.g., the right of privacy).
Selective Incorporation	Combines aspects of both "ordered liberty" and "total incorporation" interpretations of the Fourteenth Amendment. Accepts the basic premise that the due process clause encompasses *all* rights that are "fundamental to the American system of justice." Recognizes that *not all* rights enumerated in the Bill of Rights are necessarily fundamental (e.g., grand jury indictments). However, this view also recognizes that other rights may be fundamental even though not specifically enumerated in the Bill of Rights (e.g., the right to terminate a pregnancy).
Neo-Incorporation	A "half-way house" between the ordered liberty and traditional incorporation approaches. According to this view, the fact that a procedural right is incorporated into the Bill of Rights does *not* make federal procedures binding on state criminal trials (e.g., unanimous jury verdicts required in federal criminal trials, but not in state criminal trials).

*Implicit in these traditional incorporation views is the idea that once any Bill of Rights' guarantee is "incorporated," it limits state authority in precisely the same way that the Bill of Rights directly limits federal authority. This is not true for neo-incorporation.

Adapted from P. W. Lewis and K. D. Peoples, *The Supreme Court and the Criminal Process—Cases and Comments* (Philadelphia, Pa.: W. B. Saunders, 1978), p. 102, by permission of the publisher.

335[1963]), *Escobedo* v. *Illinois* (375 U.S. 902[1964]), and *Miranda* v. *Arizona* (384 U.S. 436[1966]). These cases focused on the two vitally important areas of search and seizure and the right to counsel. Collectively, the cases constitute a watershed period in the administration of criminal justice in the United States.

The Fourth Amendment: Search and seizure

The Fourth Amendment to the Constitution guarantees people the right "to be secure in their persons, houses, papers, and effects, against unreasonable searches and seizures." It was not until 1914, however, that the Supreme Court, in the case of *Weeks* v. *United States* (232 U.S. 383), established the so-called Exclusionary Rule to govern the operation of the federal courts. According to the Exclusionary Rule, evidence obtained as a result of an unreasonable or illegal search is not admissible in a federal criminal prosecution.

The Exclusionary Rule curbed, but did not eliminate, abuse of the Fourth Amendment. Evidence obtained illegally by state law enforcement officers continued to find its way into federal prosecutions on the grounds that no federal official had participated in violating the defendant's rights. This type of federal-state search and seizure became known as the "silver platter" doctrine, a name that originated in Justice Frankfurter's decision in *Lustig* v. *United States* (338 U.S. 74[1949]). Frankfurter held that "the crux of that doctrine is that a search is a search by a federal official if he had a hand in it; it is not a search by a federal official if evidence secured by state authorities is turned over to the federal authorities on a silver platter." The Supreme Court condemned this practice with regard to criminal investigations in the case of *Elkins* v. *United States* (364 U.S. 206[1960]). Writing for the majority, Justice Stewart held that the "silver platter" doctrine constituted an "inducement to subterfuge and evasion" (p. 222).

In *Mapp* v. *Ohio*, the Exclusionary Rule was extended to the state courts, a reversal of the 1949 decision of *Wolf* v. *Colorado* (338 U.S. 25); the latter decision permitted the states to establish their own procedural safeguards against unreasonable search. In *Mapp* v. *Ohio*, the court held that

> ... all evidence obtained by searches and seizures in violation of the Constitution is, by that same authority, inadmissible in a state court. Since the Fourth Amendment's right of privacy has been declared enforceable against the States through the Due Process clause of the Fourteenth Amendment, it is enforceable against them by the same sanction of exclusion as is used against the Federal Government ... (p. 655).

An even broader extension of the Exclusionary Rule is the doctrine known as the "fruit of the poisonous tree." This doctrine prohibits the admission of evidence obtained *as a result* of an "illegal or initially 'tainted' admission, confession, or search" (Kerper 1972, p. 316). Assume, for example, that the police employed coercive methods to extract a confession from a suspect who names a second party as an accomplice in the illegal sale of narcotics. Using a properly executed search warrant, the police search the residence occupied by the second party and confiscate a quantity of heroin. In this case, the fact that the search was authorized by legal warrant does not validate the admission of the heroin as evidence, because the police obtained the information leading to the search and seizure in an unauthorized, or "tainted," manner.

Many law enforcement officials maintain that the chief purpose of the Exclusionary Rule is to punish police "misconduct" involving disregard of the Fourth Amendment. Although no one defends the proposition that police officers should be free to disregard the Constitution in pursuit of a conviction, it is argued that the Exclusionary Rule punishes good-faith mistakes made by honest, conscientious officers. Such mistakes include writing the wrong address on an affidavit or warrant or writing an incomplete description of premises to be searched.

In 1980, a federal appellate court recognized an exception to the Exclusionary Rule. In *United States* v. *Williams* (622 F.2d 830 [5th Cir. 1980]), the court held that

> ... evidence is not to be suppressed under the exclusionary rule where it is discovered by officers in the course of actions that are taken in good faith and in the reasonable, though mistaken, belief that they are authorized. We do so because the exclusionary rule exists to deter wilful or flagrant actions by police, not reasonable, good-faith ones. Where the reason for the rule ceases, its application must cease also (p. 840).

Civil libertarians believe that good faith exceptions to the Exclusionary Rule will result in wholesale abuses by the police. An opposing view is offered by a group called Americans for Effective Law Enforcement (AELE):

> Visions of police harrassment of innocent persons in their homes at 3:00 a.m., however dramatic, are not in issue. The "real" issue is the good faith mistake of a professionally trained officer, or an unnoticed minor error, or the retroactive effect of an overturned court precedent, or even a 3-to-2 decision that a particular law or procedure is "unconstitutional." Defense attorneys, who sometimes constitute the largest group of state legislators, have a vested interest in perpetuating the status quo.
>
> The real goal of criminal justice should be the encouragement of professional law enforcement and to obtain convictions of the guilty. A search for technicalities does not further that end. The good faith exception, however, encourages police professionalism and still punishes intentional misconduct or an indifferent attitude to the rights of society. Good faith legislation is the modification of a rigid rule that in no way affects its principal purpose (1982, p. 3).

The AELE believes that most problems raised by opponents of the good-faith exception can be resolved by statute. The organization has proposed a model statute in that regard, maintaining that the courts should be given as much direction and as little discretion as possible.

AELE MODEL STATE STATUTE

Adopted by *Americans for Effective Law Enforcement, Inc.*, 14 July 1982.

Exclusionary Rule Limitations: Admissibility of evidence obtained as a result of an unlawful search or seizure.

A. If a party in a proceeding, whether civil or criminal, seeks to exclude evidence from the trier of fact because of the conduct of a peace officer in obtaining the evidence, the proponent of the evidence may urge that the peace officer's conduct was taken in a reasonable, good faith belief that the conduct was proper and that the evidence discovered should not be kept from the trier of fact if otherwise admissible.

B. No court shall suppress evidence which is otherwise admissible in a civil or criminal proceeding if the evidence was seized in good faith or as a result of a technical violation.

C. "Evidence" means contraband, instrumentalities or fruits of a crime, or any other evidence which tends to prove a fact in issue.

D. "Good faith" means whenever a peace officer obtains evidence:
  1. Pursuant to a search warrant obtained from a neutral and detached magistrate, which warrant is free from obvious defects other than non-deliberate errors in preparation and the officer reasonably believed the warrant to be valid; or
  2. Pursuant to a warrantless search, when:
    a. The officer reasonably believed he possessed probable cause to make the search, and
    b. The officer, possessed at least a reasonable suspicion that the person or premises searched, possessed or contained items of an evidentiary nature, and
    c. The officer reasonably believed there were circumstances excusing the procurement of a search warrant; or
  3. Pursuant to a search resulting from an arrest, when:
    a. The officer reasonably believed he possessed probable cause to make the arrest, and
    b. The officer reasonably believed there were circumstances excusing the procurement of an arrest warrant, or
    c. The officer procured or executed an invalid arrest warrant he reasonably believed to be valid; or
  4. Pursuant to a statute, local ordinance, judicial precedent or court rule which is later declared unconstitutional or otherwise invalidated; and
  5. The officer has completed a law enforcement academy or other approved prerequisite curriculum and any mandatory subsequent training or instruction in Constitutional law and criminal procedure, where required by the [State Peace Officers' Standards and Training Commission].

E. This section shall not adversely affect the rights of any plaintiff to seek special damages against a peace officer or a governmental entity, provided that the trier of fact in such civil action determines that the officer or entity conducted an unlawful search or seizure.
F. [Appropriate savings and severability clause].

The Fifth Amendment: Self-incrimination

Among the provisions of the Fifth Amendment is the right of protection against self-incrimination: "No person . . . shall be compelled in any criminal case to be a witness against himself . . ." This right goes to the very heart of the adversary system of criminal justice, because it implies that the state must prove the guilt of the accused. It has its greatest relevance in the matter of interrogation and how confessions are elicited from suspects. In *Brown* v. *Mississippi* (297 U.S. 278 [1936]), the Supreme Court ruled that confessions secured by physical abuse were inadmissible in state courts. In the cases of *Escobedo* v. *Illinois* and *Miranda* v. *Arizona,* the Court added that to secure the validity of confessions suspects must be notified of their rights against self-incrimination and for representation by counsel during an interrogation.

In March 1963, Ernesto Miranda was arrested in Arizona for kidnapping and rape. After being identified by the victim and questioned by police for several hours, Miranda signed a confession that included a statement that his confession was made voluntarily. Over the objections of his attorney, the confession was admitted into evidence and Miranda was found

Ernesto Miranda (right) with his attorney, John Flynn. The U.S. Supreme Court's reversal of Miranda's conviction established guidelines for police to follow in the interrogation of suspects. Courtesy United Press International.

guilty. The Supreme Court of Arizona affirmed the conviction and held that Miranda's constitutional rights had not been violated in obtaining the conviction; in accordance with the earlier *Escobedo* ruling, Miranda had not specifically requested counsel. The U.S. Supreme Court, in reversing the Arizona decision, attempted to clarify its intent in the *Escobedo* case by spelling out specific guidelines to be followed by police before interrogating persons in custody and using the statements as evidence. The guidelines require that after a suspect is taken into custody for an offense and prior to any questioning by law enforcement officers, the suspect must be advised of certain rights if there is intent to use his or her statements in court. These guidelines, as they have been incorporated into the "Miranda warning," have become familiar to many Americans by their frequent reiteration on police shows on television. A copy of the warning, reproduced from a card carried by urban law enforcement officers, is shown in **figure 2.2**.

The Miranda story had a violent ending. On the night of Saturday, 13 January 1976, Ernesto Miranda became involved in a fight over a card game in a skid row bar in Phoenix, Arizona. He was stabbed twice by one of the men he had beaten—an illegal alien from Mexico named Fernando Zamora Rodriguez—and was dead on arrival at the hospital. One assumes that the police officer who arrested Rodriguez remembered to read him his Miranda rights!

The Sixth Amendment: Right to counsel

No prison is without its share of "jailhouse lawyers," men and women who have become familiar with the law from first-hand experience. In the days when the right to an attorney was not available in court, much less behind the jailhouse walls, these jailhouse lawyers helped put cases together for

DEFENDANT	LOCATION

SPECIFIC WARNING REGARDING INTERROGATIONS

1. You have the right to remain silent.

2. Anything you say can and will be used against you in a court of law.

3. You have the right to talk to a lawyer and have him present with you while you are being questioned.

4. If you cannot afford to hire a lawyer one will be appointed to represent you before any questioning, if you wish one.

SIGNATURE OF DEFENDANT	DATE
WITNESS	TIME

☐ REFUSED SIGNATURE   SAN FRANCISCO POLICE DEPARTMENT   PR.9.1.4

FIGURE 2.2
Card listing Miranda warnings given to arrested individuals. Courtesy United Press International.

Police photo of Fernando Zamora Rodriquez after his arrest for the slaying of Ernesto Miranda in 1976. Courtesy United Press International.

appellate review. With time on their hands and great personal interest in their cases, these men and women paved the way for the prisoners of today. Perhaps the most famous appeal was made by Clarence Earl Gideon, referred to in chapter 1 in the discussion of prosecution and defense. An indigent prisoner in Florida State Prison at Raiford, Gideon is described by journalist Anthony Lewis in *Gideon's Trumpet* (1966, pp. 5–6):

> Gideon was a fifty-one-year-old white man who had been in and out of prisons much of his life. He had served time for four previous felonies, and he bore the physical marks of a destitute life: a wrinkled, prematurely aged face, a voice and hands that trembled, a frail body, white hair. He had never been a professional criminal or a man of violence; he just could not seem to settle down to work, and so he had made his way by gambling and occasional thefts. Those who had known him, even the men who had arrested him and those who were now his jailers, considered Gideon a perfectly harmless human being, rather likeable, but one tossed aside by life. Anyone meeting him for the first time would be likely to regard him as the most wretched of men.
>
> And yet a flame still burned in Clarence Earl Gideon. He had not given up caring about life or freedom; he had not lost his sense of injustice. Right now he had a passionate—some thought almost irrational—feeling of having been wronged by the State of Florida, and he had the determination to try to do something about it.

Gideon submitted his petition to the U.S. Supreme Court as a pauper under a special federal statute. The statute makes great allowances for those unable to afford the expense of counsel and administrative technicalities. For example, it is usually necessary to submit *forty* typewritten

Clarence Earl Gideon, who argued that his constitutional right to a fair trial was denied when he was refused an attorney. Courtesy Wide World Photos.

copies of a petition; Gideon submitted *one*, handwritten in pencil on lined yellow sheets. Although he did not have counsel in 1961 when he stood trial for breaking into a pool hall, he *did* have counsel before the Supreme Court when his petition was heard in the 1962–63 term. Abe Fortas, one of Washington's most successful lawyers (and who later became a Supreme Court justice) was appointed as Gideon's attorney for the case. In its decision of *Gideon* v. *Wainwright* (372 U.S. 902) the Court stated:

> In deciding as it did—that "appointment of counsel is not a fundamental right, essential to a fair trial"—the Court in Betts made an abrupt break with its own well-considered precedents. In returning to these old precedents, sounder we believe than the new, we but restore constitutional principles established to achieve a fair system of justice. Not only these precedents but also reason and reflection require us to recognize that in our adversary system to hire a lawyer, cannot be assured a fair trial unless counsel is provided for him (p. 796).

As if to emphasize the Supreme Court's finding, Gideon was acquitted when he was finally retried with counsel. The right to counsel has since moved rapidly in both directions along the continuum of criminal justice. In decision after decision, the Supreme Court has ruled in favor of the right to counsel at a "critical stage" in the defendant's case. This "critical stage" has been extended from initial police contact, to the preparation of briefs for appeal, to assistance in preparing transcripts of a trial. The right to counsel has moved into the prison as well as the courtroom. A milestone case decided in the 1967–68 term, *Mempa* v. *Rhay* (389 U.S. 128 [1967]), extended the right to counsel to state probation revocation hearings; these hearings were previously considered as essentially administrative. The Court held in *Mempa* that the application of a deferred sentence was a "critical point" in the proceeding.

The rule of law

In the past several decades, the U.S. Supreme Court has made more changes in criminal procedure than were made in nearly 200 years. Critics of the Court object that the changes have resulted in the "coddling of criminals" and that they reflect a permissiveness detrimental to the rights of law-abiding citizens. However, the Supreme Court has not created any new rights for criminals; rather, it has *moved toward equalizing the rights of rich and poor suspects*. The major consequence of the due-process revolution has been to extend to the poor, the illiterate, and the ignorant some of those rights that have long been enjoyed by the middle-class or upper-class defendant. But the revolution remains unfinished. Although the Court may have equalized rights on paper, many barriers still effectively bar the poor from the full benefits of due process and equal protection under the law.

Summary

To understand the problem of crime, one must examine the broader issue of deviance from societal norms. Societies attempt to contain deviance through controls (sanctions) that range from informal disapproval to the use of the police powers of the state. Antisocial attitudes, eccentricities, and various kinds of atypical behavior may all be studied for their potential value in helping to illuminate the factors involved in criminal conduct. All criminal acts are deviant, but not all deviant acts are criminal. Thus, only those deviant acts that legislative bodies have defined by statute as criminal may legitimately be considered crimes.

American criminal law as analyzed in this chapter combines the features of two systems: common law, which develops continually based on interpretation of precedents, and civil law, based on specific codes that are written and legislated. These systems are the basis of *substantive criminal law*, laws that define the necessary elements of crimes and specify the penalties for commission.

Depending on the punishment, offenses are classified as felonies or misdemeanors. Felonies are punishable by death or imprisonment. Misdemeanors are punishable by fines or relatively brief periods of incarceration.

Procedural criminal law focuses on how the criminal law is enforced, how evidence is collected, and what rights are guaranteed to persons accused of crimes. Contrary to popular belief, the Bill of Rights of the U.S. Constitution has not always provided such guarantees to people tried in state criminal courts. Not until the "due process revolution" of the 1960s were such rights made applicable to the states by means of the Fourteenth Amendment. Some people believe that the due process revolution made it possible for criminals to escape punishment; others maintain that the revolution increased the fairness of the criminal justice process by extending to the poor rights long enjoyed by the well-to-do.

issue paper

SHOULD CONSENSUAL CRIMES BE DECRIMINALIZED?

To demonstrate the futility of attempting to "legislate morality," consensual crimes are often compared with more conventional offenses against person and property. If by "legislating morality" we mean the enactment of statutes that provide legal sanctions for deviations from normative standards of conduct, then legislating morality is precisely what the criminal law seeks to do. Distinctions between legal order and moral order appear to rest primarily on the means by which conformity to normative standards is sought, rather than upon the standards themselves. Both law and morality reflect attempts to influence behavior in a desired direction.

In offenses such as robbery and rape, there is little or no conflict between morality and law, because these actions are proscribed both by moral codes and by legal statutes. But behaviors under the heading of consensual crime are sometimes proscribed by one set of rules and not the other. As a Catholic bishop visiting Boston reputedly told a Protestant minister, "Gambling in moderation is not a sin." "That may be true," the minister replied, "but in this state it is a crime."

Although few people seriously question the need for legal sanctions against offenses such as robbery and rape, many people do have serious reservations about sanctions against gambling, prostitution, homosexual behavior involving consenting adults, and abortion. In the latter case, it is argued that criminal sanctions for such behaviors constitute an unwarranted intrusion upon privacy and an indefensible extension of governmental authority into matters more properly dealt with by *informal* social sanctions. The American Law Institute, in its *Model Penal Code: Proposed Official Draft* (1964), recommended that most consensual crimes be abolished. The earlier Wolfenden Report (Committee on Homosexual Offenses and Prostitution 1964), which addressed the specific issue of consensual adult homosexuality, stated that society should not seek to equate "the sphere of crime with that of sin" and that "there must remain a realm of private morality and immorality which is, in brief and crude terms, not the law's business" (p. 24).

An intense and continuing controversy surrounds the conceptualization and legal status of "crimes against public order," societal reactions to such offenses, and the difficulties these crimes create for law enforcement, the courts, and corrections. The criminal justice system is often in the unenviable position of having to carry out conflicting policies and enforce statutes that are vague, overlapping, or even contradictory. At the same time, criminal justice personnel are subject to heated criticism for their inability to perform tasks that verge on the impossible.

Although opposition to consensual-crime laws is manifold and varied, objections concentrate on the following issues (Schur and Bedau 1974, p. 9):

1. Consensual crime laws are essentially unenforceable.
2. Apart from their failure to achieve desired ends, such laws appear to increase or worsen social ills rather than reduce them.
3. Attempts at enforcement preempt a great deal of the time, energy, and money available for other law enforcement activity.
4. Police are forced to adopt legally and morally questionable techniques in the investigation of the offenses.

5. The efforts at banning such transactions may actually encourage the growth of an illicit traffic and raise the price of the goods and services in question.
6. Some of these laws may produce *secondary crime* (i.e., other than the proscribed behavior itself) and all of them create new "criminals," many of whom are otherwise law-abiding individuals.
7. The administration of consensual crime laws is arbitrary and discriminatory; certain segments of society feel their impact a great deal more than others.
8. The largely discretionary nature of the enforcement of these laws—along with the above features of consensual-crime laws—invites corruption and exploitation and may throw the entire criminal justice system into disrepute.

Finally, there is the issue of the disposition of consensual criminals. It is difficult to fashion a compelling argument to support punishment for the drug addict; detoxification seems a more promising approach to the public inebriate than a "revolving door" of arrest-sentencing-incarceration-rearrest. The punitive response has had little success in dealing with gambling and prostitution, and the treatment approach has not yielded much gain except for a minority of self-professed compulsive gamblers or women for whom prostitution is symptomatic of serious emotional maladjustment. And even if we were able, through techniques presently available, to alter the behavior of individuals who voluntarily practice homosexual lifestyles, there are no grounds in law or morality to proceed with behavior modification without the consent of the individual. Thus, the issue of disposition may provide the most cogent and convincing arguments for the decriminalization of consensual crimes.

Winston Churchill, in volume 3 of *History of the English-Speaking Peoples* (1959), noted that the English Puritans during the Protectorate of Oliver Cromwell, like their American counterparts in Massachusetts, devoted themselves to the suppression of vice.

> All betting and gambling were forbidden. In 1650 a law was passed making adultery punishable by death, a ferocity mitigated by the fact that nothing would convince the juries of the guilt of the accused. Drunkenness was attacked vigorously and great numbers of alehouses were closed. Swearing was an offense punishable by a graduated scale of fines. Christmas excited the most fervent hostility of these fanatics. Parliament was deeply concerned at the liberty which it gave to carnal and sensual delights. Soldiers were sent around London on Christmas Day before dinnertime to enter private houses without warrants and seize meat cooking in all kitchens and ovens. Everywhere was prying and spying.
>
> All over the country the Maypoles were hewn down, lest old village dances around them should lead to immorality or at least to levity. Walking abroad on the Sabbath, except to go to church, was punished, and a man was fined for going to a neighbouring parish to hear a sermon. It was even proposed to forbid people sitting at their doors or leaning against them on the Sabbath. Bearbaiting and cockfighting were effectually ended by shooting the bears and wringing the necks of the cocks. All forms of athletic sports, horse racing, and wrestling were banned, and sumptuary laws sought to remove all ornaments from male and female attire (pp. 240–41).

The stifling effects of these innumerable petty tyrannies extended into every corner of life and made Cromwell's Protectorate despised and hated as no English government has ever been hated, before or since.

Despite its addiction to Old Testament rhetoric, Cromwell's government was a military dictatorship, with most of the characteristics of similar regimes in the twentieth century. In a dictatorship, deviance from official norms is harshly, even ruthlessly, suppressed. Dissenters may be sent to labor camps or mental hospitals. Conflicts between law and morality exhibit few of the properties associated with consensual crime in our own society. For example, it is difficult to imagine the existence of an erotic-minorities movement or C.O.Y.O.T.E. in Soviet Russia. (C.O.Y.O.T.E—Cast Off Your Old Tired Ethics—is a group favoring legal prostitution.)

In a relatively open, pluralistic society composed of groups with divergent traditions, customs, beliefs, and values, conflicts between the law and the moral views of some groups are inevitable. And although agreement on some issues is possible among groups with diverse moral and ethical convictions, certain key issues allow little or no room for compromise. It is on issues of this kind that groups are likely to seek the support of legal sanctions as a backstop for morality.

Legal scholar Herbert L. Packer has identified six conditions that ought to be present if criminal sanctions are to be imposed against conduct that engenders societal disapproval (1968, p. 296):

1. The conduct must be regarded by most people as socially threatening and must not be condoned by any significant segment of society.
2. Subjecting the conduct to criminal penalties must not be inconsistent with the goals of punishment.
3. Suppressing the conduct will not inhibit other socially desirable behavior.
4. The conduct can be dealt with through evenhanded and nondiscriminatory law enforcement.
5. Controlling the conduct through the criminal process will not expose the process to severe qualitative or quantitative strain.
6. No reasonable alternatives to the criminal sanction exist for dealing with the conduct.

We might ask whether any or all of these conditions are met by the behaviors now designated as consensual crimes.

The most reasonable conclusion about consensual crime seems to be that laws that cannot be enforced should not be enacted; the corollary to this proposition is that behavior subject to nonenforceable laws should not be legally proscribed. This does not necessarily imply, however, that certain behaviors that fit Packer's specifications should, or can be, exempt from adverse public opinion or other types of social disapproval. As Geis reminds us, "To the extent that a society trusts from its core nonconformists and then takes harsh measures to repress them, it will create a resistant force in its midst" (1972, p. 260). As an alternative, he suggests that "the most efficacious method of dealing with deviancy is to ignore, to the furthest point of our tolerance, those items which we find offensive" (p. 261). This recommendation is made in the belief that an unwillingness to isolate the deviant individual allows an opportunity for the operation of those societal values that may renew the deviant individual's "stake in conformity."

Discussion and review

1. Is *deviant* behavior more appropriate as an object of study by criminal justice professionals than the more specific study of criminal and delinquent behavior? Explain your answer.
2. How do we distinguish between *prescription* and *proscription* as forms of social sanction?
3. Compare the value consensus and value conflict models of criminal law.
4. Define and discuss *substantive criminal law* and *criminal procedure*. What are the major sources of criminal law?
5. What four characteristics of criminal law distinguish it from other rules governing human conduct?
6. What are *felonies* and how do they differ from *misdemeanors*? Why is the distinction important in the administration of justice?
7. How do crimes differ from *torts*?
8. What are the provisions of the Fourteenth Amendment which contributed so significantly to the "due process revolution"?
9. What is the Exclusionary Rule? What is considered a "good faith exception" to the Exclusionary Rule?
10. What was the significance of the U.S. Supreme Court's decision in *Gideon v. Wainwright*?

Glossary

Actus reus The conduct that constitutes a specific crime.

Common law The body of legal fact and theory that developed in England over a period of centuries and became uniform throughout the country as judges followed precedents (previous court decisions) in handling new, but similar, cases. Distinguished from code law, which seeks to lay down legal principles in the form of statutes.

Lex talionis (talion law) The "law of equivalent retaliation," which asserts that an injured party is entitled to "an eye for an eye," but no more than an eye. The aggrieved party is entitled to appropriate retaliation in kind or measure.

Mala in se Latin for "evil in itself." Refers to crimes that are considered intrinsically wrong, regardless of existing legal sanctions, (e.g., murder, rape, robbery).

Mala prohibita Refers to criminal acts that are wrong because they are prohibited by law, (i.e., declared wrong by legislative action, e.g., traffic violations, sale of liquor on Sunday).

Mens rea The "guilty mind" or criminal intent required for an accused person to be held responsible for criminal actions; the state of mind at the time a crime occurs.

Stare decisis Latin for "let the decision stand." Means that court decisions on points of law are binding on future cases that are substantially the same (i.e., where the totality of circumstances does not vary).

References

American Law Institute. *Model Penal Code: Proposed Official Draft.* Philadelphia, Pa.: American Law Institute, 1964.
Americans for Effective Law Enforcement. *Impact.* July 1982, 1–4.
Chambliss, W. J. "Elites and the Creation of Criminal Law." *Sociological Readings in the Conflict Perspective.* Edited by W. J. Chambliss. Reading, Mass.: Addison-Wesley, 1973.
Churchill, W. L. S. *A History of the English-Speaking Peoples.* The Age of Revolution, vol. 3. New York: Dodd Mead, 1959.
Cole, G. F. *The American System of Criminal Justice.* Belmont, Calif.: Brooks/Cole, 1982.
Committee on Homosexual Offenses and Prostitution. *The Wolfenden Report.* New York: Lancer Books, 1964.
"Death by Stoning for Sex Crimes." *Newsweek.* 14 July 1980, p. 40.
Durant, W. *Our Oriental Heritage.* New York: Simon and Schuster, 1950.
Eldefonso, E., and Coffey, A. R. *Criminal Law: History, Philosophy, and Enforcement.* New York: Harper and Row, 1981.
Geis, G. *Not the Law's Business.* Washington, D.C.: U.S. Government Printing Office, 1972.
Hall, J. *General Principles of Criminal Law.* Indianapolis, Ind.: Bobbs-Merrill, 1947.
Kerper, H. B. *Introduction to the Criminal Justice System.* St. Paul: West, 1972.
LaFave, W. R., and Scott, A. W. *Criminal Law.* St. Paul, Minn.: West Publishing, 1972.
Lewis, A. *Gideon's Trumpet.* New York: Random House, 1964.
Lewis, P. and Peoples, K. *The Supreme Court and the Criminal Process—Cases and Comments.* Philadelphia: W. B. Saunders, 1978.
Makielski, S. J. *Pressure Politics in America.* Lanham, Md.: University Press of America, 1980.
Packer, H. *The Limits of the Criminal Sanction.* Palo Alto, Calif.: Stanford University Press, 1968.
Perkins, R. M. *Criminal Law.* Mineoloa, N.Y.: Foundation Press, 1969.
Quinney, R. *Critique of Legal Order: Crime Control in Capitalist Society.* Boston: Little, Brown, 1974.
"Q'sas—The Law of Punishment." *Tampa Tribune.* 12 November 1982, p. 11A.
Robin, G. D. *Introduction to the Criminal Justice System.* New York: Harper and Row, 1980.
Roby, P. A. "Politics and Criminal Law: Revision of the New York State Penal Law on Prostitution." *Social Problems* 17 (1969):83–109.
Schur, E. M. *Labeling Deviant Behavior: Its Sociological Implications.* New York: Harper and Row, 1971.
Schur, E. M., and Bedau, H. A. *Victimless Crime: Two Sides of a Controversy.* Englewood Cliffs, N.J.: Prentice-Hall, 1974.
Sutherland, E. H., and Cressey, D. R. *Criminology.* Philadelphia, Pa.: Lippincott, 1978.
Swanson, C. R. and Territo, L. *Police Administration: Structures, Processes, and Behavior.* New York: Macmillan, 1983.
Tappan, P. *Crime, Justice, and Correction.* New York: McGraw-Hill, 1966.
Williams, R. M. *American Society.* New York: Alfred A. Knopf, 1970.

Cases

Brown v. *Mississippi* 297 U.S. 278, 56 S.Ct. 461, 80 L.Ed. 682 (1936).
Commonwealth v. *Welansky* 316 Mass. 383, 55 N.E.2d 902 (1944).
Elkins v. *U.S.* 364 U.S. 206, 80 S.Ct. 1437, 4 L.Ed.2d 1669 (1960).
Escobedo v. *Illinois* 375 U.S. 902, 84 S.Ct. 203, 11 L.Ed.2d 143 (1964).
Gideon v. *Wainwright* 372 U.S. 335, 83 S.Ct. 792, 9 L.Ed.2d 799 (1963).
Hurtado v. *California* 110 U.S. 516, 4 S.Ct. 111, 4 S.Ct. 292, 28 L.Ed. 232 (1884).
Lustig v. *U.S.* 338 U.S. 74, 69 S.Ct. 1372, 93 L.Ed. 1819 (1949).
Mapp v. *Ohio* 367 U.S. 643, 81 S.Ct. 1684, 6 L.Ed. 2d 1081 (1961).
Mempa v. *Rhay* 389 U.S. 128, 88 S.Ct. 254, 19 L.Ed.2d 336 (1967).
Miranda v. *Arizona* 384 U.S. 436, 86 S.Ct. 1602, 16 L.Ed.2d 694 (1966).
U.S. v. *Williams* 622 F.2d 830 (5th Circuit 1980).
Weeks v. *U.S.* 232 U.S. 383, 34 S.Ct. 341, 58 L.Ed. 652 (1914).
Wolf v. *Colorado* 338 U.S. 25, 69 S.Ct. 1359, 93 L.Ed. 1782 (1949).

3
the nature and distribution of crime

The Uniform Crime Reporting Program
Crime trends
Violent crimes
   Murder and nonnegligent manslaughter
   Aggravated assault
   Forcible rape
   Robbery
Crimes against property
   Burglary
   Larceny-Theft
   Motor Vehicle theft
   Arson

Crime data manipulation

What crime does to victims and society

Summary

Issue paper: Gun control

THE average citizen, by listening to the radio, viewing television, or reading the daily newspaper, is frequently exposed to reports about the community crime rate. Yet few people realize that news reports about the crime rate refer to only eight categories of crime: murder and nonnegligent manslaughter *(criminal homicide);* aggravated assault; forcible rape; robbery; burglary; larceny-theft; motor vehicle theft; and arson. The *crime rate* in an area is defined as the number of these offenses that occur per 100,000 inhabitants.

Crimes reported to the police extend beyond these eight categories, but only these eight are included in the crime rate or crime index reported in the *FBI Uniform Crime Reports*. The solution of crimes involving these eight offenses is an index by which the public and media can evaluate the efficiency of police departments; other indices can be used to evaluate police efficiency, but for better or for worse, this one is used most often by the media in news reports.

This chapter discusses the crime reporting system in the United States, examines each of the eight index crimes, defines and describes the elements of these crimes, and, when applicable, provides case studies of each crime. The accuracy of offenses reported to the FBI by local police is examined, and the problems of underreporting by victims and the manipulation of statistics by police are discussed. Finally, we will look at what crime does to victims and to society and will discuss the price of crime for victims as individuals and for the nation as a whole.

The Uniform Crime Reporting Program

Using crime statistics contributed by over 15,000 law enforcement agencies across the United States, the Uniform Crime Reporting (UCR) Program provides periodic assessments of crime in the nation as measured by offenses that come to the attention of the law enforcement community. The program's primary goal is to generate reliable criminal statistics for use in law enforcement administration, operation, and management. However, data from the program are also used by other criminal justice professionals, legislators, and scholars who have an interest in the crime problem. In addition, the statistics furnish the general public with an indication of fluctuations in crime levels.

The Committee on Uniform Crime Records of the International Association of Chiefs of Police (IACP) initiated the voluntary national data collection effort in 1930. That same year, Congress appointed the FBI as the national clearinghouse for statistical information on crime. Since then, a large volume of data based on uniform classifications and reporting procedures has been obtained from the nation's law enforcement agencies.

To provide a more complete picture of crime in the United States, the Committee on Uniform Crime Records of the IACP chose to use data on offenses coming to the attention of law enforcement agencies; these data are more readily available than any other reportable crime information. Seven offenses, because of their seriousness, frequency of occurrence, and likelihood of being reported to police, were initially selected to compute an

Uniform Crime Reports data can be retrieved in the form of summary tabulations by the FBI's main computer system. Courtesy FBI Law Enforcement Bulletin.

index for evaluating fluctuations in crime volume. These crimes, known as the crime-index offenses, were murder and nonnegligent manslaughter, forcible rape, robbery, aggravated assault, burglary, larceny-theft, and motor vehicle theft. By congressional mandate, arson was added as the eighth index offense in late 1978.

To provide nationwide uniformity in the reporting of data, standard definitions have been adopted for all offenses. Standardization is needed to eliminate variations in the definitions of offenses in different parts of the country. Without regard for local statutes, reporting agencies are required to submit data in accordance with the UCR definitions. Because punishment for some offenses varies among the state codes, the program does not distinguish between felonies and misdemeanors.

The IACP's Committee on Uniform Crime Records still serves in an advisory capacity to the FBI on the operation of the UCR program. In this connection, the IACP, through surveys of law enforcement records and crime reporting systems, has an active role in the program. In June 1966, the National Sheriffs' Association (NSA) established a Committee on Uniform Crime Reporting to serve in an advisory role to the NSA membership and to the national UCR program. This committee actively encourages sheriffs throughout the country to fully participate in the program. Committees on uniform crime reporting within state law enforcement associations are also active in promoting interest in the UCR program. These committees foster widespread and more intelligent use of uniform crime statistics and lend assistance to the agencies that contribute data.

Contributors to the UCR Program compile and submit their data in one of two ways: directly to the FBI or through state UCR programs. Contributors that submit directly to the FBI are provided with continuing guidance and support from the national program. At present, there are forty-seven operational state-level UCR programs; these programs have increased the coverage of agencies by instituting mandatory state reporting requirements, by providing more direct and frequent service to participating agencies, and by making information readily available at the state level. Thus, state programs have greatly increased the efficiency of operations at the national level.

When a state develops a UCR program, the FBI ceases to collect data directly from individual law enforcement agencies within that state. Instead, information from within the state is forwarded to the national program by the state collection agency. The state systems are developed to ensure the consistency and comparability of data submitted to the national program and to provide for regular and timely reporting of national crime data. Toward these goals, the following conditions must be met:

1. A state program must conform to the standards, definitions, and information in the FBI Uniform Crime Reports. However, states are not prohibited from collecting data beyond the scope of the national program.
2. The state criminal justice agency must have a proven, effective, and mandatory statewide program with acceptable quality control procedures.
3. Coverage within a state by a state agency must be at least equal to the coverage attained by FBI Uniform Crime Reports.
4. The state agency must have adequate field staff to conduct audits and to assist contributing agencies in keeping record and following established reporting procedures.
5. The state agency must furnish to the FBI all of the detailed data regularly collected by the FBI in the form of duplicate returns, computer printouts, or magnetic tapes.
6. The state must have the proven ability (tested over time) to supply all the statistical data required to meet the publication deadlines for the FBI Uniform Crime Reports.

If a state agency does not comply with these requirements, the national program may reinstitute direct collection of data from law enforcement agencies within the state (Federal Bureau of Investigation 1981, pp. 1–2).

To fulfill its responsibilities to the UCR program, the FBI edits and reviews incoming reports for completeness and quality, contacts (when necessary) individual contributors within the states (coordinating such contacts with the state agencies), and conducts training programs on state record keeping and reporting procedures.

Crime trends

The eight index crimes are frequently divided into two categories: violent crimes and crimes against property.

Violent crimes

The violent crimes among the index crimes are murder and nonnegligent manslaughter, aggravated assault, forcible rape, and robbery.

Murder and nonnegligent manslaughter Murder and nonnegligent manslaughter are defined in the UCR program as the willful (nonnegligent) killing of one human being by another. The classification of these offenses, as in all crime-index offenses, is based solely on police investigation—as opposed to determination by a court, medical examiner, coroner's jury, or other judicial body. Not included under this classification are deaths caused by negligence, suicide, or accident; justifiable homicides (the killing of felons by law enforcement officers in the line of duty or by private citizens); and attempted murder or assault with the intent to murder (classified as aggravated assaults).

Murder consistently has the highest solution rate, or *clearance rate*, of the eight index crimes (see **figure 3.1**). This high rate often surprises the average citizen, who assumes incorrectly that criminal homicides are seldom solved. Such a misconception is understandable however, considering the media attention given to unsolved murders. One merely has to recall the Boston strangler murders, the Hillside murders in Los Angeles, the murder of black children in Atlanta, or the murder of two Florida State University coeds in the Chi Omega Sorority House in Tallahassee, Florida.

The latter crimes can be accurately called media events, and both the print and the electronic media expend considerable time, money, and effort to assure that the grisly details of the crimes are brought to public attention. However, most criminal homicides are less "newsworthy"; most in-

CRIMES OF VIOLENCE

NOT CLEARED | CLEARED
- MURDER 72%
- AGGRAVATED ASSAULT 58%
- FORCIBLE RAPE 48%
- ROBBERY 24%

CRIMES AGAINST PROPERTY

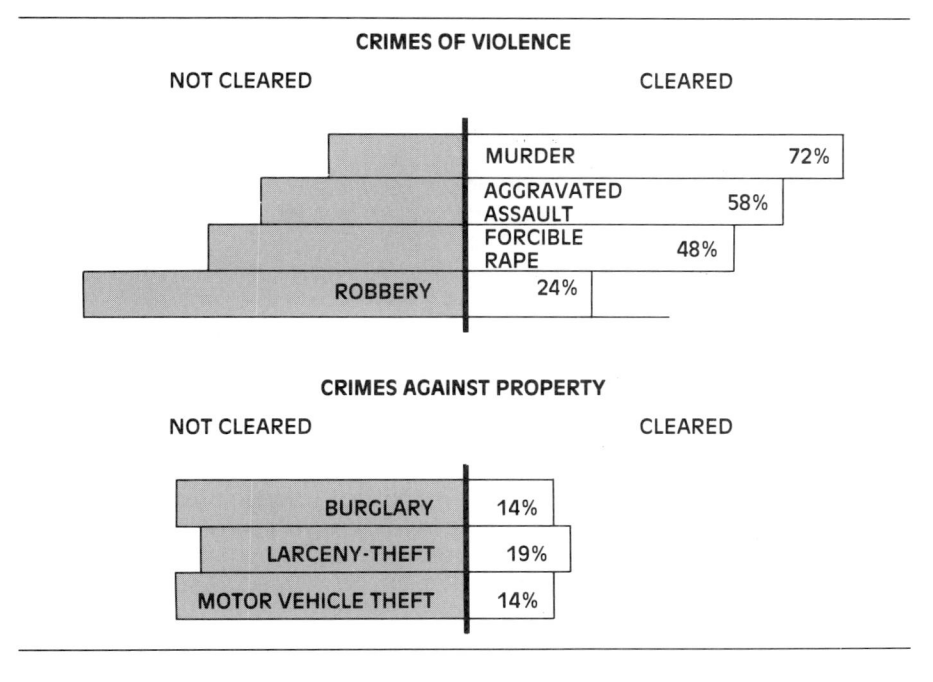

NOT CLEARED | CLEARED
- BURGLARY 14%
- LARCENY-THEFT 19%
- MOTOR VEHICLE THEFT 14%

FIGURE 3.1
Crimes cleared by arrest, 1981. Data from Federal Bureau of Investigation, Crime in the United States, *FBI Uniform Crime Reports (Washington, D.C.: U.S. Government Printing Office, 1981), p. 152.*

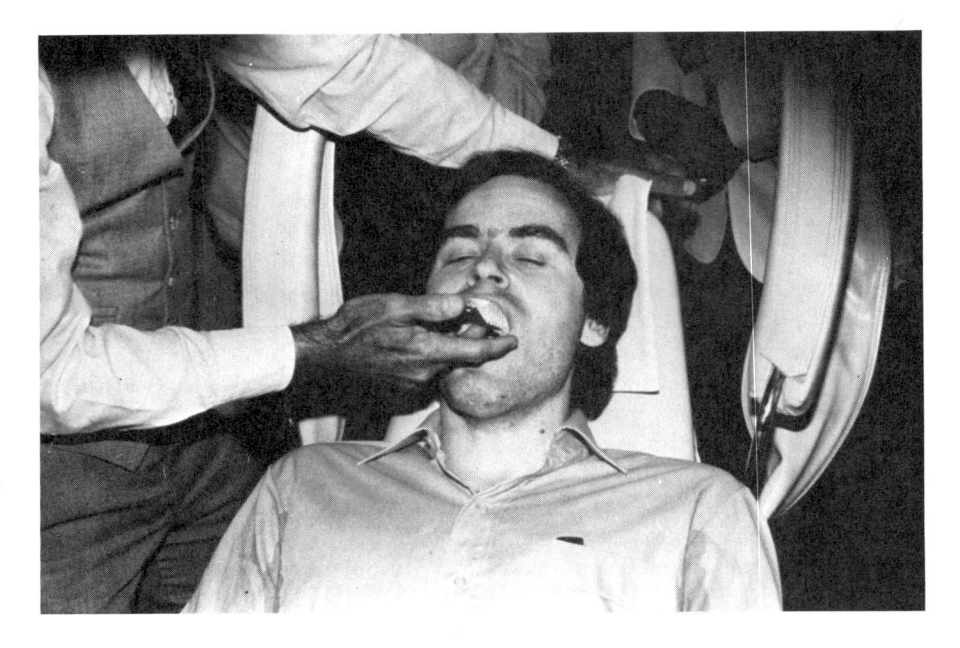

Forensic dentist obtaining dental impressions of Ted Bundy before his trial for the murder of two Florida State University coeds. Teeth marks, proven to be Bundy's, were found on one of the victims. Courtesy Ken Katsaris, former Sheriff, Leon County (Florida) Sheriff's Office.

volve individuals who live together, work together, play together, or socialize together. Such homicides are rarely carefully planned, are frequently spontaneous, and often have witnesses. This poor planning and the ineptness of assailants partially explains the high clearance rate. In addition, criminal homicides of any type are normally investigated more intensively than other index crimes.

Consider the following two murder cases involving acquaintances.

CASE 3.1

Bill and Lonnie were next door neighbors and regularly argued about the parking places in the street in front of their homes. Each man lived in his own single-family home, and each usually parked his car on the city street directly in front of his home when the parking place was vacant. Lonnie usually got home from work earlier than Bill, and if the parking place in front of his own home was taken he would park in front of Bill's home. Bill's parking place was on the city street, so neither man had a legal right to the spot.

One evening Lonnie returned home from work, found the parking place in front of his home taken, and parked in the vacant spot in front of Bill's home. When Bill arrived home and saw that Lonnie had once again parked in front of his home, he went directly to Lonnie and confronted him. Bill was verbally abusive, profane, and threatened to "beat Lonnie's ass" if he didn't move his car. Lonnie agreed, and both men then walked toward the car. When they reached it, Bill punched Lonnie in the face, knocking him to the pavement. He told Lonnie never to park in his spot again. Lonnie got up, got into his car, and drove away. The assault was witnessed by both families, including the children. (Bill was six feet four inches tall and weighed 225 pounds, Lonnie was five feet four inches tall and weighed 140 pounds.)

The following morning as Bill was exiting his home, Lonnie approached him with a razor sharp pocket knife that he had opened but concealed in his pocket. Lonnie told Bill he should not have hit him the evening before, then pulled the knife out of his pocket and cut Bill's throat. Bill fell to the pavement and bled to death. This assault was witnessed by both families, as well as by some neighbors seated on their porches. After the attack, Lonnie fled on foot. He was arrested several hours later in a nearby saloon after police were advised by neighbors that the saloon was his regular hangout.

CASE 3.2

Dave and Al, who worked together at a construction site, went to a restaurant near the site to have lunch. After examining the menu, they agreed to order the special of the day, which was actually a meal for two. One of the conditions of the special was that they would have to share one large crock of soup. The men disagreed about the type of soup they wanted, and became involved in a loud and heated argument about the matter. After several minutes, Dave pulled a pistol out of his pocket and shot and killed Al. Dave made no effort to leave the restaurant. The police were called, and Dave surrendered quietly.

These cases illustrate that—although tragic—murders involving acquaintances are rarely difficult to solve and almost impossible to prevent.

An alarming turn of events in the past decade has been the increase of criminal homicides from 8.5 per 100,000 inhabitants in 1971 to 10 per 100,000 in 1981. The clearance rate for criminal homicides decreased from 84 percent to 72 percent in the same period, in part because of an increase in homicides that involve total strangers and are committed during the commission of crimes such as burglaries, robberies, and rape. The latter homicides are infinitely more difficult to solve, and the clearance rate will likely continue to decrease as the rate of this type of crime continues to increase. The following case, although eventually solved, fits into the category of criminal homicides, committed during other crimes.

CASE 3.3

Suzanne, 26, a technician at a burn treatment center attended a musical show at a nearby university. On her way home she drove into a grocery store parking lot and mistakenly locked her car with the keys inside. Two young men helpfully unlocked the car, asked for a short lift—then forced her to drive to her apartment where they beat and raped her for several hours. The men who were later arrested after an extensive investigation advised police that they drove 50 miles to an isolated desert area and hurled Suzanne off a cliff. They heard her moaning and climbed down to her side. She pleaded with them to leave her alone because she said "I'm dying anyway" the response was swift. "Damn right you are" one of the men said and picked up a large rock and crushed her head to still her sounds (Magnuson 1981, p. 19).

Aggravated assault Aggravated assault is an unlawful attack by one person upon another for the purpose of inflicting severe or aggravated bodily injury. The crime usually involves a weapon or some means likely to produce death or great bodily harm. Attempted assaults are included in this category; if a gun, knife, or other weapon is used which could and probably would result in serious personal injury if the crime was successfully completed, it is not necessary that an injury result.

In view of the alarming increase in criminal homicides in this country, it is not surprising to find a similar increase in the occurrence of aggravated assault. There were 177 assault victims per 100,000 inhabitants in 1971, 281 assault victims per 100,000 inhabitants in 1981. Many aggravated assaults stop short of criminal homicide simply because an assailant's bullet or knife misses its target or does not strike a vital organ.

Although many victims and assailants in aggravated assaults are involved in close relationships, just as victims and assailants in criminal homicides, there is considerable difference in the clearance rates for these crimes—72 percent for criminal homicide and 58 percent for aggravated assault in 1981. The low clearance rate for aggravated assault can be attributed in part to less intensive police investigation of such crimes, especially when injuries are not serious. Also, it is not uncommon for assault victims to be uncooperative with the police—for one of the following reasons:

1. The assailant is a husband or boyfriend who is the breadwinner of the family, or is a wife or girlfriend who cares for the disputant's children. An arrest would undo an arrangement that benefits the victim.
2. The victim considers the offense to be a personal matter and wants to settle the dispute privately.
3. The victim believes that he or she got what he or she deserved, and therefore does not want the assailant to be punished.
4. The victim fears revenge if charges are pursued.

An uncooperative victim creates both legal and investigative difficulties. All states consider felony assaults to be crimes against the people of the state; thus, the state is legally the aggrieved party. Technically, the victim has no legal right to decide whether an assailant will or will not be prosecuted. Rather, the decision is made by the prosecutor; and many prosecutors are reluctant to pursue prosecution in felony assaults involving uncooperative victims. This is especially true when a victim's injuries are not critical and when the parties involved are related. This tendency not to prosecute is not commonly known among victims, however. Thus, a victim feloniously assaulted by a spouse may fear for that person's arrest and may be uncooperative or may fabricate a story about how the offense occurred.

Faced with an uncooperative victim, an officer's job is to get that victim to provide facts about the crime. This can be done, but the victim generally has to be convinced that no legal action will be taken against the assailant. The laws vary from state to state, but in many jurisdictions informal arrangements have been worked out between the prosecutor's office, the courts, and the police department to give police the authority (under carefully controlled conditions) to have a victim sign a *waiver of prosecution*. A waiver includes the name of the assailant, a statement of the victim's total satisfaction with the investigation by the police, and a statement of the victim's desire not to have the state prosecute **(figure 3.2)**.

Some people object strenuously to the practice of using waivers, because they believe that nonprosecution tends to encourage assaults. This position assumes that persons who commit assaults and are not punished are encouraged to commit similar assaults in the future. Nevertheless, overcrowded court dockets and the difficulties associated with prosecuting

---

WALTER C. HEINRICH, SHERIFF
HILLSBOROUGH COUNTY SHERIFF'S OFFICE
2008 E. 8TH AVENUE
TAMPA, FLORIDA 33605

STATE OF FLORIDA
COUNTY OF HILLSBOROUGH

CASE NO.: _____
DATE: _____

I, _____, the undersigned, do hereby:

WAIVER OF PROSECUTION

[INITIALS] _____ request the HILLSBOROUGH COUNTY SHERIFF'S OFFICE not to prosecute [NAME _____] regarding my complaint. I am satisfied with the manner in which the investigation was conducted and release the Sheriff's Office of any responsibility regarding this complaint. I request that any further investigation not be pursued.

signed this _____ day of _____, 19 __, at _____ o'clock __M.

_____
(AUTHORITY/RELATION)

WITNESSES:

_____
DEPUTY

_____

_____

_____

Courtesy Hillsborough County Sheriff's Office, Tampa, Florida. (Adapted with permission.)

FIGURE 3.2
Waiver of Prosecution Form.

cases with reluctant victims obviate any preventive or punitive benefits that might be derived from the prosecution of all assaults.

Many state and local governments have statutes and ordinances that make it unlawful to withhold intentionally information relating to a crime or to provide false and misleading information about the crime. A victim who is uncooperative or who is suspected of not being completely truthful is usually advised of such laws and the penalties associated with them (Swanson, Chamelin, and Territo 1981, pp. 202–8).

Forcible rape *Forcible rape* is defined as the carnal knowledge of a female, forcibly and against her will. Assault or attempts to commit rape by force or threat of force are included in this category, but statutory rape (without force) and other sex offenses are not.

Although the number of rapes increased dramatically between 1971 and 1981—40 per 100,000 females in 1971, 69 per 100,000 females in 1981—evidence still suggests that rape is one of the most underreported violent crimes. As victimization studies reveal, victims have specific reasons for not reporting rapes (*Rape Victimization Study*, 1975; President's Commission on Law Enforcement and the Administration of Justice (1967):

1. Lack of belief in the ability of the police to apprehend the suspect
2. Concern that they would receive unsympathetic treatment from the police and would have to go through discomforting procedures
3. Desire to avoid the embarrassment of publicity
4. Fear of reprisal by the rapist
5. Apprehension, based on television programs or newspaper reports, that they would be further "victimized" by court proceedings

Unfortunately, some complaints about the treatment of rape victims are justified; but efforts are being made to correct these deficiencies in the

Women's karate class at California State University. Courtesy Ben Martin/ TIME Magazine.

system. For example, women's groups are working with local police departments to educate the public, especially women, about the crime of rape and to correct misinformation presented in television programs and the news media.

The failure of victims to report rapes seriously diminishes the ability of the police to protect other women. A case in point occurred several years ago in San Francisco:

CASE 3.4

A young woman who was raped turned first to her friends for help and comfort, then sought aid from a local Women Against Rape group. No one encouraged her to make a police report: she was indecisive and did nothing. Several days later, she read a news account describing a rape very similar to her own. She immediately notified the police and learned that the rapist had attacked three other women. With the additional information that she provided, the police located and arrested the rapist by the end of the day (*Rape Victimization Study*, 1975, p. 86).

In an effort to combat the problems of rape and the nonreporting of rape, many police departments have implemented rape prevention programs. One hazard of such programs is that if they are successful there could be an initial increase in the number of rapes reported to the police—thus conveying an impression that the program has failed. Therefore, prior to launching a rape prevention program, a police department should make the public and the news media aware of the possibility of increased reporting.

Reported rape, like murder, frequently involves individuals who know each other casually or even very well. For this reason, rape has a fairly high clearance rate. The following case studies illustrate rapes in which the suspect and the victim knew each other prior to the rape.

CASE 3.5

Mary, an 18-year-old single woman, described being sexually assaulted by her boyfriend's uncle as follows: "I had met him three times before; I felt I knew him. He seemed like a nice man. He was taking me home from the airport and he said he had to stop and pick something up from the house and asked me to come in. Inside he told me to get into the bedroom .... I tried to get away, I cried. He was slapping me around. At one point I blacked out and when I woke up he had ripped all my clothes off. He was so brutal and degrading. He made me do things to him and it was just terrible. I could never be normal again." The offender sodomized Mary and also picked her up by her breasts. She had multiple bruises on her body and rectal bleeding. On follow-up, Mary reported that the man's wife and children had been calling her begging her not to press charges. Mary said, "I dropped the charges and then found out he raped his little girl and two other girls right in the neighborhood. He robbed a store and almost killed the man by hitting him in the head with a brick. I can't press charges. He could kill me." Mary left the state two weeks following the rape (Groth, Burgess, and Holmstrom 1977, pp. 8–9).

CASE 3.6

Shortly after midnight, Catherine, a 33-year-old mother of two, was in bed reading and waiting for her husband to return from work. A man known to the family for ten years knocked at the door and the 14-year-old son let him in. He said he was leaving town the next day and wanted to say goodbye. Catherine talked to him from the bedroom and wished him well on his trip. Suddenly the man ordered the son to his room, grabbed Catherine, and forced her to go outside with him to another building. He beat her, choked her, and sexually assaulted her. It was only after the man fell asleep that Catherine was able to escape and return home.

On follow-up, Catherine reported considerable physical pain from the beatings. She had pain and swelling to her face, neck, arms, and legs; she also reported loss of appetite, insomnia, nightmares, crying spells, restlessness, and a fear of being followed as she walked home from work. She was unable to carry out usual parenting and household tasks. There was tension within the marital relationship, delay in resuming sexual relations, and flashbacks to the assault.

Charges were pressed against the offender who "copped a plea" for the charges of rape, unnatural acts, and kidnapping. The judge sentenced him to three years probation. One year later the offender committed two rapes involving teenage girls (Groth, Burgess, and Holmstrom 1977, p. 8).

In the 1970s, two disturbing trends emerged with regard to rape. First, rapes increased almost 58 percent between 1971 and 1981; second, the clearance rate for rape decreased from 55 percent in 1971 to 48 percent in 1981. Police and social scientists can only speculate as to the reason for the dramatic increase in reported rapes, but they tend to agree that the decrease in the clearance rate is due in part to the higher percentage of rapes that involve total strangers or occur during the commission of other crimes (such as burglary or robbery).

CASE 3.7

Marcia, 30 years old, asked a woman friend to stay with her while her husband, a doctor, was out of town. She heard her two dogs barking at 2:30 a.m. outside of her second story garage apartment. She was not alarmed; there were three locks on her front door, there was no back door, and the apartment was 18 feet above ground level. But as she went to check an open window a bare chested man wearing an Arab style turban over his head pressed a knife to her throat. He ransacked the apartment, put pillow cases over both women's heads and raped the friend.

After the night of terror she began carrying a .45 caliber pistol. She and her husband put new locks on their windows and set up lights around the yard. When alone, she slept with all the lights in the apartment turned on. A few nights after the attack she returned from a brief vacation to find a make shift ladder at one of the apartment windows and the screens ripped. The prowler, whom Marcia assumed was the rapist bent on another attack, was heard by a neighbor and fled as the police arrived.

"Victims don't stop being victims when the police leave," says Marcia. "Violence is disabling. It changes your life for years." Marcia and her husband have moved from the apartment. She says, "I will never set foot there again. The danger, the dread and the fear are receding. But the rapist is still in my head. I don't think he will ever go away" (Magnuson 1981, p. 19).

Robbery *Robbery* is the taking, or the attempt to take, anything of value from the care, custody, or control of a person or persons by force, by threat of violence, by violence, or by putting the victim in fear. Because of the face-to-face confrontation between perpetrator and victim, the potential for violence is always present in a robbery; and when violence does occur, injuries can range from minor harm to loss of life. Because of its personal and often violent nature, robbery is feared greatly by the public. This fear may well be heightened by perceptions of police inability to deal effectively with the offense (only one in every four reported robberies is solved). And the robbery rate is increasing—from 187 victims per 100,000 inhabitants in 1971 to 251 victims per 100,000 inhabitants in 1981.

As already mentioned the crime of robbery requires that force or threat of force be directed against the physical safety of the victim. Thus, a threat to expose a victim as a homosexual or an embezzler would not satisfy this element of the crime. Proof that force was used—or, at the very least, that threats were made to cause the victim to fear imminent bodily harm—is essential for the successful prosecution of robberies. However, the force used in a robbery to separate victims from their property does not have to be great. When a victim *is* seriously injured, the injury is usually enough to convince an investigator or a jury that force was used. However, difficulties do arise when a victim who claims to have been robbed under the threat of force exhibits no injury. (The taking of property *without* force is the crime of *larceny.*)

In some cases, the difference between a crime classified as a robbery and one classified as a larceny is marginal. Often, the force element of robbery can be satisfied only by determining whether a victim attempted to resist the force used, and to what extent that resistance took place. A typical purse-snatching case is an example: it is generally accepted by courts that a woman who puts her purse next to her on the seat of a bus without keeping her hand on it, or loosely holds it in her hand, is not the victim of robbery if someone quickly grabs the purse and runs (neither the purse nor the woman resisted); however, if the woman were clutching her bag tightly and someone manages to grab it from her, after even a slight struggle or tug-of-war, sufficient force and resistance have occurred to constitute robbery. A good rule to follow is that the removal of an article without more force than is absolutely necessary to remove it from its original resting place constitutes larceny. If any additional force, no matter how slight, is used, the crime is considered robbery.

In addition, the force or threat of force in robbery must precede or accompany the taking. Force applied *after* the taking does not constitute robbery. Thus, victims who realize that their property has been stolen encounter force when attempting to recover that property, are not robbery victims if their property was originally taken without force. When force is not used but is substituted by a threat to the physical well-being of the victim, it is not necessary that the victim be frightened to the point of panic.

It is enough that he or she is reasonably apprehensive and aware of the potential for injury (Swanson, Chamelin, and Territo 1981, pp. 255–56).

Robbery has low clearance rate for several reasons: physical evidence may not be found; the on-scene time of perpetrators is limited; and witnesses are usually shaken, so that their information runs the gamut from minimal to completely erroneous. Physical descriptions are the most common evidence in robbery, but the descriptions are of limited use because the robbers are usually some distance away by the time the police arrive. (Swanson, Chamelin, and Territo 1981, p. 263).

Crimes against property

Among the eight index crimes, the four crimes against property are burglary, larceny-theft, motor vehicle theft, and arson.

Burglary Burglary is the unlawful entry of a structure to commit a felony or theft. The use of force is not a requirement for burglary. In the FBI Uniform Crime Reports, burglary is divided into three classifications: forcible entry, unlawful entry without force, and attempted forcible entry.

Two important aspects of burglary are its frequency and economic impact. Nationally, if reported burglaries were distributed evenly in time, a burglary would occur every ten seconds (Federal Bureau of Investigation 1981, p. 5). The offense accounts for about 31 percent of all reported property crimes. Two-thirds of all burglaries are residential burglaries, the rest being attacks on various commercial establishments **(figure 3.3)**. Although there are more residential burglaries than commercial ones, a business has the greater chance of being victimized (simply because there are fewer of them). Although burglaries of both homes and businesses occur most often on weekdays, a weekend burglary is 1.5 times more likely to occur at a business than at a residence (Pope 1977, p. 33).

The total annual loss due to burglaries is $3.5 billion, with an average loss of $924 per burglary (Federal Bureau of Investigation 1981, p. 20). In nearly two-thirds of all instances where property is stolen in a burglary, stolen items are hard-salable items such as televisions or stereos. Next in order are cash, jewelry, and furs; soft-salable items such as clothing, firearms, negotiable instruments, and drugs; and items from safes. Burglary has a low clearance rate, somewhat less than one in seven. As a rule, burglaries with very low or very high losses have greater clarance rates than the more frequent burglaries with midrange losses.

Burglaries are not the product of modern society; the tomb of the Egyptian Tutankhamen was broken into shortly after his death, and churches and abbeys were constantly victimized in the Middle Ages. Burglary does, however, change with time. Types that flourished even in the recent past have disappeared today: for example, the transom, coal-slide, and dumbwaiter burglaries are virtually extinct. Another rapidly vanishing species is the so-called step-over burglary. Apartment dwellers often place screening or other coverings on windows that open into fire escapes, but they don't cover the windows next to the escapes. A step-over burglar

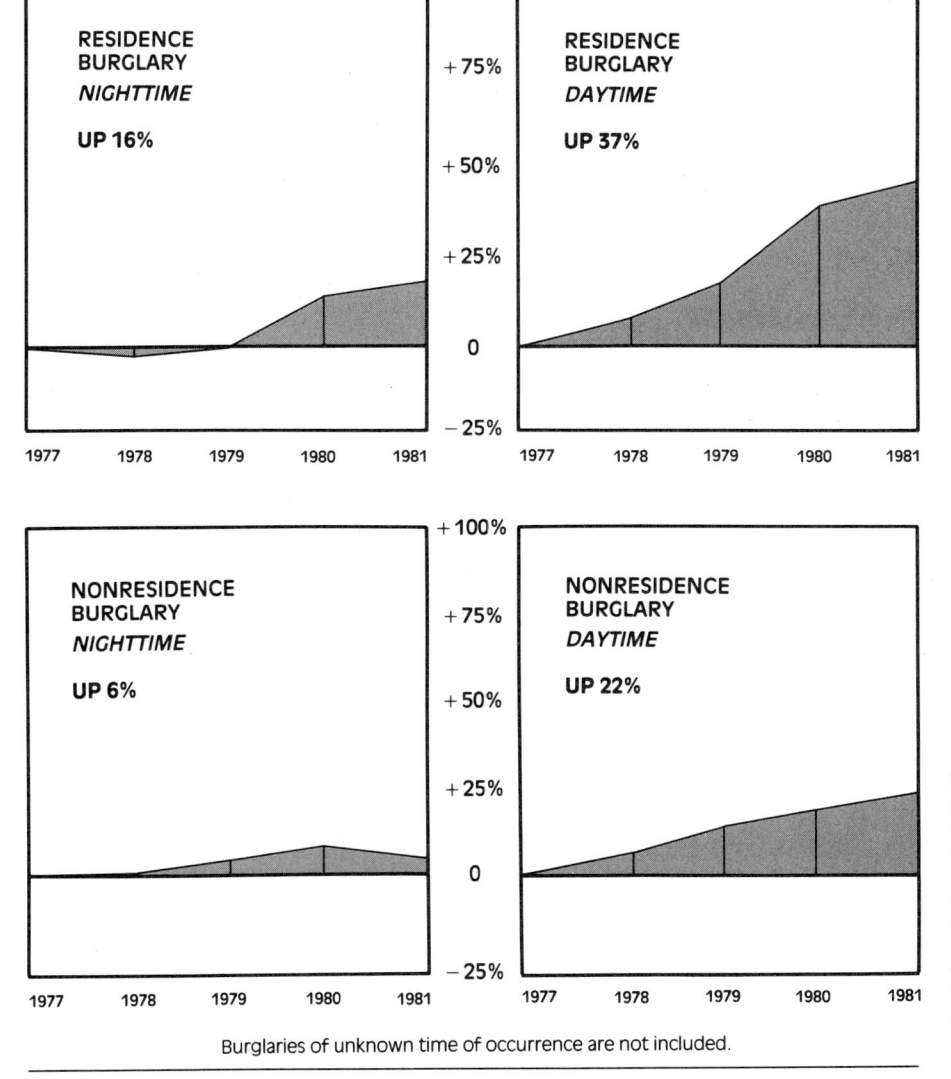

FIGURE 3.3
Percentage changes in number of day and nighttime burglarys, 1977–81.
Data from Federal Bureau of Investigation, *Crime in the United States*, FBI Uniform Crime Reports (Washington, D.C.: U.S. Government Printing Office, 1981), p. 24.

RESIDENCE BURGLARY NIGHTTIME UP 16%
RESIDENCE BURGLARY DAYTIME UP 37%
NONRESIDENCE BURGLARY NIGHTTIME UP 6%
NONRESIDENCE BURGLARY DAYTIME UP 22%

Burglaries of unknown time of occurrence are not included.

crosses from the fire escape to the ledge and enters an unprotected window. This technique has declined since the advent of interior fire escapes.

Although burglars tend to come from lower socioeconomic classes and are often not well educated, there have been notable exceptions. Burglaries have been committed by professors, probation officers, police officers, and psychiatrists. A South Carolina psychiatrist who held a law degree and earned up to $100,000 a year was once arrested, and the arresting officers recovered $500,000 in stolen property, linking the psychiatrist to 150 burglaries in a single county.

Burglars can be classified according to several variables, such as preferences for premises to be attacked and types of property they will or will not take. But the most useful classification is skill. Burglars range from the amateur to the professional, but most are unskilled at their crime.

Professional burglars may commit only four or five offenses each year. Despite the infrequency of their acts, however, they are important to the police because of the large value of cash or property taken and their intimate knowledge of sophisticated fencing systems. In addition to the "big score," the hallmark of the professional is thorough planning preceding each burglary. Professionals refuse to place themselves in jeopardy for anything other than sizable gain, and they do so only after weeks or months of painstaking study of a target. Because they know exactly what they want in advance, professionals do not ransack a premises. Thus, a stolen article may not be missed for some time. Working nationally—or, at the highest professional level, internationally—the professional burglar often operates for a long time without being arrested (Swanson, Chamelin, and Territo 1981, p. 279).

Larceny-theft *Larceny* is the unlawful taking, carrying, or leading away of property from the possession or constructive possession of another without the use of force or fear. It includes crimes such as shoplifting, pick-pocketing, purse snatching, motor vehicle theft, theft of parts and accessories for motor vehicles, and bicycle theft **(figure 3.4)**.

Larcenies make up 54 percent of the eight index crimes. Studies indicate that many offenses in this category, particularly when the value of

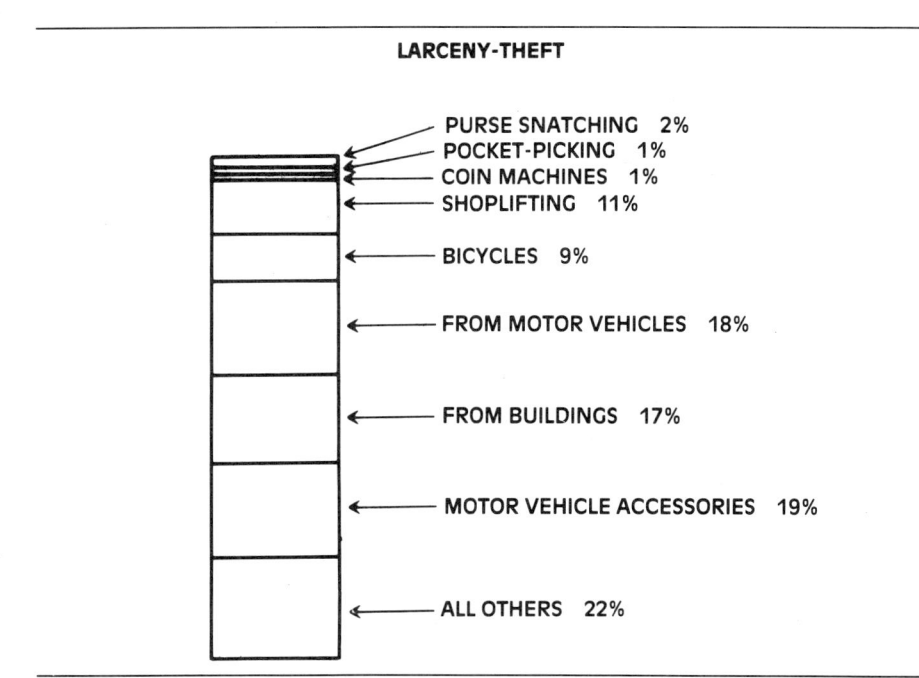

LARCENY-THEFT

- PURSE SNATCHING 2%
- POCKET-PICKING 1%
- COIN MACHINES 1%
- SHOPLIFTING 11%
- BICYCLES 9%
- FROM MOTOR VEHICLES 18%
- FROM BUILDINGS 17%
- MOTOR VEHICLE ACCESSORIES 19%
- ALL OTHERS 22%

FIGURE 3.4
Percentage breakdown of larceny, 1981. Data from Federal Bureau of Investigation, Crime in the United States, *FBI Uniform Crime Reports (Washington, D.C.: U.S. Government Printing Office, 1981), p. 28.*

stolen goods is low, never come to the attention of the police because victims do not report the thefts. In other cases, merchants and business owners are not aware of the total value of the thefts that occur; this is a common problem in the crime of shoplifting.

Most larcenies—37 percent in 1981—consist of thefts of parts, accessories, and contents of motor vehicles (Federal Bureau of Investigation 1981, p. 26). And there is reason to believe that organized crime is now involved extensively in this type of crime. In November 1979, the Senate Permanent Investigations Subcommittee held hearings to look into this problem, and a number of interesting findings emerged. For example, it was found that although a 1966 law aimed at making cars more theft resistant had been effective against teenage joy riding, the law had not stopped professional auto thieves.

The Senate subcommittee also looked into the operations of *chop shops*—garages that strip stolen cars of usable parts and sell the parts to auto repair shops. In a legitimate business, an auto repair shop will call a salvage yard to get a part. Yard owners generally have large inventories of parts obtained at auctions (insurance companies auction wrecks not worth repairing). If the yard does not have the part, it can call upon a network of other yards across the country. In an illegal operation, however, a salvage yard responds to the request for a part and offers a lower-than-cost price and a delivery date. The dishonest yard owner then contacts a thief and instructs him or her to steal the car or truck from which the part is needed. The stolen vehicle is dismantled in a chop shop in a matter of hours, and the part is delivered to the yard owner who requested it. The high cost of replacing parts for automobiles—$23,000 to buy separately what went into a $5,100 car—is considered a prime factor in the emergence of chop shops ("Senate Probing Car Theft Industry," *Atlanta Journal,* 26 November 1979, p. 24).

One law enforcement official, Vladimir Ivkovich, head of the Northern Illinois Auto Theft Unit, testified before the subcommittee that "most body parts for late model automobiles used in the Midwest are supplied by mob-dominated Chicago yards. Detroit, Kansas City, St. Louis, Iowa City, Milwaukee, Indianapolis, Cincinnati, Louisville, Nashville, and many other areas all received a large number of their body parts from Chicago" ("Witness: Chicago Car Thief Capital," *Tampa Tribune,*" 30 November 1979, p. 23A). Ivkovich went on to testify: "They operate in specific territories and specialize in specific makes and models. A thief who specializes in Cadillacs, for example, will be assigned to steal all the Cadillacs needed by a yard while another thief fills the demands for Fords" (ibid).

Bicycle theft The enormous increase in the use of bicycles for sport, transportation, and exercise has not occurred without some serious side effects for the police. The theft of bicycles, especially the more sophisticated and expensive ones, has reached almost epidemic proportions in some areas. Nationally, bicycle theft accounts for 9% of all larceny crimes (Federal Bureau of Investigation 1981, p. 26).

Despite this situation, however, many bike owners are not sufficiently aware of the problem. As a result, they fail to lock their bicycles or they use

Inside a chop shop. Late model automobiles, some of them still bearing license plates, have been partially disassembled. When this photo was taken several of the vehicles shown had not yet been reported stolen. Courtesy Samuel J. Rozzi, Commissioner of Police, Nassau County (New York).

inexpensive, minimum-security locks that only slightly deter thieves. Additionally, parking facilities for bicycles are generally in short supply and are easily compromised. Increasingly, people are buying more expensive ten-speed bicycles, starting in price at $150. This high value makes the bicycles particularly attractive to thieves. Also, the increasing demand for multigeared models makes the disposal of stolen bicycles easier; potential customers can be found almost anywhere.

In a recent national survey conducted in the fifty largest cities and on 200 college campuses, the following facts were revealed: on college campuses, 88 percent of stolen bicycles are locked; in cities, the average is 74 percent. The thief's favorite tool for locked bicycles is the bolt cutter; other tools employed, include hacksaws, hammers, pry bars, lock pliers, and vise grips.

Shoplifting The National Retail Merchants Association indicates that twelve cents of every dollar spent by consumers is an incremental cost due to shoplifting. Shoplifting accounts for 11% of all larceny crimes (Federal Bureau of Investigation 1981, p. 26), and it produces losses exceeding $3.5 billion annually (Meyer 1974, p. 34).

Shoplifters can be classified into two groups on the basis of their use of the merchandise they steal: the commercial shoplifter, or "booster," steals merchandise for resale; the pilferer takes merchandise for private use (Cameron 1964, p. 39).

Two patterns have emerged in shoplifting in recent years; both the dollar amount of the merchandise recovered and the total number of apprehensions have increased substantially. These patterns indicate that more and more people are shoplifting and that the vast majority of them are amateurs. It has been estimated that as many as 95 percent of all shoplifters apprehended are amateurs who do not sell merchandise, yet often have no personal need for it (Curtis 1972, p. 80).

As you might expect, professional shoplifters are not only apprehended less frequently than amateurs, but they also steal more per theft. The professional is frequently a member of a highly skilled and well-organized group. It is not uncommon to find teams of young men and women, ranging in number from three to five, who set out on carefully planned tours throughout the United States. Their itinerary, carefully laid out to the last detail, includes the names of stores that will be visited in various cities.

Participants in shoplifting teams are carefully trained in shoplifting techniques, and they wear special clothing to conceal and carry stolen merchandise. For example, a specially constructed unit called the "booster box" can be ingeniously designed to hold whatever kind of merchandise the shoplifter intends to steal. To an observer, the box appears to be nothing more than a package prepared for mailing; but a slot in the side or bottom allows the shoplifter to insert a stolen item swiftly and surreptitiously. *Booster skirts* or *booster bloomers* are also occasionally used by women. A booster skirt, which can be designed to match current fashion, features a hammocklike bag suspended between the shoplifter's legs. Booster bloomers (old-fashioned bloomers with double rows of tight elastic at the knees) can be worn under booster skirts; slits or pockets in the skirt or dress or an elastic waistband allow merchandise to be stuffed into the concealing recesses of the bloomers. Coat linings tailored to hold merchandise inserted through openings in the bottom of the pockets can also be adapted for men or women. A large handbag, briefcase, or shopping bag is often the trademark of the shoplifter (Cameron 1964, pp. 46–47).

The techniques employed in shoplifting are legion and the appearance and types of shoplifters innumerable. The following cases are but a sampling of the many thousands that occur each year.

CASE 3.8

A teenage girl was picked up outside a department store when a detective noticed that she seemed to have gained a lot of weight in a very short time—half an hour or so. A search revealed that the girl was wearing two bathing suits, three bras, two girdles, four dresses, and a coat. Under the coat were hidden two new pocketbooks and a jewel case.

CASE 3.9

A sixteen-year-old boy walked into a book and record store with a large paper shopping bag containing nothing but a couple of grocery items. Four minutes later he walked out with one dozen well-chosen books and eight long-playing records, more or less concealed by his grocery-store selections. He admitted modestly that he had probably the finest library and record collection of any kid his age.

CASE 3.10

Police in Philadelphia were obliged to arrest an armless man for shoplifting. What had he been stealing? Shoes, when caught, though he confessed to having stolen other items as well. Shoes had been his first choice after the sawmill accident deprived him of his arms and his livelihood. Then, as he developed new skills, he managed to get away with jackets, hats, overcoats, and yet more shoes. Sympathetic salesmen would help him try them on and give him all the time he needed to decide what he wanted. So he would admire himself in the clothes for a while, wait for a propitious moment, and then casually walk out of the store (Alexander and Moolman 1969, pp. 80–81).

Motor vehicle theft *Motor vehicle theft* is the theft or attempted theft of the motor vehicle for nontemporary use. This definition excludes the taking of a motor vehicle for temporary use by someone with lawful access. There were 1,078,988 motor vehicle thefts in 1981, accounting for 9% of all index crimes (Federal Bureau of Investigation 1981, p. 30). These thefts are generally grouped into four categories: joy riding, theft of vehicles for use in other crimes, thefts for transportation, and professional thefts (Swanson, Chamelin, and Territo 1981, p. 330).

Joy riding Car thefts for joy riding constitute the majority of motor vehicle thefts. The perpetrators are usually teenagers—fifteen to nineteen years old—who steal a car on a dare, as initiation into a gang, or for parts and accessories. Youths arrested for car theft are often repeat offenders.

Theft of vehicles for use in other crimes Criminals who plan to commit a crime often steal a vehicle that can be abandoned immediately after the crime and that cannot be traced. The perpetrator usually steals the vehicle as close to the time of the primary crime as possible; this minimizes the possibility that the vehicle theft will be reported to the police, and that a pickup order will be broadcast for the car while the thief is en route to, or departing from, the scene of the primary crime.

Thefts for transportation Thefts for transportation generally involve transients hitchhikers, and runaways. Stolen cars are abandoned when the thief reaches his or her destination or runs out of gas (Horgan 1974, p. 185).

Professional thefts The professional auto thief steals with the specific intent of making a profit, either by dismantling the vehicle for parts or by altering it for resale. Evidence suggests that organized crime is behind the growing steal-to-order car theft industry ("Senate Probing Car Theft Industry," *Atlanta Journal*, 26 November 1979, p. 24).

Arson *Arson* is defined as any willful or malicious burning or attempt to burn—with or without intent to defraud—a dwelling, public building, motor vehicle, aircraft, or personal property of another. Only fires determined through investigation to have been willfully or maliciously set are classified as arsons. Fires of suspicious or unknown origin are excluded. Because arson was not added to the list of index offenses until 1978, limited historical data are available for the crime. Some of the motivations for arson and discussed in the following paragraphs.

Revenge, spite, jealousy Arsons motivated by revenge, spite, and jealousy are often committed by jilted lovers, feuding neighbors, disgruntled employees, quarreling spouses, persons who want to get even after being cheated or abused, and persons incited by racial or religious hostility. Lovers' disputes and domestic squabbles are the greatest contributors to this category (Battle and Weston 1972). In some parts of the country, particularly in rural areas, disagreements often result in the burning of homes or barns. Alcohol consumption is often associated with this type of fire (Inciardi 1970).

Vandalism, malicious mischief Vandalism fires are set by individuals or groups who are looking primarily for excitement without any other immediate or premeditated motive. Many fires in vacant buildings can be attributed to this motive. Vandalism is also a prominent cause of fires in abandoned cars and garbage cans; these "junk" fires are often started to protest local conditions or to promote "instant urban renewal" ("The Undeclared War on the Nation's Firemen," *Parade*, 18 July 1971, p. 4). Other vandalism fires are associated with the presence of vagrants and drug users. Such fires are rapidly increasing in frequency.

Crime concealment, diversion Criminals sometimes set fires to obliterate the evidence of burglaries, larcenies, and murders. A fire may destroy evidence connecting a perpetrator to a crime, or, in the case of murder, make it impossible to identify a victim. People also set fires to destroy records containing evidence of embezzlement, forgery, or fraud. Arson has also been used to divert attention from a burglary or to cover attempted escapes from jails, prisons, and state hospitals.

Profit, insurance fraud There are many ways to profit from arson. If a property is insured and the value of the policy is greater than the sale value the owner could receive on the market, then the owner may decide to defraud the insurance company by burning the property. (Such a situation is known as a moral hazard.)

Intimidation, extortion, sabotage Striking workers and employers have used arson to intimidate each other during strikes. Criminals, particularly mobsters, have used it to intimidate witnesses and as a means of extortion.

Psychiatric afflictions: The pyromaniac and the schizophrenic firesetter. Pyromaniacs differ from other arsonists in that they lack conscious motivation for firesetting. In fact, they are considered by many to be motiveless (Rider 1980, p. 12). Lewis and Yarnell describe pyromaniacs as ". . . offenders who said they set their fires for no practical reason, and received no material profit from the act, their only motive being some sort of sensual satisfaction" (1951, p. 86).

The urge to set fires has been referred to as the "irresistible impulse." However, authorities should be cautioned about accepting this explanation. Some researchers postulate that the behavior is engaged in to release sexual tension. However, one researcher notes that although sexual tension may be a motivation in some incendiarism, it may not be a cause. And Lewis and Yarnell, in their study of pyromania, found that only a small percentage of arsonists claim to receive sexual gratification from firesetting (Gold 1962, p. 407).

Psychosis is a severe personality disorder characterized by marked impairment of contact with reality and personal and social functioning. Delusions, hallucinations, emotional blunting, and bizarre behavior may also be present. The most serious of all psychotic disorders is schizophrenia, which has been defined as "a group of psychotic disorders characterized by gross distortions of reality, withdrawal from social interaction, and disorganization and fragmentation of perception, thought, and emotion" (Lewis and Yarnell 1951, p. 118).

In one study of 1145 male firesetters, 13.4 percent (or 154) were diagnosed as psychotic. These findings indicate that psychotic firesetters are distinct from others in that (1) they set fires for suicidal purposes, (2) their motives are delusional in character, or (3) they manifest bizarre behavior either during or immediately after the firesetting (Coleman 1980, p. 395). Despite these distinctions, however, psychotic firesetters often fall within other categories as well (i.e., revenge firesetters and pyromaniacs) (Lewis and Yarnell 1951, p. 376).

Politics, terrorism Political fires are premeditated and set to dramatize an issue, embarrass authorities or political opponents, or intimidate or extort for political reasons. Fires set to protest the Vietnam War and other military activities fall into this category, along with most "bank burnings," some fires associated with racial protest, and general antiestablishment fires. Sometimes the fires are carefully planned by revolutionary groups who attack responding units, open fire hydrants to deplete water supplies, place bombs on the premises, and set diversionary fires. This type of fire increased considerably during the 1960s and was closely correlated with the rise of civil disturbances and bombings.

Vanity, heroism On occasion, the person who "discovers" a fire is the one who starts it. The motivation is to be noticed, to be a hero.

CASE 3.11

A private guard organization hired extra personnel and after a short period of time promoted one of the men to sergeant. However, after a while the company decided the extra guards were not needed and they discussed reducing the force. This would have resulted in a demotion for the sergeant. Shortly thereafter, a fire was discovered by the sergeant and as a result of his quick action and quick response by the fire department the fire was confined, although it did cause thousands of dollars worth of damage. Arson investigators became suspicious and requested the sergeant to take the polygraph. After the sergeant was examined on the polygraph, which showed reactions indicative of deception, he confessed to a police lieutenant that he had in fact set the fire. The transcript of his criminal record revealed he had recently been released from a mental institution in another state, having been sent there in lieu of going to state prison (Bates 1975, pp. 43–44).

Crime data manipulation

Although most police departments report crimes accurately to the FBI, *crime data manipulation* does sometimes occur—and for various reasons. For example, a police chief may want to convey the impression to citizens and superiors that everything is under control and that the police department is doing an effective job. Another chief, angry about potential budget reductions and personnel cutbacks, may manipulate statistics or reporting procedures to convey the impression that crime is increasing dramatically and that cutbacks will worsen the problem. And a sheriff preparing for reelection who is concerned about the effect of rising crime on his or her reputation may urge deputies to discourage citizens from making crime reports or may instruct deputies to reclassify serious crimes as less serious offenses. As Patrick Murphy, president of the Police Foundation in Washington, D.C., commented in a recent news article, "When I was a rookie in the 72nd precinct in Brooklyn, no police commander worth his salt would admit he couldn't control crime—and proved it by controlling statistics" (Magnuson 1981, p. 17).

INDEPENDENT AUDIT DEMANDED FOLLOWING CHARGES THAT CHICAGO POLICE MANIPULATED CRIME STATISTICS
Law Enforcement News

The Chicago Crime Commission has called for an independent audit of the Chicago Police Department's crime statistics after a television news report last month accused the department of covering up the true numbers of crime in the city.

In a four-part series, station WBBM-TV in Chicago alleged that Chicago police falsify reports and violate FBI standards for crime reporting in an effort to make the city appear safer.

The report said that Chicago police kill nearly half of the reports of rape it receives and nearly a third of the robbery and burglary reports. It said the percentage of reports the department declares unfounded is six times that of police in eight other cities surveyed.

Police superintendent Richard Brzeczek has promised to launch an internal investigation of the charges, saying anyone found guilty of falsifying reports will be fired.

He denied assertions that the manipulation of crime statistics is condoned by police management and said comparisons between the "unfounded" rates in Chicago and other cities is invalid because of differences in how reports are taken in various police departments.

But Brzeczek's promise of an internal audit has not satisfied the Crime Commission. Executive Director Patrick Healy said the commission will continue to push for an independent investigation.

"An independent, objective review must occur," he said. "The Chicago Crime Commission plans to take on the responsibility of keeping the issue before the Chicago community until such an audit occurs."

The WBBM-TV report focused on how Chicago police handle reports of robberies, burglaries, and rapes. Reporter Pam Zekman alleged that anywhere from 44 to 57 percent of robbery cases reported during her eight-month investigation were "literally wiped off the books." She also said nearly half of the rape cases reported during that time were not counted, and that one out of every three burglaries reported were not counted.

She said the manipulation of crime statistics occur in three ways.

The first, she said, is that police declare large numbers of crime reports unfounded, many times because the person making the complaint reportedly could not be found. Zekman located and interviewed three crime victims who claimed that the crimes they reported had been declared unfounded although no attempt was made to contact them.

Zekman claimed that Chicago police declared 9,000 robbery reports unfounded last year, one out of every three reported. She said New York, Los Angeles and St. Louis declared fewer than one out of a hundred unfounded.

But Brzeczek said comparing those statistics is "like comparing apples and oranges." He said police in other cities may exercise more discretion before taking the report, making their decisions about what reports are unfounded in a less formal way that would not show up in unfounding statistics.

Zekman also reported that Chicago police play down crime rates by reclassifying many crimes as less serious offenses. She said police killed 16,000 burglary reports last year, half of them by declaring the reports unfounded and half by reclassifying them to less serious crimes.

Police also changed or omitted evidence on crime reports to make the reports appear unfounded or less serious, Zekman alleged. She interviewed two rape victims who say medical evidence that supported their claims was omitted from the reports and their cases dropped. A burglary victim claimed that the report of a break-in at her home was changed to say the door had been left open although the door frame showed damage from the burglar's forced entry.

Brzeczek said he has no knowledge of such manipulation of reports, but that he will investigate the charges. "If it's something that some people are doing, we'll stop it," he said.

John Dineen, president of the Chicago Fraternal Order of Police, said the television reports of falsifying information on crime reports exaggerate the problem, but said he is concerned with the number of crimes that are reclassified as less serious offenses or dropped.

"If the administration continually downgrades crime, it hurts," Dineen said. "When you get a television station saying that the police department is taking burglaries and making thefts out of them, and that sort of thing, the public has to begin to wonder."

Dineen said he thinks crimes are reclassified because "no city wants to be known as a city where crime is high. No one wants that onus put on them."

But Brzeczek said the department is not playing down crime to improve the city's image and denied that manipulating the reports is "standard operating procedure," as one officer asserted in the television reports.

"It absolutely is not" Brzeczek said. "This is not something that has come down from the top."

The superintendent said that if the internal audit shows that there is a systemic problem with declaring reports unfounded or reclassifying them, he will consider hiring an outside auditor.

Brzeczek said he believes the internal audit will root out any problem. "If the internal audit can't be trusted, then you're saying I can't be trusted, and if I can't be trusted, they better find somebody else for this job."

But Healy said an independent audit must be made because any inaccuracy in crime figures would create "a myriad of problems" for the Chicago criminal justice system.

He said playing down crime could mean that city government hasn't properly allocated its resources for dealing with crime, that citizens are operating with an incorrect perception of the danger they're in, that citizens will stop calling police to report crime if they feel they are getting no response and that city officials can't accurately measure the effectiveness of the department.

"The accurate reporting of incidences of crime is central to protection of any community." Healy said.

Brzeczek challenged the Crime Commission's procedure in handling the problem. He said the commission called for an independent audit before meeting with him to discuss the television report.

"I think they should have sat down with me to talk it over before issuing their press release," he said.

Law Enforcement News Vol. VIII, No. 22, 27 December 1982

The circumstances described in the following news story suggest another reason—more economically pragmatic and self-serving—for manipulating crime statistics.

CLEVELAND MAYOR SAYS LESS CRIME PAYS

CLEVELAND, Ohio—Cleveland Mayor Ralph Perk told city policemen that if they can't cut crime by 5 per cent next month he'll cut their paychecks Jan. 1. Perk said if crime doesn't drop he'll withhold promised longevity differential and uniform allowance money until it does. The money, about $150 per man per year for uniforms and $60 to $480 for longevity, was to have been paid to policemen starting Jan. 1. The statement brought an angry response from James Magas, president of the Police Patrolmens Association, who called the Mayor's action "a political grandstand gesture."

Perk said he received telephone calls nightly at his home from citizens complaining about crime in the city. "I want the police department to reduce crime by 5 per cent in each category in the month of December," the Mayor said. "I have ordered the safety director to beef up the force to drive out the drug pushers and cut down on crime. We have 1,900 patrolmen on duty. Nine hundred of these have permission to work at least four hours overtime daily."

Safety Director James Carney said putting men on overtime should help in reducing the crime rate. Police department statistics for January through September this year show that homicides and rapes increased in the city compared with the corresponding period of last year, but there was a reduction in other major crimes.

"The Mayor is making the police department the whipping boy for the increase in crime," Magas said. He said additional policemen were needed to combat crime but that working men overtime was not the answer. Magas said the department has an authorized strength of 2,750 but that there are less than 2,400 on the force.

Crime Control Digest, 15 December 1972, p. 6. Reprinted with permission of *Crime Control Digest.*

Another technique used by police departments to manipulate crime data is a practice referred to as *clearing the books*. Although not regularly engaged in by police departments, the practice is not as uncommon as one might think. Certainly, in those communities where the practice is employed, there is a distorted picture of the crime problem and the ability of the police to solve crime.

CASE 3.12

Frank, a twenty-six-year-old previously convicted burglar, was arrested by police inside an appliance store he had broken into. There was little doubt in Frank's mind that he was going to be convicted and sent back to prison. The detectives who interrogated him realized his desperate plight and seized upon the opportunity to improve their own difficulties with a dramatically increasing burglary rate.

The detectives approached Frank with a "deal" that they described as mutually beneficial. If Frank would accept responsibility for approximately fifty unsolved burglaries, they would put in a "good word" for him with the local prosecutor, judge, and parole and probation officer who would eventually be doing his presentence investigation. Frank, of course, would only be charged with the crime he actually committed. Frank agreed, and as the detectives promised, they put in a "good word" with the appropriate people. In turn, Frank was given a lighter sentence than he might normally have received.

What crime does to victims and society

There is always a danger when studying crime to overlook the tragic impact it has on individual victims and society. Victims are too often lumped into a "victim profile," where they become part of a "crime trend." People who study crime should never lose sight of the fact that crime has tragic affects on people and their families and an equally important and profound affect upon the way we live and interact as a society. The following news story provides valuable insight into this aspect of crime.

WHAT CRIME DOES TO THE VICTIMS AND SOCIETY
By John Leo. Reported by Steven Holmes and Christopher Redman/Detroit, with other U.S. bureaus   TIME

Miami was host to a convention of travel agents last week. The city fathers, anxious to show how safe Miami really is, blanketed the better areas with extra police. Outside an elegant restaurant in Coconut Grove, four visitors witnessed a mugging. It was not an especially dramatic incident, and the visitors were not hurt or even involved. Yet afterward all four sat at their table, unable to eat because of their rage and fear. Incidents like that are common these days and so is a common feeling: no matter how many police are around, the feral youngsters who account for most U.S. crime seem to be able to strike when and where they wish. Says Criminal Justice Planner Bruce Hamersley of Miami: "The stability of the community has been destroyed. We are now living in a period where uncertainty is the rule rather than the exception."

Last September's *Figgie Report on Fear of Crime* warned that "Americans have today become afraid of one another. Confronted with this frightening new challenge, American ability to act is rendered ineffective. Fear of violent crime seems to have made the country helpless, incapable of dealing with the sources of its fear." More important, perhaps, the report says that fear "may be one of the key factors impeding society's ability to cope successfully with those problems."

That fear is measurable in the ways in which Americans are adapting to the new realities of crime—the gun sales, the overbooked karate classes, the rush to buy burglarproof locks for doors and windows. It can also be seen in the ways in which Americans have consciously changed the pattern of their lives. Wealthy businessmen, fearful of kidnapping, who drive to work by different routes each day. Ordinary citizens who learn to walk the streets turning their heads from side to side to check on who might be behind them. Joggers learn to carry at least $20 in "mugger's money," to avoid being shot.

The feeling that all citizens are vulnerable to crime is especially strong among the elderly. Says James Gilsinan, a criminologist at St. Louis University: "The elderly feel a loss of power, of control, of decision making in most facets of their lives. The feeling that they are victims in other areas spills over into crime as well. The elderly stay in a lot, and when they do go out they tend to be in group situations"—which, Gilsinan points out, reduces their chances of being victimized.

Some of the adjustments in life-styles can be quirky. Mimi Warren, 26, of Philadelphia, has developed her own "waiting for a bus behavior." If she sees anyone near a bus stop at night, she breaks into sunny chatter, on the theory that even if the person is a mugger, the conversation will reduce her chances of being attacked. Hilary Stephenson, 38, also of Philadelphia, parks illegally outside her house at night because she would rather pay the parking tickets than walk four blocks from her garage. When she was lost in an unfamiliar part of town, she purposely drove the wrong way down a one-way street to attract a policeman's attention rather than stop and ask for directions. She arranges to call a friend after arriving home from an evening out, with the understanding that the friend will summon police if there is no call. Says Stephenson, who is divorced and lives alone: "With the collapse of the nuclear family, you've got all these singles tucked away in little boxes. I think we must become each other's family."

To be sure, some people make a loud point of taking no precautions, often on the ground that criminals should not have the power to impose a quivering form of life on anyone. Former Attorney General Griffin Bell refuses to get a burglar alarm for his expensive home in northwest Atlanta. Nevenka Charia, 56, a sales clerk in New Orleans, is adamant about not changing her daily patterns out of fear of crime. "I refuse to restrict myself in my movements, day and night, or stay locked up in this house. That's not living at all." But she bought a handgun last December, and on Jan. 8, shot and killed one of two men who attacked her late at night in front of her house. She had never fired a gun before, and is now taking lessons. "It's difficult to say to anyone that they should have a gun," says Charia. "But I'll say this: by all means, fight back, resist, don't be afraid."

Police strongly disagree with her view, but people are beginning to fight back, sometimes in an organized way. At least three times in recent months, groups of subway riders in New York City have grappled with muggers and held them for police. In Memphis last month, Robert Druien, 31, happened to be in Union Planters National Bank during a robbery. He chased the robber to his car, was knocked down when the robber put the car suddenly into reverse, but then got up and joined three other citizens in a car chase through the midtown area. They got their man. Druien hit him in the face and sat on him until police arrived. In Wilmington, Del., after a woman was found dead and mutilated last year, residents of a high-rise apartment complex launched a "crime-watch program," monitoring a police radio scanner and looking out the window for signs of trouble. Richmond has a well-organized program in which neighbors agree to watch one another's homes and report suspicious behavior to police via CB radios.

"People are struggling to find a way to deal with the crime problem," says Catherine Bacharach, who has helped organize volunteer anticrime groups in Philadelphia with federal funds. "I see the rage and anger as healthy when it's channeled in a positive direction. My sense is that people who work in the system have recognized the need to work with community groups."

Not all officials feel that way. New York City authorities are ambivalent about the Guardian Angels, a group of unarmed red-bereted youngsters, mostly black and Hispanic, who patrol the subways. Though they clearly make riders feel safer, Mayor Edward Koch has labeled them "paramilitary," and the powerful transit police union regards them as amateurs. More muscular kinds of vigilante groups have begun to pop up and around the country. Frank J. Shaw, 60, a retired union organizer and one of the new breed of vigilantes, is a folk hero in Panorama City, Calif. His 40-member citizens' patrol cruises the area by car, armed with floodlights and Mace, staying in touch by CB radio. "We're not flag-waving heroes. We are angry," says Shaw. "We can put blindfolds on, close the shades, turn on the television and be in another world that we hope doesn't close in on us. Or we can face up to reality."

Part of the new reaction to crime is more attention to the victims of violent crimes. As psychologists have warned for years, a victim's lingering fear can be chronic and crippling. Ann McCaughey saw a hand reaching in the window of her Boston apartment one night. She screamed and the hand withdrew. Now she does not sleep well and the slightest noise at night can make her hyperventilate. Says her boyfriend: "It really gets to you. You don't forget." The couple are planning to move. "Being victimized is disabling, even when the crime is unsuccessful," says McCaughey's friend.

As a counselor to rape victims in southern New York State, Registered Nurse Bonnie Hollenbeck began to notice some of the hidden effects of rape and other sexual abuse—confusion, low self-esteem and an impaired ability to function in the adult world. Says Hollenbeck: "Many of these women have failed to establish a connection between their history as victims of sexual crimes and their current difficulties." She and a few colleagues have set up a volunteer crisis counseling group to move in quickly after an assault to help the victim deal with anger, depression and grief.

J. Richard Ciccone, a University of Rochester psychiatrist, thinks all victims of violent crime need that kind of help: the trauma of a beating, a stabbing or a rape requires a period of mourning, just like the death of a loved one. Says he: "Victims who do not receive appropriate understanding and treatment often fall into chronic depression, lose their ability to make their way in the world and become reclusive shadows of their former selves." Though blaming the victim often happens in rape cases, Ciccone warns that many families manage to heap blame on all victims of violence, increasing grief and guilt by saying something like "I warned you never to go into that bar." Unless society begins to do more, he warns, the epidemic of crime will be paralleled by an epidemic of psychiatric problems in victims.

In Jackson Park Highlands, an integrated neighborhood near the University of Chicago, people have begun showing up in court to support crime victims and witnesses. "There is a strong sense of community among those engaged in criminal activity," says Louise Schiff, who works with the program. "You go to court and the defendant's relatives and friends are all there. I think a person who has been victimized deserves support too." Nearby Evanston, Ill., has a more formal victim-witness program, funded through the police budget. The unit assigns social workers and other professionals to guide a victim through emotional recovery and legal complaint. Says Police Chief William C. McHugh: "It helps in a lot of ways."

Experts agree that there tends to be less crime in cohesive, closely knit communities with shared values and a strong sense of neighborhood. But artificially instilling this community spirit into a mobile society is difficult. Some psychologists believe that Americans are becoming dehumanized by crime—not just by the reality but by the fear of it, and the pervasiveness of violent scenes in newspapers and on television. Some social scientists believe that public paranoia has led not only to demands for the restoration of capital punishment and long prison sentences but also to such ugly phenomena as the resurgence of the Ku Klux Klan. "The country is becoming more conservative and punitive," says John Matthews, a sociologist for the Houston police. Indeed, some in authority envision a day when the public will want crime stopped—and will not much care how. "Frustration and fears are very natural reactions when people feel their lives are being shaped by forces beyond their control," says California Supreme Court Justice Rose Elizabeth Bird. She believes there is "great power" in such anger, but great danger as well.

Reprinted by permission from TIME, 23 March 1981, pp. 29–30.

Summary

In this chapter we wanted to accomplish a number of objectives. First, we attempted to familiarize the reader with the crime reporting system in the

United States. The Uniform Crime Reporting Program is a voluntary system established in 1930 by the International Association of Chiefs of Police, with the FBI serving as the national clearinghouse. With crime statistics voluntarily contributed by over 15,000 law enforcement agencies throughout the country, the UCR program provides periodic assessments of crime in the United States. Data from the program are widely used by criminal justice professionals, legislators, and scholars who have an interest in the crime problem.

Second, we examined the eight index crimes and defined and described the elements of each and, when applicable, provided case examples of each crime. These eight crimes are frequently divided into the following two broad categories: violent crimes (murder and nonnegligent manslaughter, aggravated assault, forcible rape, and robbery) and crimes against property (burglary, larceny, motor vehicle theft, and arson).

Murder and nonnegligent manslaughter have the highest clearance rate of all index crimes. This is in part because of the high percentage of these offenses that are spontaneous and poorly planned; in part because these crimes normally receive more intensive investigative efforts by police than the other index crimes. However, the solution rate for this category of crimes has decreased from 84 percent in 1971 to 72 percent in 1981. This is in part because an increasing percentage of these crimes involve total strangers and are committed during the commission of other crimes such as burglaries, robberies and rapes. Crimes involving strangers are typically more difficult to investigate and solve.

Aggravated assault, like murder and nonnegligent manslaughter, involve a high percentage of people who live together, work together, play together, or socialize together. Aggravated assaults also have a fairly high clearance rate—58 percent—but one quite a bit lower than the solution rate for criminal homicide. The nature of the injuries and close relationship between the victims and assailants are part of the reason. For example, if the victim's injuries are not serious, (nonlethal, or will not cause permanent injury) and if the victim and assailant know each other, there is a tendency for police not to conduct highly intensive investigations. In such cases it is also common for the victim to be reluctant to cooperate with the police, thus hampering police investigative efforts.

Forcible rapes reported to the police have increased dramatically during the past decade. In 1971 the rate was 40 per 100,000 females in the United States and in 1981 it was 69 per 100,000 females in the United States. At the same time the clearance rate for this crime decreased from 55 percent in 1971 to 48 percent in 1981. According to a number of victimization studies, rape is one of the most underreported violent crimes. Reluctance on the part of victims to report rapes results from their expectations of how they will be treated by the criminal justice system. The perceptions that most citizens have about the way victims are handled come largely from the news media and from highly dramatic television programs, both of which often focus on mistreatment of the victim by the police, prosecutors, and courts. Fortunately a variety of educational and preventive programs sponsored by police and private groups are modifying some of these distorted perceptions.

Robbery, the last in the category of violent crimes, has the lowest solution rate, 24 percent. This low solution rate results because physical evidence at the scene of the robbery is rarely present, the on-scene time of the perpetrator is limited, and witnesses are usually of little value because they are usually quite frightened and nervous at the time of the offense. Because of its personal and often violent nature, robbery is one of the crimes most feared by the public.

Two important aspects of the crime of burglary are its frequency and economic impact. Burglary comprises 31 percent of all reported property crimes, with an annual estimated loss at $2.2 billion. Burglars tend to come from lower socio-economic classes and are usually not well educated, but notable exceptions include a professor of sociology, a probation officer, police officers in several cities, and, in one case, a psychiatrist.

While burglars are classified according to a number of variables, the most useful classification is skill. This continuum ranges from amateur to professional, with most burglars falling into the latter category.

Larceny, another crime of property, contains a variety of specific offenses including shoplifting, pocket picking, purse snatching, thefts from motor vehicles, theft of motor vehicle parts and accessories, and bicycle theft. This type of crime comprises 54 percent of the total index crime with losses to victims at a very conservative estimate of $1.7 billion per year and a clearance rate of only 19 percent.

Motor vehicle theft, which comprises 9 percent of the index crime, and which has a clearance rate of 14 percent, is generally divided into four types of theft by police. These are: theft by joy riders, theft of vehicle for use in other crimes, theft for transportation, and theft by professional auto thieves.

Arson was added to the index crimes in 1978 because of the growing severity of the problem at the national level. Police generally classify arson as the result of: revenge and spiteful jealousy; vandalism and malicious mischief; crime concealment and diversionary tactics; attempts to profit through insurance fraud; intimidation, extortion, and sabotage; psychiatric afflictions; political terrorism; and vanity heroism.

The third objective of this chapter was to examine the practice found in some law enforcement agencies of manipulating crime data. Such a practice is engaged in for a number of reasons. The practice may be engaged in by police administrators to dispute reports by the public or media critical of the agency's crime fighting capabilities. In other cases police administrators may wish to pressure elected officials into allocating greater resources for personnel and equipment. Such manipulation is the exception rather than the rule.

Lastly we wanted to provide the reader with some insights into the effects of crime on both the victim and society. The individual cases discussed in the *Time* magazine article assisted in accomplishing this objective.

issue paper

GUN CONTROL

Gun control, like the death penalty, is not a single issue: it is a complicated tangle of viewpoints, positions, and opinions. Does gun control mean the total abolition of *all* firearms or merely a ban on the manufacture and sale of handguns, especially the infamous *Saturday Night Special?* Is gun registration the first step toward official confiscation of privately owned weapons? Where should the authority for gun control be placed? With the federal government? With state legislatures? With local governments? What kinds of penal sanctions should be imposed for violations of gun laws? Fines or imprisonment? These are but a few of the questions raised by the simple phrase "gun control."

As in the case of capital punishment, it is possible to identify a broad spectrum of positions on nearly every issue raised by gun control. Extreme opponents of gun control are usually against restrictions of *any* kind on the manufacture, importation, sale, ownership, or use of any firearm. Extreme advocates of gun control portray opponents as "rednecks" or cowboys (urban or Western)—or as unwashed denizens of the swamp or backwoods who drive pickup trucks adorned with squirrel tails on the aerial and bumper stickers that read, "I will give up my gun when you pry it from my cold, dead fingers." More articulate spokespersons for the side against gun control cite the Second Amendment to the U.S. Constitution as part of the rationale for opposing anything that even *suggests* the possibility of weapons confiscation. They further support their position by referring to the Soviet invasion of Afghanistan in 1978, which featured a widescale resistance movement against foreign aggressors and depended for its success on a population trained in the use of privately owned firearms.

In turn, supporters of gun control question the extent to which it is possible to draw any kind of parallel between Afghanians and Americans. Further, they cite the example of countries such as England and Japan—countries with low rates of violent crime—that have strict controls on privately owned firearms. Both extreme and moderate proponents argue that the principal source of opposition to gun control legislation is the lobbying activity of the National Rifle Association (NRA), which represents the financial interests of gun manufacturers, importers, and distributors. It is this powerful interest group, proponents maintain, that has managed for more than two decades to frustrate legislative efforts to carry out the will of the majority of the public, as expressed in poll after poll.

> **AMENDMENT II** (1791)
> A well regulated Militia, being necessary to the security of a free State, the right of the people to keep and bear Arms, shall not be infringed.

Kukla (1973), in a work copyrighted by the NRA, maintains that gun controls have historically been the forerunner of government oppression—that gun controls are a euphemism for confiscation. His argument that once a person has formed a homicidal intent, the actual instrument used to carry out the homicide is incidental, is expressed by the rather oversimplified formula, "Guns do not kill; people kill people."

Research on gun control is apt to be even less conclusive than research on the death penalty. Comparative studies of the relationship between gun control statutes and crime rates for violent offenses in the United States and other nations suffer from limitations imposed by differences in history, culture, and population composition. Comparative studies of different jurisdictions in the United States are subject to similar, though less restrictive, limitations.

Williams and McGrath (1975), in a study of the attitudes of people who own firearms in the United States, reported that liberal persons are less likely to own guns than nonliberals; that persons who are prone to violence are most likely to own guns; and that more pessimistic persons are less likely to own firearms. The study stated that people who have been victims of crime are more likely to own guns, but not to the degree expected. An additional finding was that those who fear their neighborhoods are *less* likely to own guns than those who do not fear their neighborhoods; no explanation was provided for this phenomenon.

Schuman and Presser (1977), after an analysis of public support for firearms registration as expressed in opinion polls, raised serious questions about the adequacy of traditional polling procedures. The study investigated three major hypotheses:

1 Gun registration sentiment tends to vary appreciably with the wording of a poll, and is therefore less crystallized than survey data suggest.
2 Opinions *against* registration are held with greater intensity than opinions *for* registration; thus, someone against registration is more likely to engage in political action.
3 Opposition to gun registration is found primarily among people with greater political knowledge and influence; thus, their opinions have a disproportionate impact on legislators.

Evidence was found to support the first two hypotheses, but not the third.

The weapons effect

Psychologist Leonard Berkowitz has argued that "the finger pulls the trigger, but the trigger may also be pulling the finger" (1968, p. 22). This phenomenon, which Berkowitz identified as the *weapons effect,* was shown in a laboratory situation when the mere presence of guns stimulated aggressive behavior and violence from people exposed to mild stress. In a later, more realistic study carried out in a field setting, more angry honking of horns was made by motorists who found their passage blocked at a traffic signal by a stalled truck with a rifle in a gun rack and a bumper sticker reading "Vengeance," than when an unaccoutered truck blocked the way (Turner, Layton, and Simons, 1975).

If Berkowitz's concept of the weapons effect has any validity, and guns not only permit violence but stimulate it as well, one possible approach to curbing serious or lethal interpersonal violence is to limit the availability of guns by imposing stricter gun controls. However, regardless of whether or not one accepts this premise, the fact is that if every gun in the United States suddenly disappeared (which of course they will not), the number of murders would most certainly decrease. Even if we assume that the use of guns does not increase the number of violent crimes, the fact is that most alternative weapons (e.g., knives, clubs, bottles) are less apt to inflict fatal wounds. If, for example, all of the people murdered with guns in 1981 had instead been assaulted with a knife, club, or bottle, many of them would be alive today (see **figure 3.5**).

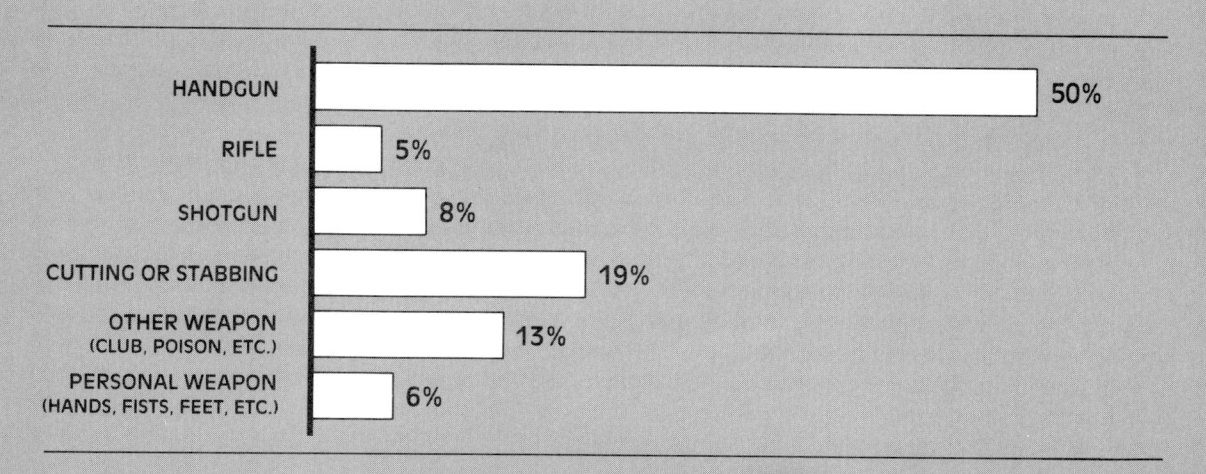

HANDGUN	50%
RIFLE	5%
SHOTGUN	8%
CUTTING OR STABBING	19%
OTHER WEAPON (CLUB, POISON, ETC.)	13%
PERSONAL WEAPON (HANDS, FISTS, FEET, ETC.)	6%

FIGURE 3.5
Weapons used in murder, 1981. Data from Federal Bureau of Investigation, Crime in the United States, *FBI Uniform Crime Reports (Washington, D.C.: U.S. Government Printing Office, 1981), p. 12.*

Gun control violations and mandatory sentencing

In 1975, Massachusetts enacted what was considered to be the nation's toughest gun control law. Among its provisions were the imposition of a one-year mandatory sentence for a conviction of carrying a gun illegally in public. An assessment of the effects of this law by *U.S. News and World Report* (Oster 1976) indicated that, although the law apparently reduced unpremeditated crimes such as passion shootings, it had little or no effect on premeditated offenses such as armed robbery.

The Massachusetts example was emulated by New York in 1980; and two Connecticut statutes that were signed into law in May 1981 provide for a five-year *extra* prison term for persons convicted of committing a felony while armed, as well as a mandatory one-year sentence for persons carrying unlicensed handguns.

Severe sentences imposed without discretion are often touted as the panacea for violent crime. Unfortunately, our experience with sentencing procedures tends to weaken, rather than strengthen, our belief in the efficacy of such measures. When laws seek to impose penal sanctions that are regarded as extremely harsh, a likely result is that prosecutors will be reluctant to indict, juries reluctant to convict, and judges reluctant to sentence. The result is nonenforcement. History tells us that at the end of the eighteenth century England had more than 200 laws prescribing the death penalty; yet relatively few executions were carried out under these provisions.

Conclusion

The National Commission on Criminal Justice Standards and Goals, in its terminal report "A National Strategy to Reduce Crime" (1973), argues that (1) the private possession of handguns should be prohibited for all persons other than law enforcement and military personnel; (2) the manufacture and sale of handguns should be terminated; (3) existing handguns should be acquired by the states; and (4) handguns held by private citizens as collector's items should be modified and rendered inoperative. These recommendations apply only to handguns, not to rifles or shotguns. The responsibility for carrying out the recommendations is left to the states, although the commission speaks of "strenuously enforcing" existing federal, state, and local laws.

When President Reagan and several members of his party were gunned down in 1981 by an emotionally disturbed young man named Hinckley, the expected cry for strict gun control legislation was heard. But opponents of gun control took heart when Reagan made it clear in his first public appearances after the shooting that he was on their side. With this kind of support, it is unlikely that the gun control situation will change in the immediate future.

Discussion and review

1. What are the two categories that encompass the eight index crimes?
2. Why is the clearance rate for murder higher than the clearance rate for the other index crimes?
3. Why is the clearance rate for aggravated assault lower than the clearance rate for murder, even though both crimes often involve close relationships between victims and assailants?
4. Why is rape one of the most underreported violent crimes?
5. What is the difference between robbery and larceny?
6. What are "chop shops"?
7. What are the four categories of motor vehicle theft?
8. What are the major motivations for the crime of arson?
9. Why would a law enforcement agency manipulate crime data?
10. What is the "weapons effect" described by Berkowitz?
11. Would the elimination of all guns in the United States reduce the number of murders committed? Why or why not?

Glossary

Aggravated assault Unlawful attack by one person upon another for the purpose of inflicting severe or aggravated bodily injury.

Arson The willful and malicious setting of fires.

Booster skirts, booster bloomers Special clothing used by shoplifters to carry and conceal stolen merchandise.

Burglary Unlawful entry of a structure to commit a felony or theft.

Chop shop Garages that strip stolen cars of usable parts for sale to auto repair shops.

Clearance rate Solution rate (percent) for crimes reported to the police.

Clearing the books Efforts by police to improve clearance rates by getting people already charged with a crime to confess to other crimes they have not committed.

Crime data manipulation Falsification of crime data submitted to the FBI Uniform Crime Reports by state and local police.

Crime rate Number of index crimes committed per 100,000 inhabitants.

Criminal homicide The willful, nonnegligent, killing of one human being by another.

FBI Uniform Crime Reports Annual reports distributed by the FBI and based upon crime data provided by state and local police.

Felony Any crime that merits a punishment exceeding one year of incarceration.

Forcible rape The carnal knowledge of a female, forcibly and against her will.

Larceny Theft of property without force or fear.

Motor vehicle theft Theft or attempted theft of a vehicle for nontemporary use.

Robbery Theft or attempted theft by use of force, violence, or threat of violence, or by putting the victim in fear.

Saturday night special An inexpensive handgun, usually a .22 caliber revolver.

Waiver of prosecution A desire on the part of a crime victim to have the state not prosecute the assailant.

Weapons effect A concept implying that the mere presence of guns can stimulate aggressive and violent behavior.

References

Alexander, A. and Moolman, V. *Stealing*. New York: Cornerstone Library, 1969.
Bates, E. B. *Elements of Fire and Arson Investigation*. Santa Cruz, Calif.: Davis Publishing, 1975.
Battle, B. P., and Weston, P. B. *Arson: A Handbook of Detection and Investigation*. New York: Arco Publishing, 1972.
Cameron, M. O. *The Booster and the Snitch*. New York: Free Press, 1964.
Coleman, J. C. *Abnormal Psychology and Modern Life*. 6th ed. Glenview, Ill.: Scott, Foresman, 1980.
Curtis, S. J. *Modern Retail Security*. Springfield, Ill.: Charles C. Thomas, 1972.
Federal Bureau of Investigation. *Crime in the United States*. FBI Uniform Crime Reports. Washington, D.C.: U.S. Government Printing Office, 1971.
Federal Bureau of Investigation. *Crime in the United States*. FBI Uniform Crime Reports. Washington, D.C.: U.S. Government Printing Office, 1981.
Gold, L. H. "Psychiatric Profile of the Firesetter." *Journal of Forensic Science*, October, 1962, p. 159.
Groth, A. N., Burgess, A. W., and Holmstrom, L. L. "Rape, Power and Sexuality." Paper presented at the LEAA Conference on Rape, March 1977, in Atlanta, Georgia.
Horgan, J. J. *Criminal Investigation*. New York: McGraw-Hill, 1974.
Inciardi, J. A. "The Adult Firesetter: A Typology." *Criminology*, August 1970, pp. 145–55.
Kukla, R. J. *Gun Control*. Harrisburg, Pa.: Stackpole Books, 1973.
Lewis, D. L., and Yarnell, H. H. "Pathological Firesetting (Pyromania)." Nervous and Mental Disease monographs, no. 82. New York: Coolidge Foundation, 1951, pp. 228–42.
Magnuson, E. "The Curse of Violent Crime." *Time*, 23 March 1981, pp. 16–21.
Meyer, S. M. "A Crusade Against Shoplifting." *The Police Chief* 41 (1974):34–36.
"National Strategy to Reduce Crime." *The National Commission on Criminal Justice Standards and Goals*, Washington, D.C.: Government Printing Office, 1973.
Oster, Patrick, R. "How One State's Gun Control Is Working." *U.S. News and World Report*, August 30, 1976, p. 35.
Pope, C. E. *Crime Specific Analysis: The Characteristics of Burglary Incidents*. Washington, D.C.: U.S. Government Printing Office, 1977.
President's Commission on Law Enforcement and the Administration of Justice. *Task Force Report: Crime and Its Impact*. Washington, D.C.: U.S. Government Printing Office, 1967.
Rape Victimization Study. San Francisco: Queens Bench Foundation, 1975.
Schuman, H., and Presser, S. "Attitude Measurement and the Gun Control Paradox." *Public Opinion Quarterly* 41 (1977–78):427–38.
"Senate Probing Car Theft Industry." *Atlanta Journal*, 26 November 1979, p. 24.
Swanson, C.R., Chamelin, N. C., and Territo, L. *Criminal Investigation*. 2d ed. New York: Random House, 1981.
Turner, C. W., Layton, J. R., and Simons, L. S. "Naturalistic Studies of Aggressive Behavior: Aggressive Stimuli, Victim Visibility, and Horn-honking," *Journal of Personality and Social Psychology*, 31:(1975) 1098-1107.
"The Undeclared War on the Nation's Firemen." *Parade*, 18 July 1971, p. 4.
Williams, J. S., and McGrath, J. *Social Psychological Dimension of Gun Ownership*. Washington, D.C.: U.S. Government Printing Office, 1975.
"Witness: Chicago Car Thief Capital." *Tampa Tribune*, 30 November 1979, p. 23A.

4
factors and theories in criminality: the search for criminal man

Economic factors

Biological factors
Nutrition
Epilepsy
Brain-wave studies
Skin-conductance studies
Toward a biosocial theory of criminality

Psychological factors
Criminality as mental illness
Psychoanalysis and criminality
    Personality structure and dynamics
    Criminality and the unconscious
The search for a criminal personality
Learning theory and criminality
Learning theory and behavior modification
    Token economies
    Aversive conditioning of deviant sexual behavior

Sociological theories
The structural approach
The subcultural approach

Sociopsychological theories
Differential association
Containment theory
The labeling perspective

Sorting it all out

Summary

Issue paper: Biotechnology and the control of criminal behavior

BEFORE the eighteenth century, criminal behavior was simply treated as moral degeneracy or "badness," without much consideration given to the reasons for its occurrence. Medieval interpretations attributed a wide range of abnormal behaviors to demonical possession—an "explanation" that could be extended to include at least some forms of criminally deviant behavior. The Supreme Court of the state of North Carolina, as recently as 1862, endorsed the notion of demoniacal possession in its declaration, "To know the right and still the wrong pursue proceeds from a perverse will brought about by the seductions of the Evil One" (Sutherland and Cressey 1978, p. 54). Offenders were to be rescued from the clutches of the Devil by being made to suffer horrible punishments. These drastic measures usually met with success, but the unfortunate offenders were often freed from possession at the expense of their lives.

More recently, the causes of crime have been looked for both within and outside the offender. Physiology and heredity, mental disorders, personality characteristics, poverty and frustration, and the criminal justice system itself—all of these factors and others have been examined as possible causes of criminal behavior. As this chapter shows, it would be nearly

Left: *Demon riding the tail of a woman's cloak.* Right: *Casting out demons by torture.* These fifteenth century woodcuts illustrate the moral tract that held misconduct attributable to demoniacal possession. From Alan C. Kors and Edward Peters, Witchcraft in Europe: 1100-1700: A Documentary History, Philadelphia: University of Pennsylvania Press, 1972.

impossible with our present knowledge to rule out any of these factors as an explanation for at least some kinds of criminality.

Economic factors

Attempts to relate crime to economic conditions have taken several approaches. The oldest approach attributes criminality to relative poverty, i.e., to how poor a person is compared with others in society who are better off economically. A second approach—the one most common to modern industrial societies—links crime to affluence. A third perspective, rooted in the works of Marx and Engels and incorporated today in the doctrine of radical criminology, views crime as the result of social circumstances produced by capitalism. Changing social beliefs and convictions have led to shifts in emphasis from one of these perspectives to another.

Understanding the relationship between crime and economic factors is complicated by the lack of precise measures of either crime or economic conditions. It may be possible to measure the economic situation in relatively simple agricultural communities such as those found in Third World countries, but it is far more difficult to do so in a society such as ours with a complex economic structure. Although one industry can serve as the economic barometer of a simple society, economic change in a complex society must be measured by a diversified index that considers all major industries. The development of such a device is a task that continues to baffle even the most expert economists.

Criminologists Sutherland and Cressey (1978) surveyed studies of crime and economic conditions both in the United States and abroad, dating back to the turn of the century. Their conclusions are as follows:

1. During periods of economic depression, the general crime rate does not rise significantly.
2. There is a slight, yet inconsistent, tendency for serious crime to increase during periods of economic depression and to decline in periods of prosperity.
3. Violent property crimes tend to increase during periods of depression. Nonviolent property crimes (such as larceny) show an extremely slight—but not consistent—tendency to rise during such periods.
4. Some studies show that drunkenness increases during periods of prosperity; yet other studies indicate that there is no correlation between drunkenness and economic conditions.
5. There is no consistent evidence that crimes against the person are affected by changes in the business cycle.
6. Juvenile delinquency has a tendency to rise during periods of prosperity and to decline in periods of depression.

Poverty is also associated with certain social conditions that may be of greater significance than economic need as a cause of crime (Sutherland

and Cressey 1978). Poverty areas in our modern cities typically occur in segregated, low-rent districts in which people are exposed to criminal behavior. And poverty usually means high unemployment with no future potential for work, loss of social status, loss of respect, feelings of powerlessness, and the attitude that there is "little to lose."

Working parents in poor areas are often away when their children are awake, and they are irritable and fatigued when at home. And approximately 43 percent of poor families are headed by women (Poplin 1978); this situation in particular adversely affects the attitudes of male children toward family responsibilities and work. Typically, a disproportionate number of children in poor areas drop out of school at an early age because they see little value in education. As a result, the jobs they hold are generally low paying, unskilled, and uninteresting, with little chance for economic advancement. Thus the cycle continues. Because the vast majority of conventional offenders come from poverty areas, it must be concluded that poverty contributes to the crime problem.

The idea of *radical criminology* takes this conclusion one step further. Radical criminologists see criminality as primarily an expression of class conflict. Behavior designated as "criminal" by the ruling classes is viewed as the inevitable product of a fundamentally corrupt and unjust society, and law enforcement agencies are seen as the domestic military apparatus used by the ruling classes to maintain themselves in power. Because the causes of crime are thought to lie within society and its legal system, it is held that crime will persist until both are changed.

Radical criminology encompasses the views of a number of contemporary criminologists whose ideas derive directly from, or have been heavily influenced by, Marxist thought. These writers have presented their approaches under a variety of designations: "new criminology," "critical criminology," "Marxist criminology," or "conflict criminology." The basic tenets of the position are outlined by Quinney (1974, p. 16):

1. American society is based on an advanced capitalist economy.

2. The state is organized to serve the interests of the dominant economic class, the capitalist ruling class.

3. Criminal law is an instrument of the state and the ruling class to maintain and perpetuate the existing social and economic order.

4. Crime control in capitalist society is accomplished through a variety of institutions and agencies established and administered by a government elite, representing ruling-class interests, for the purpose of establishing domestic order.

5. The contradictions of advanced capitalism—the disjunction between existence and essence—require that the subordinate classes remain oppressed by whatever means necessary, especially through the coercion and violence of the legal system.

6. Only with the collapse of capitalist society and the creation of a new society based on socialist principles will there be a solution to the crime problem.

Radical criminologists divide the fundamental inequities of the American criminal justice system into two categories: discriminatory treatment on the basis of class, and discriminatory treatment on the basis of race. Although race discrimination is fading somewhat in parts of the system, it is still a significant factor in the administration of justice. Class discrimination is becoming more widespread than ever today, as economic deterioration widens the gap between classes. Class and race are not, of course, mutually exclusive, as demonstrated by the position of poor blacks in the process of justice.

Radical theorists reject the concept of individual guilt and responsibility for illegal acts committed by the working class against the persons and property of the bourgeoisie. They see these crimes as wholly justified acts of rebellion by slaves against masters. This view makes the bulk of property crimes "political" crimes—morally acceptable and, indeed, almost mandatory in view of the criminal nature of society itself. Assaults and property crimes by the proletariat against members of their own class are not justified by radical theory but are understood as inevitable social distortions produced by a capitalist society that breeds racial distrust among the poor, protects the person and property of the bourgeoisie more effectively than the person and property of workers, and produces poverty and alienation.

Critics of radical criminology question the adequacy of class conflict as an explanation for a wide range of criminal behavior. As McCaghy states:

> The theory's application is actually limited to explaining legal reaction against behaviors threatening established economic interests. Thus there is no pretense at explaining such facets of the crime problem as a school janitor sexually molesting a ten-year-old student, parents brutally beating a baby because "it won't stop crying," or two friends trying to stab each other in a dispute over a fifty cent gambling debt (1976, p. 96).

He further observes that the conflict perspective is not a statement of facts or of empirically verified relationships; it is a perspective that directs attention to a *possible* interpretation of the facts.

Biological factors

An ancient and persistent notion holds that character is closely linked to physique. In Shakespeare's *Julius Caesar* (act 1, scene 2), the protagonist entreats Marc Antony:

> *Let me have men about me that are fat*
> *Sleek-headed men and such as sleep o' nights:*
> *Yon Cassius has a lean and hungry look;*
> *He thinks too much; such men are dangerous.*

In the nineteenth century, a physician named Cesare Lombroso gave this notion an intriguing twist. He suggested that criminal behavior could be explained by *atavism*—by the idea that criminals are throwbacks to some

Cesare Lombroso combined ideas from phrenology and organic evolution to develop the concept of the "born criminal." This sketch compares the head of a minister (left) with the head of a murderer to show a biological basis for criminality. Courtesy Brooks/Cole Publishing Company, Monterey, California.

earlier, more primitive forerunner of modern humans. The proof of his contention? Lombroso believed that "born criminals" could be identified by certain "stigmata of degeneracy," such as pointed ears, sloping forehead, receding chin, close-set and shifty eyes, and other physical abnormalities.

Lombroso's speculations were never proven, but later "Lombrosians" pointed to still other physical characteristics thought to be associated with criminality. Some believed that a particular body type (such as a tough, muscular physique) was characteristic of criminals; others said that criminals had glandular imbalances or abnormalities of the nervous system. To date, however, these speculations have not held up under close study. No one has identified a physical characteristic reliably found among criminals but not among noncriminals.

Still, many people believe that biology plays some role in the development of criminal behavior. Decades ago, researchers compiled family histories to show that crime "ran" in families, concluding that some people were "born" criminals, that crime was the result of "bad seed." However, because behavior is linked to upbringing, as well as to genes, family histories alone can not prove that criminality is inherited.

DO CRIMINALS HAVE "ROOTS"? THE INFAMOUS JUKES AND KALLIKAKS

Studies of the famed lineages of the Juke family by Richard Dugdale in the 19th century and the Kallikak family in the early 20th century by Henry H. Goddard supported the claim that some individuals were "born criminals" and that "bad genes" could be passed from generation to generation. Although Dugdale did not invent the Jukes, he often used his imagination when the facts failed to bolster his theory of the hereditary causes of crime. When information about individuals was difficult to obtain, Dugdale resorted to the characterizations such as "supposed to have attempted rape," "reputed sheep stealer but never caught," "hardened character."

> Goddard studied the descendants of two clans of the Kallikak family. Although both clans descended from the same Revolutionary War soldier, Martin Kallikak, the "bad" Kallikaks were attributed to the soldier's union with a feebleminded girl. There is little evidence that these families committed actual crime. In fact, Goddard found only three official cases of crime. All of the supposedly "good" Kallikas descended from the soldier's marriage with a Quaker woman. Since none of the good Kallikaks seem to have inherited any "bad genes" something rather strange must have occurred in the lineages, for we know that a certain number of the good offspring should have shown some "degenerate" traits.
>
> Alberta J. Nassi and Stephen I. Abramowitz, "From Phrenology to Psychosurgery and Back Again: Biological Studies of Criminality," *American Journal of Orthopsychiatry* 46 (1976):595–96, Reprinted by permission of the authors and the publisher.

The strongest evidence for the view of inherited criminality comes from studies of chromosomes—the structures of the cells that carry the genes. Females normally have two X chromosomes, males one X and one Y. Some males, however, have an extra Y chromosome, and several researchers have claimed that this abnormal XYY pattern—known as the *XYY syndrome*—occurs far more frequently among male prisoners than among the general population. This genetic abnormality, they say, produces tendencies toward sexual aggressiveness that leads to the commission of sexual assault. Not all criminals have XYY chromosomes however—not even all male criminals. And no one knows how many *noncriminals* possess this abnormality.

Nutrition

In 1968, Linus Pauling—twice the recipient of the Nobel Prize—coined the term *orthomolecular psychiatry*. He suggested that mental illness and behavior disorders are caused mostly by abnormal reaction rates in the body as a result of constitutional defects, faulty diet, and abnormal concentrations of essential elements. Pauling recommended that treatment of behavior disorders include the establishment of an optimal chemical state for the brain and nervous system. He attracted nationwide interest with his vigorous advocacy of massive doses of vitamin C as a remedy for the common cold.

Supporters of the orthomolecular approach maintain that various kinds of delinquent and criminal behavior are not psychosocial reactions but indications of metabolic or biochemical imbalances. That is, an adolescent youth may engage in violent behavior not because he or she is the unfortunate victim of maternal rejection, a broken home, or peer pressures, but because he or she is suffering from faulty diet, inadequate nutrition, or the presence of some toxic substance in the body (such as mercury), which adversely affects general health and functioning.

As a case in point, hyperactivity in youngsters—a syndrome characterized by restlessness, distraction, excessive physical activity, and aggressive behavior—is often regarded as antisocial or delinquent. Yet it has been suggested that hyperactivity is principally caused by nutritional deficiencies and low blood sugar (hypoglycemia). Both of these conditions may be systematically related to the "junk food" that youngsters in this country consume in large quantities and that are loaded with the processed sugar, starches, and toxic additives that produce orthomolecular imbalances. As Thornton, James, and Doerner observe:

> Children who are hyperactive often become labeled as problem cases by parents and teachers. Unable to concentrate and learn, these youth can grow into adulthood lacking a wide variety of knowledge and skills. Thus, they are prime candidates for truancy and dropping out of school, activities conducive to delinquent behavior (1982, p. 82).

Most criminologists agree that nutritional and biochemical factors influence behavior. There is much less agreement, however, as to what extent and in what specific ways these factors are involved in delinquent and criminal behavior. Arguments that low blood sugar is mainly responsible for crimes such as rape, robbery, arson, assault, and homicide, or that nearly all convicted murderers suffer from hypoglycemia or vitamin deficiencies, must be considered hypotheses that await confirmation through controlled research. Until the evidence is in, the criminological community is obliged to maintain an attitude of cautious interest toward orthomolecular claims about the causes of crime.

Epilepsy

Epilepsy—the "falling sickness" of classical reference—refers to a group of heterogenous, complex, and controversial disorders characterized by the recurrence of convulsive attacks or seizures. An alleged relationship between epilepsy and violent behavior has long been one of the popular myths relating criminality to mental illness. Batchelor feels it is more accurate to speak of epilepsies as symptoms rather than disorders: "The essential feature is not the convulsive seizure or the disturbance of consciousness, but the episodic sudden disturbance of function in the central nervous system" (1969, p. 420). Experimental studies involving brain stimulation have shown that some seizures closely resembling epileptic attacks can be elicited by electrical means.

Epilepsy has been known from antiquity, and behavioral pathologists are fond of compiling lists of world-famous figures who have been afflicted. With Alexander of Macedon, Julius Caesar, and Napoleon heading the parade, one might wonder if epilepsy and visions of world conquest go hand in hand. However, there are enough gifted artists, writers, and musicians in the tally—Maupassant, Van Gogh, and Byron, for instance—to dispel that idea.

The major types of epilepsy are grand mal, petit mal, Jacksonian, and psychomotor epilepsy. Grand mal, the most common and dramatic of epileptic reactions, is characterized by severe motor convulsions and an interruption or loss of consciousness. Petit mal, which is rare in adults over twenty-one, causes a fleeting disruption of consciousness that may go unrecognized for a long time. Jacksonian seizures, which resemble grand mal attacks in most respects, begin with a spasmodic muscular contraction in an arm or leg and usually extend to involve an entire side of the body.

Psychomotor epilepsy (or "psychic equivalents") also represents a disruption of consciousness; but the epileptic often manages to carry out some fairly complicated patterns of behavior. Among such patterns—according to standard views—are violence and aggression, up to and including mass murder (Suinn 1970). It is almost traditional in discussions of epilepsy and violence to cite the case of the Flemish painter Vincent Van Gogh, who sliced off one of his own ears with a razor, carefully packed it in cotton, and presented it to a prostitute in a provincial French bordello. Van Gogh is believed to have carried out this act of self-multilation during one of his psychomotor *fugues*.

On examination, the murderous reputation of the psychomotor epileptic is largely folklore. For example, Turner and Merlis (1962) report that only 5 out of 337 epileptics whose case records they examined exhibited antisocial behavior during their seizures. Rodin (1973) found no instances of aggressive or violent behavior in 57 patients with psychomotor epilepsy who were photographed during seizures; and he found only 34 examples of aggressive actions in 700 case histories.

Brain-wave studies

The *electroencephalograph (EEG)* is an instrument that picks up electrical activity in brain cells by means of electrodes attached to the scalp. This activity is recorded in oscillating patterns called *brain waves* by a machine connected to the electrodes. EEG studies have been used to investigate criminals since the early 1940s (Mednick and Volavka 1980). Over the years, research has indicated a rather high incidence of brain-wave abnormalities among antisocial personalities, especially in the slow-wave activity in the temporal lobe of the brain. Hare suggests that such anomalies might be a reflection of abnormal functioning of inhibitory mechanisms in the central nervous system and that "this malfunction makes it difficult to learn to inhibit behavior that is likely to lead to punishment" (1970, pp. 33–34).

Mednick, Volavka, Gabrielli, and Itil (1981) conducted a longitudinal study of 265 Danish youngsters born on approximately the same date. Seventy-two children with schizophrenic parents were matched with 72 children of "psychopathic fathers or character disorder mothers" for whom psychiatric hospitalization records were available. The control subjects were 121 children whose parents had never been hospitalized. All of the subjects were given exhaustive tests to measure psychological, neurological, and social-familial factors.

EEG results significantly discriminated delinquents from nondelinquents, although the findings did not support the hypothesis that delinquents exhibit a developmental lag. However, the fact that the testing was done well before the individuals exhibited delinquent behavior—and was therefore *predictive*—led Mednick (1979) to suggest that the EEG might be used in testing to help prevent delinquency.

Skin-conductance studies

When people are upset, anxious, fearful, or otherwise emotionally aroused, their palms perspire. This perspiration increases the electrical conductivity of the skin, which can be measured as the *galvanic skin response (GSR)*. Individuals with high levels of emotional arousal tend to show significantly higher levels of GSR reactivity than those who exhibit lower levels of anxiety, fear, or anger.

In an early study by Lykken (1957), psychopathic offenders showed low arousal as measured by the GSR and had low anxiety scores on questionnaires. Lykken concluded that psychopathic individuals have fewer inhibitions about committing antisocial behavior because they experience little anxiety over their actions. Subsequent research has consistently affirmed this finding in skin-conductance measures with criminals, especially violent offenders (Hare 1970; Lippert 1965).

Toward a biosocial theory of criminality

Mednick states that no research to date has provided conclusive evidence that genetic factors take precedence over environmental factors as a cause of criminality:

> Given the nature of the genetic and environmental facts, it is still an appropriate apriori hypothesis that *heredity and environment always interact in a dynamic fashion to bring about and shape criminal behavior*, and that both the mutual interaction and the mutual strength of the two factors form a continuous dimension from all persons and situations (1977, p. 88).

He further points out that criminality can only be studied meaningfully from a genetic perspective if it is closely associated with a "well-defined somatic or psychological state" (ibid, p. 88).

Has biocriminological research identified any such somatic or psychological states? In Mednick's judgment, the evidence from nearly thirty years of investigation indicates that deviance in the autonomic nervous system has been demonstrated to reliably differentiate antisocial individuals. Lykken (1957) reports abnormally diminished reactivity of the autonomic nervous system (ANS) and slow recovery in psychopathic offenders (as measured by the GSR). Skin-conductance measures afford a convenient method for measuring ANS activity at the surface of the body.

In 1967, Hare reported that psychopathic inmates at a maximum security prison were sluggish ANS responders. Ten years later, he found that inmates who had committed additional serious crimes exhibited the slowest recovery rates (Hare and Schalling, eds. 1978). Thus, abnormally diminished ANS reactivity and slow recovery have predictive validity in forecasting serious criminality. Further research by Bell, Mednick, Gottesman, and Sergeant (1977)—in a study of electrodermal responses of children with criminal and noncriminal fathers—demonstrated that ANS reactivity is hereditary.

Mednick has attempted to formulate a theory to explain how ANS deviance may help to account for some types of crime and some percentage of criminals. His approach seeks to understand the possible interaction of biological and social factors in the socialization process. He assumes that law-abiding behavior must be learned; that the learning of law-abiding behavior involves certain environmental conditions and individual abilities; and that the lack of any of these conditions might be responsible for some forms of antisocial behavior. An essential part of socialization involves learning to inhibit antisocial or asocial behavior such as aggression. Typically, this learning occurs when aggressive acts are followed by punishment. The child learns to avoid further punishment by suppressing or inhibiting the disapproved behavior. Fear reduction is a "powerful, naturally occurring reinforcement" in this passive-avoidance learning sequence. That is, the individual both avoids punishment and reduces fear by *learning not to do something* for which he or she was previously punished.

According to this approach, four conditions must be present for the child to learn effectively to inhibit antisocial behavior:

1   A censuring agent (typically the family or peers).
2   An adequate fear response.
3   The ability to learn the fear response in anticipation of an asocial act.
4   Fast dissipation of fear to quickly reinforce the inhibiting response.

The fourth point is critical: to be effective, reinforcement must be delivered immediately following the relevant response. The fear response, in turn, is largely controlled by the autonomic nervous system. As Mednick points out:

> If child A has an autonomic nervous system that characteristically recovers very quickly from fear, then he will receive a quick and large reinforcement and learn inhibition quickly. If he has an autonomic nervous system that recovers very slowly, he will receive a slow, small reinforcement and learn to inhibit aggression very slowly, if at all. This orientation would predict that (holding constant critical extraindividual variables such as social status, crime training, and poverty level), those who commit asocial acts would be characterized by slow autonomic recovery. The slower the recovery, the more serious and repetitive the asocial behavior predicted (1971, p. 51).

These predictions have been empirically demonstrated by research.

The central idea of Mednick's formulation has been expressed again and again in different, and less precise, language by theorists of other persuasion. Intrapsychic theorists characterize the antisocial personality as "lacking in conscience" or being "deficient in superego," while sociologically oriented theorists stress environmental factors that may lead to "defective socialization."

It is also noteworthy that Mednick refers to his formulation as a *biosocial* theory. Geneticists have cautioned repeatedly that genes are not directly responsible for the personality or characteristics of an individual;

their influence is manifested only through a chain of metabolic processes and interactions with other genes and—most importantly—through interactions with the environment. Montagu states that genes "do not determine anything—they simply influence the morphological and physiological expression of traits" (1968, p. 46). It should not be assumed that a certain chromosome structure or deviation predestines fate. Again, as Montagu points out, "Unchangeability and immutability are not characteristics of the genetic system as a whole" (ibid., p. 46). Mednick's biosocial theory is consistent with this position.

Psychological factors

If your household has been looted to your last remaining dime,
By some gentleman recruited from the serried ranks of crime,
Do not think that he was stealing that his pockets he might fill,
But remember he was feeling rather ill . . .

Men who rob you of your treasures, or who beat you out of spite,
Men who think that theft's a pleasure, and that murder's a delight,
Men who with their shell games venture to entrap the guileless hick,
Should be never named with censure; they are sick.

James J. Montague (1873–1941)
Who Can Blame Him?

Psychiatry is a branch of medicine; psychology is a behavioral science. Psychiatrists tend to interpret criminality within a *clinical* perspective. Criminal behavior is viewed as a personality disturbance or even a type of mental illness (as James Montague's satirical verses suggest). Thus, dealing with criminality is seen as a task requiring treatment or psychotherapy.

Psychologists, on the other hand, interpret criminality or criminal conduct as a problem in the acquisition or learning of behaviors that conform to the same principles governing the learning of any other kind of behavior, prosocial or antisocial. According to this perspective, coping with criminality is a matter of exchanging variables that help maintain and reinforce criminal behavior for other variables that reinforce noncriminal behavior. The laboratory is regarded as more promising than the clinic for finding explanations for criminality.

A bridge between psychiatry and psychology has been supplied by *psychoanalysis*, the body of concepts originally developed by Sigmund Freud and subsequently elaborated on and modified by Alfred Adler, Otto Rank, Karen Horney, Erik Erikson, and others. The imaginative terms and ideas used by psychoanalysts to describe the structure and dynamics of personality, its origins and development, and its sources of conflict, frustration, and motivation, gave psychiatry and psychology a common vocabulary for communication. Psychiatrists readily adopted the psychoanalytic theories that bore upon maladaptive behaviors identified as neurosis, psychosis, and character disorders; psychologists expended considerable effort attempting to reproduce, under laboratory conditions, such processes as repression ("motivated forgetting") and regression. Most importantly, psychoanalysis provided a theoretical framework for interpreting crime and delinquent behavior in terms of the same processes used to explain mental illness. The contributions of psychoanalytic criminology are discussed in this chapter.

Differences between psychiatrists and psychologists are not absolute; some psychiatrists (e.g., William Glasser) reject the "mental illness" model as a valid basis for interpreting deviant behavior, including criminality; and not all psychologists endorse the learning-theory perspective on criminal behavior. Nevertheless, the distinctions between psychiatry and psychology are extremely important to an understanding of their respective approaches to criminological theory. Unfortunately, the differences are often blurred or even ignored by some contemporary thinkers.

Criminality as mental illness

Psychiatry has been defined as "that branch of medicine whose special province is the study, prevention, and treatment of all types and degrees of mental ill health however caused" (Slater and Roth 1969, p. 6). Professional practitioners of this medical specialty have been invested with the responsibility for managing "mental ill-health" or "mental illness." The deviant behavior covered by such labels encompasses a broad range of conduct perceived as bizarre, threatening, objectionable, or merely hard to understand—including everything from the "transient situational maladjustment" of an individual experiencing the pangs of grief to the strange grimaces and antic behavior of a person labeled "schizophrenic." The psychiatrist, as a member of the medical profession, employs a vocabulary and a set of concepts that bear a strained relationship to the physical-disease models they emulate. Thus, a deviant individual becomes a "patient," the deviant behavior becomes the "symptom," and the determinants of the behavior become the "underlying pathology."

The "internal sickness" (or medical) model of criminality further strains the analogy between deviance and disease. This approach asserts that the commission of the crime is symptomatic of an offender's psychological maladjustment and an indication of a need for professional help. Halleck, in his historical review of American psychiatry and the criminal, states that the criminal offender has been a source of interest to the psychiatrist

> ... because he bears many startling resemblances to those we call mentally ill. When incarcerated (and sometimes before) the offender proved to be a miserable, unhappy person who could be observed to suffer in the same way as the mental patient. Psychoanalytic psychiatry taught us that those psychological mechanisms which produced neurotic suffering were also operant in individuals who demonstrated criminal behavior. These observations fostered psychiatry's hopes of contributing to the understanding and alteration of criminal behavior (1965, pp. 1–2).

In this passage, Halleck treads a thin line: he does not actually say that criminals *are* mentally ill, only that they bear "startling resemblances" to those who are.

Mental health and mental illness cannot be described with any of the objectivity and precision that characterize diagnoses of physical illness. Rather, as a 1973 study by Rosenhan demonstrates, psychiatric diagnoses are subject to severe problems of reliability and validity.

PSYCHODIAGNOSIS AND PSEUDODIAGNOSIS

Psychologist David Rosenhan of Stanford University conducted a study in which eight normal people—a psychiatrist, graduate student, painter, housewife, pediatrician, and three psychologists—gained admittance as pseudopatients to twelve public and private mental hospitals at various locations in the United States. Each person contacted a hospital and complained of hearing voices that seemed to say "empty" and "hollow" and "thud." Apart from accompanying indications of being nervous and ill at ease during the initial interview, the behavior of the pseudopatients was normal. They gave a fictitious name and occupation to the diagnostician; otherwise all of the life history information they provided was authentic.

Eleven of the twelve admissions received a diagnosis of schizophrenia and one was identified as manic-depressive psychosis.

These diagnostic assessments were arrived at primarily on the basis of the reported auditory hallucinations. The pseudopatients spent an average of 19 days per hospitalization, according to Rosenhan, and together they received over 2,100 pills. At discharge the diagnosis was "schizophrenia in remission." In nearly every instance, the first persons to become aware of the true identity of the pseudopatients were the real patients.

If Rosenhan had reported merely that his study had found low validity for psychiatric judgments of mental illness, it is doubtful that his article would have attracted much attention in professional circles. Instead, by making the very extreme claim that the validity of judgments of mental illness is zero, his article was given an extraordinary reception.

From David Rosenhan, "On Being Sane in Insane Places," *Science* 179(1973):250–58.

According to one view, mental illness can best be understood as a label representing societal reactions to behavior that deviates from (or in some cases, conforms to) normative standards based on cultural values. It is held that the term "mental illness" is loosely and indiscriminately applied to psychosocial problems such as crime, promiscuity, marital infidelity, political fanaticism, general unhappiness, and discontent—even to the behavior of those who manage to make themselves disliked. Those who endorse this viewpoint maintain that the term seems at times to be used as a ready explanation for almost any kind of behavior that does not make sense to the observer, reveals no clear or reasonable motivation, or merely disturbs our sensibilities.

Psychoanalysis and criminality

The founder of psychoanalysis, Sigmund Freud, had no direct contact with any criminals during his lifetime, and in his extensive writings—twenty-four volumes of *Collected Works*—there are few references to crime. Freud did not formulate a theory of criminality; psychoanalysis was intended to be a theoretical system for explaining *all* behavior. Specific applications of psychoanalytic theory were made by Freud's followers or by neo-Freudians (those who had fallen away from orthodoxy in their psychoanalytic doctrines). Such applications usually took the form of extended analyses of individual cases.

Much of psychoanalysis has entered into the mainstream, to the extent that terms such as "superego" and "Oedipus complex" have entered into pop art and culture—even into our everyday language. We speak casually of "ego trips," of "Freudian slips," and of "psychoanalyzing" our friends and relatives. Indeed, the influence of psychoanalysis in our culture and language is so pervasive that it often goes unrecognized.

Personality structure and dynamics Freud conceived that the development of each individual is dependent upon three types of factors: innate, instinctual forces, biologically determined stages of development, and environmental influences. Although all three categories were viewed as important, Freud believed the sex instinct, to which he applied the term *psychosexual development,* to be the central factor in human development. As an infant matures, the sex instinct moves from one area of the body to another, causing a series of stages, each denoted by a primary *erogenous zone,* the major area of sexual satisfaction during a stage. According to this theme, psychosexual development can be divided into three periods: infantile sexuality (from birth to approximately five years), latent phase, and puberty. Infantile sexuality can further be divided into the oral, anal, and phallic periods, the latter culminating in the Oedipus complex, and the "family romance" in which the child wishes to have intimate relations with the parent of the opposite sex and harbors antagonism toward the parent of the same sex.

Freud postulated that personality is governed by three dynamic systems, which he named id, ego, and superego. The *id* consists of instinctual sexual and aggressive drives—the substratum of personality from which all other systems develop. It operates by the "pleasure principle," seeking tension reduction through the discharge of impulses. The *ego* develops as a control system that seeks to satisfy drives through contact with reality. It functions to control the impulsiveness of the id so that drive satisfaction can be obtained; however, it operates within the limits imposed on the individual by society. The ego has control over all cognitive and intellectual functions. The *superego* is the moral element of personality: it represents all the internalized demands from parents and society.

The defense of repression is the most basic means by which the ego can control id impulses. Through repression, the ego forces emerging id impulses to remain unconscious and not function in reality. Because the direct expression of primitive impulses is forbidden by social norms, the superego and the id generally oppose one another. The struggle between the id and the superego is often an intense encounter, and anxiety is one of the by-products. Anxiety is a warning signal to the ego to take the needed steps to keep emerging impulses from overthrowing the system. Repression provides the ego with a direct mechanism for anxiety reduction: the primitive impulse is forced back into the unconscious, and the delicate balance between the id and the superego is maintained.

Criminality and the unconscious Behavior, as viewed within the psychoanalytic framework, is functional in the sense that it operates to fulfill certain needs or drives and has consequences for other aspects of personality. But Freud's emphasis on the importance of unconscious factors in mental life adds an element of complexity to the interpretation of behavior. Freud and later psychoanalysts assume that much, if not most, of the behavior exhibited by an individual possesses meaning that lies outside the range of the individual's awareness. Thus, the observable behavior of a person must be considered as merely an outward, or *symbolic*, expression of underlying (i.e., unconscious) drives and impulses. This principle implies that a focus upon the criminal action itself (manifest function) defeats any attempt to understand the etiology of the crime. Says Feldman:

> ... like any other behavior, criminal behavior is a form of self-expression, and what is intended to be expressed in the act of crime is not only unobservable in the act itself, but also may even be beyond the awareness of the criminal actor himself. So, for example, an overt criminal act of stealing may be undertaken for the attainment of purposes which are far removed from, and even contrary to, that of simple illegal aggrandizement; indeed, it may even be, as shall be seen in the sequel, that the criminal, in stealing,

A teenager's fascination with knives and guns may express hidden antisocial impulses and fantasies that can emerge later as violent behavior. Courtesy Wadsworth Publishing Company.

seeks not material gain but self-punishment. The etiological basis of a criminal act can, therefore, be understood only in terms of the functions, latent as well as manifest, which the act was intended to accomplish (1969, p. 434).

Although the specific cause of a given criminal act must be looked for in the life history of the individual offender, the general etiological formula for psychoanalytic criminology asserts that criminal behavior is an attempt to maintain or restore psychic balance. But this formula has a major flaw: neurosis is explained the same way. Therefore, what factor or factors can be identified that dispose an individual toward criminality rather than toward some other emotional or mental disorder?

One interpretation that neatly bypasses this issue is that criminality is actually a *form* of neurosis. Unfortunately, empirical data fail to support any contention that the criminal is a neurotic individual compulsively driven toward self-punishment. On the contrary, criminal offenders appear to use every effort and resource to elude capture. Moreover, empirical evidence suggests that "neurotic" personality characteristics are found in the criminal population to approximately the same degree they are found in the noncriminal population.

Equally dubious is the view of the criminal as an antisocial character who seeks immediate gratification, lives entirely in the present, and is unable to withstand tedium and monotony. Many kinds of criminal behavior require extensive training in specific skills or in systematic planning. Indeed, professional, syndicated, and white-collar crimes seem to exemplify the operation of Freud's "reality principle," (i.e., the capacity to defer or postpone gratification in order to achieve a larger gratification at some later time).

By failing to give appropriate emphasis to the fact that patterned criminality is not the spontaneous creation of the individual offender, psychoanalytic criminology minimizes the crucial importance of social learning. According to Feldman,

> ... this learning process requires the individual's participation in the formation and maintenance of relationships with others who dispose of the necessary knowledge and put it to use. It is in the context of these relationships that the individual learns his criminality and adopts for himself distinctive criminalistic attitudes and percepts. Presumably, the experiences of such a learning process must have an effect on the personality of the individual undergoing them. Yet, this reciprocating influence of criminal experience on the personality of the criminal appears to have no consideration in psychoanalytic criminology (ibid., p. 441).

Once again, the question is raised, Which comes first in the causal sequence, the personality characteristics or the criminal experience? Psychoanalytic criminology assumes it is the personality that produces involvement in criminal activity, but there is no systematic procedure available to verify this view.

In addition to the mentioned criticisms, psychoanalytic criminology possesses some serious flaws when judged as a formal theory. Psychoanalytic constructs tend to be global and all-inclusive in nature and loaded with "surplus meaning"; rarely, if ever, are they anchored in explicit, observable events. Nevertheless, such constructs have become the "facts" of psychoanalysis, upon which even more speculative and elaborate concepts have been based.

Most research generated by psychoanalytic theory is not directed at modifying the theory based on new information; rather, the goal is usually to demonstrate the essential validity of the basic postulates and assumptions of the theory. Because of the ambiguity and lack of operational specificity of the constructs in the system, however, no hypothesis derived from psychoanalytic theory can be either clearly confirmed or clearly refuted. Thus, critics of psychoanalysis have charged that the theory and its proponents do not conform to the widely accepted canons of empirical verification and refutation implicit in the scientific method.

The search for a criminal personality

Instead of pursuing criminality as a mental illness, some psychiatrists and psychologists have tried to identify a *criminal personality*. They have sought to discover some cluster of personality traits distinctive to criminal offenders, in general, or to particular categories of offenders. One approach has been to examine the results of personality tests administered to both criminals and noncriminals, with the aim of finding significant differences between them. Another approach has been to look at the incidence of psychiatrically diagnosed disorders in the criminal population. Neither method has yielded conclusive results, however. And both kinds of research present an additional serious problem: the chicken-egg dilemma. Even if investigators *did* find that certain personality traits were characteristic of criminal offenders, for example, it would still be necessary to ask which came first—the traits or the criminal behavior.

The most recent claim about the discovery of a criminal personality was advanced by Samuel Yochelson and Stanton Samenow in *The Criminal Personality* (1976). Based on a fifteen-year study of 255 criminals, the volume proposes that people become criminals early in life on the basis of choice, not accident, and that the criminal personality results more from inborn characteristics than from acquired ones. However, critics of the book have had some unkind things to say about the authors' lack of objectivity and their general disregard for accuracy. Thus, the issue of whether a criminal personality exists remains unresolved.

Learning theory and criminality

Common sense affirms the belief that aggressiveness can be taught to those who do not exhibit it in their normal behavior. From time immemorial, this belief has guided and structured basic training for military recruits. In addition to close-order drill, military etiquette, and the use and maintenance of weapons and equipment, recruits are exposed to situations intended to inculcate aggressiveness. Paul Bäumer, the protagonist of Erich

Maria Remarque's classic novel *All Quiet on the Western Front* (1929), reminisces about the training he received as a recruit in the German Army in World War I:

> We were trained in the army for ten weeks and in this time more profoundly influenced than by ten years of school.... At first astonished, then embittered, and finally indifferent, we recognized that what matters is not the mind but the boot brush, not intelligence but the system, not freedom but drill.... We became hard, suspicious, pitiless, vicious, tough—and that was good; for these attributes had been entirely lacking in us. Had we gone into the trenches without this period of training most of us would certainly have gone mad. Only thus were we prepared for what awaited us... (pp. 20–25).

Novelist John Masters—writing in *Bugles and a Tiger* (1962)—reflected similarly about the training he received one world war later, as a cadet in the Royal Military College at Sandhurst, England, in the early 1930s.

However, it is one thing to assert that a given response or pattern of behavior is learned; it is quite a different matter to describe with precision and in detail how such behavior is acquired, maintained, or modified. Yet significant advances toward accomplishing the latter objective have been made by psychologists during the past several decades. Through systematic observation of the ways in which behavior is acquired, maintained, altered, or eliminated under controlled conditions, researchers have formulated the following principles (adapted from Suinn 1970):

1. The association between a stimulus and a response is strengthened each time the response is followed by reinforcement. This is known as *acquisition*.

2. The association is weakened each time the response occurs and is *not* followed by reinforcement. This is known as *extinction*. Thus, disuse alone does not lead to extinction.

3. A response to a given stimulus may be seen to recur after complete extinction when the stimulus is re-presented. This phenomenon is known as *spontaneous recovery*.

4. Once a specific stimulus-response habit has been acquired, another stimulus that is similar in some way to the original stimulus can also elicit the learned response. This is called *stimulus generalization*.

5. Responses that occur just prior to a reinforced, learned response will also be strengthened, those nearest in time being strengthened the most. This is called the *gradient of reinforcement*.

6. Responses nearer to the time of a reinforcement tend to occur before their original time in the response sequence and to crowd out earlier, useless behaviors. This is known as the development of *anticipatory responses*.

7. Drives can act as cues and elicit specific, learned responses, or as responses and be elicited by certain cues and strengthened by reinforcement.

Learning theory and behavior modification

A program that applies learning theory with the aim of modifying criminal behavior is referred to as a *contingency management program*. A contingency, as Lillyquist notes, "is something that may or may not occur; the management aspect involves increasing the chances that it *will* occur" (1980, p. 232). In contingency management in a correctional setting, the aim is to increase the probability of occurrence of certain kinds of desired behaviors by reinforcing the behaviors when they occur. Participation in educational or vocational training programs, money management, nonaggressive behavior, and successful interviewing (for employment) are some of the behaviors that have been dealt with in contingency management programs (Braukmann, et al. 1975). Reinforcement can range from verbal praise ("Good job"; "That's fine"; "You're really getting a handle on this stuff") to release from prison. Tangible reinforcement such as candy, soft drinks, cigarettes, and snacks might be augmented with access to desired activities—such as watching television, making phone calls, and getting extra visits from family members.

Token economies An action that has no reinforcing value of its own will tend to acquire reinforcing qualities if it becomes associated with a reinforcer: it will become valuable as a medium of exchange. This principle of secondary reinforcement is basic to the idea of a *token economy*. A token is a secondary reinforcer that, like money, can be exchanged for goods or services according to a standard scale. In addition to the advantages of ease and convenience, the principal benefit of using tokens as a medium of exchange is that the system encourages stability and continuity of behavior. According to Lillyquist:

> A person in a social learning program that uses television watching and soda sipping as reinforcers is not always desirous of these rewards because appetites for all things wax and wane. But desirable behavior can be maintained if it can be made contingent on the presentation of a token that promises *future* reinforcement when the person is more in the mood for it (1980, pp. 232–33).

Token economies are particularly well suited to institutional settings, where behavior management is easier than in a free-response environment. In fact, the earliest token-economy programs were established in mental hospitals and institutions for the mentally retarded.

Aversive conditioning of deviant sexual behavior *Aversive conditioning*, a form of behavior modification, is the reduction or elimination of certain patterns of behavior by associating them with unpleasant or noxious stimuli. Variations of this method have been used to alter an individual's sexual behavior by teaching him or her to dislike and avoid stimuli that he or she regards as a source of abnormal sexual excitation. That is, the individual himself (or herself) must consider a behavior as deviant and be willing to cooperate in eliminating it; otherwise the aversive conditioning will not work and will be considered punishment.

Nausea-inducing drugs were used extensively in early experiments in aversive conditioning. The drugs were usually given by injection to induce vomiting during an undesirable behavior. This procedure, often unpleasant and traumatic, was designed to condition the sexual deviate to feel nausea whenever he or she subsequently tried to carry out the undesirable behavior. Electric shock later replaced drugs as an aversive stimuli. In the following example, an electric shock was administered to the subject, a male transvestite, through the soles of his feet. In later experiments with aversive conditioning for deviant sexual behavior, electrical shocks were applied directly to the genital organs.

> The electric grid was made from a 4 feet by 3 feet rubber mat with a corrugated upper aspect. Tinned copper wire, one-tenth of an inch thick, was stapled lengthwise in the grooves of this mat at approximately half-inch intervals.... A manually operated G.P.O. type generator ... produced a current of approximately 100 volts a.c. when resistance of 10,000 ohms and upwards were introduced on to the grid surface. Two rapid turns of the generator handle were sufficient to give a sharp and unpleasant electric shock to the feet and ankles of the person standing on the grid.... Treatment sessions were administered every half-hour, each session consisting of 5 trials with one minute's rest between each trial. A total of 400 trials was given over 6 days (average 65 to 75 per day).... The patient utilized his own clothing, which was not interfered with in any way, except that slits were cut into the feet of his nylon hose to enable a metal conductor to be inserted into the soles of his black court shoes. He commenced dressing up at the beginning of each trial and continued until he received a signal to undress irrespective of a number of garments he was wearing at the time. This signal was either a shock from the grid or the sound of the buzzer which was introduced at random into half the 400 trials. The shock or buzzer recurred at regular intervals until he had completely undressed.
>
> (Reprinted from J. C. Barker, "Behaviour Therapy for Transvestism: A Comparison of Pharmacological and Electrical Aversion Techniques," *British Journal of Psychiatry* 111 [1965]:271, by permission of the author and the publisher.)

Science fiction is replete with stories of a nightmarish future in which people are depersonalized and dehumanized. Consider Ayn Rand's *Anthem* (1961), about a world so collectivized that the very concept of self is lost and has to be rediscovered; Huxley's *Brave New World* (1978), with its test-tube genetics and mind-altering drugs; and George Orwell's *1984* (1949), with Newspeak, thought crime, and the omnipresent eye of Big Brother watching, watching, watching. Such a future seemed already upon us in 1970 when *Psychology Today* published an article making the following claim:

> I believe the day has come when we can combine sensory deprivation with drugs, hypnosis, and astute manipulation of reward and punishment to gain almost absolute control over an individual's behavior.... We have the tech-

niques to do it.... I foresee the day when we could convert the worst criminal into a decent respectable citizen in a matter of a few months—or perhaps even less time than that (McConnell 1970, p. 4).

Two years later, Schwitzgebel (1972) reported that Anectine (succinylcholine chloride) was being used in the aversive conditioning of alcoholics in California; Anectine produces a sensation of suffocation. The program in which this approach was used was singled out by Jessica Mitford in her influential book *Kind and Usual Punishment* (1974) as an example of the outrages perpetrated in the name of correctional treatment.

Behavior modification has further been criticized for making excessive claims about results, for using inmates as guinea pigs, and for opening the way for "behavior modification programs" that are actually thinly disguised programs for furthering institutional objectives at the expense of inmates. In 1974, the Law Enforcement Assistance Administration banned federal support from any and all programs using behavior modification. The ban has never been lifted.

Perhaps in response to spirited attacks from critics, proponents of behavior modification have experienced a noticeable waning in enthusiasm among their own ranks; and the techniques they use are now more sophisticated and humane. As Lazarus observes, "Behavior therapists do not deny consciousness . . . do not treat people like Pavlovian dogs . . . and are not ignorant of the part played by mutual trust and other relationship factors among our treatment variables" (1977, p. 553). Nevertheless, as a defense, many institutional authorities have dropped the term "behavior modification" from the names of their programs, knowing that the term carries with it many of the characteristics of aversive conditioning.

Sociological theories

Sociological theories about what causes crime deal with criminality in its collective, rather than individual, aspects. That is, the sociologist seeks to answer questions such as What factors are responsible for the higher crime rates among urban black males than among rural black males? Or, How can we account for the steep increase in violent crimes that has taken place in the United States during the past decade? Sociological explanations do not deny the importance of motivation in criminal acts, but they seek to tie that motivation to societal arrangements external to the individual. According to Nettler:

> A strictly sociological explanation is concerned with how the *structure* of a society or its *institutional practices* or its *persisting cultural themes* affect the conduct of its members. Individual differences are denied or ignored, and the explanation of collective behavior is sought in the patterning of social arrangements that is considered to be both "outside" the actor and "prior" to him. That is, the social patterns of power or of institutions which are held to be determinative of human action are also seen as having been in existence *before* any particular actor came on the scene. They are "external"

to him in the sense that they will persist with or without him. In lay language, sociological explanations of crime place the blame on something social that is prior to, external to, and compelling of a particular person (1974, p. 138).

Thus, Nettler identifies two sociological explanations of criminality, one *structural* and one *subcultural*. Both explanations assume that *culture conflict* is the principal source of crime; they differ, as Nettler indicates, in their evaluation of conflict and, therefore, in the societal response they prescribe.

The structural approach

The French sociologist Emile Durkheim (1858–1917) was among the first social scientists to point out the "normality" of crime. Human behavior is not inherently "normal" or "pathological"; certain forms of conduct simply are labeled as such by important or influential groups within society. Thus, in a society of saints, singing too loud in church might be punished as severely as theft would be punished in a prison society of thieves. In Durkheim's view, a society totally exempt from crime is unthinkable.

One of Durkheim's major contributions to the understanding of deviant behavior stems from his efforts to show how suicide relates to an individual's lack of integration into stable social groups. He proposed that many suicides result from *anomie*, a social condition of "normlessness" in which people experience an acute lack of meaningful rules and purpose in their lives.

The concept of anomie was extended by the American sociologist Robert K. Merton (1957) to explain deviant behavior in modern Western societies. Merton considered socially deviant behavior to be as much a product of the social structure as is conformist behavior, and he attempted to determine how the sociocultural structure of society pressures people toward deviance. Merton sought an answer to the question, Why does the frequency of deviant behavior vary with the social structure?

Societal structure is composed of various elements, but two are essential to Merton's analysis: (1) culturally defined goals—those objectives defined as legitimate for everyone; and (2) the regulatory norms that define and control the means to achieve goals. Merton maintained that deviant behavior can be regarded sociologically as a symptom of dissociation between culturally prescribed aspirations and socially acceptable avenues for realizing those aspirations.

In American society, wealth is a basic symbol of success. Money obtained illegally can be spent just as easily as hard-earned money and can be translated into the visible signs of success: expensive cars, clothes, jewelry, and luxurious apartments. Merton felt that American society placed a heavy emphasis on wealth without a corresponding emphasis on the use of legitimate means to reach this goal. Individual adaptation to this situation may take several forms, including *conformity, innovation, ritualism, retreatism,* or *rebellion*.

Merton pointed out that the greatest pressure toward deviant behavior is experienced by people in the lower class. Cloward and Ohlin, in a work appropriately entitled *Delinquency and Opportunity* (1960), expanded this idea to explain urban gang delinquency:

> The disparity between what lower-class youth are led to want and what is actually available to them is the source of a major problem of adjustment. Adolescents who form delinquent subcultures, we suggest, have internalized an emphasis on conventional goals. Faced with limitations on legitimate avenues of access to these goals, and unable to revise their aspirations downward, they experience intense frustrations; the exploration of nonconformist alternatives may be the result (p. 86).

This view holds that delinquency is partly *adaptive*, because it is instrumental in the attainment of desired goals, and also partly *reactive*, because it is prompted by a resentment of being deprived of things the delinquents believe should be theirs.

The subcultural approach

"Subculture" is a term social scientists use to refer to variations within a society on how cultural themes, patterns, artifacts, and traditional ideas are incorporated and expressed within various groups. Subcultures are presumed to have some stability and endurance. In addition, they can differ widely in the magnitude and direction of their deviation from the general culture. When the norms of a subculture impose standards of conduct

The anti-establishment behavior of some gangs reflects a subcultural form of delinquency. (Courtesy Michael Weisbrot and Holt, Rinehart, & Winston Co.)

different from those prescribed by the general culture, the resulting conflict can contribute to criminal behavior.

A principal advocate of the subcultural approach to delinquency is Walter B. Miller (1958). Miller does not go so far as to say that the lower class in the United States is a criminal class, but he does maintain that delinquency is the result of an "intensified response" of some children to "focal areas of concern" found in lower-class culture. Youths who conform to values of the lower class find themselves in inevitable conflict with the prevailing middle-class mores and the law.

Miller identifies six focal areas of concern for the lower class, discussed here in the order of their importance. *Concern over trouble* means avoiding entanglements with official authorities or agencies of the middle class. *Toughness* (bravery, body tattooing, absence of sentimentality) is viewed as the result of upbringing in female-dominated (matriarchal) homes. There is an almost obsessive concern with masculinity, and hostility toward homosexuality is expressed in "queer" baiting. The third concern, *smartness*, is defined as the ability to obtain a maximum amount of money or goods with a minimum of effort.

Traditionally, the deadening routine of lower-class life has led its members to seek relief in alcohol or evangelism; thus, Miller's delinquents seek *excitement* in "booze, bands, and broads." And related to the belief among the lower class that goal-directed efforts are futile is the concept of *fate*. Many lower-class persons see themselves as subject to a destiny over which they have no control. This attitude serves as an inhibitor to initiative and as a compensation for failure. Miller regards the lower-class emphasis on *autonomy* ("doing your own thing") as an expression of ambivalence toward authority (e.g., resenting external controls while actively seeking out a restrictive environment such as the military). The life style is summed up in the proverb, "Trouble is what life gets you into."

Cohen (1955, 1966) has tried to explain the development of a *delinquent subculture*—an antisocial way of life that has become traditional in a society. According to Cohen, a subculture develops when people with a common problem of adjustment become involved in effective interaction. The problems the delinquent subculture centers on appear to be problems of status: lower-class children are denied status in middle-class membership. The delinquent subculture deals with such problems by providing status criteria that youngsters *are* able to meet. Specifically, the subculture functions simultaneously to combat internal stress in the individual (as represented by feelings of insecurity and low self esteem) and to deal with the representatives of middle-class culture. It does so by erecting a counterculture that offers alternative status criteria in direct opposition to those of the middle class, to the extent that they impart a "non-utilitarian, malicious, and negativistic" quality to the subculture (Cohen, 1955, p. 25).

Sociopsychological theories

The sociological theories discussed in the preceding section sought to explain how people in certain social groups are subjected to pressures that produce a tendency toward criminality. As noted, however, the theories fail to account for the fact that most people exposed to such pressures *do not* become delinquent or criminal, while others not exposed *do*. This inconsistency is of major interest to sociopsychological theorists.

Sociopsychological explanations of crime center on the symbolic interactions through which people acquire the skills, techniques, values, orientations, and self-concepts essential to the criminal role. Theorists recognize that not all crime results from progressive involvement in deviant behavior; some crimes occur because of the attractions and provocations of isolated situations.

Differential association

A well-known and widely used intelligence test asks, Why should we avoid bad company? The answer—supplied by common sense and experience—is that this is the way to keep out of trouble with the law. Criminologist Edwin H. Sutherland reached the same conclusion more than a half century ago. The basic idea of Sutherland's theory of *differential association* is that people *learn* to become criminals through communication, through prolonged, intimate contact with people who are criminals themselves or who are, at least, strongly inclined to violate the law.

What, exactly, do people have to learn to become criminals? For one thing, they may learn techniques. Says Sutherland: "I worked for several years with a professional thief and had been greatly impressed by his statement that a person cannot become a professional thief merely by wanting to be one; he must be trained in personal association with those who are already professional thieves" (1973, p. 17). More importantly, in Sutherland's view, a person acquires the drives, rationalizations, attitudes, and motives that support criminal activity. These are learned in face-to-face relationships in primary groups usch as the family, gang, or play group. Criminal motives and attitudes, Sutherland stresses, precede the actual commission of criminal acts.

Containment theory

Walter C. Reckless (1973) agrees with Sutherland that some environments pressure people to engage in criminal action. Other individuals grow up in environments in which family, friends, and the community exert pressures to obey the law. Reckless calls the latter kind of pressure *outer containment*. At the same time, however, people learn to self-regulate their behavior as they grow up. This self-control, which Reckless calls *inner containment*, is a key factor in determining whether or not a person will stay within the bounds of accepted norms, values, and laws. Reckless hypothesizes that people with a poor self-concept—a negative or ill-defined view of themselves—engage in more criminal behavior than do people with favorable self-concepts. Critics of containment theory, however, point out that it is impossible to determine whether a poor self-concept is a *cause* or a *result* of criminal conduct. Moreover, the theory leaves unanswered the crucial question of why a poor self-concept would leave someone vulnerable to criminality.

The labeling perspective

When applied to crime, the labeling perspective focuses on the processes by which people are labeled as deviant and on the consequences of such processes. It switches our concern from the causes of crime and delinquency to the processes that amplify and encourage criminal and delinquent patterns. That is, once a person has been labeled as criminal or delinquent by some official agency, he or she is much more likely to be singled out for further attention by school authorities, the police, and the courts. And since misery loves company, youngsters or adults who have been labeled in this way tend to seek the company of others who have undergone the same treatment. As a result, offenders are increasingly estranged from the influence of noncriminal or nondelinquent groups.

The labeling perspective can thus be seen as a complement to other explanations of the origins and development of criminal behavior. The idea has spurred efforts to remove as many criminals as possible—and as soon as possible—from the juvenile and criminal justice systems.

Sorting it all out

Despite some progress, we are still groping to identify the causes of crime. One thing, however, seems abundantly clear: crime in general, as empha-

Boys who are disruptive and aggressive are likely to be singled out as having behavior problems. Courtesy Hiroji Kubota/Magnum.

sized by the passages quoted earlier from the President's Commission on Law Enforcement and Administration of Justice, can not be accounted for by a single factor or theory. Sunday-supplement journalists are fond of "explaining" crime and delinquency as the result of poverty, broken homes, failure of the schools, or "bad company." But "crime" is a term that embraces vastly different acts—from the vicious murders of black children in Atlanta to the greed of congressmen convicted of taking bribes in the Abscam scandal.

Increasingly, efforts to explain crime will be directed toward discovering what causes *specific* criminal or delinquent acts. Solutions to the problems posed by crime and delinquency, however, will not come automatically with the discovery of the causes of criminality. What criminologists have said about the causes of crime have affected crime policies indirectly at best. As Robert Rhodes observes:

> It is one thing to know the causes of crime; it is quite another to know how criminal justice agencies can act on these causes.... Where criminologists do agree on the social factors correlated with criminal behavior, family instability, lower-class behavior...or whatever, their conclusions lend themselves to suggesting alterations of the social structure far beyond the capacity of the criminal justice system (1977, p. 260).

Summary

The relationship between economic factors and criminality is extremely complex. Poverty can bring about crime, but its social conditions may be more important than the economic circumstances in producing crime. To the radical or critical criminologist, criminality is one of the consequences of the class struggle in a capitalist society. Criminal law and the criminal justice system are viewed as tools used by the power elites to maintain the status quo and exclude the poor and disenfranchised from sharing power and wealth.

The nature-nurture issue has never dropped entirely from criminology theories since the time of Lombroso. But genetic studies of criminality have progressed considerably since the turn of the century, when investigators traced the genealogies of families distinguished by unusually high percentages of criminals, lunatics, and mental defectives. In addition to genetic studies, researchers have conducted wide-ranging investigations of abnormal physiological structures and their possible influence on criminal behavior. Nearly four decades of research has found certain consistent patterns of abnormal functioning in the brain waves, skin conductance, and cardiovascular responses of individuals identified as having antisocial personalities.

Psychiatrists have interpreted crime as a syndrome or category of mental illness. Psychologists, on the other hand, have tended to view criminality as behavior that is acquired in the same way as other patterns of learned behavior, i.e., through reinforcement. The psychiatric approach has fostered two lines of inquiry: (1) the search for a "criminal personality", and (2) the assessment of psychiatric disorders among criminals. Both of these areas of research have failed to provide results which confirm the theories on which they are based. Neither clinical observations nor psychological tests have identified any cluster of psychological traits distinctive to the criminal. With the exception of alcoholism, drug addiction, and sociopathy or psychopathy—terms often defined with reference to the criminal behavior they are supposed to explain—psychiatric disorders appar to occur with about the same frequency in both criminal and noncriminal populations.

Approaches to criminality using learning theories, developed chiefly from laboratory studies of animal and human subjects, have provided some of the clearest theoretical accounts of how criminal behavior may be acquired, maintained, and changed. Attempts to modify criminal behavior by means of "psychotechnology," however, have generated intense opposition. Outrage over certain projects which seemed to reduce human beings to the level of animal subjects led in 1974 to the withdrawal of federal support from all projects involving "behavior modification." Current programs have dropped the language of psychotechnology and show a great deal of restraint in their claims and methods.

Sociological theories of criminality are directed toward finding answers to questions about collective rather than individual criminal behavior. There are two approaches to the exploration and interpretation of social factors in crime causation. The structural approach looks at the influence of social patterns of power or institutions on criminality. The subcultural approach emphasizes the role of conflict between the norms of the larger society and those which characterize lower class or ethnic subcultures. The latter approach maintains that when the norms of the subculture impose standards of conduct different from those prescribed by the larger culture, the resulting normative conflict can become the major source of criminal behavior.

Sociopsychological theories of criminality examine the processes by which people become delinquents or criminals, and the differential response factors that help explain why some people who are exposed to adverse environmental conditions engage in crime and delinquency while others do not. Sutherland's differential association theory suggests that crime is learned principally in primary groups. Reckless' containment theory attempts to consider both social and cultural factors (outer containment) and individual factors (inner containment) and the way these factors interact to produce crime and delinquency. Finally, the labeling perspective focuses on societal reactions to deviant behavior. The imposition of a deviant label may result in increasing, rather than decreasing, tendencies to engage in criminal behavior. According to this approach, formal treatment of deviant behavior may do more harm than good.

issue paper

BIOTECHNOLOGY AND THE CONTROL OF CRIMINAL BEHAVIOR

If criminality could be tied conclusively to some abnormal condition of the body, crime might someday be eliminated by medication, surgery, or eugenics. Thus today, whenever a new mind-altering drug, surgical technique, medical intervention, or genetic discovery is introduced to the public, there is a predictable rush to speculate that the answer to the crime problem is here at last.

In the early 1970s, for example, many researchers thought that aggressive male sexuality was causally linked to the XYY chromosome syndrome. Criminologists, however, especially those with a sociological orientation, were skeptical about the link; criminality, deviance, and various kinds of disapproved behavior have often been "explained" by defective biology. And in many cases, the defects have been attributed to racial or ethnic inferiority. So far, however, research has failed to demonstrate that a significant percentage of convicted rapists are XYY males.

In 1851, in a lecture to the Louisiana Medical Association ("The Diseases and Physical Peculiarities of the Negro Race"), Dr. Samuel A. Cartwright argued, based on "incontrovertible scientific evidence," that the "slothful negro" was biologically destined for slavery. Describing a myriad of disorders, diseases, and abnormalities peculiar to "indolent Negroes"—conditions that produced the "debasement of mind" that made the native peoples of Africa incapable of caring for themselves—Cartwright concluded that slavery was a just and human institution. Two of the "diseases" he identified would now be referred to as behavioral disorders. According to Chorover:

> Cartwright insisted that slaves who ran away from their masters were not willfully disobedient. On the contrary, they were suffering from a disease of the mind. He named this disease *drapetomania* (from the ancient Greek words *drapetes* for runaway, and *mania* for madness) and suggested that the best remedy is to treat all "Negroes with firmness and kindness, and they are easily governed."
>
> But sometimes the treatment fails, Cartwright said, because of another disease also "peculiar to Negroes." This one he named *dysaesthesia aethiopis,* or "behetude of mind and obtuse sensibility of body." He described it as one of the more prevalent "maladies of the Negro race" and expressed wonder that it had escaped the attention of his medical colleagues for so long. Afflicted individuals, he said, tended to engage in much mischief, to slight their work, to abuse tools and break them and generally to raise disturbances. Most remarkably, he saw the disease as being accompanied by an "obviously pathological" change in the functioning of the nervous system: an apparent insensibility to "pain when being punished." The treatment Cartwright prescribed included anointing the entire body with oil and, "slapping the oil in with a broad leather strap," and then putting "the patient to some hard kind of work in the open air and sunshine" (1973, p. 44).

Before dismissing Cartwright's views as hopelessly antiquated racism, consider that he spoke as a highly respected member of the medical community. Neither can his report be considered a "quaint relic of bygone days." More than a century later—not long after the Detroit riots of 1967—an echo of Cartwright's views appeared in a letter in the *Journal of the American Medical Association.* Written by Vernon Mark, Chief of Neurosurgical Services at Boston City Hospital, William Sweet, Chief of Neurosurgical Services at Massachusetts General Hospital, and Frank Ervin, a psychiatrist at Massachusetts General Hospital, the letter asserted that although the social causes of urban rioting were well known, there was "the more subtle role of other possible factors, including brain dysfunction in the rioters who engaged in arson, sniping, and physical assault" (1967, p. 895). Further, they distinguished between the majority of peaceful, law-abiding slum dwellers and the minority of violent slum dwellers—who might have been reacting on the basis of lesions in the brain.

This theme was pursued in much greater detail in *Violence and the Brain*, published in 1970 by Mark and Ervin. The authors directed attention to the *episodic dyscontrol syndrome*, a condition characterized by paroxysmal, seizurelike outbursts during which the sufferer may lose contact with the environment and commit acts of violence (including spouse and child beatings and sexual assaults). The relevance of the syndrome lies in the analogy between this condition and classical temporal lobe epilepsy. Mark and Ervin speculated that the cause of the dyscontrol syndrome is "limbic brain disease." The limbic system is a complex area of the brain that plays an important—but little understood—role in several basic functions: sleeping and waking, sitting, sexual behavior, emotional arousal, and aggression.

In the absence of any direct diagnostic tests for "limbic brain disease," Mark and Ervin relied on two indirect methods of diagnosis: first, they determined if violent persons in their study had symptoms of recognizable brain disease; second, if the first test was negative, they compared the behavior of violent subjects to the behavior of people known to have "limbic brain disease." On the basis of such shaky diagnoses, Mark and Ervin were prepared to carry out surgery on people identified as having "poor control of violent impulses." Nassi and Abramowitz (1976) and Chorover (1973) have taken Mark and Ervin to task for the numerous weaknesses and shortcomings in their work. Chorover calls their book a promotional treatise:

> It explicitly seeks to justify as "therapeutic" the destruction of brain tissue in people who exhibit allegedly unprovoked, uncontrollable, and unreasonable fits of violent behavior. They do not seriously consider the possibility that the causes of such behavior may lie elsewhere than within the brain of the individuals committing the violence. And they do not give clear and complete accounts of the symptoms that justify the use of radical physical treatments such as injections of various drugs, surgery on the limbic system, and electrical stimulation of the brain with implanted electrodes. Nor do they provide a critical assessment of a number of disastrous outcomes from their "therapeutic interventions" (1973, p. 48).

In the light of such criticism, it is interesting to find Gene Stephens, a professor of criminal justice at the University of South Carolina, suggesting that "genetic engineering could eliminate the offensive traits from future generations" (1981, p. 51). Writing in *The Futurist* about crime in the year 2000, Stephens comments:

> Microsurgery of DNA in humans may also be a possibility . . . and in the twenty-first century, gene insertion, deletion and correction surgery should be part of standard medical practice. Scientists may be able chemically to influence memory (and specific memories), intelligence, pain, pleasure, perception, and other aspects of human consciousness. . . . Computers, communications devices, and new forms of transportation may well have led to a more integrated, perhaps more controlled, society by the year 2000—the kind of society in which the use of medical technologies to control behavior would not seem particularly unusual (1981, pp. 49-50).

Civil libertarians are apt to be distressed by Stephens' position, by the bland acceptance of the proposition that we need only to find the right technique for eliminating unacceptable or objectionable behavior—or people. This position is reminiscent of earlier claims that criminal behavior is the direct result of the impact of the environment on low-grade human organisms and that certain crime patterns are characteristic of people of various races and nationalities.

PREDICTING CRIME

Should a criminal be jailed because of crimes he *might* commit in the future?

This controversial idea, called selective incapacitation, has as its goal prevention, not punishment or even rehabilitation. If John Smith is likely to commit 15 muggings, avoiding them may be worth the cost of imprisoning him.

Science, some feel, faces the major challenge of providing a way to determine how many crimes John Smith is likely to commit. Judges now make that determination by instinct and the person's record. Peter Greenwood, of Rand Corporation, on the other hand, suggests two types of research. One develops statistical profiles of many criminals' arrest histories. The other uses "self-reports" in which convicts anonymously provide data on their own criminal activities. Greenwood believes such research can lead to a reliable estimate of the number of crimes John Smith might commit annually.

American Civil Liberties Union lawyer David Landau disagrees. "Almost all social-science studies show that you cannot pedict future criminality with any accuracy," he warns. "There's also a constitutional objection. You're talking about punishing people for crimes they haven't committed."

Although he has certain reservations, Alfred Blumstein, who was the chairman of a National Academy of Sciences panel on deterrence, counters with a comparison. The idea of imposing a stiff jail sentence or even the death penalty as a deterrent to other would-be criminals is now widely accepted. Yet, he says, this amounts to punishing the criminal for *other people's* future crimes. And nobody knows how well it works. "In many respects," says Blumstein, "I feel more comfortable with the idea of putting people in jail for their own future crimes than for other people's crimes."

Most people would probably agree.

R. Coniff, "Twenty-first Century Crime-Stoppers." *Science Digest* 90 (1982):62, by permission of the author and the publisher.

The conclusion of such thought? "The elimination of crime can be effected only by the extirpation of the physically, mentally, and morally unfit or by their complete segregation in a socially asceptive environment" (Hooton 1939, p. 309). This sentiment was uttered in 1939, the year Hitler's Wehrmacht invaded Poland and ignited World War II. It was not until six years later, however, in the rubble and wreckage of the Thousand Year Reich, that the world discovered the grisly evidence of just such a program of "extirpation." But the author of the sentiment was not a Nazi working for the "Final Solution" in Europe. He was an American anthropologist named Ernest Hooton.

Discussion and review

1. Summarize the conclusions of Sutherland and Cressey in their review of research on crime and economic conditions. What are some of the factors that contribute to the complexity of the relationship between crime and economics in an industrial country like the United States?
2. How do radical criminologists view the influence of economics on crime?
3. Are there any explanations other than genetics as to why crime might "run in families"?
4. Why does Mednick refer to his theory of criminality as a "biosocial" theory? What is the significance of social learning in Mednick's formulation?
5. What are the principal weaknesses and shortcomings of the psychiatric approach to criminality as mental illness?
6. Why might you be skeptical about the prospect of identifying a "criminal personality"? What are the conclusions of research on this issue?
7. In Rosenhan's study of normal people who faked mental illness to gain entry to a mental hospital, who first became aware that the entrants were pseudopatients?
8. Why is it easier to set up and operate a token economy *within* an institution rather than outside one?
9. Describe Barker's attempt to treat transvestism by means of conditioning.
10. How does Merton explain the relationship between social structure and deviant behavior?

Glossary

Anomie A state of normlessness in society that may be caused by decreased homogeneity and that is conducive to crime and other deviant behavior.

Atavism From the Latin *atavus*, meaning ancestor. Term that implies that certain "born criminals" are an evolutionary throwback to an earlier, more primitive, human form.

Aversive conditioning Treatment in which a person is aversively (negatively) stimulated until he or she performs a certain behavior, at which time the stimulaiton is discontinued. The effect is positive reinforcement for stopping an undesirable behavior.

Contingency management program Treatment in which desirable behavior is reinforced by reward.

Criminal personality A hypothetical constellation or cluster of traits and characteristics that distinguish criminals from noncriminals.

Electroencephalograph (EEG) An instrument that picks up electrical activity in brain cells by electrodes attached to the scalp. Activity is recorded in oscillating patterns called *brain waves* by a machine connected to the electrodes. The visual recording that results is called and *electroencephalogram*.

Epilepsy A group of nervous disorders characterized by recurring attacks of motor, sensory, or psychic disturbances, sometimes accompanied by convulsive movements and loss of consciousness.

Fugue A pathological amnesic condition during which an individual is apparently conscious of his or her actions; upon a return to normal, however, the sufferer has no recollection of those actions.

Galvanic skin response (GSR) The *GSR* is a component of the polygraph, or "lie detector," apparatus. The apparatus measures minute changes in electropotential on the surface of the skin to provide an index of emotional responses such as anxiety.

Orthmolecular psychiatry Doctrine based on the belief that various kinds of deviant behavior, including delinquent and criminal activity, are systematically related to abnormal reaction rates in the body as a result of constitutional defects, faulty diet, and abnormal concentrations of essential elements.

Radical criminology An approach to crime based on the assumption that criminal law reflects the power of elite groups in society and is manifested by the use of the criminal justice system to maintain control of the production and distribution of wealth. Also known as "critical criminology."

Token economy A method of reinforcement often used in institutional settings. People are rewarded for constructive social behavior with tokens that can be exchanged for desired objects or activities.

XYY syndrome A chromosomal abnormality in males (the presence of an extra Y chromosome) that was once thought to be related to sexually aggressive behavior.

References

Barker, J. C. "Behaviour Therapy for Transvestism: A Comparison of Pharmacological and Electrical Aversion Techniques." *British Journal of Psychiatry* 111 (1965):268–276.

Batchelor, I. R. C. *Henderson and Gillespie's Textbook of Psychiatry.* London: Oxford University Press, 1969.

Bell, B.; Mednick, S. A.; Gottesman, I. I.; and Sergeant, J. "Electrodermal Parameters in Young Normal Male Twins." In *Biosocial Bases of Criminal Behavior,* edited by S. A. Mednick and K. O. Christiansen. New York: Gardner Press, 1977.

Braukmann, C.; Fixen, D.; Phillips, E.; and Wolf, M. "Behavioral Approaches to Treatment in the Crime and Delinquency Field." *Criminology* 13 (1975):299–331.

Chorover, S. L. "Big Brother and Psychotechnology." *Psychology Today* 7 (1973):43–54.

Cloward, R. A., and Ohlin, L. E. *Delinquency and Opportunity.* Glencoe, Ill.: Free Press, 1960.

Cohen, A. K. *Delinquent Boys.* Glencoe, Ill.: Free Press, 1955.

Cohen, A. K. "The Delinquency Subculture." In *Juvenile Delinquency: A Book of Readings,* edited by R. Giallombardo. New York: Wiley, 1966.

Feldman, D. "Psychoanalysis and Crime." In D. R. Cressey and D. Ward (eds.) *Delinquency, Crime, and Social Process.* New York: Harper and Row, 1969.

Halleck, S. L. "American Psychiatry and the Criminal: A Historical Review." *American Journal of Psychiatry* 121 (1965):1–21.

Hare, R. D. *Psychopathy: Theory and Research.* New York: Wiley, 1970.

Hare, R. D., and Schalling, D., eds. *Psychopathic Behavior.* New York: Wiley, 1978.

Hooton, E. A. *The American Criminal.* Cambridge, Massachusetts: Harvard University, 1939.

Huxley, A. *Brave New World.* New York: Harper and Row, 1978.

Lazarus, A. "Has Behavior Therapy Outlived Its Usefulness?" *American Psychologist* 32 (1977):550–54.

Lillyquist, M. J. *Understanding and Changing Criminal Behavior.* Englewood Cliffs, N.J.: Prentice-Hall, 1980.

Lippert, W. W. "The Electrodermal System of the Psychopath." Ph.D. dissertation, University of Cincinnati, 1965.

Lykken, D. T. "A Study of Anxiety in the Sociopathic Personality." *Journal of Abnormal and Social Psychology* 55 (1957):6–10.

Mark, V., and Ervin, F. *Violence and the Brain.* New York: Harper & Row, 1970.

Mark, V. H., Sweet, W. H., and Ervin, F. R. "Role of Brain Disease in Riots and Urban Violence." *Journal of the American Medical Association,* 1967, 201, 217.

Masters, J. *Bugles and a Tiger.* New York: Viking Press, 1956.

McCaghy, C. H. *Deviant Behavior: Crime, Conflict, and Interest Groups.* New York: Macmillan, 1976.

McConnell, J. "Stimulus/Response: Criminals Can Be Brainwashed—Now." *Psychology Today* 3 (1970):14–18, 74.
Mednick, S. A. "A Biosocial Theory of the Learning of Law-Abiding Behavior." In *Biosocial Bases of Criminal Behavior*, edited by S. A. Mednick and K. O. Christiansen. New York: Gardner Press, 1977.
Mednick, S. A. "Biosocial Factors and Primary Prevention of Antisocial Behavior." In *New Paths in Criminology*, edited by S. A. Mednick and S.G. Shoham. Lexington, Mass.: Lexington Books, 1979.
Mednick, S. A., and Volavka, J. "Biology and Crime." In *Crime and Justice: An Annual Review of Research*, edited by N. Morris and M. Tonry. Chicago: University of Chicago Press, 1980.
Mednick, S. A.; Volavka, J.; Gabrielli, W. F.; and Itil, T. M. "EEG as a Predictor of Antisocial Behavior." *Criminology* 19 (1981):219–29.
Merton, R. K. *Social Theory and Social Structure*. Glencoe, Ill.: Free Press, 1957.
Miller, Walter B. "Lower-Class Culture as a Generating Milieu of Gang Delinquency." *Journal fo Social Issues* 14 (1958):5–19.
Mitford, Jessica. *Kind and Unusual Punishment: The Prison Business*. New York: Random House, 1974.
Montagu, A. "Chromosomes and Crime." *Psychology Today* 2 (1968):43–49.
Nettler, G. *Explaining Crime*. New York: McGraw-Hill, 1974.
Orwell, G. *Nineteen Eighty-Four*. New York: Harcourt Brace, 1949.
Poplin, D. E. *Social Problems*. Glenview, Ill.: Scott, Foresman, 1978.
President's Commission on Law Enforcement and Administration of Justice. *The Challenge of Crime in a Free Society*. Washington, D.C.: U.S. Government Printing Office, 1967.
Quinney, R. *Critique of Legal Order: Crime Control in Capitalist Society*. Boston: Little, Brown, 1974.
Rand, A. *Anthem*. New York: New American Library, 1961.
Reckless, W. C. *The Crime Problem*. New York: Appleton-Century-Crofts, 1973.
Remarque, E. M. *All Quiet on the Western Front*. Boston: Little, Brown, 1929.
Rhodes, Robert P. *The Insoluble Problems of Crime*. New York: Wiley, 1977.
Rodin, E. "Psychomotor Epilepsy and Aggressive Behavior." *Archives of General Psychiatry* 28 (1973):210—13.
Schwitzgebel, R. "Limitations on the Coercive Treatment of Offenders." *Criminal Law Bulletin* 8 (1972):267-320.
Slater, E., and Roth, M. *Clinical Psychiatry*. London: Balliere and Tindall, 1969.
Stephens, G. "Crime in the Year 2000." *The Futurist* 25 (1981):48–52.
Suinn, R. M. *Fundamentals of Behavior Pathology*. New York: Wiley, 1970.
Sutherland, E. H. *On Analyzing Crime*. Chicago: University of Chicago Press, 1973.
Sutherland, E. H., and Cressey, D. R. *Criminology*. Philadelphia: Lippincott, 1978.
Thornton, W. E., James, J. A., and Doerner, W. G. *Delinquency and Justice*. Glenview, Ill.: Scott, Foresman, 1982.
Turner, W. J., and Merlis, S. "Clinical Correlations Between Electroencephalography and Antisocial Behavior." *Medical Times* 90 (1962):505–11.
Yochelson, S., and Samenow, S. E. *The Criminal Personality*. A Profile for Change, vol. 1. New York: Jason Aronson, 1977.

5
police operations and the crime laboratory

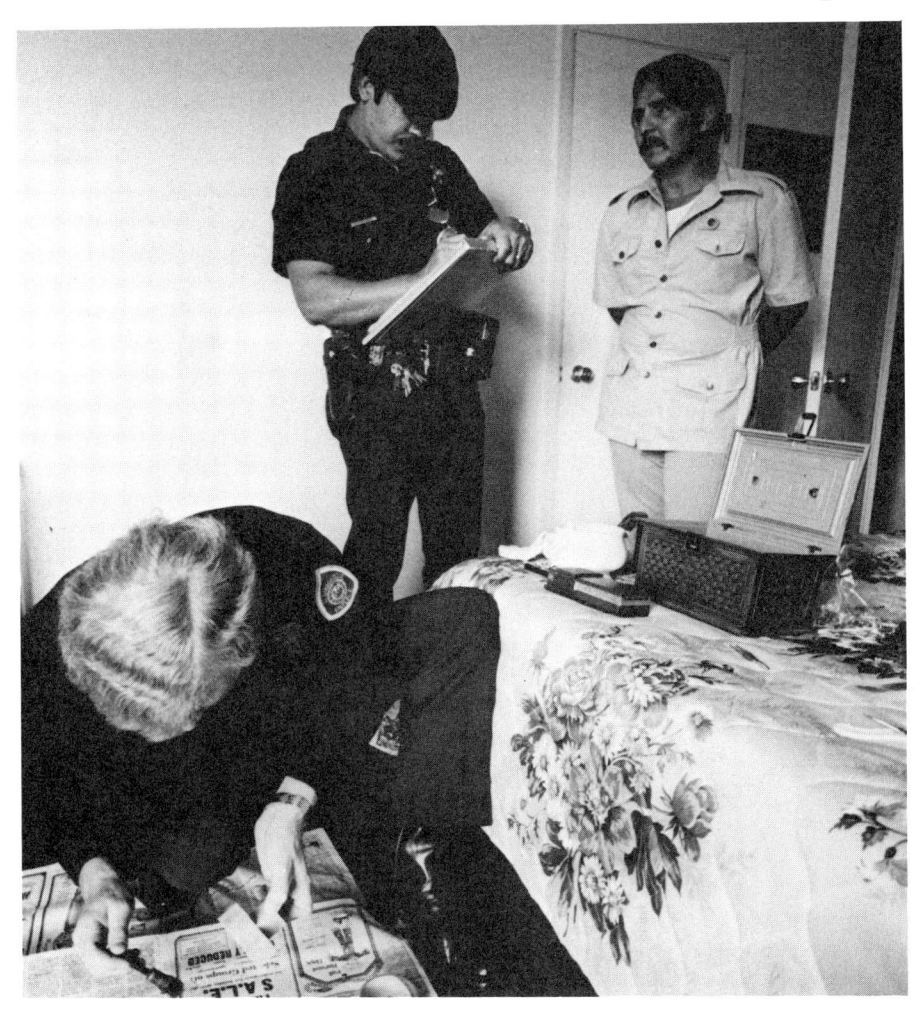

The patrol bureau: Backbone or manpower tool?
Activities of the patrol bureau
    Noncrime calls for service
    Attendance at public gatherings
    Benevolent and community services
    Preliminary investigations
    Arrests
    Traffic direction and control
    Court testimony
Team policing
    Team size
    Team supervision
    Shift schedules
    Permanency of assignments
    Blending specialists and generalists
    Community interface
    Decentralized planning
    Service orientation
    The response to team policing
The Kansas City Patrol Experiment

The traffic bureau
Activities of the traffic bureau
    Traffic control
    Accident investigation
    Traffic-law enforcement
    Selective traffic enforcement
    The quota system: Myth or reality
    Who gets the money?
Traffic enforcement policies: Police departments and sheriff's departments

The detective bureau
Activities of the detective bureau
    Incident report and preliminary investigation
    Evidence collection and processing
    Screening and case assignment
    Follow-up (latent) investigation
    Clearance and arrest
    File maintenance
    Selection, training, and supervision
The Rand Criminal Investigation Study
    The study design
    Policy recommendations
    Impact of the study
The crime laboratory
    Capabilities, limitations, and use of a crime laboratory
    Measures of effectiveness
    The FBI Crime Laboratory

Issue paper: Terrorism—the crime of the future

THE conventional approach to police operations is to briefly describe the many tasks performed by the various units of a police department. In this chapter, we instead focus on four major components of police operations—namely, the patrol bureau, the traffic bureau, the detective bureau, and the crime laboratory. When possible, we go beyond merely describing the tasks performed by these units and attempt to address issues not usually discussed in general criminal justice books.

In our discussion of the patrol bureau, we look at two specific problems common to most major patrol bureaus: first, the desire of many patrol officers to be transferred from patrol bureaus, and second, the use of the patrol bureau as a manpower pool for specialized units. We examine the sources of these problems and recommend some ways to reverse them, or at least slow them down. We also examine the team policing efforts that were so popular in the 1970s. Further, we outline the implications of the Kansas City Patrol Experiment, which sought to determine the effectiveness of the traditional strategy of routine patrol with conspicuously marked vehicles.

Our discussion of traffic bureaus focuses on traffic quotas, the impact of traffic-law enforcement on community relations, and the possible variations among the traffic-law enforcement policies of municipal police departments and sheriff's departments. Our discussion of detective bureaus seeks to dispel some of the stereotypes associated with detectives and to provide a realistic portrait of detective work. We also review the findings and policy recommendations of the *Rand Criminal Investigation Study* (Greenwood 1979), the first analytical scrutiny of police investigators nationwide. Finally, we discuss the purpose, capabilities, limitations, and use of the crime laboratory in criminal investigations.

The patrol bureau: Backbone or manpower tool?

The first assignment for almost all police officers graduating from police academies is with the patrol bureau. This assignment—for better or worse—is the foundation upon which all other police experiences are formed. Skolnick, commenting on the similarity of experiences among American police officers, states that

> the policeman's working personality is most highly developed in his constabulary role of the man on the beat. For analytical purposes that role is sometimes regarded as an enforcement specialty, but in the general discussion of the policemen as they comport themselves while working, the uniformed cop is seen as the foundation for the policeman's working personality. There is a sound organizational basis for making this assumption. The police, unlike the military, draw no caste distinction in socialization even though their order of rank title approximates the military. Thus one cannot join a local police department as, for instance, a lieutenant, as a West Point graduate joins the Army. Every officer must serve an apprenticeship as a patrolman. This feature of police organizations means that the constabulary role is the primary one for all police officers and that whatever the special requirements of roles in law enforcement specialties they are

carried out with a common background of constabulary experience (1966, pp. 43–44).

The rookie officer is usually assigned to work directly with a senior patrol officer, who bears the title *field training officer*, or *coach*. Because their job is to "break in" rookies, these senior officers are often very influential in the professional development of the new officers placed under their tutelage. The amount of time a rookie and a senior officer spend together is a function of the policy of the organization, the pace at which the new officer masters certain skills, and the needs of the organization.

The part of a community to which a new officer is assigned depends upon the personnel needs of the patrol bureau and the philosophy of the chief administrator or bureau commander. For example, one administrator might favor assigning rookie officers to high-crime areas to accelerate their experience and to allow an assessment of their ability to function under stress. This type of intensive exposure to police problems might also reduce the time a new officer has to spend under the direct supervision of a senior partner. Other administrators assign rookie officers to areas with few serious crime problems, allowing the officers to gain experience at a slower rate and in a less hostile environment.

Most patrol bureaus contain some interesting organizational contradictions that can have a negative impact on bureau operations. For example, chief administrators frequently espouse the position that the patrol bureau is the "backbone" of the agency, but they then proceed to transfer the best and brightest officers away from that bureau to other assignments, such as the detective bureau, vice squad, or training academy. This practice, which is common to many police departments, can create serious personnel problems. If continued with regularity, the practice guarantees that the "backbone" of the police department will be composed primarily of inexperienced officers and those who are average, or even below average, in ability and motivation.

Why would a police administrator employ a policy that depletes a primary operating unit of its finest people? There are several answers to this question. First, an administrator may not really believe in the importance of the patrol bureau. Second, he or she may not believe that the patrol bureau is sufficiently stimulating, rewarding, or challenging enough to keep the best, brightest and most able officers satisfied. Such officers are therefore provided with higher status and more challenging positions to keep them from resigning or becoming dissatisfied and bored with their patrol assignments. A chief of police who clings to these beliefs probably has instituted policies that do indeed make an assignment to the patrol bureau unchallenging and lacking in status. For instance, if a police chief believes that patrol officers should have no responsibility for investigating even the most routine criminal offenses and that all segments of an investigation should be conducted by a detective, then that chief has eliminated for the patrol officer one of the most interesting and challenging functions of police work—namely, criminal investigation.

Another problem in patrol bureaus is that many officers wish to be transferred to other bureaus. The environment of most patrol bureaus

Patrol officers discuss career development opportunitites with their captain. Courtesy Greensboro (North Carolina) Police Department.

probably contributes to this situation. By necessity, patrol bureaus operate twenty-four hours a day, every day of the year; and because of this schedule, officers assigned to patrol must work more weekends, nights, and holidays than many of their counterparts in other bureaus. This work schedule increases the possibility that days off will be spent making court appearances; and shift-related problems may be particularly troublesome to officers whose spouses work at regular daytime jobs with weekends off. Schedule conflicts do not promote domestic harmony and have been cited by many police officers as a prominent cause of marital discord.

The normal working day of a patrol officer is not filled with glamorous and exciting crime-fighting activities like those depicted on popular television programs. Instead, days are spent on routine patrol or performing noncriminal services for the public. However, in spite of this routine, the patrol officer's job is often far more dangerous than most people imagine. Patrol officers are the ones who are called on to respond to crimes in progress or crimes that have just been committed. Such assignments increase the possibility that a criminal will still be at the scene of the crime or in the immediate area, thereby increasing the potential for physical and armed confrontation. Thus, the job of the patrol officer has often been described as one consisting of both hours of boredom (especially on the midnight shift) and moments of terror.

Patrol officers also spend much of their day in contact with the human dregs of our society. They have to deal with drunks who have soiled themselves but who still must be searched before being transported to jail; with teenage gangs who are arrogant, disrespectful, and openly contemptuous; with prostitutes, pimps, petty thugs; and with child abusers. Patrol officers are called upon to intercede in domestic disputes in which combatting couples often turn on the officers trying to peacefully settle the dispute. With all of these problems—on top of the incredible number of written reports that patrol officers must complete—a job in the patrol bureau can be highly stressful both physically and psychologically. (Police stress is discussed in detail in chapter 6.) Thus, in spite of efforts by many progressive administrators to improve supervision and working conditions and to give greater recognition to patrol bureau officers, the ambition of many of these officers is first to become a detective and later to move into management, with its higher status, better hours, and higher pay.

Patrol officers know that the financial rewards and professional status in most police departments are reserved for managers. Persons who serve as patrol officers for twenty years and then retire are frequently considered to be "not very successful" by their peers, regardless of their accomplishments. This is a serious problem, because the organization of most police departments makes it impossible for more than 10 to 20 percent of all officers to rise above the rank of patrol officer. Thus, because of the built-in limitations of organizations, the expectations and ambitions of many officers cannot be met.

One can find among the ranks of any police department many individuals who have neither the interest nor the aptitude to become managers; yet these same individuals feel compelled to pursue managerial positions, because such positions offer the only route for achieving some degree of professional stature and monetary reward. It is apparent that new organi-

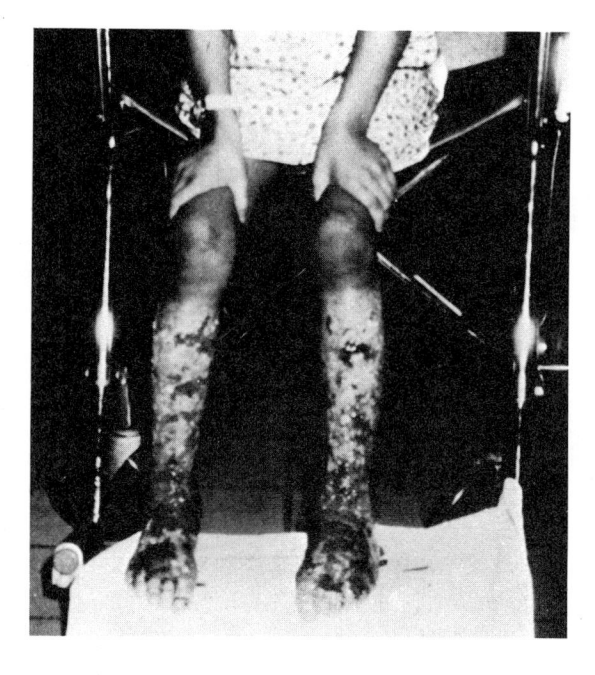

Victim of child abuse. The victim was immersed in scalding hot water by one of her parents for misbehaving. Courtesy of the Tampa (Florida) Police Department.

zational models must be considered to provide realistic and cost-effective alternatives. One possibility is a dual-career system that allows police officers to follow either a nonmanagerial, *professional officer track* or a *professional police management track* (**figure 5.1**).

A two-track system would provide a realistic and workable alternative to management. An officer could remain within the patrol ranks in a nonmanagerial role, yet still enjoy some of the professional and monetary rewards of the organization. **Table 5.1** outlines some of the recommended training and educational components that can be built into the system to assure individual development, along with quality control. Thus, all police officers would know precisely what they must do to move up the professional police officer track or the professional police management track. This dual-track model may not be appropriate in its present form to meet the needs of some police departments, but it does provide a conceptual basis from which alternative models can be developed.

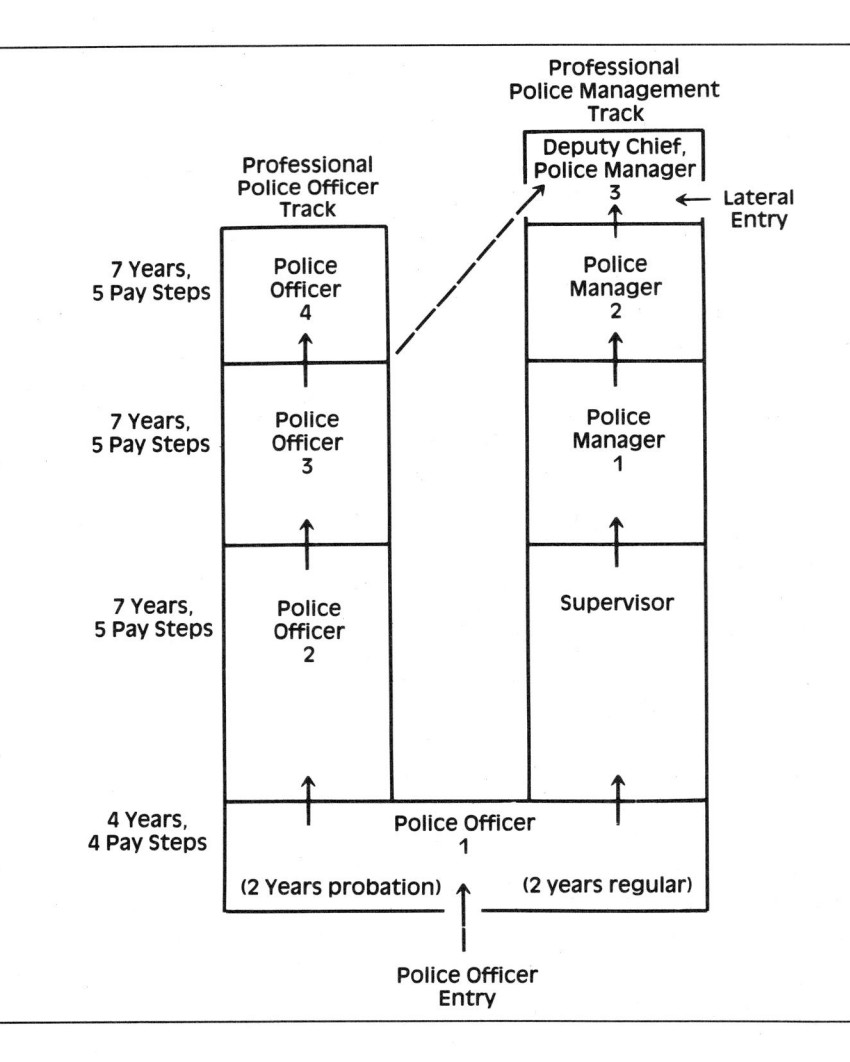

FIGURE 5.1
Professional career tracks in the police department. Adapted from P.M. Whisenand, Police Career Development (Washington, D.C.: U.S. Government Printing Office, September 1973), p. 8.

TABLE 5.1 Training and education for professional career tracks

Training step	Training requirement	Police official	Police management
5	Bachelor's degree and proven ability are the minimum qualifications. Exempt positions can be filled from one or more of the ladders or laterally from outside the agency.		Deputy chief, police manager 3
4	Bachelor's degree, 3160 training points, and seven years as a police officer 3 needed to be eligible for the three-day in-service selection and training program. If selected, a two-week in-service training program must be completed. Each person must earn 80 training points annually.	Police officer 4	Police manager 4
3	Ninety college hours (semester), 2150 training points, and seven years as a police officer 2 needed to be eligible for the three-day in-service selection and training program. If selected, a two-week in-service training program must be completed. Each person must earn 80 training points annually.	Police officer 3	Police manager 1
2	Sixty college hours (semester) and 1140 training points needed to be eligible for the three-day in-service selection and training program. If selected, a two-week in-service training program must be completed. Each person must earn 80 training points annually (1 point = 1 training hour; 15 points = 1 semester hour; 10 points = 1 quarter unit).	Police officer 2	Supervisor
1	Six-month basic academy and 24 college hours (semester)	Police officer 1	
Entry	High school diploma and the passing of other job related tests.	Police officer entry	

Adapted from P. M. Whisenand, *Police Career Development* (Washington, D.C.: U.S. Government Printing Office, September 1973), p. 15.

Activities of the patrol bureau

No two patrol bureaus perform identical tasks, although some tasks are basic to all bureaus, regardless of size. In general, patrol duties are not spelled out in great detail, except when patrol officers are assigned to a specific call for police service. Thus, the catchall phrase "routine patrol and observation" is interpreted in different ways by individual departments, supervisors, and patrol officers. For example, some patrol officers on the day shift who do not have a specific assignment might decide to concentrate on traffic enforcement; others might decide to patrol a residential area that has had a recent rash of daytime burglaries. The same variations in preference may also exist in the evening and midnight shifts; some officers might patrol a main street or business district to prevent robberies, and others might patrol a warehouse district to prevent burglaries.

Ideally, the type of routine patrol and observation engaged in by patrol officers should be the result of a collaborative effort between the patrol supervisor and the patrol officer, based on the crime data for a given patrol area. Unfortunately, such an effort is often the exception rather than the rule. Some innovative police departments have developed programs in which patrol officers who work days and are not on call are encouraged to conduct crime prevention checks of homes and businesses in their districts that are susceptible to burglaries and robberies. Such efforts usually result in more productive use of patrol time than when each officer is allowed to "do his or her own thing."

Noncrime calls for service Between 80 and 90 percent of all calls for police service are of a noncriminal nature. Many of these calls involve possession and repossession of property, landlord and tenant disputes, property-line arguments, animal control, and noise at parties. Thus, patrol officers must be knowledgeable about the civil law as well as the criminal law. Even calls for service that are clearly civil in nature must be handled promptly and tactfully, because they can quickly escalate into violent confrontation between disputants or between a disputant and an officer.

EVICTION TURNS INTO SHOOTOUT
Donna Newsome and Ferdinand Protzman   Tampa Tribune

A normally routine eviction procedure at a Davis Islands apartment complex exploded into a shootout at noon Friday that left one man dead and a Hillsborough County sheriff's deputy wounded.

The dead man was identified as 38-year-old John C. Hipson Jr. of No. 7 Island Paradise apartments, 240 Danube Ave.

Hillsborough sheriff's Cpl. Roland Corrales was listed in fair and stable condition with multiple gunshot wounds late Friday at Tampa General Hospital.

Corrales and Deputy Robin Tagliarini went to the Island Paradise at 11:30 a.m. to evict Hipson, who had missed paying rent for two months, officials said. He had written to his landlord that because he had lived and paid rent in the apartment for 13 years, he felt he "possessed and owned" it in a "real and substantial way."

When the deputies arrived, Hipson refused to come out of his apartment and threatened to barricade himself inside, according to the Tampa Police Maj. H.B. Maxey.

The deputies then called the Tampa Police Department for help.

"They (police) talked him into coming out, and when he did, Sgt. (John) Small noticed a bulge in his stomach. They asked him if they could pat him down (to check for weapons) and in the process he broke away and pulled his gun and started shooting," Maxey said.

"They (deputies and Tampa police) returned fire," he said.

Maxey said at least one police sergeant and three policemen responded to the call for help.

He said he didn't know whose bullets struck Hipson. But all the officers present did fire, a police official said.

Corrales, 45, was shot at least twice—the bullets striking him in the back and in one of his legs, hospital spokesmen said.

Hipson was shot several times by police, according to Maxey. He died in surgery at Tampa General Hospital about 12:30 p.m., according to a hospital spokesman.

Arsenio Perez, who owns the Island Paradise apartments, said Hipson had lived there for 13 years.

Until a few months ago, Hipson had been a good tenant and never caused any problems, Perez said.

The trouble began when Hipson quit paying rent, telling his landlord that he now owned his apartment, Perez said.

"He (Hipson) never gave me problems," Perez said as he stood across the street from his apartment building and watched several police officers and sheriff's deputies question witnesses. "He was a good, good tenant, but he refused to pay rent. He wouldn't talk to anybody.

"When they (deputies) came back today, he wouldn't let anyone in. The police told everyone to leave," Perez said.

Perez said he heard five or six shots a few minutes after he and the other tenants were asked to leave the building.

Perez's nephew, Gabe Perez, who had come over to help move Hipson's belongings out of the apartment, said, "When he (Hipson) fired the gun we all started scrambling. I didn't see a gun but I was standing right near the building."

Hipson's mother, who would identify herself only as Mrs. John C. Hipson Sr., said from her Bradenton home early Friday afternoon she had no idea why her son would have barricaded himself in his apartment or why he hadn't paid his rent.

She said she didn't know Hipson owned a gun.

"He doesn't work," she said. "He's on a government pension. He had been in the service."

Sheriff's spokesman Paul Marino said Corrales was conscious and talking when he was taken to Tampa General.

Corrales has been with the Sheriff's Office for eight years and has been working in the sheriff's civil division—serving court orders and eviction notices—for five years, Marino said.

He and his wife, Marie, have three children, one of whom is married and is living away from home, family members said. The couple are Tampa natives.

According to Hillsborough County court files, James Burt Inc., the company that manages the apartments for Perez, asked Hipson for $135 back rent in January. When he didn't pay, a complaint was filed in county civil court.

The court file states that Hipson owed $15 in rent from December and $240 for the months of January and February. Three days ago, County Judge Perry Little issued an eviction notice.

A letter Hipson sent to his landlord, which later was made part of the court file on his eviction notice, stated that, "My defense is essentially that I possess and own the apartment in a real and substantial way due to my having lived in it and payed for it for 13 years.

"It is an established understanding in the philosophy of law that differences and disagreements are unavoidable and necessary, and the best way of settling them is by argument rather than violence," Hipson wrote in his letter. "I would rather settle this out of court, but if you insist I'll fight to win."

Hipson also wrote in his letter that he resented involvement of the court and the Sheriff's Office in the matter, which he called "a private legal matter."

The Tampa Tribune, 20 February 1982.

Attendance at public gatherings Patrol officers are frequently assigned to work at large public gatherings such as political rallies and sporting events. Their presence is needed to assure peaceful assembly and to provide protection for those wishing to exercise their rights to peaceful assembly and free speech. An officer's presence may also prevent unlawful activity on the part of individuals or the crowd as a whole. A recent trend is for sponsors of an event to hire off-duty patrol officers, especially if the sponsors are private enterprises or individuals. For example, many sports authorities and convention centers now employ off-duty officers to work the interior and exterior of their facilities during special events and to control traffic into and out of parking areas.

Benevolent and community services Patrol officers are frequently called upon to perform tasks not in their job descriptions. They are called upon to deliver babies, to give advice to families about marital problems and problems with adolescent children, to help people who have lost the keys to their homes or automobiles, to inform people about accidents and deaths, and to deliver blood from one hospital to another. A constant complaint heard from patrol officers is that they should not have to perform so many nonpolice functions; such tasks do nothing to enhance the image of officers in the eyes of the public or in the eyes of the officers themselves. However, having reliable personnel available twenty-four hours a day to perform such services is simply too tempting for some government officials. The following examples illustrate this point.

CASE 5.1

> In one city, the head librarian of the public library contacted the city manager and asked for police assistance in recovering overdue books. The city manager agreed to help and ordered the police chief to have patrol officers go to the homes of violators (children, in some cases) and pick up books. If no one was at home, the officers were to leave a written warning on the door that arrest for larceny could result if the books were not returned immediately. Needless to say, the patrol officers were not thrilled with this task; some were, in fact, quite embarrassed by it.
>
> In another city, officers were instructed to turn on (at dusk) the Christmas tree lights in front of the homes of several influential citizens. The lights were also to be turned off at sunrise.

Preliminary investigations The patrol officer is on duty and available for all incidents that call for police service, including crimes and accidents. A patrol bureau that is adequately staffed and has properly trained its officers is in the best position to handle the *preliminary investigation* of all types of crimes. As the first police officer to arrive at the scene of a crime, the patrol officer must care for any injured persons and must apprehend the criminal if he or she is still in the immediate area. The patrol officer takes immediate steps to preserve the crime scene, then establishes communication with the dispatcher to broadcast a description of the wanted person and to request additional assistance if needed.

Because he or she has been on the scene from the beginning, the patrol officer usually continues with the initial investigation—collecting evidence, cataloguing and filing it, and preparing the necessary reports. When all leads are exhausted and further investigation would take the officer out of his or her assigned district for a long period of time, the follow-up work is usually taken over by an investigator and other specialists (Adams 1971, pp. 15–16).

Arrests Another of the many duties of the patrol officer is to arrest those who violate the law. This activity is one of the officer's primary objectives at the crime scene. Once an officer makes an arrest, several methods may be used to introduce the arrestee into the criminal justice system. These methods are defined by the laws, the courts, and the procedural manuals of various agencies. In most cases, the arrestee is taken to jail and "booked" or processed and then given an opportunity to post bail to assure his or her appearance in court at a later date (ibid., p. 17).[1]

Traffic direction and control Safe and efficient movement of pedestrians and vehicles through a community is the patrol officer's responsibility even if another division of the police department exists strictly for traffic control. (See the discussion on traffic bureaus later in this chapter.)

Court testimony Testifying in court is the patrol officer's final step in the investigative process. When an officer receives a call, he or she responds, then conducts the investigation, arrests the offender, processes the evidence, completes reports, and presents evidence and testimony in court.

Team policing

The 1960s were a time of considerable strain on our police forces; it was a period marked by urban upheavals, a burgeoning crime problem, and the due-process revolution (Phelps, Swanson, and Evans 1979).[2] As the public's anxiety grew, so did the demand for more effective police service. The police responded by attempting to provide more of their traditional services; this approach was perceived as unsatisfactory and unresponsive by many communities, however. By the late 1960s, the gulf between the police and their communities was large, a situation antithetical to the proposition that maximum citizen cooperation is fundamental to crime control in a free society. Recognizing this problem, police departments started the concept of *team policing* to "reduce isolation and induce community support in the war on crime" (National Advisory Commission on Criminal Justice Standards and Goals 1973, p. 154).

Team policing consists of five elements: (1) combining all line functions of patrol, traffic, and investigation into a single unit under common supervision; (2) blending generalists (such as patrol officers) and specialists, (such as homicide investigators) into teams; (3) establishing geographical stability by the continuous assignment of particular teams to particular areas; (4) making teams responsible for the delivery of all police services in their area; and (5) maximizing communication between team members and neighborhood residents (Sherman, Milton, and Kelly 1973, pp. 4–6). Differences between this approach and traditional policing are found in the categories of size, supervision, scheduling, assignments, coordination, community interface, planning, and service orientation (Block and Specht 1973).

Team size In the traditional organization, patrol officers are grouped by precincts or large divisions; a precinct or division usually contains 100 to 250 officers. Teams typically consist of only 20 to 40 officers.

Team supervision Team policing relies upon professional supervision characterized by the delegation of most decision making to the patrol officers. Mistakes are viewed as a learning, rather than a fault-finding, exercise; supervisors are open to suggestions and criticisms from subordinates; and interpersonal communications occur in an atmosphere of trust and confidence. In contrast, traditional supervision tends to centralize decision making; its stated preference for close supervision in the field subtly incorporates a depreciated view of the capabilities of subordinates, thereby discouraging a rich source of contributions.

Shift schedules Traditional patrol service is delivered on eight-hour tours of duty, with around-the-clock responsibility vested only in the precinct or division commander. This approach often produces unevenness in the style, level, and type of services offered. In contrast, team commanders are responsible for all police services around the clock.

Permanency of assignments The prevailing method of assigning patrol officers is to rotate geographical areas, precincts, or assignments. Team policing, because it depends upon a detailed knowledge of an area and upon maximum interaction with citizens, uses fairly stable assignments.

Blending specialists and generalists Team policing blends specialists and generalists together under the unified leadership of the team commander. The traditional method of patrol services leaves the patrol officer—a generalist—in need of support services from specialists in other bureaus; the latter situation often results in bureaucratic fencing over prerogatives and credit and fragmenting of the organizational effort.

Community interface Many police departments started community relations programs in the 1960s in an effort to lessen racial tension. Some de-

An investigator and a uniformed officer feed information into a computer. Courtesy Cincinnati Police Division.

partments did conduct meaningful programs, but others used them as a window dressing for public relations campaigns. The existence of such programs often created the attitude among patrol officers that community relations was solely, or primarily, the responsibility of a particular unit, rather than the responsibility of the entire department. In team policing, community relations is viewed as an essential, on-going effort of all officers, stressing the need for friendly contacts and attendance at neighborhood meetings.

Decentralized planning Traditional policing relies upon planning that is heavily centralized; innovation—such as may occur—flows from the top of the organization down. Team policing, on the other hand, emphasizes decentralized planning, with key contributions coming from team commanders and subordinates, subject to review and approval by senior officials.

Service orientation Team policing is proactive; maximum positive interaction with the community produces the knowledge and support necessary for crime prevention programs. Traditional policing is heavily, although not exclusively, reactive—responding to calls after the fact. It makes use of programs that are often abrasive to the neighborhood, such as aggressively conducted field interrogations or stop-and-frisk encounters.

The response to team policing Efforts to implement team policing occasionally meet with resistance from within departments. Team policing represents change, which is often threatening to senior officers. Patrol officers who see themselves as enforcers view certain elements of team policing as an attempt to make social workers out of them—a serious attack upon their perceived role. Other officers resist the idea out of a concern that informal contact with the community offers too much potential for corruption. Finally, it is argued that team policing may significantly alter the organizational structure and existing career paths; officers with a strong military orientation or heavy career investment may subvert team policing because they believe it threatens their vested interest.

The Kansas City Patrol Experiment

From 1 October 1972 to 30 September 1973, the Kansas City Police Department, with the support of the Police Foundation, conducted a study to determine if routine patrol with conspicuously marked vehicles had any measurable impact upon crime or the public's sense of security. As noted in a report on the study, "police patrol strategies have always been based on two unproven but widely accepted hypotheses: first, that visible police presence prevents crime by deterring potential offenders; second, that the public's fear of crime is diminished by such police presence" (Kelling et al. 1974, p. 42).

The study was conducted within fifteen beats in a thirty-two-square-mile area with a 1970 resident population of 148,395 **(figure 5.2)**. (*Beats* are limited geographical areas that are ordinarily patrolled by marked vehi-

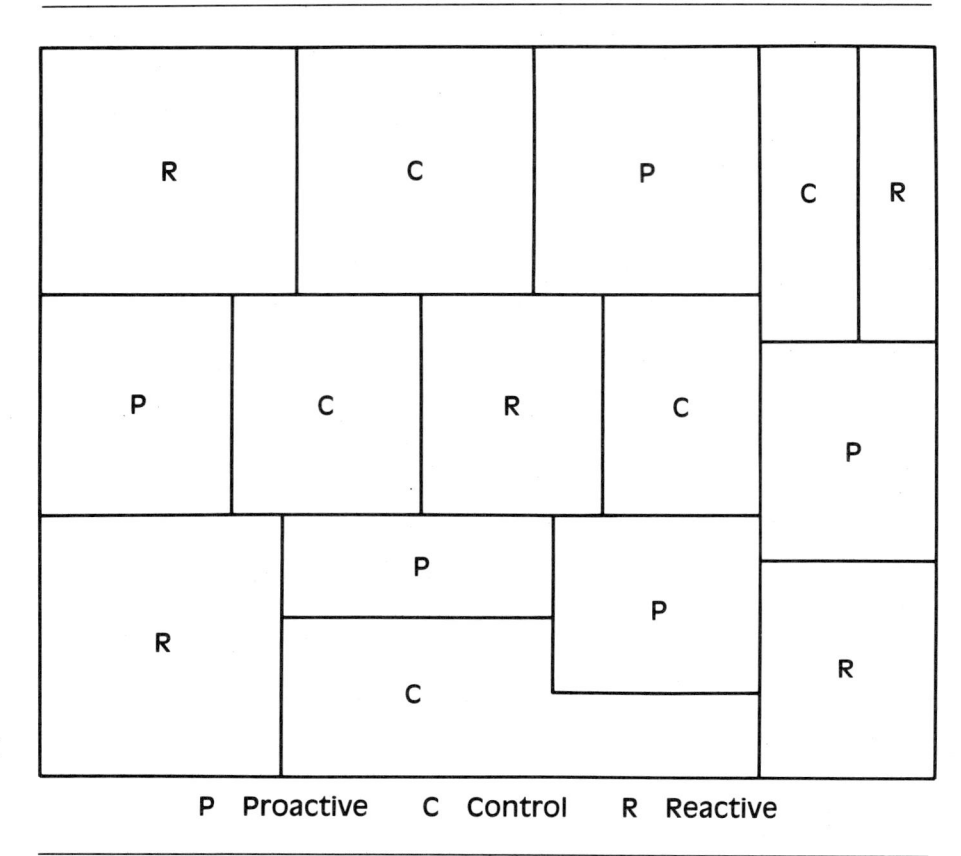

FIGURE 5.2
Schematic representation of the fifteen-beat experimental area of the Kansas City Patrol Experiment. From George L. Kelling et al., The Kansas City Patrol Experiment (Washington, D.C.: Police Foundation, 1974), p. 9.

P Proactive   C Control   R Reactive

cles operated by one or two uniformed officers.) The beats were designated as reactive, proactive, or control areas. *Reactive beats* did not have preventive patrols; officers entered these areas only upon a citizen's request for service. When not responding to calls, officers in reactive units patrolled adjacent proactive beats or the boundaries of their own beats. In *proactive beats*, routine preventive patrol was intensified to two to three times its usual level. A normal amount of patrolling was conducted in *control beats*. The following trends were noted in the evaluation of the experiment:

1. The amount of reported crime in reactive, control, and proactive beats showed only one significant statistical variation: the number of incidents in the category "other sex crimes," which excludes rape and includes such offenses as exhibitionism and molestation, was higher in reactive areas than in control areas. However, project evaluators felt that this statistical significance was probably random.

2. No statistically significant differences were found among the three types of areas with regard to fluctuations in crimes that were not officially reported to the police.

3   There was no statistically significant difference in arrests among the three types of beats.

4   Citizen fear of crime was not significantly altered by changes in the level of routine preventive patrol.

5   Variations in the level of patrolling did not significantly alter the security measures taken by citizens or businesses.

6   Little correlation was found between the level of patrol and the attitudes of citizens and businesspersons toward the policing.

7   The time taken by police to answer calls was not significantly altered by variations in the level of routine preventive patrol.

8   Level of patrol had no significant effect upon the incidence of traffic accidents.

The interpretations and findings of the Kansas City Patrol Experiment are highly controversial. Upon learning of the study, some local leaders felt that further increases in police manpower were not warranted and that decreases might even be justified. However, such persons failed to consider that just because the prevailing method of preventing crime—routine preventive patrol—was not effective, it did not follow that no strategy of prevention would work. The findings do suggest that administrators might be able to move into team policing—diverting significant manhours from routine patrol to community interface—without increasing the crime rate. This bridge between the Kansas City Patrol Experiment and team policing is tenuous, however.

The traffic bureau

Traffic is the most pervasive problem confronting police agencies. Every person who drives and every vehicle on the street is part of the problem. Because the responsibility for congestion control, traffic-law enforcement, and accident prevention can not be fixed on any single unit, traffic duty must be shared to some degree by every uniformed member of a police force. The degree to which an officer may be held accountable for traffic duties is dictated by the extent of the traffic problem.

In cities where traffic constitutes a significant problem, specific duties may be assigned to a traffic bureau to concentrate efforts. The existence of traffic specialists does not relieve the patrol officers of all responsibility for traffic, but it does free them to adjust their traffic responsibilities in relation to their other duties.

Activities of the traffic bureau

As in most areas of police activity, police departments vary as to how they structure their traffic organizations. However, most traffic bureaus are responsible for traffic control, accident investigation, and traffic-law enforcement. Some bureaus also have a safety division concerned primarily with traffic safety education. The traffic bureau shares its responsibilities with the patrol bureau, relieving the patrol officer of traffic duties that are time consuming or immobilizing, and it provides the initiative and guidance for the traffic program of the department. Traffic programs are designed by traffic specialists to concentrate on the specific needs of an area (Caldwell 1972, p. 48).

Traffic control Officers working in traffic control usually concentrate on relieving congestion by controlling intersections, parking, and emergency traffic. Intersection control requires measures to ensure a safe and continuous flow of vehicular and pedestrian traffic. Traffic signals alone can not regulate traffic flow; officers must insure that traffic signals are obeyed and that intersections are kept clear. Intersection control is usually needed only during peak traffic. Traffic-control officers also serve as a vital source of information to citizens, thus providing a rare and needed source of contact between the police and the public.

Some traffic-control officers use three-wheel motorcycles or scooters to increase mobility in congested traffic. Officers on motorcycles can patrol heavily travelled arteries, enforcing tow-away zones and removing obstacles such as stalled vehicles and illegally parked cars. Their mobility allows them to relieve congestion occasioned by changing traffic patterns throughout the day. They may also have to direct traffic at the scene of an accident or a fire, thus allowing regular patrol officers to return to their duties and the accident investigator to concentrate on the details of the investigation (Caldwell 1972, pp. 48–49).

Accident investigation Investigating traffic accidents is a vital function of the traffic bureau. Accident investigation requires skills and time commitments that preclude categorical assignment to the regular patrol officer. The extent of patrol involvement in accident investigation is determined by the demands for other patrol services.

Accident investigation is usually the responsibility of an investigator skilled in reconstructing accident scenes. Acting as evidence technicians, investigators must be able to determine why an accident occurred, how it occurred, and the extent of culpability of the parties involved. They arrive at answers by examining damages, interviewing witnesses and participants, and reviewing physical evidence. They must also render first aid and obtain medical assistance for the injured and prevent accidents from becoming worse by removing involved vehicles from moving traffic. When the investigation is complete, they must prepare a report to provide data for accident prevention efforts.

Accident investigation reports are often a vital part of civil litigation relating to accidents. The goal of such litigation is to fix civil liability for accidents and to allow injured parties to recover part of their financial losses. The accident investigator is often called as a witness in such cases (Caldwell 1972, pp. 49–50). Report data is also used by traffic engineers to correct roadway defects and by traffic researchers to determine the types of traffic violations associated with deaths and injuries.

Traffic-law enforcement Probably no other function performed by the police causes more ill will between police and the public than traffic-law enforcement. Even if community leaders, public officials, and the media lend strong support to enforcement, support is rarely found among the millions of people who receive traffic tickets each year. No particular insight is needed to understand this phenomenon; tickets can result in fines, mandatory attendance at driver education programs, and penalty points that can eventually lead to license suspension and increases in insurance premiums. Even when fairly imposed, such penalties rarely engender good will toward the police. (We do not mean to suggest, however, that traffic-law enforcement be eliminated or curtailed. But we do believe that sometimes the police may engage in practices which create more ill will than is necessary.)

Selective traffic enforcement Contrary to popular belief, the major purpose of traffic-law enforcement is *not* to fill the coffers of city, county, or state governments: it is to prevent accidents. However, this fact is rarely known by the public and is sometimes not fully appreciated by the police. The following case illustrates this point.

CASE 5.2

After having its traffic engineering department conduct a comprehensive traffic-flow study on one of its major streets, a Florida city decided to increase the speed limit on that street from thirty miles per hour to forty-five miles per hour. New speed signs were installed, but someone failed to increase the timing of one of the caution lights on a traffic signal at a major intersection. One keen-eyed motorcycle officer who noted this failure realized that motorists travelling forty-five miles per hour would have great difficulty stopping for a traffic signal that had its caution light timed to accommodate vehicles travelling at thirty miles per hour.

Based on this discovery, the officer proceeded to engage in a practice referred to professionally as "off-street observation" and informally as "bird-dogging" (the informal term is undoubtedly subject to regional variations). He wrote an average of three tickets per day for red-light violations all within a period of one hour—and thus was well on his way to meeting his quota of five citations per shift (quotas are discussed later in this chapter). His supervisor never questioned him about the inordinate number of citations given at this one intersection every day for three weeks.

As one might expect, the number of traffic accidents at this intersection also started to increase. One of the engineers employed by the city's traffic engineering department to analyze accident trends noted the dramatic increase in accidents at this intersection and, upon checking further, realized to his surprise and shock that the timing mechanism on the traffic signal had not been adjusted. The timing was quickly changed, and, as expected, traffic accidents decreased dramatically. The motorcycle officer who had been so judiciously observing this intersection lamented bitterly that his "fishing hole" had dried up. This officer and his supervisor either never learned or had forgotten that the purpose of traffic-law enforcement is accident prevention.

What should have been done or could have been done differently in the case just described? First, the supervisor had a responsibility to check data on accident patterns occurring in his area. These data were available from the traffic engineering department. Personnel should have then been deployed to high-accident areas to enforce violations that appeared to be contributing to accidents (a strategy known as *selective traffic enforcement*). In this case, the timing problem should have been promptly reported to the traffic engineering department. Traffic tickets given in high-hazard areas are certainly no more welcome than those given at safer intersections, but this type of enforcement does do more toward reducing accidents and protecting life and property than does the random issuance of tickets merely to meet a quota.

The quota system: Myth or Reality Citizens frequently ask the question, Do police departments have a traffic ticket quota? The answer in some cases is an emphatic yes; but in the final analysis, the decision to use a *quota system* depends upon the philosophy of the chief of police, command officers, and lower-level supervisors. Further, the decision can be effected by officer assignments. For example, if a police department has a traffic bureau, officers assigned to the bureau will devote most of their time to traffic responsibilities, including traffic-law enforcement. However, in patrol bureaus that have numerous other responsibilities besides traffic responsibilities, the emphasis on traffic-law enforcement may vary considerably. Police departments do not, as a rule, document how many traffic tickets they expect their officers to write; but the expected number is rarely zero. Most officers are fully aware of what is expected of them by their departments or supervisors.

Motorcycle officer as viewed by a traffic violator. Courtesy Fairfax County (Virginia) Police Department.

PATROL OFFICER SAYS FIRING IS TICKET RELATED

Leesburg, Fla. (AP)—A Florida Highway Patrol trooper says he was fired after 15 years on the force because he didn't write enough speeding tickets.

P.M. Taylor, 47, said the emphasis of the Florida Highway Patrol troopers has shifted from safety to writing speeding tickets.

Sgt. N.H. Duttenhaver, his supervisor, denied that the patrol has a ticket quota and said Taylor had not "been in keeping with department expectations."

Taylor said troopers in the Leesburg station each wrote between 25 and 80 tickets last month. He wrote 19, he said.

Taylor was suspended once this year for substandard quality of work, which Taylor also attributes to a dearth of ticket writing.

Taylor has filed two grievances with the Employee Improvement Committee, the first in February when he was suspended and the second on March 5.

The Tampa Tribune-Times, 11 April 1982.

Who gets the money? In most cases, money derived from traffic fines does not go to the agencies that enforce the traffic laws; rather, it goes into a general fund at the city, county, or state level. On occasion, a small surcharge (of one or two dollars) imposed along with a regular fine is diverted to the police department for training purposes. However, contrary to popular belief, law enforcement agencies that issue traffic citations rarely derive much financial benefit from their activities. The fee system that was common in this country about twenty years ago—in which officers got a percentage of fines—is virtually nonexistent today.

Traffic enforcement policies: Police departments and sheriff's departments

Any comparison of law enforcement agencies must be prefaced with the knowledge that because of variations in size, community expectations, geographical differences, and managerial philosophies only broad generalizations can be made. However, there are some basic differences between the enforcement policies of police and sheriff's departments.

For example, with few exceptions, police chiefs are appointed to their positions; sheriffs are elected. Thus, sheriffs are generally very sensitive about enforcement practices that might jeopardize their tenure in office. This is not to suggest that sheriffs encourage their deputies to ignore such violations as drunk driving, reckless driving, or drag racing; this is certainly not the case. But in many cases, high premiums may not be placed on the strong enforcement of less serious violations, and warnings may be issued in place of regular tickets for minor traffic infractions.

The detective bureau

Three common stereotypes influence the public's perception of investigative effectiveness in the detective bureau: the media stereotype, the historical stereotype, and the critical stereotype. Some combination of these three provides the basis for current investigative policies in most police departments (Greenwood and Petersilia 1975).[3]

The *media image* of working detectives—an image pervasive on television—is that of clever, imaginative, perseverant, streetwise cops who consort with glamorous women or handsome men and duel with crafty criminals. They and their partners roam cities for days or weeks trying to break a single case that is ultimately solved by means of the investigator's deductive powers. This is the image that many investigators prefer—although perhaps with some concessions. Most investigators concede that criminals are rarely as crafty or diabolical as depicted in the media, but they may not quarrel with the media portrayal of their own capabilities. Some current investigative practices are used mainly to preserve a media-like image or to give victims the services they expect because of that image. For example, activities such as dusting for fingerprints, showing mug shots, or questioning witnesses are sometimes done without any hope of developing leads; rather, they are done simply for public relations.

The *historical stereotype* is the image held by older police administrators of the special status of detectives in earlier times (Smith 1960). Not so many years ago, various illicit activities such as vice, gambling, prostitution, and speakeasies were openly tolerated by city governments. These illegal, but accepted, enterprises created problems for the city police. How could they control such institutions without driving them completely out of business?

Police dealings with illegal institutions were frequently handled by detectives. The detectives ensured that the businesses were run in an orderly fashion and that "undesirables" were driven out. By this delicate balance the detectives often won the favor of the business leaders and politicians involved in the illegal activities. Such political connections elevated the detective to a position of respect and influence.

The police in general also benefitted by allowing these illegal enterprises to continue. When serious crimes did occur or when public pressure was brought to bear on the police to deal with a particular problem, the illegal activities provided a valuable source of information for detectives. Not surprisingly, thieves and con men were often the customers of the vice and gambling operations, or at least had close contact with the people engaged in these businesses. If the police wanted information on a particular criminal activity, they could solicit information as a favor or extort it by threatening the safety of the illegal operations. Thus, the "effectiveness" of detective operations frequently depended on close contacts with a select group of potential informers.

Another role played by detectives of the past was that of dispensers of street-corner justice. Good cops were expected to maintain order without resorting to the courts. They did this by persuasion, by making threats, and, if necessary, by using physical force. Only when it was clear that their presence alone would not deter crime did the police bring a suspect in for criminal proceedings. Detectives played this role because they were less visible than uniformed patrol officers. Because of their experience, they were expected to be more diplomatic in handling these incidents (part of the detective's basic working knowledge was an understanding of which individuals could be treated roughly without getting the department into trouble). Detectives who could handle delicate situations without causing a commotion were highly valued by police and city administrators.

Another method once available to detectives was third-degree or extended interrogation. However, this type of activity has been limited by the Supreme Court decision on interrogations in *Miranda v. Arizona* (86 S.Ct. 1602[1966])—which increased the enforcement of civil liberties—and by the rise of community review boards. It is no longer acceptable for detectives to arrest suspects and keep them in custody simply for investigative purposes. Neither is it permissible to use physical or psychological force to extort a confession or to get information about other suspects in a case.

The *critical stereotype* of investigative effectiveness is expressed in several studies that analyze how detectives go about their work. One of the earliest critics of investigative practices and detectives was Raymond Fosdick (1921). After visiting police departments in all of the major cities of the United States, he criticized detectives for lack of civil service standards in selection; lack of training; poor coordination with patrol operation; lack of effective supervision; and lack of ordinary "business systems" for handling administrative work. More recently, analysts have made these arguments:

1 Police agencies do not routinely collect and summarize data that can be used to determine the effectiveness of investigative activities. Clearance and arrest statistics, in particular, are unsuitable because they fail to distinguish outputs of investigative efforts from those of other units in the department. Used alone, clearance data are also extremely unreliable indicators of police performance because of their subjective nature.

2 The solution rate of crimes appears to be insensitive to the number of cases assigned to each detective. This implies that detectives can accurately predict which cases can be solved and work on only those, or that some cases solve themselves.

3 A high proportion of cases are closed when a patrol officer makes an arrest at the scene of the crime.

4 Investigators make little use of physical evidence such as fingerprints or tool marks.

Uncomplimentary views of detectives have also been espoused by progressive police chiefs who have seen reforms and new initiatives in every other area of policing except the detective bureau. In such departments, an appointment to the detective bureau is no longer viewed as the best path to promotion. In other departments (the Los Angeles Police Department, for example), independent detective bureaus no longer exists, and investigators are assigned directly to local operations commanders. Many progressive police chiefs are candidly critical of the old, freewheeling style of detective work. They see detectives as trying to preserve the freedom and prerequisites of their jobs without making any effort to adapt to the shifting community and legal climate in which they work.

Activities of the detective bureau

A realistic view of investigative activities can be conveyed by describing how a typical case is handled, variations that frequently occur in the typical pattern, departmental policies that govern how cases are handled, and the supporting activities police perform to increase the likelihood of identification and apprehension.

Incident report and preliminary investigation Most cases involving the discovery of major felonies are initiated by a citizen who calls the police to report the crime or a police patrol unit that responds to evidence that a crime is in progress. In either case, the first police representative on the scene is usually a uniformed patrol officer. The patrol officer's duties are to provide aid to the victim, to secure the crime scene for later investigation, and to document the facts of the crime. In a few departments, investigators may be dispatched simultaneously with the patrol unit to begin an investigation of the crime, but in most departments, investigation by detectives does not take place until after a patrol unit files a report. The patrol officer's initial report usually contains the basic facts of the crime—the identity of the victim, a description of the suspect, the identity and location of any potential witnesses, a description of the crime scene, and any pertinent statements by witnesses or the victim. This report is passed on to the detective unit, which then continues the investigation.

Patrol units are generally under considerable pressure to cut short their investigations and get back on patrol. Thus, detectives, rather than patrol officers, are usually responsible for developing potential leads and continuing an investigation. In a few departments, however, patrol officers are encouraged to use their own initiative to continue an investigation perhaps by conducting house-to-house checks or using other means to track down suspects).

Evidence collection and processing Studies show that many crime scenes contain physical evidence linking a suspect with the crime. To collect this evidence (primarily fingerprints) many departments use trained *evidence technicians* whose sole task is to process crime scenes. Technicians may be dispatched at the time of the crime report, or they may be sent out following the initial report if the responding patrol officer feels that usable evidence might be found. Their job is to examine the crime scene, lift any latent fingerprints, and submit a report of their results to the responsible unit.

In most departments, latent fingerprints are not used unless an investigator asks the print examiner to compare them with the inked prints of a specific suspect. Occasionally, a print examiner may conduct a "cold" search, comparing lifted prints with files of known or suspected offenders.

Screening and case assignment Every morning (about seven o'clock), incident reports are assembled from the previous day and distributed to the appropriate investigative unit. The assignment of an investigator to a case is determined by the organizational pattern of the department; for example, assignments might be made by crime specialty (e.g., robbery, burglary, sex offenses) or by geographic area. Specialization might be so detailed that assignment personnel can direct an incident report to the specific investigator who will handle that case. Otherwise, the report goes to a unit supervisor who assigns the case to a detective in his or her unit, based on previous assignments or individual work loads. Each detective usually receives one or two new cases a day. Work loads are lower for detectives who handle crimes against the person, higher for those who handle minor property crimes.

In some departments, formal "solvability factors" and the judgment of the unit supervisor are used to determine if a specific case should be followed up by an investigator or suspended until new facts develop. Generally, however, every case is assigned to a responsible investigator, with some minimal attempt at follow-up expected. This minimal effort is usually an attempt to contact the victim to obtain facts in addition to those recorded in the incident report. Although most investigators have twenty or thirty open cases on their desks at any one time, only two or three cases are really considered active. Work-load data shows that most cases are closed within the first day of activity, and very few remain active after two or three days.

Follow-up (latent) investigation New cases assigned to an investigator generally fall into one of three categories. Cases that receive first priority are those in which the investigative steps are obvious, based on the facts in the incident report. These are the cases in which the victim names a suspect, gives a license number, identifies where the suspect can be found, or indicates additional witnesses who were not interviewed by the responding patrol officer.

Second in priority are those cases that require attention not because of obvious leads, but because of the seriousness of the offense or its notoriety in the press or in the community. Investigators want to avoid charges by the community that they are not doing their job, and they may simply be outraged by an offense and want to help the victim. Cases of the lowest priority are routine cases that offer no additional leads. In all departments, these cases are given only perfunctory treatment.

The first task of investigators when they come to work is to plan their activities for the day. Part of the morning is usually devoted to reviewing new cases, finishing paperwork, processing prisoners who were taken into custody the night before, and making required court appearances. Late morning and afternoon are usually free for conducting interviews or street patrol. The use of this "free" time is usually determined by a detective's own judgment; this judgement is based on a sense of priority about each case, the difficulty or attractiveness of conducting various interviews, transportation difficulties, and the activities of fellow investigators.

Investigators rarely take detailed written notes during interviews. Rather, they record only telephone numbers, addresses, nicknames, and other basic information for the official case folder. Transcripts of witness statements are made only in the most serious cases.

Clearance and arrest A major demand on an investigator's time occurs when a suspect is taken into custody—usually as a consequence of patrol activity. When an arrest occurs, an effort is often made to clear other crimes similar to the one for which the suspect was arrested. Such is the responsibility of the investigator. If the suspect is willing, the investigator may talk to him or her about similar offenses; if the suspect is not willing to talk, investigators may use their own judgment about whether the suspect might be involved in other cases. If a suspect has been identified by a victim (as often occurs in sex crimes or robberies), previous victims may be brought in to view the suspect in a lineup.

All results of a *follow-up (latent) investigation* are conveyed to the prosecutor in written reports. In many jurisdictions, prosecutors require investigators to consult them about the facts of a case at the time of filing. If an investigator helps solve a case, he or she may also have to testify in court.

File maintenance In addition to regular investigative activities, most departments expend resources to develop leads or identify suspects by alternative means. For example, all departments maintain a variety of information files that serve as sources of investigative leads. These files may include a file of crimes by type, location, or time period; a file of the addresses, descriptions, and modus operandi of known offenders; files of mug shots (usually organized by crime type and basic descriptors); files containing the fingerprints of all past arrestees; intelligence files with the names of individuals suspected of particular criminal activity; files of stolen or

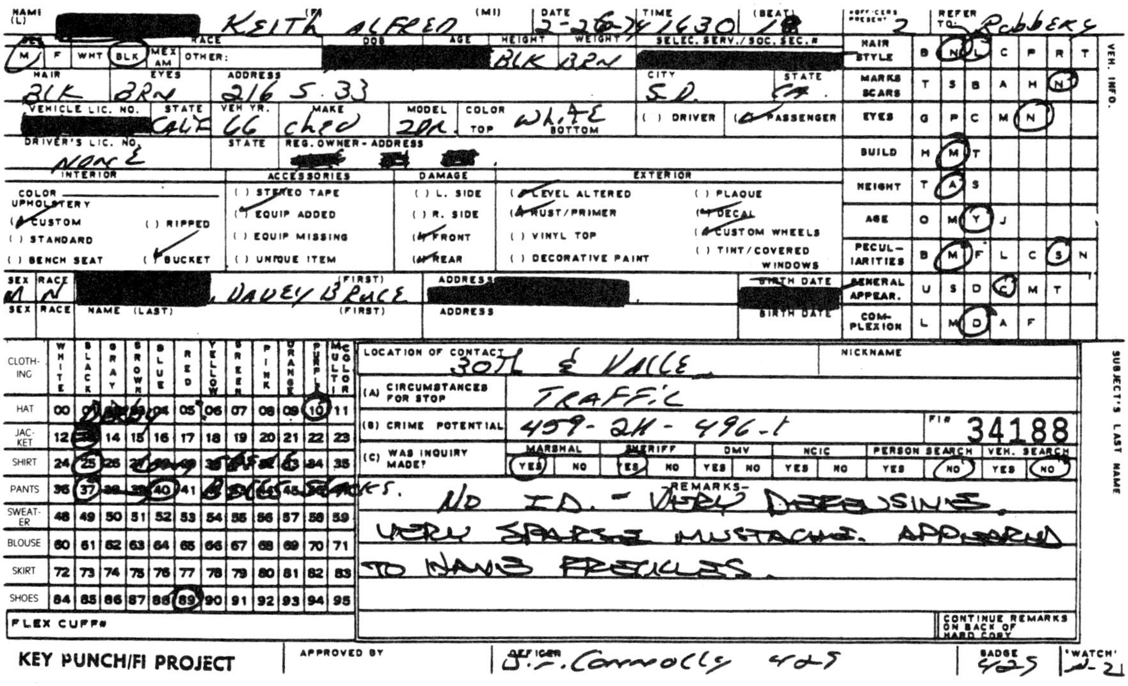

FIGURE 5.3 *Field interrogation report. Courtesy San Diego (California) Police Department.*

pawned property; and *field interrogation files* that indicate where and why certain individuals or vehicles were stopped, along with a description of the person and his or her vehicle **(figure 5.3)**. In addition, an increasing number of police agencies have highly developed crime analysis units that provide valuable information to investigators to help them narrow and focus their efforts. (Factors used in crime analysis are summarized in **table 5.2** and **table 5.3**.)

TABLE 5.2 Universal factors for crime analysis

Crime type	Burglary (class: business-commercial, residential, other) Robbery (class: armed vs. not armed) Auto theft (automobile, commercial vehicle, motorcycle, etc.) General larceny (thefts from autos, auto accessories, scrap metal, dock, etc.) Fraud (forgery, credit cards, confidence games, etc.) Rape and sex crimes (forcible rape, child molesting, indecent exposure) Aggravated assault and murder
Geography	Location offense occurred Street address or intersection Block Subreporting area or census tract Reporting area, patrol area, or beat Zone, precinct, or district
Chronology	Specific time offense occurred Time span in which offense occurred (day or night) Day of week Week of year Month of year
Victim target	Person (sex, age, race, etc.) Structure (single dwelling house, apartment, high rise, etc.) Premise (commercial, industrial, public, etc.) Purpose (sales, service, manufacturing, etc. Victim's knowledge of suspect
Suspect	Name Age Race Height Weight Clothing and unusual characteristics
Suspect vehicle description	License number Make Model and year Color Damage
Property loss description	Serial number of property loss Make of property loss (brand name, etc.) Model of property loss Type of property loss Use of the property

Adapted from George A. Buck et al., *Police Crime Analysis Unit Handbook* (Washington, D.C.: U.S. Government Printing Office, 1973), p. 33.

TABLE 5.3 Crime-specific factors for crime analysis

Residential burglary	Type of premise attacked (house, exterior or interior apartment, etc.) Occupied vs. unoccupied Point of entry (window, door, etc.) Method of entry (pry door or window, wrench door, break window, etc.) Presence of physical evidence (latent prints, etc.)
Commercial burglary	Type of business attacked (television store, clothing store, savings and loan, etc.) Alarm information (no alarm, alarm defeated, method, etc.) Point of entry (window, door, roof, wall, floor, vent, etc.) Method of entry (window smash, lock in-break out, peel wall, etc.) Safe attack method (rip, punch, peel, burn, drill, grind, etc.)
Robbery	Type of victim business (diner, bar taxi, savings and loan, gas station, etc.) Victim person descriptors (sex, race, age, occupation, etc.) Weapon used (handgun, shotgun, knife, club, etc.) Suspect mask and type (facial area covered) Suspect statement during commission; particular M.O.
Theft from person	Exact location of victim (sidewalk, park, hallway, bar, etc.) Victim person descriptors (sex, race, age, etc.) Victim condition after attack Suspect particular M.O. (approach, flight, statements, etc.) Object of theft (cash, checks, credit cards, jewelry, etc.)
Auto theft	Area stolen vs. area recovered Exact last location (on-street, parking lot, carport, sales lot, etc.) Make, year, and model of vehicle Degree of strippage and parts Presence or absence of physical evidence
Larceny	Type of victim property (business, personal, use, purpose, etc.) Location of property (left unattended, in vehicle, etc.) Specific property taken and market potential Suspect particular M.O. Presence or absence of physical evidence
Forgery	Check and credit card specifics (how obtained, type, etc.) Type of business or person victimized Document descriptors (commercial, personal, etc.) Type of identification used Confidence game specifics (ploy used, etc.)
Rape, sex offenses	Victim person descriptors (age, race, sex, occupation, etc.) Location of encounter vs. location of departure Suspect statement during commission Suspect actions or M.O. Weapon or degree of force used
Aggravated assault and murder	Relationship between victim and suspect Victim personal descriptors Motive Weapon used Physical evidence

Adapted from George A. Buck et al., *Police Crime Analysis Unit Handbook* (Washington, DC.: U.S. Government Printing Office, 1973), p. 35.

In some departments, special details or strike forces are operated to provide investigative leads that never come through in normal incident reports. The most common example of such activity is a pawnshop detail that routinely inspects items taken in by pawnshops and compares them with lists of stolen property. Another type of strike force—typically called a "sting" operation—uses investigators to buy stolen property in an attempt to identify fences and burglars. In other cases, investigators are assigned temporarily as decoys in high-crime areas.

Selection, training, and supervision Before becoming an investigator, an officer usually has to spend three to five years on patrol. Selection for investigative units is not based strictly on civil service criteria; rather, more aggressive patrol officers are often selected—presumably because an officer who makes a large number of arrests has the initiative and insight to make a good investigator.

Investigators usually get all their new training on the job. When new recruits join a detective bureau, they are given some investigative training to help them in their work, but there are rarely any special training classes. And only a few departments offer continuing education for detectives on investigative assignments.

Most investigators operate out of detective bureaus separate from the patrol bureau, except in jurisdictions where investigators are integrated into a patrol-team concept (team policing). At any rate, detective bureaus as an institution have only administrative significance: each investigator or investigator pair operates independently. Supervisors are concerned primarily with vacation schedules, the timeliness of reports, and the tidiness of paperwork, and they do not usually enter into substantive decisions about cases. In departments in which investigators are encouraged to

Property valued at $3.5 million recovered from an undercover "sting" operation coordinated between FBI and Florida state law enforcement officials. Courtesy John L. Beale, retired FBI agent.

New York detective dressed as a woman, working as a decoy in an area with a high incidence of assaults and thefts against women. Copyright New York News Inc. Reprinted by permission.

spend a good deal of their time on the street, supervisors may be only vaguely aware of what their people are doing on a day-to-day basis.

The Rand Criminal Investigation Study

In 1973, the Rand Corporation was awarded a grant by the National Institute of Law Enforcement and Criminal Justice to undertake a nationwide study of criminal investigations in major metropolitan police agencies. The purposes of the study were to describe how police investigations were organized and managed and to assess the contribution of various activities to overall police effectiveness. Prior to the Rand study, police investigators had not been subject to the type of scrutiny that was being focused on other types of police activity. Most police administrators knew little about the effectiveness of the day-to-day activities of their investigative units, and even less about the practices of other departments (Greenwood 1979).[4]

The study design The Rand study concentrated on the investigation of index offenses—serious crimes against unwilling victims—as opposed to vice, narcotics, gambling, or traffic offenses. Information on current practices was obtained by a national survey of all municipal and county police agencies employing more than 150 officers or serving jurisdictions with a 1970 population in excess of 100,000. Interviews and observations were conducted in more than twenty-five departments selected to represent different investigative styles. Data on the outcome of investigations were obtained from FBI Uniform Crime Report tapes; from samples of completed cases, which were coded for the study; and from internal evaluations or statistics compiled by individual departments. Data on the allocation of investigative efforts were obtained from a computerized work-load file maintained by the Kansas City Police Department.

Data from the national survey and the Uniform Crime Reports were combined for the purpose of analyzing relationships between departmental characteristics and apprehension effectiveness. Case samples were analyzed to determine how specific cases were solved.

Policy recommendations The first recommendation of the Rand study was that post-arrest investigation activities be coordinated more directly with prosecutors—either by assigning investigators to prosecutors' offices or by allowing prosecutors to exert more guidance over the policies and practices of investigators. The purpose of the recommendation was to increase the percentage of cases that could be prosecuted.

Secondly, it was suggested that patrol officers be given a larger role in conducting preliminary investigations, both to provide an adequate basis for case screening and to eliminate redundant efforts by an investigator. Most cases can be closed on the basis of the preliminary investigation, and patrol officers can be trained to conduct such investigations adequately. Expanding the role of the patrol officer is consistent with other trends toward geographic decentralization and job enrichment. A third recommendation was that additional resources be devoted to processing latent prints and that improved systems be developed for organizing and searching print files.

Finally, the study recommended that, with regard to follow-up investigations for cases that a department elected to pursue, a distinction should be drawn between those cases that require only routine clerical processing and those that require special investigative or legal skills. The former could be handled by lower-level clerical personnel, the latter by a separate bureau.

Impact of the study The Rand study was widely covered in the popular media and was the subject of heated controversy within the police profession. Many police officials, especially those who had not come up through the detective ranks, were sympathetic to the study in that it supported their own impressions of how investigators functioned. Others criticized it for "telling us what we already knew." Many police chiefs were hostile because the study was being used by city officials as an excuse to cut police budgets, and others refused to accept the findings because of the limited number of departments that were studied.[5]

Although there have not been any major attempts to replicate or extend the findings of the Rand study, several reports have been published with consistent findings. Bloch and Weidman's analysis of the investigative practices of the Rochester, New York, police department (1975) and Greenberg's efforts to develop a felony investigation decision model (Greenberg et al. 1977) both resulted in findings supportive of the idea that preliminary investigations conducted by patrol officers produce the majority of arrests and can provide adequate information for screening cases. A report by the Vera Institute (1977) on felony arrests in New York City indicates that a substantial portion of felony arrests for street crimes involve offenders who are known to their victims.[6] A report by Forst (1978) on the disposition of felony arrests in Washington, D.C., demonstrates the importance of physical evidence and multiple witnesses in securing convictions for felony street crimes.

The crime laboratory

To understand the role of crime laboratories, we must first understand the relationship of crime laboratories to the scientific community and to the functions of the criminal justice system (Swanson, Chamelin, and Territo 1981).[7] There are two distinct activities in laboratory work: the gathering of evidence at the scene of the crime (usually done by evidence technicians or investigators), and the scientific analysis of evidence (which usually occurs in the laboratory). The effectiveness of the latter activity depends on the efficiency of the first operation.

The terms *forensic science* and *criminalistics* are often used interchangeably to denote the same function. Forensic science is that part of science applied to answering legal questions. Criminalistics is a branch of forensics that deals with the study of physical evidence related to a crime (Safersteen 1981, p. 1–3); a crime may be reconstructed from evidence obtained in such studies. Criminalistics is interdisciplinary in nature, drawing upon mathematics, physics, chemistry, biology, and anthropology. The following case illustrates the services offered by physical anthropologists.

PERSONALITY RECONSTRUCTED FROM UNIDENTIFIED REMAINS

The badly decomposed remains of a human were found in an isolated wooded area adjacent to an industrial park. The crime scene investigation disclosed that the skeletal remains had been dragged a few feet from the location and it was suspected that this dislocation of the remains resulted from animal activities. An intensive search produced only a few strands of hair, a medium-sized sweater, and a few pieces of women's jewelry. The physical remains were taken to the medical examiner's office where the time of death was estimated to be three-to-six weeks prior to the discovery of the body. A subsequent review of missing-person reports for the pertinent time period produced no additional clues.

With the question of the victim's identity still unresolved, the remains were forwarded to the Curator of Physical Anthropology at the Smithsonian Institute in Washington, D.C. Based upon an examination of the skeletal remains, it was concluded that the skeleton was that of a Caucasian female approximately 17 to 22 years of age, who was of less than average stature. She had broader than average shoulders and hips, and was believed to be right-handed. Her head and face were long; the nose high bridged. Also noted was the subcartilage damage to the right hip joint, a condition which had probably caused occasional pain and suggested occupational stress. An irregularity of the left clavicle (collarbone) revealed a healed childhood fracture.

Local police officials then began a social and personality profile of the deceased based upon an analysis of the physical evidence obtained through the crime scene search and related photographs, medical examiner's

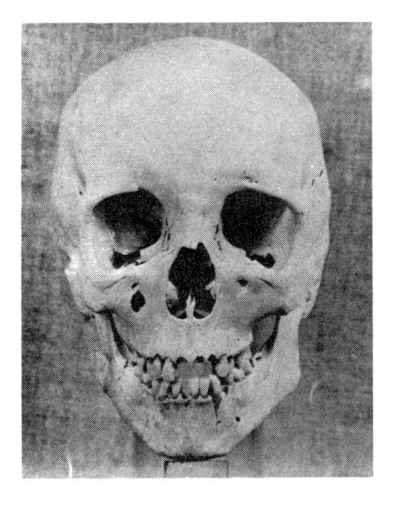

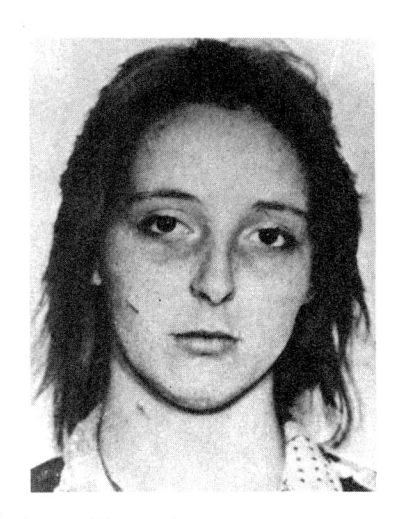

Left to right: *Skull of murdered woman; police artists's sketch of victim based on information provided by a physical anthropologist; police photograph of victim found in local police files.* Courtesy FBI Law Enforcement Bulletin.

reports, and reports from the FBI laboratory. In addition, aided by a physical anthropologist from the Smithsonian Institute, a police artist was able to sketch a photograph. The sketch was then published in a local newspaper and police officials immediately received calls from three different readers who all supplied the same name of a female whom they all knew. They advised that she resembled the sketch and they further advised that she had been missing for approximately four months.

A search of the local police files disclosed that the individual with this name had been previously photographed and fingerprinted. These prints were compared with the badly decomposed prints from one of the victim's fingers and a positive identification was made.

Further investigation by the police determined the victim was 20 years of age. Associates related that, when she was working as a nightclub dancer, she occasionally favored one leg. It was further determined that she had suffered a fracture of the left clavicle at age six.

D.G. Cherry and J.L. Angel, "Personality Reconstruction from Unidentified Remains," *FBI Law Enforcement Bulletin* 49 (1977):12–15.

The late Paul L. Kirk, a noted leader in the criminalistics movement in the United States, once remarked, "Criminalistics is an occupation that has all the responsibilities of medicine, the intricacy of the law, and the universality of science" (Kirk 1963, p. 238). One myth associated with the occupation is that its function is identification. In scientific terms, identification simply means the placing of an item in a class with other items. However, this definition is often totally insufficient for the criminalist, who must actually pinpoint the source and identity of evidence so that it can be distinguished from anything that is even remotely similar. The ability of the criminalist to do this depends largely on the resources and technology available. Because all of the needed technology does not exist at the present time, there are many things the criminalist can not do to assist the investigator. For this reason, it is essential that the investigator have an understanding of the capabilities and limitations of crime laboratories (Federal Bureau of Investigation 1981, p. 2).

Capabilities, limitations, and use of a crime laboratory The President's Commission on Law Enforcement and Administration of Justice notes that crime laboratories are the oldest and strongest link between science and technology and criminal justice (1967, p. 17). However, the growth of scientific criminal investigation in the American justice system has not been harmonious and has not been based upon a national consensus about the purpose and function of crime laboratories. Rather, most crime laboratories developed in response to a particular need in a community or region. The areas of scientific concentration in particular laboratories were, and still are, based on those needs, but have also been influenced by the interests and expertise of the people who operate them.

Not all crime laboratories have the same capabilities. Some can do much more than others, and some build up expertise in particular areas. The way in which some types of physical evidence is collected varies according to the test procedures a laboratory applies. Thus, it is important for police investigators to familiarize themselves with the capabilities of the crime laboratories in their jurisdictions, as well as with the requirements of the national forensic science laboratories. Regardless of variances in capability, all crime laboratories in the United States have a basic mission to reduce or eliminate uncertainty in the criminal investigation and to supply facts for supposition (Fox and Cunningham 1973, p. 1).

Today, there are over 300 laboratories in the United States that serve criminal justice agencies. Not all of these laboratories are publicly funded, and many have primary functions other than criminalistics. For example, private medical or hospital laboratories occasionally perform services for local police agencies.

Most crime laboratories do not have unlimited resources either in equipment, instrumentation, or human expertise to perform the vast array of scientific examinations normally identified with the FBI Crime Laboratory or the laboratories of major metropolitan law enforcement agencies. Specific laboratories may thus specialize and concentrate their analyses in one or two of the following areas: firearms identification, chemical analysis, drug analysis, photography, document examination, toxicology, microscopy, or biology.

The American Society of Crime Laboratory Directors was formed in 1974 in an effort to solve problems caused by the varying specializations and concerns of laboratories and to settle disagreements over their purpose, function, and services. The organization provides a means for laboratory directors to discuss mutual problems and work out solutions that provide the qualitative and quantitative level of service needed to support law enforcement efforts (Field et al. 1977).

Measures of effectiveness The effectiveness of a crime laboratory can be measured in terms of three criteria: quality, proximity, and timeliness (Field et al. 1977). It is widely understood, if not accepted, that it is unrealistic administratively and budgetarily for most police departments in the United States to staff and maintain a crime laboratory. However, police agencies that desire and would utilize such a facility should not be denied the opportunity to have laboratory services at their disposal. Past experience indicates that police investigators rarely seek laboratory assistance when a facility is not convenient. In some cases, technicians or investigators must travel unreasonable distances to obtain laboratory services. Evidence submission decreases sharply as the distance from the crime scene to the laboratory increases (National Advisory Commission on Criminal Justice Standards and Goals 1973, p. 302). The solution to this problem lies in adequate planning on the state level to provide needed services to agencies throughout the state.

Studies indicate that a unified statewide system can best serve the needs of the law enforcement community by providing a parent, or core, laboratory on the state level that can deliver commonly needed laboratory services. In addition, a series of regional or satellite laboratories (strategically located) should be equipped to respond to less sophisticated analytical needs and to serve as a screening agency when more sophisticated analyses are required. Texas, for example, has a central laboratory under the auspices of the Texas Department of Public Safety in Austin, with field laboratories in Dallas, Tyler, Houston, Corpus Christi, Midland, El Paso, Lubbock, and Waco. The Division of Consolidated Laboratory Services in Richmond, Virginia, serves as a parent laboratory with regional facilities located in Norfolk, Roanoke, and Fairfax. Other states using the regionalized concept are Alabama, California, Florida, Georgia, and Illinois. Regional laboratories should be located within fifty miles of any agencies they routinely serve (ibid., p. 302). Local laboratories that serve large cities can also serve as regional laboratories for nearby agencies.

Much of the current case load in crime laboratories consists of analyses of suspected or known samples of narcotics and dangerous drugs (Peterson 1974, p. 6). Even in areas where officers carry and are trained to use test kits available on the commercial market, laboratory analyses are conducted to provide conclusive evidence. Although many laboratory tests serve only to corroborate evidence, the analysis of suspected narcotics or dangerous drugs can be a key factor in successful prosecution—particularly in the early stages of judicial proceedings. Thus, the results of laboratory examinations must be made available to investigators as quickly as possible. The National Advisory Commission on Criminal Justice Standards and Goals (1973) recommends that laboratories operate round the clock when needed to handle existing case loads and that, whenever possible, analyses be completed within twenty-four hours after submission (ibid., p. 302). Of course, adequate budgeting and staffing of qualified personnel are required for such prompt action.

The FBI Crime Laboratory Of the approximately 400 employees of the FBI Crime Laboratory, the majority possess specialized technical expertise acquired through education and training. The facilities of the laboratory are available without charge to all state, county, and municipal law enforcement agencies in the United States.

Only two provisions must be met concerning the submission of evidence to the FBI Crime Laboratory. First, the evidence must be connected with an official investigation of a criminal matter and the laboratory report must be used only for official purposes related to that investigation or to a subsequent criminal prosecution. Laboratory investigations and reports can not be used in connection with civil proceedings. The second provision is that the FBI facility not be asked to make examinations if any evidence in the case has been or will be subjected to the same type of examination by another laboratory; this policy eliminates duplication of effort and ensures that evidence is received in its original condition, thus enabling laboratory personnel to interpret their findings properly and to present meaningful testimony and evidence in court. (The FBI will furnish—at no cost to local law enforcement agencies—the experts needed to testify in state or federal courts in connection with the results of their examinations.)

The FBI Crime Laboratory provides a comprehensive array of forensic services to law enforcement. Blood and other body fluids are identified and characterized in serology examinations; hairs, fibers, fabric, tape, rope, and wood are analyzed in microscopic examinations; poisons, paint, ink, tear gas, dyes, paper, blood, and urine are analyzed in chemical examinations; and soils and combinations of mineral substances (such as safe insulation, concrete, plaster, mortar, glass, ore, abrasives, gems, industrial dusts, and building materials) are analyzed in mineralogy examinations.

In addition, firearms examiners may be called upon to determine if firearms are operating properly or to determine gunpowder shot patterns. Bullets or cartridge cases may also be examined to assist in ascertaining the type of weapon used in a crime. The basic principles of firearms ex-

Examiners in the Serology Unit of the FBI Crime Laboratory prepare blood samples for analysis and record data. Courtesy of FBI.

An examiner in the FBI Microscopic Analysis Unit searches a pill box for hairs and fibers. Technician in background removes debris from a garment. Courtesy of FBI.

amination are also used to identify telltale marks left at crime scenes by punches, hammers, axes, pliers, screwdrivers, chisels, wrenches, and other objects. The explosives specialist can analyze fragments of explosives to determine the original composition and possible sources of raw materials.

The job of the FBI Metallurgy Unit is to restore obliterated or altered numbers on items such as firearms, sewing machines, watches, outboard motors, slot machines, automobiles, tools, and other metallic items. Tests can determine the possible causes of metal separation and can show if two or more pieces of metal are related in any way, or if production specifications for metals have been met.

Based on handwriting examinations by highly trained experts over many years, it is commonly agreed that no two individuals write exactly alike. Even though there can be some superficial resemblances in writing as a result of similar training, the complexity of writing is such that individual peculiarities and characteristics still appear. These characteristics can be detected by a documents expert.

The FBI Identification Division, an entity separate from the Laboratory Division, was established by an Act of Congress on 1 July 1924. The act combined the fingerprint records of the National Bureau of Criminal Identification and the Leavenworth Penitentiary—a total of 810,188 prints—into a file that serves as the national repository of criminal identification data. The file now contains over 173 million civil and criminal prints representing 64 million persons; and approximately 24,000 prints are received each day for processing. The Fugitive Program of the Identification Division goes through the file and places Wanted notices on the prints of people wanted by law enforcement agencies. Over 200,000 fugitive notices are now on file, with an average of 1,500 added each month.

The Identification Division also maintains two important reference files in its Latent Fingerprint Section. One file contains known prints of persons who have committed certain types of major crimes—such as bank robbery, bank burglary, bank larceny, kidnapping, extortion, interstate transportation of obscene materials, major theft, or check fraud. The second file, the National Unidentified Latent File, contains unidentified latent prints taken from the scene of major crimes investigated by the FBI.

Summary

In this chapter we departed somewhat from the traditional approach taken in most introductory books in addressing the topic of police operations. Rather than take a broad brush approach and briefly touch on many facets of police operations, we instead focused primarily on four areas: the patrol bureau, traffic bureau, detective bureau, and crime laboratory. We selected these areas because they are the ones which are frequently of greatest interest to the general public, the ones with which most citizens are likely to have contact, and the ones for which most of the stereotypes and misinformation exist.

The largest of the police operations bureaus and the one to which almost all new police officers are assigned is the patrol bureau. It forms the initial base upon which all future police experiences are built. When first assigned to the patrol bureau, the rookie officer typically works under the direct tutelage of a senior officer before being permitted to work alone. The patrol bureau, for better or for worse, regularly serves as a manpower pool for the other more specialized and prestigious assignments. The residual effect of this practice is a disproportionate number of patrol officers who are either relatively inexperienced or are not considered to be among the best and the brightest officers. This tendency is reinforced by the desire of many patrol officers to be transferred to other bureaus because of the difficulties associated with the environment of the patrol officer's work and the clientele they serve. We suggested the creation of a more varied gradation of classifications within the patrol officer ranks. This could reduce the need to either seek transfer or strive for a supervisory position as the sole route upward. Patrol officers might be content to remain in the patrol ranks if it offered them greater status and financial rewards.

The use of team policing in the patrol bureau was begun as a way to reduce the isolation of the police from the community and to induce the support of citizens in their efforts to reduce crime. The results of the Kansas City Patrol Experiment raised serious questions about the value of marked patrol units in reducing crime and their value in reducing the public's fear of crime. The controversy caused by these findings is still going on within the police profession today.

We hope our discussion of the traffic bureau provided the reader with greater understanding about the specific functions performed by this bureau and the relationship between enforcement, education, engineering, and traffic accidents. Traffic officers have an obligation to engage in the selective enforcement of traffic violations and not to arbitrarily write tickets just to meet some quota or to keep their sergeant happy.

The third section of this chapter discussed the detective bureau. What detectives do in their attempts to solve crimes is a crucially important part of policing. Of the three bureaus discussed, this one is surrounded by the most mystique and the most stereotypes. We have sought to convey a realistic impression of the methods that are employed in the selection, training, and supervision of detectives.

The most comprehensive study ever undertaken to analyze the day-to-day effectiveness and activities of detectives was done by the Rand Corporation in 1973. Basically, the study recommended closer post-arrest cooperation between the police and prosecutor's office, giving patrol officers greater responsibility in conducting preliminary investigations, improving the processing of latent fingerprints, improving the system to facilitate fingerprint searches, and, lastly, when a followup investigation is deemed justifiable, differentiating between those that need only clerical processing and those which need high level investigation or legal skills.

In the final portion of this chapter we discussed the crime laboratory and examined some of the major functions it can perform. There is a great deal of interest among criminal justice students and the public about the laboratory component of police work. Criminal investigations, like almost every other facet of our lives, have been beneficially affected by the technological explosion in the past 20 years.

issue paper

TERRORISM—THE CRIME OF THE FUTURE*

In the past decade, acts of terrorism have rocked the world, leaving behind a trail of death, bloodshed, and mayhem in more than a score of countries on six continents (bypassing only Antarctica). Western officials have responded with a variety of law enforcement techniques designed to eliminate revolutionary groups—and they have met with some success. Italy has shattered the Red Brigades, and West Germany has all but obliterated the Baader–Meinhoff gang. And Dutch marines, behind the advance of jet aircraft, recaptured a train and persuaded hijackers that terror would not free the Moluccan Islands from Indonesia.

The United States has not been immune to terrorist activities. The Students for a Democratic Society (SDS), active in the late 1960s, eventually gave way to the more disruptive Symbionese Liberation Army (SLA) in the early 1970s; the movement culminated in the 1980s with the capture of Weather Underground leaders in New York. Subsequent arrests cleared hundreds of crimes, ranging from murder and arson to bank robbery and burglary.

Although law enforcement has been somewhat successful in eliminating terrorist groups, police warn that new groups are springing up faster than they can track them. Indeed, terrorism may be the crime of the future. New groups are smaller, better organized, more aggressive, and much more dangerous—considering today's availability of armament and weapons. Philosophy and dedication have also changed. Yesterday's terrorists generally had a single cause arising from antiwar or civil rights sentiments in the late 1960s. For example, the Black Panthers and the Ku Klux Klan spawned from racial tensions and focused their activities on racial issues. In contrast, today's New World Liberation Front (NWLF) espouses a variety of leftist causes and directs attacks against a broad spectrum of society. Embracing the revolutionary sentiments of Karl Marx, Che Guevarra, and Carlos Marighella, the NWLF acts as an umbrella for other anticapitalist groups.

Revolution as an ideology is not new to the world—certainly not to the United States. Nor is the use of terrorist activity as a revolutionary tactic anything unusual. What is relatively new to the law enforcement community, however, is the use of guerrilla warfare by urban terrorists in the name of revolution. Terrorist activities dealt with by the police in the past generally were associated with the activities of organized criminals for whom terrorism was merely another "business tactic" in the same category as protection, muscle to take over business, or extortion ("Introduction to Terrorism," 1976, p. 1-1). In other words, prior to the late 1960s, police rarely had to contend with ideologically motivated terrorists. Rather, terrorism was what the bad guys did and was part of the overall criminal element (Jenkins 1980, p. 2); in incidents not associated with a criminally motivated element, terrorism was viewed as a manifestation of an isolated mental disorder or disease.

The same can not be said about the current terrorist problem. Individuals associated with recent international and urban terrorism are not typical of the people normally of concern to the law enforcement community—although some do fit the stereotype of traditional criminals. Terrorist groups today are fluid, task-oriented groups dedicated to political or philosophical causes (Federal Bureau of

---

*This Issue Paper contributed by Dr. Robert W. Taylor, Department of Criminal Justice, University of South Florida.

Ku Klux Klan march in Birmingham, Alabama. The Birmingham News *Staff Photo.*

Investigation Academy 1978, p. 24). Members are often bright, well-educated, strongly committed, and disciplined.

Another new facet of the terrorist problem is the dramatic increase in transnational activity within the United States. *Transnational activity* is an activity in the international arena initiated by an individual or group not controlled by a nation-state (Mickolus 1977, p. 210). Bombings in the 1980s by Croatian terrorists in New York and the shooting of diplomats by Armenian terrorists in Los Angeles are a new and unique kind of terrorism. Although transnational terrorists may act within the United States, they are often natives of citizens of different countries. For instance, the activities of two opposing groups, the Jewish Defense League and the Palestinian Black September Organization, have both been linked to terrorist activities within the United States. And although their goals and sentiments are foreign and involve geopolitical and military strategies, they nevertheless must be dealt with by American law enforcement officials.

Caribbean-oriented terrorist groups such as Omega 7—a pseudonym for the Cuban Nationalist Movement, an antiCastro group—and Fuerzas Armadas de Liberacion National (F.A.L.N.)—a Puerto Rican group seeking an independent Puerto Rico—are excellent examples of domestic groups that have caused problems for American law enforcement. These groups are well organized, well financed, and indirectly connected to foreign governments. The F.A.L.N. alone has been responsible for over seventy-five bombings in the United States since 1974. In 1980, they shocked the Wall Street financial district by bombing the New York and American stock exchanges, Merrill Lynch, and the Chase Manhattan Bank. Intelligence sources link members of the F.A.L.N. to Cuban-trained sources and sabotage agents. The group is similar to other violent Marxian revolutionary groups in that it castigates U.S. corporate structures (capitalism) as well as agencies of the U.S. government whose policies they feel exploit other nations—in this case Puerto Rico.

F.A.L.N. PUERTO RICAN TERRORISTS SUSPECTED IN NEW YEAR BOMBINGS

Robert D. McFadden New York Times

Federal and city investigators said yesterday that a Puerto Rican terrorist group was apparently responsible for a series of bombings on New Year's Eve that rocked four government buildings in lower Manhattan and Brooklyn and seriously injured three police officers.

The blasts, which struck Police Headquarters and two Federal office buildings in Manhattan and the Federal Courthouse in Brooklyn during a 90-minute period, severed a leg of one officer and injured the eyes of two bomb squad detectives.

The detectives, one of whom also lost all the fingers on his right hand and may have been deafened, were felled when one of the bombs blew up in their faces. They might have been killed had they not been wearing armored suits, the police said. A fifth bomb, made of four sticks of dynamite, was found in lower Manhattan and dismantled before it exploded.

Authorities said the explosions were believed set by the F.A.L.N.—Fuerzas Armadas de Liberación Nacional, or Armed Forces of National Liberation—which has claimed responsibility for some 100 bombings that have killed six people in an eight-year campaign of terror in the name of Puerto Rican independence.

Police Commissioner Robert J. McGuire said that at 10:20 p.m., after three of the bombs had exploded, a man called WCBS Radio and said: "This is the F.A.L.N. We are responsible for the bombings in New York City today. Free Puerto Rico. Free all political prisoners and prisoners of war."

The caller hung up after making the statement, which was recorded, the Commissioner said. Shortly afterward, at 10:27 p.m., a man called The Associated Press in New York City and claimed that the Palestine Liberation Organization was responsible for the bombings and that two more bombs would go off within an hour, Commissioner McGuire said.

Two more bombs were found at a Federal office building downtown. One exploded and the other was dismantled. However, the Federal Bureau of Investigation and Commissioner McGuire expressed skepticism about the claim on behalf of the P.L.O.

"We are definitely investigating an F.A.L.N. link," said Joseph Vallquette, a spokesman from the F.B.I.

"The type of device used is consistent with what the F.A.L.N. has previously used and taken credit for," Commissioner McGuire said at a news conference. "The type of message given is also consistent."

As word of the blasts spread, the Police Department received scores of calls warning that bombs had been planted in various locations in the city, including in the midst of the huge crowd of revelers gathered in Times Square for the New Year's Eve celebration.

Security at all public buildings was increased and searches were conducted for other bombs, but none was found, the Commissioner said. Police at the Midtown South Precinct said that officers scanned the Times Square crowd for suspicious packages but took no other precautions.

The Commissioner gave the following details of the bombings:

The first detonated at 9:27 p.m. on the north side of 26 Federal Plaza, which houses the offices of the F.B.I. and other Federal agencies. The device, made of several sticks of dynamite and a timer, knocked out windows on three floors but caused no injuries.

Four blocks away, at 9:55 p.m., a second bomb exploded on the north side of 1 Police Plaza, the city's Police Headquarters buildings, which is near City Hall and the Municipal Building. Officer Rocco Pascarella, 33 years old, who was on security detail, had heard the first blast, gone out to investigate and found the package. It exploded just as he approached, nearly severing his right leg just below the knee.

The 12-year police veteran, who is married, has one daughter and lives in Queens, was taken to Bellevue Hospital, where surgeons attempted without success to reattach the leg with microsurgery. He was listed in guarded condition late yesterday.

188 Chapter 5 | Issue paper

Examination of bomb components in the FBI Explosives Unit. Courtesy of FBI.

The third bombing occurred at 10 p.m. outside the United States District Courthouse at 225 Cadman Plaza East in Brooklyn's Borough Hall section. It shattered windows throughout the building but injured no one. "The explosion was heard all around the Brooklyn Heights neighborhood," said Officer Timothy Kane of the 84th Precinct.

At 10:45 p.m. one of two bombs exploded at 1 St. Andrews Plaza, which houses the Manhattan Federal courts and the offices of the United States Attorney for the Southern District of New York. The building is adjacent to the Metropolitan Correctional Center and just across Park Row from 1 Police Plaza.

The device blew up just as Detectives Salvatore R. Pastorella, 42, and Anthony S. Senft, 36, were trying to examine it after putting steel-mesh blankets over both bombs.

Detective Pastorella, a 15-year member of the force from Brooklyn, lost all the fingers of his right hand, sustained very serious injuries to both eyes and may have been deafened. Detective Senft, an officer for 10 years who lives in Suffolk County, suffered an injury to one eye and extensive facial and body injuries.

The two detectives were rushed to Bellevue Hospital, where they were listed later in stable but very serious condition. Commissioner McGuire said the two had been saved from death or more critical injuries by the protective suits they were wearing.

Other bomb-squad detectives at St. Andrews Plaza were ordered not to attempt immediately to remove the fifth bomb. When it had not detonated by 12:30 a.m., the detectives deactivated the device, placed it in a bomb-disposal truck and took it to the Police Department's firing range at Rodman's Neck in the Bronx.

Commissioner McGuire said that the timing and placement of the bombs suggested that the people who planted them had apparently not intended to harm ordinary citizens.

He said that 60 investigators assigned to the joint F.B.I.-Police Department Terrorist Task Force are working on the bombings.

While no suspects were named, the Commissioner said that investigators had some potentially important clues. He said several persons may have seen a man planting the last two bombs in a vicinity of St. Andrews Plaza at about 10:15 p.m.

The Commissioner said that the man was reported to be Hispanic, was carrying a package and had approached some Chinese neighborhood residents who were standing nearby and indicated to them that they should leave the area. Mr. McGuire said the police were looking for those people and he urged them, or anyone else who saw the man, to contact the police. He did not explain how the police had learned of the potential witnesses.

Investigators also had as evidence the dismantled fifth bomb. It consisted of four sticks of dynamite, each weighing about one-half pound, a blasting cap, a nine-volt battery and a pocket watch.

The other devices were believed to be similar, Mr. McGuire said. All were in "innocuous packages wrapped in newspaper," each smaller than a shoebox, the Commissioner said.

A coordinated assault on the offices of government, corporate and financial institutions has been the hallmark of the F.A.L.N., whose last bombing spree struck the New York and American Stock Exchanges, the Chase Manhattan Bank and the headquarters of Merrill Lynch & Company last March 1.

At that time, Kenneth Walton, deputy director of the New York office of the F.B.I., said that the explosions appeared to mark a resurgence of the group, which had been inactive for two years since the arrests in 1980 of 11 top members.

The New York Times 2 January 1983 p. 1A © 1983 by The New York Times Company. Reprinted by permission.

A final troublesome characteristic of modern terrorist groups is that they conduct sophisticated analyses of society and law enforcement in their areas of operation. For example, by formulating a "counterintelligence" network, groups such as the Red Army Faction in West Germany and the Tupamaros in Uruguay have evaluated the political, economic, military, and organizational conditions of their own movements and the societies in which they are enveloped. For such groups, this diagnosis provides a careful, rational analysis of the present and potential strength of their organization, as well as of the general conditions and political climate of the society involved (Wolf 1981, p. 236). With this information, a group can maximize their "terrorist effect," fostering emotional terror and social insecurity, destroying the solidarity, cooperation, and interdependence on which a society is based, and generally upsetting the framework of an active economy.

If such activity stimulates an extreme response by law enforcement, the ideological sentiments of the insurgent group are heightened. Such a strategy soon becomes a vicious cycle, wherein governments are threatened and free societies move toward repressive measures, forcing innocent citizens onto a vaguely defined battlefield (Rosenblum 1981, p. 3-1).

In summary, problems related to terrorism are very complex and quite different than criminal activities traditionally faced by the law enforcement community. The education, commitment, and sophistication of terrorists have added a new dimension to the problem, which is further compounded by the multiplicity of targets within our society and the availability of advanced weaponry.

Yet terrorism is a reality that police must face. The law enforcement community must develop intelligence and investigative units to better equip officers to apprehend and prosecute people engaged in terrorist activity. Further, law enforcement agencies must bolster their training efforts to better understand problems associated with terrorism—thus enabling themselves to develop effective countermeasures. Finally, the police must balance the effort to combat terrorism with an effort to maintain basic civil rights. The task will not be easy.

Discussion and review

1. What is the role of the field training officer?
2. What factors are involved in assigning a rookie officer to a particular geographical region of a city?
3. Why would a police administrator employ a policy that depletes the department's patrol bureau of its finest people?
4. Why do many patrol officers want to be transferred out of the patrol bureau?
5. What are the five basic elements of team policing?
6. Briefly describe the three major functions of traffic bureaus.
7. What variations sometimes exist between the traffic-law enforcement policies of police departments and sheriffs departments?
8. Describe the media image of the working detective.
9. How are detectives generally selected, trained, and supervised?
10. What policy recommendations were made based on the *Rand Criminal Investigation Study?*
11. Define the terms forensic science and *criminalistics*.
12. The effectiveness of a crime laboratory can be measured in terms of three criteria. What are they?
13. What two provisions have to be met by a police agency submitting evidence to the FBI Crime Laboratory?
14. How do terrorists of the 1980s differ from terrorists of the 1960s?

Glossary

Criminalistics A branch of forensic science that deals with the study of physical evidence related to crime.

Evidence technician A person trained to process and search crime scenes for fingerprints, tool marks, expended cartridge shells, and other physical evidence.

Field interrogation files Files that contain information on certain individuals or vehicles stopped by the police. Information includes where a vehicle or person is stopped, along with the description of the person or of the driver and his or her vehicle.

Field training officer A senior patrol officer selected to "break in" rookie officers. Also known as a "coach."

Follow-up (latent) investigation The portion of an investigation following the preliminary investigation.

Forensic science That part of science applied to answering legal questions.

Preliminary investigation The investigation generally performed by the first officer on the scene of a crime. Includes caring for any injured persons, apprehending the criminal if he or she is still in the immediate area, protecting the crime scene, and establishing communications with the dispatcher to broadcast descriptions of wanted persons.

Proactive beat An area patrolled regularly by the police. Patrols are dispatched *before* citizens call for help.

Professional officer track A career track that leads to upward mobility within the nonmanagerial ranks of the police department.

Professional police management track A career track that leads to upward mobility within the supervisory and managerial ranks of the police department.

Quota system A system requiring officers to write a specified number of traffic tickets in a given time period.

Reactive beat An area that is not patrolled until a request comes in for police service.

Team policing A system that combines all line functions (patrol, traffic, and investigation) into a single unit comprised of teams under common supervision.

Selective traffic enforcement The direction of enforcement efforts to areas experiencing the most traffic accidents. Such areas are monitored closely during peak accident periods.

References

Adams, T. F. *Police Patrol: Tactics and Techniques.* Englewood Cliffs, N.J.: Prentice-Hall, 1971.

Bloch, P., and Weidman, D. *Managing Criminal Investigations: Prescriptive Package.* Washington, D.C.: U.S. Government Printing Office, 1975.

Block, P. B., and Specht, D. *Neighborhood Team Policing.* Washington, D.C.: U.S. Government Printing Office, 1973.

Caldwell, H. *Basic Law Enforcement.* Pacific Palisades, Calif.: Goodyear, 1972.

Federal Bureau of Investigation Academy. The Terrorist Organizational Profile: A Psychological Evaluation." Mimeographed. Washington, D.C.: Federal Bureau of Investigation, 1978.

Federal Bureau of Investigation. Handbook of Forensic Science. Washington, D.C.: U.S. Government Printing Office, 1981.

Field, K. S.; Schroeder, O., Jr.; Curtid, I. J.; Fabricant, E. L.; and Lipskin, B. A. *Assessment of the Personnel of the Forensic Science Profession.* Assessment of the Forensic Sciences Profession, vol. 2. Washington, D.C.: U.S. Government Printing Office, 1977.

Fosdick, R. *American Police Systems.* New York: Century, 1921.

Fox, R. H., and Cunningham, C. L. *Crime Scene and Physical Evidence Handbook.* Washington, D.C.: U.S. Government Printing Office, 1973.

Forst, B. *What Happens After Arrest.* Washington, D.C.: U.S. Government Printing Office, 1978.

Greenberg, B.; Elliot, C. V.; Kraft, L. P.; and Proctor, H. S. *Felony Investigation Decision Model: An Analysis of Investigative Elements of Information.* Washington, D.C.: U.S. Government Printing Office, 1977.

Greenwood, P. W. *An Analysis of the Apprehension Activities of the New York City Police Department.* New York: The New York City Rand Institute, 1970.

Greenwood, P. W., and Petersilia, J. *The Criminal Investigation Process: A Dialogue on Research Findings,* vol. 1, Washington, D.C.: U.S. Government Printing Office, 1977.

Greenwood, P. W. *The Rand Criminal Investigation Study: Its Findings and Impacts To Date.* Santa Monica, Calif.: The Rand Corporation, 1979.

"Introduction to Terrorism and Intelligence Manual." Portland, Oregon Police Department, 1976.

Jenkins, B. *The Study of Terrorism: Definitional Problems.* Santa Monica, Calif.: Rand Corporation, 1980.

Kelling, G. L.; Pate, T.; Dieckman, D.; and Brown, C. E. *The Kansas City Preventive Patrol Experiment.* Washington, D.C.: Police Foundation, 1974.

Kirk, P. L. "The Ontegeny of Criminalistics." *Journal of Criminal Law, Criminology and Police Science* 54 (1963):235-238.

Mickolus, E. "Statistical Approaches to the Study of Terrorism." In *Terrorism: An Interdisciplinary Perspective,* edited by Y. Alexander and S. Finger. New York: McGraw-Hill, 1977.

National Advisory Commission on Criminal Justice Standards and Goals. Police. Washington, D.C.: U.S. Government Printing Office, 1973.

National Institute of Law Enforcement and Criminal Justice. *The Criminal Investigation Process: A Dialogue on Research Findings.* Washington, D.C.: U.S. Government Printing Office, 1977.

Peterson, J. L. *The Utilization of Criminalistics Services by the Police: An Analysis of the Physical Evidence Recovery Process.* Washington, D.C.: Law Enforcement Assistance Administration, National Institute of Law Enforcement and Criminal Justice, 1974.

Phelps, T. R., Swanson, C. R., and Evans, K. R. *Introduction to Criminal Justice.* Santa Monica, Calif.: Goodyear, 1979.

The President's Commission on Law Enforcement and Administration of Justice, *Task Force Report: Science and Technology.* Washington, D.C.: U.S. Government Printing Office, 1967.

Rosenblum, M. "Terrorism Impossible to Eliminate." *The Tampa Tribune*, 21 November 1982.
Safersteen, R. *Criminalistics: An Introduction to Forensic Science*. 2nd ed. Englewood Cliffs, N.J.: Prentice-Hall, 1981.
Sherman, L. W., Milton, C. H., and Kelly, T. V. *Team Policing*. Washington, D.C.: Police Foundation, 1973.
Skolnick, J. *Justice Without Trial*. New York: Wiley, 1966.
Smith, B. *Police Systems in the United States*. New York: Harper & Row, 1960.
Swanson, C. R., Chamelin, N. C., and Territo, L. *Criminal Investigation*, 2nd ed. New York: Random House, 1981.
Vera Institute of Justice. *Felony Arrests: Their Prosecution and Disposition in New York City's Courts*. New York: Vera Institute of Justice, 1977.
Wolf, J. "Anti-Terrorism: Operations and Controls in a Free Society." In *Critical Issues in Law Enforcement*, 3d ed., edited by H. W. More, Jr. Cincinnati, Ohio: Anderson, 1981.

Notes

1. For a further discussion of police patrols, see George L. Kirkham and Lauren A. Wollan, Jr., *Introduction to Law Enforcement* (New York: Harper & Row, 1980; George Eastman and Esther Eastman, eds., *Municipal Police Administration* (Washington, D.C.: International City Management Association, 1982); and Samuel G. Chapman, ed., *Police Patrol Readings* (Springfield, Ill.: Charles C. Thomas, 1970).

2. The discussion of team policing and the Kansas City Patrol Experiment, as well as the accompanying references, were adapted and modified, with permission, from T. R. Phelps, C. R. Swanson, and K. R. Evans, *Introduction to Criminal Justice*, (Santa Monica, Calif.: Goodyear, 1979), pp. 171–75.

3. This discussion (of the detective bureau) and the accompanying references were adapted and modified, with permission, from Peter W. Greenwood and Joan Petersilia, *The Criminal Investigation Process: A Dialogue on Research Findings*, vol. 1, (Washington, D.C.: U.S. Government Printing Office, 1977), pp. 5-11.

4. This summary and the accompanying references were adapted, with permission, from Peter W. Greenwood, *The Rand Criminal Investigation Study: Its Findings and Impacts To Date*, (Santa Monica, Calif.: The Rand Corporation, July 1979), pp. 3–7.

5. For more detailed information about objections to the findings of the Rand study, see Daryl F. Gates and Lyle Knowles, "An Evaluation of the Rand Corporation Analyses," *The Police Chief*, (July 1976), pp. 20–24, 74, 77.

6. The Vera researchers noted that in 56 percent of *all* felony arrests for crimes against the person, the victim had a prior relationship with the offender. In turn, 87 percent of these cases—as compared with only 29 percent of cases involving strangers—resulted in dismissals because the complainants refused to cooperate with the prosecutor. Once complainants "cool off," they are not interested in seeing the defendants prosecuted. Consequently, the Vera report recommends the use of neighborhood justice centers, rather than the courts, as the appropriate place to deal with most cases that involve prior relationships between victims and perpetrators.

7. This discussion (of the crime laboratory) and the accompanying references were modified and adapted, with permission, from C. R. Swanson, Neil C. Chamelin, and Leonard Territo, *Criminal Investigation*, (New York: Random House, 1981), pp. 154–61.

6
trends, issues, and problems in law enforcement

Professionalism
The rationale for collegiate standards
Determining enhanced productivity
Applying collegiate ability to the crime problem
Educational upgrading: A second rationale

Affirmative action and equal employment opportunities
Recruitment of minorities
Recruitment of women
Recruitment of homosexuals
Reverse discrimination

Officer health
Job stress
Alcoholism
Suicide
Coping with health problems

Use of deadly force

Summary

THIS chapter focuses on four topics that are of paramount concern and interest to criminal justice students, citizens, and police: professionalism in the police department; affirmative action and equal employment opportunities in law enforcement; officer health; and police use of deadly force. In the discussion on professionalism, we focus on the rationale for collegiate standards, the effect of such standards on enhanced productivity, and the application of collegiate ability to the crime problem.

The discussion of affirmative action and equal employment opportunities is directed at the recruitment of minorities and women. We address some of the reasons that minority recruitment has met with little or no enthusiasm in the minority community and look at what some police departments have done to overcome this problem. Further, we examine why women sometimes encounter unique difficulties in police work and suggest some ways police administrators can minimize these difficulties. We also touch on homosexual recruitment and the experiences of the San Francisco police department, the only major agency that has actively recruited homosexuals. We also address the allegations of some white, male officers that affirmative action programs and court mandated "quotas" discriminate against them in the promotional process.

In the discussion on officer health, we examine the unique features of police work that generate stress. We look at stress-related problems such as alcoholism and suicide and discuss some of the ways these problems can be minimized. In the last section, we discuss the use of deadly force by the police, outline limitations recommended by authorities in the field, and give some vivid examples of the unfortunate consequences that occur when police officers shoot citizens.

Professionalism

Solutions to whatever ails law enforcement have consistently been sought in the "professionalization" of policing. Thus, the term *professional* has acquired almost mystical properties in the law enforcement community. Police officers praise a fellow officer's performance by calling it "professional." Well-organized, smoothly run police departments are complimented for their "professionalism." Conduct unbecoming a police officer is criticized as being "unprofessional."

In part, the preoccupation with professionalism among police officers and administrators is directly related to a comparison of salaries and perceived position of various professions within the criminal justice system. The police perceive themselves to be near the bottom of the occupational totem pole. In almost any comparison of prestige and income with prosecutors, defense counsels, judges, physicians, psychiatrists, and expert witnesses (usually with earned doctorates), the police officer comes up short.

Formal education has traditionally been the path to both self-improvement and increased status in a particular line of work. With the passage of the Omnibus Crime Bill in 1968, public funds were made available to police personnel to pursue a college degree at federal expense—or with a partial federal subsidy. Because many officers and administrators took advantage of this assistance, today's law enforcement personnel are, on the average, much better educated than they were twenty years ago.

The rationale for collegiate standards

Do college graduates make better police officers than people who lack a college education? This question is deceptively simple. What specific criteria, for example, are involved in defining "better"? Higher arrest rates? Fewer citizen complaints? Faster promotion? In a police department with extremely low productivity in terms of arrests and clearance rates, one might expect that the infusion of college-educated officers would lead to increased productivity. If increased productivity was one of the goals of college recruiting, and if the behavior of officers was directed toward this end, then higher arrest and clearance rates certainly *would* indicate the success of higher educational requirements. However, arrest and clearance rates are often highly inflated and counterproductive. That is, arrests are made in many situations that lend themselves to alternative solutions; other arrests are made based on insufficient evidence; and some crimes are cleared based on dubious criteria. If such arrests and solutions are attributed to the competence of agency personnel—and they often are—then the infusion of college-educated officers might well result in a *reduction* in arrests and clearance rates, (even though such reductions are usually thought of as indicators of poor performance). Similarly, the crime rate might rise or fall depending upon the perceived ability of officers to establish community rapport and thus increase crime reporting.

In short, the success of any police program—including the implementation of higher personnel standards—is extremely difficult to assess. The appropriateness of a particular measure of productivity depends upon the individual agency and the characteristics of the situation. Hence, efforts to establish the credibility of higher educational standards for the police are plagued by a lack of agreement about what constitutes "good" or "bad" performance.

In some police departments, rewards are based primarily upon the ability to make arrests. In other agencies, notoriety may be obtained by becoming involved in a gun battle or making a "big bust" (note that college education contributes little to one's ability to perform either of these endeavors). On the other hand, an officer who properly refers a criminal offender to psychiatric care may go unrecognized or may even be negatively rewarded. Consider the following two situations involving officers from the same police department.

In the first case, two officers were fired upon by a man with a handgun but they did not return the fire. Instead they implored the man to throw the gun down, then chased him into a house and seized him as he reached for a loaded shotgun. Command personnel were on the scene immediately, but no commendation or verbal compliment ensued. The following month, a case occurred that involved another mental subject, a man armed with a rifle. The subject fired the rifle, then approached a police car. When he would not halt, the man was shot and killed by the two responding officers. Both of these officers received letters of commendation from the chief of police for bravery in the line of duty. The point here is not that the officers in the second incident did not deserve the letter: they held their fire for as long as they thought was reasonable. However, the officers in the first incident also acted bravely and responsibly. Thus, it appears that, at least in some police departments, rewards are available only to those involved in spectacular shootings and arrests.

Determining enhanced productivity

The problem of determining enhanced productivity is complicated by inappropriate expectations. What we fail to recognize about police training and educational programs is that some of the tasks of the patrol officer can be learned adequately only through experience. The police role involves knowledge of dozens of formulas and forms and scores of "ways of doing things." No amount of formal classroom instruction will, for instance, prevent a police recruit from being "had" a few times by con artists on the street. Some sociologists observe that a significant body of knowledge in the police service can be characterized by the term *street wisdom*. It is unfortunate that far too many administrators, and even some educators, look only to formal educational programs to enhance an officer's ability to apply street wisdom. This approach will simply not work. As a matter of fact, certain deficiencies with regard to street wisdom might be expected from middle-class college graduates. One aspect of street wisdom is a knowledge of the value systems, jargon, and customs of lower socioeconomic classes; middle-class college graduates do not normally possess such knowledge. However, experience can quickly remedy the situation.

Another serious problem in the effort to justify higher educational standards for police is that it is difficult to establish precisely what level of improved performance justifies the imposition of higher standards. That is, it is not enough merely to require that collegiate police officers perform at a higher level than noncollegiate officers. Rather, it must be established that increased productivity justifies the expense of higher salaries frequently associated with higher education. Such a determination would be difficult enough to make if police productivity could be easily measured or the goals of the police service were agreed upon by those in the field. Such is not the case, however.

The problem of determining "significant" productivity differences is compounded by the fact that the patrol officer's task is often limited in scope. If the task is merely to write traffic tickets, to shine spotlights through broken windows, or to arrest drunks, then arguments for higher educational standards are weak. However, if the task is defined at a higher level, then any standard less than an undergraduate degree might be inappropriate.

If a job involves only routine and mundane tasks, college graduates can not be expected to perform significantly better than anyone else. In fact, a college graduate with high expectations who works at a routine or mundane job, may be even less motivated than an officer without a college background. Thus, the full potential of increased educational standards in police work will be realized only when the police task is adjusted to complement the educational background of recruits.

Applying collegiate ability to the crime problem

Information from two sources—a preventive-patrol study conducted in Kansas City discussed in chapter 5 and motivation studies conducted in the last twenty years—can be used to support arguments for expanding the responsibility given to patrol officers. The Kansas City Patrol Experiment questions the value of patrol officers in crime control, since the officers often spend much of their time cruising around without specific direction or purpose. If this view is accepted as valid or is confirmed by additional research, then it behooves us to explore alternatives to current patrol patterns. For the most part, such alternatives involve the reallocation of resources to address particular offenders or classes of offenses.

For example, a principle motivation for team policing (as discussed in chapter 5) is that it allows more effective use of the patrol officer. In team policing, patrol officers have some investigative responsibility and they are responsible for establishing community contacts to aid in the control of criminal conduct. Thus defined, the police task is anything but mundane. And if we attribute any validity to the Kansas City Patrol Experiment study, then patrol officers' tasks should be changed to direct energies toward more complex activities that have greater potential for contributing to crime reduction.

More compelling reasons for expanding the role of the patrol officer come from motivational studies. These studies indicate that three characteristics of employment contribute substantially to the motivation of personnel, thus increasing productivity. The first characteristic is a management style that moves emphasis from the supervision of processes to the supervision of goals. Such a difference in style was characterized by Douglas McGregor in *The Human Side of Enterprise* (1960). The second characteristic is summarized by the term *participative management*. Research shows that whenever employees are allowed to participate in decisions about the procedures and policies that affect their work, motivation and productivity increase substantially. Participative management involves the delegation of policy-making responsibility to operational personnel. It is best described by Rensis Likert in *New Patterns of Management* (1961). The third employment characteristic related to increased motivation is the responsibility and complexity of the work. As the latter two factors increase, so increase motivation and productivity. The term *job enrichment* is used to describe this phenomenon.

Thus, research indicates that we need to dramatically alter the nature of the patrol officer's task. Police performance should be measured by the attainment of goals rather than by adherence to rules and regulations; patrol officers should be involved in the policy-making process; and the responsibilities assigned to the patrol officer should be significantly expanded. As this occurs, the police role will increasingly require professional skills, rather than the skills of a craftsman.

The importance of highly motivated personnel can not be exaggerated. A misconception that must be overcome is the illusion that patrol units function as tightly controlled, carefully directed units of a crime strike force. The illusion is perpetuated by frequent reference to fighting the "war on crime"—as if patrol units were analogous to army units fighting military battles. In fact, however, in any jurisdiction at any time, there are as many independent police units as there are patrol officers on the street.

Close field supervision of patrol units randomly roving throughout a jurisdiction is difficult. This difficulty was illustrated in one agency in which a patrol officer started a contest to determine who could drive the farthest outside the jurisdiction without being discovered. The record set was 60 miles—120 miles round trip. Although such contests are certainly not typical, the case illustrates that there is little supervisory contact with patrol officers in most jurisdictions. Because such contact is usually initiated by a radio call to set up a time and place to meet, patrol officers are generally free to do as they please. Unfortunately, that sometimes entails idleness and looking after nonpolice business.

Because supervision of patrol officers is so difficult, we must depend on the officers to internalize certain values that will direct them toward crime reduction. The desired value system is characterized as "professional"; that is, we expect police officers to be self-motivated. Unfortunately, many police agencies today are characterized by a "labor-versus-management" attitude among patrol officers and police managers. Almost all patrol officers work at some other job before joining the police agency. In most cases, the jobs held previously by officers without a college background were *working-class jobs*. The behavioral norm pervasive in such employment is that if one has free time when a supervisor is not watching, that time can be used to do anything that does not contribute to the goals of the "company." Anyone who does otherwise is regarded as a "rate buster." If we recruit patrol officer from these ranks, we should expect precisely what we get. If we expect self-motivation from police personnel, then we must draw those personnel from an employment pool that does not perceive the goals of management as existing only to be subverted.

Educational upgrading: A second rationale

Traditional police training programs emphasize the more mechanical aspects of law enforcement. By necessity, these programs deal with subjects such as preservation of crime scenes, proper collection of evidence, motor vehicle codes, and physical and firearms training. Unfortunately, some training academies have not taken the time, and too often do not have the qualified staff, to educate officers about social conflict or human behavior. Robert E. McCann, Director of Training for the Chicago Police Department, comments that "the training programs we have established teach officers how to behave for the twenty percent of the time that they have to operate in a crime situation; and eighty percent of their time we scarcely touch as far as training is concerned."

Peter P. Lejins has documented how an educational background might enhance an officer's ability to handle situations involving social conflict:

> Among the frequent disturbances to which a police officer is called are family conflicts, which often reach the level of disturbances of the peace, fights, assault and manslaughter. It stands to reason that an officer who has been exposed to some educational experience in the area of family relationships, the types of family conflict and the way they run their course, would approach this type of disturbance with a much broader and sounder perspective than someone equipped with many conventional folklore stereotypes permeated by punitive, disciplinary or ridiculing impulses. . . .
>
> An even more obvious example is a disturbance anchored in the area of ethnic relations and ethnic tensions. Exposure to the university-level study of ethnic relations, contributing an historical and broader perspective . . . again suggests itself, and again one would expect that such study would tend to diminish the effect of prejudice, racial and ethnic stereotypes, erroneous and often exaggerated, rumors, etc. . . .
>
> Still another example is the handling of disturbances for which mentally abnormal people are responsible. The use of conventional and straightforward evaluations of behavior as being or not being a violation of law, and the use of conventional law enforcement steps to arrest and secure the violator for action by the criminal justice system, would often cause unnecessary harm to the perpetrator, who is viewed by contemporary society as a sick person, and to the community itself, by injecting what basically amounts to an improper solution of the problem. . . .
>
> Whatever has been said with regard to the above three categories of disturbances could be properly restated with regard to the handling of drunks and drug addicts. . . .
>
> And finally, let us take the so-called area of civil rights and contemporary struggles for them, which often express themselves in disturbances and so-called riots. Here again the quick and sharp discernment between permissible actions in terms of freedom of speech, and freedom of demonstration, and actions that violate the individual rights of others and have all the characteristics of plain criminal acts, presupposes alert and sophisticated individuals. Persons without any higher education, acquired either in their college-age period or subsequently by means of adult education and in-service training, can hardly be cast in the role of the wise law enforcement officer who manages to lessen the tensions between ideologically antagonistic mobs, protects the rights of innocent bystanders and would-be victims, and contains the amount of violence . . .(1970, pp. 13–16).

It is true that many police officers perform mundane tasks such as directing traffic, issuing parking tickets, conducting permit inspections, and driving tow trucks. Such tasks obviously do not require college training. However, many routine tasks are rapidly being turned over to civilian employees and other governmental agencies. Thus, police officers are going back to more essential tasks, which include social control in a period of increasing social turmoil, preservation of our constitutional guarantees, and exercise of broad discretion—sometimes in life and death situations. The Education and Training Task Force of the Police Foundation comments that "the job defining that delicate balance between liberty and order, of applying wisdom, of being flexible, of using discretion and, most particularly, of seeing the mundane and trivial in a broader legal and moral context is an intellectually and psychologically awesome one" (1972). If the tasks performed by police are those normally performed by professionals, and if other professionals normally prepare for their roles by academic study, then so ought the police to prepare.

Thus, the police function, as it relates to conflict resolution and order maintenance in urban society, involves both social work and law enforcement techniques. Whether or not these techniques are employed at an appropriate time and in an appropriate way can mean the difference between successful and unsuccessful resolution of conflict. Unsuccessful resolution extols a human cost whether or not criminal behavior results.

The self-concept of the police officer as a crime fighter inhibits the ability of officers to resolve situations that can be handled by social counseling. This situation is the basis for a second rationale for educational upgrading—that college-educated individuals are more able to cope with role conflict, and a college education provides officers with a social perspective and abilities more conducive to conflict resolution.

Affirmative action and equal employment opportunities

The traditional argument for increasing minority recruitment on the police force is that such recruitment increases the effectiveness of the force. Police officers can not be effective in a hostile environment—an environment where they are unfamiliar with the culture of the community or where they feel alien, frightened, belligerent, or awkward. Citizens will not cooperate with them, will not report crimes, and will not aid in their investigations. One solution to this problem is to assign police officers that have the same ethnic background as the residents. Thus, Chicanos police Chicanos and blacks police blacks. Evidence shows that racial or ethnic similarity on the police force can indeed improve community relations and reduce tensions. Dozens of cities—including Detroit, Baltimore, Washington (D.C.), and New Orleans—have improved community relations by staffing troubled areas with police of the same racial or ethnic character as the neighborhood population (Wasserman, Gardner, and Cohen 1973, p. 41).

Recruitment of minorities

One of the difficulties that even well-intentioned police administrators encounter in attempting to assign officers based on ethnic or racial background is the lack of sufficient personnel to fill such assignments. And minority recruitment, although not nearly as difficult as some contend, is not a simple matter. After decades of exclusion, suspicion, and discrimination, a passive "open-door" policy of recruitment is not enough. Peer-group pressure—strong among young blacks—will work against it. So will fear of failure, nonacceptance, and even outright discrimination. Furthermore, job opportunities for minorities in other fields are often more attractive than those offered by the police department.

In spite of such obstacles, however, minority recruitment can be improved. First, a department must initiate a strong recruitment program. Recruitment left to a civil service board will probably not be successful. Such boards have many other responsibilities, and few have the time or skills needed to attract the kind of candidates police departments require. Thus, the department itself must assume the major responsibility.

The department must also demonstrate a commitment to internal equal opportunity. Applicants are being asked to commit themselves to a new career, and they need to know that the department recruiting them is dedicated to helping them advance. Many departments—such as those in Boston, New Orleans, Dayton, New York City, Miami, and St. Louis—have demonstrated such commitment by appointing qualified minority individuals, both from within and outside the department, to high positions. Most of these departments are also taking the important step of removing discrimination from their promotional systems.

The most effective recruiters of minority applicants are successful minority officers. Such officers should be asked to direct or assist in the development of the recruitment program, and they should be given the on-duty time to do so—along with whatever other support might be required. Appearances at high schools, community groups, veterans centers, and other gathering places for minority individuals of suitable age have been especially helpful. In addition, recruiting officers should encourage other officers to be alert for qualified applicants. The patrol car itself can be an excellent recruiting tool if officers are willing to expend the effort and are encouraged to do so. Some cities, such as St. Louis, provide up to five days paid vacation to any officer who successfully recruits a new officer. The response to such programs has been positive.

Targeting individuals as prospective officers can be accomplished in much the same manner as the department "targets" an individual criminal. Potential applicants can be assigned to individual police officers, who then visit the applicants' homes, maintain regular contact with them, and help them prepare for their examinations, maintain their determination through the waiting period, and get through training and probation. This technique has been used successfully in private industry and by the Massachusetts State Police (Wasserman, Gardner, and Cohen 1973, p. 41).

It has often been said that minority recruitment is unsuccessful because police departments refuse to lower their standards for minorities. One of the difficulties in discussing personnel standards is that the issue is seen in terms of "raising" or "lowering" requirements. Code words like these really do not address the issue. Higher or lower standards are not at stake; rather, the goal is to establish standards that are relevant to the functions for which they are designed (Territo, Swanson, and Chamelin 1977, pp. 40–47).

Recruitment of women

Not so many years ago, it was common for police administrators to dismiss the idea that women could adequately perform the functions within the exclusive domain of male officers—patrol work, nonfamily crime investigations, motorcycle riding, and so on. However, legislative, administrative, and judicial action have long since resolved the question of whether or not women should be permitted to perform these functions, and women have put to rest questions about their ability to handle such tasks. Empirical evidence supports the proposition that carefully selected and carefully trained females are as effective as carefully selected and carefully trained males. And although not all women are suited for police work, neither are all men. This is not to suggest, however, that women have been universally and enthusiastically accepted by their male counterparts—only that their employment and career advancement opportunities have improved immeasurably in the past decade.

The first women assigned to all-male operating units are faced with unique problems. These women are subject to psychological pressures that are not encountered by men and that will not be faced by those women who follow them months or years later. For example, the first female officer in a department must often perform her duties in an atmosphere of disbelief on the part of supervisors and peers who doubt her ability to physically and emotionally deal with the rigors of street work. And it must be remembered that peer acceptance is one of the greatest pressures operating within the police organization (Washington 1981, p. 142). The desire to be identified as a "good officer" is a strong motivating force, and a failure to achieve that goal in one's own eyes—as well as in the eyes of one's peers—can be devastating and demoralizing.

For the rookie female officer, attaining the approval of her peers can be an even more frustrating task than it is for her male counterparts. Like them, she must overcome doubts about her own ability to perform her duties effectively; but unlike the men, she must also overcome prejudice stemming from societal influences that depict the female as the "weaker sex" (Washington 1981, p. 143). And she will very likely receive little support from her family, friends, and male companions.

LATIN POLICEWOMEN
Bill Gjebre   Cox News Service

MIAMI—When Elizabeth Martin told her family she was going to become a Miami police officer, her mother was stunned. She told Martin the family had sent her to a private school "to make you a lady."

When Andrea Landis informed her family of her plans to become a Miami police officer, her mother tried, unsuccessfully, to change her mind.

Elizabeth Alvarez didn't receive any direct family pressure to keep her from joining the Metro Public Safety Department. The pressure was cultural. Alvarez said the traditional Hispanic upbringing discourages women from becoming police officers.

The three women are part of a small group in the two departments who have broken with their Latin backgrounds to enter police work. To Latins, the police force is a man's world.

Police recruiters for the city and the county—both of which are in the throes of heavy recruitment efforts—say the most difficult group to attract as job applicants are Latin females.

Of 122 females in the Public Safety Department, only 12 are Latin. In the Miami Police Department, the ratio is even smaller: Only four of 51 female officers are Latin. Of the nine females now in training, one is Latin.

With the city under a federal mandate to promote Latins, blacks and women, the city's female Latin officers appear to have good chances of moving up. Landis, for example, is No. 11 on the promotion list, and is likely to move up before the list expires.

"In the Hispanic culture, (police work) is not considered appropriate for women—it's not a feminine occupation," says Manny Mendoza, an associate professor of political science and sociology at Miami-Dade Community College.

Police work is considered a "macho job" for males, says Mendoza, who is of Cuban descent. Mendoza is a member of the city of Miami's Affirmative Action Advisory Board.

Females are supposed to be "mothers and homemakers" and if they go to work they are supposed to go into the professions, such as law and medicine, Mendoza adds.

Carlos Arauz, assistant director of the Miami Human Resources Department, adds this: "In a majority of countries in Latin America, police officers are not seen as community servants, but as oppressors. . . . The image of police officers is not something a Latin woman associates with."

In the Latin family, the "woman always had the housewife role," says Randy Eques, Human Resources coordinator for the Public Safety Department.

Latin families "do not perceive (females) being police officers," says Miami police Maj. Robert Alba. "They place daughters on pedestals, think of them as mothers and housekeepers. Women are to bear children, not be police and firemen. And what the community perceives you as is the way you feel."

"There is a basic misconception among Latins that being a police officer is anti-feminine," says Martin, 29.

That was another argument her Cuban mother used six years ago to try to dissuade her from joining the force, she said.

"Latin females are raised to be feminine, and not to do anything without asking the man," says Martin. "The husband makes the decisions. Latin females stay at home, raise kids and get office jobs, if they work."

Martin tried the traditional route first. She got married right out of high school. But that ended in divorce and she went to work as a stewardess.

But when she lost her stewardess job because of a Pan Am cutback, she applied, with some encouragement from a Miami police officer, to the city's police department. She was single at the time.

She says that she probably would have had a difficult time joining the department had she been married to a Latin male. "Latin men couldn't handle women being police officers," Martin says.

"Latin women think you go out there and are kicking and fighting all the time." But of course that's not so. "You're not out there every day battling. More often than not, you are out there doing social work.

"There are times when I have had to fight," she says. But she adds that males tend to be less hostile toward female police officers.

"Latin women aren't into fighting," she says. "I don't want to get hurt. I try to use my head. Sweet talk is the best way to get them into my back seat.

"Usually I say, 'Come here and sit in my car and tell me all about it.'" With such a large Latin population, Martin says Latin females are valuable as translators and in certain sensitive assignments. One time, she adds, a male officer called her at home and asked if she would tell a Latin woman that her daughter had been killed in an accident.

For Martin, there is one male in her life who likes what she does: her 9-year-old son, who "thinks it's neat to have me as a police officer."

Andrea Landis, a Peruvian who came to the United States 13 years ago, didn't want a desk job. Six years ago, she decided against becoming a stewardess and became a Miami police officer because "it's different and challenging."

Her mother "had a fit. She thought it was dangerous." Her father was not alive when she applied for the job. Had he been, Landis says, he "would have killed me."

Latin families instill in females that they should "get married and raise a family," Landis says.

During the past six years, Landis has spent most of her time on patrol work, on the 3 p.m. to 1 a.m. shift.

Speaking Spanish helped Landis on one occasion. She does not look typically Hispanic and was in the company of several Latin suspects who didn't know she could speak their language.

The two men were talking to each other in Spanish, and one told the other he was armed, Landis recalls. "I didn't wait to see what they were going to do," Landis says. She got the drop on them.

Landis' husband of two years, Vince Landis, is a Miami police sergeant who has no problem with his wife being a policewoman.

"She is a grown person and knows what the job entails," says Landis, who is of Irish and Italian decent. "I have no hangups about it. Women have their place in this world—whatever the calling is. I am encouraging her to go as high as she can."

Landis soon will return to work after a leave to have a baby, Tiffany Leigh, 2 months old.

"I'll let (Tiffany) make her own decisions" about her future, says her father. "If she wants to be a cop, that's OK; whatever the Lord wants her to be."

From *The Tampa Tribune,* 29 November 1980.

Administrators can take several steps to facilitate the entry of females into their operating units. For example, when policewomen, are first introduced into patrol activities, the move should be discussed in advance with male patrol officers, emphasizing that female officers will be given neither preferential treatment nor preferential assignments. Also, field training officers and supervisors of rookie female officers should be individuals who will fairly and accurately assess performance without considering sex. A chief administrator should also issue a general order outlining the administrative expectations of women assigned to previously all-male units. For example, one chief of police issued a written order with nineteen guidelines to set the stage for the entry of women into the patrol force. Some of these guidelines were: women should be given the same assignments, privileges, and considerations as men; no special scout cars or special assignments should be created for women; women should be given a full range of assignments, including assignments to scout cars, foot beats, station duty, and traffic duty; and women should be considered for certification to patrol alone when they have the necessary experience (Washington, D.C., Police Department 1972). A written order will affirm a chief's full support of women in patrol work and have an undeniable impact on the treatment of female patrol officers (Block, Anderson, and Gervais 1973).

Recruitment of homosexuals

One of the most controversial personnel practices employed in recent years has been the active recruitment of homosexuals by the San Francisco Police Department. Although it seems unlikely that many police departments will voluntarily follow the San Francisco precedent, the federal courts may be called upon by gay rights activists to intervene on their behalf, as the courts have done for minorities and women.

SAN FRANCISCO RECRUITS HOMOSEXUAL POLICE OFFICERS

Susan Cohen

SAN FRANCISCO—One clue to John Abney's survival as a San Francisco sheriff's deputy is this piece of philosophy: "You have to learn to laugh at the fag jokes."

Abney is one of more than a dozen openly homosexual deputies in the sheriff's department, which guards the city's jails. He also is one of more than 350 homosexuals who've applied to join the San Francisco Police Department, which patrols the city's streets.

At a time when it still is routine in most jurisdictions to fire police officers for homosexuality, San Francisco has become the first city in the country to actively recruit gay cops.

"Every police force in the United States has had a policy of barring gays from the force. But in five years there won't be a major urban area without gay officers," predicts Les Morgan, who at one time headed gay recruitment for the sheriff's and police departments.

For the last six months, Morgan, a social scientist who is homosexual, has been a volunteer for the police, meeting with gays and cooperating with the city's civil service system, which has been testing and screening applicants. The department, however, no longer is seeking applicants.

The campaign to hire gays was embraced by Police Chief Charles Gain, but Morgan admits it was greeted with less than total enthusiasm by the rank and file of San Francisco's finest.

"I'm told originally there was sort of a siege mentality, like the Russians were invading the U.S.," is the way Morgan describes it. "But when they saw we're not going to have a bunch of drag queens coming in here, the tension eased off."

The tension has not eased off enough, however, for a single San Francisco police officer to dare to acknowledge being gay, even though the chief and the head of the Police Officers Association state that there are homosexuals on the force.

"To have them come out of the closet and have them subjected to pressures, there's no point," argues police association president Bob Barry. "It will only raise a lot of moral questions in other officers' minds."

But Morgan disagrees. He hopes that with a big enough influx of gay recruits, no one rookie will be singled out for pressures, and attitudes will change among police as they have in the sheriff's department.

"Gays pay a lot of taxes in this city and they shouldn't be discriminated against in hiring," he says. "It's important that the community be adequately represented for the same reasons there should be blacks, women, Asians, and Chicanos."

The acceptance of homosexuals in the sheriff's department happened as gradually as their general acceptance as a sizable and politically influential part of San Francisco.

In 1961, when Undersheriff Charles Smith entered the department, he remembers there was a fellow rookie with an unfortunately high voice. Unfortunate because, Smith says, it led to the deputy being "terminated from the department on suspicion of being gay, even though he was married."

In 1972, Rich Hongisto was elected sheriff with the strong support of the gay community and a pledge to liberalize the department. It gave one new deputy the courage to allow a local gay newspaper to take a picture of him in uniform and write about his homosexuality.

The reaction among other deputies was mostly grumbling about the public nature of the disclosure, Smith recalls. But at the Alameda County Sheriff's Academy where the officer was sent for training, worse was in store.

"He was singled out," Smith says, "They tried to wash him out with a phony charge that he had cheated, and it took an investigation to show he had not."

It was in that atmosphere that Morgan was hired by Hongisto in 1974 as a civilian administrator and liaison to the gay community. One thing Morgan discovered was that even though homosexuals often were assaulted by gangs of roving punks in San Francisco, they were afraid to report it to the police.

One answer, he thought, was more gays in law enforcement.

The recruits who responded to Morgan's Outreach drive did not all identify themselves as being homosexual during the hiring process or even later, in the department. Someone posted a list of the new recruits with those suspected of being gay marked in red. The list was torn down.

There were jokes and jibes, but gradually most of the deputies found they were more comfortable telling others they were gay than concealing their personal lives.

"I was really petrified. I didn't know what was going to happen at all," says Sgt. Connie O'Connor of her decision to tell the sheriff she was a lesbian. "I had just never really talked about my personal life too much, although I'm sure people suspected."

But, sitting on a review board screening applicants for the department, O'Connor heard some recruits state that they were gay.

"It was a little embarrassing. Here I was judging them and I'm closeted and they're open," she says.

Her decision not to conceal her sexual preference had no ill effects for O'Connor, 32, who today is in charge of one of the city's women's jails. But she believes lesbians in law enforcement have an easier time than homosexual men, because women officers "usually get called dikes even if they're not."

It took Sgt. Zapata a year of soul searching before he took aside some friends at a departmental Christmas party and said, "Hey, did you know I'm gay?"

"Some said, 'no,'" some said 'thought so,' but generally they all said it didn't make any difference," Zapata says. "I did it mostly to ease the pressures on me because I can't feel I'm being deceitful."

If to the public the image of homosexuals as effeminate and police as the ultimate in machismo are incongruous, they are not to Zapata. He thinks both stereotypes are incorrect.

Not only is there a wide range of behavior within the gay community, he says, but also "the macho image should be changed in any law enforcement agency anyway."

"It's not real. How can you fairly deal with people when you're spending all your time proving how tough you are?"

But Zapata believes deputies must be able to convince suspects and the community that they are capable of handling tough situations and that "affected people or flamboyant people" wouldn't fare well as deputies.

Abney, 30, dark-haired and deep-voice, has a no-nonsense way about him and says that he is probably more conservative than his non-gay fellow deputies. He wants to join the police not only to do patrol work, but also to breach another barrier for homosexuals.

Abney says that the deputies who entered the sheriff's department as a result of the gay recruitment—90 per cent of whom remain—have blended into the agency. He, for instance, takes a female date to departmental get-togethers, explaining: "Why make some guy explain to his wife why two guys are there together."

"If somebody wants a cop, they don't care if it's a gay cop or a straight cop. It doesn't make any difference when you're on the job who you go to bed with at night."

From *The Tribune* (Chicago), *7 May 1979.*

Reverse discrimination

Departments that enjoy a high degree of success in recruiting minority and women officers sometimes encounter an unfortunate and unanticipated side effect when these officers are later promoted or placed in desirable assignments: white, male officers resent being passed over for promotions or desirable assignments because of the department's affirmative action goals. This problem is referred to as *reverse discrimination*. Traditionally, police officers have been told that promotions and assignments are given based on level of performance, promotional examinations, education, and years of experience. Now they are being told that sex, race, and ethnic background are also factors. And although such policies are in keeping with legally mandated federal guidelines and federal court edicts and are the most expeditious way to rectify years of blatant discrimination, it should not come as a surprise that some resentment occurs on the part of those officers who are passed over specifically because of sex, race, or ethnic origin.

One of the side affects associated with this problem is that personal antagonisms are created between white male officers and officers given preferential treatment. Further, even when a clearly superior officer from a special class is promoted, there will be those who will denigrate the officer's professional accomplishments and attribute the promotion solely to sex, race, or ethnic background. However, there are indications that preferential treatment will be slowed down in the future as police forces become more balanced.

U.S. ASKS FEDERAL COURT TO OVERTURN NEW ORLEANS POLICE PROMOTION PLAN
Associated Press

WASHINGTON—In a groundbreaking appeal, the Reagan administration asked a federal appellate court on Friday to overturn a court-approved agreement under which the city of New Orleans promised to promote equal numbers of black and white police officers.

It marked the first time the Justice Department has ever challenged in court what it called a "race-conscious quota system" designed to remedy past discrimination, department spokesman John Wilson said.

Technically, the Justice Department asked the 5th U.S. Circuit Court of Appeals in New Orleans for permission to intervene in a 10-year-old case and to have the full circuit court overrule a Dec. 16, 1982, judgment by three members of the court.

The Reagan administration argued that the promotion system agreed to by the city violated Title VII of the 1964 Civil Rights Act, inequitably infringed "on the interests of innocent non-black employees" and violated the equal protection guarantees of the Constitution.

New Orleans City Attorney Salvador Anzelmo called the move "incredible." He said it "raises very serious questions about the attitude of the present Justic Department on matters of civil rights and efforts to end discrimination."

"It is the city's position that the Justice Department has no logical nor legal basis for becoming involved in this case at this time," Anzelmo said.

The case began in 1973 when 13 black police officers sued the city, charging it with racially discriminatory employment practices. Before the case went to trial, the city and the black plaintiffs agreed to a consent decree to settle the suit. Under the agreement, the city will promote one black officer for each white officer promoted until blacks constitute 50 percent of the supervisors in the police department. New Orleans' population is 55 percent black.

A U.S. district court in New Orleans approved all parts of the consent decree except the promotion quotas, which were objected to by groups of female, Hispanic and white police officers. They intervened in the case, contending that the promotion quotas adversely affected them.

The black plaintiffs appealed to the 5th Circuit and on Dec. 16, 1982, the 5th Circuit panel ordered by a 2-1 vote that the promotion system be approved by the district court.

The Justice Department asked the full 5th Circuit to rehear the case and reverse that ruling.

Numerous U.S. cities are under court "affirmative action" orders to give racial minority members and women special consideration in promotional policies to make up for past bias.

In court papers, Assistant Attorney General William Bradford Reynolds, head of the department's civil rights division, said, "The district court's rejection of the race-conscious promotion quota at issue in this case was compelled by Title VII (of the 1964 Civil Rights Act), by fundamental principles of equity and by the equal protection guarantee of the United States Constitution."

In line with Reagan administration policy on job discrimination remedies, Reynolds argued that the 1964 Civil Rights Act "expressly prohibits courts from ordering specific affirmative relief for persons who were not actual victims of the defendant's unlawful employment practice."

He said that the most the court could approve would be an order that granted victims of past discrimination the seniority and promotions they would have had but for that discrimination.

"The racially preferential quota contained in the proposed consent decree would have operated to prefer black officers without regard to whether they had actually been discriminatorily denied promotions in the past," Reynolds said.

He added that the decree would thus have "required innocent nonblack police officers to surrender their legitimate promotion expectations to black officers who have no 'right place' claim to promotion priority."

Finally, he said that the Constitution prohibits the government from enforcing such a decree because there is no compelling interest in giving preference to people who are not victims of discrimination at the expense of innocent third parties.

Wilson said the department's arguments based on treatment of third parties and the 1964 Civil Rights Act would apply to such an agreement whether it was in a government job or in a private job. The government said that its position on the Constitution would apply only to government jobs in light of the Supreme Court's 1979 decision in the Weber case.

From *The Tampa Tribune*, 8 January 1983.

Officer health

Historically, business and industry in the United States have been slow to identify and provide for the needs of workers. Largely because of labor unions, however, the U.S. worker has attained a variety of benefits, ranging from increased wages to comprehensive medical care to retirement programs. The evolution of mental health compensation as a significant management issue occurred through a combination of union pressures and simple economics. A healthy, well-adjusted worker means increased efficiency and higher production from the corporation. As a consequence, *job stress* "has moved from the nether world of 'emotional problems' and 'personality conflicts' to the corporate balance sheet. . . . Stress is now seen as not only troublesome but expensive" (Slobogin 1977, p. 48).

Police work is highly stressful. It is one of the few occupations in which employees continually face physical dangers and may be asked to put their lives on the line at any time. The police officer is exposed to violence, cruelty, and aggression and must often make critical decisions in high-pressure situations.

IF YOU EVER HAVE TO KILL A MAN, NEVER LOOK AT HIS FACE
United Press International

MEMPHIS, TENN.—Eight years ago, patrolman John Thomas Cursey, 33 killed two holdup men during a liquor store robbery.

He shot one when the man turned on him with a gun, and the other when he ran. The second man did not die instantly.

"I heard him gasping for breath as he died," Cursey recalled. From this, he learned a lesson: "If you ever have to kill a man, never look at his face."

A few days after the killings, Cursey's buddies presented him with a fifth of whiskey. Over the label, they pasted a police photo of one of the dead bandits sprawled on the liquor store floor.

Six months later, Cursey was an alcoholic. He relived the killings night after night in his dreams. His wife left him and in 1976 the police department fired him because of his "uncontrollable" drinking. He couldn't hold a job.

Thurday, the city of Memphis' pension board awarded Cursey a lifetime disability pension of $5,500 a year—the first it has ever granted for psychological injuries.

Cursey, who reportedly collapsed in tears at the hearing, could not be reached for comment.

E. W. Chapman, Memphis' police director, said the board's decision was an indication that more and more people "have reached the realization that the psychological strain of being in police work is immense."

In an interview two years ago, Cursey recalled that the department had put 20 men on stakeout after a series of liquor store heists.

"The lieutenant called in eight of us and stood us up in front of him while he said, 'I want you to go out and kill those bastards. Don't come back until you've killed 'em.'"

It was Februrary 3, 1970, when two men entered the liquor store where Cursey was watching from a back room. One, armed with a pistol, demanded cash. He struck the storekeeper over the head and Cursey burst in and leveled his shotgun at them.

"The guy with the pistol turned and started to aim at me. That was when I cut loose on him. I had to do it. It was either him, or me, or the manager." The man died instantly and the second robber was wounded.

"The other robber hesitated a moment and I begged him to give up. I said 'Please don't run or I'll have to kill you.'" He ran and I shot him just as he went out the door." He died 30 minutes later.

A psychologist, Dr. Lindley Davis Hutt, Jr., told the pension board Cursey was "what I would describe as a stable, hard working, family-oriented type of fellow with a good circle of friends," Hutt said. "His reaction to the incident was very severe anxiety and depressive neuroses, insomnia and a lack of concentration."

Reprinted by permission of United Press International.

Stress produces many varied psychophysiological disturbances that, if intense and chronic enough, can lead to demonstrable organic disease. It can also result in physiological disorders and emotional instability, manifested in alcoholism, broken marriages, and, in the extreme, suicide. Three fourths of all heart attacks suffered by police officers are caused by job-related stress. As a result, courts have ruled that a police officer who suffers a heart attack (even off duty) is entitled to worker's compensation (Washington Crime News Service 1975). Thus, even a superficial review of the human, organizational, and legal impacts of stress-related health problems should sensitize every police administrator to the need for preventing, treating, and solving these problems.

Job stress

Stressors in law enforcement have been identified by various methods (Stratton 1978). Researchers such as Kroes (1974; 1976), Eisenberg (1975), Reiser (1970; 1972; 1974; 1976), and Roberts (1975) have all studied occupational stress in law enforcement. And although these researchers do not group stressors into identical categories, they do follow similar patterns. Thus, most of the stressors can be grouped into four categories: (1) organizational practices and characteristics; (2) criminal justice system practices and characteristics; (3) public practices and characteristics; and (4) police work itself.

Kroes, Margolis, and Hurrell (1974) asked 100 Cincinnati patrol officers about the elements of their jobs that they believed were stressful. Foremost on the list were the courts (scheduling appearances and leniency), police administration (undesirable assignments and lack of backing in ambiguous situations), faulty equipment, and community apathy. Items listed less frequency were changing shifts, relations with supervisors, nonpolice work, other officers, boredom, and pay.

A later survey of twenty police chiefs in the southeastern United States confirmed these findings (Somodevilla et al. 1978, p. 6). When asked about situations they believed were stressful for line personnel, the chiefs listed lack of administrative support, role conflicts, public pressure and scrutiny, peer group pressures, the courts, and imposed role changes.

Working with the San Jose Police Department, one researcher (Eisenberg 1975) identified numerous sources of physiological stress that reflected his personal observations and feelings experienced as patrol officer for approximately two years. Some of these stress sources were poor supervision; absence or lack of career development opportunities; inadequate reward systems; offensive administrative policies; excessive paperwork; poor equipment; unfavorable court decisions; ineffective corrections agencies (inability to rehabilitate or warehouse criminals); misunderstood judicial procedures; inefficient courtroom management; distorted press accounts of police incidents; unfavorable public attitudes; derogatory remarks by neighbors and others; adverse government decisions; ineffective referral agencies; role conflict; adverse working conditions; exposure to people suffering physical and mental anguish; concern over the consequences and appropriateness of their own actions; and fear of serious injury, disability, or death.

Alcoholism

Alcoholism in government and industry is not only widespread but is also extremely costly—a fact established by many independent researchers. Some 6.5 million employed workers in the United States today are alcoholics. Loss of productivity because of alcoholism has been computed at $10 billion (Dishlacoff 1976, p. 32).

Although precise figures are not available, department officials report informally that as many as 25 percent of their officers have serious alcohol

Wife of a Cincinnati police officer at her husband's burial. The officer and his partner were killed by a robbery suspect. Courtesy The Cincinnati Post.

problems (Hurrell and Kroes 1975, p. 241). These problems manifest themselves in a number of ways: higher than normal absentee rates prior to and immediately before regular days off, complaints of insubordination by supervisors, complaints by citizens of misconduct in the form of verbal and physical abuse, intoxication during regular working hours, involvement in traffic accidents while under the influence of alcohol on and off duty, and reduced overall performance.

It has been suggested that police work is especially conducive to alcoholism. Because police officers frequently work in an environment where social drinking is common, it is relatively easy for them to become social drinkers. The nature of the work and the environment in which it is performed are the stress stimuli (ibid.). Traditionally, however, police departments adhere to the "character flaw" theory of alcoholism. This philosophy calls for the denunciation and dismissal of an officer with an alcohol problem; to recognize the officer as a symptom of underlying problems would reflect negatively on the department. But this approach does not consider that alcoholism may result from the extraordinary stress of the job and that eliminating the officer does not do away with the source of the stress (ibid.).

There is no single "best way" for a police department to assist an officer with a drinking problem, but some agencies have enjoyed a fair degree of success in their efforts. For example, the Denver Police Department now utilizes a closed-circuit television system to reach officers who are problem drinkers and to encourage them to join an in-house program. The in-house program is designed to persuade the problem drinkers—after they have been sufficiently educated about their problem—to enter the Mercy Hospital Care Unit for recovering alcoholics (Dishlacoff 1976, p. 39).

Dishlacoff concludes that it is the responsibility of the individual police agency and its administrators to recognize and accept alcoholism as a disease and to create a more relaxed atmosphere and an in-house program to disseminate information about the problem. Police chiefs should neither tolerate nor ignore the unsatisfactory performance, excessive cost, and near-certain progressive deterioration of the individual officer (to the point of unemployability) that occur if the illness goes unchecked (ibid.). If drinking affects an officer's health, job, or family, immediate action is essential: the officer is probably an alcoholic.

Reports from the Denver Police Department indicate that the department has benefitted greatly from its alcohol abuse program. Some of the benefits are (ibid.):

1. Retention on staff of most officers who suffer from alcoholism
2. Solution of complex and difficult personnel problems
3. Realistic and practical extension of the police agency's program into the entire city government
4. Improved public and community attitudes for officers and their families
5. Elimination of the dangerous and antisocial behavior of officers in the community
6. Full cooperation with rehabilitation efforts from police associations and unions that represent officers
7. Development of a preventive influence on moderate drinkers

Suicide

Suicide as a problem for police officers can best be understood by examining the differences between younger and older officers. Suicide among young officers is not particularly common, but when it does occur it is often associated with divorce or other family problems. Among older police officers, however, suicide is more common and is often related to alcoholism, physical illness, or impending retirement (Schwartz and Schwartz 1975, p. 136). And although hard data are not readily available, some researchers speculate that suicides immediately after retirement are not uncommon. It is widely known within police departments that police officers do not adjust well to retirement. It is not surprising to see newly retired officers become depressed and allow their physical condition to deteriorate. Like individuals in other occupations, police officers in general do not plan realistically for retirement. However, unlike other occupations, police officers are often deeply involved with their work up until the actual day of retirement. It is a shock to suddenly be estranged from a job that has occupied a major portion of one's life and has been the source of many social activities (ibid., p. 136). Such losses can be devastating for retiring or retired officers. But unfortunately, most police departments—unlike many major industries—have not yet addressed the problem.

One study concludes that male police officers are more likely to kill themselves than men in other occupations (Lester 1970, p. 17). For example, the annual suicide rate for members of the New York City Police Department from 1960 to 1967 was 21.7 officers per 100,000; the annual rate from 1950 to 1965 was 22.7 per 100,000. Both rates were higher than the suicide rate of 16.7 per 100,000 for all males in the United States during the same periods (Friedman 1967). In reported suicide rates for males in various occupations in the United States in 1950, police officers had the second highest rate out of thirty-six occupations: 27.6 per 100,000 per year. Only self-employed manufacturing managers and proprietors had a higher rate; at 10.6 per 100,000, clergymen had the lowest rate (Labovitz and Hagedorn 1971).

Six possible reasons have been identified for the high suicide rates among police (Nelson and Smith 1970):

1. Police work is a male-dominated profession, and males have a higher suicide rate than females.
2. Firearms are available, and officers know how to use them.
3. Police suffer psychological repercussions from being constantly exposed to death.
4. Long and irregular working hours make strong friendships difficult and strain family ties.
5. Officers are constantly exposed to public criticism and a dislike for "cops."
6. Judicial contradictions, irregularities, and inconsistent decisions tend to negate the value of police work.

Some authorities believe that aggressive behavior does not stem from internal drives, but from societal frustration. In this sense, suicide and homicide are different manifestations of the same phenomenon. As acts of aggression, suicide and homicide cannot be differentiated with respect to the source of the frustration that generates the aggression. Homicide occurs when aggression legitimized by the aggressor is directed outward. Suicide, or self-oriented aggression, occurs when outward expression of frustration is deemed inappropriate (Henry and Short 1954, p. 15).

In one study of the suicides of twelve Detroit police officers who killed themselves between February 1968 and January 1976, Danto found that the group consisted of

> ... young men, married and for the most part, fathers, ... with backgrounds of unskilled employment prior to their police appointment or mil-

itary service, high school education or better, and some stable family life as measured by parents who were married and who had created families. The majority of the officers were white and had not been employed as police officers for many years. . . .

The officers who committed suicide . . . used firearms and fatally shot their heads and abdomens. Carbon monoxide was the second most common cause of death and many of the suicides, regardless of method, occurred in an automobile. . . .

The officers of the Detroit Police Department who committed suicide were different from the New York Police Department suicides. The Detroit group was younger, had less service time with the department, had a lower suicide rate within a police department, and less physical illness and police medical consultation histories, and fewer were single. In some respects they were similar: many had a history of alcohol abuse and dependency, had picked primarily firearms as their suicide method, and had suffered marital disharmony prior to their deaths.

Neither study proves that the police officer is any more prone to choose his profession because of its opportunities to express aggression than anyone else in society. The rising suicide and homicide rates for nonpolice persons should attest to that (1978, p. 36).

The most upsetting problem for the suicidal male officer is his marriage. Officers sometimes commit suicide following the death of a significant person, or they kill themselves at a location near the persons they care for. To some extent, marital problems may be connected to the job, because hours are erratic and subject to change and officers are subjected to dangers not always understood by civilians.

Police suicide should be viewed from a psychological basis that emphasizes both the unique and multideterminant aspects of an individual's behavior and the societal influences on that behavior. The human being is a frustrated and status-oriented social animal who is not isolated from peers. In fact, in many ways the American police officer is like a health professional. As part of their life's work, officers frequently are in contact with the behaviorally different and socially ill citizens of our cities. When they themselves suffer unrelenting anguish, they often fear the loss of their jobs if they seek treatment (and perhaps realistically so) because of parochial attitudes toward mental health in many departments. Unfortunately, however, the closest analogy between the police and health professionals is the reluctance to get a fellow worker into treatment, probably because they feel it is none of their business. But a troubled police officer, like a troubled health professional, is of no use to the public or to the profession if he or she does not seek treatment (Heiman 1975).

Coping with health problems

There are many ways to reduce stress and to cope with health problems on the police force. The following methods and programs have been recommended in recent years (International Association of Chiefs of Police 1978, p. 3):

1. Using efficient preemployment screening to weed out persons who can not cope with high stress
2. Increasing practical training for police on the subject of stress, including the simulation of high-stress situations
3. Increasing support from police executives with regard to the stress-related problems of patrol officers
4. Instituting mandatory alcoholic rehabilitation programs
5. Providing immediate consultation to officers involved in traumatic events such as justifiable homicides
6. Providing complete false-arrest and liability insurance to keep officers from worrying about their decisions
7. Providing psychological services to police officers and their families

Whatever the methods, a firm commitment is required from both the individual officer and the department. Any effort to increase effectiveness in coping with stress will be less successful in the absence of close cooperation between these parties.

Use of deadly force

No aspect of police work elicits more passionate concern or more divided opinion than the use of deadly force. Many community groups and minority organizations believe that police killings of civilians are excessive and often unjustifiable. Police agencies, on the other hand, are sometimes apprehensive and angry about unprovoked assaults on patrol officers (Wilson 1980, p. 16).

Few would argue with the idea that police officers have the right to use deadly force to protect their own lives or the lives of innocent persons. In many states, however, the law and departmental policies allow officers discretion that goes far beyond the simple edicts of self-defense or the defense of others. Many laws and policies are still modeled after English common law, which allows a police officer to use deadly force to apprehend someone reasonably believed to have committed a felony. The rationale for this formula is based on the fact that, until the early 1800s in both the United States and England, virtually all felonies were punishable by death. A felon was someone who, by his or her act, had forfeited the right to life (Milton et al. 1977, p. 39).

Although many states still retain the *common-law rule* (or some variation of it), lawmakers have increasingly questioned the rule as a basis for authorizing the use of deadly force. As a result, some legislatures have enacted stricter statutes. Some statutes vary in terms of the degree of knowledge an officer must have to justify killing a suspected felon: some require a "felony in fact"; others call for "resonable belief." Other statutes limit the kinds of felonies that justify the use of deadly force, and some distinguish between an arrestee and an escapee. In general, the modern trend is toward the adoption of both statutes and departmental policies that control and narrowly define the circumstances under which an officer may use deadly force.

In 1962, the American Law Institute proposed a model penal code that included the following section on policy for the use of deadly force in law enforcement (American Law Institute, p. 3-07):

> The use of deadly force *is not* justifiable under this section unless:
> 1. the arrest is for a felony and
> 2. the person effecting the arrest is authorized to act as a peace officer or is assisting a person whom he believes to be authorized to act as a peace officer;
> 3. the actor believes the force employed creates substantial risk of injury to innocent persons; and
> 4. the actor believes that: the crime for which the arrest is made involves conduct including the use or threatened use of deadly force; or there is substantial risk that the person to be arrested will cause death or serious bodily harm if apprehension is delayed.

In 1968, the University of Wisconsin Institute of Government Affairs published another model for policy on deadly force. The model contains the following provisions (Wileman, sec. 800):

Firearms training on a police shooting range. Courtesy Sergeant Robert Phillips and Deputy Martin Wolinski, Erie County (New York) Sheriff's Department.

Deadly force can be used only as a last resort and then only:

1. when an officer reasonably believes that he or others are threatened by death or great bodily harm; or
2. to make a legal arrest for a felony which normally causes or threatens death or serious bodily harm to the officer or others or which involves the breaking and entering of a building, and the officer reasonably believes that the arrest cannot be made, of custody otherwise retained or regained....

An officer may use deadly force in self defense only as a last resort and only if he reasonably believes that such force is necessary to prevent death or great bodily harm.

An officer is privileged to defend a third person from real or apparent unlawful interference by another under the same condition and at the same means applicable to the privilege of self defense.

Further, the FBI's policy on the use of firearms and force directs that (Federal Bureau of Investigation 1979):

1. special agents can use firearms only in defense of themselves of others where in it reasonably appears that they are in danger of death or grievous bodily harm;
2. special agents will use force as necessary to expeditiously make an arrest but no force in excess of that which is actually required;
3. special agents may draw a firearm to the ready when making an arrest if it appears reasonably or likely under the specific circumstances that they might be confronted with existing deadly force;
4. special agents may not fire a warning shot to stop a fleeing person or for any other purpose

Such recommendations that restrict police discretion in the use of deadly force are becoming increasingly common in law enforcement agencies. For example, the research findings and reports of the Police Foundation (Milton et al. 1977) and the International Association of Chiefs of Police (Matulia 1982) indicate that these groups support the present trend in many cities to limit the use of deadly force to situations involving self-defense, defense of others, and the apprehension of suspects involved in violent or potentially deadly felonies.

In addition to humanitarian reasons, there are legal, political, and social reasons for controlling police use of deadly force. For example, commissions established to study the causes of urban rioting have pointed out that the event that triggers violence is often the shooting of a young, minority male by a police officer (Kerner 1968).

ONE KILLED, SEVEN INJURED IN MIAMI MELEE

MIAMI—A rock- and bottle-throwing mob, angered over the shooting of an armed black man by police, besieged a pool hall and trapped two officers inside for 30 minutes Tuesday night before they were rescued, authorities said.

Violence erupted in the Overtown section of Miami after the shooting of a black man by police officers. Courtesy Wide World Photos.

Hospital officials said one man was shot to death in the incident, and seven others were injured, four with gunshot wounds. Two other motorists said they were hurt when rocks crashed through the windshield of their car in the street violence.

At least three police cars were set on fire and other scattered blazes were burning in the Overtown area, a predominantly black section of Miami. Crowds estimated at up to 150 blacks milled the streets during the disturbance, which was quelled within an hour, said Miami Police Chief Kenneth Harms.

"The situation is well under control and well in hand," Harms said at an 11 p.m. news conference. Nine people were arrested on "assorted charges," he said, and up to 200 officers had ringed the troubled area at one time.

United Press International reported that after Harms spoke to reporters, police said they had killed one of a band of looters trying to break into National Freezers Inc. in Overtown after someone opened fire on them.

The disturbance began shortly after the two police officers, whom Harms identified only as Hispanic males, entered a pool hall called the Game Room about 6:30 p.m., the police chief said.

One of the officers "saw a bulge" on a pool hall customer, Harms said, and when he asked what it was, the man replied: "That's a gun."

As the officer moved to arrest the man, he moved suddenly and "the officer's gun discharged," Harms added. Police spokesman Jack Sullivan said earlier that the man was shot in the head.

Shortly afterward, a crowd of about 150 people surrounded the pool hall and "became hostile and refused to let the officers exit," he said.

The man shot by police was identified as Neville Johnson Jr., 21. He was listed in critical condition at Jackson Memorial Hospital.

Another man whose identify wasn't released was killed by a gunshot wound to the chest, said hospital spokeswoman Betty Baderman.

"Eight victims have been brought to the hospital, four with gunshot wounds," she said.

Among the wounded were four black males, one white female and three white males, the spokeswoman said.

Shortly after 8 p.m., 15 squad cars assembled at a northwest Miami intersection and officers buckled on riot helmets and hefted billyclubs in preparation for an assault into the area, Sullivan said.

Miami City Commissioner J.L. Plummer said three special weapons teams in combat gear and the entire shifts from the central and south precincts, totaling more than 100 officers, were moved into an 84-block area around the beseiged building before the officers were freed.

At about 9:30 p.m., most of the uniformed officers had been pulled out of the area as public safety officials met to discuss the disturbance.

The police chief said a full review of the shooting would be conducted. City Commissioner Miller Dawkins said, "If anything is found wrong, we will act accordingly."

Several vehicles outside the pool hall, including unmarked police cars and television news vans, were set afire by the mob.

About 50 officers were pulled back to protect Miami police headquarters and a gunshop near the tense area. Traffic was detoured away from the 72-block warehouse district.

From *The Tampa Tribune* 29 December 1982.

Financial liability might also result from the use of deadly force. Deaths occurring from police action often result in substantial judgments against financially hard-pressed cities.

OVER MILLION DOLLAR JUDGMENT GIVEN YOUTH SHOT IN STORE BEING LOOTED DURING 1967 DETROIT RIOT.

A six-member Wayne County Circuit Court jury awarded a judgment of $875,000 plus over $150,000 in back interest to a young black high school student who was shot during the Detroit riot of 1967. The youth, then 13, alleged he was shot after entering a closed five-and-dime store to warn others "that the police were coming." The decision is unusual because the boy was unable to identify the officers who came to the scene "brandishing rifles," according to his testimony. Detroit police denied any knowledge of the shooting there and stated they had not themselves fired any shots in the vicinity. Attorneys for Albert Wilson, now 18, said the verdict against the City of Detroit is the largest ever awarded in Michigan for an injury to one person.

Wilson and two other witnesses testified that before the shooting they saw Detroit policemen, carrying rifles, arrive at the scene. The plaintiff stated that he was crouching behind a partition and looking through a small space when he saw a police officer aim at him. He "saw a flash, heard a pop and felt a slug hit him before he fell unconscious." A bullet entered the boy's left side, destroyed a kidney, left him paralyzed below the waist and confined to a wheelchair."

The policeman who allegedly fired the shot was never identified and the bullet that struck Wilson was determined to be 30 caliber, but was so badly damaged that ballistics tests could not be made. City attorneys denied that a Detroit policeman was guilty and contended that Wilson was not wounded in the store.

The original suit asked for $750,000 in damages, but Wilson's attorney, in his closing statement, requested that the sum be increased "to a reasonable amount, not to exceed $1.7 million." In addition to the tax free $875,000, Wilson is to be paid six percent annual interest on that amount from the time the suit was filed in April, 1969.

Reprinted from *AELE Law Enforcement Liability Reporter* (sample issue), p. 5.

In other cases, individual police officers have been held responsible for injuries to persons they have shot.

OFFICER HELD LIABLE FOR SHOOTING 17-YEAR OLD

A police officer was ordered to pay $45,000 to a 17-year-old youth he shot as the youth was escaping through the window of a house he was burglarizing. The youth was not armed at the time, but guns had been observed at the scene. The jury found that the shooting was justified, but the officer was found negligent for violating a regulation that prohibits firing at a suspect unless the officer believes that life is in danger. The jury also found that the youth had suffered $74,000 in damages, but this was reduced to $45,000 because he was 40% contributorily negligent.

Reprinted from *AELE Law Enforcement Liability Reporter*, Februrary 1979, p. 9.

In the final analysis, it appears that the incentive to restrict police use of deadly force far outweighs arguments for keeping that use broad and ill defined. It is likely that by the end of the 1980s, many departments that now adhere to the common-law rule will move toward more restrictive policies, in great part to avoid some of the unfavorable consequences of police shootings.

Summary

In this chapter we have focused on four issues we believe were deserving of special attention, namely: professionalization of the police; affirmative action and equal opportunities in law enforcement; police officer stress; and police use of deadly force.

Police leaders believe that moving towards professionalization of the police would eventually allow them to enjoy the prestige, respect, and high salary normally accruing to those who are considered professionals. Linked to this pursuit of professionalization is the need for police officers to have a college degree. We have suggested that the acquisition of a college degree by police officers will not necessarily lead to greater productivity or a reduction in the community crime rate. Much of what police officers do, however, is not related to the "crime fighting" function, but rather involves delivering social services, resolving conflicts, and maintaining order. It may indeed be that the greatest benefits police and citizens will derive from the professionalization of the police is not so much improvements in their technical skills, but improvements in their human relations skills.

The affirmative action and equal employment opportunity programs pursued by police departments have met with marginal success. Recruitment of minority men, especially black males, has encountered some resistance, in part because of the negative image some police departments have in their communities. However, some police departments have implemented innovative recruiting programs that have met with considerable success. The recruitment of females has been successful by and large, but women first entering traditionally all male organizations have not always been accepted by their male counterparts. Some have even encountered resistance or lack of support from their families and friends. In this chapter, we have outlined some recommendations that should rectify or at least minimize some of the problems that they encounter.

Affirmative action programs engaged in by police departments have not always been met with enthusiasm by all members of the force. White male officers have alleged that they have been passed over for promotion by less qualified officers because the officers were either members of a minority group or women. These beliefs have resulted in antagonisms between white male officers and those persons perceived as being given preferential treatment. There is some evidence that we may see a slowing down of this trend in the near future.

In our discussion of police officer stress we have tried to identify some of the major features of police work that are perceived by officers and administrators as being the most stress-inducing. Further, we discussed alcoholism among police officers and reviewed the efforts of one police department to help its officers with this problem and some of the benefits derived from these programs by the officer and the police department. We also tried to identify some of the major reasons for the high frequency of suicide among younger and older police officers. Also described were the numerous organizational and individual programs which can be quite useful to officers in their efforts to cope with job stress.

The use of deadly force by a police officer can create serious problems for the individual police officer, the police department, citizens, and the community at large. It is our belief that the present trend of many police departments to restrict the use of deadly force by their officers will continue well into the 1980's. These restrictions generally prohibit the use of deadly force except in those instances where the officer's life or the life of some innocent person is threatened.

Discussion and review

1 What is the principle motivation for police administrators and officers wanting to achieve the status of a professional?
2 What two factors strengthen arguments to change and expand the responsibility of patrol officers?
3 What have some police departments done to enhance the recruitment of black males?
4 What obstacles not faced by men do women sometimes encounter upon entering police work?
5 Why are minorities, females, and members of certain ethnic groups sometimes given preference in promotional policy?

6 What are the four categories of stress in law enforcement?
7 What benefits do Denver police derive from their alcohol abuse program?
8 What can be done to help police officers reduce stress or learn to cope with it?
9 What is the English common-law rule regarding the use of deadly force by police officers?
10 What is the latest trend in departmental policy regarding the use of deadly force?

Glossary

Common-law rule (on use of deadly force) Policy by which police officers are allowed to use deadly force to apprehend someone reasonably believed to have committed a felony.

Job enrichment Steps taken to create an environment in which employees have a highly developed sense of satisfaction about their work.

Job stress Factors associated with police work that may lead to physical disorders, alcoholism, marital disharmony, and suicide.

Participative management The involvement of subordinates in making decisions that affect the work environment.

Reverse discrimination Within the context of police work, *reverse discrimination* involves allegations by white male officers that departmental affirmative action policies discriminate against them in assignments and promotions.

Street wisdom Knowledge gained primarily from working the streets as a law enforcement officer.

Working-class jobs Those jobs that do not require a college degree or any highly developed entry-level skills.

References

American Law Institute. *American Law Institute Model Penal Code.* Proposed official draft 3-07. 1962.
Block, P., Anderson, D., and Gervais, P. *Policewomen on Patrol: Major Findings.* Vol. 1. Washington, D.C.: Police Foundation, 1973.
Danto, B. L. "Police Suicide." *Police Stress* 1 (1978):32.
Dishlacoff, L. "The Drinking Cop." *Police Chief* 43 (1976):32.
Eisenberg, T. "Labor Management Relations and Psychological Stress." *Police Chief* 42 (1975):54–58.
Federal Bureau of Investigation. An unsigned letter to Ronald L. Gaines, Acting Deputy Assistant Attorney General, U.S. Department of Justice, 23 November 1979.
Friedman, P. "Suicide Among Police." In *Essays in Self Destruction,* edited by E. Schneidman. New York: Science House, 1967.
Heiman, M. F. "The Police Suicide." *Journal of Police Science and Administration* 3 (1975):267–73.
Henry, A., and Short, J. "Suicide and Homicide." Glencoe, Ill.: Free Press, 1954.
Hurrell, J. J., and Kroes, W. H. "Stress Awareness." In *Job Stress and the Police Officer: Identifying Stress Reduction Techniques,* edited by W. H. Kroes and J. J. Hurrell, pp. 234–46. Washington, D.C.: U.S. Department of Health, Education, and Welfare, 1975.
International Association of Chiefs of Police. *Training Key.* Gaithersburg, Md.: International Association of Chiefs of Police, 1978.
Kerner, O. *Report of the National Advisory Commission on Civil Disorders.* New York: Bantam Press, 1968.
Kroes, W. H. *Society's Victim—the Policeman.* Springfield, Ill.: Charles C. Thomas, 1976.
Kroes, W. H., Margolis, B. L., and Hurrell, J. J. "Job Stress in Policemen." *Journal of Police Science and Administration* 2 (1974):145–56.

Labovitz, S., and Hagedorn, R. "An Analysis of Suicide Rates Among Occupational Categories." *Sociology* 17 (1971):67–72.
Lejins, P. P. *Introducing a Law Enforcement Curriculum at a State University.* Washington, D.C.: U.S. Government Printing Office, 1970.
Lester, D. "Suicide in Police Officers." *Police Chief* 45 (1970):17.
Likert, R. *New Patterns of Management.* New York: McGraw-Hill, 1961.
Matulia, K. J. *A Balance of Forces.* Gaithersburg, Md.: International Association of Chiefs of Police, 1982.
McGregor, D. *The Human Side of Enterprise.* New York: McGraw-Hill, 1960.
Milton, K.; Halleck, J. W.; Lardner, J.; and Abrecht, G. L. *Police Use of Deadly Force.* Washington, D.C.: The Police Foundation, 1977.
Nelson, Z., and Smith, W. "The Law Enforcement Profession: An Incidence of Suicide." *Omega* 1 (1970):293–99.
Police Foundation. "Education and Training Task Force Report." Mimeographed. Report of the Police Foundation, a subsidiary of the Ford Foundation, 1972.
Reiser, M. "A Psychologist's View of the Badge." *Police Chief* 37 (1970):24–27.
———. "Some Organizational Stress of Policemen." *Journal of Police Science and Administration* 2 (1974):156–65.
———. "Stress, Distress, and Adaptation in Police Work." *Police Chief* 43 (1976):24–27.
Reiser, M., Sokol, R. J., and Saxe, S. J. "An Early Warning Mental Health Program for Police Sergeants." *Police Chief* 29 (1972):38–39.
Roberts, M. D. "Job Stress in Law Enforcement: A Treatment and Prevention Program." In *Job Stress and the Police Officer: Identifying Stress Reduction Techniques*, edited by W. H. Kroes and J. J. Hurrell. Washington, D.C.: U.S. Department of Health, Education, and Welfare, 1975.
Schwartz, J. A., and Schwartz, C. B. "The Personal Problems of the Police Officer: A Plea for Action." In *Job Stress and the Police Officer: Identifying Stress Reduction Techniques*, edited by W. H. Kroes and J. J. Hurrell. Washington, D.C.: U.S. Department of Health, Education, and Welfare, 1975.
Slobogin, K. "Stress." *New York Times Magazine*, 20 November 1977, pp. 48–55.
Somodevilla, S. A.; Baker, C. F.; Hill, W. R.; and Thomas, N. H. "Stress Management in the Dallas Police Department." Dallas, Tex.: Psychological Services Unit, Dallas Police Department, 1978.
Stratton, J. G. "Police Stress: An Overview." *Police Chief*, 45 (1978):58.
Territo, L., Swanson, C. R., and Chamelin, N. C. *The Police Personnel Selection Process.* Indianapolis, Ind.: Bobbs-Merrill, 1977.
Washington, B. "Stress and the Female Police Officer." In *Stress and Police Personnel*, edited by L. Territo and H. J. Vetter. Boston, Mass.: Allyn and Bacon, 1981.
Washington Crime News Service, "Compensation for Police Heart Attacks Allowed." Crime Control Digest, 9 (1975):3.
Washington, D.C., Police Department. "Utilization of Police Women on Patrol." Circular 57, 17 April 1972.
Wasserman, R., Gardner, M. P., and Cohen, A. S. *Improving Police Community Relations.* Washington, D.C.: U.S. Government Printing Office, 1973.
Wileman, J. A. *Model Policy Manual for Police Agencies.* Institute of Government Affairs, Univ. of Wisconsin, 1968: Sec. 800.
Wilson, J. Q. "Police Use of Deadly Force." *FBI Law Enforcement Bulletin*, August 1980, pp. 16-20.

7
prosecution and defense

The adversary system

The prosecutor
The prosecution function
Election of the prosecutor
Power of discretion

Defense
The legal aid system
Strengths and weaknesses of the public defender system
Strengths and weaknesses of the assigned counsel system

Summary

Issue paper: Court of first resort—The neighborhood justice center

THE image of prosecutors and defense attorneys in popular television programs, movies, and novels gives a somewhat distorted and oversimplified view of the functions these people perform. There are no real-life counterparts to television's popular defense attorney Perry Mason, who somehow always manages to have his client acquitted ten minutes before the end of the program. Nor are there prosecutors like Perry Mason's protagonist, Hamilton Burger, who manages to lose every case—a fact, incidentally, that would most likely jeopardize the continued employment of even the most charming prosecutor.

Our system of justice and the roles played by attorneys tend to mystify the average citizen, who often has great difficulty understanding why or how anyone could defend certain classes of criminals. There is even greater confusion as to why individuals who have obviously committed crimes are sometimes released on "technicalities." Further, it appears to the layperson that prosecutors and defense attorneys are often more concerned with winning their cases than in seeking truth or justice, and that the final outcome of the criminal trial is affected more by the skills, personalities, and theatrics of attorneys than by the merits of the case.[1]

In this chapter, we address some of the public's concerns and misconceptions and provide the reader with an overview of the rationale underlying our system of criminal justice. Further, we outline the functions and discretion of the prosecutor in the criminal justice system and discuss the implications of this discretion. Lastly, we examine the role of the defense attorney and the pros and cons of various legal assistance programs available to citizens.

The adversary system

To the layperson, and perhaps even to some social scientists, the role of all lawyers is to see that justice is done. Anyone who has been educated in our legal traditions, however, knows that justice must be done according to law and within the procedures of the *adversary system* (American Bar Association Project on Standards for Criminal Justice 1974).[2]

The adversary system central to the administration of criminal justice is not the result of abstract thinking about the best way to settle disputes of law and fact. Rather, it is the result of a slow evolution from trial by combat or by champions to a less violent form of testing by argument and evidence. An atmosphere of contention still marks our way to justice, however, and for that reason, the adversary system has received much criticism.[3]

One criticism is that the system does not provide the best setting for discovering the facts of a particular case or for resolving legal policy. However, it must be recognized that the presentation of opposing views in vigorous debate as a prelude to decision is a feature also found in the legislative and executive branches of government. By contention—provided it is kept within proper bounds—a dispute is narrowed, and arguments that appear to be correct and logical, but are not, are exposed in the course of debate. Contest spurs each side to greater intellect and imagination so that, in the words of the 19th century statesman Thomas B. Macaulay, "it is certain that no important consideration will altogether escape notice."

Cross-examination has proved to be an effective means to expose not only false testimony but, more frequently, inaccurate testimony. Two adversaries, approaching the facts from entirely different perspectives and functioning within the framework of an orderly set of rules, will uncover more of the truth than investigators would seeking to compose a picture of the event. Scientists may quarrel with this technique for discovering facts, because their approach is properly one of discovering absolute truth. But lawyers know that our legal system is man-made and does not exclusively seek absolute truth. Rather, it is subject to limiting rules directed at higher values and larger purposes than would be a system that guarantees the conviction of every transgressor. Just as we reject, for example, torture and other inhumane techniques, so also we reject certain modes of investigation that, although not inhumane, are incompatible with the values of a free people. Moreover, a man-made system, inevitably finite and fallible, must provide safeguards to account for its fallibility. Because some error is inevitable, the adversary system deliberately chooses to err on the side of the guilty in order to protect the innocent.

Government under law, Lord Coke long ago declared, means that even the king is subject to law. For that reason, in a criminal prosecution in which one adversary is the government, the state is not above the law, but is simply one of the contending parties subject to the law. It is symbolic that, in common-law systems, with rare exception, counsel for the government and for the accused sit in equal positions in the courtroom; prosecutors do not sit at or near the judge's bench as they do in some civil-law courts. As a public officer, the judge has an obligation to do justice "according to law," rather than to decide always "in the best interest of the state."

The neutrality of the judge and jury reflects the historical wisdom of our mode of justice: parties who bring a matter to the attention of the courts are likely to accept the decision of a neutral tribunal. In the context of a criminal case, this means that the victim and the public must accept the finality of an acquittal or a disposition less harsh than they desired. For the *defendant*, neutral tribunal provides assurance of fair treatment and establishes confidence that encourages them to stand trial rather than to flee or otherwise seek to subvert the legal process. If found guilty, the defendant must then accept the penalty in a spirit conducive to rehabilitation.

Each adversary in a situation must have ample opportunity to present information relevant to the final court decision. The rules of procedure and evidence are designed to protect that opportunity within the bounds of time and the judge or jury's capacity to absorb information—as well as to preclude (so far as is possible) the introduction of material that does not contribute to the rational disposition of a case.

As limited by rules and procedures, the adversary system is also designed to ensure that the goals of finding the facts and treating everyone justly and fairly are not achieved at the expense of human dignity. Common-law legal institutions long ago decided that the system must permit (but not require) the accused to compel the state to establish their guilt under the rules of procedure and evidence—even though the accused may privately admit facts that, if shown, would warrant a guilty verdict. Thus, lawyers are often asked to defend a person who has admitted guilt.

Traditionally, guilt is something ascertained only at the conclusion of the court process. Our purpose "is not merely to protect the innocent person from the possibility of an unjust conviction, precious as that objective is, but to preserve the integrity of society itself. It aims at keeping sound and wholesome the procedures by which society visits its condemnation on an erring member" (Fuller, 1960). The essence of the adversary system is challenge. The survival of our system of criminal justice and the value that it advances depends upon a constant, searching, and creative questioning of official decisions and authority. It is this function that lawyers serve when they secure the acquittal of defendants, undeserving though they may be, when conviction is sought by methods repugnant to basic values protected by the constitution. This is the rationale behind the suppression doctrine, an essentially American invention, by which reliable evidence may be excluded from a trial because of the manner in which it is acquired. In sum, the adversary system seeks to accomplish justice by eliciting facts that can be proven under fixed rules of procedure. This policy, evolved largely by judges, is designed to ensure that trials are conducted fairly in both reality and appearance.

The prosecutor

The *prosecutor* in the American criminal justice system differs markedly from prosecutors in the systems from which our legal institutions sprang—Roman law and English common law. In continental Europe, prosecutors are appointed career officials that have a close relationship to the court; thus they have, in some respects, certain advantages, and in other respects, less autonomy, than American prosecutors. They are generally not considered part of the practicing bar, nor do they participate in lawyer associations. Although like their American counterparts they are key figures in the criminal justice system, their authority stems from being part of a central, rather than a local, government (American Bar Association Project on Standards of Criminal Justice 1974.)

In England, prosecution is administered by a Director of Public Prosecutions—a career official and subordinate of a cabinet minister. The actual trial of cases is assigned to private-practice barristers designated as Crown Counsel. A British barrister may prosecute for the Crown in some cases and act for the defense in others. However, the Crown Counsel has no part in preliminary decisions about whether to prosecute or what crimes are to be charged; in court, they function as professional advocates. The Crown Counsel's relationship to the Director of Public Prosecutions is essentially like that of a barrister to the solicitor in a civil case. Justices of the Peace and other courts of limited jurisdiction handle the bulk of all criminal prosecutions—95 percent or more; solicitors, private parties, police, or other administrative officials conduct the prosecutions in these courts. The rate of guilty pleas in all courts in England is substantially higher than in the United States, and appeal is not allowed in England as a matter of right.

The prosecution function

American prosecutors, representing the executive branch under a system of divided powers defined in a written constitution, are officers of the court only in the same sense as other lawyers are. They are career officials or civil servants, and relatively few of them devote their entire professional lives to this work. Prosecutors are usually elected local officials, largely autonomous and generally having no ties with the state attorney general or the chief officer of the executive branch of which they are a part.[4]

Whatever their precise title and jurisdiction, American prosecutors are invariably drawn from the practicing bar, and they usually return to private practice or seek other public office after a few years. They are generally active participants in *bar associations* and other lawyer groups. In most respects, including their autonomy, they are more like the British barrister than like the prosecutor in continental Europe. However, they are different from their counterparts in both England and continental Europe in that they are local, elected officials. American prosecutors derive important strengths from this unique characteristic of the office, but also certain weaknesses and burdens that sometimes encumber and impair their function.

The political process has played a significant part in the shaping of the American prosecutor. Experience as a prosecutor is a typical stepping stone to higher political office. The *district attorney* has long been glamorized in fiction, films, radio, television, and other media; many political leaders were first exposed to public notice and political life in this office. Many executive and legislative officials, as well as judges, have served as prosecuting attorneys at some point in their careers.

The political involvement of the prosecutor varies with jurisdiction. In some jurisdictions, prosecutors are required to run with a party designation; other prosecutors are elected on a nonpartisan basis. The powers of prosecutors are formidable, and these men and women are important in their communities. If they are not truly independent and professional, their powers can be misused for political or other improper purposes. Perhaps even more than other public officials, the prosecutor's activity is largely open to public gaze—as it should be—and spotlighted by the press.

Election of the prosecutor

The popular election of prosecutors came about as a result of a deep concern that the enormous power of the prosecutor be vested in a public officer who is directly responsible to the voters. Although ultimate fact finding rests with jurors, the power of prosecutors to institute criminal prosecution vests in them an authority at least as sweeping as, and perhaps greater than, the authority of the judge who presides in criminal cases. In short, the prosecutor is vested with virtually unlimited power as to deciding who will be prosecuted.

The prosecutor has a dual role that reflects the ambivalence of public attitudes toward law enforcement. On the one hand, prosecutors are the leaders of law enforcement in the community. They are expected to participate actively in marshaling society's resources against the threat of crime. When a crisis in enforcement arises in the community, the press and others clamor for a "war against crime," and the prosecutor may be drawn into the political controversy by the demand that he or she "stamp out the criminals." Prosecutors are called upon to make public statements, to propose legislative reforms, and to direct the energies of the law enforcement machinery of the community. On the other hand, the office demands—and the public expects—that the prosecutor respect the rights of persons accused of crime. Our nation began with resistance to oppressive official conduct, and our traditions, embodied in national and state constitutions, demand that the prosecutor be fair to all. Yet conflicting demands exert pressures on prosecutors that try their sense of fairness as lawyers. Nevertheless, both their public responsibilities and their obligations as members of the bar require that they be something more than a partisan advocate intent on winning a case.

Many observers of our criminal justice system who have also studied the British system comment on the importance of the professional independence of the barrister. Because the barrister plays both prosecution and defense—depending on the assignment—traditions have grown that blunt excessive zeal and improve the quality of advocacy. Also, because of its bifurcation, the British system encourages harmony within the bar and is conducive to strong traditions of internal and external discipline, traditions that temper the flamboyant and irrational partisanship so often exhibited in American courtrooms. Thus, American prosecutors might profit by an exchange of roles. For example, experienced criminal defense lawyers might, from time to time, be appointed as special prosecutors. Some younger prosecutors are already moving in this direction by doing private defense work or working on defender programs.

Because prosecutors are lawyers as well as public officers, they must answer not only to the electorate or appointing authority but also to the professional control and discipline of the bar and the courts. Because of the nature of the prosecutor's function and the right to appellate review, the prosecutor's conduct at trial is called into question more often than the conduct of defense counsel. By no means, however, do trials represent the major activity of the American prosecutor. The vast majority of criminal cases are disposed of without trial as a result of negotiated guilty pleas (see chapter 8).

Power of discretion

Under American law, criminal litigation generally does not occur until action is initiated by a prosecutor. The prosecutor has the *power of discretion*—the power to investigate citizens, order arrests, present one-sided arguments to the grand jury, and recommend sentences to the court. It is the prosecutor's decision whether a charge shall be pursued, reduced, plea bargained, or dropped altogether—and these choices are made with little or no statutory or case-law guidance (Lewis, Bundy, and Hague 1978).[5] The duties and responsibilities of the prosecutor are generally not specifically defined by law—other than by state statutes and constitutions that require the "prosecutor to proceed with litigation against those who transgress the jurisdiction's laws," or by case law that describes the prosecutor's duties in equally general terms (Lewis, Bundy, and Hague 1978).

When a case is brought to the attention of a prosecutor, he or she may simply refuse to proceed. Even after charges are filed or a grand jury indictment is in, the process can be stopped by the principle of nolle prosequi, the halting of prosecution. A prosecutor may even request the court to dismiss charges. One basis for the decision to prosecute is whether there is sufficient evidence to proceed with litigation. Beyond this, there are other concerns:

> It is said, for example, that the prosecutor must be allowed to consider whether prosecution will promote the ends of justice, instill a respect for law, and advance the cause of ordered liberty, and to take into account "the degree of criminality", the weight of the evidence, the elements of public opinion, timing and relative gravity of offense (La Fave 1970, p. 532).

Prosecutorial discretion is not a modern-day invention or an accommodation to the stresses of an urban society. This kind of power has always been accorded the prosecutor, as was observed in 1931 by the National Commission on Law Observance and Enforcement: "The prosecutor is the real arbiter of what laws shall be enforced and against whom, while the attention of the public is drawn rather to the small percentage of offenders who go through the courts" (p. 7).

Discretion is not solely the province of the prosecutor, however. Police officers exercise discretion in deciding to write a ticket, make an arrest, issue a warning, or allow an offender to go free. Nevertheless, the police officer's discretionary power is neither as broad nor as well accepted as the prosecutor's. Judges use discretion in dismissing cases, suspending sentences, or sentencing offenders to incarceration. They rule on motions during trial and they play an important role in determining parole dates. Even the jury has discretion—the power to acquit a defendant in spite of his or her guilt.

What makes the prosecutor's discretion so important is that all other segments of the criminal justice system are directly affected by the decisions of this office. On occasion, policy shifts in prosecution are made deliberately to effect change in other areas. For example, prosecutors may dismiss most of some types of cases because they consider police conduct to have gone beyond reasonable limits. Because police efficiency is usually measured by the number of cases closed, the police usually comply with a prosecutor's wishes and redirect their efforts. The prosecutor's decisions also affect the work of the judge. Decisions to proceed with one type of case but not another, to reduce charges and negotiate a guilty plea, or to proceed with an original charge, affect the type and number of cases reaching judges.

Why do we give so much power to one office? For one thing, not every violation of the law needs to be pursued. If every case were prosecuted, the system would be rendered helpless within a short time. Thus, someone has to decide which cases are most important. In addition, wholesale prosecution would not consider individual circumstance and would therefore be arbitrary and unfair in many cases.

The crucial issue to be explored is under what circumstances the prosecutor should choose not to prosecute or to pursue an alternative less than the maximum penalty. As the following example shows, this can be an issue even when a serious crime has been committed:

> A man telephoned the police, reporting in a semihysterical state that his wife had just shot and killed herself. When the police and an ambulance arrived, the victim was dead of a bullet wound in the upper left temple. The husband was holding the gun with which he alleged his wife had shot herself. He stated that he had arrived home from work just prior to the incident, but neither his wife nor their three preschool-age children were there. His wife arrived home a short time later and she had been drinking heavily. When he questioned her about the whereabouts of their three children she told him they were at her mother's home. A heated argument then followed about her neglect of their children, her drinking, and her seeing other men. According to the husband, his wife then slapped him in his face and he slapped her back. At that point, she walked over to a nearby desk drawer where he kept a revolver. She removed the revolver from the desk drawer, placed the barrel against her head, fired a single shot, and fell to the floor. No one else was home at the time this incident occurred.
>
> The relatives of both the victim and her husband provided the police with the following information.
>
> To their knowledge the victim had not been despondent, nor had she ever previously attempted to discuss suicide.
>
> The victim and her husband had been having serious domestic difficulties because she was seeing other men, spending the house money on liquor, and not properly caring for their three young children.
>
> Both parties were known to have assaulted each other in domestic disputes in the past.
>
> These facts tended to indicate that the victim's death was perhaps not a suicide but a criminal homicide. An interrogation of the husband established what the facts suggested. The husband related that he had been truthful about the events leading up to the argument, but after his wife slapped him, he angrily knocked her to the floor, removed the revolver from the desk drawer, and went back over to his wife, who was now on her knees. Standing over her, he fired a single shot into her head. After shooting her, he became frightened and fabricated the story of his wife's committing suicide (Swanson, Chamelin, and Territo 1981, pp. 205–6).

The investigation of the husband's background by the prosecutor's office revealed several interesting facts. First, he had never before been in trouble with the police (he was in his late forties). Second, he had been steadily employed at the same business for over twenty years, and his employer indicated that he was an honest and hard-working employee. Third, the victim's mother and father testified that their son-in-law was a devoted father, loving husband, and generous provider, and, although they grieved over the loss of their daughter, they felt no good purpose would be served by putting the man in prison. Fourth, the police officers involved felt that the accused would not be a danger to the community when he was eventually released, and, in fact, they were sympathetic about the tragic series of events leading up to the victim's death. After considering all the facts, the prosecutor agreed to accept a guilty plea to the charge of manslaughter and recommended probation for a period of ten years. The judge agreed and the sentence was imposed; the man successfully completed his probation.

Sometimes, the personality of the person charged may influence a prosecutor's decision. And there are categories of crimes and offenses that can be more effectively disposed of by some means other than prosecution. In many cases, it is apparent that winning in court is doubtful. By refusing to proceed with a case that does not clearly show the defendant to be guilty beyond a reasonable doubt, prosecutors save themselves and the court expense and time. And prosecutors are aware that a winning record is important for a positive public image at election time.

When theft or property damage have occurred, suspects sometimes agree to pay the victim or take care of the damage in some other way. In such cases, the prosecutor may drop charges. The attitude of the victim is also a factor. Field studies show that in many communities victims consistently refuse to prosecute (Miller 1969, p. 174). In domestic disturbances, for example, few of the original charges made by husbands and wives against each other are ever carried through.

Charges may also be dropped if alternatives to prosecution are sufficient. In the case of an offender that commits a crime while on probation or parole, for example, probation or parole can be revoked instead of charging the offender. If a suspect is mentally ill, it might be better to require commitment under civil procedures; sex deviates and other mentally disturbed persons are often handled in this way. In other cases, suspects (such as drug users) may be persuaded to work as informers for the police. If a suspect agrees to act as a witness against other defendants, charges are often dropped or sharply reduced.

Laws also exist that few citizens expect prosecutors to rigorously enforce. These laws may have been passed long ago and have become meaningless to modern society. Or they may be laws pertaining to fornication or adultery, laws that exist only to maintain the moral tone of the community. Prosecutors would generally lose favor with their communities if they insisted on full enforcement of such statutes: thus, neither the police nor prosecutors usually enforce them.

Prosecutorial discretion allows the office to respond directly to the particular requirements of the community. This factor is important, because prosecutors are usually elected. The danger is that in times of severe public pressure a prosecutor may overstep the bounds of legality to satisfy the momentary desires of the community. On the positive side, however, those laws that relate to more serious crimes and areas that the community feels must be dealt with vigorously can be given greater attention.

The prosecutor's office is generally considered a stepping stone to higher political office. Thus, there is obvious benefit to keeping oneself before the public, and how this is done can have an effect on cases. To present their best profile, prosecutors may reduce charges unnecessarily just to gain sure convictions. And cases that would ordinarily be handled expeditiously and quietly are sometimes dredged up for public view. The public interest is not served in either of these instances.

One effective way to control discretion is to make it more visible. Prosecutors should be required to publish policy statements about what circumstances affect their discretion, including which cases and offenders are mostly likely to be prosecuted and which cases and offenders may expect *plea bargaining*. Circumstances that affect discretion should be spelled out, and guidelines should be written for everything from pretrial screening to sentencing recommendations.

Defense

Because of the crime explosion, both private and public *defense attorneys* (especially in urban areas) face immense *case loads* that severely limit the quality of the services they are able to provide. The "sausage factory" character of many urban criminal courts creates strong pressures on defenders to process cases rapidly. And the interpersonal relationships between prosecutors and defenders combine with court pressures to motivate the defense to "keep the assembly line moving." Thus, the strongest pressure on a defendant to plea bargain may come not from the prosecutor but from

Defense attorney and prosector conferring with the judge during a trial. Courtesy Michael Heron/Woodfin Camp & Associates.

the defense lawyer. In this way, private and public defenders contribute to a decline in the quality of justice dispensed by the criminal courts (Willard 1976).[6]

Even a defendant who can afford private counsel is not guaranteed competent or interested representation. Many lawyers who station themselves outside municipal courtrooms and offer their services to people brought in by officers have a vested financial interest in encouraging their clients to plead guilty. Few such lawyers are willing or able to conduct extensive investigations on behalf of their clients or to engage in intensive pretrial preparation. The best (i.e., most competent and interested) criminal lawyers are more expensive; and there is frequently a direct correlation between a defendant's ability to pay and the quality of representation he or she receives. For the *indigent*, private counsel is not a viable option, and the only avenue for their defense is through public defenders or court-appointed attorneys.

The legal aid system

Prior to the signing of the Constitution, it was not uncommon for criminal courts to deny the right to counsel to some defendants, putting them at the mercy of the judge and the prosecuting agent of the state. In the late 1700s, however, the importance of legal counsel in criminal proceedings came to be widely acknowledged, and many then-independent states acted to provide a legislative guarantee of access to counsel through their constitutions (National Legal Aid and Defender Association 1969, p. 2). This right was extended to all states through the Sixth Amendment, which states that "in all criminal proceedings, the accused shall enjoy the right . . . to have the assistance of counsel for his defense." A strict reading of this amendment guarantees only the right to use an attorney in the preparation and delivery of one's defense. However, a less strict interpretation is needed to guarantee an ability, regardless of wealth, to acquire counsel. To give someone the right to counsel without removing the financial stumbling blocks to the use of that right is to really give nothing at all. (Similarly, freedom of speech can be said to be meaningless without the ability to speak.)

Unfortunately, acceptance of the implied right to afford counsel was long in coming. Until 1932, only New Jersey and Connecticut had provisions for appointing counsel for the poor—and then only for capital offenses (ibid.). The federal government wasn't much more responsive to the needs of the poor; it assigned counsel only in capital cases in which defendants were incapable of defending themselves (ibid., p. 3). Under such arrangements, most poor defendants really had no right to counsel.

In 1932, the Supreme Court ruled in *Powell* v. *Alabama* (287 U.S. 45) that all states were required to assign counsel to poor defendants in capital cases, thus extending the practice of New Jersey, Connecticut, and the federal government to all states (National Legal Aid and Defender Association 1969, p. 3). The first major step toward expanding the provision of counsel occurred six years later: in 1939, the court in *Johnson* v. *Zerbst* (304 U.S. 458) expanded the provision of counsel at the federal level beyond capital cases to include all felonies. A similar move on the state level was gaining momentum, but in 1942 the court ruled in *Betts* v. *Brady* (316 U.S. 455) that the states were not required to extend the provision of counsel beyond capital cases. The *Betts* decision was not unequivocal in its denial of expansion, however; the court added that the states must provide counsel if it is necessary to ensure a fair trial.

Legal scholars generally agree that the *Betts* decision was a judicial mistake: the court was soon inundated by case appeals, all claiming that the denial of counsel in each case was unconstitutional because of complex issues of fact. Essentially, the court had placed itself as the final arbitrator in every felony prosecution on the state level, a task beyond the capabilities of nine justices. Strangely enough, the court was long in remedying its error; not until 1963, in *Gideon* v. *Wainwright* (372 U.S. 335) did the court move to change the precedent. In *Gideon*, the court extended the precedent of *Johnson* v. *Zerbst* to the state level, requiring assigned counsel for indigent accused felons. *Gideon* proved to be the first drop of water over the dam. In the three or four years after the decision, the assignment of counsel was recognized to include delinquency proceedings (*In re Gault*[387 U.S. 1 (1967)]), police interrogations (*Miranda* v. *Arizona* [384 U.S. 436 (1966)]), postindictment lineups (*U.S.* v. *Wade* [388 U.S. 218 (1967)]), probation revocations (*Mempa* v. *Rhey* [389 U.S. (1967)]), and preliminary hearings (*Hamilton* v. *Alabama* [368 U.S. 52 (1962)]).

The final judicial precedent on the subject is found in the Supreme Court's 1972 decision in *Argersinger* v. *Hamlin* (407 U.S. 25 [1972]). Approaching *Gideon* in importance, the *Argersinger* decision provided that, on the state and federal levels, counsel must be provided in all cases where the defendant is threatened with a loss of liberty, whether indicted for a misdemeanor or a felony. The importance of this decision lies largely in the number of defendants it affects: approximately 5,000,000 people a year, or 84 percent of all those arrested, are charged with misdemeanors (Silverstein 1965, p. 1).

The legislative contribution to the right to assigned counsel has not been as significant as that of the judicial branch. In fact, the sole legislative contribution is the Criminal Justice Act of 1964 (Cappelletti and Gordley 1972, p. 2). Essentially, the act provides defendants in all federal courts with counsel at all stages of the criminal process. Furthermore, it provides that attorneys for the indigent be members of the local bar that specialize in criminal law. The practical impact of this act has been a reduction of the parameters of discretion in the American criminal justice system. At least in theory, no jurisdiction can now deny a defendant legal advice merely because he or she is indigent. For nearly all categories of offenses, a defendant is accorded an almost absolute legal right to representation.

Legal aid to indigent defendants has consistently taken two forms: the *assigned counsel system* or the *public defender system*. The assigned counsel system is the most prevalent system in the United States, being utilized in 2,900 of the 3,100 American counties (Cappelletti and Gordley 1972, p. 377). In this system, members of the local bar association are appointed to serve as counsel for indigent defendants at little or no compensation and without support services such as investigators and secretaries. In some jurisdictions, appointed attorneys are paid by the court on a set fee or sliding scale basis.

The public defender system is the system used most often in large cities and major jurisdictions. The office of public defender may be either private, public-private, or public in sponsorship, depending on the source of funding (Silverstein 1965, p. 46). Newer offices tend to be public, reflecting increased governmental commitment to legal aid (Cappelletti and Gordley 1972). And older offices, most of which were initially private, are becoming increasingly dependent on public sources for support. Attorneys in the public defender's office are full-time employees who, unlike assigned counsel, are helped by office investigators or law students.

Thus we are faced with two fundamentally different systems for providing legal aid to the indigent. Is one system preferable over the other?

Strengths and weaknesses of the public defender system

The public defender system offers three benefits to a jurisdiction. First, it insures that the indigent receive competent legal counsel. Many stories have been told about public defenders who are supposedly young lawyers getting experience before they join criminal law firms, or old lawyers not competent enough to support themselves in private practice. But there are good reasons to question these stories: a variety of studies report favorably on the competence of public defenders (Silverstein 1965, p. 47).

Some studies point to statistics showing a higher percentage of guilty pleas for defendants represented by public defenders; however, this percentage is probably related more to the class of defendants that use public defenders than to the competence of the defenders themselves (Wice and Suwak 1974). More often than not, the clients of public defenders are poorly educated, unaware of their rights, and apt to make self-incriminating statements to the police—conditions that might well make a guilty plea the only practical alternative for the defender. Public defenders also handle many clients who are (1) guilty, (2) repeat offenders, and (3) relatively experienced in legal matters. Such individuals may know that the prosecutor has a strong case against them, and, quite intelligently, they regard plea bargaining as the best way to resolve their problems. The high percentage of guilty pleas from the clients of public defenders is directly related to the fact that a higher percentage of persons who plan to plea bargain select public defenders (as opposed to private attorneys). If defendants know they are going to plead guilty, why should they pay for an attorney when equally competent representation may be obtained without cost? As a rule, then, it is unlikely that the percentage of guilty pleas is a serious reflection on the quality of services from the public defender. Rather, public defenders generally provide high-quality legal assistance for indigent defendants.

A second advantage of the public defender system is that public defenders are not strongly motivated to solicit money from the families of their clients. Most or all public defenders are paid fixed salaries, frequently at civil service wage scales. Conversely, appointed counsel is under considerable pressure to secure additional funds, because court fees are relatively nominal. All investigative expenses come out of the court fee, so the margin of profit for an appointed attorney is often small. The public defender, in contrast, pays nothing for office and secretarial support, and expenses for research or investigation come out of a general office fund. Although few public defender offices are sufficiently funded, the financial pressures on the individual defender are not as great as those facing the appointed attorney.

Efficiency is another benefit of the public defender system. As a rule, defenders are able to handle comparatively large case loads more efficiently and less expensively than private attorneys. Why? First, defenders benefit from group research and investigation. Second, they deal from day to day with similar kinds of cases—cases for which they are well prepared. Thirdly, defenders benefit from an ability to recruit highly motivated and well-qualified law school graduates. Such attorneys are frequently excellent trial lawyers who are motivated to work in a defender's office to gain experience. Because they are fresh out of law school, they are frequently more up-to-date on the state of the law than are their older colleagues. In sum, there are good reasons to believe that public defender systems are the most efficient way—from a financial standpoint—to provide high-quality legal aid to the indigent.

The efficiency advantage, not surprisingly, has been the subject of strong criticism. Some critics argue that efficiency is irrelevant to justice, that it is not a valid criterion for evaluating legal assistance. The best criterion, they say, is the quality of justice attained for the defendant. Thus, critics conclude that public defenders sacrifice justice in the interests of efficiency as they try to deal with their excessive case loads. Defenders, like all other judicial actors, *are* overloaded; and it is not surprising that they may be as willing as prosecutors to plea bargain, rather than to see a case through in court.

Many critics believe that some public defenders are not sufficiently independent from prosecutors. The public defender and the prosecutor who meet one another in the court day after day form interpersonal bonds that affect their behavior in important ways. One critic compares this relationship to "two professional wrestlers who fight one another every night in a different town, and after a while, get so that they do not want to hurt each other much" (Silverstein 1965, p. 47). And similar bonds may develop between the judge and the defender. The defender learns what kind of behavior the judge approves of and what kind of pleas the judge likes to hear. In this way, the defender serves as a representative of the judge to the client. Defenders gradually acquire a vested interest in keeping the assembly line moving and are loath to "rock the boat" in the interests of one client. To do so might harm their chances in future cases.

Defenders themselves are quick to point out that the personal and professional pride of each public defender may work against a cozy relationship with the prosecutor and the judge. Defenders want to have a successful case record to the same degree that prosecutors do, they are frequently drawn to their positions by a concern about the welfare of indigent defendants, and they are often highly motivated to provide their clients with the best representation possible.[7]

As a practical matter, the central determinant of the quality of a defender's services is the size of his or her case load. A proper case load for legal aid attorneys has been set at roughly thirty-five cases per attorney per year (Wice and Suwak 1974, p. 178). By this criterion, many legal aid offices are badly overloaded, and others (by far in the minority) are operating at or below the proper level. When case loads become unmanageable, public attorneys must accommodate their professional pride to the needs of efficiency. Because plea bargaining is the most rapid way to dispose of cases, defenders must sometimes encourage their indigent clients to plead guilty for reduced sentencing considerations. Too, as case loads become too large, the ability of public defenders to properly interview clients and to pursue legal research and investigation declines. Thus, the legal advice they give to their clients may be of poor quality (ibid., p. 165).

Low-quality legal representation can have irreparable consequences. For example, the Supreme Court has ruled that guilty pleas incorrectly advised by legal aid attorneys are not grounds for new trials (*Chambers* v. *Maroney*, 399 U.S. 52 [1970]). The victims of incompetent lawyers, then, must bear the burden of that incompetence, often for many years in prison. One legal resource for the convicted defendant may be a *legal malpractice* suit against the attorney to gain financial compensation. Malpractice suits against attorneys are increasing each year for a variety of reasons, although the bulk of these suits stem from civil actions (*Time*, 1976, p. 53). There is little evidence that the incidence of malpractice suits against criminal lawyers has had much influence on the diligence with which these lawyers work for their clients.

The main impetus for malpractice suits against lawyers is money. Civil cases sometimes involve huge sums of money, and when these cases are handled incompetently, clients are able to claim large financial losses. The financial incentives for criminal cases are not as attractive, however, and there is a natural reluctance on the part of lawyers to sue other lawyers for incompetence (or simple procedural mistakes) on the basis of a small claim. In a sense, however, the field of legal malpractice is "wide open," and it may well have important effects on the future conduct of criminal law.

Strengths and weaknesses of the assigned counsel system

Some jurisdictions prefer the assigned counsel system to the public defender system. In small jurisdictions, for example, the assigned counsel system is less expensive in the long run, because public funds are needed for only a small number of cases that can be parceled out to a variety of private attorneys. These attorneys are customarily chosen from the local bar association's membership rolls. Of course, this system places more of the burden for public assistance upon individual lawyers and their staffs. As a general rule, each lawyer is paid a set fee for specific services—a fee that is usually too small even to cover expenses. This benefits the government, which does not have to pay for extensive services.

Cost is not the only benefits of the assigned counsel system, however. Supporters of the system also claim that there are psychological benefits to the defendant. Because one lawyer is assigned for the entire judicial proceeding, the traditional lawyer-client relationship is preserved, even though the defendant may not be able to pay for the services. Thus, defendants feel that they have received the best personal attention, rather than being processed through the public defender's "assembly line." This benefit, of course, is based more on personal feelings than on any real state of affairs. For one thing, the "assembly line" character of the public defender's office cannot be equated with low-quality legal service. Indeed, quite the opposite may be true. And although clients may feel that they have been treated well by an individual lawyer, that lawyer may well have shortchanged the client in terms of research, investigation, and trial preparation. Thus, it is not always true that private attorneys give superior service; it is only true that clients may *feel* better about the service because they have been represented by a single person.

Another advantage frequently claimed for the assigned counsel system is that it involves a wide spectrum of the legal community, that it makes available to the defendant a vast array of legal talent. But this situation may not be desirable in some cases, especially if corporate lawyers are assigned to criminal cases for which they have no experience. Such a problem can be prevented, however, if judges—as mandated in the federal courts by the Criminal Justice Act of 1964—assign lawyers from a list of attorneys who do have criminal experience.

The strongest claims for the assigned counsel system are usually made on behalf of small jurisdictions. Small jurisdictions often can not justify a full-time legal aid office: the number of indigent defendants does not warrant the spending required to provide office space and support services for a public defender. Thus, for the few indigent defendants in these jurisdictions, it is more cost-effective to assign a lawyer. In addition, many small jurisdictions have local bar associations that view public service as an important part of the organization. Presumably, the members of these associations—as long as they are not terribly overburdened by appointed cases—do not view court-appointed work as too onerous. Thus, they will probably provide high-quality legal assistance to their clients.

An important criticism of the assigned counsel system is that lawyer selection is frequently open to abuse. In some cases, judges appoint friends who need income. One such example was noted in Boston:

> [One judge] . . . chose to call on about half a dozen regular lawyers . . . when indigent defendants asked to be represented in court. He parcels out the assignments one-here-one-there so that each lawyer picks up a hundred and fifty to two hundred dollars a week from the state. . . . They get the assignments as long as they do things the way [the judge] . . . wants—with dispatch (Harris 1973, p. 45).

Thus, a judge who is overly concerned with processing a large number of cases might select lawyers who either advise their clients to plea bargain or who do not cause too many problems during trial. To circumvent this situation, some assigned counsel systems use computers to match lawyers and defendants. This approach has already met with success in Houston (National Legal Aid and Defender Association 1969, p. 19).

Some theorists criticize the assigned counsel system for a feature also found in the public defender system: young, inexperienced lawyers frequently assigned as counsel are thought to be less competent than more experienced colleagues. This can be viewed as a positive feature of the system, however, in that it provides opportunities for experience. Yet, as one author remarks, "Experience is valuable only for those who need it" (Silverstein 1965, p. 19). To ask the indigent to serve as human hamsters in legal education may well be to deny the central value of the criminal justice system—equal justice to all.

Another very serious criticism of the assigned counsel system is that it is subject to extralegal pressures. For example, the plea that a defendant is advised to enter by assigned counsel may not be in the defendant's best interests; rather, it may be a reflection of the desires of the counsel. Youthful attorneys may advise a plea of not guilty solely because they desire trial experience. Older attorneys may advise guilty pleas only because they wish to return to their more profitable private practices. In all such cases, the needs of the defendant are essentially irrelevant to the conduct of the case. Private attorneys, it is claimed, sacrifice the best interests of their clients to the administrative or financial needs of their own practices. Of course, there are no reliable statistics to indicate the extent of this problem; and the short-changing of clients may not be unique to assigned counsel, as the same pressures can bear upon private attorneys that represent paying customers. Yet, the critics say, the pressures to short-change clients are especially strong for private attorneys representing indigent defendants, simply because the public fees are so low. An obvious solution to this problem is to increase fees, but in some jurisdictions this would be politically infeasible or fiscally impossible.

The financial pressures on private attorneys are often severe; and many of these attorneys are unable to expend large amounts of money for investigation or for expert testimony. In such cases, a defendant may be convicted on erroneous testimony that the defense lawyer could not afford to rebut. In one case, a defendant was cleared of a previous conviction when it was discovered that, contrary to expert testimony, the person the convict was alleged to have killed actually died of a heart attack. Unfortunately, this information came out ten years after the defendant's conviction (Silverstein 1969, p. 29).

Summary

Our system of criminal law is based upon the adversary system—the presentation of opposing views in vigorous debate as a prelude to decision-making. It is not a system designed to discover the ultimate truth in the absolute sense, but rather to protect the people against the abuse of governmental power, and to assure that no innocent person is found guilty of a crime they did not commit. Cross-examination is used to determine the facts and has historically proved to be the most effective means of exposing false testimony and inaccuracies in testimony. Our system also rejects the practice of torture and other inhuman practices incompatible with the values of free people. In summary, the adversary system seeks to accomplish justice by illiciting provable facts under fixed rules of procedure.

In America, prosecutors represent the executive branch of the government. Their powers are formidable and they exert considerable influence upon and within the criminal justice system. Their power to institute criminal prosecution vests in them an authority in the administration of criminal justice as large, or perhaps greater than, the authority of the judge who presides in criminal cases. They may initiate criminal charges, stop the charging process, or request that the court dismiss the charges. Thus, the powers within the prosecutor's office in this country are indeed quite formidable.

On the opposing side of the prosecutor is the defense counsel. The courts have mandated that counsel be provided at both the state and federal level, in all cases where the defendant is threatened with loss of liberty, whether the accused is charged with a misdemeanor or felony. Legal assistance may be provided by private counsel, public defenders, or counsel assigned by the courts. Each alternative has its strengths and weaknesses. For example, hiring a private attorney does not guarantee competent or interested representation. The best criminal lawyers are expensive and frequently there is a direct correlation between the defendant's ability to pay and the quality of representation received.

The merits of the public defender system include the assurance that the indigent receives competent legal counsel. It avoids some of the worst excesses of the appointed counsel system (such as soliciting money from the families of clients), because most or all are paid constant salaries. Public defenders are able to handle comparatively large case loads more efficiently and less expensively than private attorneys. Critics of the system contend that public defenders are often not completely independent from prosecutors because of their close day-to-day working relationship. Further, their heavy case loads reduce public defenders' ability to properly interview their clients and to pursue legal research.

The last legal defense system discussed in this chapter, assigned counsel, also has strengths and weaknesses. It is psychologically beneficial to the client because the defendant sees the traditional lawyer-client relationship preserved. Also, a wide spectrum of the legal community is involved in the process. This method of providing counsel is the most practical and cost effective for jurisdictions too small to justify a full-time legal aid office. The critics of the system claim that it is subject to abuse because judges may appoint their friends who need the income. Others believe that judges concerned with processing large numbers of cases will appoint attorneys who either encourage their clients to plead guilty or do not raise too many difficulties during the trial.

Further, some critics believe that it is the young and inexperienced—and less competent—attorneys who are the ones assigned counsel work. Lastly, the assigned counsel system has been criticized because the pleas that defendants are advised to enter may not be in the defendant's best interests, but rather a reflection of the desires of the assigned counsel.

issue paper

COURT OF FIRST RESORT—THE NEIGHBORHOOD JUSTICE CENTER

In 1971 in Columbus, Ohio, City Attorney James Hughes and Professor John Palmer (Capital University Law School) developed a dispute-settlement program for resolving citizen conflicts and averting serious crimes. Called the Night Prosecutor Program, the model was intended to provide a means for coping with disputes in which the parties had a long-standing personal relationship with one another (e.g., married couples, relatives, and friends). Hughes and Palmer regarded the courts, with their formal structure and rigid procedures, as more suitable for the adjudication of guilt or innocence in felony offenses than as an appropriate forum for dealing with personal fights, vandalism, petty thefts, wife and child abuse, disputes over parking spaces, barking dogs, loud stereos, and television sets—the kinds of cases the criminal justice system is often nearly powerless to handle effectively. Hughes and Palmer sought to offer an alternative to the courtroom and trial as an approach to conflict resolution.

Although many citizen disputes seem minor or trivial, they represent potential sources of conflict within the home, school, or neighborhood. Assault and homicide frequently occur as the result of petty conflicts between people who are close to each other. And serious juvenile crimes sometimes follow minor abuses that nobody bothers to address.

The procedure adopted by the Night Prosecutor Program has been widely emulated in the more than 200 neighborhood justice centers around the country, which together handle over 200,000 cases a year. In a typical case, a hearing officer opens the proceedings by giving a brief explanation of the purposes of the program. Complainants and respondents are then allowed to present their versions of the specific incident without interruption by the other party. After these initial presentations, the hearing officer encourages the two parties to discuss the basic causes of the dispute. Questions are asked of complainants, respondents, and witnesses (who, in many instances, are friends of both parties). The hearing officer's emphasis is to explore the negative and hostile feelings, attitudes, and experiences behind the specific incident, with the goal of arriving at a mutually acceptable resolution of the dispute. If the opponents are unable or unwilling to reach a compromise, the hearing officer may suggest alternatives. Disputants are sometimes nudged toward resolution when the mediator informs them of the possible legal sanctions that could be applied if they fail to resolve the dispute on their own.

Mediation affords direct, face-to-face communication and an opportunity to ventilate pent-up frustrations and anger—activities that formal court proceedings simply do not permit. There are no judgments of guilt or innocence; rather, an agreement is reached that, although it does not have the force of law behind it, is backed up by the pressure of friends, family members, and neighbors. Consider, for example, a case handled by the Milwaukee Mediation Center:

DISPUTE RESOLUTION: SEEKING JUSTICE OUTSIDE THE COURTROOM
J.J. McCarthy   Corrections Magazine

A cook had been fired from his job in a Milwaukee chain restaurant. A few days later, he met two of his former supervisors and their district manager in a local bar. The cook threatened to "blow them away," and proceeded to rough them up; he punched one of his ex-bosses in the face before stalking off into the night.

The three men filed a complaint with the district attorney's office. The cook could have been charged with battery, which carries a maximum penalty of nine months in jail and a $10,000 fine. The assistant district attorney, however, strongly suggested that the men take their case to the Milwaukee Mediation Center. This center, and scores of others like it around the country, tries to resolve disputes without expensive and time-consuming litigation. Proponents of this approach aim to reduce court backlogs and even jail populations, for while most of the cases submitted for mediation do not involve criminal matters, they are often the kind of problem that can fester for years. By producing a true solution to a dispute, rather than a mere determination of who is at fault, mediators hope to reduce the tensions that can lead to violence and criminal behavior.

In the Milwaukee incident, the mediator (a trained volunteer who asked to remain anonymous because of the confidentiality of the proceedings) remembered the session well. The restaurant employees were nervous before the meeting, he recalled. "They kept looking out the window," he said. "They even told me I should search the guy when he came."

When the cook showed up, the mediator continued, "his appearance did nothing to calm their fears. He was a big guy in his mid-thirties, with gold chains around his neck and a shirt unbuttoned down to his navel. He wore a huge 'Greek Afro' with a headband and a full black mustache."

The mediator opened the session with an explanation of the process: first the three complainants would tell their stories, without interruption, and then the cook would have his turn. After that, the mediator would try to find a common ground on which both sides could agree.

"The restauranteurs launched into their typed two-page account of the incident, listing the statutes they thought the cook violated," the mediator recalled. "Then the cook spoke. He said his father had died three weeks before and that he supported both his mother and two younger brothers. He hung his head and talked slowly, as he told how the Greeks were a proud people and how his mother had yelled at him when he lost his job, and made him feel not like a man but a little kid. He said he acted like a little kid in the bar. Finally, he said he was sorry, real sorry that the whole thing happened."

Then the mediator met privately with each side to find out what they wanted. One of the restaurant employees said that the ex-cook was dangerous and belonged in jail, but the mediator explained that this might not happen, even if they took the matter to court. Besides, the mediator says, "all of them had been affected by the cook's apology. But when I asked them, 'What do you want out of this?' they just gave me blank looks. They didn't know there was an alternative to sending him to jail. So I said that if the cook would agree to never harass them or even approach them again, would they need anything else from him? They couldn't think of anything."

When he met with the ex-cook, the mediator recalled, "He said he'd never been in this kind of situation and that he felt helpless—this big, macho guy felt helpless. He said he'd been drinking, and apologized again. He said he'd agree to just about anything to resolve this."

The man quickly agreed to the complainant's proposal. The mediator wrote an agreement that neither side would approach or harass the other, and all the parties signed it. The mediator said he stressed that the district attorney would not be happy if the matter returned to his office, and that the center would contact the men in the future to make sure that they stuck to their word. He did not mention that the agreement was unenforceable in court.

Reproduced from J.J. McCarthy, "Dispute Resolution: Seeking Justice Outside the Courtroom," *Corrections Magazine* 8 (1982):33–34. Copyright 1982 by Corrections Magazine and Criminal Justice Publications, Inc., 19 W. 34th St., New York, N.Y. 10001.

Dispute-settlement programs have been praised by a diverse group, from Chief Justice Warren Burger of the U.S. Supreme Court to consumer advocate Ralph Nader. Daniel McGillis, a criminal justice researcher who studies neighborhood justice centers, believes that such programs herald a major shift in American jurisprudence (McGillis and Mullen, 1977). As an alternative to formal litigation, the neighborhood justice center boasts these following advantages:

1. Cases are handled much faster than in the courts. Hearings are conducted within ten days of referral, as compared with four to five months for court hearings.
2. The settlement process is handled by nonprofessional volunteers; thus, the system is far less expensive than formal legal proceedings.
3. Both parties are able to accept the settlement reached in the mediation process. The settlement is theirs: they participated fully in the decision-making process. As McCarthy points out,

> the most basic distinction between the courts and dispute resolution is that dispute resolution minimizes the differences between the disputants, while the court process exaggerates them. Both parties to a mediation must share responsibility for the dispute and give as well as take, and both sides can't "win." The court's adversary system locks the two sides into their set positions and guarantees a winner-take-all fight to the finish (1982, p. 36).

Neighborhood justice centers are not without their critics, however. For example, some people question the adequacy of training provided for volunteer mediators. It has even been suggested that mediators should be licensed and certified to ensure that they will be properly prepared for their responsibilities. Other questions are directed toward the confidentiality of the proceedings. For example, could the mediator and case records be subpoenaed? Most concerns, however, focus on cost-effectiveness and the reduction of case loads in the criminal justice system. Supporters of neigh-

Two adversaries in a neighborhood dispute agree to settle their difficulties with the assistance of a mediator. Courtesy Corrections Magazine.

borhood justice centers claim that it is much less expensive to process a dispute through mediation than by adjudication, but there are no data to confirm this contention.

Another hope of Hughes and Palmer was that mediation would significantly reduce the number of misdemeanants jailed before trial. There are no data to indicate that this has been the case, however. And a study conducted by the Brooklyn Dispute Resolution Center indicates that mediation does little to reduce future violence. In that study, selected felony cases were randomly assigned to mediation or court processing. Researchers reported little or no difference between mediated cases and court cases in the stability of agreements or the emergence of new problems between disputants (McCarthy 1982).

Despite such disappointing conclusions, however, enthusiasts of the mediation concept continue to be optimistic. They feel that time will vindicate their hopes and aspirations for dispute-settlement programs throughout the country. They remain confident that neighborhood justice centers will eventually meet their expected goals.

Discussion and review

1. Why is cross examination an effective way to expose false or inaccurate testimony?
2. How does the prosecutor in the American criminal justice system differ from prosecutors in continental Europe and England?
3. What factors can affect the decision by a prosecutor to prosecute a case, reduce charges, or dismiss charges?
4. Why is the prosecutor's office a good stepping stone in American politics?
5. What was the significance of the Supreme Court's *Gideon* v. *Wainwright* decision?
6. What are the major strengths and weaknesses of the public defender system?
7. What are the major strengths and weaknesses of the assigned counsel system?
8. What are the most frequently cited advantages of neighborhood justice centers?

Glossary

Adversary system A system of criminal justice characterized by the testing of propositions by argument and proof.

Assigned counsel system System in which members of the local bar association are appointed to serve as counsel for indigent defendants for little or no compensation.

Bar association A statewide association that is responsible for licensing attorneys, developing and enforcing ethical standards, and examining and making final decisions about charges brought against attorneys.

Case load The number of cases being defended or prosecuted by an attorney at a given time.

Defendant A person charged with a crime.

Defense attorneys Attorneys retained or appointed to defend individuals charged with committing criminal offenses.

District attorney, state attorney Common titles for the position of prosecutor.

Indigent A person that can not afford legal counsel.

Legal aid Legal assistance paid for by the state and made available at little or no cost to defendants unable to afford an attorney.

Legal malpractice Civil action taken against an attorney, usually for some serious failure in the attorney-client relationship (e.g., dishonesty, incompetence, or other acts of misconduct).

Plea bargaining The interaction of the prosecutor, defense counsel, and judge in negotiating a final charge and sentence without resorting to trial.

Power of discretion The legal power inherent in the position of the prosecutor to decide whether or not to initiate criminal action in a case.

Prosecutor An attorney (usually elected) in public office who presents the state's case against individuals charged with crimes against the state.

Public defender system A publicly funded system with a staff of full-time attorneys available to defend indigent persons accused by the state of committing crimes.

References

American Bar Association Project on Standards for Criminal Justice. *Standards Relating to the Administration of Criminal Justice.* Washington, D.C.: American Bar Association, 1974.
Cappelletti, M., and Gordley, J. "Legal Aid: Modern Themes and Variations." *Stanford Law Review*, 24 January 1972, pp. 347–421.
Fuller, L. L. "The Adversary System." In Harold J. Berman (ed.) *Talks on American Law.* New York: Vantage Books, 1960, pp. 30-43.
La Fave, W. L. "The Prosecutor's Discretion in the United States." *American Journal of Comparative Law*, 18 (1970):532–548.
"Lawyers v. Lawyers." *Time* 12 January 1976: 53-55.
Lewis, M., Bundy, W., and Hague, J. R. *An Introduction to the Courts and Judicial Process.* Englewood Cliffs, N.J.: Prentice-Hall, 1978.
McCarthy, J. J. "Dispute Resolution: Seeking Justice Outside the Courtroom." *Corrections Magazine* 8 (1982):33–40.
McGillis, D., and Mullen, J. *Neighborhood Justice Centers: An Analysis of Potential Models.* Washington, D.C.: U.S. Government Printing Office, 1977.
Miller, F. W. *Prosecution: The Decision to Charge a Suspect with a Crime.* Boston, Mass.: Little, Brown, 1969.
National Legal Aid and Defender Association. *Report to the National Defender Conference.* Washington, D.C.: National Defender Project, 1969.
National Commission on Law Observance and Enforcement. *Report on Prosecution.* Washington, D.C.: U.S. Government Printing Office, 1931.
Silverstein, L. *Defense of the Poor in Criminal Cases in American State Courts: A Field Study and Report.* Chicago: American Bar Foundation, 1965.
Swanson, C. R., Chamelin, N. C., and Territo, L. *Criminal Investigation.* 2d ed. New York: Random House, 1981.
Wice, P. B., and Suwak, P. "Current Realities of Public Defender Programs: A National Survey and Analysis." *Criminal Law Bulletin*, 10 (1974):161–83.
Willard, C. A. *Criminal Justice on Trial.* Skokie, Ill.: National Textbook Company, 1976.

Cases

Argersinger v. *Hamlin* 407 U.S. 25, 92 S.Ct. 2006, 32 L.Ed. 2d 530 (1972).
Betts v. *Brady* 316 U.S. 455, 62 S.Ct. 1252, 86 L.Ed. 1595 (1942).
In re Gault 387 U.S. 1, 87 S.Ct. 1428, 18 L.Ed. 2d 527 (1967).
Gideon v. *Wainwright* 372 U.S. 335, 83 S.Ct. 792, 9 L.Ed.2d 799 (1963).
Hamilton v. *Alabama* 368 U.S. 52, 82 S.Ct. 157, 7 L.Ed.2d 114 (1962).
Johnson v. *Zerbst* 304 U.S. 458, 58 S.Ct. 1019, 82 L.Ed. 1461 (1938).
Mempa v. *Rhay* 389 U.S. 128, 88 S.Ct. 254, 19 L.Ed.2d 336 (1967).
Miranda v. *Arizona* 384 U.S. 436, 86 S.Ct. 1602, 16 L.Ed.2d 694 (1966).
Powell v. *Alabama* 287 U.S. 45, 53 S.Ct. 55, 77 L.Ed. 158 (1932).
Wade, U.S. v., 388 U.S. 218, 87 S.Ct. 1926, 18 L.Ed.2d 1149 (1967).

Notes

1. Readers interested in the topics of lawyer training, bar associations, admission to the bar, and so on may wish to review J. J. Bonsignore et al., *Before the Law*, Chap. 3 (Boston, Mass.: Houghton Mifflin, 1977), pp. 173–218, and Herbert Jacob, *Justice in America: Courts, Lawyers, and the Judicial Process*, chap. 4 (Boston, Mass.: Little, Brown, 1978), pp. 45–78.

2. This discussion of prosecutors and the adversary system was adapted, with permission, from the American Bar Association Project on Standards for Criminal Justice, *Standards Relating to the Administration of Criminal Justice*, (Washington, D.C.: American Bar Association, 1974), p. 56. Additional information may also be found in *American Bar Association Standards for Criminal Justice*, second edition (Boston: Little, Brown, 1980).

3. For a more comprehensive treatment of the adversary system and its historical development, see Blair J. Kolasa and Bernadine Meyer, *Legal Systems*, chap. 10 (Englewood Cliffs,

N.J.: Prentice-Hall, 1978), pp. 266–301; Gilbert Stuckey, *Procedures in the Justice System*, chap. 2 (Columbus, Ohio: Charles E. Merrill, 1980), pp. 14–33; and Walter F. Murphy and C. Herman Pritchett, *Courts, Judges and Politics*, chap. 11 (New York: Random House, 1974), pp. 355–79.

4. An interesting treatment of the role of the prosecutor may be found in Edward Eldefonso and Alan R. Coffey, *Criminal Law*, app. B (New York: Harper and Row, 1981), pp. 284–89, and Sheldon Goldman and Austin Sarat, eds. *American Court Systems*, chap. 3 (San Francisco: W. H. Freeman, 1978), pp. 92–121.

5. This discussion of prosecutor discretion was adapted with permission, from the work and references in M. Lewis, W. Bundy, and J. R. Hague, *An Introduction to the Courts and Judicial Process* (Englewood Cliffs, N.J.: Prentice-Hall, 1978), pp. 246–49.

6. This discussion of defense and the accompanying references were adapted, with permission, from the work of C. A. Willard, *Criminal Justice on Trial*, (Skokie, Ill.: National Textbook Company, 1976), pp. 111–21.

7. For an in-depth examination of the public defender system, see Jonathan D. Casper, *American Criminal Justice: The Defendants Perspective*, chap. 4 (Englewood Cliffs, N.J.: Prentice-Hall, 1972), pp. 100–125; Abraham S. Blumberg, ed., *Law and Order: The Scales of Justice* (New Brunswick, N.J.: Transaction Books, 1973), pp. 159–72; and Robert Herman, Eric Single, and John Boston, *Counsel for the Poor* (Lexington, Mass.: Lexington Books, 1977).

8
pretrial procedures

Initiating prosecution in misdemeanor offenses
The complaint
The magistrate

Initiating prosecution in felony offenses
Preliminary hearing
Arraignment

The grand jury

Pretrial motions

Bail or jail?
Types of bail
Conditions of bail
Forfeiture of bail
Defects in the bail system
Bail reform
The issue of preventive detention

Plea negotiation
The negotiation process
Inducement for plea bargaining
Factors in plea negotiation
Reforming plea negotiation

Summary

Issue paper: The bounty hunters and the bail jumper

HOWEVER important the criminal trial[1] by jury may be to the novelist or dramatist, it occupies a relatively minor position in the administration of justice in the United States. In any given year, less than 10 percent of suspects apprehended for serious crimes go through the formal steps of a criminal trial. Thus, much of the criminal process is administrative rather than judicial. That is, the process flow is accomplished through negotiation rather than adversarial proceedings.

The fact that this administrative model is inconsistent with the traditional model of litigated criminal prosecution should not be viewed with alarm. Given the enormous number of cases that must be processed, particularly in metropolitan areas, the resources of the criminal justice system would be strained beyond the breaking point if most cases were not dropped or carried to a negotiated conclusion. The administration of justice would not merely be slowed, it would come to a complete halt. In addition, the facts in many criminal cases are not disputed. The suspect either clearly did or clearly did not commit the offense with which he or she is charged. If the facts are beyond dispute, there is no need for a time-consuming, expensive, and laborious criminal trial.

Most of the important decisions that affect the disposition of a case and the fate of the accused are made during the pretrial period between arrest and trial or plea. By posting bond or by *release on his or her own recognizance (ROR)*, (i.e., a promise to appear at a later date to stand trial) the defendant may be released from custody pending trial. A defendant who is unable to post bail may face the prospect of remaining in detention until the case is tried—a period of weeks or months. The attorney for the defendant may negotiate with the prosecutor during this period to secure a reduced charge or other advantages for the client. Such negotiations—including the practice of plea bargaining—are the topic of fierce debate and continuing controversy within the criminal justice system.

Initiating prosecution in misdemeanor offenses

The process of bringing a criminal offender to justice is put into motion by an arrest. *Arrest* refers to the apprehension or detention of an individual so that he or she is available to answer for an alleged crime. An arrest on a criminal charge can be made upon the issuance of a *warrant*, but a warrant is not absolutely necessary. In fact, most arrests are made without them. A valid warrant may be executed by any law enforcement agent or private citizen to whom the warrant is directed.

A misdemeanor, as we noted in chapter 2, is a less serious offense that may be punished by a fine or incarceration in a city or county jail for a period of less than one year. Prosecution for a misdemeanor is usually initiated by the issuance of a *complaint*. The complaint is usually made by a victim of, or a witness to, the crime. Often, the arresting officer is the complaining witness. After a suspect is arrested, he or she is brought to the police station, detained, and interrogated. Following interrogation, he or she may be released (for lack of evidence of wrongdoing) or *booked* (pressed with formal charges). Following booking, a suspect may be released on his or her own recognizance with a signed promise to appear in court, released on presentation of bail, or locked up to await trial. The choice is made based on the suspect's reputation and the seriousness of the offense.

The complaint

As mentioned, the issuance of a complaint is the basis for proceeding with the prosecution of misdemeanors following arrest. The word *complaint* is somewhat misleading, because it suggests an action taken by the injured party or victim of a crime. Although the victim of the crime may be the complainant, the plaintiff is actually the *people of the state* acting through their lawful representative, the district attorney. It is the public prosecutor, therefore, who issues the complaint in a criminal proceeding. The formal complaint is a written document that (1) alleges the commission of an offense and the aim of the defendant, (2) identifies the time, place, and jurisdiction of the court involved, and (3) is sworn to and signed by the complainant.

A complaint is essentially a justification for the arrest of a defendant so that he or she can be *arraigned*—that is, allowed to enter a plea. There are four questions a prosecutor must ask to determine if a complaint should be prepared:

1 Has a crime (public offense) been committed?
2 Did a particular individual whose identity is known commit the crime?
3 Is there sufficient legally admissible evidence to ensure a conviction?
4 Are there adequate alternatives to prosecution available that are preferable to the formal processing of the offender through the criminal justice system?

Unless the answer to all of these questions is yes a complaint should not be prepared.

The magistrate

In theory, a suspect should be brought before a magistrate or justice of the peace within a "short time" after the arrest. How short is a "short time"? The President's Commission on Law Enforcement and Administration of Justice (*Task Force Report: The Courts*, 1967) reports that, in 1965 in the District of Columbia, 20 percent of the defendants were detained for more than one day between arrest and the initial appearance in court. A study conducted in 1969 by the American Civil Liberties Union (ACLU) indicates that people at that time were still being illegally detained for excessive periods of time without either formal booking or appearance before an inferior court. Even today, it is difficult to claim with assurance that such practices do not occur. Recognizing that there are sometimes plausible reasons for delays—if the arrest occurs on a weekend or holiday, for example—the President's Commission recommended a *maximum* delay of twenty-four hours between arrest and initial appearance. Extensive delays can be grounds for later actions against the state by defendants.

A magistrate has *summary* jurisdiction; that is, he or she is empowered to determine guilt or innocence and can impose minor sentences for petty offenses. In many states, the accused can request a jury trial. For more serious crimes, the magistrate holds a preliminary hearing to determine if sufficient evidence has been presented to justify holding the suspect for further action. Overall, the setting within which misdemeanor justice is administered is not likely to inspire much respect for law or confidence in the impartiality of justice. As Bloch and Geis remark:

> Misdemeanor justice in its usual form is meted out by magistrates or justices of the peace who as often as not appear to have secured their positions because of their political coloration and activity rather than because of their legal acumen, human compassion, or social insight. Misdemeanor justice usually takes place in rather sordid surroundings and involves in many instances defendants who through considerable exposure to its operation have become familiar as the bailiff with its routine. Guilty pleas are the rule (1962, p. 464).

Initiating prosecution in felony offenses

Felony offenses are serious crimes that are punishable by incarceration for a year or more in a state prison or by death in the case of capital offenses (see chapter 2). Some felony offenses are settled by dismissal or by the entrance of a guilty plea at an early stage in the criminal justice process. Cases not settled in one of these ways progress through a series of stages, beginning with the *preliminary hearing* (see **figure 8.1** for a flow chart of the process).

Preliminary hearing

Following arrest, a suspect accused of a felony offense is brought before a lower court for a preliminary hearing. At this point, the state is constrained to show "probable cause" for binding the accused over for trial. The expression "probable cause" has the flavor of legal cant, because it is highly *improbable* that a prosecutor would initiate judicial proceedings without a reasonably strong case. Nevertheless, the legal view persists that the preliminary hearing is of benefit to the accused.

On occasion a prosecutor may ask for a *nolle prosequi*, which signifies that there will be no further action by the prosecution. A "nol pross," as it is known informally, is usually regarded as an acknowledgment that the prosecutor's case has collapsed (perhaps a crucial piece of evidence was lost or stolen, or a key witness died or disappeared before making a deposition).[2] For whatever reason, the prosecutor decides not to pursue the prosecution.

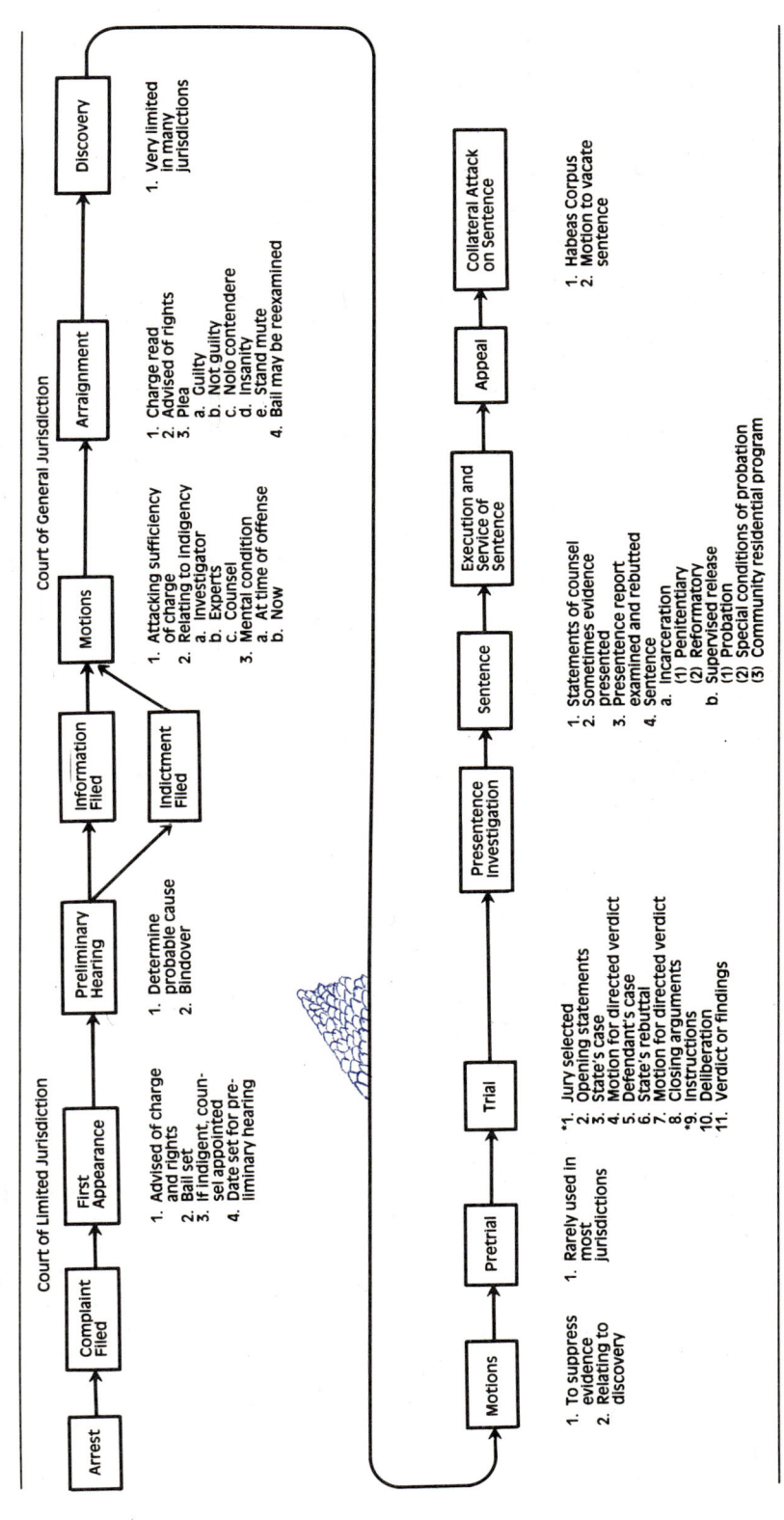

FIGURE 8.1 *Typical progression of criminal felony litigation. Reprinted from H. Ted Rubin, The Courts: Fulcrum of the Justice System (Pacific Palisades, Calif.: Goodyear, 1976), p. 189.*

The state seeks to reveal only enough of its evidence against the accused to support the contention that further prosecution is warranted. Defendants fortunate enough to be represented by alert and experienced counsel may be able to extract additional information from the preliminary hearing, such as the strength of the case presented by the state. Some jurisdictions still fail to provide free attorneys for indigent clients at this early stage of the judicial process, and most unrepresented defendants are not equipped to take full advantage of hearings. Thus, the preliminary hearing tends to weigh heavily on the side of the prosecution. For these and other reasons, the preliminary hearing has been criticized as a moribund procedure that is little more than a dress rehearsal for the prosecution.

After evidence is presented by the prosecution, a judge decides whether there is probable cause to believe that the accused person committed the alleged crime. If the answer is yes, the defendant is bound over for trial; if the answer is no, charges are dismissed and the defendant is released from custody. If the former is the case, the prosecutor files an *information* with the court where the trial will be held. The time period allowed for filing varies from jurisdiction to jurisdiction, but fifteen days from the preliminary hearing is a typical period.

Arraignment

Arraignment refers to the process in which an accused person is brought before the court to answer an indictment or for information. The term has acquired the informal meaning of any appearance before a magistrate or trial court for the purpose of entering a plea. More precisely, it should be restricted in meaning to the appearance of an accused person in a felony case before the magistrate who has the power to receive the defendant's plea. Arraignment usually takes place in the court where a case will be tried. Thus, a defendant usually appears before a different magistrate than the one who handles the case in a lower court.

The prosecutor formally reads in open court the bill of indictment that specifies the charges brought against the accused by the state. The accused is informed again of the constitutional right to be represented by an attorney; if the defendant is indigent and has not already been assigned counsel, an attorney will be appointed at this time.

The defendant may enter a plea of either guilty or not guilty. In some states, other options may be available: not guilty by reason of insanity, former jeopardy, and *nolo contendere*, for example. The plea of nolo contendere in a criminal proceeding is generally regarded as a guilty plea, although in some states it means simply that the defendant does not understand the charges. The chief advantage of a nolo contendere plea is that is may spare the defendant from certain civil penalties that might follow a guilty plea. Thus, a nolo contendere plea is likely to be entered in situations in which, in addition to criminal sanctions, the defendant is liable to prosecution for civil damages, (e.g., cases involving embezzlement or fraud). The nolo contendere plea can only be entered at the discretion of the prosecutor and the judge. Another option available to the defendant is "standing mute." However, in many jurisdictions, the court will automatically enter a plea of guilty if the accused fails to enter a plea.

Before a plea of guilty will be accepted by the court, certain conditions must be met. The plea must be entered voluntarily and the defendant must be aware of the implications of the plea. *A guilty plea is considered equivalent to a verdict of guilty.* The court may deliver a sentence at the time of the plea or set a date for sentencing.

The grand jury

The function of the *grand jury* is to investigate criminal charges to determine if a defendant should be brought to trial. The Fifth Amendment states that "no person shall be held to answer for a capital or otherwise infamous charge unless on a presentment or indictment of a grand jury." According to Bloch and Geis, "grand juries were intended to allow the defendant to avoid a public accusation and the trouble and expense of a public trial before establishing the likelihood of his having committed the crime. They were also intended to prevent hasty, oppressive, and malicious prosecutions" (1972, p. 481).

The grand jury does not seek to determine guilt or innocence; rather it duplicates in many respects the function of the preliminary hearing. The only major difference is that the defendant has no legal right to be present at grand jury deliberations. Thus, the decision to indict or not to indict is made solely on the evidence presented by the prosecuting attorney.

If a grand jury is convinced by the prosecutor's evidence that a *prima facie* case has been made (i.e., that so far as can be judged on its face value, the evidence will prevail as proof of the facts in issue unless or until it is contradicted or overcome by other evidence) a "true bill" of indictment will be returned, indicating probable cause to proceed to trial. If, on the other hand, the grand jury is not persuaded by the prosecutor's evidence, it can ignore the charges by returning a "no bill" finding, in which case the prosecutor may charge the defendant with a lesser offense. In the majority of indictments, the grand jury follows the inclination of the prosecutor. Most states require a preliminary examination prior to charging in felony offenses. Grand jury indictments are a statutory requirement in about half the states.

Pretrial motions

It is fairly standard for defense attorneys to move for the dismissal of charges against their clients even before a plea is entered. The general strategy is to attack the information or indictment, claiming improprieties in the organization or methods of the grand jury. Other possible grounds for a motion to dismiss are prior jeopardy and the statute of limitations (the latter is used if the law under which the accused has been charged is no longer valid).

A more effective pretrial motion is one requesting the state to reveal information or evidence that the prosecution has gathered against the defendant. This is called a motion for a *bill of particulars.* If some or all of the evidence was obtained illegally—as has been the case in a number of prosecutions involving drugs—there is a good chance that the case will be thrown out.

If, because of adverse pretrial publicity, the accused and the defense attorney believe it is impossible to receive a fair trial in the area where the crime was committed, the defense attorney may move for a *change of venue.* Despite the attention paid to such motions in media coverage of criminal trials—sensational ones—this motion is made rather infrequently. Equally infrequent are motions seeking a separate trial in cases with codefendants.

Bail or jail?

Once it has been determined that there is probable cause to bind a defendant over to the grand jury, it is the function of the lower-court magistrate to set bail. *Bail* is a legal procedure for securing temporary liberty following arrest through a written promise to appear in court as required. In support of this promise, it may be necessary to provide cash bail, post a surety bond, or supply evidence of an equity in real property, together with the written assurance of another person or persons.

The basic purpose of bail is to furnish a means for the release of a detained individual while his or her case is pending, provided the accused is ready to give reasonable and sufficient assurance of a willingness to appear in court at the appropriate time. In providing for release on bail, the presumption of innocence goes beyond its well-known place in trial proceedings (i.e., the necessity for proof of guilt beyond a reasonable doubt), emphasizing that, in American criminal jurisprudence, guilt is the decision of the court and is not inherent in prosecution. At the federal level, release on bail in noncapital cases is a constitutional right.

Types of bail

Release on bail may involve the posting of a formal bond for the amount of the bail (along with sureties as "guarantors"), the deposit of cash bail without sureties, or release upon personal recognizance. These forms of bail have been around since colonial times. The so-called schedule of bail contains a list of misdemeanors and the amount of bail required for release. It may also specify a standard amount of bail for release or for all misdemeanor offenses not listed in the schedule.

Conditions of bail

During the post-arrest period of detention, the amount of bail depends upon the severity of the offense, whether the arrest was made with or without a warrant, and whether or not the defendant has been arraigned. When an arrest is made on a warrant alleging a public offense, bail should be in the amount specified on the warrant's endorsement by the issuing magistrate. When the arrest is for a misdemeanor, the amount of bail should be fixed by the magistrate at the time of arraignment. Prior to arraignment, bail should be set as fixed in the arrest warrant. If arrest is made without a warrant, the amount of bail should coincide with the nationwide schedule of bail for misdemeanors. For a felony arrest, bail should be fixed by the judge before whom the prisoner is arraigned upon the formal complaint; prior to the arraignment, bail should be set as stated on the arrest warrant. If, without sufficient excuse, a defendant fails to appear as required in the bail agreement, or upon any other occasion when his or her presence in court is required by law, the court will enter the fact in its minutes and will declare forfeited the undertaking of bail or the cash bail deposited. If the amount of the bail or deposit exceeds fifty dollars, the bondsman or depositor must be notified.

Forfeiture of bail

After a forfeiture of bail, the bondsman or depositor has 180 days in which to adjust the forfeiture. One of three procedures can be followed: (1) the defendant and the bondsman or depositor appear in court and provide an acceptable explanation or justification for the defendant's neglect, or satisfactorily indicate to the court that the absence was not with the connivance of the bondsman or depositor; (2) the bondsman may appear in court and certify that the defendant is dead or physically unable to appear during the time period allowed; and (3) the defendant may be turned over to the court.

Defects in the bail system

When an accused person lacks financial resources, the bail system adds a discriminatory element to the administration of criminal justice. In his 1964 review of major findings about the bail systems of New York and Philadelphia, Johnson noted that many defendants were unable to furnish bail, especially when bail was set above $1,000. Bail usually was set so high for serious offenses that few defendants in the cases obtained pretrial release. And from 10 to 20 percent of defendants incarcerated pending trial were not convicted. For similar crimes, Johnson noted that jailed offenders were more likely to be convicted and to receive longer sentences than offenders released on bail. Why? The indigent defendant is unable to hire a lawyer, locate witnesses, and pay for the investigation necessary to present his or her case adequately, especially when incarceration pending trial interrupts normal earnings. The appearance of the defendant in court under guard may have an adverse effect on the jury. Even when convicted, the bailed defendant has the advantage of showing evidence of steady employment and good conduct while awaiting trial. Such evidence supports a plea for probation.

Another defect in the bail system is that it encourages criminality: bondsmen are willing to set bail for thieves, even if they lack the cash or collateral to pay it back. This puts a thief in the position of having to acquire a large sum of money in a very short time after having been arrested. Thus, bond money is not always come by honestly. For short-term bail bonds, a bondsman is usually permitted to charge an interest rate of 10 to 20 percent, depending on state regulations. Thus, if a person is arrested and bond is set at $25,000, he or she must pay the bondsman between $2,500 and $5,000 for the "loan" (surety) of $25,000. This money may also be raised by illegal means.

And there is yet another way that the bail system encourages crime. Persons arrested, even professional thieves, do not always know where and from whom to get bond. Because jailers, sheriffs, and police officers are in a position to recommend bondsmen, the stage is set for an escalating system of gifts and payoffs for the recommendation of one bondsman over another (Chambliss 1969). However, many progressive law enforcement agencies prohibit this dubious practice.

Bail reform

In 1961, a wealthy New York businessman named Louis Schweitzer visited the Brooklyn House of Detention, one of the city's largest jails. Appalled by the number of people who were incarcerated pending trial because they were too poor to afford bail, Schweitzer created the Vera Foundation (named in honor of his wife). Using his own money, he set out to provide assistance for defendants who were unable to post bail. Within six months, the Vera Foundation—later renamed the Vera Institute of Justice—launched the Manhattan Bail Project. According to Thomas, "the idea behind the project proved as powerful in practice as it was simple in concept. The project was to provide information to the court about the defendant's ties to community and thereby hope that the court would release the defendant without requiring a bail bond" (1976, p. 4).

Schweitzer's project was administered in cooperation with the Institute of Judicial Administration and student assistants from New York University Law School. Originally, the plan had been to provide a revolving bail fund for indigent defendants; but this plan was soon rejected on the grounds that it merely perpetuated reliance upon money as the criterion for pretrial release. In its place, the Vera Institute sought to expand the idea of release on recognizance by implementing appropriate controls and screening techniques.

The process worked like this: When a prisoner was brought in for booking and detention prior to the first court appearance, a staff member of the institute checked his or her previous record and current charge with the arresting officer to see if bail was possible in the initial arraignment. Crimes considered not bailable included homicide, most narcotic offenses, and certain sex offenses (Sturz 1965). If the offense was bailable, the defendant was interviewed to determine if he was working, how long he had held the job, whether he supported a family, whether he had contacts with relatives in the city, how long he had lived in the city, and how long he had lived at his present address.

Based on the interview, the accused was scored on a point-weighting system. If he or she appeared to be a good risk for release on recognizance, the rating and a summary of the information were provided to the bench at the initial arraignment. Thus, release rested finally with the judge. (See **figure 8.2** for a sample form granting release on recognizance.) When a defendant was released, a staff member of the institute would notify him or her in writing of the date and location of subsequent court appearances. If the defendant was illiterate, he or she was notified by telephone and a follow-up letter was sent to establish an official record of the transaction.

During the first year of the project, half of the cases recommended for release on recognizance were set aside as a control group and were not recommended to the court. This was to determine how accused persons who met the institute's release standards fared without a recommendation. The court granted release on recognizance in 60 percent of the cases in which an actual recommendation was made and in only 14 percent of the control cases. In the next two years of operation, the number of releases increased because of two factors: (1) greater proficiency in screening with a more subjective set of standards; and (2) greater reliance by the court upon the institute's recommendations (Sturz 1965).

By 1965, the Manhattan Bail Project was considered so successful that it was transferred to the New York City Office of Probation and made a part of routine court procedure. The work of the Vera Institute generated nationwide interest in bail reform. In 1964, with the endorsement of Attorney General Robert F. Kennedy and Chief Justice Earl Warren of the U.S. Supreme Court, the National Conference on Bail and Criminal Justice was convened in Washington, D.C. On the eve of the conference, Senator Sam Ervin introduced a series of bills intended to reform bail practices in the federal courts. The resulting passage of the federal Bail Reform Act of 1966, the first major change in national bail policy since 1789, led to the revision of bail laws in at least a dozen states within five years. Today, release on recognizance is a standard form of pretrial release in jurisdictions throughout the nation.

In 1963, dissatisfied with the commercial bail system in Chicago, the state of Illinois initiated legislation known as the Illinois Ten Percent Deposit Plan. This legislation retained money as the prevailing form of surety release, but it required that a defendant pay the 10 percent bonding fee directly to the court rather than to a commercial bail bondsman. Upon completion of the case, the money was refunded to the defendant, minus a service fee of only 1 percent. The result, as Thomas (1976) notes, was the complete demise of professional bail bondsmen in the state of Illinois.

The issue of preventive detention

One of the continuing impediments to bail reform is the fear that individuals charged with serious crimes, especially crimes against the person, will be free to commit further crimes if they are released on bail or upon their

IN THE CIRCUIT/COUNTY COURT OF THE SIXTH JUDICIAL CIRCUIT
OF THE STATE OF FLORIDA IN AND FOR PINELLAS COUNTY

COURT NO. _____

STATE OF FLORIDA

VS.

_____

I, _____, do hereby request that I be released on my own recognizance with the understanding that I will appear at any time or place the Court or its official may direct. Further, I agree to comply with the following conditions:

(a) I agree not to leave Pinellas County, Florida, or change my residence without first getting permission of the Court Investigator.

(b) I will notify my attorney of my release on my own recognizance immediately upon release.

(c) I will report to the Court Investigator, Room #A-207, Criminal Courts, 5100 144th Avenue North, Clearwater, Florida, as directed on each <u>Monday</u> preceding a final disposition in all cases. PHONE: 530-6410.

(d) Further, I hereby agree to any and all other conditions that the Court may see fit to impose, as listed below:

(e) Gainfully employed.

(f)

(g)

I understand that any violation of the above conditions of release under this Order will be punishable as a Contempt of Court, and that I will also be subject to being recommitted to custody. I also understand that being arrested while released on my own recognizance may result in my Release on Recognizance being revoked.

I understand that criminal charges arising from and related to my arrest may be prosecuted by the State of Florida in the Circuit and/or County Court in and for Pinellas County, Florida and that I must, and will, appear in either Court as may hereafter be required by either Court.

I have read the above conditions and fully understand them, and agree to abide by them, and to be in Court on the day indicated below.

DUE IN COURT: On Call of Court.

_____
DEFENDANT

WITNESS: _____
_____
DATE

<u>ORDER GRANTING RECOGNIZANCE</u>

The Court after being advised concerning the above matter does hereby Order the above named defendant to be released on the defendant's own recognizance this _____ day of _____.

_____
CIRCUIT/COUNTY JUDGE

cc: State Attorney
    Sheriff
    Defendant
    Court Investigator

(rev.) 4-82

FIGURE 8.2 *Sample order for release on recognizance*

own recognizance. It was this kind of fear that led Congress in March of 1970 to pass a bill authorizing preventive detention in the District of Columbia—where crime had been depicted by the news media as being "out of control"—for a period of up to sixty days without bond for defendants charged with crimes of violence and "dangerous" crimes. The bill drew the wrathful thunder of Senator Sam Ervin, long recognized as a staunch opponent of preventive detention:

> Preventive detention is not only repugnant to our traditions, but it will handicap an accused person and his lawyer in preparing his case for trial. It will result in the incarceration of many innocent persons.
>
> If America is to remain a free society, it will have to take certain risks. One is the risk that a person admitted to bail may flee before trial. Another is the risk that a person admitted to bail may commit a crime while free on bail.
>
> In my judgment, it is better for our country to take these risks and remain in a free society than it is to adopt a tyrannical practice of imprisoning men for crimes which they have not committed and may never commit merely because some court may peer into the future and surmise that they may commit crimes if allowed freedom prior to trial and conviction (*Hearings on Preventive Detention*, p. 3, 1970).

In a study of Washington's preventive detention law, Bases and McDonald (1974) report that, during the first ten months of operation, the program resulted in the detention of only 10 of 6,000 felony defendants. And at present, when jails throughout the country are under pressure to reduce overcrowding, it is not likely that many jurisdictions will advocate more of such legislation.

Plea negotiation

Prosecutors are legally empowered to negotiate with defendants and their attorneys. These negotiations are likely to be much more informal during the pretrial period than at a later stage when the court becomes officially involved via the trial. Plea negotiation fulfills various purposes, the most important of which are (1) improving the administrative efficiency of the courts, (2) lowering the cost of prosecution, and (3) permitting the prosecution to devote additional time to more important and more serious cases (Wheatley 1974).

As mentioned earlier, prosecutors prefer to pursue cases that have a good chance for conviction. Thus, because many major crimes include the elements of lesser crimes (e.g., murder and manslaughter), prosecutors with shaky cases may accept a guilty plea to "lesser included offenses" to save the time, money, and risk of a trial for a major crime. They may also offer various incentives to the accused to elicit information about other offenders or to induce them to give testimony that will help the prosecution. One such incentive is an offer to accept a plea of guilty to a lesser charge (called *reduction in charge*); another is immunity from further prosecution on the incidental charge. Thus, a number of misdemeanors begin as felony charges: drunken driving may be reduced to "reckless driving," or statutory rape may be reduced to "contributing to the delinquency of a minor." At arraignment, the defendant and counsel may attempt to bargain for a *reduction in sentence*. Other types of plea negotiation or plea bargaining include bargaining for concurrent charges, and bargaining for dropped charges.

> 1. *Bargain Concerning the Charge.* A plea of guilty was entered by the offenders in exchange for a reduction of the charge from the one alleged in the complaint. This ordinarily occurred in cases where the offense in question carried statutory degrees of severity such as homicide, assault, and sex offenses....
>
> 2. *Bargain Concerning the Sentence.* A plea of guilty was entered by the offenders in exchange for a promise of leniency in sentencing. The most commonly accepted consideration was a promise that the offender would be placed on probation, although a less-than-maximum prison term was the basis in certain instances. All offenses except murder, serious assault, and robbery were represented in this type of bargaining process....
>
> 3. *Bargain for Concurrent Charges.* This type of informal process occurred chiefly among offenders pleading without counsel. These men exchanged guilty pleas for the concurrent pressing of multiple charges, generally numerous counts of the same offense or related violations such as breaking and entering and larceny. This method, of course, has much the same effect as pleading for consideration in the sentence. The offender with concurrent convictions, however, may not be serving a reduced sentence; he is merely serving one sentence for many crimes....
>
> 4. *Bargain for Dropped Charges.* This . . . involved an agreement on the part of the prosecution not to press formally one or more charges against the offender if he in turn pleaded guilty to (usually) the major offense. The offenses dropped were extraneous law violations contained in, or accompanying, the offense alleged in the complaint such as auto theft accompanying armed robbery and violation of probation where a new crime had been committed.... (Reproduced from D. J. Newman, "Pleading Guilty for Considerations: A Study of Bargain Justice," *Journal of Criminal Law, Criminology, and Police Science* 46 [1956]:787, by permission of the author and the publisher.)

The practice of plea bargaining has been both attacked and defended by a wide variety of legal and criminal justice authorities. In 1973, the National Advisory Commision on Criminal Justice Standards and Goals referred to it as a "notorious" practice and recommended that it be completely abolished by 1978.[3] The U.S. Supreme Court, on the other hand—in *Santobello* v. *New York*, 404 U.S. 257 (1971)—held that plea negotiation is a legitimate means to secure a guilty plea from a criminal defendant.

Plea negotiation has defenders among criminal justice personnel and legal authorities for many reasons: society's need to dispose of criminal charges without incurring the expense of a trial; a defendant's willingness to plead guilty; the administrative burden that would be imposed by a large number of trials if plea negotiation were not permitted; the enhanced opportunity for rehabilitation of the offender in the event of an agreed-upon disposition; and the chance to individualize punishment, thus lessening the bitterness felt by many defendants after trial. And plea negotiation is also attractive to the defendant. For a guilty party, a negotiated plea may prevent a long stay in jail awaiting trial, the notoriety and stigma of a criminal trial, and, most importantly, the chance for a minimum sentence.

The negotiation process

Some prosecutors claim that they never allow a plea to be negotiated until or unless they have decided that the defendant is guilty. This reflects a sense of responsibility on the part of the prosecutor that precludes the use of plea bargaining to coerce or pressure an innocent defendant into pleading guilty. However, because a prosecutor is a lawyer who is responsible for representing the state in its prosecution of criminals, a determination should be made not with regard to a defendant's *guilt*, but with regard to a defendant's *innocence*. If the defendant maintains innocence and the prosecutor believes him or her, plea bargaining should not be used to induce the defendant to take the easy way out.

Inducement for plea bargaining

Prosecutors frequently charge the accused with as many offenses as possible. This has been called "horizontal overcharging." Another device, "vertical overcharging," is the practice of charging a suspect with a higher offense than is warranted by the evidence. The practice of overcharging is thought to be widespread, because it allows the prosecutor an advantage: in reality, the prosecutor is not bargaining anything away. If the offense charged does not reflect what the prosecutor really intends to pursue, then it can be argued that the prosecutor is negating the defendant's rights. The defense attorney may be aware that the client is being overcharged, but is nevertheless unable to predict the outcome if he or she decides to recommend that the client stand trial.

Factors in plea negotiation

According to Mather (1979), the following variables are most frequently identified as having a significant influence on case disposition:

1. Case load of the prosecutor
2. Strength or weakness of the case
3. Type of defense attorney
4. Personal characteristics of the defendant (e.g., age, race, prior record, bail status)
5. Type of crime

What is not clear from research is the relative importance of these factors in determining case disposition; nor is it clear how these factors are weighted when seen from the different viewpoints of perspectives of the principals in the negotiations: the prosecutor, the defense counsel, and the defendant.

In 1970-71, in an effort to clarify these issues as they affect the dynamics of plea bargaining, Mather conducted an empirical study of case dispositions in Los Angeles County Superior Court. She found that decisions by prosecutors in Los Angeles were based primarily upon substantive concerns for appropriate punishment or an interest in securing convictions. And she stressed the *un*importance of case load as a factor in plea negotiation, a finding consistent with the studies of Eisenstein and Jacob (1977), Feeley (1975), Heumann (1975), Levin (1977), and Rosett and Cressey (1976). Mather also noted that the type of attorney—whether a public defender or a private lawyer—did not appear to make a difference in the decision to plea bargain or to stand trial. In 1974, Lehtinen and Smith analyzed felony dispositions in Los Angeles and found only marginal differences in sentences. In addition, they suggested that "it does not really matter in the actual results whether convicted offenders are represented by public defenders or private attorneys" (p. 17). (See chapter 7 for a further discussion of this issue.)

Based on these studies, the two factors that appear to have the greatest influence on case disposition are the seriousness of the case and the strength of the case. "Serious" cases are distinguished from "light" cases on the basis of the likelihood that the defendant will receive a severe sentence. Says Mather:

> There are two attributes by which cases are routinely identified as "serious." First, a mandatory felony offense creates a presumption of seriousness because lenient sentences are less common on these offenses. More specifically, those mandatory felony offenses which *typically* receive severe sentences are generally described as "serious." This includes homicide, robbery, kidnapping, sale of opiates, forcible rape, and lewd acts with child. Second, a bad criminal record for a defendant (particularly a prior felony conviction) indicates that his case is "serious," regardless of his charged offense (1979, p. 40).

In Mather's study, the strength of the prosecution's case was based on the amount and type of evidence in relation to how such evidence would be perceived by the judge and jury with regard to the issue of reasonable doubt. Thus, three kinds of cases were identified based on chance of conviction:

1. *"Dead bang" cases.* Cases in which there was a very high probability of conviction because the prosecution possessed physical evidence such as fingerprints, contraband found on the defendant, stolen goods, and canceled checks (in forgery cases).
2. *"Overfiled reasonable doubt" cases.* Cases in which the defendant was charged in the first degree, but where the evidence was only strong enough to convict in the second degree. For example, a public defender said, "On murder cases, there may be reasonable doubt on first degree, but they're definitely gonna get him on second degree or manslaughter. It's the same with first degree burglary or robbery" (Mather 1979, p. 43).
3. *"Reasonable doubt" cases.* Cases in which there was insufficient evidence to connect the defendant with the crime or to prove that any crime had been committed. Included in this category were cases where

the reputation and demeanor of the defendant and victim were crucial to the determination of credibility (e.g., sex offenses [rape, sex perversion, child molestation] and assault cases). Such cases present good prospects of acquittal because the conflict typically is between the testimonies of the victim and the defendant.

Table 8.1 shows the disposition of cases in Mather's study as they were affected by the strength and seriousness of the case—together with the convergence of views between the prosecutor and defense counsel.

Reforming plea negotiation

Suggested reforms in plea negotiation—as contrasted with the complete elimination of the practice as recommended by the National Advisory Commission on Criminal Justice Standards and Goals (1973)—generally emphasize the formulation of explicit guidelines for the negotiations. Here is one prosecutor's version of such guidelines:

1. General principles under which plea negotiation is to be conducted should be stated, preferably in writing, and should include how and why plea negotiation is to be carried out.
2. The prosecutor will discuss the possibility of plea negotiation with each defense counsel, recognizing that plea negotiation may not be appropriate in every case.
3. Plea negotiation should be conducted between the defense counsel and the prosecutor without direct intervention of the defendant, except for those rare cases in which the defendant chooses to represent himself or herself.

TABLE 8.1 Recommendations by defense attorneys on method of disposition as a function of strength of prosecution's case, seriousness of case, and convergence of district attorney and defense attorney views

Strength of prosecution's case (prediction of conviction or acquittal)	"Light" case	Seriousness of case (prediction of severity of sentence) "Serious" case — If district attorney and defense attorney views converge	"Serious" case — If district attorney and defense attorney views diverge
"Dead bang" case	Negotiated disposition (implicit bargaining)	Negotiated disposition (explicit bargaining)	Trial
"Reasonable doubt"—chance of conviction on lesser charge	Negotiated disposition (implicit or explicit bargaining)	Negotiated disposition (explicit bargaining—convergence more likely here than above)	Trial
"Reasonable doubt"—chance of complete acquittal	Indeterminate	Negotiated disposition (explicit bargaining)	Indeterminate

Adapted from L. M. Mather, *Plea Bargaining or Trial?* (Lexington, Mass.: Lexington Books, 1979), p. 66, by permission of the author and the publisher.

4 Plea negotiation should be accompanied by full disclosure, with the exception that, in the event that negotiation does not lead to an agreement, the information discovered will not be used subsequently to the detriment of the defendant.

5 Time requirements should be established to encourage negotiation and agreement before a case is set for trial.

6 A prenegotiation report should be prepared by the office of the prosecutor to determine whether negotiation would serve any useful purpose in the particular case.

7 The prosecutor must determine which charges may be reduced and to what degree.

8 Overcharging to force defendants to enter a guilty plea should be eliminated.

9 Judicial participation in the negotiation process should be prohibited.

10 The defendant must acknowledge his or her guilt in open court before the plea will be accepted.

11 The agreement must be reduced to writing and submitted to the court for acceptance or rejection.

12 Trial court must have available all of its discretion in accepting or rejecting a plea.

Mather feels that most proposals of this kind fail to reach the core of the negotiating process: "the discussions of the defendant's character and the interpretation of his offense to reach decisions on the proper sentence" (1979, p. 146). Efforts to formalize and legalize plea negotiation, as Rosett and Cressey observe, ensure "that defendants are not openly told lies about the consequences of a guilty plea, but [do not] ensure that the punishments they receive are either appropriate or fair" (1976, p. 172).

THE VICE PRESIDENT OF THE UNITED STATES COPS A PLEA

In October of 1973, Vice President Spiro T. Agnew became the first Vice President of the United States to leave office under a cloud of criminal charges. The judicial settlement of the Agnew case was brief but dramatic. At the same time the Vice President's resignation was being announced in Washington, he was appearing in person before U.S. District Court Judge Walter E. Hoffman in a Baltimore courtroom. Mr. Agnew pleaded *nolo contendere*—no contest—to one charge: that he had failed to report some $29,500 of income received in 1967 while serving as Governor of Maryland, and thus evaded paying taxes of some $13,500. In return for that plea, all other charges were dropped.

Judge Hoffman, stating that the plea of *nolo contendere* "is the full equivalent of a plea of guilty," promptly sentenced Mr. Agnew to pay a fine of $10,000 and to be placed under probation—without supervision—for three years. No prison sentence was imposed. It was Attorney General Elliot L. Richardson who formally recommended that the sentence "not include confinement" of the Vice President, and the judge agreed. Usually, the judge commented, he would impose a prison term in a case such as that of Mr. Agnew. "However," Judge Hoffman said, "I am persuaded that the national interests in the present case are so great and so compelling . . . that the ends of justice would be better served by making an exception to the general rule. I therefore approve the plea agreement between the parties." That agreement, the judge said, "provides that the Federal Government will take no further action against the defendant as to any federal criminal charge which had its inception prior to today."

The next day, Maryland Attorney General Francis C. Burch announced that he would recommend no prosecution be undertaken against Mr. Agnew in State courts. Mr. Agnew "has suffered enough," he said. Thus Mr. Agnew was virtually assured that he will never go to prison for any of the charges to far made against him. . . .

Reprinted from U.S. News and World Report, 22 October 1973, p. 18, by permission of the publisher.

Mather advocates any reforms in criminal procedure that might help to lessen the isolation and alienation of defendants in court. She was disturbed by the exclusion of defendants from active participation in the "court culture": "Despite the court's ostensible focus on the 'rehabilitation' of the defendant through extensive use of probation and other alternatives to incarceration, the defendant himself was seen as an outsider" (1979, p. 147). Her recommendation that the defendant should be allowed to participate actively in the plea bargaining process in suported by Norval Morris, who believes that plea bargaining should involve the judge and the victim. Bringing the accused and the victim together has the obvious advantage, according to Morris, of permitting them to see one another as human beings, not faceless entities: He views a pretrial settlement in which the victim takes part as an opportunity for the convicted criminal, in or out of prison, to get an immediate start in the process of self-reformation.

Summary

During the past two decades it has been recognized that the period from arrest to trial (or acceptance of a guilty plea) is perhaps the most crucial phase in the criminal process. This pretrial period is the time when many important decisions are made about what will happen to the defendant. If the grand jury proceeding or preliminary hearing results in sufficient evidence to charge the individual with a crime (i.e., a finding of "probable cause"), the defendant is arraigned and given the opportunity to enter a plea to the charges. He is informed of his constitutional rights, particularly as to representation by counsel, and may be placed in confinement, freed on bail, or released on his own recognizance.

The two critical issues which arise during the pretrial period both involve discretion. The first of these is pretrial release. A defendant who is detained in jail suffers adverse consequences from the experience, but his individual plight has to be weighed against the possibility that his release will result in further danger to society. The second issue is plea negotiation. Since the criminal justice system lacks the resources to try every person accused of a crime, the practice of plea negotiation—despite its critics and detractors—is seen as an essential element in the administrative disposition of a large percentage of cases.

issue paper

THE BOUNTY HUNTERS AND THE BAIL JUMPER

Most Americans think that the bounty hunter is a relic of the frontier. However, there is a modern counterpart to this figure from Wild West movies: the bail bondsman in hot pursuit of the bail jumper. On 7 February 1983, CBS's "Sixty Minutes" related the tale of two present-day bounty hunters whose exploits in retrieving a fugitive from Canada caused an international incident.

The story began in Palatka, Florida, where a real estate entrepreneur named Sidney Jaffe was arrested for illegal land dealings. Prosecutors charged him in April 1981 with twenty-eight violations of Florida law for giving quitclaim deeds rather than warranty deeds to people who bought lots in a development in Putnam County near Palatka. The quitclaim deeds were no protection against mortgages that still encumbered the land, as outraged buyers soon discovered. Jaffe's lawyers claimed that the case should have been treated as a civil dispute rather than a crime, especially because Jaffe did not own the real estate company at the outset of the transactions.

Jaffe posted a $137,500 bond and returned to Canada, where he had lived since 1966. (He was granted citizenship not too long after the Florida charges were filed.) He failed to show up for trial in May 1981, sending a physician's statement that he was unable to travel. Circuit Court Judge Robert Perry refused a continuance and declared the bond forfeited. Prosecutors then asked Governor Bob Graham to seek Jaffe's extradition, but the governor's office turned them down twice on the advice of the Florida Attorney General, who stated that the applications for extradition had not been filled out properly.

At this point, according to sworn testimony from a Palatka lawyer named Miller (who was representing the bail firm), two assistant state attorneys encouraged the bondsmen to take the law into their own hands. "Why don't y'all go get him?" was what the prosecutors were supposed to have said. At any rate, the bail firm sent two experienced bounty hunters named Timm Johnsen and Daniel Kerr to Canada to bring Jaffe back.

In Toronto, the bounty hunters grabbed Jaffe at the entrance to his apartment and hustled him into the back seat of a rented Datsun from which the inside door handles had been removed. They they whizzed across the U.S.-Canadian border to a waiting airplane and took off for Orlando, Florida. Jaffe was tried and convicted in February 1982 and was given sentences totaling 145 years, 35 of them to be served consecutively. This is a harsher sentence than is received by many armed robbers. Jaffe's lawyers subsequently argued in federal court, without success, that the state had no right to try Jaffe because of the way he was returned to Florida. According to a traditional tenet of American law, however, it does not really matter *how* a defendant is dragged into court.

Nevertheless, the issue of Jaffe's guilt or innocence quickly took second place to the fact that he was seized and brought back to the United States in flagrant violation of Canadian law. The Canadian government in Ottawa reacted with understandable indignation and demanded the extradition of the bounty hunters, Johnsen and Kerr, for trial in Canada as kidnappers. U.S. Secretary of State George Schultz asked Florida to release Jaffe from prison, claiming that his incarceration is deleterious to U.S.-Canadian relations. Today, as Florida continues to be the target of bad publicity in the Canadian press, Jaffe languishes in Avon Park Correctional Institution in Avon Park, Florida. And state and federal officials continue to disclaim responsibility for rectifying Jaffe's abduction. In this bizarre affair, Florida justice has managed to make Jaffe look like a martyr.

Apart from the complex tangle of legal issues involved in extradition, the Jaffe case provides a graphic demonstration of the almost complete immunity enjoyed by the bail bondsman in the retrieval of fugitives who flee to avoid prosecution. Incredible though it may sound, the bondsman wields extraordinary powers to arrest a fugitive defendant (bail jumper) and to surrender the defendant to the custody of a law enforcement officer. This power is not based on any authority given to the bondsman by the state in the form of police powers; instead, it derives from the private contract between the accused and the bondsman (in the form of surety on the bail bond). Compared with the severe constraints under which sworn police officers must operate in the retrieval of fugitives, the bondsman's power to arrest, imprison, and transport an accused person across state lines is practically unlimited.

Murphy refers to the arrest and custody power of bondsmen as "a degenerate vestige of a bail relationship between defendant and surety that either perished or never gained footing in this country" (1975, p. 40). Nevertheless, the courts have consistently upheld this power in cases where fugitives have been taken at gunpoint, handcuffed or shackled to the floor of an automobile, beaten severely, and driven long distances without food or water in order to secure the remission of a $100 or $200 misdemeanor bond.

Bondsmen have contended that they perform a valuable service to the state by functioning as custodians of released defendants and hunters of fugitive defendants at no cost to the public. This contention, Murphy claims, is myth. The interest of the bondsman in retrieving fugitives is financial, not judicial. If that interest can be served by some means other than tracking down and returning the fugitive, the bondsman is unlikely to have any strong inclination to see that the defendant appears for trial.

Whenever bail bondsmen are prosecuted for such abuses as fee splitting, bribery, and "fixing" of minor criminal cases, a fine or some other punitive action soothes the public and presumably restores the theoretical purity of the bail system. However, reformers such as Thomas (1976) maintain that it is not abuses in the bail system that constitute the problem: it is the system itself. In Murphy's (1975) view, any reform that leaves the bondsman with undiminished powers of arrest and custody is an exercise in futility. He argues that the answer lies in adjusting the official retrieval system to increase efficiency without causing a corresponding loss of civil liberties—a move that could encourage the final replacement of bondsmen with police officers, a socially acceptable goal.

Discussion and review

1. How is prosecution initiated in felony cases? How is prosecution initiated in misdemeanor cases?
2. What are the four basic questions a prosecutor must answer to determine if a complaint should be prepared?
3. What is summary jurisdiction?
4. Are there any advantages for the defendant in the preliminary hearing? What are the advantages for the prosecution?
5. What are the major functions and responsibilities of the grand jury?
6. Describe the principal alternatives to pretrial incarceration (such as bail, or release on recognizance).
7. What are some of the major inequities of the bail system?
8. Briefly describe the Manhattan Bail Project. What was its significance for bail reform in the United States?
9. What is a plea of nolo contendere? How does it differ in consequence from a guilty plea?
10. What are the four types of plea negotiation described by Newman?
11. What are some of the important advantages of plea bargaining for the prosecutor and the defendant?
12. What are the principal factors that appear to affect plea bargaining? How significant were these factors in the findings of Lynn Mather?
13. In terms of the Jaffe case, discuss the issues raised by the actions of bondsmen ("bounty hunters") in retrieving fugitives.

Glossary

Arraignment The event that formally initiates the trial process. The first official occasion in which the accused is given an opportunity to establish his or her identity and enter a plea in response to the accusation. *Arraignment* takes place in the court where the case is to be tried.

Arrest The taking of a person into legal custody for the purpose of holding or detaining him or her to answer to a court of law for an offense with which he or she has been charged.

Bail A system of posting a bond to ensure that a defendant will appear at trial, while allowing him or her to remain free until that time.

Complaint A charge stated before a magistrate of jurisdiction that a person named has committed a specified criminal offense.

Felony A criminal offense punishable by death or by incarceration for a year or longer in a state prison.

Grand jury A jury of inquiry whose duties are to receive complaints in criminal cases, to hear the evidence produced by the state, and to indict in situations where a trial is warranted.

Information An accusation against a person for an alleged criminal offense. An *information* differs from an *indictment* in that it is presented by a competent public officer rather than by a grand jury.

Misdemeanor A less serious crime which is punishable by a fine or by a period of incarceration of up to one year in a city or county jail.

Nolle prosequi Latin for "I refuse to prosecute." Refers to the discretionary authority of the prosecution to refuse to file a charge against a defendant, even though the evidence supports such a charge.

Nolo contendere Latin for "I will not contest it." A plea in a criminal action that has the same legal effect as a plea of guilty with respect to all proceedings on the indictment and on which the defendant may be sentenced. A plea of nolo contendere, however, may spare the defendant from certain civil penalties that might follow a plea of guilty.

Preliminary hearing Hearing in which the accused is advised of his or her constitutional rights, in which the *judge* determines if there is probable cause to bind the defendant over to an appropriate court for trial.

Pretrial motion Motion made by the defense counsel to suppress the introduction at trial of incriminating evidence, alleging the evidence was acquired illegally. Pretrial motions are often made to suppress evidence obtained by police in violation of the Fourth or Fifth Amendments.

Release on recognizance (ROR) The release of a defendant, by permission of the court, which permits the defendant to be at liberty upon his or her own agreement and without furnishing sureties for appearance at a pending trial.

Warrant A legal document, issued by a court, that authorizes specific acts by law enforcement officers (e.g., the arrest of a person named in the warrant, or the search of a specific place).

References

American Civil Liberties Union. *Secret Detention of the Chicago Police.* New York: Free Press, 1969.
Bases, N. C., and McDonald, W. F. *Preventive Detention in the District of Columbia: The First Ten Months.* New York: Vera Institute of Justice, 1974.
Bloch, H. A., and Geis, G. *Man, Crime, and Society.* New York: Random House, 1962.
Chambliss, W. J. *Crime and the Legal Process.* New York: McGraw-Hill, 1969.
Eisenstein, J., and Jacob, H. *Felony Justice: An Organizational Analysis of Criminal Courts.* Boston: Little, Brown, 1977.
Hearings on Preventive Detention Before the Subcommittee on Constitutional Rights of the Senate Committee on the Judiciary. 91st Cong., 2d Sess. (1970) (Statement of Senator Sam Ervin).
Feeley, M. "The Effects of a Heavy Caseload." Paper delivered at the annual meeting of the American Political Science Association, San Francisco, 2–5 September, 1975.
Heumann, M. *Plea Bargaining.* Chicago: University of Chicago Press, 1978.
Johnson, E. H. *Crime, Correction, and Society.* Homewood, Illinois: Dorsey Press, 1964.
Kerper, H. B. *Introduction to the Criminal Justice System.* St. Paul, Minn.: West, 1972.
Lehtinen, M., and Smith, G. W. "The Relative Effectiveness of Public Defenders and Private Attorneys: A Comparison." *Legal Aid Briefcase* 34 (1974):12–20.
Levin, M. A. *Urban Politics and the Criminal Courts.* Chicago: University of Chicago Press, 1977.
Mather, L. M. *Plea Bargaining or Trial?* Lexington, Mass.: Lexington Books, 1979.
Morris, N. *The Future of Imprisonment.* Chicago: University of Chicago Press, 1974.
Murphy, J. J. *Arrest by Police Computer.* Lexington, Mass.: Lexington Books, 1975.
National Advisory Commission on Criminal Justice Standards and Goals. *Courts.* Washington, D.C.: U.S. Government Printing Office, 1973.
Newman, D. J. "Pleading Guilty for Considerations: A Study of Bargain Justice." *Journal of Criminal Law, Criminology, and Police Science* 46 (1956):780–90.
President's Commission on Law Enforcement and Administration of Justice. *The Challenge of Crime in a Free Society.* Washington, D.C.: U.S. Government Printing Office, 1967.
President's Commission on Law Enforcement and Administration of Justice. *Task Force Report: The Courts.* Washington, D.C.: U.S. Government Printing Office, 1967.
Rosett, A., and Cressey, D. R. *Justice by Consent.* Philadelphia, Pa.: Lippincott, 1976.
Sturz, H. J. *National Conference of Bail and Criminal Justice.* Washington, D.C.: U.S. Government Printing Office, 1965.

Thomas, W. H. *Bail Reform in America*. Berkeley: University of California Press, 1976.
Wheatley, J. R. "Plea Bargaining—A Case For Its Continuance. *Massachusetts Law Quarterly* 59 (1974):31–41.

Notes

1. There are criminal trials by jury and civil trials by jury. This chapter is about the former.

2. A "nol pross" may also be requested if it is determined that a defendant is not guilty.

3. The commission's recommendation was not followed, however, and plea negotiation continues today.

9
the courts

What is a court?
The federal court system
The U.S. Supreme Court
The U.S. Courts of Appeal
The U.S. District Courts

State and local courts
Courts of last resort
Intermediate appellate courts
Trial courts
Lower courts

The judiciary
Selection of judges
"Courthouse culture" and the socialization of judges
Job stress and the judiciary

Court administrative personnel
The bailiff
The court reporter
The court clerk
The court administrator

Summary
Issue paper: Judging the judges—Dealing with judicial misconduct

THE court system in the United States is more complex than any other judicial system in the Western world. Some of this complexity in structure and operations exists because the nation's founders adopted a federal form of government with powers constitutionally divided between two levels of authority. Thus, some arrangement was needed to handle cases that might arise under two distinct sets of laws—the laws of the national government and those of the individual states. To solve this problem, two separate court systems were established, each complete with trial and appellate courts. Each state was free to fashion its own judicial apparatus. As a result, the federal court system is now comprised of over 100 district and appellate courts, as well as the individual judicial systems of the fifty states, (each with its own organization, personnel, and rules of procedure). Constitutionally, the national and state court systems are independent and equal in their respective spheres of authority.

In this chapter, we examine the dual court system and describe the organization and functions of the individual courts at both the federal and state levels. First, however, we look at what a court is and define some of the terms used throughout the chapter.

What is a court?

The term *court* can refer to a particular person (a judge) or a number of persons (a judicial assembly), to a room or building where a tribunal meets to hear the adjudicate cases, or to a session of some judicial assembly. A *judge* is an officer who presides in a court of law. In some courts (for example, the U.S. Supreme Court), a judge may be called a *justice*. A *magistrate* is a judge who performs a variety of judicial functions other than trial or appellate duties. Magistrates may be regular judges acting temporarily in the capacity of magistrate, or they may be elected or appointed to their positions.

The authority of a court, as established by the legal limits within which it is empowered to handle cases, is referred to as the court's *jurisdiction*. Kerper identifies the following courts in terms of their various jurisdictions (1972, p. 210):

1   *Trial court*. A court that has authority to try cases. A trial court impanels a jury, hears the evidence and arguments of counsel, receives the verdict, and sentences the defendant. Such a court has *original jurisdiction* of a case.
2   *Appellate court*. A court that reviews cases that have originally been tried in a trial court. An appellate court is also called an *appeals court* and is said to have *appellate jurisdiction*.
3   *Court of Record*. A court whose decisions are reviewed *on the record*. This means that an appellate court does not hear the testimony of witnesses and the arguments of counsel. Instead, the court reads the

written transcript (or record) of what went on in the original trial and bases its findings and decision on that record.

All courts that try felonies and most that try serious misdemeanors (those that carry possible jail sentences) keep records of court activity in each case. Thus, the term *court of record* is used to distinguish such courts from *courts of limited jurisdiction* (i.e., courts such as magistrate or justice of the peace courts that do not hold jury trials or handle appeals).

A *court of original jurisdiction* is authorized to try cases; a *court of general jurisdiction* can hold jury trials, hear the arguments of counsel, examine evidence, and listen to testimony from witnesses; a *court of appellate jurisdiction* has the authority to hear a defendant's appeal to set aside a conviction. Courts with original jurisdiction seldom have appellate jurisdiction, and never with regard to a case they have already tried. Cases can be appealed to a *court of intermediate appeal* in a state, but the highest tribunal to which a case can be appealed is the *court of last resort*—the state equivalent of a supreme court.

It is common practice to refer to "lower" courts, or *inferior courts*, and to "higher" courts, or *superior courts*. The former include courts of limited jurisdiction; the latter include the appellate courts, especially courts of last resort. The status of trial courts (courts of general jurisdiction) in this hierarchy is variable: they are sometimes included among the lower courts, sometimes among the higher courts. Such distinctions are largely the result of custom and usage—a reflection of the prestige accorded to the various courts by the legal profession.

The federal court system

The U.S. Supreme Court is the only federal court specifically mandated by the Constitution. Other federal courts were established by legislative action. Article III, section 1 of the Constitution states that "the judicial power of the United States shall be vested in one Supreme Court, and in such inferior courts as the Congress may from time to time ordain and establish."

The federal court system is a hierarchy with the U.S. District Courts at the base, the U.S. Courts of Appeals at the intermediate level, and the U.S. Supreme Court at the apex. Also a part of the federal judiciary are the U.S. Magistrates, formerly called U.S. Commissioners, and a variety of specialized courts. Among the latter are the U.S. Court of Military Appeals, the U.S. Court of Claims, and the U.S. Custom Court.

The U.S. Supreme Court

The U.S. Supreme Court, often referred to simply as "the Court," consists of nine judges called *justices*. The justices are appointed by the president, subject to confirmation by the Senate. The president also appoints one member of the Court to act as chief justice. As the chair of the Court, the chief justice has no formal powers of coercion over other justices, but he or she may apportion case loads or direct the writing of a judicial decision.

There is no formal requirement in the Constitution (or anywhere else) that a Supreme Court justice must have a background of distinguished judicial service. For that matter, a justice is not required to have any legal training whatsoever. Earlier in our national history, appointment to the Supreme Court was a reward for political prominence or party loyalty. Earlier still, nomination to the court was a dubious distinction: George Washington had difficulty finding candidates with suitable qualifications or enthusiasm for the position, and in 1795, Chief Justice John Jay left the Court—firmly convinced that it would never attain equal status with the executive and legislative branches of government.[1] It is fortunate for the nation that in subsequent years the Supreme Court benefited from the wisdom, insight, scholarship, and philosophy of some of the most distinguished legal minds in the country, leaders like Marshall, Brandeis, Cardozo, Holmes, Hughes, and Warren.

Justices hold their tenure for "life or good behavior," as provided by the Constitution. A justice can only be removed by voluntary retirement or impeachment. The Constitution also denies Congress the authority to reduce the salaries of justices. The term of the Court is variable. Although statutory law requires that the term begin each year on the first Monday of October, it does not set a closing date. Thus, the Court continues in session as long as it has business to transact. The work load has steadily increased with the expansion of the federal and state judiciaries. Although the Supreme Court gets most of its cases on appeal from these courts, the number of justices on the Court has not changed to meet the growing case load. Each term, the Court handles approximately 3,000 cases.

Technically, the Supreme Court has both original and appellate jurisdiction. As specified in the Constitution, it is the *court of first instance* in cases involving diplomatic representatives of foreign powers and in controversies in which a state is a party. Virtually all cases heard under the Court's powers of original jurisdiction relate to disputes between two states—usually over water rights—or between the federal government and a state.

The appellate jurisdiction of the Court accounts for the overwhelming bulk of its business. The Court reviews cases from lower federal courts and from state tribunals when issues are involved that pertain to the Constitution or to laws of the United States. The Court has almost absolute power to control its agenda, thus enabling it to be highly selective and to assume jurisdiction only in cases that raise an issue it wishes to consider. Over half of the requests for Court time come from losing parties in the U.S. Courts of Appeal; most of the remainder come from disappointed litigants in the state tribunals of last resort.

Only at the level of the Supreme Court is there a bridge between the federal and state judicial structures. No path of appeal exists from a state court to any federal tribunal at lower levels in the hierarchy. If the Supreme Court grants *certiorari* (accepts jurisdiction), it will scrutinize the constitutional issue at stake and either sustain the state tribunal's finding or reverse the decision and release the appellant who had the appeal accepted. The Supreme Court reverses rulings in about two thirds of the cases it hears, partly as a result of the careful screening by the Court for cases that have "rightness"—that is, cases that involve the specific issues the Court wishes to address.

The U.S. Courts of Appeal

The U.S. Courts of Appeal—designated as lower federal courts—were established in 1891 to lighten the Supreme Court's case load from appeals from federal district courts.[2] Until 1948, the U.S. Courts of Appeal were known as the U.S. Circuit Courts of Appeal. They are characterized as *intermediate appellate courts* because they stand between the U.S. District Courts, the U.S. Magistrates, and the specialized federal courts on one hand, and the Supreme Court on the other hand. They have the principal responsibility for reviewing judicial decisions in the lower courts (Klein, 1977).

There are eleven U.S. Courts of Appeal (including one for the District of Columbia), each with jurisdiction over a particular geographical section of the country—a so-called judicial circuit. The number of judges in each court of appeals ranges from three to fifteen, depending on the size and population of the area served. At least two judges must sit on each case, but decisions are normally made by a panel of three. The composition of these groups varies from case to case, with the presiding judge in each court making the assignments. On occasion, when disagreement arises among the judges on an important point of law, the matter may be decided by the full court in an *en banc decision*. Judges of the U.S. Courts of Appeal, like Supreme Court justices, hold their appointments for "life or good behavior."

The U.S. District Courts

The ninety-three U.S. District Courts are trial courts in the federal system. There are eighty-nine of these courts within the fifty states, and one each in the District of Columbia, Guam, Puerto Rico, and the Virgin Islands. Until sovereignty of the Canal Zone reverted to the government of Panama in 1979 there was a U.S. District Court in the Canal Zone. The federal district courts are tribunals of original jurisdiction or first instance. It is in these courts that the majority of noncriminal (civil) suits arising under federal law are initiated and terminated—actions on patent rights, postal problems, copyright violations, bankruptcy, and so on. Here also are tried crimes committed against the federal government (i.e., those that involve conduct prohibited by Congress and that are punishable by the federal government). Each state contains no less than one federal district court (some having multiple divisions); sixteen states have two tribunals, eight have three, and New York and Texas have four each. Every district has at least one judge, depending on the work load, and some districts have as many as twenty-four. A single judge conducts the trials in these lower tribunals, except in cases that involve the constitutionality of national and state statutes. In the latter type of case, three judges must preside at the trial.

State and local courts

No generalizations can be made regarding the jurisdictions, functions, and titles of state and local courts. Although there are structural parallels between state court systems and the federal judicial system, as shown in **table 9.1,** the hierarchy in any given state may include two, three, four, or even more levels of courts. To confound matters further, many persons in the criminal justice system often forget that the nomenclature for courts is rather arbitrary. Consequently, courts are often referred to by title rather than by jurisdiction or function.

Courts of last resort

Each state has an appellate tribunal that serves as the court of last resort. In New York, Kentucky, and Maryland, the court of last resort is known as the court of appeals. In other states, it is called the supreme court of appeals, supreme court of errors, court of criminal appeals, or supreme judicial court. Whatever its title, the court of last resort is the final authority in cases involving issues of state law.

Courts of last resort relate to the lower state courts in much the same way that the U.S. Supreme Court relates to the lower federal courts. As the highest judicial body of the sovereign states, these tribunals have discretionary power to decide which cases they will hear. For this purpose, the court uses a writ of certiorari—a writ of review commanding a lower court to "send up the record" of a case for consideration. (The Supreme Court

TABLE 9.1 Parallels between the state and federal court systems

	State court system	Federal court system
Court of last resort	Supreme court, court of criminal appeals, supreme court of appeals, supreme judicial court, etc.	U.S. Supreme Court
Intermediate appellate courts	Superior court, district court of appeals, appellate court, supreme court, etc.	U.S. Courts of Appeal
Trial courts (Courts of general jurisdiction)	Circuit court, district court, state court, county court, etc.	U.S. District Courts
Lower courts (Courts of limited jurisdiction)	Municipal court, small claims court, traffic court, justice of the peace, etc.	U.S. Magistrates and specialized courts (e.g., U.S. Customs Court)

uses the writ of certiorari in much the same way.) Courts of last resort are presided over by three to nine judges (usually seven).

Intermediate appellate courts

Twenty of the most heavily populated states have an intermediate level of appellate courts that corresponds to the U.S. Courts of Appeal. As in the federal system, these intermediate courts provide relief for overburdened state supreme courts and serve as courts of last resort for the majority of appeals received from the courts of original jurisdiction. New York was the first state to create a system of appellate courts (it did so shortly before the turn of the century).

Some of the names given to intermediate appellate courts are superior court, appellate court, and supreme court. In some states, courts of appeal may have both original and appellate jurisdiction; in others, jurisdiction may be restricted to particular kinds of cases. Some states assign the defendant the right to appeal, regardless of whether or not the court wants to hear the case. Following a conviction for a criminal offense, an individual may appeal the decision arrived at by the court. The appeals process is highly fragmented and cumbersome, but there is a basic model that applies to most jurisdictions.

The first step in the process is the finding of *guilt* by some court system at the municipal, county, state, or federal level. In each case, the procedure for appeal is determined by the court of record. Appeals are usually made by the defendant, because the states are highly restricted in their ability to appeal decisions. The effect of an appropriately introduced appeal is a stay in the execution of the original sentence until the appeal is decided. As soon as possible, if not immediately after the sentence is pronounced, the defendant's attorney must either move for a new trial or make an appeal on some grounds. And although appellate courts usually make short work of frivolous appeals, the courts must be careful not to go too far in the other direction:

> Appellate courts . . . do not reverse decisions simply because they disagree with them. Reversal must proceed from error of law and such error must be substantial. But if this account is to be veracious I must call attention to a fact familiar to every experienced lawyer, yet not apparent in the classical literature of the law, and probably not consciously admitted even to themselves by most appellate judges. By that I mean practically every record contains some erroneous rulings [and] they can nearly always find some error if they want grounds for reversal (Ulman 1933, pp. 265–66).

In most state systems, courts of appeal review the decisions of the trial courts for judicial error. The facts of a case are not questioned, and all of the trial court's decisions on facts are binding on the appellate court. Thus, evidence is not presented to the court of appeals; rather, the review is accomplished from the trial record. An appellate court can not reverse the factual findings of the trial court unless they are totally erroneous. In states where there is a second level of review, the trial record and the intermediate court's decision are examined. Usually, the refusal to hear an appeal of a lower appellate court's ruling is the same as upholding the decision; the case stops there unless an appeal is filed separately in federal court on a constitutional issue.

Trial courts

Trial courts are also known as courts of general or original jurisdiction. They are the courts that have original jurisdiction in most criminal cases, and they are the lowest courts of record at the state level. These courts are referred to as district, circuit, or superior courts, or courts of common pleas, and they are structured differently from state to state. Some systems provide for separate criminal and civil divisions; a few retain equity or chancery tribunals; and others have special probate and domestic relations courts. Regardless of how they are structured, however, the trial courts handle the bulk of major litigation under state law. All important civil litigation originates in these courts, and persons accused of criminal offenses—other than petty crimes—are tried in them. These tribunals also serve as appellate units for cases instituted in courts of limited jurisdiction. However, because such cases are tried *de novo* (as though they had not previously been heard), further appeal normally lies with a higher court.

Lower courts

At the bottom of the hierarchy are the lower courts, also known as courts of limited and special jurisdiction. According to a national survey of court organizations conducted by the Law Enforcement Assistance Administration (1972), there were 12,636 lower courts in the United States in 1971. These minor tribunals of local character are identified by titles such as justice of the peace, magistrate, municipal, police, and small claims courts. These courts have various duties and jurisdictions. They are not courts of record, so appeals from them are usually appeals for a completely new trial before the next level of courts in the state system. The jurisdiction of justices of the peace and other lesser courts is confined to minor infractions of the law—such as disorderly conduct, vagrancy, traffic violations, and civil suits involving small sums of money. In some states, justices of the peace and magistrates also conduct preliminary hearings in criminal matters to determine whether accused individuals should be bound over for trial in higher tribunals.

Historically, the American experience with lower courts has not been reassuring. It was once common practice (and still is in some areas) for laypersons with no formal legal training and little judicial aptitude to preside over lower courts. Considering this background, the following comment of a justice of the peace about defendants brought before him is hardly surprising: "I don't ever remember having one who *wasn't* guilty. If the sheriff picks up a man for violating the law, he's guilty or he wouldn't bring him in here. Anyway, I don't get anything out of it if they aren't guilty" (Banks 1961, p. 188). The following excerpt from the *Task Force Report: The*

Courts, authored by the President's Commission on Law Enforcement and Administration of Justice, conveys something of the atmosphere that characterizes the functioning of the lower courts:

> An observer in the lower criminal courts ordinarily sees a trial bearing little resemblance to those carried out under traditional notions of due process. There is usually no court reporter unless the defendant can afford to pay one. One result is an informality in the proceedings which would not be tolerated in a felony trial. Rules of evidence are largely ignored. Speed is the watchword.... Traditional safeguards honored in felony cases lose their meaning in such proceedings; yet there is still the possibility of lengthy imprisonment or heavy fine.
>
> In some cities trials are conducted without counsel for either side; the case is prosecuted by a police officer and defended by the accused himself.... Short jail sentences of one, two, or three months are commonly imposed on an assembly line basis ... (1967, pp. 31–33).

An offender subjected to a process of this kind is not likely to emerge changed for the better. Rather, he or she will return to the streets to begin the cycle again in all of its futility.

The Judiciary

The symbolism and rituals of the judicial process are summarized in the figure of the goddess of justice, Astraea, who stands blindfolded with scales suspended in one hand and a sword in the other. The scales signify the weighing of evidence; the sword implies the power and authority of punitive sanction; and the blindfold indicates that justice is oblivious to temptation or bribery.

This is an inspiring and ideal image, but it has little to do with reality. For one thing, courts are an integral part of the political system and they perform policy-making functions not unlike those of legislative bodies and executive agencies (Peltason 1955). As such, they are often the target of furious controversy, their decisions eliciting both praise and damnation. There is a great contrast between the dignified chambers of the U.S. Supreme Court and the television editorials on the evils of school busing, between the silver-haired Chief Justice and the tirades of antiabortionists, between the solemn enclave of the Supreme Court and the vituperation of proponents of school prayer.

Legal realists such as Benjamin Cardozo, Jerome Frank, and Thurman Arnold helped dispel the myths of judges as automatons and of the law as a system of definite and consistent rules readily discoverable by reason alone. When people become judges, they are not suddenly cleansed of all their prejudices or given immunity against social pressures. How they act depends on their personality, background, attitudes, beliefs, and values. In a statistical analysis of the split decisions of the 1960 term of the U.S. Supreme Court, Schubert found that almost all votes could be explained by the justices' attitudes or preferences: "A justice reacts in his voting behavior to the stimuli presented by cases before the Court, in accordance with his attitudes toward the issues raised for decisions" (1962, p. 91).

Other scholars believe that judges make decisions according to conflicting principles and interests because they are guided by what they think will be the decision's impact on society and by what they perceive as its advantages to society. Proponents of this thesis deny that jurists decide questions according to personal preference and point out that, as trained lawyers, judges are influenced by the doctrine of *stare decisis* ("let the decision stand") and wish to achieve as much stability in the law as possible (Miller 1965). When societal considerations are reconciled with the doctrine of stare decisis, the resulting judicial decisions are, in effect, compromises.

MEET THE JUDGE

Courts and the judicial process usually bring to mind a picture of a judge, draped in a black robe, overseeing a trial. When a judge enters a courtroom, everyone rises and stands quietly until he or she sits behind the elevated bench and raps the gavel to start the proceedings. In courts composed of a number of members, it is common for judges to march in together quickly as if choreographed on cue to take their seats in a flourish of flowing robes. Loud talking or even whispering among court spectators is not permitted. At the U.S. Supreme Court severe-looking ushers holding long sticks roam the aisles, and they poke these sticks at individuals who talk too loudly or distract others from focusing on the front of the large courtroom. Called "the Marble Palace," the U.S. Supreme Court building is very ornate, with high ceilings and decorated walls, polished floors, and long benches that resemble pews in a church. Reverence and respect are expected and enforced. Other courtrooms are less magnificent, but the floor plan, furniture arrangement, and the judge raised above everyone else are similar and clearly show who is in charge and what goes on.

The odds are good that few of us picture a black or a woman presiding over a court. There is an increasing number of female and black judges in the United States, but chances are most of us still envision a middle-aged white man, perhaps slightly overweight, with graying or white hair. Judges are thought to be slightly aloof, but patient, understanding, and unlikely to lose their tempers. They also run their courts firmly but fairly. Judges are not too tall or short or thin or bald, and they do not sport beards or styled haircuts. Of course, judges *do* come in all shapes, shades, and sizes, but Chief Justice Warren Burger *really looks* like a judge.

Reproduced from H. R. Glick, *Courts, Politics, and Justice* (New York: McGraw-Hill, 1983), p. 1, by permission of the author and the publisher.

Selection of judges

In selecting judges, it is necessary to distinguish between formal procedures and requirements (as specified by constitutional or statutory law) and actual practice. The former provide the legal specifications to be followed in choosing judicial personnel, but leave an undefined area in which informal practices develop. State law may call for the popular election of judges, but who runs may be determined by the political parties. The law may provide for gubernatorial appointments, but the choice of candidates may actually be dictated by political leaders or bar associations.

In the judicial system of most European nations, the office of judge is treated as a profession distinct from lawyers. Those who aspire to judgeship must meet rigid qualifications and undergo special training. They usually begin their service as apprentices and are promoted within the judicial hierarchy. This procedure is alien to the United States, where we have opted for what Neubauer describes as "essentially amateurs . . . who have no practical experience or systematic exposure to the judicial world" (1979, p. 168). Judges are chosen from the bar, and there is nothing in law school or in the practice of law that prepares judges to assume their extensive power. A judge may be trained in the rules of evidence and courtroom procedure, but he or she may know little or nothing about criminology, psychology, and the prevailing theories and practices in corrections. Too often, new judges assume their positions with little knowledge of the technicalities of their jobs or the magnitude of their influence on the criminal justice system.

Until recently, few formal requirements—other than those of age, residency, citizenship, and admission to the Bar—were prescribed for judicial selection. Candidates with prior experience on the bench do not necessarily have a better chance of appointment or selection than those without such qualifications. For example, since the Supreme Court was established in 1790, only 40 percent of all nominees to the Court have had prior judicial careers. And the percentage is no higher for the appellate tribunals of most states. Only in the case of the U.S. Courts of Appeal does experience appear to give a candidate a decided advantage; in recent decades, more than 60 percent of the nominees to these have courts had extensive experience on the bench before their appointments.

There are various methods for selecting judges, and each has its own advocates and supporting arguments. The selection procedures used in the United States may be grouped into three general categories: elective, appointive, and appointive with modifications. The method of election prevails in thirty-three states, with nearly equal numbers of partisan (in which the nominee declares a party affiliation) and nonpartisan elections. Appointments are used in the federal judiciary and in somewhat less than one fourth of the states. The third method of selection, sometimes referred to as the Missouri plan or the nonpartisan court plan, is used in five states—Alaska, Iowa, Kansas, Missouri, and Nebraska. Some of the major features of this method also apply to judicial selections in several other states, including California and Illinois.

Popular election of judicial personnel did not occur in the United States until the rise of Jacksonian democracy shortly before the middle of the nineteenth century. According to those who support this concept, judges should be politically responsible for the conduct of their offices. However, proponents of the appointive system decry the need for judicial candidates to compete with one another for popular favor in partisan, or even nonpartisan, campaigns. They maintain that the average voter is ill equipped to assess the technical fitness and judicial aptitude of the individuals who seek judgeships. Further, they contend that judges who are dependent on popular support for their office incur political obligations that may affect their decisions.

Popular election of state court judges is actually not as predominant as statistics suggest. Numerous vacancies on the bench occur through the death, resignation, or retirement of an incumbent before the expiration of a term. When this occurs, the governor of a state usually has the power to fill the judgeship for the remainder of the term or until the next election. In other words, governors select a substantial number of judges, even in states that have elective systems. Individuals so appointed have a distinct advantage in later elections, because they enter the elections as incumbents.

The modified appointment plan, developed by the American Bar Association and the American Judicature Society, was first adopted in Missouri in 1940. This plan combines restricted executive selection with popular approval. In Missouri, for example, the governor fills judicial vacancies on the supreme court and on the circuit courts of Jackson County (Kansas City) and St. Louis County (the intermediate appellate tribunals) from lists submitted by nonpartisan nominating commissions. These commissions are composed of gubernatorial appointees, lawyers selected by the state bar, and the presiding judge of one of the appellate courts. The commission in Jackson County, for example, includes two laypersons, two lawyers elected by members of the local bar association, and the presiding judge of the Kansas City Court of Appeals. After newly appointed judges have served on the bench for one year, their names are submitted on ballots to area voters, who determine if the judges should be retained in office. A similar referendum is held every six years thereafter for circuit court judges and every twelve years thereafter for appellate justices.

An examination of the selection process in the federal court system should dispel any illusions about the apolitical character of judicial appointments. When a vacancy occurs on the federal bench, a set procedure is followed. Names of nominees are submitted by senators to the attorney general's office, which serves as a clearing house or screening agency for all appointments to the national judiciary. Informal discussions then take place among members of the Department of Justice, White House staff, senators, and party leaders from the state where the vacancy exists. When the choice is narrowed, the Committee of Federal Judiciary of the American Bar Association is invited to comment on the candidates (this practice was initiated during Eisenhower's administration).

The bar association's committee does not initiate or suggest prospective nominees; it simply gathers recommendations on the names submitted by the attorney general. In this capacity, however, the committee exerts its influence by deterring the nomination of individuals it deems unqualified. Simultaneously with the bar committee's review, a full field investigation of the potential nominees is conducted by the FBI. At the conclusion of these activities, the attorney general makes a recommendation to the president. By this time, the acceptability of a candidate to the state senators (of the President's party) has been established. Only rarely does a president submit the name of a judicial nominee over the objection of these officials.

Experience has demonstrated the difficulty of excluding politics from the selection process—even under a restrictive appointment method. This was shown in Missouri under the nonpartisan court plan during the plan's first twenty-five years: of the sixty judges appointed during this period, over 70 percent belonged to the same political party as the governor. Charges have been made that governors may attempt to influence the choice of names on the nominee lists through their appointees on the nominating commissions. These allegations have led to proposals to take the appointment of lay members of such commissions out of the governor's hands (Roberts 1965).

To what degree can the selection process be removed from politics? To deny a governor any voice in the composition of the nominating panel would further strengthen the role of the bar associations in the choice of judicial appointees. For example, Hearnes reported in 1965 that over one half of the members of the Missouri bar believed that the nonpartisan court plan substituted bar politics and gubernatorial politics for the traditional politics of party leaders and political organizations. Few members, however, regarded this development unfavorably, and some suggested removing the element of gubernatorial politics altogether by eliminating the governor's power to appoint part of the nominating panel. If this happened, only bar politics would influence the decision. In the final analysis, any selection method—no matter how it is designed—includes a political decision at some point in the process.

The relationship between the method of selection and the caliber of judges who staff the courts remains more a matter of individual perception than of systematic study. Does the appointive process produce better judges than popular election? Or is the Missouri plan superior to either appointment or election? The subject has been debated for some time. Proponents of executive selection point to the experience of the federal bench, which has traditionally enjoyed a higher reputation for competency than its state counterparts. How much of this relative superiority can be attributed to the mode of selection is not known, however. The greater benefits of federal judgeships—lifetime tenure, better pay, and higher prestige—are probably much more important factors. It can be assumed that the more attractive a position is made because of money, security, and prestige, the more the position will appeal to persons with ability and talent.

"Courthouse culture" and the socialization of judges

Rosett and Cressey describe the complex of shared values, attitudes, and informal norms of cooperation that make up what they call a "subculture of justice within the courthouse":

> Even in the adversary world of law, men who work together and understand each other eventually develop shared conceptions of what are acceptable, right and just ways of dealing with specific kinds of offenses, suspects, and defendants. These conceptions form the bases for understanding, agreements, working arrangements and cooperative attitudes.... Over time,

these shared patterns of belief develop the coherence of a distinct culture, a style of social expression peculiar to the particular courthouse (1976, pp. 90–91).

Newcomers to the bench undergo a process of on-the-job learning that transforms them into jurists. During this process, judges are exposed to and absorb various aspects of the "courthouse culture" that pertain to organizational goals, preferred means for achieving these goals, role responsibilities, required behavior, and rules for maintaining the court as an organization (Schein 1968).

Alpert (1981) has identified five stages in the occupational socialization of trial court judges: professional socialization, initiation, resolution, establishment, and commitment. Professional socialization is a stage that occurs prior to judicial selection. This period covers both formal legal training in law school and informal training that occurs in legal practice. It also includes experience in public office (e.g., as a prosecutor or city attorney) that may help prepare an individual for the bench. Initiation is described by Alpert as a period of bewilderment and confidence building. The newcomer learns how to behave in court, manage the docket, make proper rulings, and maintain order in trials and hearings. Resolution, which occurs in about years one through four in judicial experience, completes the transformation of the newcomer from advocate to arbiter. The judge reaches a level of comfort in which he or she begins to handle the isolation and the external pressures endemic to the job.

Establishment follows resolution and covers a period of approximately four years. During this time, many judges are susceptible to midcareer crises, as personal and family needs conflict with organizational demands. Judges face the decision of whether to remain on the bench or to seek more lucrative opportunities in nonjudicial pursuits. It is a period of introspection and rumination about the future. Commitment, the final stage in the socialization process, is marked by a deep-seated identification with the court, an increase in personal satisfaction, and a growing sense of dedication to a judicial career.

Carp and Wheeler (1972) note that a judge's colleagues are the foremost training agents in the process of judicial socialization. They accomplish this task through formal meetings and seminars and by informal exchanges during the work day. A second major source of information is attorneys who appear in the courtrooms and persons on the judge's staff: law clerks, secretaries, court administrators, and bailiffs. These people supply the judge with critical advice on procedural and administrative matters (Blumberg 1967). But in the end, as Neubauer (1979) concludes, the judicial socialization process is largely a matter of self-education in which judges spend a lot of time reading in law libraries, seeking out the counsel of knowledgeable people, and learning by doing.

Job stress and the judiciary

In chapter 6, we discussed how job stress and anxiety affect the job performance and personal lives of police officers and administrators. In much the same way, occupational and social stresses result from the pressures and conflicts experienced by members of the judiciary.

One source of job stress for judges is the cases they encounter. For example, consider judges who are confronted regularly with jury trials involving gruesome accounts of violent crimes. The judges must try to act impartially, even though they are bombarded with facts that would upset the average person. Judges have direct, meaningful, and unending daily contact with crisis situations that they can not escape as long as they remain in their jobs.

Another job stress for judges is public image. The public traditionally views judges as people equipped to handle situations and make consequential decisions swiftly and correctly. Judges are expected to move from one emotionally charged situation to the next, while remaining aloof and detached. They are expected to be fair and impartial, regardless of the choices they must make. They must have the ability to use emotional control and shut off or suppress emotional responses to provocative situations. To meet these demands, a judge may "keep too tight a rein on his emotions, and over a period of time isolate his feelings or become uncomfortable in expressing them. This can be analogized to a pressure cooker that has its top spout tightened down so that the steam which builds up cannot escape. Eventually with the constant buildup of steam the pressure cooker will explode" (Stratton 1978, pp. 60–61).

People who decide to seek a career as a judge are sometimes attracted by the rewards of independence; thus, they often refuse to admit their dependence upon others, because this dependence is inconsistent with their self-concept. Unless they stay within the confines of their role, they may have feelings of uncertainty about their status as perceived by others. Thus, the job can be a lonely one. This same point has been made about executives with regard to leadership: "I have watched executives curse in desperation the forces which, in moments, vitiated years of their efforts. I have listened to them protest the loneliness of their sometimes opulent offices, the distance from old friends. I have seen them cry out their pent-up fury . . . and disguise their tears with alcohol" (Levinson 1970, p. 127).

Political pressures are another source of stress for the judiciary. Anthony Lewis (1978) describes a regrettable situation that occurred during a Supreme Court election in California in which Judge Rose Bird, who was up for re-election, became the target of an ugly political campaign.[3] Judge Bird's decision to reverse an appellate court decision and provide the possible release of a defendant accused of a brutal rape was based on a point of law, rather than on her personal feelings about the crime. She could not use her repugnance toward the crime and the criminal as a basis for rewriting the statutes—and political conservatives agreed with her. However, unfair publicity and slanted editorializing put the election in jeopardy. The result was a heavily ideological campaign that had a broader target than a single judge: the campaign was designed to exert pressure on all the judges in the state to conform with reactionary views on matters involving criminal law.

Proposals for sentencing reform have often called for judges to provide reasons in writing for decisions made in difficult, complex, or unusual cases. Judges are pressured to document the reasons for particular sentences because of the "increase in appellate review and reversal, the heightened criticism by the press and the public, and consequent diminution of the judiciary's role" (Robin 1975, p. 201). Robin feels that this pressure is intrinsically threatening and stress producing, because discretion contributes significantly to the self-concept and occupational satisfaction of judges. Further, judges rejection of sentencing accountability "is rooted in the recognizably human and pervasive aversion to being criticized, countermanded, and sanctioned" (ibid., p. 204). "Viewed publicly, every formalized judicial statement accompanying sentencing is perceived as a justification of action taken and thus invites evaluation and criticism from all sources" (ibid., p. 205).

Most of the stress encountered in an occupation detracts from job satisfaction. However, one study indicates that there are four types of occupational stress that may actually *increase* job satisfaction (Burke 1976). Three of these—too much responsibility, too heavy a work load, and feelings of not being fully qualified—are associated with a demanding, challenging job and the high organizational expectations of the employee. The implication is that a job that can be enlarged or enriched may lead to increased satisfaction, but also to an increase in certain pressures. The fourth occupational stress that Burke found positively related to job satisfaction involves decisions that affect the lives of others. Because all four of these stress factors apply to the judiciary, it may be assumed that not all stresses produce negative effects and that some may lead to greater job satisfaction.

Perhaps the most direct way to understand the stress and anxiety judges experience is to follow a judge through a typical day in court. Judge Lois G. Forer provides such an opportunity in an article entitled "View from the Bench: A Judge's Day" (1975). She allows a glimpse of a routine day through her eyes and the frustrations and anxieties so typical in the life of a trial court judge.

A long day on the bench begins at 9:30 in the morning, and frustrations mount as overloaded public defenders arrive late, witnesses can not be found, and defendants are forgotten at the jail rather than being brought to court when they are needed. Cases have to be continued, and judges are asked to decide on bail for men and women they can not see or talk to and who the public defender knows nothing about. They are asked to sentence people using only two alternatives: prison or the streets. What is often needed instead is a drug program or a hospital plan, but these alternatives are seldom available. Judges must sit through five-hour sanity hearings and decide which team of psychiatrists is correct about a defendant. They are frustrated by jail overcrowding, but they face harsh public and self-criticism if they release anyone who commits another crime. They encounter seemingly unsolvable cases in which there are simply no resources to provide for the needs of defendants.

Judges experience the computerization of human beings and the trappings of the bureaucracy when a defendant is "lost in the system" or "forgotten" in a jail for five months without ever appearing before a judge. They must accept negotiated guilty pleas from defendants who have only talked with their court-appointed attorney for five minutes; they wonder if such defendants would have been convicted had they gone to trial. And then there's the "batting average": "Woe betide those who fail to keep pace in getting rid of cases" (Forer 1975, p. 39). Feeling the frustration of being bound by the iron laws of economics, without knowing how to replace the present system, Judge Forer sums up her feelings this way:

> At the end of a day in which as a judge I have taken actions affecting for good or ill the lives of perhaps 15 or 20 litigants and their families, I am drained. I walk out of the stale-smelling, dusty courtroom into the fresh sunshine of a late spring day and feel as if I were released from prison. I breathe the soft air, but in my nostrils is the stench of the stifling cell blocks and detention rooms. While I sip my cool drink in the quiet of my garden, I cannot forget the prisoners, with their dry bologna sandwiches and only a drink of water provided at the pleasure of the hot and harried guard (ibid.).

The judge, then, is seen "not as a cold fish but as a warm-blooded mammal, not as a rational calculator always ready to work out the best solution but as a reluctant decision maker—beset by conflicts, doubts, and worry, struggling with incongruous longings, antipathies, and loyalties, and seeking relief by procrastinating, rationalizing, and/or denying responsibility for his own choices" (Janis and Mann 1977, p. 15).

Court administrative personnel

The complex and demanding business of the courts could not be conducted without the administrative services performed by the *bailiff*, the *court reporter*, and the *court clerk*. And these criminal justice professionals have been joined in recent years by a specialist who bears the title *court administrator*. In this section, we briefly examine the tasks, duties, and responsibilities of each of these important officers of the court.

The bailiff

The bailiff is charged with the responsibility of maintaining the order, security, and decorum of the court. In a large metropolitan court that meets daily, the bailiff is generally a permanent employee. In smaller or rural communities, a bailiff may be appointed by a judge to serve only for the duration of a trial.

The duties of the bailiff vary. As sergeant-at-arms within the courtroom, he or she keeps watch over defendants and suppresses disorderly behavior among spectators. He or she summons witnesses when they are called to testify and maintains the legal proprieties pertaining to the actions of jurors and witnesses. When the jury is sequestered on the order of the judge, the bailiff accompanies the jurors and guards to prevent violations of trial secrecy—such as making unauthorized phone calls, reading an unedited newspaper, or listening to accounts of the trial on the radio or television. It is also the bailiff's job to see that the jury is suitably housed and fed during a trial.

The court reporter

Court reporters take down a verbatim account of the proceedings in all cases conducted within a court of record. Most of these highly proficient reporters use a stenotype recorder—a mechanical device that types shorthand symbols. At the close of each day in court, or at the conclusion of the entire trial, the reporter's notes are transcribed. In most courts, in addition to salary, the court reporter is paid by the page for the preparation of the record. Consequently, as Chamelin, Fox, and Whisenand observe, "it is not rare to find triple spaced, wide margined transcripts" (1979, p. 278).

The court clerk

The court clerk keeps all of the records of the court. In federal or appellate courts, court clerks are appointed; in lower courts, they are elected. In many areas, the duties of county clerk and court clerk are combined into a single office.

The court clerk has the authority to handle nearly all of the paperwork that accompanies a judicial proceeding. Returns of arrest and search warrants, indictments, informations, all pleadings filed by the prosecutor and defense counsel, instructions to the jury, verdicts, and sentences are filed by the clerk or are transcribed into the permanent court record. Subpoenas for witnesses, notices regarding jury service, and records of all cases filed, dismissed, tried, and appealed are the responsibility of the court clerk.

The task of the court clerk is made unnecessarily arduous and complex by the fact that judicial record keeping is a bewildering hodgepodge of diverse procedures. Despite continuing efforts by professional organizations of court clerks, there is little in the way of uniformity or standardization. It is not unusual to find that a particular criminal justice agency (e.g., a correctional facility) receives more than a dozen different forms of the same document from the various courts within a state, at an annual cost to the taxpayers of thousands of dollars.

The court administrator

The new and challenging position of court administrator was mandated at the Federal level by the Ninety-first Congress. In H.R. 17906, the court administrator is assigned duties that include exercising administrative control over all nonjudicial activities of the court of appeals in the circuit to which the administrator is appointed; formulating and managing a system of personnel administration; preparing the budget; maintaining a modern accounting system; collecting, compiling, and analyzing statistical data for reports; and other activities relating to the business and administration of the courts. The court administrator—a skilled professional trained in systems analysis, budgeting procedures, the use of computers, and modern techniques of office management and personnel administration—may well prove to be the best hope for bringing efficiency and order to the overburdened courts.

Summary

The American judicial system is extremely complex. It is more accurate, in fact, to speak of judicial *systems,* because there are courts at the federal, state, county, and municipal levels of jurisdiction. The state operates trial courts, intermediate appellate courts, and courts of last resort, (i.e., the highest tribunals to which cases can be appealed). This pattern is repeated at the federal level. Federal appellate courts, however, can rule on state cases, and the U.S. Supreme Court is the court of last resort for all cases decided in the United States.

Direct supervision of the courts is the responsibility of the judiciary. Judges are either appointed or elected. As public officials, they are involved in political issues and controversies that are an inseparable feature of public life. Coming from a variety of backgrounds and experiences, newcomers to the bench undergo a process of learning that gradually accommodates them to the role of judge. The human side of judging is nowhere more clearly revealed than in the job-related stresses that affect members of the judiciary.

Other members of the judicial staff include the bailiff, court clerk, court reporter, and court administrator. These members of the judicial team provide expert assistance and counsel, without which the judicial process would barely function. The court administrator, in particular, is beginning to emerge as a focal figure in easing the administrative and management burdens of the judge.

issue paper

JUDGING THE JUDGES—DEALING WITH JUDICIAL MISCONDUCT

Clark Mollenhoff, a journalist and Pulitzer Prize winner who spent several years investigating the federal bench, claims that the problems caused by unfit judges amount to a national scandal at present ("Judging the Judges," *Time*, 1979, p. 52). Until October of 1981, when a new system of discipline took effect in the federal courts under an act of Congress, ridding the federal judiciary of unfit judges could only be done by impeachment, a time-consuming and cumbersome procedure. This may help account for why only eight federal judges in our history have been impeached by the House of Representatives, and, of these, only four have been convicted by the Senate and removed from office (Mollenhoff and Rushford, 1980, p. 39). Following the passage of the new legislation noted above, 89 grievances were filed in a nine-month period, resulting in corrective action in 11 cases and the retirement of a judge in a 12th case (Gest, 1983, p. 42).

A growing number of state judges are being charged with misconduct. Cases range from the California judge who was removed from office after staging a "bargain day" on which those pleading guilty received light sentences, to a Missouri judge who drew a nine-year prison term for conspiring to make illegal drugs (Gest, 1983, p. 42). A judge in Ohio was convicted on criminal charges of keeping weapons seized as evidence, seeking sex from female defendants, and attempting to block an investigation of his misconduct. In New York, a judge was removed from the bench after bringing a coffee vendor before the court in handcuffs and bawling him out because he had served "His Honor" a lousy cup of coffee (David and David, 1980, p. 105).

Commissions on judicial misconduct have been operating now for about twenty years and can be found in all fifty states and the District of Columbia. They are composed of laypersons, attorneys, and judges, and their mission is to investigate complaints about judicial misconduct on or off the bench. According to Gest (1983), 3,500 complaints were lodged against judges in 1981. During that year, sixteen judges were removed from office; fifty-five were admonished or censured; and seventy judges resigned or retired while under investigation.

It is not surprising that many complaints against judges are made by disgruntled defendants or plaintiffs who are displeased with the decisions made in their cases. About three quarters of these complaints are dismissed, because they are based on judicial rulings rather than on charges of misconduct. For legitimate complaints, however, commission investigators who are, for the most part, lawyers or retired judges, review transcripts and preside over hearings. The commission then either dismisses the charges, issues an informal warning to the judge, or recommends disciplinary action to the state supreme court. Disciplinary matters involving federal judges are dealt with by a panel of peers.

Judges may complain that they are held to a higher standard of conduct than other professionals, but this view is not likely to generate much sympathy. After all, if judges are going to sit in judgment on their fellow citizens, at the very least they should provide a model of intelligence, fairness, and honesty for the rest of us. Thus, if a judge's public behavior discredits the office, people feel entitled to question the fitness of that judge to serve as a member of the judiciary.

Commissions also take actions against judges for medical reasons (alcoholism, for example). When a judge has a drinking problem, a commission may refer him or her to a treatment program rather than recommending removal from office.

Judges who are not alcoholics may do other things on occasion that raise questions about the limits of judicial decorum. Former Los Angeles Municipal Court Judge Noel Cannon painted her chambers pink, kept a pet Chihuahua by her side, and was called the "Dragon Lady." She once threatened to give a traffic officer "a vasectomy with a .38" ("Judging the Judges," 1979, p. 49). Brill (1979) describes federal district court judge Irving Ben Cooper, who called Puerto Rican defendants who could not speak English "the slime of the earth" and accused a newly hired bailiff who mistakenly opened a broom-closet door, thinking it led to the judge's chambers, of being assigned to humiliate him because he (the judge) is short (p. 22). The conviction of twenty-four-year-old Eric Michael of New York for robbery, rape, and sodomy was overturned because he had been tried twice for the same crime. According to *Time*:

> The first trial had been terminated by Criminal Judge Arnold G. Fraiman. Why? Because continuing the trial would have interfered with the vacation plans of the judge and some jurors. Judge Fraiman, who had once before ended a trial rather than forego a holiday, this time offered to postpone his plans, but he did not order the jury to do so; instead, he declared a mistrial ("Judging the Judges," 1979, p. 47).

Judge Thomas Wicker, chair of the ethics committee of the National Conference of State Trial Judges, conducted a nationwide survey that indicates that nine out of ten judges across the country believe that judicial commissions protect the rights of the public. Nevertheless, many judges are critical of what they regard as unwarranted intrusions into their personal lives. While acknowledging that their position requires them to conform to more exacting standards than apply to many other professions and careers, they question the kinds of behavior that are labeled misconduct. They maintain that misconduct should be tied directly to what happens on the bench. It was in this spirit that the Montana Supreme Court halted proceedings against a judge, having decided that the judge's wife's sixty unpaid parking tickets had nothing to do with judicial misconduct.

Some judges also complain that they are treated unfairly once misconduct charges are filed against them. Justice Edwin Kassoff of the New York Supreme Court says that judges are not protected by a statute of limitations and do not have adequate opportunities to confront their accusers or present an effective defense. In effect, he ways, judges are denied due process.

An especially critical issue is the effect of adverse publicity on a judge's career. Even when a judge is found innocent of misconduct, his or her reputation may already have fallen victim to newspaper and television publicity. In many states and the District of Columbia, misconduct charges are made public either when the judicial commission finds probable cause for misconduct or when the commission makes its recommendations for action to the state supreme court. A remedy for this situation might be to impose penalties for disclosing news about on-going commission investigations until *after* disciplinary measures have been taken (if, in fact, the commission reaches a decision that misconduct has occurred).

Discussion and review

1. What distinguishes a court of record from a court of limited jurisdiction?
2. Why are state supreme courts sometimes called courts of last resort?
3. What are the principal areas of jurisdiction of the U.S. Supreme Court? How does the Court obtain its cases?
4. What are the areas of jurisdiction of the U.S. District Courts? What kinds of cases reach the U.S. Courts of Appeal?
5. Discuss parallels in the structure and operations of the federal and state judicial systems.
6. What are some of the characteristics of lower courts that earn these courts the reputation of "the weakest link in the administration of justice"?
7. What were some of the major problems in the judicial selection process that the Missouri plan sought to overcome?
8. Describe the duties and responsibilities of the bailiff, the court clerk, and the court administrator.
9. Discuss some of the principal sources of job-related stress that judges encounter.
10. Is it possible to separate effectively the trivial and the important kinds of judicial behavior that lead to charges of judicial misconduct? What, in your opinion, are some types of misconduct that would justify removing a judge from the bench?

Glossary

Appellate court A court that reviews cases that have been tried in a trial court. Except in special cases in which original jurisdiction is conferred, an *appellate court* is not a trial court or a court of first instance.

Bailiff An officer of the court whose principal duty is to maintain the security and decorum of the court. He or she is responsible for keeping an eye on defendants delivered to the court and for assuring the legality of actions involving witnesses and jurors. He or she summons witnesses when it is their turn to testify, and sees that witnesses and jurors do not discuss cases when they are not supposed to. The bailiff is also responsible for maintaining the secrecy of jury deliberations and for arranging food and lodging for the jury.

Certiorari Latin for "to be informed of, to be made certain in regard to." *Certiorari* is a writ of review or inquiry directed by a superior court to an inferior court, asking that the record of the case be sent up for review. This method of obtaining a review of a case is used by the U.S. Supreme Court.

Court of first instance A court to which a case must originally be brought; usually a trial court.

Court of general jurisdiction The largest jurisdiction a court of first instance can have in a given political unit (i.e., state, federal, district, circuit, county).

Court of intermediate appeal A court of appeals established in several states to lessen the work load of the highest reviewing tribunal. Ultimate review can still be held in the highest court by that court's permission or, in limited cases, as a matter of right.

Court of last resort A court from which there is no appeal to a higher court in the same jurisdiction.

En banc decision Judicial decision rendered by the whole court with all members sitting as a body.
Inferior court In the federal system, all courts created under Article III, section 1 of the U.S. Constitution, except the U.S. Supreme Court; in the state systems, all courts of limited original jurisdiction.
Stare decisis Latin for "let the decision stand." A doctrine holding that the courts will abide by the rulings of prior court decisions when dealing with cases in which the facts are substantially unchanged.

References

Alpert, L. "Learning about Trial Judging: The Socialization of State Trial Judges." In *Courts and Judges*, edited by J. A. Cramer. Beverly Hills, Calif.: Sage, 1981.
Banks, L. "The Crisis in the Courts." *Fortune* 64 (1961):186–89.
Blumberg, A. *Criminal Justice*. Chicago, Ill.: Quadrangle, 1967.
Brill, S. "Benching Bad Judges: Should It Be Easier Than It Is To Remove Federal Judges?" *Esquire*, 10 April 1979, pp. 20-21.
Burke, R. J. "Occupational Stresses and Job Satisfaction." *Journal of Social Psychology* 100 (1976):235–44.
Carp, R., and Wheeler, R. "Sink or Swim—Socialization of a Federal District Judge." *Journal of Public Law* 21 (1972):359–93.
Chamelin, N. C., Fox, V. B., and Whisenand, P. M. *Introduction to Criminal Justice*. Englewood Cliffs, N.J.: Prentice-Hall, 1979.
Cohen, M. R. *Law and Social Order*. New York: Harcourt Brace, 1933.
David, L., and David, I. "The Crime of America's Justice." *Good Housekeeping*, August 1980, pp. 105, 191–3.
Forer, L. G. "View from the Bench: A Judge's Day." *The Washington Monthly*, February 1975, pp. 33–39.
Gest, T. "Crackdown on Judges Who Go Astray." *U.S. News and World Report*, 28 February 1983, p. 42.
Hearnes, W. E. "Twenty-Five Years Under the Missouri Plan." *Journal of the American Judicature Society* 49 (1965):100–104.
Janis, I. L., and Mann, L. *Decision Making*. New York: Free Press, 1977.
"Judging the judges." *Time*, 20 August 1979, pp. 48–55.
Kerper, H. B. *Introduction to the Criminal Justice System*. St. Paul, Minn.: West, 1972.
Klein, F. J. *Federal and State Court Systems—A Guide*. Cambridge, Mass.: Ballinger, 1977.
Law Enforcement Assistance Administration. *National Survey of Court Organization, 1971: Preliminary Report*. Washington, D.C.: U.S. Government Printing Office, 1972.
Levinson, H. *Executive Stress*. New York: Harper & Row, 1970.
Lewis, A. "Curious Things a Campaign Brings . . . Including Virulence in California." *St. Petersburg Times*, 31 October 1978, p. 6D.
Miller, A. G. "On the Need for 'Impact Analysis' of Supreme Court Decisions." *Georgetown Law Review* 53 (1965):365–401.
Mollenhoff, C., and Rushford, G. "Judges who should not judge." *Readers Digest*, February 1980, pp. 39-47.
Neubauer, D. *America's Courts and the Criminal Justice System*. North Scituate, Mass.: Duxbury, 1979.
Peltason, W. J. *Federal Courts in the Political Process*. New York: Random House, 1955.
President's Commission on Law Enforcement and Administration of Justice. *Task Force Report: The Courts*. Washington, D.C.: U.S. Government Printing Office, 1967.
Roberts, L. E. "Twenty-Five Years Under the Missouri Plan." *Journal of the American Judicature Society* 49 (1965):92–97.
Robin, G. D. "Judicial Resistance to Sentencing Accountability." *Crime and Delinquency* 21 (1975):201–12.
Rosett, A. I., and Cressey, D. R. *Justice by Consent: Plea Bargains in the American Courthouse*. Philadelphia, Pa.: Lippincott, 1976.
Schein, E. H. "Organizational Socialization and the Profession of Management." *Industrial Management Review* 9 (1968):1–16.
Shubert, G. "The 1960 Term of the Supreme Court: A Psychological Analysis." *American Political Science Review* 56 (1962):90–107.
Stratton, J. G. "Police Stress—An Overview." *Police Chief*, April 1978, p. 38.
Ulman, J. *The Judge Takes the Stand*. New York: Alfred Knopf, 1933.

Notes

1. The lack of enthusiasm was understandable. Supreme Court justices in Washington's administration were required to hear cases in widely scattered and remote locations. To reach these places, they had to endure exhausting trips on horseback and the culinary horrors of wilderness inns and taverns.

2. Federal courts other than the U.S. Supreme Court are often referred to collectively as "lower federal courts." U.S. District Courts are included in this category.

3. A detailed account of Judge Bird's ordeal is given in Preble Stoltz, *Judging Judges: The Investigation of Rose Bird and the California Supreme Court*. (New York: Free Press, 1981). Despite the biased campaign, Judge Bird retained her position on the bench.

10
the criminal trial

Rules of evidence
Privileged and confidential communications
Opinion and expert testimony
Hearsay

Anatomy of a trial
The jury
  Scientific jury selection
  Jury size
Opening statements
  The case for the state
  Motion for dismissal or directed verdict
  The case for the defense
Rebuttal and surrebuttal
Closing arguments
Charging the jury
Jury deliberations
Sentencing and appeal

Summary
Issue paper: Mad or bad? The insanity defense

THE importance of the criminal trial in the criminal justice system has been identified by Kaplan, who refers to the trial as the "balance wheel of the entire process" (1973, p. 337):

> Although . . . relatively few cases are disposed of after full trial, it is the threat of exclusion of evidence at trial that is the basis of the exclusionary rule's effort to control the police; it is the projected result of a trial which influences the exercise of the prosecutorial discretion and it is the chance of success at trial which determines the bargaining positions of the lawyers attempting to dispose of the case through negotiations for a guilty plea (ibid.).

Frank (1949), referring to the adversary nature of American criminal jurisprudence, calls the jury trial a "sublimated brawl" (p. 7). Smith and Pollack seriously question the generality and validity of the public image of the courtroom as a place where "truth is discovered through . . . trial by combat between two equally armed lawyer-gladiators, with the struggle presided over by the judge (as repository of the wisdom of the community)" (1972, p. 137). Despite criticisms, however, the adversary model of courtroom procedure is one of the most cherished legacies of English common law and a symbol of the freedoms guaranteed to American citizens under the U.S. Constitution.

While it can not be denied that drama is inherent in adversarial proceedings, the jury trial has proven—over centuries of evolution to its present form—to be a reliable means of uncovering the truth. It accomplishes this by following a formal set of rules for presenting evidence, rules that seek to deny advantage to either the prosecution or the defense. Much of what laypersons might regard as a fussy preoccupation with procedural details or interpretations of legal precedent is, in fact, the expression of a painstaking effort to eliminate bias.

Rules of evidence

Rules of evidence govern the presentation of evidence at a trial in much the same way that the rules of a game govern the conduct of the players. According to this analogy, the judge acts as impartial referee or umpire. Evidence consists of legal proofs presented to the court in the form of witnesses, records, documents, objects, and other means, for the purpose of influencing the opinions of the judge or jury toward the case of the prosecution or the defense. The four kinds of evidence are;

1. *Real Evidence.* Objects of any kind (weapons, clothing, fingerprints, and so on).
2. *Testimony.* Statements of competent, sworn witnesses.
3. *Direct Evidence.* The observations of eyewitnesses.
4. *Circumstantial Evidence.* Any information that tends to prove or disprove a point at issue.

To be accepted by the court, evidence must be relevant, competent, and material. Relevant evidence is evidence that directly pertains to the issue in question. That is, evidence is relevant not only when it tends to prove or disprove a fact in issue, but also when it establishes facts from which further inferences can be drawn. As Kerper points out,

> ... if the defendant is charged with murder, and the issue is his ability to commit the offense, his opportunity to commit the offense, and his intention to commit the offense, are all relevant evidence. His fingerprints on the murder weapon, his sudden wealth after the deceased was robbed, the threats he made against the deceased, his attempt to flee or commit suicide, are also relevant evidence, as the proof of these facts would tend to prove the guilt of the defendant. Lawyers often speak of the "chain of evidence," which refers to the fact that evidence tends to develop bit by bit with one piece of evidence supporting and tending to prove another (1972, pp. 306–7).

Relevance is determined by contrast with the concept of *materiality of evidence*. Material evidence is evidence which relates to the crime charged or which has a legitimate and effective bearing on the decision of the case (22A C.J.S. § 637., 1961). Evidence is sometimes held to be inadmissible because it does not tend to prove the specific issue (i.e., is immaterial). Evidence may be logically relevant but not necessarily material. For example, evidence that a defendant purchased a .38 caliber revolver and ammunition shows that he possessed a weapon. But if the defendant is accused of burglary, not robbery, evidence that he owns a gun is not material to this trial. The trial judge possesses considerable latitude in the determination of materiality of evidence and doubts should be resolved in favor of admission of evidence unless some definite rule makes it impossible (22A C.J.S. § 637, 1961).

Competent evidence is evidence supplied by a competent witness. Very young children, mental retardates, and persons classified as mentally disturbed may be considered by the court as incompetent witnesses. Competence, however, is a complex and controversial issue. Just how old must children be before they can distinguish between right and wrong? Before they are able to understand the meaning of what they have seen or heard? If a witness has been institutionalized or treated for mental illness, is this incontrovertible proof that he or she is incapable of giving reliable and competent testimony on a specific question?

Competency is no guarantee that the evidence will carry *weight* with the jury. Although a convicted felon may be a competent witness, the mere fact of his or her conviction may discredit the testimony. Similarly, a wife's testimony on behalf of her husband may be competent—but worthless in terms of influencing a juror's opinion. At any rate, *competency* of evidence is a matter for the judge to decide; the weight of the evidence is a matter for the jury.

Privileged and confidential communications

The distinction between privileged communications and confidential communications is often confused by laypersons. *Privileged communications* are those protected by law (e.g., those that occur between attorney and client, between physician and patient, or between priest and penitent). The person receiving the communication cannot be compelled to divulge the contents of the communication unless the person making the statement waives the legal right to secrecy. Communications between husband and wife are also privileged. In some states, however, a person may be permitted to testify *for* his or her spouse.

Confidentiality refers to an ethical obligation on the part of a professional person to safeguard the privacy of communications made by a client within the context of the professional relationship. But confidential communications have no legal protection in the courts. A marriage counselor, for example, is bound by the ethics of the professional relationship to maintain the confidentiality of statements made by the client. Nevertheless, such statements do not constitute privileged communications, and a counselor could be ordered to reveal the statements or risk a citation for contempt of court.

Opinion and expert testimony

A cardinal rule of evidence restricts lay (nonexpert) witnesses to testimony based on the direct evidence; their opinions, speculations, or conclusions are not valid. Exceptions to this rule cover situations in which an opinion can be supported by observation of facts that fall within the realm of common experience. Thus, a witness' opinion that a defendant was drunk may be accepted by the court on the basis of testimony that the witness smelled alcohol on the defendant's breath, heard his slurred speech, saw him down several drinks in rapid succession, and observed him walking with an unsteady gait.

Unlike the eyewitness or the alibi witness, *expert witnesses* do not have to have any first-hand knowledge of the crime, nor are they restricted by the rules of evidence from expressing their opinions. In fact, expert witnesses are summoned for the specific purpose of expressing opinions. The court can accept any person as an expert witness whose credentials establish an expertise in a particular field or discipline. Fingerprint specialists, handwriting specialists, crime lab technicians, or criminal investigators may act as expert witnesses. Psychiatrists and psychologists may be asked to give expert testimony on the mental status of the defendant; a ballistics specialist may testify regarding the identification of a murder weapon; an art dealer may be asked to appraise the value of a stolen painting introduced as evidence. Even merchants, artisans, and skilled workers (electricians, plumbers, locksmiths), whose long experience in their field qualifies them as experts among their peers, may be called in specific cases.

Specialists must first be qualified by the court to act as expert witnesses. The side that calls the expert—the prosecution or the defense—

must convince the court that the witness is, in fact, an expert and is therefore capable of expressing a valid and reliable opinion. Opposing counsel may shorten the inquiry considerably by agreeing that the witness is acceptable as a qualified expert. This is often done when the expert's credentials are well known to both sides. In some instances, the opposing counsel may object to qualifying the witness and may attempt, through cross-examination, to disqualify the individual as an expert. If the witness is discredited, the judge will rule that he or she can not testify as an expert in the trial.

Hearsay

Another important rule of evidence excludes *hearsay* as admissible evidence in a court of law. Hearsay is knowledge or information that a witness acquires second-hand (i.e., facts he or she is told by someone else). The court views such evidence as a denial of the defendant's right to confrontation, because there is no opportunity to establish the truth of hearsay through the cross-examination of actual witnesses.

A major exception to the hearsay rule involves *res gestae*, a Latin phrase meaning "the things that happened." As Kerper explains, "If an event is under investigation, then the entire transaction and every part of it may be introduced into evidence, even though some of the statements made at the time would ordinarily be barred by the hearsay rule" (1972, p. 312). Thus, the investigation of an incident of forcible rape might include in the testimony and evidence this statement from the victim's roommate: "I've told her a hundred times not to go walking in the park at night."

Other exceptions to the hearsay rule include admissions against interest, confessions, and statements made from the deathbed. An admission ties the defendant to the crime. For example, in a case involving homicide, the accused may tell the investigator, "Yes, I was there in the apartment when the shooting took place." This admission places the accused at the scene of the crime. A plea of guilty may be accompanied by a written confession, which the prosecutor can read to the court. The prosecutor strongly desires a confession, because the Constitution provides safeguards against self-incrimination, and the defendant is not required to take the witness stand. The defense counsel is equally concerned with keeping the confession *out* of evidence. If the defendant is incriminated by his or her own statements, it is obviously difficult to get a *verdict* of not guilty. In any event, the judge carefully examines the circumstances under which a confession is made (i.e., if it was given voluntarily and without coercion) before he or she allows the confession to be read to the jury.

The admissibility of deathbed statements is based on the belief that a person aware of impending death has no motive to lie. Thus, deathbed declarations must include evidence of the declarer's *knowledge* of impending death. In many cases involving deathbed statements, the victim has suffered gunshot or stab wounds and the witness to the statement is a police officer or detective.

Anatomy of a trial

The U.S. Constitution guarantees a defendant's right to trial before an impartial jury. Unless a defendant waives this right, the trial in a felony case and in many serious misdemeanors is held before a jury. In some states, defendants must file a request for a jury trial when they enter a plea or at some time specified before the beginning of the court term in which a jury will be impaneled. Failure to file a request for a jury trial constitutes a waiver of the right. In other states, an *express* waiver of jury trial is required.

Criminal trials in the United States conform to the following outline (Wells and Weston 1977):

1. Jury selection, impaneling, and administration of oath
2. Opening statements by both sides (facts only)
3. The state's case
4. The defense case
5. Rebuttal (state)
6. Surrebuttal (defense)
7. Closing arguments by both sides
8. Charge to the jury (instructions on law)
9. Verdict
10. Judgment

The jury

The jury in a criminal trial is chosen by a complex—and often time-consuming—process. Because the prosecution and the defense both rely upon the jurors for a favorable decision, the factors involved in jury selection are of extreme concern to both parties in the proceedings. So important is the issue of jury selection that the methods of social science and psychiatric research have been applied to the process (with results we consider when we discuss scientific jury selection later in this chapter). When an offense is involved that has acquired great notoriety—such as the case of John Wayne Gacy, the man accused of more than thirty homosexually motivated murders of youths in Illinois—the time required to impanel a jury may stretch into months, and hundreds or even thousands of prospective jurors may be examined.

Eligible voters or taypayers make up the list from which a group of potential jurors, called the jury panel, or venire, is selected. This group meets the qualifications for jury duty as set by statute in the jurisdiction of the court. (In federal cases, the members of the jury are drawn from the entire jurisdiction of the district court trying the case.) State laws may exempt certain categories of individuals from jury duty: people with defective vision or hearing, persons over age sixty-five, and members of particular occupations or professions (e.g., attorneys). Physicians, clergymen, and women with infants or small children may also be excluded at their own request.

A group of veniremen (sometimes called the *array*) is summoned from the panel of potential jurors to appear in a given case. The veniremen are questioned in open court to determine their general qualifications for jury duty. Can they comprehend the English language? Are they citizens of the state? Are there any problems involving health or personal hardship that might interfere with the performance of their duties as jurors? Have they ever been convicted of a felony offense? (This last question is asked in those states in which a felony conviction disqualifies a person from jury duty.) The trial judge hears requests for exemption and dismisses veniremen with legitimate reasons for being excluded from jury duty.

The names of the prospective jurors are randomly selected from the veniremen that remain after questioning. A fairly common procedure is to write the names on slips of paper and place the slips into a revolving drum; the court clerk then draws names out one by one. As a juror's name is read, he or she takes a place in the jury box and is questioned by both the defense counsel and the prosecutor in the so-called *voir dire*. The voir dire (usually translated as "to speak the truth") is a procedure by which potential jurors are examined as a group and individually with regard to their eligibility as jurors. They are questioned about their knowledge of a case and whether that knowledge might affect their ability to hear the evidence impartially. They are asked about their acquaintance with the participants in the trial (the defendant, judge, attorneys, and witnesses) as a possible source of bias in their judgment of the evidence. And they are asked whether they are already formed an opinion of the facts or issues involved in the case. If the answer to any of these questions is yes, the panel member may be dismissed "for cause" by the judge. The prosecution and the defense each have an unlimited number of *challenges for cause* and the widest latitude in questioning. They may query the prospective juror on almost any matter that bears on that person's ability or willingness to reach an impartial decision. In addition, the judge may exercise an option to examine the potential jurors. (Note that dismissal from a jury panel in one case does not exclude a venireman from selection for service on another trial jury during his or her term of jury duty.)

At this point, each side is allowed a specified number of *peremptory challenges*—requests to the court to exclude a prospective juror without reason. For example, the prosecutor may decide that he or she does not want a woman under forty-five or a man over fifty on the jury; or the defense attorney may feel uneasy about a potential juror on the basis of his or her facial expression, clothing or demeanor. These reasons, whatever they are, do not have to be justified—or even stated—to the court.

If a juror is dismissed by peremptory challenge, the court clerk draws another name from the drum. The person whose name is drawn replaces the excused juror and is then questioned by the prosecutor and the defense counsel. This procedure continues until both parties have used up or waived their peremptory challenges and a jury of twelve has been accepted by both sides. In some states, alternate jurors are also selected. Alternates attend the trial but do not participate in the deliberations of the jury unless one of the original jurors is unable to continue in the proceedings. When the jurors have been selected, the whole panel is sworn in and one of their members is chosen as foreman.

A JURY OF YOUR PEERS???

The following is an excerpt from a book titled *Prosecution Course* published and distributed by the Dallas County District Attorney's office. The book was developed as part of a course for new prosecuting attorneys in this state. The section we quote is out of the chapter on "Jury Selection in a Criminal Case" by Jon Sparling, an assistant D.A. in Dallas. Sparling was the first Dallas prosecuter to get a 1,000 year sentence for a convicted felon; he is also known for his prosecution in the Guzman-Lopez case involving the killers of two Dallas County sheriff's deputies. . . . Who you select for the jury is at best a calculated risk. Instincts about veniremen may be developed by experience, but even the young prosecutor may improve the odds by the use of certain guidelines—if you know what to look for.

The following outline contains very little substantive law because I presume that any prosecutor is as able to look it up as I. The outline does, however, contain one prosecutor's ideas on some things that need to be said to the panel, and some things to look for in a juror . . .

III. What to look for in a juror.
   A. Attitudes.
      1. You are not looking for a fair juror, but rather a strong, biased and sometimes hypocritical individual who believes that Defendants are different from them in kind, rather than degree.
      2. You are not looking for any member of a minority group which may subject him to oppression—they almost always empathize with the accused.
      3. You are not looking for the free thinkers and flower children.
   B. Observation is worthwhile.
      1. Look at the panel out in the hall before they are seated. You can often spot the show-offs and the liberals by how and to whom they are talking.
      2. Observe the veniremen as they walk into the courtroom.
         a. You can tell almost as much about a man by how he walks as how he talks.
         b. Look for physical afflictions. These people usually sympathize with the accused.
      3. Dress.
         a. Conservatively, well dressed people are generally stable and good for the State.
         b. In many counties, the jury summons states that the appropriate dress is coat and tie. One who does not wear a coat and tie is often a non-conformist and therefore a bad State's juror.
      4. Women.
         a. I don't like women jurors because I can't trust them.
         b. They do, however, make the best jurors in cases involving crimes against children.
         c. It is possible that their "women's intuition" can help you if you can't win your case with the facts.
         d. Young women too often sympathize with the Defendant; old women wearing too much make-up are usually unstable, and therefore are bad State's jurors.

Reprinted from *The Texas Observer*, 11 May 1973.

Scientific jury selection During the 1970s, scientific jury selection attracted a great deal of interest from both the mass media and the legal community. But once the glare of publicity dimmed, skepticism about the success of the method and a concern for ethical issues focused professional interest on the technical details (sampling procedures, questionnaires, and behavior checklists for observing prospective jurors). According to Ellison and Buckhout (1981), one of the factors that limited enthusiasm for this approach to jury selection was cost.

Scientific jury selection is the application of tools and techniques that have long been familiar in social science research—questionnaires, interviews, attitude scales, public opinion surveys, and careful sampling procedures—to the detailed examination of information about prospective jurors. Data obtained from field research are analyzed to identify key variables that may affect the jury's decision-making process. (The methods of the attorney and the social scientist in jury selection are compared in **table 10.1**.)

Critics of scientific jury selection charge that it represents "sophisticated jury tampering, seeks to identify jurors who are not simply impartial but partial to the defendant, replaces trial by jury with 'trial by social scientists,' and discriminates against the ordinary defendant who cannot even afford the cost of a lawyer, let alone that of consultants and surveys" (Robin 1980, p. 276). Proponents of scientific jury selection claim that it provides a means to detect covert biases among prospective jurors that would not be uncovered during the voir dire examination; thus, the method supports a defendant's constitutional right to a fair trial by an impartial jury.

Indications are that scientific jury selection may spell the difference between conviction and acquittal in cases where the evidence presented in the trial is less important than the attitudes and personalities of the jurors. Also, as Robin states, "whenever there are sound reasons to believe that a defendant would be denied a fair trial by virtue of locale, pretrial publicity, the method of drawing the jury pool, or the identity of the individual jurors, then scientific jury selection is an appropriate tool for responding to the challenge of guaranteeing fair trials in a free society" (ibid.).

TABLE 10.1 Comparison of the methods of lawyers and social scientists in jury selection

Area	Social scientists	Lawyers
Jury panel characteristics	Surveys and demographic studies	Experience with previous jury pools
In-court observations	Systematic ratings	Intuition based on experience
Reputations of jury pool members	Information networks	Informal contact
Jury composition	Use of findings from small group research	Selection of key jurors
Follow-up	Systematic interviews of jurors and peremptory challenges	Informal feedback

Reproduced from Katherine W. Ellison and Robert Buckhout, *Psychology and Criminal Justice* (New York: Harper and Row, 1981), p. 177, by permission of authors and publisher.

SCIENTIFIC JURY SELECTION: THE JOAN LITTLE CASE

On 27 August 1974, a young black woman named Joan Little (who was being held in Beaufort County Jail, North Carolina, pending appeal on a conviction for burglary) killed a sixty-two-year-old white jailer and escaped. A little over a week later, she surrendered to the state police and was subsequently indicted for first-degree murder. Her defense was that the jailer had forced her to have oral sex with him by threatening her with an ice pick. According to her account, he dropped the ice pick in the heat of passion, whereupon she grabbed it and used it as a weapon to defend herself.

Psychologists conducted a public opinion survey among the residents of two dozen counties in the Beaufort area to determine attitudes toward race and justice. Results indicated that racial prejudice among the predominantly white inhabitants of this conservative Southern community had already decided the case against Joan Little. A *change of venue* was granted and the trial was subsequently held in Raleigh (the state capital) in Wake County.

The researchers constructed a psychological profile of the kind of juror who would most likely be sympathetic to the defendant. They also came up with a series of questions for the defense attorneys to use in spotting prejudiced jurors and exercising challenges to remove these persons from the array. Nearly 150 veniremen were examined over a ten-day period before the jury was finally impaneled. The trial jury finally selected included six blacks and six whites. Prior to retiring to deliberate their verdict, the members of the jury were informed by the judge that the charge of first-degree murder was reduced to second-degree murder because the prosecution had failed to prove premeditation.

On 15 August 1975, after seventy-eight hours of deliberation, the jury returned a verdict of not guilty. The circumstantial evidence in the case failed to convince the "scientifically" selected jury of Joan Little's guilt "beyond a reasonable doubt." Chief counsel for the defense credited scientific jury selection with the acquittal.

Jury size Nothing in the U.S. Constitution expressly mandates that a criminal trial jury must consist of "twelve good men and true." The significance of the figure twelve has been attributed to the Twelve Apostles, the Twelve Tribes of Israel, and the Twelve Patriarchs, but these theories are purely conjecture. About all we say with certainty is that the jury of twelve is a tradition whose origins are lost in antiquity (Klein 1977).

Although few states have altered the right of a person accused of a serious crime to demand a trial by a jury of twelve, some states have amended their constitutions to permit variations in civil cases and in criminal cases involving misdemeanors. Six-person juries were introduced into the federal court system in 1971. A year earlier, in *Williams* v. *Florida* (399 U.S. 78 [1970]), the U.S. Supreme Court upheld the right of state courts to try individuals charged with serious felony offenses by juries of six persons. In stating that the main purposes of the jury are to act as a group of fact finders, to exercise common sense judgment, and to ensure community participation and shared responsibility in the determination of guilt or innocence, the Court did not believe that the fulfillment of these purposes depends on the particular number of people that make up the jury:

> To be sure, that number should probably be large enough to promote group deliberation, free from outside attempts at intimidation, and to provide a fair possibility for obtaining a representative cross-section of the community. But we find little reason to think that these goals are in any meaningful

sense less likely to be achieved when the jury numbers six, than when it numbers 12—particularly if the requirement of unanimity is retained. And, certainly the reliability of the jury as a factfinder hardly seems to be a function of its size (p. 1906).

In 1973, in *Colgrove* v. *Battin* (413 U.S. 149), the Court extended the six-member jury prerogative to civil suits in federal courts.

As Ellison and Buckhout (1981) point out in their discussion of six-person and twelve-person juries, social scientists and legal scholars have repeatedly criticized the validity and reliability of research that reports no significant differences between the two types of juries. In 1978, the U.S. Supreme Court, in *Ballew* v. *Georgia* (435 U.S. 223) took a closer look at older studies and conducted a thorough review of newer empirical evidence on jury size. The Court concluded that (1) smaller juries are less likely to foster effective group deliberation, (2) twelve-person juries are less likely to reach "extreme compromises" in verdicts than are six-person juries, (3) smaller juries tend to hurt the defense more than the prosecution, and (4) a jury of less than six persons substantially threatens Sixth Amendment and Fourteenth Amendment guarantees. Ellison and Buckhout regard the *Ballew* decision as a "landmark in the application of psychological research to the rendering of a Supreme Court decision that will directly affect policy in the courtrooms of the United States" (1981, p. 163).

Opening statements

After the jury is impaneled, the trial opens with a reading of the indictment or information. Then the prosecution presents its opening statement. (The order in which the defense and prosecution present their cases varies from state to state, but each state follows a legally established procedure. Generally, the prosecution goes first.) The prosecutor, in his or her address to the jury, explains the charge, describes the crime the defendant is alleged to have committed, and draws a general picture of what the state intends to prove "beyond a reasonable doubt." The purpose of the opening statement is to provide the members of the jury—who lack familiarity with legal matters and procedures of criminal investigation—with an outline of the major objectives of the prosecution's case, the evidence it plans to present, the witnesses it intends to summon, and what it will seek to prove through the testimony of those witnesses. The idea is to make it easier for jurors to grasp the meaning and significance of evidence and testimony, and to keep them from becoming confused by the complexities of the case.

One thing the prosecution must *avoid* doing in the opening statement, however, is to promise evidence that it can not deliver. Deming points out that in the 1968 murder trial of William Anthony Clinger in Los Angeles, the prosecutor outlined the expected testimony of a witness named Mrs. Dorothy Casto. When the prosecution was subsequently unable to locate Mrs. Casto, the verdict of guilty that the jury returned was set aside "on the grounds that the outline of the expected testimony of the witness who failed to appear had been prejudicial" (1970, p. 115).

When the prosecutor concludes his or her opening statement, the defense can either follow with its opening statement or defer its presentation until later in the case. The usual procedure is for the defense to describe how it plans to expose the weaknesses or inadequacies of the prosecution's case and to demonstrate to the jury the defendant's innocence. In no state is the defense *compelled* to make an opening statement.

The case for the state After opening statements are concluded, the prosecution calls its first witness. The witness takes an oath or affirmation to tell the truth. The prosecutor then begins the presentation of evidence by *direct examination* of the witness—a question-and-answer procedure designed to elicit information from the witness about the case. According to LeGrande:

> Witnesses are required to respond directly to the question asked, and attempts to avoid the direct thrust of the question or to volunteer additional information beyond the question's scope are strongly discouraged. The basic reason for requiring direct responsiveness is that a witness, if given freedom to do so, might blurt out material which is legally objectionable, and if highly prejudicial might constitute reversible error. The procedural restrictions upon the methods of receiving testimony are designed, insofar as possible, to assure that objectionable material is not received by the jury (1973, p. 128).

Only the prosecutor, and the defense counsel, and the judge can ask questions of a witness. Although some states allow jurors to ask questions through the judge, this practice is not prevalent.

On many occasions, the prosecutor's first witness is the arresting officer. In such a case, direct examination might go like this:

PROSECUTOR: Would you please state your name and occupation for the court.

WITNESS: My name is Sergeant James Brown. I am employed as a detective with the Hillsborough County Sheriffs Department.

PROSECUTOR: On the night of 15 January 1983 were you directed to investigate a homicide reported at 10:00 P.M.?

WITNESS: Yes, sir.

PROSECUTOR: Please describe your investigation.

The witness would then describe the details of the investigation as he or she conducted it. Physical evidence is introduced by a witness under oath. It is not enough for the prosecutor to say, "This .38 caliber revolver was found in the defendant's bedroom." The evidence must be validated by a witness who can explain to the court how he or she determined that the evidence is what the prosecutor (or defense counsel) claims it to be.

When the prosecutor finishes with a witness, the defense attorney has the option to conduct a *cross-examination* of the testimony. Cross-examination is designed to test a witness' powers of observation and recollection, truthfulness, and possible bias against the cross-examiner's side. On cross-examination, the witness can be asked only about things to which he or she testified on direct examination, but the cross-examiner is permitted to ask *leading questions* (i.e., questions that suggest the answers). A skillful cross-examiner attempts to confuse, fluster, anger, or frighten the witness, causing him or her to lose self-control and composure. The result may be that the witness is *impeached*—meaning that the testimony is discredited. Impeachment may also occur by introducing testimony from other witnesses to challenge the version of events as related by a previous witness. The right to impeach a witness is restricted to the opposing side in cross-examination. Thus, an attorney can not attempt to impeach his or her own witness.

Upon completion of cross-examination, the prosecutor may conduct a *redirect examination* to clarify some point or issue raised during the cross-examination. The defense counsel may then carry out a *recross-examination*. These examinations are restricted to matters dealt with in the immediately preceding examination. Subsequent witnesses are called by the prosecution, and the procedure outlined above is followed with each of them. The prosecution presents all of its witnesses before any witnesses are called by the defense. After the last witness for the prosecution has testified, the prosecution rests its case.

Motion for dismissal or directed verdict At the conclusion of the prosecution's case, the defense attorney asks—almost as matter of routine—for the jury to be sent out of the courtroom while he or she moves for a dismissal of the case or a *directed verdict* of innocence from the judge. Such motions are usually based on one of three grounds:

1 The prosecution failed to show that a crime was committed.
2 The prosecution failed to show that the defendant had anything to do with the commission of the crime.
3 The prosecution failed to demonstrate the guilt of the defendant beyond a reasonable doubt.

In practice, these motions are rarely granted; the prosecution rarely takes a case to trial if it is not convinced of its own ability to prove the guilt of the defendant beyond a reasonable doubt. If the state fails to meet the burden of proof, however, the judge may grant the motion and acquit the defendant. If the motion is denied, the defense proceeds with its case.

The case for the defense Presentation of the case for the defense is similar to that of the prosecution. The defense counsel calls witnesses and directly examines them, then turns them over to the prosecutor for cross-examination. The following procedural considerations apply to the defense:

1 The defendant is not required by law to present witnesses; rather, defense can be based entirely on the evidence and testimony presented by the state.

2. The defendant is not required to give personal testimony. A defendant's refusal to take the stand can not be called to the attention of the jury by either the prosecutor or the judge. If he or she *does* choose to take the witness stand, a defendant faces the same hazards of cross-examination as any other witness.

3. The defense is not obligated to prove the innocence of its client, but merely to show that the state has failed to prove guilt.

When the testimony of the last defense witness is completed and all of the evidence has been introduced, the defense rests its case.

Rebuttal and surrebuttal

At the conclusion of the defense's case, the prosecution is given an opportunity for *rebuttal*. That is, it may summon additional witnesses to buttress its case, which may have been weakened by evidence and testimony presented by the defense. Testimony offered in rebuttal must be limited to matters covered in the defense's case. In addition, if the prosecutor chooses to conduct a rebuttal, the defense may summon surrebuttal witnesses to bolster its case.

Closing arguments

Closing arguments, or *summations*, provide the defense counsel and the prosecutor with an opportunity to summarize evidence and testimony and persuade the jury to accept their interpretation of the case. At one time, the summation was a theatrical display of forensic eloquence, as the opposing attorneys sought to influence the emotions of the jury. Hence, the old adage for trial lawyers: If the law is against you, pound the facts; if the facts are against you, pound the law; if both the law and the facts are against you, pound the table. At present, table pounding is considered in poor taste by most judges, and excessive flamboyance on the part of either counsel is apt to draw a rebuke from the bench.

Charging the jury

When all of the evidence has been presented and both sides have rested their cases, it is the responsibility of the judge to instruct the jury. As already noted, it is the prerogative of the jury to decide the facts, but the court must instruct the members of the jury on those aspects of the law that apply to the case. For example, if the defense is based on insanity, the judge must explain to the jurors how insanity is determined in that particular state.

Both the prosecutor and the defense are given the opportunity to submit instructions for the jurors. These instructions incorporate the theories of the respective attorneys as to the interpretation of the facts of the case. The judge selects from the instructions suggested by the attorneys or prepares his or her own instructions. In the absence of specific instructions, the judge may use a standard set of instructions that apply to cases of a similar nature. After the instructions are prepared, the judge reviews them with both attorneys in the judge's chambers. The final instructions are then prepared and the attorneys are given the opportunity to enter any objections to them as grounds for possible appeal.

The final instructions read to the jury in open court relate to specific issues of evidence or testimony in the case and traditionally cover the following areas:

1. The definition of the crime with which the defendant is charged.
2. The presumption of the defendant's innocence.
3. The fact that the burden of proof is upon the prosecution.
4. That if, after consideration of all the evidence, there remains reasonable doubt as to the defendant's guilt, he or she must be acquitted.
5. Procedures for electing a foreman and returning a verdict.

In many jurisdictions, jurors are given written instructions to take with them into the jury room during deliberations.

Instructions are also offered to the jury concerning the possible verdicts they may render. Guilty and not guilty are the usual alternatives in a criminal case, but the jury may also be given an option to decide on the *degree of the offense* in a particular case (e.g., murder in the first degree, murder in the second degree). The court supplies a written form for each verdict, along with the instruction that the appropriate form be returned to the court as soon as an agreement is reached.

Jury deliberations

After receiving their instructions, the jurors retire to the jury room to begin their deliberations in an effort to arrive at a verdict. The conduct of jurors and the procedures governing jury deliberations are established by local statutes and court rules. Generally, such rules restrict the members of the jury from communicating with anyone except the bailiff or the judge during their deliberations. And most jurisdictions do not allow the jury to separate once deliberations have begun. If it appears that deliberations might continue for more than several hours, arrangements may have to be made to sequester the jury in an adjacent hotel or motel. During the ensuing deliberations, jurors will be fed and housed together and will be prohibited from reading newspapers or watching television accounts of the trial.

Early in deliberations, the foreman of the jury may call for a vote. On rare occasions, this first vote may result in a unanimous verdict. More generally, however, the first vote reveals a three-way split among jurors, with some voting guilty, some voting not guilty, and some undecided. (If the case presents difficult and complex issues, the latter category may include the majority of the jurors.) The jury then discusses the case, with the foreman acting as a moderator or discussion coordinator. Sometimes a jury asks to review a particular piece of evidence or line of testimony or requests further instructions from the court on a point of law.

A unanimous verdict in criminal cases has been a basic requirement of common law since the fourteenth century. The U.S. Supreme Court upheld this requirement in both the nineteenth and twentieth centuries, and most states have endorsed this position in their provisions for jury trials. In *Johnson* v. *Louisiana* (409 U.S. 1085 [1972]), however, the Court held that Louisiana's use of 9–3 verdicts in major criminal cases was constitutional; and a similar decision was made in *Apodaca* v. *Oregon* (406 U.S. 404 [1972]), regarding Oregon's use of 10–2 verdicts in serious criminal cases. More recently, the Court dealt with the issue of less-than-unanimous verdicts in cases involving juries with fewer than twelve persons. In *Burch* v. *Louisiana* (441 U.S. 130 [1979]), the Court held that a 5–1 vote for conviction *does* fail to satisfy the minimum constitutional requirements.

If a jury is hopelessly deadlocked after prolonged deliberations, it may return to the courtroom, where the judge will instruct the members to go back to the jury room for a final effort to arrive at a verdict. The judge usually sets a specific time period for this to be done. If all reasonable methods are exhausted without reaching unanimity—resulting in a hung jury—the judge dismisses the jury, declares a mistrial, and schedules a retrial of the case with a new jury.

When the jury does return a verdict, the defense counsel or the prosecutor may request that the jurors be polled. Each juror is asked individually by the court clerk or the judge if the verdict announced is his or her verdict. The rationale for this procedure is to determine whether the juror is voting freely according to the dictates of conscience or if he or she is responding to pressure from fellow jurors. If polling discloses a less-than-unanimous verdict where one is required by law, the jury may be instructed to return to the jury room and continue its deliberations, or it may be dismissed and a mistrial declared. A mistrial places the defendant in the same position as if no trial had occurred, and proceedings may be reinstated against that defendant. If the verdict is not guilty, the defendant is discharged.

Sentencing and appeal

Before the sentencing stage of the criminal justice process, the defendant has either pled guilty to, or been found guilty of, a criminal offense. The court must then decide an appropriate disposition for the individual—a decision that is often complex and difficult for the judge. In earlier times, the imposition of sentences was cut and dried. Specific punishments for specific offenses were laid down by the law, and once a verdict of guilty was returned, the judge merely ordered the appropriate sentence to be carried out. The focus of attention was the offense, not the offender. However, this situation has changed as a consequence of societal reaction to crimes and criminals. Sentencing today involves a broader range of alternatives for the offender. Many of these alternatives involve rehabilitation and call for the assistance of professionals in psychology, sociology, education, and social welfare.

Sentencing is regarded, with justification, as one of the most significant stages in the administration of justice. For criminal offenders, it represents the determination of how they are going to spend the coming months and years, or—as in the case of capital punishment—whether they will face death. For society, as Reid observes, it is "a time of decision that necessitates not only action in a particular case but recognition of that society's philosophy of punishment and rehabilitation" (1982, p. 434). (In chapter 11, we explore the questions and issues raised by our present philosophical orientation toward punishment and its impact on the entire criminal justice system.)

A basic tenet of the criminal justice process in the United States is that every person accused of a crime is presumed innocent until proven guilty. And the system also requires that the proof be obtained legally. Appellate review acts as a shield for an individual caught up in the processes of criminal trial, incarceration, or supervision in the community. The power of the state is great and citizens must be protected against the capricious and arbitrary exercise of such power. The right to appeal the verdict in a criminal trial is one of the most important aspects of *due process,* although it is not spelled out in the Bill of Rights.

Summary

Compared with the total volume of cases entering the criminal justice system, relatively few cases are disposed of by trial. Nevertheless, the criminal trial is an indispensable feature of our system. The accused is brought to trial under a presumption of innocence; it is the task of the prosecution to prove beyond a reasonable doubt that the defendant is guilty of the crime with which he or she is charged.

The adversary concept of criminal justice is most clearly exhibited in the trial. The prosecutor uses the authority and resources of the state to gather enough evidence to convince the court and jury of the guilt of the defendant. The defense counsel attacks the weaknesses of the prosecution's case, seeks to impeach the testimony of state witnesses, questions the validity and reliability of the prosecution's evidence, and is alert to any tactics of the opposing counsel that violate the constitutional rights of the defendant.

An extremely important aspect of the trial is the selection of people to serve on the jury. Jurors are chosen by a procedure called voir dire, which assigns the prosecution and defense a number of challenges for cause (stated reason or reasons why a particular person is unfit to serve and a juror) and peremptory challenges (challenges for which no reasons need be given). In recent years, there have been some noteworthy attempts to use the methods of the social scientist to pick jurors who would be inclined to favor the defendant. This process of scientific jury selection has been attacked as "jury stacking" and defended as a guarantor of fairness. Whatever its defects or merits, however, the expenses involved in its use will probably keep it from becoming a routine procedure in criminal trials.

Trials are governed by rules and procedures that have evolved over many years and are enforced by the judge, who acts as an arbiter or referee. The order of a criminal trial may vary somewhat from one jurisdiction to another, but it generally conforms to a standard pattern. After a reading of the formal charges against the defendant, the prosecution presents its case by introducing evidence and witnesses whose testimony is subject to cross-examination by the defense. At the conclusion of the prosecution's case, the defense presents its case, including evidence and testimony, and may call the defendant to testify on his or her own behalf. Following closing statements by both sides, the judge instructs the jury on points of law, and the jury is then sequestered until it reaches a verdict or finds itself hopelessly deadlocked.

issue paper

MAD OR BAD? THE INSANITY DEFENSE

Under our system of criminal justice, there are two methods by which an offender can be absolved of criminal responsibility for his or her behavior. The first method involves being declared incompetent to stand trial; the second method is to be found not guilty by reason of insanity. Both of these defenses grew out of the overuse of the death penalty in England. The issue of competency to stand trial rests upon the common-law criteria that a defendant must be able to understand the charges and be able to cooperate with defense counsel in the preparation of his or her own defense. The insanity defense is based on the proposition that the defendant did not have the capacity to understand the nature of the criminal act or to know that the act was wrong. The common-law development of the insanity plea was a major shift away from the harsh punitive practices of the early nineteenth century.

Laws on competency provide that a person accused of a crime may be tried only if he or she is able to understand the nature of the charge and aid counsel in preparing a defense. As the U.S. Supreme Court ruled in *Dusky* v. *United States* (362 U.S. 402 [1960]), it is not sufficient that the defendant be oriented with regard to time and place or have some recollection of events. The test must be "whether he has sufficient present ability to consult with his lawyer with a reasonable degree of rational understanding—and whether he has a rational as well as a factual understanding of the proceedings against him" (*Dusky* at 402). A defendant found incompetent to stand trial is usually committed to a mental institution (e.g., state hospital) until such time as he or she is certified to be competent by medical or psychiatric authorities. During this period, the defendant remains under the jurisdiction of the court. The significance of the competency issue has generally been obscured, because it is often confused with the insanity defense. Yet far more persons are confined in mental hospitals on the basis of incompetency than as a result of a finding of not guilty by reason of insanity.

The insanity defense raises the issue of criminal responsibility. Is the defendant capable of making distinctions between right and wrong or good and evil, as these terms are defined in codes of social conduct? The general view within the law is that wrongdoing must be conscious to be criminal. The fundamental link between moral knowledge and free choice is indicated by the legal principles that allow for the diminution or elimination of responsibility under certain conditions that lessen or destroy a person's capacity to discriminate between right and wrong and to act in accordance with such discriminations.

A variety of tests or formulas have been developed over the years to help the jury in a case involving the insanity defense. The best known of these tests is the M'Naghten Rule, which is used in about twenty states. This rule is named after Daniel M'Naghten, a psychotic individual who murdered the secretary of Prime Minister Robert Peel in the mistaken belief that he was actually assassinating Peel. M'Naghten was probably a paranoid schizophrenic; he was entangled in an elaborate system of persecutory delusions and believed he was being pursued by government spies. M'Naghten was acquitted on the grounds that he was insane at the time he committed the murder. The basis for the decision is incorporated in the following statement that has come to be known as the M'Naghten Rule:

> Every man is presumed to be sane, and . . . to establish a defense on the grounds of insanity, it must be clearly proved that, at the time of the committing of the act, the

party accused was labouring under such a defect of reason from disease of the mind, as not to know the nature and quality of the act he was doing; or if he did know it, that he did not know he was doing what was wrong *(Daniel M'Naghten's Case,* 10 C.&F. 200, 210-211, 8 Eng. Rep. 718, 722-723 [1843]).

As used here, *insanity* is a legal and philosophical term; it is not a synonym for psychosis or mental illness. When psychiatrists or psychologists testify in cases involving the insanity defense, the best they can do is to give evidence or opinions about the possible influence of mental conditions on the capacity of the accused to form criminal intent. The judgment of criminal *responsibility* is a matter for the jury. If the jury decides that a defendant is, in fact, not guilty on the grounds of insanity, the defendant is committed to a mental institution where he or she remains under the jurisdiction of the court until institutional authorities certify a recovery. The subsequent disposition of the individual is up to the court of original jurisdiction.

The intense publicity generated by such cases as that of John W. Hinckley, Jr., the attempted assassin of President Reagan, is out of proportion to the handful of cases in which insanity is actually used as a plea. And as Kaufman (1982) points out, a successful insanity defense is even more rare. In New York, for example, it is estimated that the insanity defense is involved in no more than 1.5 percent of all felony indictments, with success in only about one quarter of the cases. The problem, as Kaufman observes, is that acquittals by reason of insanity tend to undermine public faith in the ability of the criminal justice system to deal rationally and equitably with crime. Many people, he feels, conclude that the insanity defense is a cop-out that allows dangerous criminals to be released to commit further criminal acts after a brief period of psychiatric confinement.

Unfortunately, such cases do occur. As a teenager, Edmund Emil Kemper III murdered his grandparents and was sent to a psychiatric hospital. He was subsequently released, subject only to the requirement that he return periodically for psychiatric examination. After leaving the hospital, Kemper murdered eight more people, including his mother and a fifteen-year-old girl (who he dismembered). A few days later, while driving around with the girl's remains in the trunk of his car, Kemper visited his psychiatrist, who pronounced him "safe."

An issue that came up again and again in the heated discussion that followed the Hinckley case was the inability of psychiatrists and psychologists to predict whether individuals such as Hinckley and Kemper will pose a threat to society if released from psychiatric confinement. (There is the additional issue of whether such persons represent a threat to *themselves,* but this is less likely to trigger public indignation than the danger posed by the homicidal individual.) Research consistently demonstrates that predictions of dangerousness are beyond the capacity of contemporary psychiatric and psychological expertise.

The American Psychiatric Association (APA) issued a policy statement in January 1983 on the insanity defense that recommends a narrower application of the plea. In addition, the APA has criticized a series of legal rulings that authorized findings of insanity for persons with abnormal personalities—such as antisocial individuals who commit crimes of violence with no show of concern or remorse for their victims. The insanity defense, according to the APA, should apply only to persons who are pyschotic or who have a severely distorted perception of reality. This limitation, it seems, would exclude President Reagan's would-be assassin, John Hinckley, Jr.

The APA also recommends tighter supervision of persons who commit violent acts but are acquitted by reason of insanity. It is strongly critical of procedures that permit the release of such individuals just because psychiatrists are unable to certify that they pose a danger to themselves or others.

The APA's position is not quite as extreme, however, as a Reagan administration proposal to do away with the insanity plea. The proposal limits the insanity defense to people who do not know that they are doing when they commit an illegal act, and it calls for a verdict of guilty but mentally ill. Several states have already barred the insanity defense or extensively curtailed its use, and the APA's policy statement may offer an acceptable middle ground for legislative action in other states.

THE INSANITY DEFENSE AND ME

Last week, in a radio speech to the nation broadcast from Camp David, Ronald Reagan announced that he is sending a new anticrime package to Capitol Hill that will include "common-sense revisions of the insanity defense, a defense that has been much misinterpreted and abused." By far the most notable recent controversy over that defense centered on the case of John W. Hinckley Jr., who was acquitted in June of the attempted assassination of Reagan—by reason of insanity. Coincidentally, Hinckley himself offered Newsweek *a manuscript on the subject of the insanity defense and his own experience with it. Hinckley's article—written at Washington's St. Elizabeths Hospital, where he has been treated since the end of his trial:*

I don't feel guilty for being found not guilty by reason of insanity. It was the proper verdict and, although I was surprised by it, my fragile conscience is clear of useless guilt. The American people are angry with me, my parents' money and my fame. They are jealous and just drooled at the thought of me spending the rest of my life in some wretched prison in the backwoods of North Carolina. But here I am, in this insane asylum in southeast Washington, D.C., surrounded by the criminally insane, and everyone on the outside can't stand the thought of my innocence.

Those people who wish to abolish the insanity defense are a little nuts themselves. I wish they would move to Iran or Turkey, where defendants are shot in record time. America has the insanity defense because it is a compassionate and fair country. The passions of the mind separate the mental case from the criminal, and thank God we make such a distinction in this country.

The 12 people who sat on my jury deserve the Congressional Medal of Honor. Their bravery is worthy of great respect, and I admire them for their decision to ignore the public pressure to find me guilty and return a controversial not-guilty-by-reason-of-insanity verdict. They saw all of the evidence, listened to all of the doctors and concluded that I was mentally ill on March 30, 1981. As a result, I was not responsible for my actions on that day.

The public outrage over the verdict is disturbing to me because it truly demonstrates the vindictive nature of many Americans. These same people that curse my name and the insanity defense did not spend one minute in the courtroom during the trial. They may have read the newspapers and watched television accounts of my trial, but this is a very unfair way to judge a man's innocence or guilt. Based solely on media reporting, the American public found me guilty of the worst crime in the world.

Perhaps the uproar is for the belief that a person can shoot the president of the United States and not be punished for it. To hell with the mental state of the defendant; throw him in jail, so say the disgruntled masses. I can only respond with a shake of my head and the wish that society will someday show some compassion for its disturbed outcasts. Sending a John Hinckley to a mental hospital instead of prison is the American Way.

As things stand right now, it takes a near miracle to win with an insanity defense, and very few people actually attempt it. In order to convince 12 people that a particular person was "insane" at the time of a crime, a staggering amount of evidence must be presented to back up such a claim. My own attorneys had the benefit of dragging my past life in front of the jury, and a virtual gold mine of "bizarre" actions were revealed. The defense doctors found me to be delusional, psychotic, schizophrenic and perhaps the most alienated young man they had ever examined. On the other hand, despite evidence to the contrary, the prosecution doctor said I merely had some personality problems and deserved to be punished with imprisonment. The jury thought long and hard about everything they saw and heard and acquitted me. I had a fair trial with a fair judge and received a fair verdict. Only in America could this have happened.

A basic fact of my case which nobody knows is that I never wanted a trial in the first place. My attorneys and I tried desperately to plea bargain with the government and avoid a trial altogether. But the attorney general demanded that I be put on trial. Both pleas were flatly rejected. In return for four concurrent life sentences and a parole possibility in 15 years, I would have pleaded guilty. Incredibly, the government turned this offer down. Even more astounding is the fact that I was not allowed to simply plead guilty, without any sort of plea bargain. By January of 1982, I was so tired of waiting for a trial that I wanted to plead guilty and put an end to the charade. I was informed that this proposal was unacceptable to the judge and Justice Department. So I waited and went to trial and was acquitted. The public outrage over the verdict should be directed at the government for forcing me to go to trial.

Insanity trials are so painful. My life has become an open book, with my most intimate secrets now public knowledge. At times the testimony was almost unbearable. Anything said about my girlfriend Jodie Foster [the actress and Yale student] was upsetting to me, and I was compelled to leave the damn courtroom on a few occasions when my emotions got the best of me. But the trial and verdict were fate, and I suppose the emotional pain of sitting in that courtroom day after day was the price I had to pay.

To abolish the insanity defense would be a travesty of justice. Now we have the proposal by legislators that a not-guilty-by-reason-of-insanity verdict should be changed to a guilty-but-mentally-ill combination. The advocates of this idea want the disturbed defendant to be treated for his illness and, once he is cured, to be sent to prison to be punished for his crimes. This is an atrocious idea for two reasons: first, we would still be in the sorry position of wanting to punish a mentally ill person for his sickness, and, secondly, once the "cured" person is sent to prison, he is just going to get sick all over again, because prisons don't rehabilitate, they breed sociopaths.

Let's leave the insanity defense alone and accept the fact that, every once in a while, someone is going to use this "defense of last resort" and win with it. I was acquitted not because of my parents' money, or my attorneys, or the black jury; I was found not guilty by reason of insanity because I shot the president and three other people in order to impress a girl.

From *Newsweek*, 20 September 1982.

Discussion and review

1. Why has the jury trial been referred to as a "sublimated brawl"?
2. How does competent evidence differ from relevant evidence? From material evidence? How is the competency of a witness established?
3. Distinguish between privileged communications and confidential communications. Which type of communication is protected by law?
4. What are some of the exceptions to the rules of evidence against the admissibility of hearsay?
5. Briefly describe the selection process for jurors. What are some of the major issues raised by the process of scientific jury selection?
6. What do the opposing counsels seek to accomplish in their opening statements? Which side goes first?
7. Distinguish between direct examination and cross-examination. What limitations are imposed on cross-examination?
8. What are some of the major rights enjoyed by the defendant with respect to evidence and testimony in a criminal trial?
9. What are the principal matters covered by the judge in instructions to the jury?
10. What is the significance of the rulings in *Apodaca* v. *Oregon* and *Johnson* v. *Louisiana*? What are the pros and cons of the unanimous jury verdict?
11. Distinguish between incompetency and insanity. Why is the insanity defense so controversial if it is used so sparingly in criminal trials?
12. Who was Daniel M'Naghten and what is the significance of the M'Naghten Rule?

Glossary

Array (Veniremen)   The whole body of potential jurors summoned to court as they are arranged or ranked on the panel.

Challenge for cause   An attempt by the prosecutor or defense counsel to exclude a prospective juror during the voir dire examination by pointing out to the court why the person in question is unfit to serve or would not be impartial.

Change of venue   Moving a trial to a jurisdiction other than the one in which the crime was committed to guarantee the accused a fair trial.

Circumstantial evidence   All evidence of an indirect nature; circumstances from which the court or jury may infer a principal fact in a case.

Competency   In the law of evidence, the presence of those characteristics that render a witness legally fit and qualified to give testimony.

Cross-examination   The questioning of a witness in a trial or in a deposition by the party opposed to the one that produced the witness.

Directed verdict   An instruction by the judge to the jury to return a specific verdict.

Direct evidence   Proof of facts by witnesses who saw acts done or heard words spoken, as distinct from circumstantial evidence.

Direct examination   The first interrogation or examination of a witness by the party (defense or prosecution) who calls the witness.

Expert witness   A person who testifies in relation to some scientific, technical, or professional matter (i.e., persons qualified to speak authoritatively by reason of their special training, skill, or familiarity with a subject).

Hearsay Second-hand evidence of which the witness lacks personal knowledge. The witness merely repeats something that someone else said.

Impeachment of witness An attack on the credibility of a witness by the testimony of other witnesses.

Leading question A question that suggests to the witness the answer desired. *Leading questions* are prohibited in direct examination.

Material evidence Evidence that is relevant and bears upon the substantial issues in dispute.

Peremptory challenge A challenge that the prosecutor or defense counsel may use to reject prospective jurors without stating a cause for the rejection.

Rebuttal The introduction of rebutting evidence; arguments showing that statements of witnesses are not true; the stage of the trial at which rebutting evidence may be introduced.

Verdict In practice, the formal finding or decision made by a jury, reported to the court, and accepted by the court.

Voir dire French for "to speak the truth." Refers to the examination of prospective jurors by the prosecutor, defense counsel, and (sometimes) the court to determine their fitness to serve as jurors in a trial and to eliminate persons who would not be impartial. Also refers to the questioning of a witness to ascertain potential bias or, in the case of an expert witness, to determine qualifications and competence.

References

Coffey, A., Eldefonso, E., and Hartinger, W. *An Introduction to the Criminal Justice System and Process.* Englewood Cliffs, N.J.: Prentice-Hall, 1974.

Corpus Juris Secundum, vol. 22A. Brooklyn, N.Y.: The American Law Book Company, 1961.

Deming, R. *Man and Society: Criminal Law at Work.* New York: Hawthorn, 1970.

Ellison, K. W., and Buckhout, R. *Psychology and Criminal Justice.* New York: Harper & Row, 1981.

Frank, J. *Courts on Trial: Myth and Reality in American Justice.* Princeton, N.J.: Princeton University Press, 1949.

Kaplan, J. *Criminal Justice.* St. Paul, Minn.: West, 1973.

Kaufman, I. R. "The Insanity Defense." *New York Times Magazine,* 8 August 1982, 16-21.

Kerper, H. B. *Introduction to the Criminal Justice System.* St. Paul, Minn.: West, 1972.

Klein, F. J. *Federal and State Court Systems—A Guide.* Cambridge, Mass.: Ballinger, 1977.

LeGrande, J. L. *The Basic Processes of Criminal Justice.* Beverly Hills, Calif.: Glencoe, 1973.

Reid, S. T. *Crime and Criminology.* New York: Holt, Rinehart and Winston, 1982.

Robin, G. D. *Introduction to the Criminal Justice System.* New York: Harper & Row, 1980.

Smith, A., and Pollack, H. *Criminal Justice in a Mass Society.* New York: Holt, Rinehart and Winston, 1972.

Wells, K. M., and Weston, P. B. *Criminal Procedure and Trial Practice.* Englewood Cliffs, N.J.: Prentice-Hall, 1977.

Cases

Apodaca v. *Oregon* 406 U.S. 404, 92 S.Ct. 1628, 32 L.Ed.2d 184 (1972).
Ballew v. *Georgia* 435 U.S. 223, 98 S.Ct. 1029, 55 L.Ed.2d 234 (1978).
Burch v. *Louisiana* 441 U.S. 130, 99 S.Ct. 1623, 60 L.Ed.2d 96 (1979).
Colgrove v. *Battin* 413 U.S. 149, 93 S.Ct. 2448, 37 L.Ed.2d 522 (1973).
Dusky v. *United States* 362 U.S. 402, 80 S.Ct. 788, 4 L.Ed.2d 824 (1960).
Johnson v. *Louisiana* 409 U.S. 1085, 93 S.Ct. 691, 34 L.Ed.2d 672 (1972).
M'Naghten, Daniel, Case of 10 C&F 200, 210-211; 8 Eng. Rep. 718, 722-723 (1843).
Mapp v. *Ohio* 367 U.S. 643, 81 S.Ct. 1684, 6 L.Ed.2d 1081 (1961).
Williams v. *Florida* 399 U.S. 78, 90 S.Ct. 1893, 26 L.Ed.2d 446 (1970).

11
sentencing and after

Punishment
Retribution
Deterrence
Incapacitation (Restraint)

Rehabilitation: The treatment perspective
The prison system
Issues in correctional treatment

Sentencing
Sentencing structures
Balancing release rates and sentencing
Sentencing disparities
Sentencing reforms
   Penal code reforms
   Sentencing guidelines
   Sentencing councils and institutes

Appeal and postconviction remedies

Summary

Issue paper: The death sentence

THE traditional role of the criminal justice system has been to apprehend, convict, and punish offenders. Although many changes have occurred in our society in the last century, the orientation of the criminal justice system is still primarily punitive. Based on the historical systems that have shaped our ideas of law and justice, it is difficult to see how it could have been otherwise; and it is almost impossible to imagine any fundamental changes in the administration of justice without sweeping changes in the basic nature of our society and culture. At the same time, it must be emphasized that punishment for the sake of vengeance alone has never enjoyed unqualified support in this country. Since colonial times, a substantial minority has sought the goals of reform and *rehabilitation* for the criminal offender. And even when these goals have clashed with those of social defense and the maintenance of public order, rehabilitation has remained as an ideal of the American criminal justice system.

If sentences were intended merely to mete out punishment to criminal offenders, the task of judges would be much simpler and less controversial than it is. But sentencing—at least in modern times—has also been viewed as the cornerstone of rehabilitation. These broadly divergent objectives constitute part of the dilemma faced by many judges: Is it possible simultaneously to punish and to rehabilitate an offender?

In many jurisdictions, decisions about where and how people may spend years of their lives are made by a judge whose discretion is virtually unchecked or unguided by criteria, procedural constraints, or review. Often a sentence is meted out by a judge who has no information except the offender's name and the crime of which he or she is guilty. The reliability and accuracy of information provided to the court by presentence investigation reports often goes unchallenged. And the laws in many states about the selection of sentences are chaotic. In some states, mandatory "flat-time" sentences allow the court no discretion; in others, judges have full discretion as to the nature and extent of the sentences imposed. Disparity of sentences has been cited as one of the major causes of unrest leading to prison violence.

Punishment

Punishment is familiar to us in all aspects of life. We are acquainted with its use in the family and in the school; we employ punishment of various kinds with our pets, our children, and with one another; we believe that we understand the operation of punishment, and we can generally foresee its effects when it is employed. Through the use of positive sanctions (such as rewards or reinforcements), groups and societies seek to encourage conformity to various norms; by means of negative sanctions (punishments), attempts are made to discourage deviant behavior.

Reward and punishment, two of the principal techniques or processes for affecting behavior, have been familiar to the philosopher—or indeed to any person with an inquisitive mind—since time immemorial. The notion that people seek to maximize pleasure and avoid pain or discomfort was already ancient when it found its way into Jeremy Bentham's *hedonistic calculus*. Similar ideas had been expressed by the ancient Greek philosophers; and Freud's *Pleasure Principle* and *Reality Principle*, and B. F. Skinner's views on reinforcement did little more than restate the idea in a more sophisticated form (Smith and Vetter, 1982).

As a technique for modifying behavior, neither reward nor punishment is exact and unvarying in its effect. Punishment is often no more successful in discouraging some kinds of deviation than reward is in encouraging conformity to various norms. The persistence of these techniques in human affairs, however, indicates that they serve an important function other than merely altering behavior.

The use of punishment to deal with norm violators is traditionally justified by one of three rationales:

1. *Retribution*. "You're going to get what's coming to you."
2. *Deterrence*. "We're going to punish you so that you won't do it again." And a variation: "We're going to punish you so that *others* won't do the same thing."
3. *Incapacitation*. "As long as we're punishing *you*, you won't be out doing something to *us*."

As you might expect, these rationalizations leave considerable room for overlap. For instance, locking a naughty child in his or her room without supper may serve all three functions simultaneously. That is, it may communicate to the child that acting naughty will bring down the wrath of the parents and family; second, that it is no fun being locked up without supper, which gives one something to think about the next time an opportunity to act naughty presents itself; and third, that as long as one is locked up, there is little chance for further naughtiness. If a thoughtful brother or sister draws an appropriate conclusion from watching a sibling being punished in the above manner, the punishment may even manage to serve as a deterrent. These points should be kept in mind when considering the use of punishment for official purposes. The seriousness and magnitude of the punishment may differ, but the principles are the same.

Retribution

The punitive response is rooted in tradition and buttressed by common sense. Retribution—which means "something for recompense"—is a rather primitive (one hesitates to call it natural) human reaction: people who get hurt want to hurt back. It is not difficult, therefore, to understand why this justification for punishment ("the law of just deserts") has received a good deal of popular support throughout the ages. During the Iranian crisis in 1980, for example, practically every newspaper in the country received letters suggesting that the United States round up an equal number of Iranian hostages (from among the Iranians here on student visas) and hold them under exactly the same conditions that U.S. embassy personnel endured in Teheran. And similar messages, some of which verged on the obscene, festooned the bumpers of automobiles from Maine to California.

Deterrence

Deterrence has both a *specific* and a *general* aspect. When we punish subject A by imprisonment, we wish to deter A from committing further offenses, not only during A's period of incapacitation, but also following release from confinement. Our desire is reinforced by the belief that punishment brings about beneficial changes in the behavior of the person who is punished. We also believe that punishing A will deter B and C from committing criminal offenses similar to those committed by A. Optimistically, we hope that the example provided by A's punishment will have even broader effects in terms of deterring the commission of offenses *other than* those for which A was punished.

Psychologists, sociologists, economists, and other specialists have experimented extensively with the deterrent effects of punishment. Psychologists have looked at both animal and human subjects and have generated a large volume of conflicting and often contradictory results. This is quite understandable, given the complexity of even the simplest experiment on punishment; but it offers little help to the judge or correctional administrator. It is particularly difficult to understand how criminal justice authorities can be expected to place much confidence in research involving animal subjects when a crucially important element in deterrence is the human capacity for reasoning about the probable outcome of one's actions (Newman 1978).

Some sociological studies of the effectiveness of punishment as a deterrent deal with variations in recidivism (repeat crimes) in relation to the type and severity of sentencing. Sociologists have also focused on the issue of capital punishment as it affects homicide rates. Economists, too, have devoted considerable attention to capital punishment as a deterrent to violent crime, but they tend to employ extremely sophisticated mathematical models that are beyond the comprehension of almost everyone (except other economists or mathematicians). Despite the sophistication and complexity of the methodology, however, economists' results have not been appreciably different from those reached by psychologists—namely, that some research supports the idea of deterrence, and some does not.

Experts on punishment stress that several factors seem to have a significant effect on the results or outcome of punishment. That is, the factors are related to the success, partial success, or failure of punishment as an approach to deterrence. These factors are the speed, severity, and certainty of punishment. Evidence from both informal anecdotes and laboratory experiment indicates that certainty is a more influential variable than severity or speed, but it is difficult to arrive at an unqualified conclusion. All three factors are rarely present in any real-life situation; and even in the controlled environment of the laboratory, it is nearly impossible to conduct a rigorous and exacting comparison of the relative efficacy of one variable with respect to the others.

According to Grünhut, three components must be present if punishment is to operate as a means for curbing crime. First, "speedy and inescapable detection and prosecution" must convince the offender that crime does not pay (Grünhut 1948, p. 3). Second, after punishment has been meted out, the criminal must have a fair chance for a fresh start. Third, "the state which claims the right of punishment must uphold superior values which the offender can reasonably be expected to acknowledge" (ibid.).

Incapacitation (Restraint)

Punishment that involves imprisonment is justified on the grounds that as long as an offender is being held in confinement he or she is not free to commit more crimes. This rationale is regarded by both supporters and critics of the punitive approach as the most plausible argument in favor of punishment.

Extreme forms of punishment, such as execution or life imprisonment, constitute total incapacitation. Implicit in incapacitation is the belief that past behavior is the best basis for predicting future behavior. In the case of criminal behavior, the presumption is that a person who commits a particular type of crime is likely to commit more of those crimes or crimes of some other type. As Packer points out:

> This latter justification does not seem to figure largely in the justification for incapacitation as a mode of prevention. To the extent that we lock up burglars because we fear that they will commit further offenses, our prediction is not that they will if left unchecked violate the antitrust laws, or cheat on their income taxes, further burglaries, or other crimes associated with burglary, such as homicide or bodily injury. The premise is that the person may have a tendency to commit further crimes like the one for which he is now being punished and that punishing him will restrain him from doing so (1968, p. 50).

In every case, Packer reminds us, whether or not the prediction is valid is something that can only be determined by the subsequent actions of the offender.

Disillusionment with the rehabilitative ideal in corrections has led some influential authorities in criminal justice (e.g., Van den Haag 1975; Wilson 1977) to argue strongly for swift, certain, and severe punishment to remove habitual and serious offenders (particularly juvenile and youthful offenders) from circulation. This position is supported by research that demonstrates rather conclusively that a small number of offenders accounts for a large percentage of criminal offenses (Petersilia, Greenwood, and Lavin 1977; Wolfgang, Figlio, and Sellin 1972). What would happen to crime rates if the suggested strategy was followed?

Petersilia, Greenwood, and Lavin (1977) claim that it is counterproductive to incapacitate older habitual offenders when data suggest that individual offense rates decline substantially with age. In a study of a birth cohort by Wolfgang and his associates (Wolfgang, Figlio, and Sellin 1972), approximately 6 percent of 10,000 male subjects in the cohort committed five or more offenses by the time they were eighteen years old; this 6 percent was responsible for about two thirds of the violent crimes committed by the entire group. The implication is that if these individuals had been removed from circulation at some early point in their criminality, society would have been spared considerable grief and damage.

The principal stumbling block facing proponents of incapacitation is the fact that those who are incapacitated by being placed in confinement do not stay there: they are eventually released from prison or training school, and their subsequent behavior inevitably reflects the consequences of their experience during confinement. Vachss and Bakal (1979), for example, contend that confinement of criminality-prone delinquents has the effect of *increasing*, rather than decreasing, the commitment to a criminal career. Their argument is not directed toward the ineffectiveness of incapacitation, but toward the adverse results of confinement in existing correctional institutions.

There is nothing novel in the discovery that imprisonment has a deep effect upon those who undergo confinement. But it is necessary to point out that a substantial body of opinion within corrections supports the belief that those effects are beneficial for the inmate and society; that those effects are, in fact, the primary purpose for incarcerating an individual in the first place.

Rehabilitation: The treatment perspective

Treatment, according to the general dictionary definition, connotes the manner in which a person or thing is handled, used, or processed. In the context of mental health, the goal of treatment or therapy is to help an individual who has been diagnosed as emotionally disturbed or mentally ill to attain some level of improved functioning. In chapter 4, we documented some of the problems encountered in the application of the medical model to a wide range of psychosocial problems, many of which have little or no resemblance to conditions that can reasonably be expected to fit some model of a disease or illness. If the same is true for much of what psychiatry has claimed for the province of mental illness, the mischief wrought in corrections by the extension of these ideas is well-nigh incalculable.

The idea of rehabilitation in corrections began as a matter of moral redemption of the offender. It was gradually co-opted by psychiatry, however, and transformed into a problem for psychotherapy. The goal of correctional treatment became the changing of the personality of the criminal to achieve improvements in social behavior and personal adjustment. This was a praiseworthy objective; unfortunately, it had to be pursued within a system whose practitioners and representatives are charged with a responsibility for defending society that takes precedence over the rehabilitation of offenders. Consider the issue of incarceration.

The prison system

Prisons are the most visible manifestation of the corrections component of the criminal justice system. Critics of the penal institution consider the prison a monument to society's failure to devise more effective and humane methods for dealing with criminals. This viewpoint deserves careful consideration, but it is only a part of the story. The righteous indignation directed against prisons is singularly misdirected, especially by critics who fail to offer realistic alternatives for coping with the problems that prisons are compelled to handle.

Prisons today house a disproportionately high concentration of people who are socially deviant, emotionally unstable, psychologically disturbed, mentally retarded, and prone to aggression and violence. No longer are prison populations composed primarily of nonviolent offenders. Our search for alternatives to imprisonment has become focused on probation and other community-based correctional programs for first offenders, minor property criminals, drug offenders, and similar types of persons, leaving behind those who are perceived as a threat to public safety. Thus, we have loaded our prisons with the highest concentration of dangerous offenders in the entire history of penology.

The evidence speaks for itself. In 1974, one American prison witnessed eighty-seven stabbings and twelve inmate fatalities. This was not some backward bastion in the boondocks. It was San Quentin, California—a correctional institution in a state that boasts of having the most progressive correctional system in the country. The following year, ten inmates were slain in Florida prisons in explosive outbursts of violence triggered by some trifle—an argument over a bar of soap, an alleged insult, the theft of a cigarette.

Tensions in prison are elevated by racism. Inmates practice an informal, self-imposed segregation: whites and blacks stand in separate lines for meals, and whites, blacks, and Hispanics rarely sit together in the mess hall. Black convicts with hostile attitudes towards whites and Hispanics band together, and Hispanics with an antiblack or antiwhite bias do likewise. The result is that everyone is constantly struggling over the spoils of prison enterprises and over violations of the prisoner code that constitute slights against each group's honor. This internecine strife creates potentially explosive conditions within the institution that can be fused by a single incident.

Involvement of the New Left in American prisons during the protest years of the late 1960s and early 1970s was reflected in the demands of rioting Attica prisoners for guarantees of "asylum and safe passage to some nonimperialist country" ("Prisons: Uprising in Attica," *Time*, 1971). Eldridge Cleaver, George Jackson, Huey Newton, and Malcolm X were militants who developed their political consciousness while "doing time." It is not hard to understand how people with a background of social and economic deprivation readily accept the argument that they are political prisoners of a racist, capitalist system that has provided them with no alternative to a life of crime. And it is equally easy to comprehend how such views can make hash out of treatment or rehabilitation. For nonwhite inmates, participation in programs sponsored by "The Man" is the rough equivalent to collaboration with the enemy. For example, George Jackson was contemptuous of the efforts of California prison authorities to turn him into what he called "a good nigger."

The authors of a leading textbook in corrections (Allen and Simonsen 1981) observe that many criminal justice practitioners view any program or institution that is not punitive in its approach as "being soft" on criminals or "operating a country club for cons." These practitioners believe that the implementation of a treatment ideology does not mean coddling inmates or allowing them free run of an institution. In fact, they maintain that some form of treatment can be applied even within the strictest and most custody-oriented institutions.

> The major difference between the treatment and punishment ideologies is that in the former, offenders are assigned to the institution for a correctional program intended to prepare them for readjustment to the community, not just for punishment and confinement. There is room for punishment and for security in the treatment approach, but little room for treatment in the punitive approach. The more humane treatment methods are intended to be used in conjunction with the employment of authority in a constructive and positive manner, but inmates must be allowed to try and to fail. Authoritarian procedures, used alone, only provide the offender with more ammunition to support a self-image as an "oppressed and impotent pawn of the power structure" (ibid., p. 84).

In sharp contrast, Alberta Nassi (1980), on the basis of her experiences within the California prison system, is very skeptical that treatment can be carried out in the punitive context of a state prison. Rather, she sees an almost insurmountable role conflict between the objectives of treatment and custody.

Issues in correctional treatment

Three fundamental issues have to be addressed with regard to treatment of the criminal offender: an offender's right to treatment; an offender's right to *refuse* treatment; and the ability of the criminal justice system to provide *effective* treatment. The right to refuse treatment might be alternatively phrased as the right to receive punishment rather than treatment. The first and second of these issues raise significant questions in terms of constitutional law. The third issue involves a searching appraisal of people-changing capabilities as they relate to contemporary intervention techniques.

A series of legal decisions has affirmed the right to treatment on both constitutional and statutory grounds for persons who have been committed to mental hospitals on the basis of a civil commitment rather than a criminal proceeding (*Rouse* v. *Cameron* [373 F.2d 451 (1966)], *Donaldson* v. *O'Connor* [493 F.2d 507 (1974)], *Wyatt* v. *Stickney* [344 F.Supp. 373 (1972)]). The position of the courts has been that confining a person for the primary purpose of securing treatment for that individual in cases where there are unmistakable symptoms of severe psychiatric disturbance carries with it an obligation to provide such treatment. If this obligation is not met—that is, if no treatment is available—the quid pro quo for confinement has been violated and the individual has been deprived of his or her liberty in violation of due process.

Attempts to extend this right to treatment to incarcerated felons who do *not* exhibit signs of psychiatric disorder raise questions and issues that are different from those that pertain to the civil commitment of mentally disturbed persons. The rationale for confining criminal offenders is punitive rather than therapeutic, despite the belief of many criminal justice practitioners that rehabilitation is a more defensible goal than punishment, deterrence, or incapacitation. A much clearer case can be made for the right of juveniles to treatment, because the doctrine of *parens patriae* (i.e., the juvenile court acting in the role of "kind and loving parent") implies an obligation to provide treatment rather than punishment. As the U.S. Supreme Court pointed out in the Gault decision (*in re Gault* [387 U.S. 1 (1967)]), depriving a juvenile of rights guaranteed to adults under the process can only be justified if the procedural informality of the juvenile court operates in favor of youngsters to secure access to treatment.

Of even greater significance to the incarcerated criminal offender, however, is the right to refuse treatment. When treatment is aimed at changing the mind or thought processes of the recipient, the right to refuse treatment is based on the First Amendment right to free speech. The First Amendment has been interpreted to support an individual's right to "mind freedom" and "privacy of the mind." The right to have private thoughts and ideas is fundamental. The courts have been careful not to interfere in the fundamental rights of individuals except where such interference can be justified—as being in the vital interest of the state, for example. If the right to think, or even to have delusional thoughts, is protected by the First Amendment, the use of coercive treatment to change the mind can thus be justified *only* in cases where there is a clear and compelling state interest.

Case law has held the more experimental the treatment, the greater the responsibility of the physician to completely inform patients of alternatives and consequences. In *Mackey* v. *Procunier* (47 F.2d 877 [1973]), District Appellate Court Judge Merrill addressed Mackey's contention that he had been subjected to a traumatic administration of succinylcholine, a drug used in aversive therapy, without his informed consent. An inmate of the California prison system, Mackey, contended that he had consented to electroshock therapy, *not* the experimental aversive therapy. Judge Merrill wrote that if Mackey's contention was true, there was a serious question of "impermissible tinkering with the mental processes."

The concept of a right to choose punishment over treatment may seem absurd on first consideration, but there is a plausible argument for such a right. The right to treatment was first claimed on the basis of statutory law, rather than on constitutional grounds; the right to punishment can be argued on a similar basis. Although it is not directly applicable to the circumstances of the individual diagnosed and confined as mentally ill or incompetent, the statutory interpretation is relevant to the situation of an offender who is criminally responsible for his or her conduct, (e.g., the antisocial [sociopathic] person). The criminal could object to treatment based on the First Amendment right to privacy of the mind and could support this objection by referring to a statutory right to punishment based on a state criminal code that designates a specific period of imprisonment as punishment for the crime committed (Toomey, Allen, and Simonsen 1974). A case of this kind has not been decided thus far, but offenders sentenced to indeterminate incarceration may eventually raise this issue.

These considerations notwithstanding, however, the most important issue in correctional treatment is whether the state—operating through the formal agencies of the criminal justice system or through the vast informal network of social service and mental health referral agencies—has the *ability* to provide effective treatment for criminal offenders. However "effective treatment" is defined, its objective has to be some demonstrable or measurable decrease in antisocial conduct, particularly as indicated by a decrease in recidivism.

A number of publications have raised the public consciousness with respect to charges that the rehabilitative goals of corrections are a widespread and massive failure. As a result, critics of the treatment approach have been all too simplistically labeled "hardliners," presumably to set them off from those who continue to advocate treatment in corrections. James Q. Wilson, author of the widely read and much-discussed book *Thinking About Crime* (1977), assesses the correctional treatment approach and its results this way:

> It does not seem to matter what form of treatment in the correctional system is attempted—whether vocational training or academic education; whether counseling inmates individually, in groups, or not at all; whether therapy is administered by social workers or psychiatrists; whether the institutional context of the treatment is custodial or benign; whether the person is placed on probation or released on parole; or whether the treatment takes place in the community or in institutions. Indeed, some forms of treatment—notably a few experiments with psychotherapy—actually produce an *increase* in the rate of recidivism (Wilson 1977, p. 159).

Equally pessimistic about the effectiveness of correctional treatment are Lipton, Martinson, and Wilks (1975), who conducted a massive review of over 200 correctional treatment projects spanning nearly twenty years. The projects were classified according to the intervention techniques or methods employed—including milieu therapy, group therapy, individual counseling, parole supervision, and medical treatment. Treatment outcomes were assessed based on recidivism, personality and attitude change, and community adjustment. According to Martinson, the principal conclusion that could be reached from this survey was that, *"with few and isolated exceptions, the rehabilitative efforts that have been reported thus far have had no appreciable effects on recidivism"* (1974, p. 25).

Dissent with these negative evaluations has been registered by Glaser (1975), who concludes from a survey of correctional treatment studies that certain programs do have some success with particular categories of offenders. And Adams (1970) reports that an intensive counseling program at a California penal institution—the so-called PICO (Pilot Intensive Counseling Organization) program—appeared to produce positive results with selected offenders. Shireman, Mann, Larsen, and Young (1972), based on a review of a dozen treatment studies conducted in various institutions, conclude that certain types of institutional therapy (e.g., short-term milieu therapy), coupled with high staff morale, can yield results that are sufficiently strong to carry over into the postrelease period. They also found some evidence that positive results are associated with treatment programs aimed at youthful offenders—programs such as intensive milieu therapy, group counseling, and plastic surgery for individuals with psychological problems related to facial deformation or disfigurement.

Further, Gibbons and his colleagues maintain that correctional treatment has not yet been given a fair trial. At the same time, they contend, "it is likely that intervention efforts will need to move away from many of those earlier stratagems that were based on psychiatric images of offenders and on efforts to tinker with their mental health through some kind of individual counseling or therapy" (Gibbons et al. 1977, p. 106). This approach seems to be an excellent first step toward divesting corrections of its overload of psychiatric jargon and illness models. Terms such as "treatment" should be reserved for medical procedures, and psychiatrically neutral terms such as "intervention technique" should be used in their place. A meaningful and financially rewarding job or the chance to acquire further education are probably more valuable than short-term or long-term psychotherapy in encouraging prosocial behavior in criminals, because such techniques increase the criminal's stake in conformity.

At present, there is no tried and proven way to "treat" antisocial behavior. Most research that has concerned itself with the durable effects of behavior change has involved relatively stable, reasonably motivated, middle-class patients or clients who have voluntarily sought therapy. Even under these favorable circumstances, it has proven exceedingly difficult to achieve successful therapeutic outcomes, at least in terms of measures for which there is some professional consensus. To extrapolate these findings to some of the clientele of the criminal justice system is out of the question. As Silber reminds us, most of the prisoners in correctional institutions

> . . . are hostile, suspicious, and immature and tend to identify with subcultural values that are legally proscribed. They usually perceive their personality functioning to be acceptable. They are not, in general, likely to clamor for individual psychotherapy and usually are seen on referral. Thus, there is no strong, sustained interest on the part of the prisoners themselves for treatment (1974, p. 242).

Sentencing

Sentencing reflects a blend of policies and procedures that derive from legislative, judicial, and administrative authorities (Reid 1982). In some cases, legislatures enact laws that fix penal sanctions for various criminal offenses; in other cases, judges exercise their discretion within limits established by law.

Sentencing structures

If a legislature fixes the length of a sentence by statute (e.g., a term of fifteen years for armed robbery), the sentence is called a *definite* or *flat-time* sentence. Thus, neither the trial judge nor administrative agencies (such as the parole board or the department of corrections) are permitted any discretion in assigning such sentences. Other jurisdictions allow judges to fix sentences within a range of minimum and maximum sentences established by the legislature. Thus, armed robbery may carry a sentence of five to fifteen years. The judge imposes a *determinate sentence* within the limits set by statute. In this scheme, administrative authorities have no discretion to reduce the sentence fixed by the court. (The *minimum* term generally refers to the earliest time at which an imprisoned offender can be considered for release.)

According to a third scheme, an administrative model, judges impose minimum sentences within a wide range of possible sentences for a given crime. For example, the crime of armed robbery may carry a sentence from as low as one year up to a maximum of life imprisonment, with a ten-year minimum being the most common sentence imposed by judges. Then, as Reid notes,

> the decision to release the inmate is later determined by an administrative agency, usually a parole board. The type of sentence imposed in this model is called the *indeterminate sentence*. The idea is that the offender should remain incarcerated only as long as necessary for rehabilitation, but neither a legislature nor a judge can tell in advance how long a sentence should be for a particular individual (1982, p. 444).

In addition, some states have passed laws that impose *mandatory sentences*. For example, a Florida law requires a minimum sentence of three years for conviction of any crime involving the use of firearms. Mandatory sentencing statutes usually specify that the offender can not be considered for probation, parole, or any other form of conditional release until the minimum sentence is completed. Mandatory sentences have been established for crimes such as rape, robbery, murder, and repeated violations of drug laws.

Another approach is *presumptive sentencing*. Earlier in this chapter, we discussed retribution as one of the justifications for punishment. Bayley distinguishes retribution from vengeance as follows:

> Unlike vengeance, retribution is imposed by the courts after a guilty plea, or a trial, in which the accused has been found guilty of committing a crime. Prescribed by the law broken and proportioned to the gravity of the offense committed, retribution is not inflicted to gratify or compensate anyone who suffered a loss but to enforce the law and vindicate the legal order (1976, p. 551).

It is Bayley's view that the primary purpose of sentencing is to punish the offender. Hirsch (1976) believes that punishment is the *only* legitimate goal of sentencing.

A system of law that allows each offender to know what he or she faces is more fair than one based on the offender's social background, personality, or other factors. Bayley calls for the establishment of a range of authorized punishment. For example, a legislature would create a standard or presumptive sentence with a range of authorized variations to guide judges in sentencing. Sentences would be determined by the nature of the crime and the offender's criminal history. Judges could deviate from the presumptive sentence to the extent allowed by the legislation only if there are mitigating factors defined by law. The punishment would be primarily the loss of liberty (i.e., the physical custody of an individual for a substantial portion of every day). This system of presumptive sentencing would still give the court some discretion (Bayley 1976, p. 555).

Bayley also believes that, although there is still a need for rehabilitation, rehabilitation should not be the controlling factor in sentencing. Rather, he feels that the term of a sentence should be fixed in advance so that an offender knows how long he or she will be under state control. In addition, the offender should not have to spend all of his or her time in confinement, but should be offered a graduated release program involving lesser degrees of custody:

> Rehabilitation could be facilitated within the framework of a certainty of punishment model. Defendants would know their exact status at all times and yet be without incentive to engage in the dramatic acts which so often characterize attempts to convince parole boards that rehabilitation has taken place. The opportunity for gradual reentry into society would exist because the defendant is entitled to it, but not because he or she has earned it (ibid, pp. 561–62).

The characteristics of various sentencing structures are summarized in **table 11.1.** It must be pointed out, however, that many states employ sentencing procedures that vary from these models and approaches. Senna and Siegel caution that it is difficult to find precise meanings for such terms as "definite sentence," "indefinite sentence," and "determinate sentence": "The situation is further confused because what one state may designate as a indefinite sentence may be called a definite sentence in another state" (1981, p. 424).

Finally, variations in sentencing can occur as a consequence of multiple convictions. That is, if defendants are convicted of more than one offense, or on more than one count of the same type of offnese, they may be given either *concurrent* or *consecutive* sentences. Time served for concurrent sentences begins on the same day, regardless of how many sentences are imposed. For consecutive sentences, time served on the second sentence begins *after* the first sentence is completed. When an offender is sentenced to terms that add up to a ridiculous total such as 400 years in prison, media attention may be attracted and the judge may gain a reputation as being "tough on criminals"; but is the terms are to run concurrently, they will have the same net effect as if the offender had received a single sentence for all of the crimes with which he or she is charged.

Balancing release rates and sentencing

Because the state and federal correctional systems are finite in size, sentencing decisions are affected by the release rates at correctional institutions. If more sentences are imposed than releases are granted, dangerous

TABLE 11.1 Common sentencing structures

Sentencing structure	Characteristics
Indeterminate	Minimum and maximum terms prescribed by legislature; place and length of sentence controlled by corrections and parole; judge has little discretion over time served; goal is rehabilitation; sentence to fit offender; uncertainty and disparity in sentencing is major problem.
Indefinite	Similar to indeterminate sentence in some states; minimum and maximum terms, or only maximum term prescribed by legislature; sentence to match offender's needs; judge has some sentencing discretion; wide disparity in sentences imposed; parole used for early release.
Definite	Fixed period prescribed by legislature and imposed by judge; goal to punish and deter offender from further crime; allows for same sentence to apply to all convicted of particular offenses; eliminates disparity; judge has no discretion over length of sentence, but only over choice of sentence; offender required to serve entire sentence; no parole, inflexibility and rigidity is major problem.
Determinate	Similar to definite sentence; has one fixed term of years set by legislation; offender required to serve entire sentence where no parole exists.
Mandatory	Fixed term set by legislature for particular crimes; sentence must be imposed by judge; judge has no discretion in choice of sentence; goal is punishment and deterrence; contrary to individualized sentence; no sentencing disparity; no parole.
Presumptive	Legislatively prescribed range of sentences for given crimes; minimum and maximum terms with judge setting determinate sentence within these bounds; judge maintains some discretion; guidelines and use of mitigating and aggravating circumstances established by legislature; goal is justice, deterrence and individualization in sentencing; "just desserts."

Adapted from J. J. Senna and L. J. Siegel, *Introduction to Criminal Justice* (St. Paul, Minn.: West, 1981), p. 431, by permission of the authors and the publisher.

overcrowding results. Such was the case in Florida in 1972 and in 1974 when Director of Corrections Louis Wainwright refused to admit any more prisoners to the state prison system. His action produced results: the courts diverted prisoners to other facilities, and the parole board went to work to clear out the prisons. Thus, sentencing—unavoidably—is the sum of decisions that affect the number of prisoners in institutions and the balancing of limited resources for handling persons sentenced to serve terms.

Sentencing disparities

Do offenders who commit similar crimes under comparable circumstances generally receive similar sentences? Impressionistic accounts (Frankel 1973) and systematic research (Partridge and Eldridge 1974; Diamond and

Zeisel 1975; Diamond 1981) confirm that they do not. In fact, disparities in sentencing are one of the most serious shortcomings of our criminal justice system. As Kneedler points out, sentencing disparity has adverse effects upon: (1) prisoners, who know many of the facts surrounding their fellow prisoners' convictions and do not understand why they are being treated differently; (2) the public, which is more aware of disparities in the sentencing process than is sometimes acknowledged, and which, as a result, questions the integrity of the entire criminal justice system; and (3) judges themselves, who have no guidelines for comparison and who thus find it difficult to remove the disparities (1979, p. 18).

Criticisms of sentencing variations are increasing, and statistical studies show that there is a wide range of dispositions for identical offenses. The indeterminate sentence, once thought to be a solution to the disparity problem, has been questioned on both philosophical and constitutional grounds. McGee (1974) claims that the only valid arguments remaining for indeterminacy in the sentencing of felony offenders are the injustices and inconsistencies that arise from disparities among judges in the same jurisdictions who administer the same laws and dispose of offenders to the same correctional institutions. Pejorative terms such as "hanging judge," "softy," and "Maximum John" (the nickname given to federal Judge John Sirica of Watergate fame) make the same point: namely, that judges vary considerably along a continuum from leniency to severity in sentencing.

One form of sentence disparity is the minimum sentence that adversely affects the parole eligibility of the offender. Also, some trial judges use consecutive sentences to create minimum terms; this type of sentencing can prevent otherwise eligible offenders from being paroled. Unduly long sentences demoralize offenders and threaten their chances for successful reintegration.

In daily court business, trial judges often lack sufficient time to consider all of the crucial elements of an offense and the special characteristics of the offender before imposing a sentence. And some judges have a tendency to standardize their decision making, announcing sentences to fit certain categories of crimes without paying too much attention to the particular offender. This is especially true in cases involving minor violations. Although individuals convicted of minor offenses are good candidates for reform, they are frequently sentenced immediately after being found guilty or when they enter a guilty plea. And if counsel requests a presentence report before the sentence is imposed, a defendant may have to remain in jail during the delay, a price many defendant's are not willing to pay.

Differences in the sentencing tendencies of judges fascinate social scientists. The disparities may be ascribed to a number of factors: the conflicting goals of criminal justice, the fact that judges are a product of different backgrounds and have different social values, the administrative pressures on judges, and the influence of community values. Each of these factors structures, to some extent, the judge's exercise of discretion in sentencing. In addition, a judge's perception of these factors is dependent on his or her own attitudes toward the law, toward a particular crime, or toward a certain type of offender. Gaylin relates an amusing and instructive anecdote on this subject:

> A visitor to a Texas court was amazed to hear the judge impose a suspended sentence where a man had pleaded guilty to manslaughter. A few minutes later the same judge sentenced a man who pleaded guilty to stealing a horse and gave him life imprisonment. When the judge was asked by the visitor about the disparity of the two sentences, he replied, "Well, down here there is some men that need killin', but there ain't no horses that need stealin'" (1974, p. 8).

Kneedler notes that, at a sentencing seminar he conducted, a group of trial court judges from several states listed more than thirty factors (collectively) that they took into account in sentencing decisions. Among the factors identified were prior criminal record, drug history, age, education, economic problems, family problems, attitude toward the offense, health, religious convictions, cultural differences, race, sex, and the judge's personal impression about the defendant's experience as a criminal. Unfortunately, none of the judges took all thirty factors into account, and "the degree to which particular factors influenced their decisions differed widely" (Kneedler 1979, p. 18).

Sentencing reforms

Attempts to rectify sentencing disparities to follow one of four approaches. The first approach involves legislative overhaul of criminal statutes; the second seeks to establish sentencing guidelines for trial court judges. A third approach seeks to organize sentencing councils or institutions that afford judges an opportunity to meet and discuss the factors that influence their decisions—with the goal of developing sentencing norms for similar offenses and offenders within a given jurisdiction. Finally, some efforts at reform are directed toward the appellate review of sentencing in jurisdictions where sentences have not been subjected to review in the past. (This approach is discussed later in this chapter under "Appeal and Postconviction Remedies").

Penal code reforms The penal codes of most jurisdictions are a potpourri of social thinking from ages past. Historically, criminal statutes have been enacted as ad hoc responses to specific events, often without relating a crime to similar offenses in the penal code. If an event is particularly heinous or repugnant, the public may pressure legislators to create a new law with a formula for punishment attached. Unfortunately, such laws—with punishments that are often irrationally severe—remain on the books for decades long after the causative event and the legislators are forgotten.

State criminal codes are, at times, illogical in the kinds of sentences they mandate for some offenses. In California, for example, the maximum penalty for breaking into a car to steal its contents is a prison term of fifteen years; stealing the car itself only nets a maximum term of ten years. In two states, bribing a witness, juror, or judge carries with it a maximum sentence of five years, whereas bribing a football player carries a maximum sentence of ten years (National Advisory Commission on Criminal Justice Standards and Goals, *Corrections*, 1973, p. 146).

The President's Commission on Law Enforcement and Administration of Justice noted that severe sentences for nearly all felony offenses were characteristic of American penal codes and that "prison sentences in America are, as a general rule, longer than those elsewhere" (1967, p. 142). One reason for such harsh sentences for certain crimes is that many laws imposing extremely long sentences were passed following a criminal incident that shocked the public; a legislature quickly passed a law to protect society by putting the offender away for a long time. Yet only a small portion of the criminal population is responsible for such incidents. The sad fact is that long maximum penalties tend to drive up sentences in cases where long sentences are unwarranted. One judge might choose five to eight years as an appropriate sentence under a twenty-year maximum statute. Others might back away from the minimum end of the range and impose as much as fifteen years for the same offender. Thus, the drafter of penal statutes is in a quandry. He or she must provide a sentence stiff enough to handle the occasional "worst offender," but short enough to be applied to offenders who are not unusual risks.

The American Law Institute's *Model Penal Code: Proposed Official Draft* (1962) addresses the problem of severity and nonuniformity in current penal codes with regard to sentencing. Imprisonment is seen as a last resort and is used only when (1) there is undue risk that during the period of suspended sentence or probation the defendant will commit another crime; (2) the defendant is in need of correctional treatment that can be provided most effectively by his or her commitment to an institution; or (3) a lesser sentence will depreciate the seriousness of the defendant's crimes (ibid., p. 106). These criteria are intended only as guide for extreme cases. The *Model Penal Code* envisions that priority will be given to the use of all alternatives to imprisonment before the criteria are applied in a specific case.

The *Model Penal Code* also recommends that all crimes be reduced to five grades, three for felonies and two for misdemeanors. A maximum penalty—shorter than those now used by most states—would be assigned to each grade. Minimum sentences would be set at one year for all felonies and at three years for the most serious felonies. If a particular offense was to strike great fear in the community and if the offender was especially dangerous, a judge would be allowed to extend the maximum sentence. Judges would be granted flexibility to fit a sentence to a particular case. Nevertheless, although the *Model Penal Code* appeals greatly to practitioners in corrections, it has not been widely accepted among legislators—men and women who must face the outcry of enraged citizens when harsh "law-and-order" statutes are struck down.

Sentencing guidelines Sentencing guidelines are developed empirically by examining past judicial decisions within a jurisdiction. In a manner comparable to the development of the actuarial tables used by the Federal Parole Board, a grid is constructed based on two scores. One of these, the *offender score*, is derived by assigning points to such factors as the number of convictions for juvenile crimes, adult misdemeanors, and adult felonies; the number of times imprisoned; escapes from prison; whether probation or parole has been granted; and occupational and educational status. The *offense score* is based on the severity of the crime. As shown in **table 11.2,** the scores are arranged so that a judge can consider the likelihood that a given individual will recidivate.

Sentencing guidelines represent a summation of the collective experience of a given city or state in dealing with various kinds of offenders. Although judges are not compelled to use them, the guidelines provide a means by which a judge can sense how defendants with similar characteristics and offenses were sentenced in the past. Thus, a number of cities and states have already adopted such guidelines.

Sentencing councils and institutes The sentencing council is a group of judges who sit regularly in a particular court. The work of the council is described by Smith as follows:

> The judges meet in panels of three, each judge having the presentence investigation report from the probation department and having prepared a study sheet, not only for the offenders he must sentence, but also for those who are the primary responsibility of the other two judges. Customarily the one judge will call his first case, merely stating the name of the offender and giving a brief statement of the offense. He will then state to his brother judges the factors, in his judgement, believed to be controlling as to disposition, and will recommend a disposition to be made. Each of the other two judges will then give, in turn, the factors believed by him to be controlling, together with his recommended sentence.... It is in the discussion following the recommendation as to sentencing that the Council performs its most useful function.... [P]oints are emphasized or subordinated according to the judgement of the individual judges, with the result that there is a close approach to a common meeting ground (1971, p. 551).

According to Senna and Siegel, sentencing councils have three advantages: they make judges aware of their sentencing philosophies; they provide an opportunity for judges to debate their differences; and they provide a forum for periodic evaluation of a court's sentencing practices (1981, p. 437). To date, three U.S. District Courts have used sentencing councils.

Frankel (1973) reports that sentencing councils cause judges to give shorter prison sentences and to make fuller use of probation as an alternative to incarceration. And Kratcoski and Walker claim that such councils are educational: "Judges who serve on them are made aware of the sentencing practices of their colleagues; the council discussions may bring out information from the presentence reports which could well have been overlooked by a judge acting alone" (1978, p. 186). Despite these advantages, however, sentencing councils are still not popular with the states as an approach to resolving sentencing problems.

Sentencing institutes, which originated in federal legislation in 1958, provide a mechanism whereby judges can be brought together in a seminar or workshop to discuss sentencing problems. As stated in the American Bar

TABLE 11.2 Suggested sentencing guidelines for Colorado (felony 4 offenses)[1]

	_ Offender score (probability of recidivism)[2]				
Offense score (severity of offense)[3]	−1–−7	0–2	3–8	9–12	13+
10–12	Indeterminate minimum; 4–5 year maximum	Indeterminate minimum; 8–10 year maximum	Indeterminate minimum; 8–10 year maximum	Indeterminate minimum; 8–10 year maximum	Indeterminate minimum; 8–10 year maximum
8–9	Out[4]	3–5 month work project	Indeterminate minimum; 3–4 year maximum	Indeterminate minimum; 8–10 year maximum	Indeterminate minimum; 8–10 year maximum
6–7	Out	Out	Indeterminate minimum; 3–4 year maximum	Indeterminate minimum; 6–8 year maximum	Indeterminate minimum; 8–10 year maximum
3–5	Out	Out	Out	Indeterminate minimum; 4–5 year maximum	Indeterminate minimum; 4–5 year maximum
1–2	Out	Out	Out	Out	Indeterminate minimum; 3–4 year maximum

[1]The Colorado Penal Code contains five levels of felonies (Felony 1 is the most serious) and three levels of misdemeanors. The Felony 4 category includes crimes such as manslaughter, robbery and second-degree burglary. The legislated maximum sentence for a Felony 4 offense is ten years. No minimum period of confinement is to be set by the court.
[2]The higher the offender score, the higher the probabilty of recidivism.
[3]The higher the offense score, the more serious the crime.
[4]"Out" indicates a noncarcerative sentence such as probation, deferred prosecution, or deferred judgment.
Adapted from J. M. Kress, L. T. Wilkins, and D. M. Gottfredson, "Is the End of Judicial Sentencing in Sight?" *Judicature* 60 (1976):221, by permission of the authors and the publisher.

Association's *Standards Relating to Sentencing Alternatives and Procedures*, these proceedings are intended "to develop criteria for the imposition of sentences, to provide a forum in which newer judges can be exposed to more experienced judges, and to expose all sentencing judges to new developments and techniques" (1968, p. 299). Once again, as in the case of sentencing councils, there has been no pell-mell rush on the part of the states to emulate the federal practice. At present, only three states—California, Massachusetts, and New York—use sentencing institutes.

Appeal and postconviction remedies

A few decades ago, very few criminal cases were appealed. Since *Gideon* v. *Wainwright* (1963), however, the picture has changed dramatically. The right to counsel for all defendants was secured by the *Gideon* decision, opening the floodgates in appellate courts all across the country. *Collateral attack*—the filing of an appeal in federal court before a state case is decided (a procedure almost unknown prior to the 1960s)—the filing of an appeal in federal court before a state case is decided (a procedure almost unknown prior to the 1960s)—is now almost routine in state courts. As a result, the review system is overloaded, and judges have experienced an unprecedented increase in case loads. And litigation has often been drawn out over a long period of time, thus eroding the public belief in the finality of convictions for criminal offenses.

According to the National Advisory Commission on Criminal Justice Standards and Goals, the major steps in the review process are (*Courts*, 1973, p. 113):

1. A motion for a new trial is filed in the court where the conviction was imposed.
2. An appeal is made to the state intermediate appellate court (in states where there is no intermediate appellate court, this step is not available).
3. An appeal is made to the state supreme court.
4. The U.S. Supreme Court is petitioned to review the state court's decision on the appeal.
5. Postconviction proceedings are initiated in the state trial court.
6. The postconviction proceedings are appealed to the state intermediate appellate court.
7. An appeal is made to the state supreme court.
8. The U.S. Supreme Court is petitioned to review the state court's decision on the appeal from postconviction proceedings.
9. A *habeas corpus* petition is presented in U.S. District Court.
10. An appeal is made to the U.S. Court of Appeals.
11. The U.S. Supreme Court is petitioned to review the U.S. Court of Appeals decision on the habeas corpus petition.

It is easy to see why the review process can take so long, especially when some steps may be used several times in a single appeal, with review taking place consecutively in more than one court system. Thus, due process may be a long and complicated procedure, and appeals may become part of a long, drawn out, and seemingly endless cycle.

In the 1960s, a series of appellate decisions were made in favor of the incarcerated offender. These decisions had diverse effects on the criminal justice system. On the positive side, the protections of the Fourth, Fifth, Sixth, and Eighth amendments were extended to incarcerated offenders through a series of appeals that were based on the due process and equal protection clauses of the Fourteenth Amendment. The success of such appeals has encouraged more and more defendants to go the appeal route, and the result has been an increase in the appeal rate in some jurisdictions. In some areas, the appeal rate has grown from less than 10 percent to a rate of 90 percent in recent years.

In the past, few states permitted appellate review of sentences. At present, however, slightly more than half of the states do allow the merits of a sentence to be reviewed upon appeal. According to Kratcoski and Walker (1978), review has not been available in many jurisdictions because of fears of increased litigation, concern that appeallate judges are less qualified than trial judges to determine appropriate sentences, and the belief that sentencing is a matter of judicial discretion rather than a matter of law. On the other hand, the American Bar Association (through its Committee on Minimum Standards for Criminal Justice) maintains that "judicial review should be available for all sentences imposed in cases where provision is made for review of the convictions" (1968, p. 7).

Sentencing review is one of several *postconviction remedies*—"procedural devices available to a person who, after conviction and sentence, wants to vacate or reduce the sentences imposed, invalidate his pleas of guilty, or set aside his conviction" (Popper 1978, p. 1). For example, consider an individual who is not represented by counsel at trial but has not waived the right of representation; such a defendant might claim that his or her sentence or plea was defective and might seek redress by a postconviction proceeding. Popper notes that petitions filed in U.S. District Courts (including civil rights cases) by state and federal prisoners rose from 2,177 in 1960 to 19,307 in 1975, an increase of nearly 800 percent. Further, he notes:

> As impressive as these figures are, they do not even reflect the number of prisoner petitions filed in state courts. It is this burgeoning post-conviction activity which, in past, accounts for pleas by court administrators, judges, and some communities to put a lid to litigation by cutting back on the chances for post-conviction relief (ibid., p. 4).

In its assessment of the appellate process, the National Advisory Commission on Criminal Justice Standards and Goals expresses doubt that any lasting benefits will result from efforts to speed up the existing review apparatus. Instead, the commission recommends a restructuring of the entire review process: ". . . there should be a single, unified review proceeding in which all arguable defects in the trial proceeding can be examined and settled finally, subject only to narrowly defined exceptional circumstances where there are compelling reasons to provide for a further review" (*Courts*, 1973, p. 113). This unified review would combine into one proceeding all of the issues presently litigated on the basis of motions for new trials, direct appeals, and postconviction proceedings. Thus, the motion for a new trial would be abolished, and the traditional distinction between direct appeal and collateral attack would be abandoned. Unfortunately, the self-evident merits of the commission's proposal have not yet brought the establishment of a unified review. In some states, however, sentencing review has been instituted by means of special panels of trial judges who meet to examine the propriety of sentences in individual cases. After reviewing a case, a panel may decide to decrease or increase the original sentence. In eight states, appeals for sentence review can be brought to a regular appellate court.

Summary

Sentencing is perhaps the most important phase of the criminal process, for it is in this stage that the disposition of the criminal offender is decided. In earlier periods, offenders were subject to retaliation and physical abuse as a punishment for wrongdoing. The contemporary criminal justice system is still punitive in its orientation, but the punishment is justified on several utilitarian grounds, including deterrence and incapacitation. In recent years, support has grown for the position that retribution ("the law of just deserts") is an appropriate objective of sentencing. Traditional dispositions include fines, probation, and imprisonment, with probation being the most common choice.

One of the most significant features of the sentencing process is its tripartite structure involving the legislature, a judge, and correctional agencies. The actions of each of these parties affect the type and length of sentence imposed on the offender. Thus, the system often results in sentence disparity with courts seeking to fit the sentence to the individual offender rather than to the crime. To make dispositions more uniform, some states now allow appellate review of sentences and use sentencing councils and institutes.

issue paper

THE DEATH SENTENCE

At the end of 1982, the population on death row in the United States reached 1,137—the largest figure since record keeping began in 1953. Southern states held three quarters of the condemned, including eight women, and Florida, Georgia, and Texas accounted for more than half of the total.

In 1972, when the death row population stood at 631, the U.S. Supreme Court ruled in *Furman* v. *Georgia* (408 U.S. 238) that "the imposition and carrying out of the death penalty in the instant cases constitutes cruel and unusual punishment in violation of the Eighth and Fourteenth Amendments." As a result of the *Furman* decision, the death sentences of the 631 inmates on death row were set aside.

Had the Supreme Court struck a mortal blow to the advocates of capital punishment? No. There was no consensus by the Court in *Furman*. The decision was 5–4, and each of the nine justices wrote an opinion expressing his view on the constitutionality of the death penalty. Four of the justices stated that the imposition of the death penalty did not run afoul of the Constitution. Only two justices (Brennan and Marshall) stated that capital punishment was unconstitutional under all circumstances. And three justices agreed that the death penalty had historically been arbitrarily and capriciously imposed—especially against blacks, the poor, and men. However, they did not decide in *Furman* whether the death penalty could *ever* be imposed, given new legislative guidelines.

The legislative response to *Furman* was swift. Thirty-six jurisdictions (including the U.S. Congress) passed new legislation to remove the discrimination that had permeated the death penalty for many years. But the legislative packages were anything but uniform. Some states made the death penalty mandatory for a conviction of first-degree murder. Others left sentencing exclusively to the jury. And others permitted a sentencing recommendation from the jury, but left the final decision with the trial judge. However, most states did provide legislative guidelines to the juries and judges as to their sentencing authority in capital cases.

All of the occupants now on death row in the United States were convicted under post-*Furman* statues. However, opponents of the death penalty, including the American Civil Liberties Union and Amnesty International, contend that sentencing under the new laws is as arbitrary and racially discriminatory as that which occurred before the *Furman* decision. One study—based on statistics from Texas, Ohio, Florida, and Georgia from 1972 through 1977—concluded that blacks convicted of murdering whites were sentenced to death eighteen times as frequently as whites convicted of murdering whites. And 170 of the 1,015 blacks convicted of murdering whites were sentenced to death, while only 3 of 341 whites convicted of murdering blacks received the death penalty.

Discussions about capital punishment are usually dominated by emotional, rather than intellectual, considerations. The issues raised by the death penalty tap deep levels of primitive belief. Our answers to questions about the taking of human life in socially sanctioned circumstances are thus likely to express our primitive beliefs; and the intellectual arguments we use to justify our attitudes amount to rationalizations.

One of the principal forms of rationalization involves the deterrence argument. As noted earlier in this chapter, the rationale for deterrence is that people will refrain from committing criminal acts because they fear the consequences of punishment. Supporters of the death penalty might argue, therefore, that because a fear of death is one of the most powerful motivations in human behavior, capital punishment provides a powerful defense against any crime that incurs the death penalty. But opponents of the death penalty maintain that this position is based on a simplistic idea of human conduct—one that views human beings as rational creatures who can weigh the potential consequences of their actions and make informed choices among alternatives. (Note that this position comes very close to the doctrine of free will upon which criminal law is based).

In the end, the issue of capital punishment is fought on the question of whether the evidence supports or refutes the contention that the death penalty deters people from committing certain crimes. Supporters of capital punishment take refuge from accusations that they are barbaric and bloodthirsty by claiming that the death penalty works to reduce the incidence of heinous murders. And abolitionists, with Jove-like objectivity, ask for satisfactory scientific evidence that the death penalty is an effective deterrent against crime. Scores of studies by criminologists, psychologists, and economists have thus far failed to produce convincing scientific evidence, however, and some claim that such evidence is beyond the reach of scientific verification—now or ever.

At times, the discussion of capital punishment brings out irrelevant or misleading arguments. For example, Ellison and Buckhout claim that "murder is seldom a cold-blooded crime but is nearly always committed in the heat of violent passion, when the murderer is obviously incapable of rationally considering the consequences of his or her act" (1981, p. 267). This description fits the kind of homicide that typically involves people who are closely, even intimately, involved with or related to one another—husband, wife, and lover (the "eternal triangle"), or friends, neighbors, and close acquaintances. But these "crimes of passion" usually result in indictments for *second-degree murder*, not murder in the first degree. And persons convicted of second-degree murder do not end up on death

Deterence or cruelty? Electric chair used in executions in Illinois (left photo); California gas chamber. (Left photo courtesy Illinois Department of Corrections; right photo courtesy of California Department of Corrections.

row; it is the person who, in the overwhelming majority of instances, is convicted of first-degree murder under the *felony murder doctrine* (that is, the murder is committed during a rape, robbery, kidnapping, burglary, or other type of felony).

Some occupants of death row have committed crimes so far outside the bounds of normal human experience that the perpetrators seem to belong to another species. Consider Lawrence Bittaker, who was sentenced to death for kidnapping and murdering five teenage girls. According to an account in *Time*,

> he and a partner raped and sodomized four of them first, for hours and days at a time, sometimes in front of a camera. But that is not all. He tortured some of the girls—pliers on nipples, ice picks in ears—and tape-recorded the screams. But that is not all. The last victim was strangled with a coat hanger, her genitals mutilated and her body tossed on a lawn so that he could watch the horror of its discovery (Andersen 1982, p. 39).

Bittaker's prosecutor coined the term "mutants from hell" for Bittaker and his partner.

In December 1982, Charlie Brooks, Jr., was put to death in Texas, the first American ever to be executed by a lethal drug injection. The execution released a flood of speculation that we might be on the brink of a large-scale resumption of executions that could boost the execution rate to the level of the 1930s. These speculations are buttressed by public opinion polls that indicate a major shift from the 1960s, when only a minority of the public favored the death penalty. Today, a majority support capital punishment. The editorial comments that accompany poll results convey the impression that most people are fed up with delays and are impatient to push on with the distasteful but necessary task of executing condemned murderers.

However, before concluding that capital punishment will be resumed in the 1980s on a large scale, we must give some thought to how recent public opinion polls arrived at their findings—and what those results actually mean. For example, consider a study conducted by Patricia Keeley (1976), in which students in four different colleges of the University of South Florida—business administration, engineering, education, and social and behavioral sciences—were asked to select from four options a penalty for each of seventeen specific offenses. The four options were the death penalty, life imprisonment with no parole, life imprisonment with possible parole, and twenty-five years with possible parole. The crimes included murder, kidnapping, skyjacking, rape, armed robbery, treason, and drug dealing, and all were based on actual offenses. Circumstances varied as to whether or not the offense resulted in the death or serious injury of a victim or victims.

Keeley found that criminal justice and engineering majors favored the death penalty for various offenses more than students majoring in education or the social and behavioral sciences (e.g., psychology or sociology). But students in all

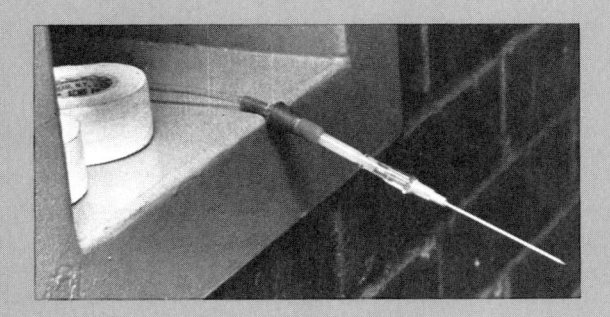

Convicted murderer Charlie Brooks was put to death with a lethal dose of pentothal injected with this hypodermic needle. Courtesy Huntsville Item/Gamma-Liaison.

disciplines expressed more support for the death penalty when a victim was killed as a consequence of the criminal act; and they were also harsher in their penalties when the victim was a child. Of much greater significance, however, was the finding that misleading (if not totally erroneous) data resulted from general questions such as, Are you in favor of the death penalty? For example, most education majors answered no to this question, yet they chose the death penalty overwhelmingly for kidnapping when the victim was murdered, for forcible rape of a juvenile when the victim was murdered, for mass murder, and for murders committed by a repeat offender. Criminal justice and engineering majors, on the other hand, answered yes to the general question on the death penalty, then rejected the death penalty in favor of a lesser penalty for seven of the seventeen offenses.

Keeley's study suggests that public opinion polls should be interpreted cautiously when general questions are asked. A better question might be, Would you be in favor of the death penalty as a possible option? Then the poll could state precisely the circumstances and nature of a particular offense and the sentencing options available to the court. As Keeley's study clearly illustrates, different crime scenarios can produce different sentencing choices from the same people.

Discussion and review

1. Why is sentencing such an important phase of the criminal process?
2. What are some of the factors that significantly affect the success or failure of punishment as an approach to deterrence?
3. How do we distinguish between general and specific deterrence?
4. Does research support the argument that incapacitation or restraint of serious offenders is a sound rationale for imprisonment?
5. On what principle is an offender's right to treatment based? Is there any valid legal basis for claiming a right to *refuse* treatment?
6. Discuss the counterarguments to Martinson's claim that "nothing works" in correctional treatment.
7. What is the distinction between a definite sentence and a determinate sentence? Between a definite sentence and a mandatory sentence?
8. What is the distinction between concurrent sentences and consecutive sentences?
9. What are some of the adverse effects of sentence disparities. What are the major causes of such disparity?
10. How are sentencing guidelines developed empirically for a particular jurisdiction? What is the relationship between offender scores and offense scores in arriving at an appropriate sentence?
11. Discuss the significance of the *Gideon* v. *Wainwright* decision in terms of its impact on the filing of appeals from "behind the walls."
12. How does the National Advisory Commission on Criminal Justice Standards and Goals propose to reform the appellate process?
13. Why were the sentences of more than 600 inmates on death row set aside as a result of the *Furman* v. *Georgia* decision?
14. Discuss Patricia Keeley's research and outline its implications for public opinion polls on the death penalty.

Glossary

Collateral attack   A challenge against the legality of confinement as opposed to an appeal based on the merits of the conviction. A writ of federal habeas corpus is the principal method used by state prisoners seeking review of their convictions.

Deterrence   A justification for punishment based on the idea that crime can be discouraged or prevented by instilling in potential criminals a fear of punishing consequences. Punished offenders, it is hoped, will serve as examples to deter potential criminals from antisocial conduct.

Habeas corpus   Latin for "you have the body." A writ of *habeas corpus* orders a person who is holding another person in confinement to produce the person being detained.

Incapacitation   A theory of punishment and a goal of sentencing; generally implemented by imprisoning an offender to prevent him or her from committing further crimes.

Indeterminate sentence   An indefinite sentence of "not less than" and "not more than" certain numbers of years. The exact term to be served is determined by parole authorities within the minimum and maximum limits set by the court or by statute.

Parens patriae   Latin for "father of his country"; a doctrine specifying that the juvenile court treat youngsters as if it were a "kind and loving parent."

Rehabilitation   A rationale for the reformation of offenders based on the premise that human behavior is the result of antecedent causes that may be identified and controlled by objective analysis. The focus is on treatment of the offender, not punishment.

Retribution   A theory of punishment that maintains that an offender should be punished for the crimes he or she commits because he or she *deserves* the punishment.

References

Adams, S. "The PICO Project." In *The Sociology of Punishment and Corrections*, edited by N. Johnston, L. Savitz, and M. E. Wolfgang. New York: Wiley, 1970.
Allen, H. E., and Simonsen, C. E. *Corrections in America*. New York: Macmillan, 1981.
American Bar Association. *Standards Relating to Sentencing Alternatives and Procedures*. New York: Institute of Judicial Administration, 1968.
American Law Institute. *Model Penal Code: Proposed Official Draft*. Philadelphia, Pa.: American Law Institute, 1962.
Andersen, K. "An Eye for an Eye." *Time* 24 January 1983: 28–39.
Bayley, C. T. "Good Intentions Gone Awry—A Proposal for Fundamental Change in Criminal Sentencing." *Washington Law Review* 51 (1976):529–56.
Diamond, S. S. "Exploring Sources of Sentence Disparity." In *The Trial Process*, edited by B. D. Sales. New York: Plenum, 1981.
Diamond, S. S., and Zeisel, H. "Sentencing Councils: A Study of Sentence Disparity and Its Reduction." *University of Chicago Law Review* 43 (1975):109–49.
Ellison, K. W., and Buckhout, R. *Psychology and Criminal Justice*. New York: Harper and Row, 1981.
Frankel, M. E. *Criminal Sentences—Law Without Order*. New York: Hill and Wang, 1973.
Gaylin, W. *Partial Justice*. New York: Vintage, 1974.
Gibbons, D. C.; Thurman, J. L.; Yospe, F.; and Blake, G. F. *Criminal Justice Planning: An Introduction*. Englewood Cliffs, N.J.: Prentice-Hall, 1977.
Glaser, D. "Maximizing the Impact of Evaluative Research in Corrections." In *Criminal Justice Research*, edited by E. Viano. Lexington, Mass.: Lexington, 1975.
Grünhut, M. Penal Reform. London: Oxford, 1948.
Keeley, P. A. "Students' Attitudes Toward Capital Punishment as a Function of Training in the College of Their Major." Master's thesis, Department of Criminal Justice, University of South Florida, 1976.
Kneedler, H. L. "Sentencing in Criminal Cases: Time for Reform." *The University of Virginia Newsletter* 55 (1979):17–20.
Kratcoski, P. C., and Walker, D. B. *Criminal Justice in America: Process and Issues*. Glenview, Ill.: Scott Foresman, 1978.
Lipton, D., Martinson, R., and Wilks, J. *The Effectiveness of Correctional Treatment—A Survey of Treatment Evaluation Studies*. Springfield, Mass.: Praeger, 1975.
McGee, R. A. "A New Look at Sentencing." Part I. *Federal Probation*, 37 (1974):3-8.
Martinson, R. "What Works? Questions and Answers About Prison Reform." *The PUblic Interest*, Spring 1974, pp. 22–54.
Nassi, A. J. "Therapy of the Absurd: A Study of Punishment and Treatment in California Prisons and the roles of Psychiatrists and Psychologists." In *Contemporary Perspectives on Forensic Psychiatry and Psychology*, edited by H. J. Vetter and R. W. Rieber. New York: John Jay, 1980.
National Advisory Commission on Criminal Justice Standards and Goals. *Corrections*. Washington, D.C.: U.S. Government Printing Office, 1973.
National Advisory Commission on Criminal Justice Standards and Goals. *Courts*. Washington, D.C.: U.S. Government Printing Office, 1973.
Newman, G. *The Punishment Response*. Philadelphia, Pa.: Lippincott, 1978.
Packer, H. *The Limits of the Criminal Sanction*. Palo Alto, Calif.: Stanford, 1968.

Partridge, A., and Eldridge, W. *The Second Circuit Sentencing Study: A Report to the Judges of the Second Circuit.* Washington, D.C.: U.S. Government Printing Office, 1974.

Petersilia, J., Greenwood, P. W., and Lavin, M. *Criminal Careers of Habitual Felons.* Santa Monica, Calif.: Rand Corporation, 1977.

Popper, R. *Post-Conviction Remedies.* St. Paul, Minn.: West, 1978.

President's Commission on Law Enforcement and Administration of Justice. *The Challenge of Crime in a Free Society.* Washington, D.C.: U.S. Government Printing Office, 1967.

"Prisons: Uprising in Attica." *Time* 20 September 1971:12–14.

Reid, S. T. *Crime and Criminology.* New York: Holt, Rinehart and Winston, 1982.

Senna, J., and Siegel, L. *Introduction to Criminal Justice.* St. Paul, Minn.: West, 1981.

Shireman, C. H., Mann, K. B., Larsen, C., and Young, T. "Findings From Experiments in Treatment in the Correctional Institution." *Social Service Review* 46 (1972):38–59.

Silber, D. E. "Controversy Concerning the Criminal Justice System and Its Implications for the Role of Mental Health Workers." *American Psychologist* 29 (1974):239–44.

Skinner, B. F. *Science and Human Behavior.* New York: Macmillan, 1953.

———. *Beyond Freedom and Dignity.* New York: Harper and Row, 1971.

Smith, B. D., and Vetter, H. J. *Theoretical Approaches to Personality.* Englewood Cliffs, N.J.: Prentice-Hall, 1982.

Smith, T. "The Sentencing Council." In *The Criminal in the Arms of the Law,* edited by L. Radzinowicz and M. E. Wolfgang. New York: Basic, 1971.

Toomey, B., Allen, H. E., and Simonsen, C. E. "The Right to Treatment: Professional Liabilities in the Criminal Justice and Mental Health Systems." *The Prison Journal* 54 (1974):43–56.

Vachss, A. H., and Bakal, Y. *The Life-Style Violent Juvenile.* Lexington, Mass.: Lexington, 1979.

Van den Haag, E. *Punishing Criminals: Concerning a Very Old and Painful Question.* New York: Basic, 1975.

Von Hirsch, A. Doing Justice: The Choice of Punishments. New York: Hill and Wang, 1976.

Wilson, J. Q. *Thinking About Crime.* New York: Vintage, 1977.

Wolfgang, M. E., Figlio, R. M., and Sellin, T. E. *Delinquency in a Birth Cohort.* Chicago: University of Chicago, 1972.

Cases

Donaldson v. *O'Connor* 493 F.2d 507 (5th Cir. 1974).
Furman v. *Georgia* 408 U.S. 238, 92 S.Ct. 2726, 33 L.Ed.2d 346 (1972).
In re Gault 387 U.S. 1, 87 S.Ct. 1428, 18 L.Ed.2d 527 (1967).
Mackey v. *Procunier* 477 F.2d 877 (9th Cir. 1973).
Rouse v. *Cameron* 373 F.2d 451 (D.C. Cir. 1966).
Wyatt v. *Stickney* 344 F.Supp. 373 (D.C. Ala. 1972).

12
jails and detention

The American jail system
Types of jails
Purpose of jails
Jail populations

Care of special prisoners
Alcoholics
The mentally ill
Drug addicts
Sex offenders

Jail security
Counts
Shakedowns
Frisks
Tool control
Key control
Cutlery control
Narcotics control
Visitation control

The role of the jail in the criminal justice system
Jails and the police
Jails and the courts
Jails and corrections

Summary

Issue paper: Suicides in jail

BECAUSE they are remote from public view, jails have evolved more by default than by plan. Perpetuated without major change from the days of Alfred the Great, these institutions have been a disgrace to every generation. Colonists brought to the New World the concept of the jail as an instrument for confining, coercing, or correcting people who broke the law or were merely nuisances. In the early nineteenth century, with the American innovation of the state penitentiary, punitive confinement became the principal response to criminal acts and removed the serious offender from the local jail. Gradually, with the building of insane asylums, orphanages, and hospitals, the jail ceased to be the repository for all social casualties. But it continued to house minor offenders, the poor, and the vagrant, all crowded together in squalor and misery, without regard to sex, age, or criminal history.

Many European visitors admired the new American penitentiaries. Two observers—de Beaumont and de Tocqueville—also saw, side by side with the new penetentiaries, jails in the old familiar form. They noted that ". . . nothing has been changed; disorder, confusion, mixture of different ages and moral characters, all the vices of the old system still exist" (de Beaumont and de Tocqueville 1964, p. 49). In an observation that should have served as a warning, they continued: "There is evidently a deficiency in a prison system which offers anomalies of this kind. These shocking contradictions proceed chiefly from the want of unison in the various parts of government in the United States" (ibid).

By and large, the deficiencies these two travelers found remain today; the intervening decades brought little but the deterioration of jail facilities from use and age. Changes have been limited to variations in clientele, and jails have become residual organizations for handling the vexing and unpalatable social problems in each locality. (The most conspicuous additions are the homeless and the drunks.) Thus, "the poor, the sick, the morally deviant, and the merely unaesthetic, in addition to the truly criminal all end in jail" (Mattick and Aikman 1969, p. 114).[1]

The American jail system

Jails are primarily a function of local government. Approximately 85 percent of our jails are operated by counties, but some large cities do operate their own. And a few cities and counties operate a separate department of corrections. Prisons are operated by the states. A few states—Connecticut, Delaware, Hawaii, Rhode Island, and Vermont—have an integrated jail-prison system. Alaska has a partially integrated jail-prison system with six locally operated jails (United States Department of Justice 1980).[2] (See **table 12.1** for a differentiation of jails and prisons.)

In some major metropolitan areas (Chicago, New York, and San Diego, for example), the Federal Bureau of Prisons operates metropolitan corrections centers for people awaiting trial on federal charges. In places where there are federal courts but no federal detention facilities, the U.S. Marshal's Service arranges for local jails to care for and detain federal prisoners; There are about 800 such arrangements, housing some 5,000 federal detainees (i.e., more than 70 percent of all federal detainees).

TABLE 12.1 The differences between jails and prisons

Jails	Prisons
Usually operated by a local unit of government.	Operated by the state.
Holds pretrial detainees and sentenced petty offenders, usually misdemeanants.	Principally for the confinement of felons.
The population changes frequently, perhaps as much as 70 percent within seventy-two hours.	The population is relatively stable.
Located in population centers.	Historically located in rural areas.
Tend to have smaller populations than prisons.	Tend to have larger populations than jails.
Usually have limited inmate programs.	Have diverse inmate programs.
Have traditionally been ignored by scholars and researchers.	Have received considerable attention from scholars and researchers.

Data from Charles Swanson, "Overview of Jails," *Jail Operations* (Athens, Ga.: Institute of Government, University of Georgia, 1983), p. 24.

Types of jails

There are three types of jails in the United States—*pretrial detention facilities, sentenced facilities,* and *combination facilities*. The pretrial detention facility is used solely to confine persons awaiting trial. The sentenced facility is where convicted persons serve their sentences; inmates in these facilities are usually misdemeanants, although a few such facilities may house felons with short sentences. If operated by a city or county, a sentenced facility may be called a city or county farm, a city or county prison, or a city or county correctional facility. To some observers, these facilities are not jails, because they contain no pretrial detainees and some of the inmates in them are serving long sentences. Thus, it can be said that although they technically meet the definition of a jail, sentenced facilities are actually correctional facilities. Combination facilities house pretrial detainees and some convicted persons, usually misdeameants—although again, in a few states, felons serving shorter sentences may be housed there. The combination facility is the most common type of jail.

Purpose of jails

First, they enhance public safety by segregating persons deemed a criminal threat to people and property, and then ensure that persons charged with crimes appear at trial. Second, they are expected to effect some measure of positive behavioral-attitudinal change—the rehabilitative function. And third, they serve as a form of punishment.

Most jails in the United States are quite old. At present, 3 percent of the daily jail population is housed in facilities built before 1875. Further, 14 percent of all jail facilities were built between 1875 and 1924; 24 percent were built between 1925 and 1949; 43 percent were built between 1950 and 1969; and only 16 percent were built between 1970 and 1978. It would be inaccurate, however, to say that a jail is inadequate simply because it is old. Obnoxious conditions may exist in a facility of any age, depending on the resources available and the attitudes of jail administrators and jailers.

In general, though it is fair to say that an old facility is more likely than a new facility to have deficiencies. Unrenovated, uncared for, mismanaged, or misoperated jails present problems for the jailers, and persons confined in them are frequently in danger. Such facilities—with their noxious odors, dirty lavatories, and dirty floors and walls—are offensive to the eye and nose. In addition, some jails are fire hazards, some have inadequate lighting, ventilation, and bedding, and some are vermin infested and overcrowded.

To a great extent, however, the physical conditions of a jail are affected more by the professional competency and philosophy of the sheriff or the jail director than by the age of the facility (Territo 1983). The following case illustrates this point and also shows that even carefully made plans can take some interesting and unanticipated turns.

> As frequently happens every four years there was a hotly contested sheriff's race between a couple of men who were remarkably different in many personal and professional respects. Prior to being elected the incumbent sheriff had very little formal education and no prior administrative experience or professional training to administer the county jail. His opponent had a master's degree in criminology and broad ranging experience in criminal justice. The incumbent was defeated and when the newly elected sheriff took office, one of his first tasks was to conduct a systematic inspection of all parts of the sheriff's department's facilities which naturally included the county jail.
>
> Upon his inspection of the county jail, the new sheriff was shocked at its general state of disrepair and poor sanitary conditions. Puzzled at the obvious long term neglect of the facility the sheriff started questioning some of the jail personnel about it. He learned from them that the former sheriff placed his highest priority on the law enforcement component of the agency and almost no importance on the jail. The former sheriff also believed that jail inmates were criminals, and the jail should be as unpleasant a place as possible to discourage them from ever wanting to return to it.
>
> As a result of this attitude the following conditions existed at the jail:
>
> ☐ No part of the facility had been painted since it opened fifteen years earlier;
> ☐ Approximately 25% of all the lights in the cell block area were burned out, in addition, the cell block area was painted black;
> ☐ The showers would not drain properly because they were plugged up with human hair and inmates frequently had to stand in at least six inches of dirty water while showering;
> ☐ No cleaning material was provided to clean the commodes in the cell block area, thus they were not only stained with human waste but also emitted a very unpleasant odor;
> ☐ The jail was overrun by roaches, mice, rats and other vermin;
> ☐ The kitchen area, including the stove, had not been cleaned in years;
> ☐ The front lobby area where people waited to either conduct some business at the jail or visit inmates contained furniture that was so decrepit and

damaged that the chances of being impaled by one of the springs from these worn out couches was considerable.

Interestingly, all of these things existed in a state which is alleged to have very strict state controlled jail inspections, yet the facility was always given a satisfactory rating.

The new sheriff felt that such conditions were intolerable not only for those who were confined in the jail, but also because his employees had to work there, a point the former sheriff seemed to overlook. Thus, a massive housecleaning effort and repairs were undertaken by the county maintenance department at the request of the sheriff. In addition, an exterminator was employed to eliminate all of the unwelcome guests and some decent furniture was purchased, at cost, for the lobby area of the jail.

A couple of months after the cleanup and repairs were underway, some anonymous phone calls were made to the local newspapers and TV stations and complaints were lodged that the sheriff was spending the tax payers' dollars to convert the county jail into a luxury hotel for criminals. Media representatives contacted the sheriff and requested access to the jail to see if in fact it was as elegant and luxurious as some callers had described. There was some speculation that these anonymous phone calls may have been made by some supporters of the former sheriff who were not particularly happy with the defeat of their man. The sheriff agreed, but was concerned that the media might present a distorted or inaccurate picture of what it was that he wanted to accomplish. Nevertheless, the doors were opened and representatives of both the local newspapers and television stations were invited in. When they arrived, the planned changes were approximately half completed thus providing a realistic "before and after" contrast. All employees of the jail and inmates were encouraged to speak freely and openly to the media representatives. A series of totally unplanned but very pleasant side effects occurred as a result of the interviews conducted by the media representatives. For example, they interviewed people in the jail lobby area waiting to visit inmate relatives, attorneys visiting clients, jail officers and inmates. When some of the jail visitors who had witnessed the changes were interviewed their comments were quite favorable. One of them commented that it was unpleasant enough just having to come to the jail to visit a loved one, but when the place also looked like a dungeon as it previously had the experience was even more unpleasant. The attorneys who were waiting to see their clients were also quite pleased with the changes. The visitation rooms they used to talk to their clients no longer had broken tables, ripped up floor tiles, broken acoustical tiles, and half of the lights burned out. One attorney commented that the facility now gives the impression that "it was being administered by a professional administrator, and not the Marquis de Sade."

The response from the jail officers was also quite positive, and many commented that it was much more pleasant to come to work in a facility that "looked clean and smelled clean." They also appreciated the special attention that the new sheriff had shown them and the jail and had a renewed sense of pride in their work.

The last group of people to be interviewed were the inmates. This brought to light one of the most startling unplanned side effects of the planned change. Since at that point only half of the cell blocks had been repainted, or had the lights and plumbing repaired, the media was exposed to a vivid "before and after" contrast. The first set of cell blocks visited had been repainted light green, the burned out lights had been replaced and all of the plumbing repaired. As the media representatives walked along the catwalk they would stop and interview some of the inmates. In some cases, the inmates would even call out to the media representatives and request to talk to them. Both inmates and media representatives had access to each other, but the inmates were not permitted out of their cells. The inmates were questioned about their confinement and asked if they had any complaints about the facility. There were some minor complaints about needing more access to a telephone, and there were the normal amount of protestations about their innocence, but all in all, there were no serious complaints.

The second set of cell blocks visited were still in the original state of disrepair, but had basically the same classification of inmates as the previous cell blocks visited. As the heavy steel door to the cell block area was opened, the contrast in lighting and odor was startling. The group entered, and the inmates immediately started complaining about the food, abuse by jail officers, limited recreational opportunities, poor mail service and so forth. These complaints were made even though there was no difference between any of the cell blocks in terms of the quality of food, jail officers, recreational opportunities, mail service, and so forth. The only real difference between these cell blocks were the ones previously discussed. Interestingly, the jail officers also reported far more disciplinary problems in the unrepaired and unpainted cell blocks than in the newly renovated ones.

The cost of these changes were negligible to the taxpayers since all of the work was done by the county maintenance department as part of its regular responsibilities. All of these facts were accurately reported by the media and the criticism subsided (Territo 1983, p. 11-25).

Jail populations

As of February 1978, an estimated 158,000 persons were being held in the country's 3,500 local jails. Of this total, four out of every ten had been charged with, but not convicted of, a crime. The 1978 inmate population was a 12 percent increase over the population recorded by a similar survey in 1972. This increase was actually lower than expected, because of two factors unique to the 1970s—the backlogging of convicted felons in local jails to relieve overcrowded state prisons, and the entry of the baby-boom generation into the prime age bracket for offenders (eighteen to thirty-four). Indeed, the number of persons confined in prison rose approximately 40 percent from 1972 to 1978. Criminal justice reforms—such as the exclusion of juveniles from adult detention facilities, reduced incarceration rates for nuisance offenses, and the imposition of probation rather than confinement for some crimes—were in part responsible for the smaller relative increase in jail populations.

In both 1972 and 1978, males predominated the jail population. The proportion of women was the same in both years, and blacks and young people were represented disproportionately. The jail population in 1978 was even more youthful than in 1972, but the number of juveniles held in jails dropped sharply—a reflection of legislation prohibiting the joint housing of adult and juvenile offenders (U.S. Department of Justice, 1980, pp. 1-2).

Single persons—those who had never married or were divorced or separated—made up about three fourths of the inmate population in 1978 (single persons account for only one third of the total U.S. population). And three out of every five inmates lacked a high school diploma, compared with only one of every four persons in the general population. Military veterans were less numerous in the jail population than in the national population, and people with low incomes were present in higher numbers than in the general population. The average predetention annual income was only $3,700, and the percent of persons employed was much lower than in the general population. At least one in every four inmates was financially dependent on welfare, social security, unemployment benefits, or family and friends (rather than on a wage or salary).

The proportion of female inmates subject to economic disadvantage was particularly high and, to some extent, the same was true for blacks. Not surprisingly, therefore, black female inmates were the most likely of the four largest race-sex groups to be living in poverty. Drug and alcohol abuse also played a significant role in the lives of many inmates. About four out of every ten inmates used some drug daily prior to incarceration, and one fourth of all women inmates were herion addicts—far more than the proportion for men. About a fifth of the convicted inmates were under the influence of drugs when they committed the offense for which they were convicted. And an additional one fourth of the convicted inmates drank heavily just before they committed their offense (whites outnumbered blacks in the latter category by two to one) (ibid.).

Care of special prisoners

Alcoholics, diabetics, epilectics, the mentally ill, drug addicts, *sex offenders*, and other *special prisoners* present unique problems for the jailer. Such prisoners often require professional attention. And although jail officers are not expected to serve as physician, psychiatrist, or psychologist, they do need to have some knowledge of problems involved in supervising various types of special prisoners (Pappas 1971).[3]

A jailer deals with people from a wide range of backgrounds, in varying stages of health, and with needs ranging from simple housing with minimal security to tight security with continual supervision and care. The first decision a jailer must make is whether to admit a person brought to jail for detention. This decision is based on the policy of the jail administrator and the laws of the jurisdiction in which the jail is located. If the law requires that every person brought to the jail be admitted, the jail must then assume responsibility for any necessary medical care. And if the jail can not refuse persons who are ill, injured, or otherwise in no condition to be confined, then the jailer must be able to evaluate the prisoner's condition. In either case, the jailer must be able to recognize the unusual and be aware of the consequences of his or her actions. The safety and welfare of all prisoners may depend on the jailer's ability to recognize illness and injury. Furthermore, the jailer has both a moral and legal responsibility for the health and welfare of prisoners. Increasingly, the courts have recognized the legal rights of prisoners and have, in some instances, permitted civil

Alcoholics

The special prisoner seen most often by the jailer is the alcoholic. The familiar symptoms of intoxication include shakiness, staggering, thick speech, and a blank, glassy-eyed look. However, because other conditions can produce the same symptoms, it would be a mistake to assume that anyone who exhibits them is drunk. Multiple sclerosis, for example, is a disease that sometimes causes a person to stagger. Persons suffering from this disorder have been arrested for drunkenness despite protests that they have had nothing to drink.

The symptoms of a head injury can also be confused with the effects of excessive drinking. A person who has been hit over the the head or who strikes his or her head in a fall may appear intoxicated. Such a person should receive immediate medical attention. And someone in a diabetic coma may resemble a drinker who has passed out; if the diabetes goes untreated, the person may die. Thus, even when jailers are virtually certain that they are dealing with a simple case of intoxication, they should make sure that the prisoner in question is checked regularly. A person who has consumed a large amount of alcohol might first show typical signs of drunkenness, but might later lapse into deep unconsciousness and die.

JAIL BLAMED FOR DIABETIC'S HOSPITALIZATION
Cella W. Dugger   The Atlanta Journal

A DeKalb County prisoner who claims jail authorities refused to give him insulin and the special diet he needs was treated for a "critical" diabetic condition at Grady Memorial Hospital and is still listed in poor condition at the hospital.

The jail's physician denies the allegations, saying the inmate, Walter Jones, is lying.

Two doctors who treated Jones at Grady said his condition indicated that he may not have received the insulin.

Jones, 28, of 2369 Columbia Wood Court, Decatur, was arrested Nov. 2 and charged with the armed robbery of a 7-Eleven store at 2381 Columbia Drive, Decatur, and with aggravated assault on DeKalb police officers G.M. Fahey and M.L. Sharkey.

DeKalb police spokesman Chuck Johnson said Jones "fired shots at two officers outside the 7-Eleven as they were attempting to arrest him."

Jones was admitted to Grady Friday morning, five days later, in critical condition with pneumonia and an abnormally high blood sugar level, according to Dr. Mark Goldfarb. Goldfarb said this condition can result from a diabetic not getting enough insulin.

He said he didn't know why Jones—"a young healthy man" despite his diabetic condition—has pneumonia, but said a lack of insulin could have put Jones into a "stuporous state" in which he might have contracted pneumonia. Noting that Jones' blood sugar was 10 times the normal level, Goldfarb said, "I would assume he hadn't been getting his insulin, but I don't know."

Ralph Jackson, the other physician treating Jones, said "either he wasn't getting insulin or he had an infection. If he had been taking his regular dose of insulin, I don't think his glucose (sugar) would have been that high, but I can't be sure."

Jones, a construction worker, told both his brother and the medical student with primary responsibility for his care at Grady that while in custody he had been denied insulin and had been given the same diet as the other prisoners. Diabetics require a special diet to maintain their blood sugar level.

Jones could not be interviewed because of tightened security measures at Grady brought about by the rash of escapes from the hospital this year.

Dr. Charles Allard, who was in charge of the case at the jail, refused to describe the treatment he had prescribed for the patient.

"I don't give any information to anybody over the telephone. He [Jones] is lying. I won't tell you nothing," Allard said.

A doctor and a nurse are on duty 24 hours a day for the jail's more than 500 inmates, according to a DeKalb County Sheriff's Department spokesman. "We feel good about our medical team," Lt. Winston Pittman said.

"We have some people who come in there and don't tell us what's wrong with them and we get the blame," Pittmann said.

Jones' brother Tommy, of the same address, said he received a call from the prisoner on the afternoon of his arrest.

"I called them (the jail) and told them he was a diabetic. He had already told them. And they didn't give him insulin or the right food or anything," Tommy Jones said.

On Wednesday, Tommy Jones said, an inmate called him to tell him his brother was sick. "He said he was out and about to go into a coma," Jones said.

Jones said he then went to the jail, and that the "jailers told me there wasn't nothing wrong with him."

When he got back home, he said, another inmate called telling him his brother was "bad off sick. The inmates must have been passing the phone around.

Thursday morning at about 9:30, Jones said, he went back to the jail to try to see his brother, and was told that "he was fine." Jones said he hired an attorney, Donald J. Stein, who went to the jail that afternoon.

Stein said those in charge wouldn't let him see Walter Jones because "he was doing too badly and they were giving him a hypodermic to sedate him."

Friday morning, Jones was admitted to Grady.

Ken Dobson, the medical student responsible for Jones' care, said he asked Jones, who Dobson said could not speak coherently until Sunday morning whether he had been getting his insulin and what he had been eating in the jail.

"He said he had asked for it (insulin) and they wouldn't give it to him. And he said, "I'm having to eat the same food as the other men," Dobson said.

Reprinted from the *Atlanta Journal,* 12 November 1980.

The mentally ill

Mental illnesses that are least understood are likely to be the most frightening. The behavior of the mentally disturbed person is often strange and alarming. The term *mental illness* is also misleading, because it covers a wide range of complicated emotional disorders that may involve physical, mental and behavioral disturbances. A disorder may be relatively mild and difficult to detect, and it may not seriously handicap the individual. At the other extreme, a condition may be so obvious and serious that the sufferer requires constant care and may even present a danger to himself and others.

Some behavior that results from mental illness is dramatic and attracts immediate attention. Individuals who insist that they see or hear things that do not really exist are readily recognized as emotionally disturbed. But other signs of mental illness may be difficult to detect; for example, people who assert that someone is plotting against them may sound quite convincing, even though their belief is wholly without basis.

When people hear, see smell, or taste something that is not really there, they are experiencing *hallucinations.* Hallucinations usually indicate a serious mental disturbance. Continuous heavy use of alcohol, drugs, and other chemical substances may also produce hallucinations. The most common hallucinations involve hearing. For example, a person might report that a voice is telling him or her to do "bad" things. A person who shows clear signs of mental illness should be referred immediately to a physician (preferably a psychiatrist) or a clinical psychologist.

Drug addicts

When long-time drug users are brought to jail, they may appear normal and be difficult to recognize as addicts. Nevertheless, cautious jailers should watch for signs of drug intoxication and withdrawal and examine prisoners for needle marks and scars over the blood vessels of the arms and legs. Weight loss and loss of appetite are also signs of drug addiction.

Jail personnel should watch prisoners closely to prevent them from obtaining unauthorized drugs. Jailer's are responsible for keeping the addict safe from self-imposed injuries during drug withdrawal and to assist with the medical aspects of the process. The jail physician is responsible for the addicted prisoner's medical care, although most of the care is actually given by the jail staff. If a prisoner becomes seriously ill during withdrawal, the physician may recommend a short period of controlled hospitalization.

Sex offenders

The jailer also sees a wide variety of sex offenders, including persons accused of indecent exposure, window peeping, child molestation, and rape. Despite popular belief, these offenders are quite different from one another and they each present unique problems. Not all of them require the same

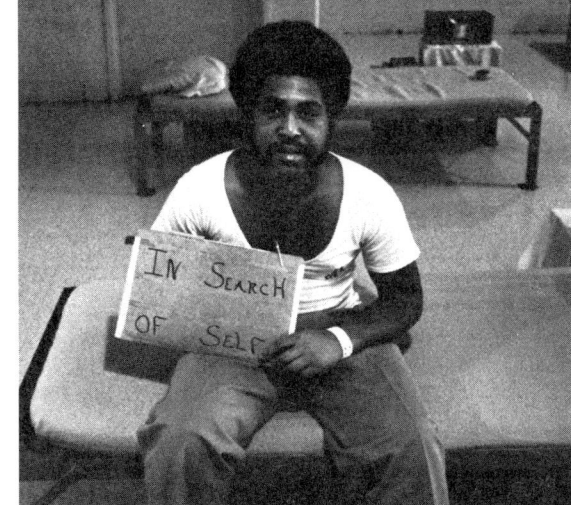

An inmate in the residential unit of the Cook County (Illinois) Jail. The jail provides comprehensive treatment for inmates with mental health problems. Courtesy Tony O'Brien/ Corrections Magazine.

degree of supervision or segregation, for example. Consider a prisoner charged with molesting a child: such a prisoner usually poses no sexual threat to adults, but he (or, rarely, she) may have to be protected from other prisoners. Anger toward the child molester and other sexual criminals is sometimes very intense. In general, most sex offenders are passive persons who pose no major problems in a jail setting; only a few are violent or dangerous. However, because some such offenders become depressed and suicidal, close observation is required. (Suicidal inmates are discussed in the Issue Paper at the end of this chapter).

Jail security

In the real world of jail administration, security is given marked priority over rehabilitation. Although the two goals are often mentioned in the same breath, there is little question that security comes first. In most institutions, virtually all other activities and functions are subordinated to security. The reason is quite simple: no jail administrator has ever been fired for failing to rehabilitate an inmate; but many have been dismissed following prisoner escapes or disturbances (Miller 1978).[4] Some of the common security techniques and procedures used throughout the nation are counts, shakedowns, frisks, tool control, key control, cutlery control, narcotics control, and visitation control.

Counts

During a *count*, institutional activities are temporarily halted and all inmates are counted. It is hoped that the total will equal the number of people who are supposed to be in confinement. If it does not, at least one recount is taken, and an attempt is made to identify and locate the missing inmate or inmates. If the count still comes up short, escape procedures are implemented. In the event an escape does occur, routine counts provide some knowledge of the time frame within which the escape took place.

Shakedowns

A *shakedown* is a thorough search of a jail or any part thereof for *contraband* (anything an inmate possesses in violation of institutional rules and regulations). The definition of contraband varies from jail to jail, but weapons, alcohol, and narcotics not prescribed or approved by the jail physician are universally prohibited. Prisoners often employ ingenious methods to conceal contraband and to modify available objects for use as weapons or tools for escape.

> **Case 12.1**
>
> In a county jail in Washington state, U.S. marshalls discovered the following items in the inner compartments of a prisoners rubber-soled shoes: two razor blades, five double-edged razor blades, one fingernail clipper (file and

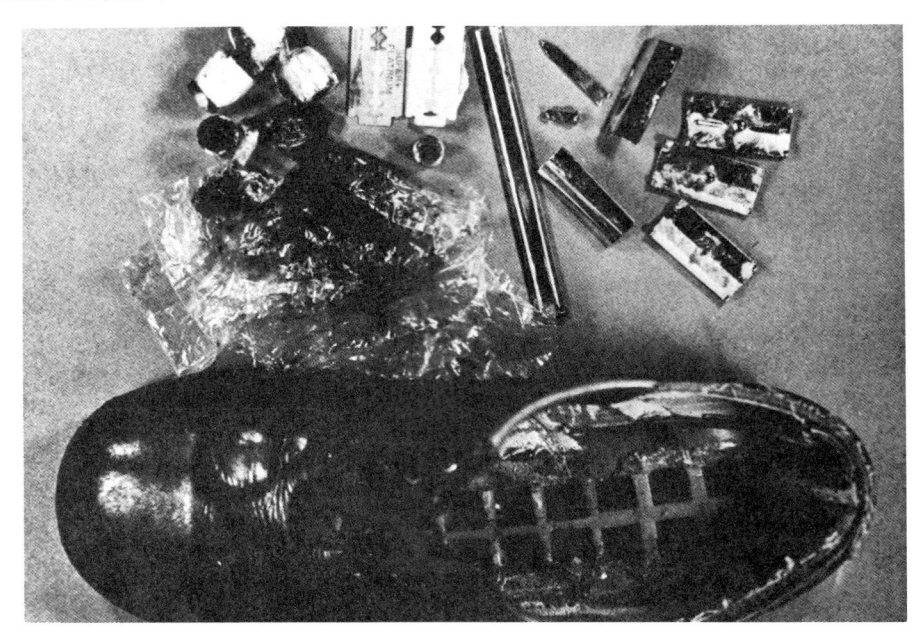

Shoe containing contraband. Courtesy Pierce County (Washington) Sheriff's office.

case), one handcuff key (fabricated from a double-edged razor), and six metal tubes containing a black, paintlike substance.

Case 12.2

Upon searching a cell, officers in a New York State correctional facility found a crude, concealed weapon, handmade from a twelve-inch brass lavatory valve rod. The rod, which normally has a time-release push button at one end, extends downward through the fixture into the wall. The opposite end is linked by a cotter key to internal plumbing. Once the key is broken, however, the rod can be extracted and easily honed to a point by manually rubbing it against an abrasive surface (such as a concrete floor).

Case 12.3

Correctional officers in the Westchester County (New York) Jail found a shank—fabricated from a tray—in the possession of a prisoner. The tray had

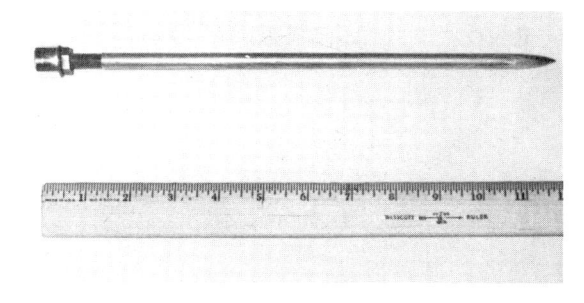

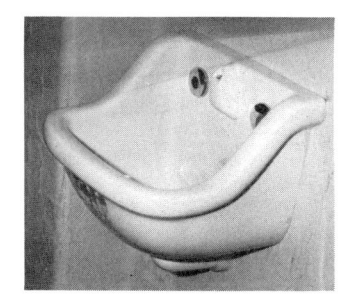

Weapon (left photo) fashioned from valve rod taken out of a jail cell sink. Courtesy Westchester County Department of Correction, Valhalla, New York

been previously tested and was believed to be unbreakable, but it was discovered that the tray weakened over time.

✃ Frisks

A *frisk* is a "pat search" of an inmate; officers run their hands along the outside of the inmate's clothing to detect concealed contraband. The frequency of frisks depends upon the security classification of the inmate and the areas to or from which the inmate is coming or going. For example, if a maximum security prisoner is leaving an area where there are usually tools (i.e., potential weapons), a frisk would be an appropriate, if not a mandatory, security procedure. Some jails use metal detectors instead of, or in addition to, standard frisking.

Case 12.4

Officers in an Oregon correctional facility discovered that a prisoner had developed a zipper tab into a screwdriver. The prisoner first worked the tab loose from the zipper, then ground down each side. The result was a custom-made screwdriver that could remove security screws from windows.

Case 12.5

At one jail, only one of sixteen prisoners taken from the jail to court for trial was searched. As a result, the inmates brought a hacksaw blade with them and sawed through one of the bars of their holding cell. Three inmates squeezed through an eight-by-twelve-inch hole, jumped to a lower level outside the building, then dropped to the ground. One inmate broke his ankle and was recaptured on the scene. During the next ten hours before recapture, the remaining two inmates murdered six people.

Shank fabricated from tray. Courtesy Westchester County Department of Correction, Valhalla, New York.

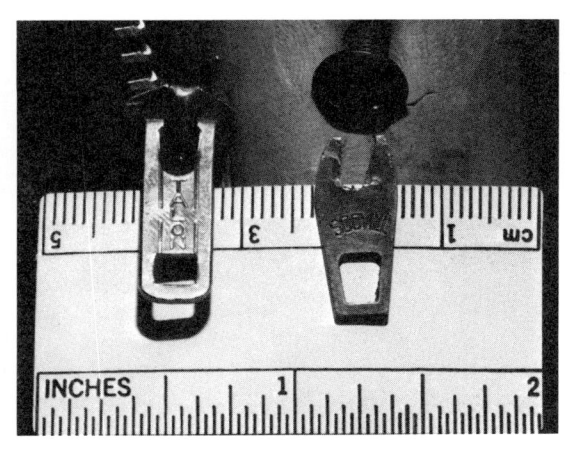

Zipper screwdriver. Courtesy Douglas County Sheriff's Department, Corrections Division, Roseburg, Oregon.

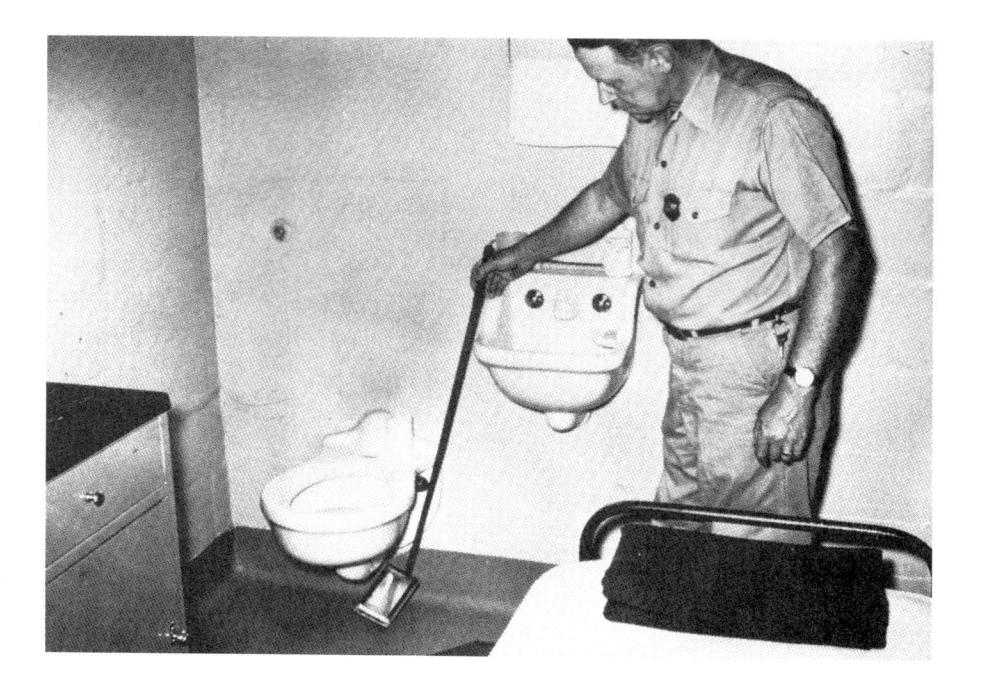

A guard searching a jail cell for contraband, using a mirror mounted on a rod. Reprinted from Nick Pappas, editor, The Jail: Its Operation and Management, Washington, D.C.: U.S. Bureau of Prisons.

Tool control

Tool control is system of accounting for all tools available in a jail. Tight control is essential, because tools can be—and often are—used as weapons or as an aid in escape. Because proper tool control requires up-to-date inventory surveys, all tools should be stored in secure places and be fully accounted for at the end of each workday.

One of the best methods of assuring adequate tool control is the use of a "shadow board" (for tool storage.) The outline of each tool is painted on the board, so that a tool-crib operator can tell at the end of the day if tools are missing. When tools are checked out, a receipt is completed and attached to the board in place of the tool to ensure accountability.

> **Case 12.6**
>
> An inmate escaped from a third-floor rooftop and recreation area, even though the area was completely screened by a heavy-gauge wire fence and cover. A jail officer supervised the area but could not see one corner of the yard from his position. The inmate used a pair of wire cutters inadvertently left behind by a workman, cut through the fence, and climbed down a building drain pipe (The National Sheriffs Association 1974, p.70).

Key control

Despite its obvious importance, *key control* is less than effective in many jails. There is often no central control system, and those that do exist may

Shadow board used for tool control. Reprinted from Nick Pappas, editor, The Jail: Its Operation and Management, *Washington, D.C.: U.S. Bureau of Prisons.*

be ineffective because of the casual attitudes of jail officers. Control is particularly difficult in jails that have a different key for every door. A jailer who carries both cell keys and keys to cell blocks risks assault from prisoners attempting to escape. Once prisoners have the keys to their cell block, it is a simple matter for them to get to and open the door leading out of the jail.

Case 12.7

A jail officer asked an inmate to get cleaning supplies from a furnace room; he gave the inmate the keys to the security door. The inmate got the supplies and returned the keys, but left the door to the furnace room open. Three inmates then simply walked out, because the furnace room was outside the security portion of the jail and led directly to the street. The jail officer was subsequently tried in court and fined for negligence, although the court decided not to give him a jail sentence (ibid., p. 73).

Cutlery control

Cutlery control is a system of accounting for all eating utensils used in a jail. Normally, kitchen equipment such as butcher knives and other potentially dangerous items are monitored under an institution's tool control program. But special measures are needed to ensure that the cutlery used at meals is not "borrowed" and used for illegal purposes. A table knife is an obvious weapon, and a fork or a spoon that has been sharpened at one end can be equally dangerous.

When inmates eat in communal dining halls, cutlery control is rather standard. When the inmates enter the dining room, they are each handed eating utensils for that meal. At the end of the meal, as the inmates leave via a main exit, they must deposit into a large receptacle under the obser-

Key control board. A metal tag bearing the officer's name is used as a receipt when keys are withdrawn. Reprinted from Nick Pappas, editor, The Jail: Its Operation and Management, *Washington, D.C.: U.S. Bureau of Prisons.*

vation of an officer the same number and type of utensils they were initially issued. If an inmate fails to do this he or she is detained in the dining hall. After everyone has deposited their used cutlery as required, the silverware is again counted before it is taken back into the kitchen for washing. If any cutlery is missing at that point, a search or shakedown is conducted to recover the missing items.

When inmates eat in their cells, a common practice in many jails, officers must again be careful to supervise the dispensation and return of silverware. If anything is missing a search of the area involved should be started promptly. The silverware should also be counted again when it is returned to the kitchen: there is always the possibility that trustees or other inmates will pilfer one or more items during the transit from the cells to the kitchen. Why not use plastic utensils? Because plastic items are difficult to clean properly (given the equipment in most jail kitchens), and it would be extremely expensive and inconvenient to replace utensils after each meal.

Case 12.8

Two prison transportation officers were attacked by an inmate with a knife that was stolen from the jail kitchen by another inmate and concealed in the prisoner-transport vehicle. One officer was killed. The incident occurred on a busy highway, and motorists were in substantial danger because of an exchange of gunfire after the inmate took the gun of the dead officer. Matters worsened when the second officer, already seriously wounded, was shot and wounded again by an off-duty police officer in foot pursuit of the escapee (ibid, p.73).

Narcotics control

Narcotics control is a major problem in many jails, particularly in metropolitan areas, because of the high number of addicts confined on criminal charges. This situation creates an immediate and substantial demand for illicit drugs. Again, good control procedures start with an accurate and up-to-date survey of inventory. All narcotics should be stored securely in an area not readily accessible to inmates. And medication prescribed for inmates should be prepared by qualified medical personnel, not by jail officers. In most jails, medication is dispensed in the cell block, because too many problems are involved in moving prisoners to and from an infirmary. Medication should be dispensed personally by an officer, and inmates should be required to swallow the medication in the presence of that officer. A guard should check under the tongue to ensure that the medicine has been consumed and not "saved" for purposes of hoarding or sale within the institution. Certain types of medication can be dissolved in water first to get around this problem. Jail personnel also have to be alert to the possibility that drugs might be mailed or smuggled into the jail.

Visitation control

Any time people from the "outside" come into or go out of a jail, a threat is posed to the security of the institution. This is especially true today, because of narcotics smuggling. Thus, *visitation control*—the control of visiting procedures and facilities—requires careful attention on the part of prison administrators.

A common form of visitation control is the enclosed booth with a plexiglass or bullet-resistant glass front. Inmates sit in the booth and communicate with their visitors via voice-powered telephone. Some jails use a less structured arrangement and allow inmates to sit across a table from their visitors (with or without a screen between them). A third visitation mode is an informal, quasi–living room setting—sofas, easy chairs, coffee tables—with few, if any, physical barriers. Another type of visit, one that is currently a source of controversy in some jurisdictions, is the "contact" visit. In such visits, the inmate and his or her spouse are allowed to kiss hello and good-bye and to hold hands during the visit. The purpose of this approach is to make visits as normal as possible.

A key to maintaining proper security during visits is the careful screening of inmates. For example, a maximum security prisoner who poses and imminent escape risk or is otherwise considered dangerous should be allowed to visit only in the booth arrangement. On the other hand, a minimum security prisoner who has demonstrated his or her trustworthiness should be allowed to visit in a more relaxed atmosphere. Under any visiting format, however, officers should be present and alert to any sign of trouble or any attempt to pass contraband. To further ensure security, many jails frisk inmates after visits before returning them to their housing or work areas; some jails even perform a complete strip search of every inmate.

Case 12.9

One inventive young woman who visited her boyfriend at a county jail in Florida left a felt-tipped pen and some writing paper for him after each visit.

The pen was always checked by correctional personnel before it was turned over to the prisoner, and each time it appeared to be nothing more than a pen. In fact, it *was* a pen, but it was also used as a container to smuggle marijuana into the jail. Before the start of each visit, the woman would remove the pen's plastic top and take out the cartridge. She would then stuff the pen with enough marijuana for two cigarettes. She added black paper on top of the marijuana to block the view of anyone who might remove the top of the pen for inspection. The scheme was discovered only because another inmate informed correctional personnel. The next time the girlfriend visited, she was searched and the marijuana was found. The woman was arrested for attempting to smuggle drugs into the jail.

Case 12.10

A state jail inspector informed a particular jail administrator that his facility had inadequate security procedures and staffing. The jail administrator disagreed with the inspector and released a story to the press that appeared on the front page of the Sunday newspaper. That same Sunday night, the lone officer on duty (for thirty-eight inmates) was called to a cell block area by an inmate, who shot him with a gun smuggled in by a female visitor in a candy box with a fake bottom. (The officer was over seventy years old and had just retired from another job two months before.) The inmate took the dying officer's keys and opened his cell door. The jail administrator, who lived in adjacent quarters, heard the gunshot, rushed to the scene and was also shot. The escapee dashed down a stairway into the courthouse lobby, broke a window in the front door, and drove off in a waiting car with an accomplice (ibid., p.72).

The role of the jail in the criminal justice system

As indicated in Chapter 1, the criminal justice system is an arrangement of four working parts: the police, the prosecution, the courts, and corrections. The police force is responsible for criminal investigation and apprehension, the prosecution for the prosecution of offenses against the state, the courts for determination of guilt, and corrections for confinement and rehabilitation. The system will not work at all if any of the parts is missing, and it will work at a low level of efficiency if any of the parts is not operating well (Pappas 1971).

The jail is important as evidence of society's interest in justice, punishment and rehabilitation. Anyone who has been found not guilty by a court has had first-hand experience with our system of law and justice. And anyone who is awaiting trial or serving a sentence will get a long and intensive exposure to the values of society with regard to crime and punishment. The jail has an extremely important place in the criminal justice system, both because it is the most common type of confinement and because more persons pass through the jail than through any other agency in the system.

Jails and the police

The relationship of jails to the police is one of accommodation and cooperation. Jails must accept any prisoner who is legally detained and who can be legally received. (In some jurisdictions, however, jails can not admit juveniles, even if the arrest is legal). Jails are passive, and to some extent, the jail population reflects this. For example, if the police have periodic clean-up campaigns to remove drunks and vagrants from the streets, the jails will soon contain many such persons. And because arrest policies are not a matter of police determination alone, but are a reflection of community attitudes and governmental policy, complaints from local business people may be enough to initiate a clean-up policy.

NORTH FRANKLIN POLICING HIT
Ivan Hathaway   Tampa Tribune

Claiming that panhandlers are running rampant and "women have to walk out into the street to avoid being molested," a group of North Franklin Street merchants charged yesterday that police are not providing adequate protection.

The charge was leveled by a group of about 25 businessmen at a morning meeting at Todd's Restaurant, 208 E. Cass Street, which was attended by City Councilmen Joe Kotvas and Lee Duncan, Deputy Police Chief Allison Wainwright and Police Maj. J. W. Morton.

Making the strongest complaints was Harry Arkus, who told the city officials that customers entering stores on Franklin and its stores for 30 minutes or longer, saying that police response was slow.

Addressing Wainwright, Arkus said, "We see an officer walking the beat once in a while, and then we don't see him again for a few days and don't know where he is when we need him. We want to be protected."

Responding to the complaints, Wainright said police officials already were aware that side streets have to make their way past panhandlers begging for money.

"These bums line the sidewalks, alienating customers. I've seen two women who had to walk out onto the street to avoid being molested," Arkus said.

One merchant told of being robbed in his store five times in recent years and of being mugged and robbed on the sidewalk only a week ago.

He said, referring to the most recent case, that had there been a policeman on the street the robber could have been caught.

Others complained of "drunks" being allowed to lie on the streets in front of their downtown merchants "have a problem."

"The only answer to this problem you're having seems to be in assigning more officers to patrol the area. But we just don't have the men to do this," he said.

From *The Tampa Tribune,* 16 January 1973.

POLICE CRACK DOWN ON PANHANDLERS
Ivan Hathaway   Tampa Tribune

A crackdown on "nuisance violations," aimed particularly at the growing number of panhandlers in the downtown area, has resulted in 10 arrests within a 24-hour period, Tampa police said yesterday.

Jail dockets indicated the 10 men were charged with "begging." They were held in lieu of $25 bond each.

The arrests came shortly after a meeting in which North Franklin Street merchants criticized the policing in their business area.

Col. Allison Wainwright, deputy chief of police, said the meeting did not bring about the crackdown, "though it may have been a contributing factor."

We've always been interested in protecting the downtown area. Because of a shortage of officers and the crime rate, we have not had the opportunity to enforce the ordinance as we would have liked to," Wainwright said.

But the panhandling has had a gradual increase and is now a major problem. "People are being pushed around and verbally abused. Panhandlers are even approaching our plainclothes detectives."

To cope with the problem, officers who had been assigned to other Tampa areas have been called in to patrol the "entire downtown area," and policemen are doubling up on their assignments, he said.

"It has been our experience that as soon as we apply enforcement in an area, we begin seeing results and the problem begins decreasing," Wainwright said.

The crackdown will continue "as long as possible," he said.

"With these additional men in the downtown area we have a hairline balance of manpower. We'll keep them there as long as we can. If a need for additional manpower arises in another part of the city, we will have to pull them out for reassignment," Wainwright said.

From *The Tampa Tribune*, 18 January 1973.

The important point here is that the jails feel the effects of community and police policy. They are not independent units in the community, uninfluenced by events around them. Rather, they are part of a larger system, and what the rest of that system does affects them. And the way the jails operate will, in turn, affect the community and the rest of the criminal justice system.

Jails hold the accused until the formal machinery of criminal justice begins to move. While an accused person is in a jail, coordination is often required between the police and jail personnel. Some exchange of information is necessary, particularly when there is a need to keep accomplices separated. When a long-term investigation is required, the police and the jail may need to coordinate efforts to schedule interviews or to otherwise make the accused available to the police, the prosecuting attorney, and the defense counsel. The need for information exchange and coordination is equally important when the jail is holding a material witness (a vital service to the police).

Jails and the courts

Jails and the courts must cooperate closely if both are to complete their work. The courts influence the jail's activity and, in turn, are dependent on the jail's successful handling of the court-imposed work load. And the jail has a scheduling and coordinating function with regard to the courts. The jail must follow trial schedules and be aware of trial results and orders to produce or release prisoners. To a great extent, these functions make the jail a department of the court.

Sentencing decisions clearly demonstrate the extent of interdependence between jails and the courts. The courts can sentence an individual to jail, modify the sentence before its completion, place an offender on probation, and, in some jurisdictions, sentence offenders to work release. These decisions influence the jail population and its composition and the extent of program activity. For example, misdemeanants may be sentenced to jails instead of to workhouses or work farms, thus increasing the number of prisoners in jails. Or the court may decide to sentence prisoners to a county correctional institution, thus reducing the jail population. In some cases, the courts may decide to use probation, a suspended sentence, or a fine. And court decisions against the arrest of drunks may reduce the number of drunks among the jail population.

Although some bail is routine, all bail is a matter of court supervision. Until recently, jails were passive in bail proceedings; if an accused person made bail, he or she was released from jail. Today, however, bail projects have expanded the role of the jail. In addition to detention and confinement, the jail is now involved in selecting persons for release on their own recognizance. The selection may be done by jail personnel, although it is usually done by employees of the probation department. Where such programs do not exist, traditional bail procedures require that the jail work within court and statutory requirements to develop bail procedures.

Because of the need for close coordination, courts and jails are often located in the same building. Although it is possible to operate a jail at some distance from the court, such an arrangement is inconvenient in terms of moving prisoners back and forth to the court. In general, coordination between a court and a jail becomes more difficult as the distance between them increases. A jail outside the immediate vicinity of the court is isolated, and jail personnel may begin to feel that the jail has little to do with the court.

The decisions of the court relative to convicted offenders make it necessary for the jail to serve as a distributor to the system. The jail is the transfer point for prisoners who have been sentenced to a workhouse, county farm, or correctional institution. In some instances, the transfer is a procedural matter handled by notifying the proper agency. Depending on the case, prisoners may be delivered to the receiving institutions either by that institution or by the jail. If large numbers of prisoners are involved in a transfer, the jail may serve as a collection point.

Jails and corrections

Many people view the jail as primarily a law enforcement operation, probably because the chief administrator of the jail is usually a law officer (namely, a sheriff). However, jails do not have specific law enforcement functions. They are not a base of operations for criminal detection or apprehension, although they may be located in a department where these activities go on. Jail personnel may be formally connected with the law enforcement organization and may, in fact, be deputy sheriffs; but their specific duties in the jail are not in the area of law enforcement.

The jails have more than a passing responsibility for the care of prisoners who are serving sentences. In essence, jails are in the business of corrections. Today there is increased recognition that the jail must serve many functions in the community. And correction is one of these functions. The jail is called upon by the courts and the community to become involved in correctional programs and to concern itself with the rehabilitation of prisoners who are serving sentences. Some authorities even recommend that the jail become the focus of the community correctional effort.

The fact that most sentenced prisoners are not felons does not divorce a jail from the rehabilitative effort. Rehabilitation does not begin with the felon; rather, it is needed most for the misdemeanant. And it is an area in which jails have a particular advantage: they are located in the community and can coordinate community resources to develop an effective program.

Aside from their rehabilitative function, jails play a role in the general correctional effort in the state. In this regard, the jail must develop close and effective ties with the state correctional program. This will result in a shared effort between the jail and the larger system—to the benefit of both. In program planning, the jail may be able to benefit by the state's experience with certain rehabilitative techniques. And personnel training can be shared, especially when a jail has too few personnel or resources to develop its own training program. The expert help needed to plan new construction or renovation can also be provided by the state. Finally, local and state facilities can coordinate prisoner statistics to get a statewide picture of jail and correctional needs.

Summary

Jails are the intake point of our entire criminal justice system and are the most prevalent type of correctional institution. They are primarily a function of local government, and they are as diverse in size, physical condition, and efficiency as the units of government that operate them. The three types of jails are pretrial detention facilities for persons awaiting trial, sentenced facilities for persons serving sentences, and combination facilities for pretrial detainees and some convicted persons.

Jails in the United States are quite old and are frequently in need of extensive repair. In addition, many are offensive to the eye and nose because of noxious odors, dirty lavatories, dirty floors, stained walls, and vermin. Many jail facilities also contain fire hazards that endanger both inmates and correctional staff. In all fairness, however, it must be noted that there are also many jails that are clean and well maintained. Often, the major difference between a poorly run and poorly kept jail and one that it well maintained is the attitude, philosophy, and priorities of the local sheriff or jail administrator. For example, it is rarely expensive to keep a jail clean and free of vermin, but if such activity is not viewed as being very important by the person in charge, then poor conditions may not get the attention they need.

An estimated 150,000 people were being held in 3,500 jails in the United States in 1978; and the evidence suggests that the jail population will continue to increase at a much faster rate than new jails are built or old ones expanded. The population in these jails is comprised overwhelmingly of males, with black males and young persons represented disproportionately. Further, jail inmates tend to be single or divorced and poorly educated. Special prisoners that present problems for the jailer include alcoholics, the mentally ill, drug addicts, sex offenders, injured persons, and depressed or suicidal prisoners. Jail personnel must be properly trained to recognize and supervise such prisoners, and, when necessary, to provide them with special care. The failure to do so might result in the death of a prisoner and a lawsuit against those responsible for jail administration and operation.

When hard choices must be made between security and rehabilitation in the jail, security is always given priority. This is not surprising, considering that jail administrators can be fired and sheriffs defeated at election time if a dangerous or infamous prisoner escapes. To ensure the integrity of jail security, several measures are employed: shakedowns, which involve a thorough search of a jail or any part thereof for contraband; regular frisking of inmates, especially when they are moved from one part of the jail to another; tool control; key control; cutlery control; narcotics control; and visitation control.

Overall, the jail plays an extremely important role in the criminal justice system. Because of its strategic location, many citizens come into contact with the jail each year and form their first impressions about the quality and fairness of the system. And jail personnel are involved in a close working relationship with the police, the courts, and corrections. The extent to which these other parts of the criminal justice system are effective is sometimes quite dependent upon the quality of the jail and its personnel.

In spite of the bleak picture often presented of American jails, evidence suggests that the quality of jail personnel and jail facilities will steadily improve throughout the 1980s. This will occur in part because of pressure imposed by the federal courts in rulings relating to prisoners' complaints about overcrowding, unsanitary conditions, poor health care, and physical abuse. Other improvements will occur because the states are now taking a more active role in requiring minimum qualifications and training for jail personnel. Finally, there is reason to believe that the chief administrators of our local jails—whether they are sheriffs or civilian administrators—are better educated, better trained, and generally more professional than their predecessors.

issue paper

SUICIDES IN JAIL

According to a recent study completed by the National Center on Institutions and Alternatives in Alexandria, Virginia, there were 419 reported jail suicides in the United States in 1979. There is some speculation, however, that the figure is probably closer to 1000, because there is no master list of jails. Due to the less than enthusiastic cooperation from some jail authorities, totally accurate figures are not available (Michaels 1982, p. 4). In this issue paper, we focus on two dimensions of jail suicides—the psychological factors of the suicidal inmate and the management of the suicidal inmate. Further, we give several examples of actual jail suicides.

The psychology of the suicidal inmate

Bruce L. Danto (1971), a nationally recognized authority on suicide and suicide prevention, concludes that certain types of persons are likely candidates for suicide in jail. One such person is the inmate who has had no previous experience with incarceration. In some cases, such an individual may not have been arrested for a very serious crime, but nevertheless may have strong feelings of depression, shame, and guilt.

> **Issue Paper Case 12.1**
>
> On June 6, 1981, James Kiley was jailed at 3:10 A.M. in the Haverhill, Massachusetts County Jail on charges of drunk driving. He had been drinking with friends at a beach and his vehicle struck a telephone pole while he was driving home. He was arrested shortly thereafter for drinking and driving. At 4:45 A.M. the police say their television monitor showed him asleep in his cell. Ten minutes later he was found dead—hanged with his shirt-sleeves. The victim's mother said, "We just don't understand what happened. He was an easygoing nineteen-year-old boy with a brand new car, a plumbing job he liked, and a girl he loved. He left home whistling that night" (Michaels 1982, p. 4).

> **Issue Paper Case 12.2**
>
> On Thursday morning, August 13, 1981, Risa Boltax was riding her bike to a job interview in Scotch Plains, New Jersey, when she was stopped by the police. They took her into custody in connection with a previous incident involving possession of marijuana. Around lunchtime, Risa's mother, Yetta Boltax, visited her at the Union County Jail in Elizabeth and, she says, found her confused and upset. Some time near midnight, the police said nineteen-year-old Risa stood up on her bunk, twisted the sheet around her neck, tied each end of the sheet around the top bar of her cell, and stepped off the bunk (ibid.).

Some first-time offenders do commit very serious crimes—murder, a highly publicized sex offense, a white-collar crime (such as embezzlement), and so on. This type of inmate, according to Danto, is highly subject to suicide soon after admission to the jail.

Another type of person likely to commit suicide in jail is the inmate who has resided in a holding or postsentence center for weeks, months, or even years, and has developed a feeling of hopelessness and futility about the future. This type of person frequently has spent previous time in penal confinement.

> **Issue Paper Case 12.3**
>
> A forty-three-year-old inmate in a county jail who had just been transferred from a federal prison for court proceedings was found dead hanging from the neck by strips of sheets in his cell. The inmate had been serving time in a federal prison for killing a law enforcement officer in a gunfight. The man—a hardened convict experienced in the ways of prisons and jails—soon found himself a niche in the county jail. During his confinement, several inmates heard him say that he was never going back to federal prison, even though his date for transfer was approaching. On the day of his suicide, the inmate received copies of divorce papers from his former wife's lawyer. The man left a note making some practical requests concerning his burial, the disposition of his death benefits, and a note cursing his wife "until my dying breath." His suicide, although quite likely triggered by the receipt of the divorce papers, was merely the culmination of his total loss of hope for the future (Fawcett and Marrs 1973, pp. 93–94).

The third type of person prone to suicidal behavior is the antisocial person who tries to manipulate others. Such inmates choose nonlethal forms of suicide in an attempt to manipulate guards and other officials. They characteristically make superficial cuts on their wrists or swallow glass (or at least say they have). Experience shows that this type of person can, indeed, kill himself or herself if pushed and goaded enough by others (ibid., pp. 96–97).

Management of the suicidal inmate

Jail suicides are not only tragic, but they can also be quite costly to the taxpayer. For example, the parents of James Kiley have notified the city of Haverhill that they intend to file a negligence suit for $100,000 (Michaels 1983, p. 5). As a result of such lawsuits, jail administrators are now training jail personnel in suicide prevention. The following suggestions are becoming a routine part of all such programs:

- The jail officer must take all threats of suicide seriously.
- Inmates who threaten or attempt suicide should not be kept in isolation, but should be housed with inmates who are willing to assist jail officers in watching them.
- Medical treatment for actual or claimed injury is essential.
- If depression and suicidal thoughts or behavior occur in relation to the falling off of contact with relatives or friends, correctional officers should arrange for a quick phone call or a visit between the involved parties.

Mr. and Mrs. John Kiley of Methuen, Massachusetts, picket outside Haverhill Jail where their nineteen-year-old son died. Courtesy Lawrence (Massachusetts) Eagle Tribune.

- ☐ If jail doctors prescribe tranquilizers for disturbed inmates, the jail officer must make certain that the medication is taken. Further, efforts should be made to ensure that the inmate does not roll the pill back under the tongue and spit it out later or save it for a suicide attempt.
- ☐ Jail officers should be sensitive to inmates who abruptly withdraw from activities, suffer a loss of appetite, have sad facial expressions, or suddenly slow down in their thoughts or actions. Such signs are typical of depression.

The proper training of jail personnel and the use of mental health specialists for the screening and aftercare of suicidal inmates and for the reevaluation of jail directives can go a long way toward reducing the rate of jail suicide. In Los Angeles, for example, drunks are no longer jailed; rather, they are sent to a detoxification center run by the Volunteers of America. This policy change is credited as a major factor in suicide reduction in the Los Angeles County Jail. And the Pima County Jail in Tuscon, Arizona, recently adopted a pretrial release program for certain types of nonviolent offenders; as a result, the jail has experienced a 90 percent decrease in both attempted and successful suicides.

Conclusion

Jail suicide is one of the most serious and potentially costly problems facing jail administrators today. The tragedy is that most jail suicides are preventable: the information and procedures needed for prevention are readily available. However, we will reduce jail suicides only if jail administrators make use of mental health specialists, train jail officers in suicide prevention, and implement specific policies and procedures to address the problem.

Discussion and review

1. How did American colonists perceive the function of the jail?
2. What are the three types of jails?
3. What are the three fundamental objectives of jails?
4. According to the most recent demographic information, what are some of the major characteristics of the jail population?
5. What types of custodial problems are typically associated with alcoholics, the mentally ill, drug addicts, and sex offenders?
6. What is the purpose of a count?
7. What is one of the best methods for tool control?
8. What is the most basic rule of key control?
9. How are jails affected by community and police policy?
10. What type of coordinating function do jails play in relation to the courts?
11. Why is there considerable support and pressure for jails to get involved in the correctional effort?
12. According to Danto, three types of persons are most likely to commit suicide in jail. Briefly describe each type.
13. What can jail officers do to reduce inmate-suicides?

Glossary

Contraband Anything possessed by an inmate in violation of institutional rules and regulations.

Combination facility A facility that houses pretrial detainees and some convicted persons, usually misdemeanants; the most common type of jail.

Count A method of accounting for all prisoners to be sure that none have escaped; usually conducted on a regular basis.

Cutlery control A system of accounting for all eating utensils in a jail.

Frisks Individual "pat searches" of inmates in which officers run their hands along the outside of the inmate's clothing to detect concealed contraband.

Hallucinations The hearing, seeing, smelling, or tasting of something that does not really exist.

Key control A system that assures that no jail officer has keys that would allow inmates to escape if the officer is overpowered.

Mental illness A wide range of complicated emotional disorders that may involve physical, mental, or behavioral disturbances.

Narcotics control A system that involves storing drugs in secure areas not readily accessible to inmates, and keeping an up-to-date record of drug inventory.

Pretrial detention facility A facility used solely to confine persons awaiting trial.

Sentenced facility A facility where convicted persons serve their sentences.

Sex offenders Persons arrested for indecent exposure, window peeping, child molestation, and rape.

Shakedown A thorough search of a jail or any part thereof for contraband.

Special prisoners Jail prisoners that require special care and attention; generally includes alcoholics, diabetics, epileptics, the mentally ill, suicidal persons, drug addicts, and sex offenders.

Tool control A system of accounting for all tools within a jail.

References

Blumer, A. H. *Discipline*. Washington, D.C.: U.S. Government Printing Office, 1971.
———*Correctional History and Philosophy*. Washington, D.C.: U.S. Government Printing Office, 1971.
———*Jail Climate*. Washington, D.C.: U.S. Government Printing Office, 1971.
———*Jail Operations*. Washington, D.C.: U.S. Government Printing Office, 1971.
———*Supervision*. Washington, D.C.: U.S. Government Printing Office, 1971.
———*Special Prisoners*. Washington, D.C.: U.S. Government Printing Office, 1971.
Danto, B. "The Suicidal Inmate." *The Police Chief*, August 1971, pp. 64–71.
de Beaumont, G., and de Tocqueville, A. *On the Penitentiary System of the United States and Its Application in France*. Carbondale, Ill.: Southern Illinois University, 1964.
Fawcett, J., and Marrs, B. "Suicide at the County Jail." In *Jail House Blues* edited by B. L. Danto. Orchard Lake, Mich.: Epic, 1973.
Mattick, H. W., and Aikman, A. "The Cloacal Region of American Corrections." *Annals of the American Academy of Political and Social Science* 381 (1969):109–18.
Michaels, M. "Why So Many Young People Die in Our Jails." *Parade*, 23 May 1982:4–7.
Miller, E. E. *Jail Management*. Lexington, Mass.: Lexington, 1978.
National Sheriffs Association. *Jail Administration*. Washington, D.C.: The National Sheriffs Association, 1974.
Pappas, N. ed. *The Jail: Its Operation and Management*. Washington, D.C.: U.S. Bureau of Prisons, 1971.
Territo, L. "Planning and Implementing Change in Jails." In *Jail Management*, edited by C. R. Swanson. Athens, Ga.: Institute of Government, University of Georgia, 1983.
U.S. Department of Justice. *Profile of Jail Inmates*. Washington, D.C.: U.S. Government Printing Office, 1980.
Ward, D. A. and Schoen, K. F. eds. *Confinement in Maximum Custody: New Last-Resort Prisons in the United States & Western Europe*. Lexington, Mass.: Lexington, 1981.

Notes

1. For a more thorough examination of jail operations and administration, review the following works of Alice H. Blumer: *Correctional History and Philosophy; Jail Operations; Personnel and Fiscal Management; Jail and Community Corrections; Community Relations; Legal Problems;* and *Supervision, Discipline, and Jail Planning*. All of these works were published in Washington, D.C., by the U.S. Bureau of Prisons in 1971.

2. This discussion of demographic data on American jails was obtained and modified with permission from the U.S. Department of Justice, *Profile of Jail Inmates* (Washington, D.C.: U.S. Government Printing Office, 1980).

3. This discussion of special prisoners and the relationship of the jail to the criminal justice system was obtained and modified from N. Pappas, ed., *The Jail: Its Operation and Management* (Washington, D.C.: U.S. Bureau of Prisons, 1971), p. 9.

4. Much of this discussion on jail security was obtained and modified with permission from E. E. Miller, *Jail Management* (Lexington, Mass.: Lexington, 1978), p. 33.

13 correctional institutions

Historical perspective
Maximum security prisons
Maxi-maxi prisons
Population
Institutional models
   Alcatraz
   Marion (Illinois) Federal Correctional Center
   Minnesota Correctional Facility at Oak Park Heights
   Butner: A new facility for violent offenders
Medium security correctional centers
Minimum security correctional centers
Reception and classification centers
Institutions for women
Youth corrections centers
Summary
Issue paper: Homosexual rape in correctional institutions

IN this chapter, we discuss the development of correctional institutions in the United States, starting with the late 1600s and proceeding through the nineteenth century. This should provide the reader with a historical framework to understand how we got where we are today. We then move into the twentieth century and discuss maximum, medium, and minimum security institutions—even though it is difficult to make clear-cut distinctions. All three classifications may be used (and usually are) in the same institution, and what may be considered maximum security in one state may be considered medium security in another. In general, however, the terms refer to the relative degree of security. We also devote considerable attention to a fourth classification: the maxi-maxi prison designed for the hard-core, violent prisoner.

Further, we discuss a relatively new addition to the corrections scene—the reception and classification center. The final portion of the chapter is devoted to a discussion of some of the major features of institutions created specifically for women, and for youthful offenders (sixteen to thirty years of age). Institutions and facilities for juveniles (persons under sixteen years of age are discussed in chapter 16.

Historical perspective

Institutionalization as a primary means to enforce customs, mores, or laws is a relatively modern practice. In earlier times, restitution, exile, and a variety of corporal and capital punishments—many of them unspeakably barbarous—were used. Confinement was used only for detention (National Advisory Commission on Criminal Justice Standards and Goals 1973).[1]

The North American colonists brought with them the harsh penal codes and practices of their homelands. It was in Pennsylvania, founded by William Penn, that initial attempts were made to find alternatives to the brutality of British penal practice. Penn knew the nature of confinement well, because he had spent six months in Newgate Prison in London for his religious convictions. In the *Great Law of Pennsylvania*, enacted in 1682, Penn made provisions to eliminate to a large extent the *stocks, pillories,* branding irons, and *gallows.* The Great Law directed ". . . that every county within the province of Pennsylvania and territories thereunto belonging shall . . . build or cause to be built in the most convenient place in each respective county a sufficient house for restraint, labor, and punishment of all such persons as shall be thereunto committed by laws." (Dunn and Dunn 1982, p. 206) In time, Penn's jails, like those in other parts of the New World, became places where the untried, the mentally ill, the promiscuous, debtors, and various petty offenders were confined indiscriminately.

In 1787, when the Constitutional Convention was meeting in Philadelphia (and people were thinking of institutions based on the concept of the dignity of man), the Philadelphia Society for Alleviating the Miseries of Public Prisons was organized. The society believed that the sole purpose of punishment is to prevent crime and that punishment should not destroy the offender. The society, many of whose members were influential citizens, worked hard to create a new penology in Pennsylvania, a penology that largely eliminated capital and corporal punishment as the principal sanction for major crimes. The penitentiary was invented as a substitute for these punishments.

In the first three decades of the nineteenth century, citizens in New York, Pennsylvania, New Jersey, Massachusetts, and Connecticut were busy planning and building monumental penitentiaries. These were not cheap installations built from the crumbs of the public treasury. In fact, the Eastern State Penitentiary in Philadelphia was the most expensive public building constructed in the New World up to that time. States were proud of these physical plants. Moreover, they saw in them an almost utopian ideal. They were to become stabilizers of society, laboratories committed to the improvement of all humanity (Rothman 1971).

At the time these new penitentiaries were planned and constructed, practitioners and theorists believed that criminal behavior was primarily caused by three factors. The first factor was environment. Report after report pointed out the harmful effects of family, home, and other aspects of environment on the offender's behavior. The second factor was the offender's lack of aptitude and work skills, a problem that led to indolence and a life of crime. The third factor was seen as the felon's ignorance of right and wrong because of a lack of knowledge of the Scriptures.

The social planners of the first quarter of the nineteenth century designed prisons and programs to create an experience for the offender in which (1) there would be no injurious influences, (2) the offender would learn

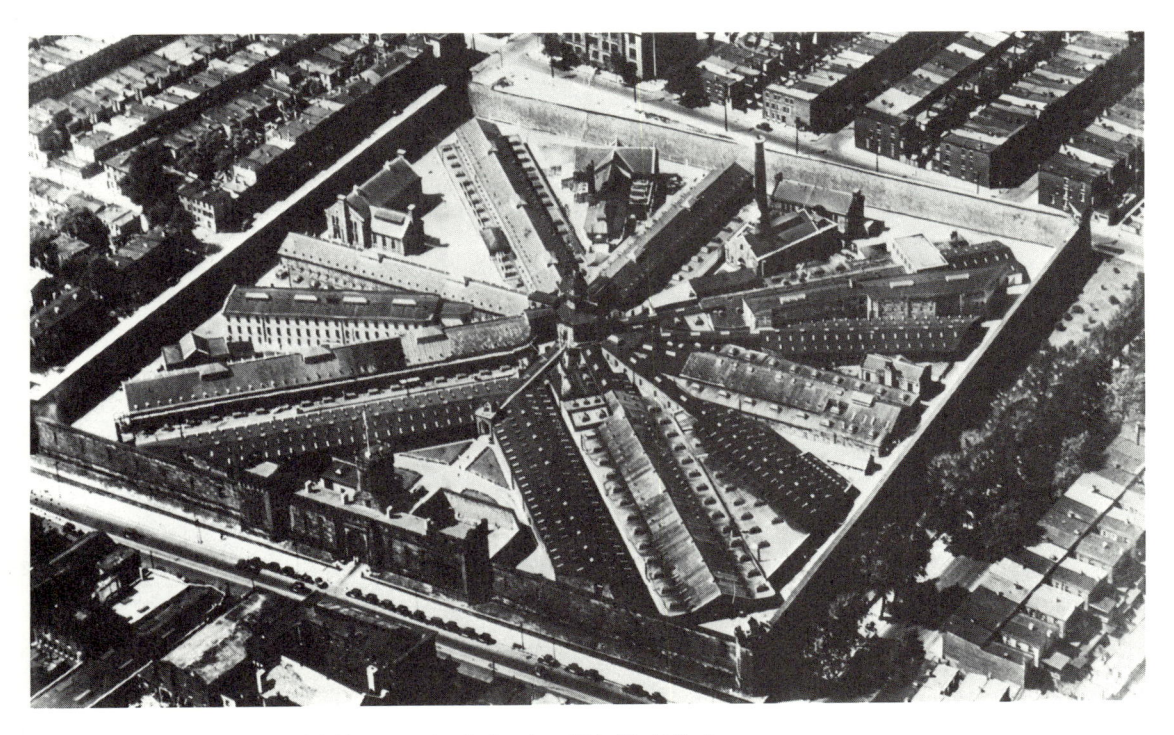

Eastern State Penitentiary, Philadelphia, Pennsylvania. Courtesy Wide World Photos.

the value of labor and work skills, and (3) the offender would have the opportunity to learn about the scriptures and the principles of right and wrong. Various states pursued these goals in one of two ways. The *Pennsylvania system* was based on solitary confinement, accompanied by bench labor within the offender's cell. The offender was denied all contact with the outside world except through religious tracts and visits from specially selected, exemplary citizens. The prison was painstakingly designed to make this kind of solitary experience possible. The walls between cells were thick, and the cells themselves were large, each equipped with plumbing and running water. Each cell contained a work bench and tools and a small, walled area for solitary exercise. The institution was designed magnificently to eliminate external influences and to provide work and the opportunity for penitence, introspection, and religious learning (Barnes 1972).

New York's *Auburn system* pursued the same goals by a different method. As in the Pennsylvania system, offenders were isolated from the outside world and were permitted virtually no external contact. However, convicts were confined to their small cells only on the Sabbath and during non-working hours. During working hours, inmates labored in factorylike shops. The "contaminating effect" of the congregate work situation was eliminated by a rule of silence: inmates were not allowed to communicate in any way with one another or the jailers.

Auburn (New York) State Prison cells: 1928 (left photo) and today. Courtesy Robert J. Henderson, Superintendent, Auburn State Prison.

The relative merits of these two systems were debated vigorously for half a century. The Auburn system ultimately prevailed in the United States, because it was less expensive and because it lent itself more easily to the production methods of the industrial revolution. But both systems were disappointments almost from the beginning. The solitude of the Pennsylvania system sometimes drove inmates to insanity. And the rule of silence in the Auburn system became increasingly unenforceable, despite regular use of the lash and a variety of other harsh and brutal punishments.

As instruments of reform, prisons were an early failure. But they did have notable advantages. They rendered obsolete a myriad of inhumane punishments, and their ability to separate and hold offenders gave the public a sense of security. Imprisonment was also thought to deter people from crime. But imprisonment had disadvantages, too. For one thing, many prison "graduates" came back. The prison experience often further reduced the offender's capacity to live successfully in freedom. Nevertheless, prisons have persisted, partly because our nation could neither turn back to the barbarism of an earlier time nor find a satisfactory alternative. For nearly two centuries, American penologists have sought a way out of this dilemma.

Maximum security prisons

For the first century after penitentiaries were invented, most prisons built were in the category of *maximum security prisons*—facilities characterized by high perimeter and internal security and operating procedures that curtail movement and maximize control. The early zealots who dreamed of institutions that would not only reform the offender but would also cleanse society itself were replaced by a disillusioned and pragmatic leadership that saw confinement as a valid end in itself. Moreover, the new felons were seen as outsiders—Irish, Germans, Italians, and blacks; they did not talk or act like "Americans." The prison became a dumping ground where foreigners and blacks who could not adjust could be held outside the mainstream of society. The new prisons, built in the most remote areas of the country, became asylums—not only for the hardened criminal but also for the inept and unskilled "un-American." Although the rhetoric of reformation persisted, the be-all and end-all of the prison was detention.

From 1830 to 1900, most prisons built in the United States reflected the ultimate goal of security. Their principal features were high walls, rigid internal security, cagelike cells, sweat shops, a bare minimum of recreation, and little else. Prisoners were kept in, the public was kept out; and that was all that was expected or attempted. Many of these prisons were constructed well and lasted long, and they form the backbone of our present-day correctional system.

It is nearly impossible to describe the "typical" maximum security prison. The largest such prison confines more than four thousand inmates; another holds less than sixty. Some contain massive, undifferentiated cell blocks, each housing as many as five hundred prisoners. Others are built in small modules that house less than sixteen inmates each. The industries in some prisons are archaic sweat shops; in others, they are large, modern factories. Many facilities have no space inside for recreation, and only a minimum of such space outside; others have superlative gymnasiums, recreation yards, and auditoriums. Some are dark, dingy, and depressing dungeons; others are windowed and sunny. An early warning system in one prison consists of cowbells strung along chicken wire atop a masonry wall, yet other facilities have closed-circuit television and electronic sensors to monitor corridors and fences.

Maximum security institutions are geared to the fullest possible supervision, control, and surveillance of inmates. The architecture of such institutions and the work and recreational programs they provide are largely dictated by security considerations. Buildings and policies restrict the inmate's movement and minimize control over the environment. The prisons are usually surrounded by masonry wall or a double fence with manned towers. Inside, prisoners live in windowless cells, not rooms. Doors that might afford privacy are replaced by grilles of tool-resistant steel. Toilets are unscreened, and showers are supervised. And control is not limited to structural considerations. All activity—including dining—is weighed in terms of its relationship to custody. Prisoners often sit on fixed, backless stools and eat without forks and knives at tables devoid of condiments. In spite of such control, however, contraband and weapons still find their way into many American prisons.

To prevent security breaches by intrusions from outside, special devices are built to prevent physical contact with visitors. Relatives often communicate with inmates by telephone and see them through double layers of glass. Contact is allowed only under a guard's watchful eye. And body searches usually precede and follow all visits. Internal movement is limited by bars and grilles that define precisely where inmates may go. Areas of inmate concentration or possible illegal activity are monitored by

Weapons confiscated from inmates in an Indiana prison over a period of several months. Courtesy David Agresti, Department of Criminal Justice, University of South Florida, Tampa, Florida.

correctional officers or by closed-circuit television. Blind spots—areas that can not be supervised—are avoided in the building design.

Maxi-maxi prisons

At present, there are few facilities to house hard-core, violent, and incorrigible prisoners—the group responsible for instigating most of the disruption and damage that occurs in correctional institutions. But there is growing public support for building new facilities of this kind, because the facilities are viewed as investments in community protection. Correctional administrators see such facilities—called *maxi-maxi prisons*—as a solution to the problem of troublesome prisoners in regular maximum security institutions.

Population

The maxi-maxi prison houses the most dangerous offenders. An individual is usually considered dangerous because of the nature of the offense for which he or she was convicted. Thus, "dangerous" likely refers to persons who have perpetrated violent crimes against the person (such as homicide, forcible rape, robbery, or aggravated assault). It may also refer to individuals involved in persistent property offenses such as residential burglary, racketeering, or the sale of hard drugs. In the former case, the heinous nature of the offense may be the deciding factor in making the appraisal of dangerousness; in the latter case, the deciding factor may be the extent of the offender's past criminal activity. The judgement of dangerousness is invoked to support the decision to confine an offender for the purpose of preventing further crimes (that is, to justify incapacitation).

Institutional models

The structural and procedural controls used at Alcatraz (San Francisco, California), the Marion (Illinois) Federal Correctional Center, the Minnesota Correctional Facility at Oak Park Heights, and the federal correctional facility at Butner, North Carolina, are typical of controls used at maxi-maxi prisons throughout the country. These four facilities are described in the following paragraphs.

Alcatraz For thirty years, Alcatraz served as a last resort in the federal prison system. The purpose of the facility—which was closed in 1963—was to punish and incapacitate violent and persistent offenders. In addition to notorious criminals, Alcatraz housed inmates who were management problems at other institutions (i.e., those who were involved in escapes, riots, protests, work stoppages, assaults on staff, and strong-arm gangs). Ward and Schmidt (1981) note that a transfer to Alcatraz was often seen as an honor: in the view of some inmates, Alcatraz housed "the elite" of the system; to be sent there, you had to be among the "baddest." (This attitude

Maxi-maxi prison: Alcatraz Federal Penitentiary, San Francisco, California. Courtesy Federal Bureau of Prisons.

suggests that the threat of transfer to a last-resort prison might actually be an *incentive* for further misconduct).

Security at Alcatraz was multifaceted. Alcatraz is an island in the middle of San Francisco Bay, waters that are swept by treacherous, icy currents, and are often enveloped in fog. The island itself was controlled by a system of gun towers connected by overhead walks, and inside security was provided by gun galleries at each end of the cell block (Bates 1936). Despite this rather formidable security system, a major preoccupation of inmates on the "rock" was escape, perhaps because of the long sentences the vast majority had to serve. Only 8 out of the 1,500 inmates who served time on Alcatraz actually succeeded in getting off the island, however; and only three of these inmates were not recaptured. (The story of these three men was portrayed in the Clint Eastwood film *Escape from Alcatraz*.)

In line with the custodial philosophy, the limited programs available at Alcatraz reflected the institution's emphasis on discipline and punishment. Inmates could participate in the work program, but the program was not mandatory. Inmates could stay in their cells all day. Communication with the outside world was limited, and inmates were not allowed access to the press, newspapers, and telephones. Not until the 1950s were inmates allowed to have radios. Visits with wives or blood relatives were allowed once a month for one hour, with inmates and visitors separated by bulletproof glass and conversing over guard-monitored telephones. There were no treatment programs or educational and vocational training programs.

Despite the restrictive and punitive atmosphere, however, inmates at Alcatraz generally settled down rather than lashing out at their environment. This response was probably due to several factors, including the constraints of the institutional regimen and the recognition by inmates

Exercise yard at Alcatraz. Courtesy Federal Bureau of Prisons.

that Alcatraz was the end of the line (Ward and Schoen 1981). In other words, inmates knew that because they would be in Alcatraz for a long time, acting up would only be to their detriment. They also knew that rule infractions at Alcatraz would be written up and punished. And by the time offenders reached Alcatraz, many had calmed down simply because they had grown older and recognized the futility of troublesome behavior.

Ward and Schmidt (1981) provide some interesting insights into the positive effects of a structured, secure, and predictable prison environment. Alcatraz inmates who were transferred to Atlanta, Georgia, when the institution closed in 1963 regarded Atlanta as a very dangerous environment "full of violence and unpredictable people" (Ward and Schmidt 1981, p. 67). To insulate themselves from such dangers, former Alcatraz inmates organized their lives to avoid as much contact as possible with other inmates. These former Alcatraz inmates felt that Atlanta would be a better place if it was managed more like Alcatraz; at least in a controlled environment, the inmates did not have to worry about living through the day.

Marion (Illinois) Federal Correctional Center Another model of a super-secure or maxi-maxi prison is the federal prison at Marion, Illinois. The facility was constructed in 1963.

THE END OF THE LINE: MARION, ILLINOIS
Michael Satchell   Parade

Behind the walls of the U.S. government's top security penitentiary are confined 520 of the nation's most dangerous—and clever— criminals. They are exiled here because other prisons can't handle them, can't hold them, or don't want them. Some are sent to Marion for committing murder or other acts of violence behind bars. Others are escape artists, gang leaders, and troublemakers of every stripe. All are leaders—not followers—men considered too vicious, incorrigible, or criminally sophisticated to be safely housed even in the maximum security sections of other federal or state prisons. Says Marion's crew-cut warden Harold Miller: "Judges sentence criminals to prison to protect society. Wardens send prisoners to Marion often to protect other prisoners. . . ."

Unlike other major prisons, Marion has no trustees behind the walls, no honor cells, no prison newspaper, no entertainment visits from outside groups, and few vocational training programs. "There's little point in teaching a man front-end alignment or transmission repair when he's doing three consecutive life terms," notes Warden Miller laconically. . . . Marion remains a prison where rehabilitation necessarily takes a back seat. This is primarily a place for the discipline and punishment of men who refuse to reform and who have rejected many opportunities to do so. And nowhere inside these walls is this better illustrated than in the control unit.

Officially, this is the worst punishment the American penal system can administer to a man, short of execution. Inmates are referred to the unit from other prisons, or from inside Marion, and it may take six months of hearings and review before a man can be placed in here.

To enter the main part of Marion penitentiary, you must pass through a metal detector and five sets of electronically controlled steel gates. The control unit is at the end of a separate wing, fortified by five more steel gates. Pass through these, tracked all the time by television cameras, and you reach a steel door. Ring the bell. A pair of eyes peers through a viewing slit, the door is opened, and you are inside the prison-within-the-prison—the ultimate "hole" where the average inmate spends ten months in solitary, but with continued bad behavior, can spend years.

For twenty-three hours each day, up to sixty men sit in cells that are 8 feet deep, 8 feet high and 6 feet wide. The other hour is for showering, a suspendable privilege, or for exercise—one hour a week outside in a tiny courtyard, the rest in a caged area within the cell block.

The only time a man is allowed out of the unit is to go to the prison hospital, or to see a visitor. To leave the unit, he is handcuffed while in his cell and strip-searched on leaving and returning. He talks to visitors by telephone from behind a plexiglass screen. He is not allowed to go to the chapel or to the library.

His cell, equipped with a television, bed, toilet and washbasin, is his world. More than half of the cells, known as "boxcars," have doors on the front that can be closed to increase the isolation.

For some men, particularly those who have been locked up in here for a year or longer, the control unit becomes a pressure cooker. Behavior sometimes is irrational. Passions may explode at the slightest provocation. A harmless insult called to a prisoner in the next cell may later cost a man his life.

Security is paramount. Men exercise alone, occasionally in carefully selected groups of two or three—a necessary precaution because the men sometimes attack each other. One control-unit inmate who managed somehow to fashion a rudimentary knife stabbed another inmate twenty times and killed him before guards could get to them. Prison officials have no idea what triggered the attack.

The unit has a long history of violence on both sides of the bars. In the past, guards have been fired for throwing urine on inmates in retaliation for prisoners throwing the same—and worse—on them. . . .

Prison reform groups have tried unsuccessfully to get the courts to order the control unit closed, calling it a violation of the constitutional right against cruel and unusual punishment. But prison officials argue convincingly for retaining it as the last resort for controlling men whose continual violence and escape attempts can't be controlled in other ways. . . .

Warden Harold Miller, who began his career as a guard on Alcatraz, believes Marion is necessary. "We have some in here who are so dangerous and who have refused all attempts to help them, that they must stay in Marion until the very last day of their terms. Even though they may be almost through serving their time, we daren't release them into another prison to smooth their transition."

"It's not an easy thing to do, releasing a man like that into the community. You wonder what he'll do. And you know he'll be back.

No matter what you try to do, some men will always get into trouble. That's why we need Marion.".

Reproduced by permission from *Parade*, 28 September 1980, pp. 4–6.

Minnesota Correctional Facility at Oak Park Heights The new maxi-maxi prison at Oak Park Heights, Minnesota, is perhaps the most up-to-date, state-of-the-art installation built to date. This all-male facility was developed on the premise that the quality of the prison environment is determined by management, available resources, and the physical facility, rather than by the nature of the offenses committed by its population (Ward and Schmidt 1981).

Designed and conceived specifically to stablize the inmate population at other Minnesota facilities, the Oak Park Heights facility houses inmates who are chronic management problems, extremely predatory, or high risks for escape. Despite this highly volatile population, the objective is still to create as normal an environment as possible, keeping in mind the need for maximum security. Security is designed to protect the public from these offenders and to provide a safe environment for both staff and inmates.

Community protection is accomplished by a combination of external and internal security measures; but unlike other high security facilities, the institution does not have a system of external towers or an expensive electronic system. Instead, security is based on a system of two fences with coils of razor wire between them and a pit to serve as a vehicle trap. Further, there is an alarm device atop one of the fences to serve as a first warning. However, it is doubtful that an inmate would ever reach the fence. An escapee would first have to get out of his room or living area and onto the institution's common green, scale one of the walls of the three-story buildings surrounding the green, and cross an open area of approximately 100 yards and to climb the double fences. It is estimated that it would take an inmate fifty seconds longer to get out of this institution than to get through the federal government's tightest security system.

The institution's four hundred plus inmates are housed in eight separate units of fifty-two inmates each. This division of the population into relatively small, manageable, and compatible groups improves security, safety, and control, and provides a better climate for communication and interaction between staff and residents. Moreover, because each housing has its own work program and outdoor recreational facilities, the units can be operated separately—although it is not planned that they will be. The housing units themselves are broken down into smaller units of six or seven rooms, each with its own activity area. This provides a defensible space, where staff and inmates can feel a sense of security and control.

A common green large enough for a football field and several baseball fields is located in a central area accessible to all housing units. This area also contains a town center that serves as congregation area for leisure-time activities and provides access to the visiting area. Because of the cen-

Minnesota Correctional Facility, Oak Park Heights, Minnesota. Courtesy Frank W. Wood, Warden, Minnesota Correctional Facility at Oak Park Heights.

tral location of the green, the staff can allow residents from all or some of the housing units to move freely from one unit to another.

The facility has one special unit designed to handle the most severe disciplinary cases. Following the model of older maximum security facilities, this unit is under the supervision of staff specially trained to manage difficult inmates. Unit inmates are allowed to leave their rooms only on a controlled basis. In general, however, the management of inmates in the Oak Park Heights facility does not depend upon segregation and sophisticated electronic devices; rather, it is based on programming.

The institution operates a full day program (sixteen hours) that encompasses both leisure time and working hours and furnishes a full range of program options for inmates. This programming includes industrial work, education, group therapy, and chemical dependency counseling. Although it is not a major focus of the institution, education is available to inmates through both traditional and computer-based approaches.

A major concern of the facility is to enable the offender to earn a legitimate living and to develop a realistic view of the world of "paid work." Inmates experience real work situations such as getting a job, earning wages, and assuming responsibility for on-the-job conduct. They are exposed to hiring and firing, productivity standards, job variety, job progression, and discipline in the work place (Ward and Schoen 1981). Industries include microfilming, commercial sewing, production of office and educational supplies (folders, notebooks, etc.) bookbinding, and general shop. Evening activities include sex offender groups, education, chemical dependency groups, recreation, religion, and organized leisure.

This full-participation program is designed to prepare the inmate for a transfer to one of Minnesota's other adult facilities and to improve his ability to succeed upon returning to the community. It is recognized that some inmates will not participate in any of the programs available. For such inmates, the facility provides the needed supervision and control to ensure that they do not interfere with or obstruct other inmates who want to take advantage of program options.

The construction cost of the Oak Park Heights facility was $32 million, and the annual operating budget is estimated at $12 million. These costs may seem high, but the alternative may be even more costly. Without new prisons, the only option we have is to continue to place violent and unmanageable offenders in archaic, warehouse-type facilities that are already overcrowded. (In some facilities, inmates are confined two or three to a cell, or in tents and trailers.) The result of such a policy is, as Wood suggests, "widespread institutional disturbances, surpassing those of the late 60s and early 70s".[2] Recall the brutality and damage of the riots at the New Mexico State Penitentiary on February 2–3, 1980: thirty-three inmates were killed (see **table 13.1**), and the cost of repairing the damage and settling claims from the riot was $82 million (Bingham 1980). With this in mind, the Minnesota Correctional Facility probably represents a major cost savings.

TABLE 13.1 Inmates killed in the February 1980 riots at the New Mexico State Penitentiary

Name	Age	Ethnicity	Hometown	Crime/Sentence	Housing unit	Where found/Condition
Briones, Michael	22	Hispanic	Albuquerque, N. Mex.	Criminal Sexual Penetration, 10–50 yrs.	CB4	Basement, CB4; foreign object through head.
Cardon, Lawrence C.	24	Hispanic	Las Cruces, N. Mex.	Car Theft, 1–5; Failure to Appear, 1–5 yrs.	CB3	CB3, cell 32; multiple stab wounds, neck and chest.
Coca, Nick	30	Hispanic	Taos, N. Mex.	Burglary, 2–10; Kidnapping, life; Criminal Sexual Penetration, 10–50; Aggravated Battery, 10–50 yrs.	CB3	Officer mess hall; carbon monoxide poisoning.
Fierro, Richard J.	26	Hispanic	Carlsbad, N. Mex.	Forgery, 1–5; Possession and Sale of Narcotics, 1–5; Escape, 1–5 yrs.	F1	Carried to Tower 1; stab wounds.
Foley, James C.	19	White	Albuquerque, N. Mex.	Armed Robbery, 15–55; Car Theft, 1–5; Murder (1st) life.	A1	Carried to Tower 1; cranocerebral injuries.
Gossens, Donald J.	23	White	Farmington, N. Mex.	Possession and Sale of Narcotics, 2–10 yrs.	CB4	CB4 basement, cell 35; cranocerebral injuries.
Hernandez, Phillip C.	30	Hispanic	Clovis, N. Mex.	Breaking and Entering, 1–5 yrs.	CB4	CB4 basement; blunt trauma to head, stab wounds.
Jaramillo, Valentino E.	35	Hispanic	Albuquerque, N. Mex.	Possession and Sale of Narcotics, 1–5, 2–10 yrs.	CB4	CB4, mid-tier, cell 23; hanged.

Data from the Report of the Attorney General on the February 2-3, 1980 riot at the Penitentiary of New Mexico, pp. J-1 through J-4. (Santa Fe, New Mexico: Office of the Attorney General of the State of New Mexico, June 5, 1980.)

406 Chapter 13 | Crime and justice in America

The 1980 riot at New Mexico State Penitentiary began on the morning of February 2, when inmates overpowered four officers during a routine inspection of a crowded dormitory floor similar to this one, shown as it appeared after the riot. Courtesy Dennis Dahl.

This double-sliding security grill, which separates the south wing from the administrative area of the penitentiary, was left open during the morning watch, contrary to prison policy. The open grill allowed inmates to reach the Control Center and take over the entire building. Courtesy Attorney General collection, New Mexico State Record Center and Archives.

New Mexico - Riot

TABLE 13.1 Inmates killed in the February 1980 riots at the New Mexico State Penitentiary—(continued)

Name	Age	Ethnicity	Hometown	Crime/Sentence	Housing unit	Where found/Condition
Johnson, Kelly E.	26	White	Albuquerque, N. Mex.	Forgery, 2–10 yrs, 6 mo.	CB3	Gymnasium; burned.
Lucero, Steven	25	Hispanic	Farmington, N. Mex.	Aggravated Battery, 5 yrs.	AD	School corridor; blunt trauma to head, stab wounds.
Madrid, Joe A.	38	Hispanic	Albuquerque, N. Mex.	Possession and Sale of Narcotics, 1–5 yrs.	B1	Near control center; blunt trauma to head, incision in neck.
Madrid, Ramon	40	Hispanic	Las Cruces, N. Mex.	Possession of Burglary Tools, 1–5; Possession and Sale of Narcotics, 1–5; Burglary, 1–5 yrs.	CB4	CB4, cell 25; burned.
Martinez, Archie M.	25	Hispanic	Chimayo, N. Mex.	Escape, 10–50; Violation of Suspended Sentence, 1–5; Escape, 2–10 yrs.	CB3	Carried to Tower 1; trauma to the head.
Mirabal, Joseph A.	24	Hispanic	Alamogordo, N. Mex.	Assault and Battery on a Peace Officer, 1–5; Receiving Stolen Property, 1–5 yrs.	A2	CB4 basement; blunt trauma to the head.
Moreno, Ben G.	20	Hispanic	Carlsbad, N. Mex.	First-degree Murder, life.	F1	Carried to Tower 1; blunt trauma to head.
Moreno, Gilbert O.	25	Hispanic	Carlsbad, N. Mex.	Robbery, 2–10; Armed Robbery, 50–150; Escape, 10–50 yrs.	F1	Near control center; stab wound in chest, trauma to head.

TABLE 13.1 Inmates killed in the February 1980 riots at the New Mexico State Penitentiary—(continued)

Name	Age	Ethnicity	Hometown	Crime/Sentence	Housing unit	Where found/Condition
O'Meara, Thomas	25	White	Albuquerque, N. Mex.	Armed Robbery, 10–50; Assault and Battery on a Peace Officer, 1–5; Escape, 1–5 yrs; Contempt of Court, 6 mos.	CH2	Gymnasium; burned.
Ortega, Filiberto M.	25	Hispanic	Las Vegas, N. Mex.	Burglary, 2–10 yrs.	B1	Gymnasium; burned.
Ortega, Frank J.	20	Hispanic	Las Vegas, N. Mex.	Second-degree Murder, 10–50; Burglary, 1–5 yrs.	B1	Carried to Tower 1; incised wound to head and neck.
Paul, Paulina	36	Black	Alamogordo, N. Mex.	Armed Robbery, 2–10; Aggravated Battery, 10–50 yrs.	CB4	Brought to front gate; multiple stab wounds, decapitated.
Perrin, James	34	White	Chapparal, N. Mex.	First-degree Murder, life.	CB4	CB4 basement at entry; trauma, burned, stabbed.
Quintela, Robert F.	29	Hispanic	Carlsbad, N. Mex.	Burglary, 2–10; Escape 2–10 yrs.	F1	Near control center; blunt trauma to head, stab wounds.

Panels of two-way bullet-resistant glass in the New Mexico Penitentiary Control Center were smashed in minutes by inmates wielding pipes and canister fire extinguishers. The glass had been installed three weeks before, replacing steel grills and small panes of glass. Courtesy Attorney General collection, New Mexico State Record Center and Archives.

One room of the main penitentiary building destroyed by rioting inmates. Courtesy Attorney General collection, New Mexico State Record Center and Archives.

TABLE 13.1 Inmates killed in the February 1980 riots at the New Mexico State Penitentiary—(continued)

Name	Age	Ethnicity	Hometown	Crime/Sentence	Housing unit	Where found/Condition
Rivera, Robert L.	28	Hispanic	Albuquerque, N. Mex.	Burglary, 1–5; Escape 2–10, 1–5; Theft, 1–5 yrs.	F1	Corridor dorms A-F; stabbed in the heart.
Romero, Vincent E.	34	Hispanic	Albuquerque, N. Mex.	Armed Robbery, 10–50 yrs.	CB4	CB4 basement, cell 41; cranocerebral injuries, wounds in the neck.
Russell, Herman D.	26	Indian	Waterflow, N. Mex.	Rape, 5–10 yrs.	CH6	Dorm A1, bottom floor; burned, carbon monoxide poisoning.
Sanchez, Juan M.	22	Hispanic	Brownsville, Tex.	Aggravated Battery, 2–10 yrs.	CB3	CB3, lower tier, cell 12; shot by tear gas gun, head trauma.
Sedillo, Frankie J.	31	Hispanic	Santa Fe, N. Mex.	Burglary, 1–5 yrs.	CH6	Carried to Tower 1; carbon monoxide poisoning.
Smith, Larry W.	31	White	Kirtland, N. Mex.	Armed Robbery, life.	CB4	CB4, front entry; cranocerebral injuries.
Tenorio, Leo J.	25	Hispanic	Albuquerque, N. Mex.	Contributing to the Delinquency of a Minor, 1–5; Escape, 1–5 yrs.	CB4	CB4, front of cell 76, basement level; stab wound to heart.
Tenorio, Thomas C.	28	Hispanic	Albuquerque, N. Mex.	Robbery, 2–10 yrs.	CB4	CB4, basement, cell 41; stab wounds, neck and chest.
Urioste, Mario	28	Hispanic	Santa Fe, N. Mex.	Receiving Stolen Property, 1–5; Shoplifting, 2 yrs.	CB4	CB4, main entry; blunt trauma to head, rope around neck.
Waller, Danny D.	26	White	Lubbock, Tex.	Credit Card Fraud, 1–5 yrs.	A1	Tower 1; multiple stab wounds, cranocerebral injuries.
Werner, Russell M.	22	Hispanic	Albuquerque, N. Mex.	Armed Robbery, 15–55, 1–5 yrs.	F1	Catholic chapel; carbon monoxide poisoning, burned, blunt trauma to head.

Butner: A new facility for violent offenders The federal correctional facility at Butner, North Carolina, represents much of the new thinking about how facilities for violent offenders should be designed and operated. Butner has a population of four hundred males who are typically multiple offenders with a record of at least one violent offense. The inmates are divided into three groups according to the institution's three major functions: research (150); mental health (100); general population (150).

Security at Butner is external. The forty-two-acre site is surrounded by two twelve-foot-high fences with seven rolls of concertina wire between them and barbed wire on top. Mobile patrols of armed correctional officers are present at all times. On the inside, the institution is an open facility that emphasizes a relaxed atmosphere. During the day and early evening, inmates move unrestricted throughout the facility. Inmates are also permitted to wear civilian clothing.

Ingram (1978) reports that most inmates at Butner feel safe and comfortable and want to stay. Thefts are almost nonexistent, and inmates report that they are free of the pressures of homosexuality. Moreover, the buildings are arranged to give the appearance of a small town or a college campus, rather than a prison. The feeling of normality is further enhanced by making inmates responsible for getting to work and school on time. And when not involved in programs, inmates are free to mingle on the common greens between buildings.

Inmates are housed in seven one-story buildings with sun roofs that provide ample light. Each housing unit has several wings that contain either single rooms or cubicles. (Although not as good as private rooms, the cubicles do provide more privacy than dormitories.) Within policy and fire safety limitations, inmates are allowed to decorate their own rooms. However, overcrowding has forced Butner to use double-bunking in many of its housing areas.

As in many other federal institutions, each housing unit at Butner is supervised by a unit team. A team consists of a unit manager, a case manager, a psychologist, a counselor, an educational representative, and several inmates (Lansing, Bogan, and Karacki 1977). Ingram (1981) considers the inmates to be the most important part of the team. This approach to inmate management is designed to provide better control and to improve relationships by dividing large prison populations into smaller, more manageable groups.

Twenty-three percent of the staff, including 15 percent of the correctional supervisors, and two of the lieutenants at Butner are female. Women officers have the same duties as male officers. Only a few inmates object to taking orders from women officers. (One inmate commented, "I have been away from a woman for forty years; I don't want anything to do with women" [Ingram 1981, p. 104].) Ingram feels that women officers can maintain the necessary control over male inmates and that they provide a steadying influence in the institution.

Butner Federal Correctional Facility, Butner, North Carolina. Courtesy Federal Bureau of Prisons.

Inmate room at Butner Federal Correctional Facility. Courtesy Federal Bureau of Prisons.

    The research project at Butner is modeled after the ideas of Norval Morris, as outlined in *The Future of Imprisonment* (1975). Morris contends that forced rehabilitation is unworkable and that inmates should instead be provided with opportunities and resources for *voluntary* self-improvement. To test Morris's approach, all inmates in Butner's research population are told upon admission when they are going to be released. A contract worked out with each inmate includes a graduated release plan that specifies such things as when the inmate will be permitted to go into the community, when he will receive his first furlough, and when he will be released to a halfway house. Participation in self-improvement programs does not affect an inmate's release or his privileges; the latter are influenced only by the inmate's compliance with regulations, his behavior on mandatory work assignments, and his seniority (Ingram 1978). Although inmates in the research experiment do not have any choice as to whether they are sent to Butner, they do have an option to transfer to another institution at the end of their first ninety days. This assures that inmates in the Butner program are there because they want to be. The success of the program is being evaluated by comparing project inmates with a similar group of inmates housed in traditional institutions.

    The only difference between inmates in the Butner research project and those in Butner's general population is that the latter can not transfer to another institution after ninety days. For both populations, participation in self-improvement programs is voluntary, but there are constraints on what inmates have to do. First, all inmates must work for at least half a day, obey institutional regulations, and either participate in available programs or work for an additional four hours; thus, they can not choose idleness. Ingram (1981) notes that it would be interesting to experiment with

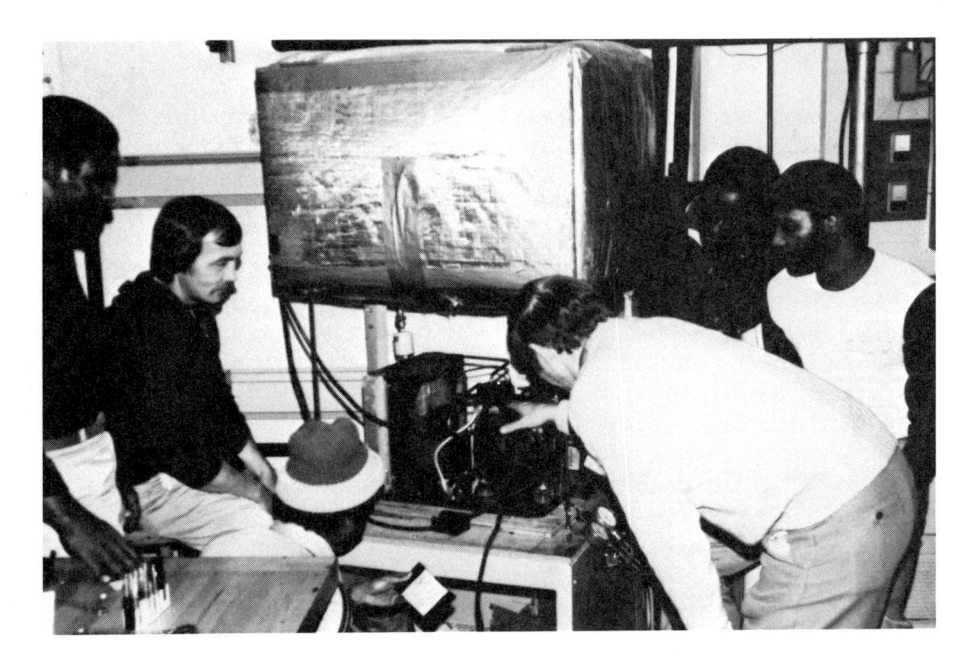

Vocational training in heating and air conditioning at Butner Federal Correctional facility. Courtesy Margaret C. Hambrick, Warden, Butner Federal Correctional Facility.

a completely voluntary institution in which inmates could choose idleness, work, or program participation.

Inmates in the mental health group at Butner are suicidal or psychotic inmates who are referred from other institutions or who come directly from the courts. An attempt is made to screen out offenders who only *appear* to be disturbed—perhaps because they do not abide by institutional rules and regulations. The primary goal of the program is to provide inmates with the treatment they require within the context of a normal routine. This goal is based on the premise that if inmates are *expected* to act normally, they will try to meet this standard. Thus, inmates in the program are all expected to hold regular jobs and to participate in educational and other activities in the company of other inmates. When an inmate can no longer handle a normal routine, he can be placed in a seclusion room—a kind of "time-out" environment for those experiencing difficulties. The mental health program at Butner is intended only as a short-term intervention program; its objective is to return inmates to their regular institutions as soon as possible. And although most inmates do not want to leave the program, Ingram (1981) reports that there have been few repeat referrals.

Butner offers several vocational programs and a range of academic programs for all inmates. Because the institution operates on an optional programming model, a program is only offered if there is sufficient inmate interest to justify it. And like other institutions, Butner has traditional recreational programs, arts and crafts, and facilities for basketball, outdoor track, softball, and miniature golf. Butner has a limited industry program, including has a part-time textile products industry that employs 55 men and a glove factory that employs 125. The top wage for inmates in these industries is about $120 a month.

Medium security correctional centers

Since the early twentieth century, developments in the behavioral sciences, the increasing emphasis on education, the dominance of the work ethic, and changes in technology have led to modified treatment methods in corrections. Parole and probation have increased, and institutions have been set up to handle special inmate populations. Pretrial holding centers, or jails, are now separate from facilities receiving convicted felons, and different levels of security have been developed: maximum, maxi-maxi, medium, and minimum. Most of the correctional construction in the last fifty years has been medium security. In fact, 51 of the existing 110 *medium security correctional centers* were built after 1950.

Today, medium security institutions embody most of the ideals and characteristics of early attempts to reform offenders. It is in these facilities that the most intensive correctional and rehabilitative efforts are conducted. Inmates are exposed to a variety of programs intended to help them become useful members of society. The predominant consideration is still security, however, and inmates are confined where they can be observed and controlled. All facilities have perimeter security, either in the form of masonry walls or double cyclone fences. Electronic sensors may also be used. Perimeter towers are staffed by armed guards and equipped with spotlights.

Internal security is usually maintained by locks, bars, and concrete walls; clear separation of activities; defined movement both indoors and outdoors; tight scheduling; head counts; visual observation; and electronic monitoring. Housing areas, rooms for medical and dental treatment, schoolrooms, recreation and entertainment facilities, counseling offices, vocational training and industrial shops, administrative offices, and maintenance facilities are usually clearly separated. Some activities are located in individual compounds complete with their own fences and sally ports. Barred gates and guard posts control the flow of traffic between areas. Central control stations track movement at all times. Circulation is restricted to certain corridors or outdoor walks, with certain areas designated out of bounds. Closed-circuit television and alarm networks are used extensively. Doors are made of steel (and kept locked), and all external windows, and some internal ones, are barred. Bars or concrete walls line all corridors and surround control points.

Housing units in medium security institutions vary from crowded dormitories to private rooms with furniture. Dormitories may house as many as eighty persons or as few as sixteen. Some individual cells have grilled fronts and doors. Variations among medium security institutions are not as extreme as those among maximum security facilities, perhaps because the former developed in a shorter period of time.

In recent years, campus-type medium security facilities have been designed to eliminate the cramped, oppressive atmosphere found in most prisons. Buildings are separated by meandering pathways and modulated ground surfaces to break the monotony. Attractive residences house small groups of inmates in single rooms. The schools, vocational education buildings, gymnasiums, and athletic fields at these facilities compare favorably with the best community colleges. Nevertheless, adequate external and internal security are provided to protect the public.

Minimum security correctional centers

Minimum security correctional centers range from large drug rehabilitation centers to small farm, road, and forestry camps in rural America. The facilities are diverse, but they generally have this in common: they are relatively open, and they house inmates that are considered to be nonviolent and low risk for escape.

Most, but not all, minimum security facilities serve the economic needs of society and institution. Cotton is picked, lumber is cut, livestock is raised, roads are built, forest fires are fought, and parks and public buildings are maintained. Remote facilities have major deficiencies, however. They seldom provide education or services (other than work), and the predominantly rural labor bears no relationship to work skills needed for urban life. The prisoners are separated from their real world almost as much as if they were in a penitentiary.

One unusual minimum security correctional center—a branch of the Illinois State Penitentiary—was opened in 1972 at Vienna, Illinois. Although large, the facility approaches the environment of a nonpenal institution. Buildings resemble garden apartments built around a "town square" complete with churches, schools, shops, and a library. Paths lead to "neighborhoods" where "homes" provide private rooms in small clusters. Extensive indoor and outdoor recreation is provided, and the academic, commercial, and vocational education facilities equal or surpass those of many technical high schools.

Reception and classification centers

Reception and classification centers—facilities that examine new inmates and assign them to appropriate institutions—are recent additions to the correctional scene. In earlier times, there were no state correctional systems, no central departments of corrections. Each prison was a separate entity, usually managed by a board that reported directly to the governor of a state. If a state had more than one institution, either geography or a judge determined where an offender would go. As the number and variety of institutions increased, however, classification systems and agencies for central control evolved. Eventually, the need for reception and classification centers seemed apparent.

Not all of these centers operate as distinct and separate facilities, however. In most states, the reception and classification function is performed in an existing institution—usually a maximum security facility. Thus, most new prisoners start their correctional experience in the most confining, most severe, and most depressing part of the system. After a period of observation, testing, and interviewing, an assignment is made that supposedly reflects the best marriage between the inmate's needs and the system's resources.

Inmates in corridors at the Lake Butler Reception and Medical Center, Lake Butler, Florida. Courtesy Florida Department of Corrections.

Security in reception and classification centers is based on the premise that "a new fish is an unknown fish." Nowhere on the current correctional scene are there more bars, more barbed wire, more electronic surveillance devices, more clanging iron doors, and less activity and personal space. All of this is justified on the grounds that the nature of the residents is unknown and that their stays will be short.

A notable exception to this type of security exists at the Reception and Medical Center at Lake Butler, Florida (opened in 1967). This campus-style facility has several widely separated buildings on a fifty-two-acre site enclosed in a double cyclone fence with towers. Inmates circulate freely between the classification building, gymnasium, dining room, clinic, canteen, craft shops, visiting area, and dormitories. Three quarters of the inmates are assigned to medium security units scattered around campus. One quarter are housed in a maximum security building.

Inmates not specifically occupied by the demands of the classification process at Lake Butler are encouraged to take part in recreational and self-improvement activities. Visits are allowed in an open-air patio and an indoor visiting facility (ordinarily used only in inclement weather). The relationships among staff and inmates are casual, and movement is not regimented. Morale is high, and escapes are rare. However, overcrowding has become a problem in recent years.

Diagnostic processes in reception centers range from a medical examination and a single inmate-caseworker interview (without privacy) to a full battery of tests, interviews, and psychiatric and medical examinations (supplemented by an orientation program). The process can take from three to six weeks.

Institutions for women

The changing role of women may profoundly influence the future of corrections. Women have always been treated differently than men by the criminal justice system, in part because they commit fewer crimes, especially *serious* crimes. Six men are arrested for every woman. The ratio is still higher for indictments and convictions, and thirty times more men than women are confined in state correctional institutions.

Because of the rebirth of the women's liberation movement in the late 1960s and 1970s, social scientists speculated that more and more women would get involved in crimes typically committed by males: robbery, burglary, auto theft, and so on. The most recent data do not support this theory, however—although women do continue to be arrested and convicted for the same offenses they have traditionally been involved in (shoplifting, passing bad checks, forgery, fraud, and prostitution, for example) (Silverman 1981).

Correctional institutions for women are a microcosm of the American penal system. In one state, some women offenders are thought to be so dangerous that they are confined in a separate wing of the men's penitentiary. There they are shut up in cells and cell corridors without recreation, services, or meaningful activity. In other states, new (but separate) facilities for women have been built based on the philosophy, operational methods, hardware, and tight security of the state penitentiary. Such facilities are surrounded by concertina fences, and movement is monitored by closed-circuit television. Inmates spend much of their time playing cards or sewing. The contrasts among women's institutions demonstrate our confusion about what criminals are like and what correctional responses are appropriate: in six states, all female offenders are housed in maximum security prisons; at least fifteen other states house them exclusively in "open" institutions.

Youth corrections centers

With the advent of the penitentiary in the early nineteenth century, corporal punishment for the youthful offender (aged sixteen to thirty) was replaced with the reformatory concept of incarceration with rehabilitation. The keystone of this reform movement was education and vocational training to enable the offender to make a living in the outside world. The concepts of parole and indeterminate sentences were introduced, and inmates who progressed satisfactorily could reduce the length of their sentences.

The physical plant in the early reformatory era was highly secure—perhaps because the first such facility (located in Elmira, New York) was actually a converted maximum security prison. Huge masonry walls, multitiered cell blocks, "big house" mess halls, and dimly lit shops were all part of the model. Several of these early reformatories are still in use. Then, in the 1920s, youth institutions adopted the telephone-pole design developed for adult institutions: in this design, housing and service units pass through an elongated inner corridor. More recently, campus-type plants—some of which resemble new colleges—have been constructed. Most new reformatories, now called *youth correction centers* or youth training centers, provide only medium or minimum security. They emphasize academic and vocational education and recreation, supplemented with counseling and therapy (including operant conditioning and behavior modification).

In terms of physical environment, security, education, and recreation, most youth centers are similar to adult centers of comparable custody classification. The only major difference is that some youth institutions have more space to accommodate more programs. Some youth centers have highly screened populations and only one goal—to increase educational levels and vocational skills. The effectiveness of such centers is highly dependent on inmate selection and classification. Facilities and programs available in youth corrections centers vary widely. Some centers provide many positive programs; others emphasize the mere holding of the inmate, offering few rehabilitative efforts, sparse facilities, inadequate recreational space, and a generally repressive atmosphere.

Youth institutions include at least two types of minimum security facilities—work camps and training centers. Outdoor labor in work camps is useful for burning up youthful energies, but these camps are severely limited in their capacity to meet other important needs of the youthful offender. Moreover, they are usually located in rural America, which is predominantly white; many youthful offenders belong to minority groups. The second type of youth center has complete training facilities, fine buildings, attractive surroundings, and extensive programs; but these, too, are often remote from population centers. And because many states are finding it difficult to choose youthful inmates who are stable enough to handle minimum security facilities, many such centers are operating far below capacity. Because walk-aways are a serious problem, some centers have been forced to develop internal controls, in addition to visible external controls (such as wire fences).

Summary

The North American colonists brought with them the harsh penal codes of their homelands. Not until the late 1600s did William Penn take the initial steps that would eventually lead to more humane penal practices and eliminate capital and corporal punishment as sanctions for major crimes.

The monumental penitentiaries still common today in the United States got their start in the first three decades of the nineteenth century. The social planners who designed these prisons had three goals in mind: to remove bad influences; to teach the offender the value of labor and work skills; and to teach the offender about the Scriptures and the principles of right and wrong. The two systems which emerged for meeting these goals were the Pennsylvania system and New York's Auburn system. The Pennsylvania system was based on solitary confinement with bench labor within the offender's cell. The Auburn system housed inmates in small cells but confined them only during nonworking hours and on the Sabbath. During working hours, inmates labored in factorylike shops. The Auburn system ultimately prevailed in the United States.

The major classifications of correctional institutions are maximum security, maxi-maxi security, medium security, and minimum security. Maximum security institutions employ full supervision, control, and surveillance of inmates. Security is the highest priority, as reflected by the architectural design and the types of work and vocational programs available. Maxi-maxi institutions house the hard-core, violent, and incorrigible prisoners. Most have high perimeter security, high internal security, and operating regulations that curtail movement and maximize control.

Medium security institutions, on the other hand, embody most of the ideals and characteristics of early attempts to reform offenders. Although the top priority in such facilities is still security, intensive rehabilitative efforts are made. Minimum security facilities, although quite diverse in purpose and location, have one common feature: they are relatively open and they house inmates that are considered nonviolent in their actions and low risk for escape.

Reception and classification centers are relatively recent additions to the correctional scene. Some are part of larger facilities, and some are completely separate. Most are maximum security facilities, because the propensity of new inmates for escape or violence is generally unknown. The diagnostic processes in reception centers include medical examinations, psychological testing, and interviews by caseworkers.

Women's prisons are as diverse in their physical security and philosophy as men's prisons. Yet many have the trappings of maximum security facilities, even though women are generally not considered high risks for escape. And women are less frequently involved in the violent acts characteristic of men's prisons. Thus, the need to house women in maximum security facilities has been questioned.

Youth corrections centers house offenders between the ages of sixteen and thirty. Most such facilities provide medium or maximum security. Some emphasize academic and vocational education and recreation; others emphasize the mere holding of inmates. One of the difficulties some states face with this type of institution is in identifying those youths who are stable enough to handle open facilities: walk-aways are not at all uncommon.

issue paper

HOMOSEXUAL RAPE IN CORRECTIONAL INSTITUTIONS

William Laite, a businessman and former Georgia legislator, was convicted in Texas of perjury in connection with a contract he negotiated with the Federal Administration Housing Authority. Laite was sentenced to a term in the Tarrant County Jail in Fort Worth, Texas. The minute he entered the "tank," or dayroom, of the jail, he was approached by five men. Said one of them: "I wonder if he has any guts. We'll find out tonight, won't we? Reckon what her name is; she looks ready for about six or eight inches. You figure she will make us fight for it, or is she going to give it to us nice and sweet like a good little girl? Naw, we'll have to work her over first, but hell, that's half the fun, isn't it?" (Laite 1972, p. 42).

Laite was terrified. "I couldn't move. This couldn't be happening to me," he recalled (ibid., p. 42). But Laite was saved from forcible homosexual rape: a seventeen-year-old youth was admitted to the dayroom just as the five men were about to begin their assault. The men turned on the youngster viciously, knocking him unconscious. They were on him at once "like jackals, ripping the coveralls off his limp body. Then as I watched in frozen fascination and horror, they sexually assaulted him, savagely and brutally like starving animals after a raw piece of meat. Then I knew what they meant about giving me six or eight inches" (ibid., p. 42).

But the attack did not end there. While the youth was still unconscious, the attackers jabbed his limp body with the burning tips of pencil erasers, making it twitch—and thereby increasing the sexual excitement of the rapists. In a final sadistic gesture, one of the attackers "shoved his fingers deep into the boy's rectum and ripped out a mass of bloody hemorrhoids" (ibid., pp. 42–44).

It is noteworthy that this homosexual rape occurred in a jail setting. Rape is much more pervasive in jails, detention centers, and training schools than in prisons—where control is tighter and prisoners are subjected to greater physical restraint. Jails typically contain both inmates who are serving sentences of less than one year for misdemeanor offenses and those who are awaiting trial for serious felony offenses such as murder, attempted homicide, robbery, and rape. Also housed in jails are "bound-overs," offenders who have been sentenced to prison terms and are waiting to be transferred. Homosexual rapists in the jails are chiefly found among the latter two categories of prisoners.

Davis (1968) interviewed 3,304 inmates out of 60,000 who passed through the Philadelphia prison system in a two-year period (1966–1968). He also interveiwed custodial employees. The study revealed that sexual assaults were epidemic: approximately 2,000 of the inmates interviewed admitted to being victims of homosexual rape. Of this number, only 156 cases were documented; and of those 156 cases, only 96 had been reported to the prison authorities and a mere 26 had been reported to criminal justice agencies outside the prison. Reporting is discouraged by unwritten laws of prison culture and the fear of brutal reprisal.

Davis observes that sexual assaults, as opposed to consensual homosexuality, are *not* caused by sexual deprivation: "They are expressions of anger and aggression prompted by the same basic frustrations that exist in the community, and which very probably were significant factors in producing the rapes, robberies, and other violent offenses for which the bulk of the aggressors were convicted" (1968, p. 16). Rather, as Scacco (1975) points, racism is the central factor in sexual assaults within correctional institutions. Black aggressors and white victims are found in disproportionate numbers in every study of sexual assault in jails and prisons. Blacks rape whites to humiliate and degrade them—to give members of the white majority a taste of what blacks experience as members of the minority community. The same pattern is evident with respect to Hispanic minorities and whites. Rarely do blacks and Hispanics rape one another.

Studies also indicate that whites rarely band together to resist attacks or to protect each other. They are also more conscious than minorities of the punishment they are likely to incur from the correctional staff if they fight to defend themselves against sexual aggression. Scacco notes that

> . . . most whites did not have the verbal ability and street savvy to ward off the baiting techniques of their aggressors. The latter were familiar with institutional settings and knew how to set up any white they chose for sexual acts. This was true since most of the aggressors had been returned to the same institution for their second or third time. Thus, they knew how to take what they wanted in the form of sexual gratification. The whites usually had little or no experience with institutional subcultures and were at a loss as to how to counteract even the slightest act of intimidation directed against them (1975, p. 55).

Status also plays a major role in rape. Status in prison is a mark of survival. (It was not uncommon in Biblical times for an invading army to sodomize males in the conquered land to demonstrate their dominance.) The higher an inmate's status, the lower the incidence of attack against that inmate. Status in prison is usually related to the type of offense for which the individual was convicted and the length of time he or she has to serve. Lockwood (1980) found that men who were imprisoned for homicide, aggravated assault, and larceny were not likely to be raped. Why? These men commanded respect because they were in for the long term. In contrast, white-collar criminals had more than a 60 percent chance of being raped. Such criminals were usually white, nonviolent, short term, and nonaffiliated. But the inmates most likely to be assaulted (and to be murdered) were sex offenders. These men are at the bottom of the prison totem pole; they are considered scum and are treated accordingly. Sex offenders are usually labeled the minute they arrive in prison.

Thus, it appears that homosexual rape is not committed for sexual relief. Rather, inmates rape each other for the same reason that men rape women—to exert control and dominance and to degrade the victim. Race is a major factor in homosexual rape, and certain types of inmates are more likely to get raped than others. The only practical solution might be to isolate probable victims from the predatory inmates. Because of prison overcrowding, however, such action may be impossible on any wide scale.

Discussion and review

1. What are the basic differences between the Pennsylvania system of corrections and the Auburn system?
2. Why is it so difficult to describe the "typical" maximum security facility?
3. What are the characteristics of maxi-maxi facilities?
4. How did some inmates react when they were transferred to the federal prison in Atlanta when Alcatraz closed in 1963?
5. What is the philosophy behind the Minnesota Correctional Facility at Oak Park Heights?
6. What are the major features of the federal correctional facility at Butner, North Carolina? How does the facility differ from other maximum security prisons?
7. What are the major characteristics of medium security correctional centers?
8. Describe a typical minimum security correctional center.
9. What is the major purpose of a reception and classification center?
10. For what crimes are women typically arrested and convicted?
11. When did the reformatory movement start, and what did it hope to accomplish?
12. What two inmate characteristics are primary factors in homosexual rape in correctional institutions?

Glossary

Auburn system A corrections system in which inmates labored in factorylike shops during working hours and were confined to their cells on the Sabbath and during nonworking hours; started in about 1830.

Gallows An upright frame with a crossbeam for hanging a condemned person.

Great Law of Pennsylvania Law enacted in 1682 that largely eliminated the use of stocks, pillories, branding irons and gallows.

Maxi-maxi prisons Facilities characterized by high perimeter security, high internal security, and operating regulations that curtail movement and maximize control; inmates include persistent property offenders, troublesome inmates, and individuals considered to be dangerous because of the nature of their offenses.

Maximum security prisons Facilities geared to the fullest possible supervision, control, and surveillance of inmates; usually surrounded by a masonry wall or double fence with gun towers, electronic sensors, and good lighting.

Medium security correctional centers Facilities in which the most intensive correctional or rehabilitation efforts are conducted. The primary consideration is still security, however, and many centers have the same features as maximum security facilities (i.e., gun towers, masonry walls, and electronic sensors).

Minimum security correctional centers Range from large drug rehabilitation centers to small farms, road, and forestry campuses in rural America; inmates are considered nonviolent and low risk for escape.

Pennsylvania system A corrections system based on solitary confinement with bench labor in each inmate's cell; started in about 1830.

Pillory A wooden frame with holes for the head and hands of offenders; offenders were locked in and exposed to public scorn.

Reception and classification centers Facilities (usually maximum security) where most new prisoners are sent for observation, testing, interviewing, and eventual assignment to a state prison.

Stocks A heavy wooden frame with holes to confine offenders' ankles and (sometimes) wrists.

Youth corrections centers Facilities designed to house youthful offenders (ages sixteen to thirty); built to provide medium to minimum security.

References

Barnes, H. E. *The Story of Punishment.* Chapter 6. Montclair, N.J.: Smith, Patterson, 1972.
Bates, S. *Prisons and Beyond.* Freeport, N.Y.: Books For Libraries, 1936.
Bingham, J. *Report of the Attorney General on the February 2-3, 1980 Riot at the Penitentiary of New Mexico.* Part 1. Santa Fe, N. Mex.: Office of the Attorney General of the State of New Mexico, 1980.
Davis, A. J. "Sexual Assaults in the Philadelphia Prison System and Sheriffs' Vans." *Trans-Action* 6 (1968):9–17.
Dunn, R. S. and Dunn, M. M. eds. *The Papers of William Penn: Volume II 1680-1684.* Philadelphia: Univ. of Pennsylvania, 1982.
Ingram, G. L. "Butner: A Reality." *Federal Probation* 42 (1978):34–39.
Ingram, G. L. "The Federal Correctional Institution at Butner, North Carolina: An Experimental Prison for Repetitively Violent Offenders," In *Confinement in Maximum Security,* edited by D. A. Ward and K. F. Schoen. Lexington, Mass.: Lexington, 1981.
Laite, W. *The United States vs. William Laite.* Washington, D.C.: Acropolis, 1972.
Lansing, D., Bogan, J. B., and Karacki, L. "Unit Management: Implementing a Different Correctional Approach." *Federal Probation* 41 (1977):43–49.
Lockwood, D. *Prison Sexual Violence.* New York: Elsevier, 1980.
Morris, N. *The Future of Imprisonment.* Chicago, Ill.: University of Chicago Press, 1975.
National Advisory Commission on Criminal Justice Standards and Goals. *Corrections.* Washington, D.C.: U.S. Government Printing Office, 1973.
Rothman, D. *The Discovery of Institutions: Social Order and Disorder in the New Republic.* Chapters 3 and 4. Boston, Mass.: Little, Brown, 1971.
Scacco, A. M. *Rape in Prison.* Springfield, Ill.: Charles C. Thomas, 1975.
Silverman, I. J. "Female Criminality: An Assessment." In *The Mad, The Bad, and the Different: Essays in Honor of Simon Dinitz,* edited by I. L. Barak and C. R. Huff. Lexington, Mass.: Lexington, 1981.
Ward, D. A., and Schoen, K. F., eds. *Confinement in Maximum Security.* Lexington, Mass.: Lexington, 1981.
Ward, D. A., and Schmidt, A. K. "Last-Resort Prisons for Habitual and Dangerous Offenders: Some Second Thoughts About Alcatraz." In *Confinement in Maximum Security,* edited by D. A. Ward and K. F. Schoen. Lexington, Mass.: Lexington, 1981.

Notes

1. Portions of this chapter were adapted from National Advisory Commission on Criminal Justice Standards and Goals, *Corrections.* (Washington, D.C.: U.S. Government Printing Office, 1973), pp. 341–49.

2. F. W. Wood, 16 October 1981; personal communication.

14
social, political, and racial forces in American prisons

The inmate social system before 1960
The black prisoner movement
Black is beautiful
Black separatism
Racial gangs in prison
Black gangs
Chicano gangs
White gangs
Socialization and recruitment
Gang services
Impact of gangs on prison systems
Evolution in prison management
Restoring legitimate control
Increase work and activity
Increase staff
Reduce unit size
Develop an intelligence system
Encourage a lawful community
Increase program participation by minority leaders
Avoid recognition of gang leaders
Keep power away from the gangs
Prevent the introduction of contraband
Summary
Issue paper: The socialization of prison guards

This chapter focuses on social, political, and racial forces that have been at work in many of our largest and most dangerous prisons since the 1960s. We examine how these forces have changed and how they have impacted correctional administrators, correctional officers, and inmates. Further, we discuss how philosophical changes in prison management have affected the social, political, and racial environment in prisons. Finally, we recommend ways to restore legitimate control in prisons where certain inmates have gained sufficient power to undermine the authority of prison officials.

The inmate social system before 1960

Because a number of important social and political changes occurred in American prisons in the 1960s and 1970s, it is useful to examine the inmate social system both before and after the 1960s. In the 1970s, a substantial number of minorities from lower socioeconomic classes in urban areas entered the prisons, substantially changing the prison environment.

Observers of prison populations prior to 1960 report one common value system among prison inmates: a code of conduct that defined relationships among inmates and between inmates and correctional officers. The code was usually rigidly reinforced by the inmate population, and violators were either ignored by other inmates or subjected to acts of violence (Sykes and Messinger 1960).[1] The chief tenets of the code fall into five categories:

1. *Maxims that caution:* don't interfere with inmates' desires to serve the least possible time and to enjoy the greatest number of pleasures and privileges possible while in prison. The most flexible directive in this category was concerned with the betrayal of a fellow prisoner to institutional officials: never rat on a con. In general, no qualification or mitigating circumstances were recognized, and no grievance against another inmate—even though it was justified in the eyes of the inmate—was to be taken to officials for settlement. Other specifics included don't be nosy, don't have a loose lip, keep off a man's back, don't put a guy on the spot, be loyal to your fellow prisoners, and present a unified front against the guard (no matter how great the personal sacrifice.

2. *Injunctions to refrain from quarrels or arguments with fellow prisoners:* don't lose your head; play it cool; and do your own time. (Exceptions were made for inmates subjected to legitimate provocation, however.)

3. *Assertions that inmates should not take advantage of each other by means of force, fraud, or chicanery:* don't exploit inmates; don't break your word; don't steal from cons; don't sell favors; don't be a racketeer; don't welch on debts. Inmates were expected to share scarce goods, rather than to sell to the highest bidder or to selfishly monopolize amenities.

4. *Rules that stress the maintenance of self:* don't weaken; don't whine; don't cop out (cry guilty); don't suck around; be tough; be a man. Dig-

nity and the ability to withstand frustration or a threatening situation without complaining or resorting to subservience were wildly acclaimed. The prisoner was to be able to "take it" and to maintain his or her integrity. When confornted with wrongfully aggressive behavior, the prisoner was to show courage. And although starting a fight ran counter to the inmate code, retreating from a fight started by someone else was equally reprehensible.

5. *Maxims that forbid according prestige or respect to custodians or the world for which they stand:* don't be a sucker. Guards were to be treated with suspicion and distrust. In any conflict, officials were automatically considered to be in the wrong. Furthermore, inmates were not to commit themselves to the values of hard work or to submit to duly constituted authority.

An inmate who betrayed a fellow prisoner was labeled a *rat* or a *squealer* and was universally scorned and hated. Prisoners who exhibited highly aggressive behavior and who quarreled easily and without cause were often referred to as *toughs*. An individual who used violence liberally was called a *gorilla* (gorillas often used force against other prisoners in violation of the inmate code). The term *merchant*, or *peddler*, was applied to inmates who exploited fellow inmates by manipulation and trickery and who sold or traded goods in short supply. A prisoner who was unable to withstand the general rigors of prison was referred to as a *weakling* or a *weak sister*. An inmate who entered into homosexual activity was labeled a *wolf* or a *fag*, depending on whether the inmate's role was active or passive. An in-

Informers, as this sign in a Rhode Island state prison illustrates, are regarded with contempt by other inmates. Courtesy Corrections Magazine *and* Criminal Justice Publications.

mate who continued to plead his case was sarcastically known as a *rapo* (from bum rap), or an *innocent*. And an inmate who allied himself with prison officials or expressed the values of conformity was ridiculed as a *square John*.

Inmates who carefully followed the norms of prison society—who celebrated the inmate code rather than violated it—were known as *right guys*, *real cons*, and *real men*. These inmates were heroes of the inmate social system, and their existence gave meaning to the prison villains: the rats, the toughs, the gorillas, and the merchants. A right guy was always loyal to his fellow prisoners. He never let them down no matter how rough things got. He kept his promises; he was dependable and trustworthy. He wasn't nosy about other inmates' business, and he didn't shoot off his mouth about his own. He didn't act stuck up, but he didn't fall all over himself to make friends either—he had a certain dignity.

A right guy never interfered with other inmates who were conniving against officials. He didn't look for a fight, but he never ran away from one when he was in the right. Anyone who started a fight with a right guy had to be ready to go all the way. When a right guy got extras in prison—cigarettes, stolen food, and so on—he shared them with his friends. He didn't take advantage of prisoners who didn't have much, and he didn't strong-arm other inmates into fagging for him. Instead, he acted like a man. When dealing with prison officials, a right guy never acted foolishly. When he talked about officials with other inmates, he was sure to say that even the *hacks* (guards) with the best intentions are stupid, incompetent, and not to be trusted; the worst a con could do was to give the hacks information (they'll only use it against you when the chips are down.)

A right guy stuck up for his rights and he didn't ask for pity: he could take everything the *screws* (guards) could hand out—and more. He didn't "suck around" the officials, and the privileges he got were deserved. Even if a right guy didn't look for trouble with the officials, he would go to the limit if they pushed him too far. He realized that there were just two kinds of people in the world: those "in the know" and suckers. Those "in the know" skim pleasures off the top; suckers work.

As suggested earlier, the inmate social system that existed before 1960 has undergone considerable change. And the changes are more dramatic in some states than in others. Thus, we focus in the rest of this chapter on two prison systems—California and Illinois—that provide some vivid examples of changes in prison life after the 1960s.

The black prisoner movement

Racial tensions in prisons began when the number of black prisoners increased and the attitude of black prisoners shifted (Irwin 1980).[2] Although linked to the civil rights movement outside, the latter change had unique qualities. For example, the tactics of civil rights protestors were too gentle to catch the imagination of black prisoners, and the central issue of civil rights—equal treatment under the law—was not critical in prison. Thus, the "black is beautiful" movement and *black separatism* played a more important role in prison than did civil rights.

Black is beautiful

After World Warr II, because of the large migration of southern blacks to northern and western cities (and some measure of educational and occupational progress), many black Americans developed a new sense of worth. This new pride focused on two qualities that blacks in the United States believed were related to the Negro race: *soul* and masculinity. Soul involved spontaneity, the capacity to relate to others with more ease, and special expressive abilities—particularly as revealed in music. Masculinity was related to athletic and sexual prowess. Many of the early believers in these new definitions came to prisons in the late 1950s and early 1960s, spreading among black prisoners the idea that "black is beautiful." Not until the late 1960s and early 1970s, however, did the idea really take hold.

Black separatism

The *Black Muslims* emerged as the major separatist organization in the early 1950s and found its way into the prisons in the mid-1950s. *Malcolm X*, who more than any other individual personified the development of black separatism, describes the growth of Muslim faith in prison:

> You let this caged up Black man start thinking, the same way I did when I first heard Elijah Muhammad's teachings. Let him start thinking how with better breaks when he was young and ambitious he might have been a lawyer, a doctor, a scientist, anything. You let this caged up Black man start realizing, as I did how from the first landing of the first slave ship, the millions of Black men in America have been like sheep in the den of wolves. That's why Black prisoners become Muslims so fast when Elijah Muhammad's teaching filters into their cages by way of other Muslim convicts. "The white man is a devil" is a perfect echo of that Black convict's lifelong experience (1965, p. 183).

Black Muslim prisoners recruited other black prisoners, and the organization grew throughout the 1950s. Members followed a nonviolent, separatist course and clashed with prison administrations only over restrictions of religious practices. They asked to receive copies of the Koran and Muslim newspaper *Muhammad Speaks*, to hold meetings, to meet with outside representatives of the organization, to be served pork-free meals, and to be segregated from other prisoners. All prison administrations resisted these requests and suppressed the organization, which they perceived as a threat to prison peace and administrative authority. But the Muslims were tenacious: they formed groups of highly disciplined black prisoners who shaved their heads, kept themselves impeccably neat, maintained a cold but polite attitude toward other prisoners, refused to eat pork, congregated whenever possible, and listened to each other deliver the teachings of Elijah Muhammad. Although their rhetoric was hostile, the Muslims seldom precipitated violence. However, they were occasionally involved in violence initiated by someone else—perhaps by a guard firing on a group of Muslims or on a group of Muslims and other prisoners. Eldridge Cleaver describes the aftermath of one such shooting, revealing the essentially nonviolent posture of Muslims:

> After the death of brother Booker T. X., who was shot dead by a San Quentin guard and who at the time had been my cell partner and the inmate minister of the Muslims at San Quentin, my leadership had been publicly endorsed by Elijah Muhammad's West Coast representative, minister John Shabazz of Muhammad's Los Angeles mosque. This was done because of the explosive conditions in San Quentin at the time. Muslim officials wanted to avert

Wallace Muhammad, standing before a portrait of his father, Elijah, in 1975. Courtesy Wide World Photos.

any Muslim initiated violence, which had become a distinct possibility in the aftermath of brother Booker's death. I was instructed to impose iron discipline on the San Quentin mosque, which had continued to exist despite the unending efforts of prison authorities to stamp it out (1968, p. 63).

Elijah Muhammad's teachings did condemn and vilify whites and white society, however, a situation that antagonized, threatened, and frightened white inmates and prison administrators. As a result, many administrators tried to suppress the organization by introducing rules against membership. One prison even adopted a rule prohibiting more than two black prisoners to congregate. In response, the Muslims carried their fight to the courts, and in 1965 they won the right to exist as a religious organization in prisons.

By the time of their court victories, the Muslims were losing momentum in California prisons. Malcom X left the outside organization in 1963 and was later assassinated. Malcolm X's departure, his political vision, and his homicide—which many believe was perpetrated by the Muslims—turned many Muslim prisoners in California away from the organization. Some followed Malcolm X's route to political organization. Cleaver responded to Malcolm X's assassination this way:

> What provoked the assassins to murder? It bothered them that Malcolm was elevating our struggle into the international arena through his campaign to carry it before the United Nations. Well, by murdering him they only hastened the process because we certainly are going to take our cause before a sympathetic world. Did it bug the assassins that Malcolm denounced the racist straight-jacket demonology of Elijah Muhammad? Well,

Muslim organizations in many prisons offer Islamic studies to their members. Here an inmate studies the Koran. Courtesy Tony O'Brien/Criminal Justice Photos

we certainly do not denounce it and will continue to do so. Did it bother the assassins that Malcolm taught us to defend ourselves? We shall not remain a defenseless prey to the murder, to the sniper, and to the bomber. In so far as Malcolm spoke the truth, the truth shall triumph and prevail and his name shall live; and in so far as those who opposed him lied, to what extent will their names become curses. Because truth crushed to earth shall rise again (1968, pp. 65–66).

In California during the late 1960s and early 1970s, ex-Muslims and other black prisoners followed a variety of courses until the Black Panther Party came into prominence on the outside, supplying black prisoners with the new, dynamic black nationalistic organization. In this phase of separatism, black prisoners who identified with the Black Panthers or similar organizations were more politically radical (and more prone to violence than their forerunners (at least they were much more prepared to respond to threats with violence).

Racial gangs in prison

The hate between white and black prisoners is the most powerful source of division in prisons. Gangs of various types—including white, black, and chicano—inhabit many state prison systems. The gangs in Illinois are generally acknowledged to be the largest.

Black gangs

Black gangs in Illinois prisons are an extension of Chicago street gangs. The most famous (and probably still the largest) of the street gangs is the Black Stone Rangers, which had 3,000 to 5,000 members in the early 1970s. The Rangers later changed their name to the Black P Stone Nation, and to A Neo-Islamic *El-Rukns* in 1979. Other large gangs are the *Vice Lords*, the *Latin Kings*, and the *Disciples*.

In the 1970s, hundreds of gang members were sent to prison for involvement in drugs and prostitution. Most were sent to the Illinois State Penitentiary at Stateville, near Chicago, and the second largest group went to the state prison at Pontiac. Although these arrests neutralized much of the gang activity on the street, the gangs emerged as a powerful force in prisons (Krajick, 1980, p. 11).[3] Young, militant blacks carried racial hostility with them into the prison system, resulting in clashes among blacks, whites, and custodial personnel. Robinson describes the attitude of black prisoners this way:

> In the prison, the Black dudes have a little masculinity game they play. It has no name, really, but I call it Whup or Fuck a White boy—especially the White gangsters or syndicate men, the bad juice boys, the hit men, etc. The Black dudes go out of their way to make faggots out of them. And to lose a fight to a White dude is one of the worst things that can happen to a Black dude. And I know that, by and far, the White cats are faggots. They will

drop their pants and bend over and touch their toes and get had before they will fight. So, knowing this, what kind of men did this make us? They told us where, how, and when to shit, eat, sleep (1971, p. 29).

In the face of such treatment, white prisoners tend to reciprocate with racial hostility—regardless of their attitudes *before* entering prison (Irwin 1980, p. 183).

Upon entering the Illinois prison system, black gangs organized massive resistance to prison administration. Prisoners seized hostages, set fires, organized boycotts, refused to be locked up in their cells, and assaulted and intimidated guards. They quickly gathered power by recruiting inmates who had not been gang members on the outside. (Prison officials estimate that at least half of gang members today join in this way.) The advantages of joining up immediately were obvious: anyone who didn't join would be beaten, raped, robbed, or killed, and members would be protected from attack by nonmembers.

The testimony of dozens of prisoners over the last decade indicates that most prisons "offbrand" inmates who are either rejected by the gang or who choose not to join. (Offbrands pay protection money to one or more gangs.) Only the most highly respected offbrands—most of them longtime convicts—escape gang terrorism. For the rest, the complexion of prison life has changed radically. "You used to know what to expect and you could do your time in peace," said one older white prisoner. "Now I don't know what the hell is going to happen next. I'm more afraid of these bangers [the name for the most vicious gang members] than I am of the screws [guards]."

Chicano gangs

Gang types vary from state to state, depending on the background of the young hoodlums that arrive at adult prisons (Irwin 1980). In California, the gang takeover began in San Quentin in 1967, when a click of young Chicanos—youths who had known each other in other prisons and on the streets of Los Angeles—began to take drugs forcefully from other prisoners (mostly Chicanos). This tough group was labeled the *Mexican Mafia*. According to rumor, Chicano hoodlums aspiring to Mafia membership had to murder another prisoner for initiation. This rumor aroused many "independent" Chicanos to group together to eliminate the Mafia. On a planned day, this group of Chicanos pursued known Mafia members through San Quentin and attempted to assassinate them. Several dozen prisoners were seriously wounded and one was killed in the daylong battle; but the Mafia held its ground and was not eliminated.

After this unsuccessful attempt, some non-Mafia Chicanos—particularly those from Texas and from small towns in California who had been in conflict with Los Angeles Chicanos for decades—formed the counter group *La Nuestra Familia*. In the ensuing years, the conflict between the two Chicano gangs increased and spread to other prisons and even to the outside, where gangs tried to penetrate drug trafficking. The attacks and counterattacks between members of the two gangs have become so frequent that prison administrators have attempted to segregate the gangs, designating two prisons for the Mafia—San Quentin and Folsom—and two for La Nuestra Familia—Soledad and Tracy.

The escalation of robbery, assault, and murder by Chicano gangs served to consolidate and expand black and white groups, some of which were already involved in violent activities on a small scale. Two gangs, the white-dominated Aryan Brotherhood and the Black Guerilla Family, rose in prominence, and the Aryan Brotherhood eventually formed an alliance with the Mexican Mafia. When the Black Guerilla Family allied with La Nuestra Familia, a very hostile stalemate prevailed (although peace did not return). Racist clicks among black and white prisoners still occasionally attack other prisoners; Chicano gangs still fight each other; and some Chicano gangs fight among themselves. Thus, although the California prisons have passed their peak of violence, the violence and fear that remain are intense.

White gangs

White gangs in prison are primarily an outgrowth of violence against white inmates by organized blacks and Hispanics. There is little evidence to suggest that white prison gangs are in any way an extension of street gangs in cities. Some white prisoners may belong to the same gang in a city that they belong to in prison, but there is no large-scale white counterpart to the development of black and Hispanic gangs in prisons. Individuals who belong to motorcycle clubs may form coalitions inside prison, but it is doubtful that these gangs recruit individuals who are members of their clubs outside of prison.

White gangs are generally as violent, aggressive, and cohesive as their black and Hispanic counterparts. For example, in the state prison at Menard in southern Illinois on the fringes of Appalachia, half of the twenty-six hundred inmates are white and heavily racist. Many belong to a white gang known as the White Citizen Council. Members of the Council, the Aryan Brotherhood, and various offshoots of the Ku Klux Klan have battled with black groups in Menard's yard in recent years. Nevertheless, racial conflict at Menard has declined, probably because of increased security.

Socialization and recruitment

Gangs are a significant reality behind prison walls. The unaffiliated convict fears that his life may be endangered by gangs and that he will be shaken down for commissary and sex. Unfortunately, the security staff can offer little protection. To survive, a white inmate might become a "punk" for one of the gangs. Some whites also maintain physical security by demonstrating fighting ability or by boasting of connections with organized crime (Jacobs 1977).[4]

The Latin Kings and Vice Lords are skeptical of penitentiary dwellers and do not recruit in the prisons; but the El-Rukns and the Disciples do recruit vigorously in prisons, just as they do on the street. Solicitation is frequently forceful and highly sophisticated. New prisoners are usually confronted by both a "hard" and a "soft" sell.

In contrast to the unaffiliated convict, the gang members that enter prison from the street have no trouble adjusting to their new environment. As the warden of Pontiac (Illinois) penitentiary once said, "When a guy comes up here it's almost a homecoming—undoubtedly there are people from his neighborhood and people who know him." The chief of the Disciples claims that he knew seventy-five Disciples at Stateville Prison when he arrived. And a young leader of the Latin Kings claims that he knew all but two of the Kings at Stateville when he arrived; the first afternoon, he received a letter from the ranking chief welcoming him into the family (Jacobs 1977, p. 152).

B. P., Chief of the Vice Lords, explains that when a young Vice Lord comes into prison, the man is set up immediately with coffee, tea, deodorant, and soap. Visitors and correspondence are arranged for Vice Lords who have been deserted by their families. Normally, the cell-house chief provides an elaborate orientation. The Disciples distribute the following rules to incoming members:

1. Degradation of another Disciple will not be tolerated at any time.
2. Disrespect for any governing body of said cell house will not be permitted.
3. There will not at any time be any unnecessary commotion while entering the cell house.
4. Homosexual confrontation toward another Disciple will not be tolerated.
5. Dues will be paid up on time on any designated schedule.
6. Fighting another Disciple without consulting a governing chief will result in strict disciplining.
7. Upon greeting another Disciple, proper representation will be ascertained.
8. There will never be an act of cowardice displayed by another Disciple, for a Disciple is always strong and brave.
9. There will not be any cigarettes in the hole for those who relentlessly obstruct the rules and regulations of the organization or the institution.
10. Anyone caught perpetrating the above rules and regulations with disorder and dishonesty will be brought before the committee and dealt with accordingly (Jacobs 1977, p.152).

The parallels between these rules and the general inmate code are striking. In fact, Irwin and Cressey (1964) maintain that the inmate code can be described by reference to the norms of certain criminal subcultures.

Gang services

The prison gang meets many of the material and psychological needs of its members. In addition to providing physical security, some organizations buffer members from poverty within the institution. At Stateville, for example, each gang has a poor box. Cell-house chiefs in each gang collect cigarettes from members and store them for those who have legitimate need. When a member makes a particularly good "score" or deal, he is expected to share the bounty with the leaders and to donate to the poor box. Although skeptics claim that these boxes are often depleted and that many benefits do not filter down, one observer has seen gang leaders giving cigarettes away. Furthermore, when a gang member is placed in isolation, he can always expect cigarettes and food to be passed in to him.

Gangs also function as communication networks. If McCleery (1960) is correct in asserting that a crucial concern of new inmates is their lack of information about prisons, then gangs function to keep their members informed and to provide guidelines for all situations and events within the institution. By assigning "soldiers" to jobs in the administration building, as runners, as yard workers, and as house help, gangs insure that information will flow with great precision.

Gangs also provide a distribution network for contraband. One Latin King informant explains that where an independent might hesitate to attempt a score (fearing that he might not be able to hide the stolen items), a gang member knows that he can divest himself of most contraband within minutes. The role of the gangs in organizing illicit activities is unclear, but it *is* clear that no illicit activities operate without the approval of gang leaders. Gang affiliation enables young inmates to establish connections in illegal trafficking and to muscle in on independents who are not already paying off one of the other gangs.

By far, however, the most important function of the Disciples, the Latin Kings, the Vice Lords, and the El-Rukns at Stateville is psychological support. Whether one subscribes to the theories of Cohen (1955) or Miller (1958) to account for the origin of gangs, the important point here is, as Thrasher (1963) notes, that the gang serves as a membership and reference group to provide the delinquent with status and a positive view of himself. As B. P., the leader of the Disciples, explains, "These guys in my branch [of the Disciple Federation] are closer to me than my own family. Anything I do around them is accepted—for stuff that my parents would put me down for, these guys elevate me to a pedestal" (Jacobs 1977, p.153).

Over and over again, inmate informants, gang members, and off-brands express the opinion that gangs provide an identity, a feeling of belonging, and an air of importance:

> It's just like a religion. Once a Lord always a Lord. Our people would die for it. Perhaps this comes from lack of a father figure or lack of guidance or from having seen a father beaten up and cowering from the police. We never had anything with which to identify. Even the old cons like me—they are looking for me to give them something they have been looking for for a long time (Jacobs 1977, p.153).

Gang members consistently explain that it is the gang—both on the street and within the prison—that allows you to feel like a man; it is a family with which you can identify. Several informants state that the organization is the only thing worth dying for. With their insignias, colors, salutes, titles, and legendary histories, the group provide the only meaningful reference group for their members. Gang "soldiers" live by specific rules and aspire to succesive levels of status.

Impact of gangs on prison systems

According to prison officials and police, gangs are organized into paramilitary heirarchies. Each gang has an identifiable leader or group of leaders who command a chain of "colonels," "enforcers," "ambassadors," "lieutenants," and "soldiers" (also known as "indians"). Gang leaders are revered and often have other prisoners opening cell doors for them, serving them special food, and accompanying them as bodyguards (Krajick 1980).

At the height of their power in the last few years, gangs have controlled cell and job assignments and access to foods at the commissary; some even control certain areas of their prisons. Such control is gained by intimidating poorly trained and outnumbered guards. According to prisoners, officials, and outside observers, much of this control (as well as the extortion of offbrands) has been undermined by better trained and more numerous guards; but this administrative control is tenuous. "We sent a message to the gangs that we were taking back control," says Mike Lane, assistant director of the Department of Corrections in Illinois. "But it is nonsense to say that we can break them up. The gangs are there and they're a hell of an influence." And Marvin Redd, Warden of Stateville, adds, "Things are quiet now, but the gangs can influence and disrupt anything we've got going whenever they want" (Krajick 1980, p.12).

Administrators have been criticized in the past for not aggressively controlling gangs. "They've been applying traditional methods (lockdowns, informants) to situations where they're not fitted anymore," notes prison authority John Conrad. "The gangs have shown that inmates can trust each other and overwhelm the administration" (ibid.). Conrad suggests punishment and improved living conditions and programs as a way to control gang activity.

Current attempts by prison administrators to regain control of Stateville Penitentiary started with a big shakedown at the prison in February 1979. The most powerful gang leaders were transferred to a federal holding facility in Chicago. Prison officials wanted to transfer the leaders permanently to out-of-state federal prisons, but the gang leaders sued—claiming that they were being denied due process in the transfer. They were held in Chicago pending the outcome of the suit.

Gail Franzen, Director of the Illinois Department of Corrections asked Norman Paulsen, head of the Federal Bureau of Prisons, to take more gang members; but he was turned down. "He [Paulsen] didn't want them any more than I do," said Franzen. Anyway, Franzen knew that more transfers would not solve the problem. Removing the leaders would not cure gang infestation. A charismatic leader can issue orders (through intermediaries) from wherever he is. Or new leaders might arise. A follower of Disciple leader Dirk Acklin once said, "Sure he was leader. But you get rid of him, somebody else comes up. They can't do nothing to stop us" (ibid. p.14).

Prison officials in Illinois have tred to recognize and work with the gangs to keep them under control. The Stateville chapel was once set aside on certain days for gang meetings, and leaders were allowed to move freely throughout the institution to collect information and keep order. But the leaders did not keep order, although veteran administrators do credit some of them with trying. Today, administrators avoid officially recognizing gang leaders as representatives of other inmates. They do not give them special privileges, and they do everything they can to prevent organized gang activity.

The El-Rukns are now petitioning the courts for religious status. They claim to be an offshoot of the Moorish Science Temple, a black Islamic sect. This initiative worries prison administrators. Religious status would guarantee the El-Rukns harrassment-free meetings, access to outside clergy, and the right to recruit members openly. In a landmark case in 1964 the U.S. Supreme Court gave the Black Muslims similar rights, recognizing them as a bona fide religious organization.

The El-Rukns and other gangs claim that they are misunderstood and maligned. Members say that the gangs have evolved from criminal enterprise into political and social organizations. One prisoner who joined the Disciples in 1967 when he was eleven asserts: "Sure we were robbing and killing and beating back in the 60s. We all did. I did it. But now we've learned better.... We were fighting for justice.... We're not a gang any more. We're an organization" (ibid.).

Nevertheless Chicago police say that the gangs are as heavily into criminal activity as ever. Prison officials regularly receive death threats from gang members inside and outside prison, and guards who enforce rules too strictly against the wrong people get phone calls in the middle of the night at their homes. During his first few months as warden at Stateville, Alvin Reed carried a .357 magnum revolver outside the prison because of threats. And Charles Row, director of the Illinois Department of Corrections, stepped down from his post on December 1978 with relief: gang members had threatened to kill his two-year-old daughter unless he gave up efforts to crush a narcotics smuggling ring at Stateville. Because of threats, the family of another high administrator at Stateville is accompanied around the clock by armed guards supplied by the state. One Disciple expresses this attitude about threats: "They beat on us, we'll get back, it doesn't matter whether they're wearing bars or stars on their shoulders, or three-piece suits. We'll get them back. It's only right" (ibid.).

So far, gangs have not made good on any threats against high officials at Stateville. However, guards are periodically stabbed and beaten at the prison, and gang members on the outside have dramatically demonstrated their solidarity with their imprisoned comrades on several occasions. One Sunday morning in August 1979, for example, 150 El-Rukns drove up to the Stateville gates in a caravan of Cadillac limousines. Wearing ceremonial fezes, they supposedly came to visit friends and relatives. Administrators had heard rumors that the El-Rukns planned to take over the visiting room, so guards and state police armed with shotguns tried to turn the caravan away. Many El-Rukns refused to leave, however, and police had to tow their cars away. Several visitors were arrested for carrying guns.

Evolution in prison management

Dinitz (1980), in a paper presented to the John Vincent Barry Memorial Lecture at the University of Melbourne, Australia, provides an interesting and insightful look into the evolution of prison management.[5] Early in this century (and in the Texas prison system today), the staff of a prison was wholly dependent on the whims of the administrator and was wholly loyal, as in any paramilitary setting, to the maintenance of the system. It helped to have a mentality in which the locking and unlocking of cells and the counting of bodies five or more times a day was considered a "calling"—a quasi-religious experience. It helped to define reality in terms of "good guys" versus "bad guys." It helped to be somewhat paranoid, because the caged were always plotting to escape to contravene the system.

The study of paranoia increased with the introduction of teachers, doctors, nurses, counselors, chaplains, legal aids, and defenders into the prison system. How could a prison be run when every custody decision could be challenged as antitherapeutic or, at the very least, capricious? Treatment and due process became clubs with which to beat underpaid custodial people. Understandably, these workers felt inadequate, demeaned, and powerless in the face of the new penology. In the riots in the 1950s and again in the last half of the 1960s were often triggered by custodial losses in this treatment-custody conflict.

Today, the battle is over. Martinson's idea that nothing works (1974), and the writings of Wilson (1975), Van Den Haag (1975), Von Hirsh (1976), and Morris (1974), have buried the ideal of rehabilitation. Even so, a prison staff may feel isolated and unappreciated. Many correctional officers are so poorly paid that their families are on food stamps. Many are overworked and abused and mocked by inmates, and their decisions are scrutinized by lawyers and prison masters appointed by distant judges. As a result, correctional officers desert their jobs and succumb to stress or *burnout* at a high rate.

Recently, correctional officers have joined labor unions and pressed their interests through collective bargaining. In this process, institutional loyalty has disappeared. With a voice of their own, correctional officers in many states are now bargaining, rather than begging, for improved working conditions (Irwin 1980, pp. 220-22). For example, sick-outs have been used to close entire institutions to draw attention to staff demands. In such confrontations, the staff is likely to emerge as the power center in the threefold struggle among staff, inmates, and prison administration. What a judge orders in his or her chambers is ultimately obeyed or rejected on the line. Thus, guards have become the final decision makers inside the walls, despite all the due process on the books. The guard is the sovereign—at least until his or her decisions are reversed by riots, hunger strikes, or disturbance, or appealed by jailhouse lawyers or court-appointed overseers (Freeman, Dinitz, and Conrad 1977). Despite the enormity of this power, however, custodial officers still feel isolated, estranged, and embittered. The reason for this is not hard to find. In guard mythology, there is a conspiracy involving do-gooders, defense attorneys, the courts, and spineless prison managers to promote the interests of the inmate—the wrongdoer. These conspirators have tried and failed to turn the prison into an asylum. Yet guards have not promised the public a hospital or offered themselves as attendants. Nor have they promised that prisons, through due process, would be fair communities. Occasionally, a dissident guard, captain, or associate warden will view the prison as a therapeutic community or a lawful community and will try to implement these views. But the rank-and-file officer has no need for such vision. What he or she wants—and is within striking distance of getting—is a quiet day with some overtime pay and no lip from inmates or their defenders.

Dinitz (1980) notes that even wardens have changed dramatically in the past twenty years. Wardens were once full-fledged autocrats endowed with unlimited power and authority over all persons—guards and prisoners—in their territories. Riots or spectacular escapes might topple them, but wardens were generally accountable only to the governor of a state

Striking prison guard is carried to an ambulance after being struck accidentally by a car. Courtesy Wide World Protos.

(who was usually interested in other things). Wise wardens mixed terror, incentives, and favoritism to keep their charges fearful but not desperate, hopeful but always uncertain. Their absolute power extended to the guards, who were dependent upon their favor for employment security and advancement. An experienced warden kept some power in reserve, never depending on intimidation alone, and he or she usually atomized the prison community. Groups were never permitted, and silence systems were used to assure that prisoner solidarity did not develop.

After the silence rule went out of fashion, wardens used intelligence systems to maintain control. Stool pigeons were everywhere, and no one could trust anyone else. When uprisings occurred, the warden (or a successor) could regain control by finding and punishing ring leaders. This unregulated authority often led to grotesque abuses of power and privilege by wardens, captains, and con bosses. When a warden boasted that he or she was represented wherever any three prisoners gathered in the prison, the claim was not an exaggeration. A warden had to know how to gather information and use it to achieve the desired degree of atomization (Barak 1978).

After World War II, the centralization of power in the bureaucracy of state prison systems reduced wardens to field managers and made them accountable to a commission of corrections in the state capitol. Through such commissions, wardens were accountable to the governor and the legislature. Many positive results have come from this shift in authority, but there have also been negative consequences. Violence has increased, contraband comes in freely in some prisons, and authorities are often impotent to act.

Restoring legitimate control

Conrad offers six principles of action and three principles of avoidance that can be used to return control now held by gangs to prison authorities (1979, pp. 141–45).[6] The principles of action are to increase work and activity, to increase staff, to reduce unit size, to develop an intelligence system, to encourage a lawful community, and to increase program participation by minority group leaders. The principles of avoidance are to avoid recognition of gang leaders, to keep power away from gang members, and to prevent the introduction of contraband.

Increase work and activity

Because it serves to relieve boredom and inactivity, the slum gang thrives on unemployment. One participant in a slum gang in Glasgow, (Scotland) reports this experience:

> Life with the gang was not all violence, sex, and petty delinquency. Far from it. One of the foremost sensations that remains with me is the feeling of unending boredom, of crushing tedium, of listening hour after hour to desultory conversation and indiscriminate grumbling. Standing with one's

back against the wall, with one's hands in one's pockets ... was the gang activity ... (Patrick 1973, p. 8).

The prison gangster standing with back against a wall and hands in pockets—and sharing complaints with comrades—becomes committed to the gang. The gang promised relief: Narcotics may be on the way, or there may be a punk to rape or a score to settle with a rival gang. The prison provides the basic necessities for survival, but the gang offers life. (Part of this life is the business of waiting; authorities should not mistake the waiting for tranquility.) Full employment in prison will not solve the problem, but without meaningful work and activity, it is inconceivable that gangs will ever be reduced in influence and number.

Increase staff

The prevailing style at maximum security facilities is to pair off guards so that one can protect the other. This system is necessary, given the hazardous conditions in these prisons, but staff working in pairs have little contact with prisoners. They will see and be seen, but they will be impersonal in their communications. Two officers patrolling together can cover less of a cell block or an activity than can two officers patrolling separately. Correctional officers can not be everywhere, but the more they get around the more likely it is that violence will be prevented or minimized.

Reduce unit size

By their nature, large prisons are limited to reactive control. There are places that must be prepared for the worst—because the worst is certain to happen. Neither correctional officers nor prisoners can know each other or initiate activities to relieve hostilities. Unfortunately, smaller prisons can be terrible places, too: some of the worst prisons are relatively small. The key to preventing violence is to provide units of no more than thirty inmates (and preferably less). This measure can be used in both small and large prisons.

Develop an intelligence system

It is unlikely that informants can be found to infiltrate prison gangs, and it is not recommended that efforts be made to do so. However, this does not mean that prison officials can or should give up trying to find out what is going on. The patrol guard is around not only to see and be seen, but also to hear and be heard. An officer trained to interact informally but significantly with prisoners will eventually be entrusted with information that can be used for control. This will probably not happen if officers are always in pairs, but it can happen if an officer is in regular contact with a small unit. A decent person who is seen every day and understood by those he works with may become a confidant of some inmates and will at least be respected by most inmates in his charge.

Encourage a lawful community

A prison should be lawful, and all persons working in a prison should enforce the law. All violations must be investigated and prosecuted. The unwillingness of district attorneys to add to their work loads, and the reluctance of criminal investigators to engage in the unrewarding work of crime detection in the prison yard, must give way to a rigorous policy of law enforcement. Prisons will become less dangerous only if the consequences of law violations are clear. Wrongdoing must have adverse consequences wherever it occurs, especially in prison. All available resources should be used to increase the effectiveness of investigations and prosecutions. Statutes that set the penalties for felonies committed in prison should be harsh. Incentives to prisoners who supply information leading to convictions must be administered carefully to ensure the safety of the informants.

Increase program participation by minority leaders

Gang leaders still use the rhetoric of the civil rights movement and the language of the political prisoner. Thus, organizations such as the National Association for the Advancement of Colored People, the Urban League, and the United Farm Workers should be actively encouraged as alternatives to gang activity. It is doubtful that the "hard core" would participate in such groups, but many minority inmates might be drawn in by legitimate minority leadership.

A national prisoners' union has also been suggested as a way to offset the power of gangs. However, the introduction of a union would only complicate the problem. The role of the union would be uncertain, its leaders would be inexperienced, and gangs might even gain control.

Avoid recognition of gang leaders

Prison administrators should never negotiate with gang leaders or make concessions to them. Gang leaders can not be co-opted, and any attempt to establish a laissez-faire policy toward them is doomed to failure. Gang leaders should not be arrested or held on mere suspicion, but they should be punished when they violate prison rules. In addition, gang insignias should be confiscated, gang meetings should be forbidden, communications should be carefully controlled, and all mail to and from active gang members should be censored.

By necessity, prison management will have to have some contact with gang leaders. These contacts may be unwitting, because the identity of leaders is not always known. However, if a council of prisoners is assembled for management purposes, gang leaders will probably be present. But such a council should not be a forum for negotiations on gang terms. Rather, it should be an occasion for the articulation of community relations acceptable to management.

Keep power away from the gangs

Prison officials must be careful not to assign any advantages to gang members. Rather, it should be made clear that unaffiliated prisoners are favored. Known gang members should not be assigned to privileged jobs, and reports of intimidation should receive intensive investigation. Anyone making threats should be placed under strict control.

Prevent the introduction of contraband

The importation of narcotics and other contraband into a prison is undesirable—even without considering the fact that contraband assures the power of gangs. Gang life depends, in part, upon contraband rewards. Current efforts to keep forbidden articles out of the prison should be reviewed to determine their effectiveness. Prosecution of anyone engaged in contraband traffic should be swift, and conviction should automatically bring a prison term. A prison in which narcotics traffic flourishes is a prison with tenuous official control. Gangs have management about where they want it to be—in a condition of relative impotence.

Summary

The social, political, and racial forces within America's largest and most dangerous prisons have changed dramatically in the past two decades. The inmate social system and codes of conduct described by Sykes and Messinger (1960) are no longer accurate. A new type of inmate has entered prisons in large numbers since the 1960s, and many political changes have occurred in society since that time.

One of the most significant changes in prison life has been the emergence of gangs. These gangs are generally divided among blacks, whites, and Chicanos. Black gangs emerged in the 1950s as an outgrowth of the civil rights and black movements outside of prisons. White gangs developed largely as a result of violence directed against them by black and Chicano gangs. Chicano gangs were an extension of street gangs operating in the cities and towns of California and Texas; hostilities that existed between these groups on the streets carried over into prison. At one point, the attacks and counterattacks between gangs in California prisons were so frequent that authorities segregated gangs by assigning them to different prisons. Gang affiliation is frequently viewed by inmates as necessary and desirable—necessary for personal safety and desirable because of services provided by the gangs.

Prison management has also changed since the sixties. People concerned with treatment have come into the system and have been vocal about antitherapeutic or capricious decisions made by administrators. Under strict administrative control, custodial workers felt inadequate, demeaned, and powerless in their jobs, and their decisions were constantly scrutinized by lawyers, prison masters, and others. As a result, officers and guards often dropped out at a very high rate. Recently, however, prison workers have joined labor unions and pressed their claims through collective bargaining. Dinitz (1980) points out that even wardens have not escaped the changes of prison management. They once enjoyed almost limitless power within the prison walls, but such power has all but disappeared. State bureaucracies have reduced wardens to field managers and made them accountable to legislatures and governors.

Conrad (1979) recommends six principles of action and three principles of avoidance to restore legitimate control in prisons. The principles of action are to increase work and activity for inmates, to increase staff, to reduce unit size in prisons, to develop an intelligence system, to encourage a lawful community, and to increase program participation by minority group leaders. The principles of avoidance are to avoid the recognition of gang leaders, to keep power away from gang members, and to prevent the introduction of contraband into the prison.

issue paper

THE SOCIALIZATION OF PRISON GUARDS

Prison guards live and work in a world that is less familiar to most Americans than the interior regions of Australia or Borneo. Unlike other careers and professions that have been studied exhaustively by scholars and depicted in some detail by the popular media, the occupation of prison guard has been almost totally neglected. Movies and television portray guards in crude caricatures and stereotypes: the brutal sadist, the rigid bureaucratic automaton, the kindly but ineffective humanitarian. There has been little or no effort to deal with prison guards in realistic terms—as people working at difficult and demanding jobs.

There is nothing very remarkable or original about the observation that captives and captors often share the unpleasant aspects of captivity. Nevertheless, a casual remark by a Florida State Prison guard—"We're doing time just like the inmates, only we don't get any gain time"—has important implications for the careers of correctional officers. In this issue paper, we examine three dimensions of the correctional officer's job: staff culture and the socialization of correctional officers; relations with inmates; and the outcome of officer socialization.

Staff culture and the socialization of correctional officers

Even before they finish their first day on the job, new correctional officers are exposed to influences that play an important part in their role conceptions and job orientations. Just as new inmates shape their attitudes and behavior as a consequence of exposure to the convict culture, officer recruits are indoctrinated into the staff culture of the prison by means of their relationships with veteran officers. These veteran guards are the recruit's most important reference group. According to Crouch and Marquart, veterans physically back up the recruit, offer advice and reinforcement, and communicate the values of the guard subculture. They tell the new officer what is expected in three areas: how to perceive inmates, how to anticipate trouble, and how to manage inmates (1980, p. 79). In many prisons, the staff culture depicts convicts as lazy, morally deficient individuals who freely chose crime as a way of life.

The most important message the new officer receives, both from formal training and from veteran guards, is that prisoners must always be controlled and dominated—by words and by behavior. Through observation and imitation of experienced guards, the new officer learns informal strategies for maintaining order and control—such as maintaining social distance from inmates, using profanity and bluster, saying no to inmate requests, and keeping prisoners "off balance."

The latter can be done by staring at an inmate, thus keeping him or her wondering what the officer is thinking.

Crouch and Marquart have identified what they refer to as "the several tenets of subcultural wisdom which define acceptable guard behavior" (1980, p. 89). These aspects of the guard role are gradually revealed to the new correctional officer through advice from fellow officers and encounters with inmates. The first of the tenets is that security and control are paramount. Anything that threatens the custodial routine—visits from volunteers, sports figures, or evangelists, or the presence of treatment personnel—should be viewed with suspicion and hostility.

A second tenet is that officers must maintain social distance from prisoners. Recruits are told about officers who made the mistake of trusting inmates and ended up getting "burned." The third tenet is that guards must be tough, knowledgeable, and able to handle prisoners. Veteran guards stress the importance of being authoritative with inmates—even to the extent of using profanity and obscenity when addressing them.

The prison lore transmitted to the new officer—often by a veteran guard (sometimes referred to as a "maggot stomper")—largely consists of stories that emphasize the brutality, depravity, bestiality, or stupidity of convicts. Thus, the recruit hears about the four prisoners who "got loaded" on raisin jack and killed and sodomized the body of a fellow inmate; about the "queen" (male prostitute) who tried to perform a sex-change operation on himself with a razor blade and bled to death; about the inmate who inserted a cola bottle in his rectum and required an emergency operation to remove it; and about the inmate currently in "the hole" (solitary confinement) for knifing a guard with a homemade shank. These stories heighten feelings of solidarity among correctional officers by emphasizing or exaggerating the negative characteristics of convicts.

Learning to anticipate trouble—escapes, attempted escapes, riots, hostage seizures, drug use, or use of homemade intoxicants—is a skill that can take a long time to acquire. Experienced correctional officers, like veteran police officers, insist that the necessary savvy comes only from exposure to inmates and sensitivity to subtle cues. Informal discussions among guards—similar in form and content to "choir practice" among street cops—offer opportunities to share experiences, swap insights and observations, and sharpen the awareness of the new officer. In addition, officers must become familiar with both the formal and informal rules that guide institutional life. They must be able to spot any deviation from the rules, regardless of how well the deviation might be disguised.

Relations with inmates

The most important aspect of prison life for the correctional officer is his or her relationships with prisoners. As already mentioned, recruits are subject to influences from veteran officers and staff culture that stress dominance and authority. In practice, this influence translates not into the development of the hard-hosed, bull-headed James Cagney stereotype, but into an officer who can be described as "firm but fair."

Unlike the police, whose first-hand contacts with crime victims tend to "bring home" society's quarrel with a criminal, correctional officers see criminals under circumstances where they are likely to be perceived as sick, inadequate, stupid, or degenerate. Although the staff culture depicts the inmate population in such terms, exceptions are made in individual cases. "Good" inmates differ from "bad" inmates not on the basis of their instant offense or previous record but on their willingness to conform to authority. The attitude of one correctional officer on Florida's death row is rather typical:

> I don't know anything about what they did that brought them here. And I don't want to know. That might change the way I deal with them. As far as I'm concerned, if they do what they're told and obey the rules, they get a fair shake from me. The ones that make my job tough are the smart asses, the troublemakers. The ones that are always trying to do a number on you. Those are the sons of bitches you have to step on—hard (Personal conversation).

The ultimate show of officer authority was once apt to be a taste of corporal punishment—a rap along side the head. This treatment was often carried out in the privacy of a cell or in a segregation wing. Is such abuse still a problem in American prisons? Do reported beatings or other abuses represent institutional policy, or are they individual acts of brutality?

According to May (1976), overt guard violence is extremely rare. One of the nation's senior prison ombudsmen, Theartrice Williams of Minnesota, investigated about forty-five hundred inmate complaints over a four-year period and found that fewer than six complaints involved correctional officer violence. Similarly, Connecticut's prison ombudsman, James T. Bookwalter, found only a handful of charges of correctional officer brutality in more than one thousand complaints handled over three years. Bookwalter doubts that inmates are taken out and deliberately worked over in today's prisons, but excessive force may sometimes be used: "When there is a physical conflict between an inmate and an officer and force is required to bring an inmate under control, the inmates believe that the officer gets in a few extra licks" (May 1976, p. 40).

The outcome of officer socialization

Whatever they bring to the job in the way of personality characteristics, attitudes, and values, officer recruits undergo changes in attitude and behavior once they are on the job. One type of change involves *role conflict,* which is common among recruits who enter maximum security prisons with aspirations of helping prisoners. Rookies discover that inmates regard such aspirations as a sign of weakness, and they are quick to exploit the attitude to their own advantage. Recuits are also frustrated by their inability to operate effectively within the paramilitary structure of the prison system. As a result, new officers either quit and look for a different line of work or they reevaluate their original aspirations in light of the reality of prison life. If they stick it out, recruits are subject to the kind of cynicism that Niederhoffer (1967) identifies as an occupational disease among police officers.

Another useful concept from the study of police officers which can help us to understand the socialization of the correctional officer is the *working personality,* a configuration of attitudes and behaviors that result from learning the police role (Skolnick 1966). As an occupational group, police officers perceive and respond to their work based on two variables—danger and authority. According to Skolnick, "the element of danger isolates the policeman socially from that segment of the citizenry which he regards as symbolically dangerous and also from the conventional citizenry with whom he identifies" (1966, p. 44). Required continually to assert their authority, police officers develop a heightened alertness to potential threats and dangers; thus, they become suspicious persons, always on the lookout for violence and lawbreaking. The same is true of correctional officers.

PRISON GUARD: SLAIN OFFICER KNEW THE UNIFORM WOULDN'T SAVE HIM FROM DANGERS IN "PRETTY SICK ENVIRONMENT"

Jon East St. Petersburg (Florida) *Evening Independent*

Steve Dennard, a Union Correctional Institution guard stabbed to death by inmates last week, told of the dangers he faced when interviewed by the St. Petersburg Evening Independent *earlier this year. Here is a condensed version of a March 15 profile of Dennard, who was buried Monday in Jacksonville.*

When Steve Dennard does a good job, the people with whom he works would rather break his hand than shake it.

Dennard is a correctional officer at Union Correctional Institution in Raiford. And his daily companions are some of the most hardened criminals in Florida.

For the past three of his five years at Union, Dennard has been a member of the Inside Security Squad. For officers, it's a position of prestige. The squad members roam the institution each day, acting as trouble shooters. For the inmates, though, the squad represents trouble. To them it's the "Goon Squad," and the officers on it are targets.

Dennard knows it, too. He knows if he turns his back at the wrong moment, someone is liable to insert a handsculpted dagger into it.

"Okay, let's see the passes. Yeah, that means you. Get over here."

The three men, all in their 20s, stop. One turns his back and shakes his head in disgust. Dennard finds out none is in the proper assigned work area.

"Where are you supposed to be?" he asks.

"The Man sent me to the library," one responds. "He said it was okay."

"That ain't what this says. You know he's supposed to give you a pass."

"Aw, come on, man. Why you want to give me s—?"

"You looking to sleep in the Cage (solitary confinement) tonight? You'd better get all of your a— the hell out of here and back to where you supposed to be. I don't want to see you around here again."

The three walk away, talking to each other as they do. Dennard turns to a companion for the day.

"I guess that sounds kind of harsh to you," he says. "(But) you've got to be that way. When I'm on the yard I will act just as crazy as I need to be. They respect that. They know just how far they can push you."

He pauses, thinking about what he has described. "That sounds perverse, don't it? Maybe it is . . . This is a pretty sick environment in here."

Dennard went looking for a job as a correctional officer five years ago, when he found he could get paid tuition for college courses. Since then, he has lived in an environment far different from the academic world. The students on his campus all try to cut class, and he is the teacher they have been trained to hate the most.

To survive in that setting, Dennard, 29, 6 feet tall, 200 pounds, must prove himself. The uniform does not earn respect. His actions must. So Dennard says he is tough with inmates.

He also tries to be fair and reasonable. He could spend his entire day writing disciplinary reports (called DRs) if he wanted to trap every inmate on every infraction. Instead he tries to head off the major problems and help the inmates who are simply trying to do their time and get out.

"I feel like you've got a responsibility to the inmate," he says. "They'll respect you if they know you're tough—as long as you're fair."

Dennard is involved in calming some disturbance nearly every day. That sometimes means approaching two inmates battling with knives and trying to stop them without having a weapon himself. Dennard and the other guards are not even allowed to carry nightsticks.

But after five years, most of his fears have subsided. Most of them—but not all.

"It's not the loud ones . . . They're not the ones that bother me. They're just talk. It's the one who's just sitting over there not saying anything. He's the one who scares me."

Like most correctional officers, Dennard is shouted at, hit, and abused almost daily. He sometimes wonders what he's supposed to do about it. He threatens many inmates with the Cage. But some laugh, because they know they still get three good meals there and don't have to work. For some, its even a status symbol.

Dennard himself knows inmates won't stay in the disciplinary confinement cells for more than a few days because overcrowding means they must make way for more discipline problems.

So Dennard just exercises self-control. His fortitude is sometimes tested to its limit.

"Okay, let's say you've got a guy in the Cage and you know you've got to go back there and check every hour. So, the first time you go back there, he spits on you. What do you do? Do you write a DR? He's already in the Cage. That's the worst you can do to the man. So, maybe you wipe if off and walk away. That's professional, right?

"The next time you go back there and he throws a cup of urine on you. So what do you do? Well, maybe you're professional again and you clean yourself up and walk away. So the next time, he's waiting and he throws feces on you. What do you do?

"Let me ask you. What's your limit?"

From the Tampa *Tribune*, 10 May 1983.

Monday May 11 9:00 am

Discussion and review

1. What were some of the major features of the inmate social system before 1960?
2. Why did the inmate social system change dramatically starting in the 1960s?
3. When did the black prisoner movement begin, and what was its major impetus?
4. What was the early effect of the Black Muslim movement on white prisoners and prison administrators?
5. What is the connection between prison gangs and street gangs?
6. How did California prison authorities try to neutralize gang conflicts in their system?
7. Why do white gangs develop in prisons?
8. What services do prison gangs sometimes offer their members?
9. How do gangs impact informal and formal prison systems?
10. What are some of the recent changes that have occurred in prison management?
11. What are the tenets of subcultural wisdom that define acceptable guard behavior?
12. What changes in attitude and behavior do new correctional officers experience as a consequence of their exposure to veteran guards, inmates, and superiors?

Glossary

Aryan Brotherhood A prison gang of white inmates.
Black Muslims The major black organization espousing the philosophy of black separatism; considered to be responsible for the black prison movement in the 1950s.
Black separatism A movement that gained popularity in the 1950s and 1960s; espouses the political, social, and economic separation of black Americans from mainstream white America.
Burnout A condition of depleted energy; to fail, wear out, and exhaust one's physical and mental resources.
Disciples A black street gang found on Chicago streets and in Illinois prisons.
El Rukns A black street gang found on Chicago streets and in Illinois prisons; formerly called the Black Stone Rangers and the Black P Stone Nation.
Gorilla Prisoners who use violence liberally to gain their ends.
Hacks or screws Derogatory terms used by inmates to refer to correctional officers.
La Nuestra Familia A prison gang of Chicanos from Texas and small towns in California; formed to counter the activities of another Chicano prison gang, the Mexican Mafia. Gang members are usually confined at Soledad State Prison or Tracy to avoid conflicts with the Mafia.
Latin Kings A black street gang found on Chicago streets and in Illinois prisons.
Malcolm X A leader of the Black Muslim movement who personified the philosophy of the organization in the 1950s.
Merchant or peddler An inmate who exploits fellow prisoners by manipulation and trickery and who typically sells or trades goods in short supply.

Mexican Mafia A prison gang of young Chicanos who know each other from the streets of Los Angeles and from other prisons. Gang members are usually confined to San Quentin and Folsom to avoid conflict with their chief rivals, La Nuestra Familia.

Rat or squealer An inmate who betrays a fellow prisoner.

Right guy An inmate loyal to fellow inmates who keeps his promises, minds his own business, does not discuss his own business, defends himself, and doesn't look for trouble.

Sick-out A labor tactic in which large numbers of employees fail to report to work because of alleged sickness.

Soul A quality of spontaneity, of having the capacity to relate to others with ease, and of having special expressive abilities (particularly as revealed in music).

Toughs Prisoners who exhibit highly aggressive behavior, quarrel easily, and fight without cause.

Weakling or weak sister A prisoner unable to withstand the general rigors of life in custodial institutions.

White Citizen Council A white inmate gang.

Wolf or fag An inmate unable to endure prolonged deprivation of heterosexual relationships who consequently enters into homosexual activity. The *wolf* plays the active role, the *fag* the passive role.

Vice Lords A black street gang found on Chicago streets and in Illinois prisons.

References

Barak, I. "Punishment to Protection: Solitary Confinement in the Washington State Penitentiary, 1966-1975." Ph.D. dissertation, Ohio State University, 1978.

Cleaver, E. *Soul on Ice*. New York: McGraw-Hill, 1968.

Cohen, A.K. *The Culture of the Gang*. New York: Free Press, 1955.

Conrad, J.P. "Who's in Charge? The Control of Gang Violence in California Prisons." In *Correctional Facility Planning*, edited by Robert Montilla and Nora Marlow, pp.135–47. Lexington, Mass.: D. C. Heath, 1979.

Crouch, B. M., and Marquart, J. W. "On Becoming a Prison Guard." In *The Keepers: Prison Guards and Contemporary Corrections*, edited by B. M. Crouch. Springfield, Ill.: Charles C. Thomas, 1980.

Dinitz, S. "Are Safe and Humane Prisons Possible?" Paper presented to the John Vincent Barry Memorial Lecture, University of Australia, 8 October 1980.

Freeman, R., Dinitz, S., and Conrad, J. P. "The Bottom Is in the Hole." *American Journal of Corrections* 39 (1977): 25–31.

Irwin, J. *Prisons in Turmoil*. Boston: Little, Brown, 1980.

Irwin, J. and Cressey, D. R. "Thieves, Convicts and Inmate Culture. In *The Other Side*, edited by Howard S. Becker, New York: Free Press, 1964.

Jacobs, J. B. "Street Gangs Behind Bars." In *The Sociology of Corrections*, edited by Robert G. Leger and John R. Stratton, pp.148–161. New York: Wiley, 1977.

Krajick, K. "The Menace of Supergangs." *Corrections Magazine*, June 1980, pp. 11–14.

Malcolm X. *The Autobiography of Malcolm X*. New York: MacMillan, 1965.

Martinson, R. "What Works? Questions and Answers About Prison Reform." *The Public Interest* 35 (1974): 22–54.

May, E. "Prison Guards in America: The Inside Story." *Corrections Magazine* 1976, 2, pp. 4–5, 12, 36–40, 44–48.

McCleery, R. "Communication Patterns as Bases of Systems of Authority and Power." In *Theoretical Studies on Social Organization of the Prison*, edited by G. M. Sykes and S. L. Messinger, pp. 49–75. New York: Social Science Research Council, 1960.

Miller, W. B. " Lower-Class Structure as a Generating Mileau of Gang Violence." *Journal of Social Issues* 14 (1958): 5–19.

Morris, N. *The Future of Imprisonment*. Chicago: University of Chicago Press, 1974.

Niederhoffer, A. *Behind the Shield*. New York: Doubleday, 1967.

Patrick, J. *A Glasgow Gang Observed*. London: Eyre-Methuen, 1973.

Robinson, B. "Love: A Hard-Legged Triangle." *Black Scholar*, September 1971, pp. 29–48.

Sheehan, S. "Annals of Crime: A Prison and a Prisoner." *The New Yorker*, 24 October, 31 October, and 7 November 1977.
Skolnick, J. H. *Justice Without Trial*. New York: Wiley, 1966.
Sykes, G. M. and Messinger, S. L. "The Inmate Social System." In *Theoretical Studies in Social Organization of the Prison*, edited by G. M. Sykes and S. L. Messinger, pp. 5–19. New York: Social Science Research Council, 1960.
Thrasher, F. M. *The Gang*. Chicago: University of Chicago Press, 1963.
Wilson, J. Q. *Thinking About Crime*. New York: Basic, 1975.
Van Den Haag, E. *Punishing Criminals*, New York: Basic, 1975.
Von Hirsh, A. *Doing Justice*. New York: Hill and Wang, 1976.

Notes

1. This discussion of the inmate social system was adapted, with permission, from G. M. Sykes and S. L. Messinger, "The Inmate Social System," in *Theoretical Studies in Social Organization of the Prison*, by Richard A. Cloward, et al. (New York: Social Science Research Council, 1960), pp. 5–19.

2. The discussions of black and Chicano prisoners, (and the accompanying references) were adapted, with permission, from J. Irwin, *Prisons in Turmoil* (Boston: Little, Brown, 1980), pp. 66–70, 189, 191.

3. Portions of the discussion of black and white gangs in the Illinois prison system and the impact of gangs upon informal and formal prison systems were adapted, with permission, from K. Krajick, "The Menace of Supergangs," *Corrections Magazine*, June 1980, pp. 11–14.

4. The discussion of gang socialization and recruitment and services performed by gangs, along with accompanying references, was adapted, with permission, from J. B. Jacobs, "Street Gangs Behind Bars," *Social Problems* 21 (1974): 395–409.

5. The discussion of prison management was adapted, with permission, from Simon Dinitz, "Are Safe and Humane Prisons Possible?" Paper presented to the John Vincent Barry Memorial Lecture, University of Australia, 8 October 1980, pp. 13–18.

6. The discussion of restoring legitimate control to prisons was adapted, with permission, from J. P. Conrad, "Who's in Charge?" In *Correctional Facility Planning*, edited by Robert Montella and Nora Marlow (Lexington, Mass.: D. C. Heath, 1979), pp. 141–45.

15
alternatives to confinement

Probation
The suspended sentence: Birthplace of probation
John Augustus: Father of probation
Imposing probation
    Probation without adjudication
    Presentence investigation reports
    Conditions of probation and parole
Revocation of probation
Role conflict and the probation officer
Success rates in probation
Probation in retrospect

Conditional and graduated release
Parole
    Parole selection
    Conditions of parole
    Enhancing parole prediction: Actuarial tables
    Innovations in parole
    The effectiveness of parole
    The beleaguered status of parole
Other forms of conditional release
    Work release
    Study release
    Furloughs
    Graduated release
    Halfway houses
    The PORT program
Diversion
Alcohol and drug abuse programs
    Detoxification centers
    DWI offenses
    Addiction treatment
Community correctional centers

Summary
Issue paper: Community corrections—in anyone's community but ours!

Although the law requires that violators receive specific penalties, it also provides for the mitigation of severe sentences. A person convicted of a crime may be placed on *probation* rather than being incarcerated, may be *paroled* from prison prior to the expiration of his or her sentence, may have his or her prison sentence or fine commuted to a lesser penalty, or may receive a full or conditional pardon (with a restoration of civil rights). A fifth method of mitigating the full force of legal sanctions is called *amnesty*—a group pardon.

Offenders sent away to prison return, sooner or later, to free society. But imprisonment may not only fail to rehabilitate many offenders, it may also exacerbate their criminal tendencies. Criminal justice authorities, therefore, have long sought realistic, workable alternatives to confinement. In recent years, the emphasis has been upon involving offenders in programs and facilities based within the community. Such programs allow society to provide offenders with only the amount of supervision they require. And because crime has its roots in the community, it is reasonable that the community assume some responsibility for dealing with offenders. This approach also minimizes the problem of reintegration.

Probation and parole are the two methods most often used to replace imprisonment with community supervision. More than half of all persons convicted of felonies each year are placed on probation. The number of prisoners released on parole is currently declining, however, because of dissatisfaction with selection procedures and skepticism about parole effectiveness. Strictly speaking, parole is not an alternative to confinement in the same sense as probation; it is actually a form of conditional release for someone already serving a prison term.

In addition to probation and parole, we briefly consider *work release*, study release, home *furloughs*, *halfway houses*, detoxification and drug abuse programs, and *diversion* as alternatives to incarceration. We also discuss the concept of the community correctional center as a multipurpose facility that can provide human services in a community setting.

Probation

Probation has been called "the least visible, least studied, most diffuse and most underfunded part of the criminal-processing apparatus" (Krajick 1980, p. 7). Yet probation is the sanction that a criminal court is most apt to impose on offenders. Between 60 and 80 percent of sentences meted out by the courts involve probation, and on any given day, there are about one million persons on probation in the United States. This figure is, at best, an estimate, because probation services are spread among many agencies and facilities, from the municipal level to the federal level. According to a count by the National Council on Crime and Delinquency (1981), there are about twenty-four hundred probation offices administering adult probation services in the United States. But the authors of the report acknowledge that the actual figure is probably much higher. Some jurisdictions practice "postcard probation," in which clients report their activities once or twice a month by sending in preaddressed postcards.

Probation is intended as a combination of treatment and punishment. An offender is actually serving time on probation, but he or she is also supposed to be treated in the context of community-based supervision. Ideally, probationers receive counseling and guidance to insure their adjustment to free society. But probation is also punitive, because restrictions are placed on the probationer. (Many authorities deny the punitive aspects of probation and claim that their policies are strictly rehabilitative.

Liberal and conservative critics of the criminal justice system agree that placing an offender on probation without using private community services is equal to doing nothing. Such action is neither treatment nor punishment. As a criminal court judge observes: "The offender continues with his life style . . . . If he is a wealthy doctor, he continues with his practice; if he is an unemployed youth, he continues to be unemployed. Probation is a meaningless ritual; it is a sop to the conscience of the court" (Krajick 1980, p. 7).

A major problem in probation is the built-in role conflict experienced by probation officers. Are they police officers or counselors? Is their responsibility primarily surveillance, or should they be agents of active social change? Many of the other difficulties that plague probation—high staff turnover, low morale, and burnout—stem from this basic conflict. There are also critical problems in trying to evaluate the effectiveness of probation as an alternative to confinement. However, some innovative and experimental approaches have been proposed to augment traditional probation programs in an attempt to deal with these problems.

The suspended sentence: Birthplace of probation

Probation is derived from the suspended sentence, handed down indirectly from our judicial past. Both a suspended sentence and probation are a form of mitigating punishment through judicial procedure. Their earliest antecedent is the Right of Sanctuary, which is frequently cited in the Bible; holy places and certain cities were traditionally set aside as places of sanctuary.

The practice of Right of Sanctuary was written into Mosaic law. To escape the vengeance of a victim's family, a killer could go to a sanctuary and find refuge. In the Middle Ages, many churches offered sanctuary to persons hiding from harsh secular laws. The practice of sanctuary disappeared in England in the seventeenth century and was replaced with "benefit of clergy." This practice, originally reserved for clerics, was eventually extended to those who could pass the "Psalms 51" test, which required the ability of the offender to read the verse beginning "Have mercy upon me . . ." The result was a form of suspended sentence that allowed offenders to move about in society without undue fear of retribution.

The suspended sentence differs from probation, even though the terms are sometimes used interchangeably. The suspended sentence does not require supervision and usually does not specify a particular set of goals for the offender. It is merely a form of quasi-freedom that can be revoked at the discretion of the court. The practice of suspended sentence, like the right of sanctuary, has outlived its usefulness in the United States and has generally been replaced by supervised probation.

John Augustus: Father of probation

A nineteenth century Boston cobbler named John Augustus is regarded as the father of probation. Augustus spent much of his leisure time in the courts and was distressed that common drunks were forced to remain in jail because they had no money to pay their fines. A humane, sympathetic man, he convinced authorities to allow him to pay offenders' fines; after their release, he provided offenders with friendly counsel and supervision. From 1841 to 1848, Augustus bailed out nearly two thousand men, women, and children. Barnes and Teeters describe his approach:

> His method was to bail the offender after conviction, to utilize this favor as an entering wedge to the convict's confidence and friendship, and through such evidence of friendliness as helping the offender to obtain a job and aiding his family in various ways, to drive the wedge home. When the defendant was later brought into court for sentence, Augustus would report on his progress toward reformation, and the judge would usually fine the convict one cent and costs, instead of committing him to an institution (1959, p. 554).

Augustus's efforts encouraged his home state of Massachusetts to pass the first probation statute in 1878. Five more states followed suit before the turn of the century. In 1899, with the creation of the first juvenile court, probation was established as a legitimate alternative to penal confinement. The need to supervise troubled youths and to keep them out of adult prisons provided strong motivation toward developing probation in the United States.

Imposing probation

Probation can be implemented in three ways. First, the law may allow the trial judge to suspend the execution of sentence and to place the offender on conditional probation. Second, a state statute may require sentencing but may permit suspension. Finally, sentencing and probation may be left to the discretion of the trial judge. If a probationer violates the conditions of his or her probation, the trial judge usually orders the execution of the sentence originally imposed. If a judge has suspended sentencing, a probation violation might result in a stiffer prison sentence than would have been imposed earlier.

Probation without adjudication Once the court has decided to grant probation, the sentencing judge must decide whether the offender should be adjudicated guilty and labeled a convicted felon, or whether he or she should be placed on probation without adjudication. This decision is outlined by Murchek:

Although adjudication of guilt may provide certain safeguards to society such as: requiring criminal registration, serving notice to prospective employers that the applicant has been convicted of a criminal offense, preventing the offender from voting, holding public office, serving on a jury and perhaps making it more difficult to obtain firearms, it appears to provide very little appreciable effect in providing protection to society. It does, in fact, seriously hamper the offender's chances of rehabilitation.

The withholding of adjudication of guilt, on the other hand, is consistent with the philosophical concepts of probation which combine community-based treatment with the full utilization of available community resources as a viable alternative to imprisonment and the accompanying degradation and stigma associated with same. (1973, p. 27).

Actually, probation without adjudication was practiced at the time of John Augustus. Augustus convinced judges to withhold sentencing on offenders released to him for a period of three weeks, after which the offenders returned for sentencing. This procedure gave offenders a chance to prove themselves, and it usually resulted in offenders being fined rather than imprisoned. This system of delayed or postponed sentencing kept the offender in the community, under supervision and without the handicap of a criminal record. The ability to function in the community without the stigma of a criminal conviction often provides a psychological uplift to the offender that may contribute to a desire for self-improvement and reform.

Presentence investigation reports To determine which offenders are good candidates for probation, sentencing judges rely heavily upon presentence reports. Information secured in presentence investigations can be used at almost every stage in the criminal justice process: by the courts in deciding the appropriate sentence; by the prison classification team in assigning custody level and treatment; by the parole board in determining when an offender is ready to be returned to the community; by probation and parole officers in helping offenders readjust to free society; and by correctional researchers in identifying the characteristics of successful probation (Carter and Wilkins 1976). The primary purpose of presentence investigations is not to determine the guilt or innocence of defendants, but rather to give insights into their personalities and lives.

Some type of a presentence investigation report should be made in every case. Objectivity is essential in the preparation of this document; probation officers must see things as they are, not as they would wish them to be. Under our adversary system of justice, the district attorney and the defense counsel are committed to particular points of view, but the preparer of the presentence investigation report is free to include all facts pertinent to the case. The report should include a description of the offense, including statements of co-defendants; the defendant's own version of the offense; prior record; family and marital history; description of the neighborhood in which the defendant was reared; and facts about the defendant's education, religion, interests, mental and physical health, employment history, and military service. Optional information might include the attitude of the defendant toward arresting officers, the amount of bond, and the attitude of arresting officers.

The evaluative summary is the most difficult and important part of the presentence report. It is this summary that separates professional probation officers from fact-gathering clerks. Probation officers need considerable analytic skills and an understanding of human behavior to interpret the facts in a presentence report and to make a meaningful recommendation to the court. Many judges ask these officers to recommend sentencing alternatives, or, if the defendant is placed on probation, to recommend a plan of treatment.

Conditions of probation and parole Although probation is usually managed by the courts and parole by an executive department of government, the conditions of both alternatives are similar. These conditions are generally fixed jointly by the legislature, the court, and the probation and parole departments. Some general regulations—such as requirements that probationers live law-abiding lives, that they not leave the state without the court's consent, that they report periodically to their probation or parole officer, and that they pay court costs—may be fixed by statute; no allowances are made for discretion by the trial court or the parole board. However, unique conditions may be applied in individual cases. For example, probationers may be required to either stay home or leave home, to support their parents, to get a steady job working days, to make restitution to their victims, or to attend church regularly.

Some conditions of probation and parole have been unfair and unrealistic. When this occurs, a probation officer may choose to enforce the conditions selectively, thereby muting their effect in the interest of common-sense justice. The concerned probation officer should ask, Are these rules reasonable? Are they effective? Do they serve the best interests of the individual and the community?

Revocation of probation

There are no uniform criteria for revoking probation throughout the country—not even among judges in the same district courts. Conditions of probation should be realistic, and they should be applied fairly. Unrealistic conditions frustrate the offender and may lead to further violations. For example, it is pointless to fine a probationer if financial problems caused the original violation. Similarly, compulsory church attendance might create resentment on the part of the probationer. Thus, conditions of probation should be guidelines to assist the probationer in leading a law-abiding life—not rigid vows of chastity and obedience that only the most disciplined can endure.

When probationers violate the conditions of their probation, care must be taken to determine whether the violation is the result of unrealistic probation rules or the attitude of the probationer (DiCerbo 1966). The probation officer must ask, To what extent is this violation a reflection of deep-seated hostility? To what extent is the behavior symptomatic of a person trying to find himself or herself? Revocation of probation is justified only when probationers defy the courts or when they become a threat to the community. In cases involving restitution, if a probationer is sentenced to prison, the crime victim loses out. No violation should result in automatic revocation. Probation officers should ask themselves how they would respond to the probationer's acts if he or she was *not* on probation. For example, we do not sentence people to prison for losing or quitting their jobs. Thus, all violations should be judged in light of the probationer's total adjustment to society.

Role conflict and the probation officer

Probation and parole both involve community supervision of the offender. The offender is required to conform to certain conditions as a basis for securing an alternative to imprisonment. The probation officer is the person who must see to it that the offender lives up to and carries out the terms imposed by the court or by probation authorities. Thus, the probation officer has the task of surveillance, which is basically a police function.

However, the probation officer is also expected to provide a variety of human services to the probationer or parolee. That is, the officer is expected to perform as a social caseworker. The influence of social work has had a profound effect on the development of probation services. In the past, an overemphasis on casework and the medical model—which conceived of the criminal offender as a "sick" person—resulted in a narrow focus on the relationship between the probationer and the probation officer. This led, in turn, to a tendency to overlook the connection between crime and contributing factors such as poverty, racism, unemployment, poor health, substandard housing, and poor education.

One drawback in the model of the probation officer as a caseworker is that officers may have to assume functions not related to probation. Placement in foster homes, operation of shelters, alcoholism, drug addiction, and mental illness may be more properly handled by community mental health agencies. No one probation officer has the background required to deal with all the problems of probationers. Yet probation officers are accountable for probationers that get into trouble again. The first question asked by the court in this situation is usually, When did you last see your client? As a result, probation officers tend to overextend themselves to prevent or justify client failures.

In our discussion of parole in this chapter, we briefly examine how probation officers have fared in California's approach to conditional release. For many officers, the role conflict of "cop or counselor" is a major source of job stress.

Success rates in probation

It generally costs about ten times more to place a person in prison than to put the person on probation for a comparable period. But even though probation is more economical than incarceration, is it successful in rehabilitating the offender? How can success or failure be identified?

Allen, Carlson, and Parks (1979) point out that surprisingly few studies compare probation with other sentencing alternatives with regard to effectiveness. Available research can be divided into three categories: studies that compare the performance of probationers with the performance of offenders that receive alternative dispositions; studies that measure probation outcomes without comparison with other forms of sanction; and studies that measure probation outcomes and attempt to isolate characteristics that contribute to the success or failure of probation. The results of ten of the latter studies are summarized in **table 15.1.** As a rule of thumb, if 30 percent or more of those on probation successsfully completed their probation, a program was considered to be effective. If the figure was less than 30 percent, probation was judged to be ineffective or of limited success.

Allen and his colleagues note that, because of wide disparities in method and approach, "it is nearly impossible, not to mention inappropriate, to draw any conclusions from these studies about the effectiveness of proba-

TABLE 15.1 Studies reporting recidivism rates for probationers

Study	Instant offenses[1]	Failure[2]	Follow-up[3]	Failure rate (%)
Caldwell, 1951	Internal Revenue laws (72%)	Convictions	Postprobation: 5½-11½ years	16.4
England, 1955	Bootlegging (48%); forgery and counterfeiting (9%)	Convictions	Postprobation: 6–12 years	17.7
Davis, 1955	Burglary; forgery and checks	Two or more violations and revocation (technical and new offenses)	To termination; 4–7 years	30.2
Frease, 1964		Inactive letter, bench warrant, and revocation	On probation: 18–30 months	20.0
Landis, 1969	Auto theft; forgery and checks	Revocation (technical and new offenses)	To termination	52.5
Irish, 1972	Larceny and burglary	Arrests or convictions	Postprobation: minimum of 4 years	41.5
Missouri Division of Probation and Parole, 1976	Burglary, larceny, and vehicle theft	Arrests and convictions	Postprobation: 6mo.-7 years	30.0
Kusuda, 1976	Property	Revocation	To termination: 1–2 years	18.3
Comptroller General, 1976		Revocation and postrelease conviction	Postprobation: 20-month average	55.0
Irish, 1977	Property	Arrests	Postprobation: 3–4 years	29.6

[1] *Instant Offense*: the crime for which the individual was convicted at the time the study was conducted
[2] *Failure*: the reason(s) for the termination of probation, ranging from technical grounds for revocation to arrest and conviction on further crimes
[3] *Follow-up*: period ranging from several months to many years following the initial data collection period

tion compared to other alternative dispositions" (1979, p. 33). In particular, there are discrepancies in the way recidivism, the crucial factor in the success or failure of probation, is defined. Given these differences and variations in the follow-up period used in the various studies, the one characteristic most consistently associated with probation failure was the probationer's previous criminal history. Persistent law violators, regardless of the type of violations, appear to be poor probation risks. Probation is most likely to have a significant impact on first offenders.

Probation in retrospect

Probation is sometimes viewed as a bright hope for corrections. It is generally conceded, however, that the full potential of this alternative to confinement will not be attained without some attention to two major issues: the need to develop an effective system for determining which offenders should receive probation, and the need to provide community support and services to probationers to allow them to live independently in a socially acceptable way. To be coherent, probation services need better organization, staffing, and funding. Shifting money and resources to community-based projects is fundamental if probation is to become a realistic and effective alternative to confinement. The National Advisory Commission on Criminal Justice Standards and Goals (1973) officially endorses probation as the recommended disposition, preferably without adjudication of guilt. It also recommends that the probation program, which started as a volunteer service, again seek out volunteers to serve in all capacities.

Arguments favoring probation over imprisonment focus on reduced stigma, community help, and other benefits to the offender. However, one of the strongest arguments is cost. The taxpayer can easily appreciate the fact that while it costs about $3,500 a year (excluding capital costs) to keep the average adult offender in prison, probation costs only about $350 a year. If you include in the former cost the capital cost of $25,000 per bed for an average correctional institution, plus the cost of welfare, the loss of tax revenue, and broken homes, the difference in dollars and cents is even greater.

Conditional and graduated release

As noted earlier, all offenders except those who are executed or committed to prison for "life certain" terms will eventually be released. How well they fare once they return to society—whether they successfully reintegrate or commit further offenses that lead back to prison—depends on many complex factors, one of which is the length of time they spend in prison. Reid cites the case of Ralph Lobaugh, who was released in 1977 after spending thirty years in an Indiana prison:

> The freedom for which he had fought during 14 years, however, was too much for him. After two months, Lobaugh decided he could not cope with

life outside the walls and went back to prison. According to Harold G. Roddy, director of the work-release program in Indiana, Lobaugh "just wanted to live in a cell again and be with his old friends" (1981, p. 282).

The Lobaugh case may be extreme, but the problem of readjustment to free society for a released prisoner is not unusual.

Parole

Parole is the conditional release, under supervision, of offenders from correctional institutions after they have served part of their sentences. It is the way in which the majority of incarcerated felons are released from prison each year. The concept of parole has its roots in military history; the practice of releasing a captured officer on his word of honor that he will not take up arms against his captors is called *parole d'honneur*. Similarly, inmates are released to free society on their word of honor that they will not again violate the law. Parole differs from probation, because it implies that the offender has served time. Administratively, parole is a function of the executive branch of government, and probation is a judicial act of the court. Selection, supervision, regulations, revocation, and release procedures are similar for parole and probation, however, and the two kinds of release are often confused by the public.

Prisoners have always been released on their *mandatory release date*—that is, on the termination date of their sentence. In inmate terms, this is referred to as serving "flat time" or "day to day." Parole is conditional release. Inmates who make genuine progress toward rehabilitation are selected to serve a final part of their sentence under some form of community supervision.

Parole selection Prisoners seeking to be released on parole must follow a procedure of recommendation and review to determine their readiness. Review and selection are subject to the decision-making authority of a *parole board*, which generally includes representatives from the prison, the state department of corrections, and other professionals qualified to assess an inmate's eligibility for parole.

Most parole boards assign cases to individual board members who review the cases in detail; the members then make recommendations to the full board when it meets. The recommendations of board members are usually accepted, but sometimes the full board will ask for more details. Some states even send parole board members into the prisons to interview inmates and institutional staff; other states convene their entire boards at individual institutions on a regular schedule. If inmates do not meet board criteria, their sentences are continued and they are "flopped." If parole is granted, the inmate is prepared to be turned over to the adult parole authority for the period of supervision determined by the parole board.

A major problem with parole decisions is that offenders often do not know the criteria they are expected to meet and the reasons that parole might be denied. Porter comments on this aspect of the decision-making process:

> It is an essential element of justice that the role and processes for measuring parole readiness be made known to the inmate. This knowledge can greatly facilitate the earnest inmate toward his own rehabilitation. It is just as important for an inmate to know the rules and basis of the judgment upon which he will be granted or denied parole as it was important for him to know the basis of the charge against him and the evidence upon which he was convicted. One can imagine nothing more cruel, inhuman, and frustrating than serving a prison term without knowledge of what will be measured and the rules determining whether one is ready for release.... Justice can never be a product of unreasoned judgment (1958, p. 227).

Correctional staff should also be told the "rules of the game" so that they can guide inmates toward desirable behavior.

Four inmates at the Indiana State Penitentiary have described three aspects of parole decisions that candidates resent. First, most parole boards emphasize a candidate's prior record:

> What is so frustrating to men who keep getting rejected for parole because of "past record" is that there is obviously nothing that the individual can do about it. It cannot be changed, it cannot be expunged. It therefore generates a feeling of helplessness and frustration, especially in men who take seriously what they are told about rehabilitation and perfect institutional records. These men cannot understand the rationale behind parole denials based on past records if the major goal of the correctional system is rehabilitation and if they have tried to take advantage of every rehabilitation program offered by the institution. The men know that merely serving another two or five years is not going to further the "rehabilitation" process (Griswold et al. 1970).

Second, many parole boards believe that their principal responsibility is to protect society, not to rehabilitate the offender. With this attitude, boards are reluctant to release offenders who are considered poor risks. Rather, they prefer to let such offenders serve their full sentences and return to the community without supervision. This practice may reduce the recidivism rate for offenders on parole, but it may not affect nonparoled inmates' chances for successful reintegration. For some, the wait might be positive: the sheer passage of time seems to mature some people. For most inmates, however, the longer they remain in prison, the more likely they are to absorb the values, techniques, and rationalizations of the criminal subculture. Finally, inmates believe that parole boards are more responsive to public opinion and political pressure than to the record and behavior of the individual applicant. This feeling adds to cynicism about the entire parole process.

Another aspect of parole that has come under attack is the inmate's inability to appeal an unfavorable decision. Parole decisions are often subject to question, especially when an inmate is denied knowledge as to why he or she was denied parole. Future parole selection *must* include self-regulating and internal appeal procedures. If such procedures are not provided, case after case will be sent to court, and the U.S. Supreme Court will eventually step in and establish rules and procedures based on the Fourteenth Amendment. Some states have seen the handwriting on the wall and have started to formalize selection criteria and to develop appeal procedures.

Conditions of parole Many of the first parole procedures imposed unreasonable restrictions on the released offender. Too often the rules were simply a convenient pretext for returning the parolee to prison—which was often done if the parolee created even the slightest fuss for the parole officer. As recently as twenty years ago, it was not uncommon for the conditions of parole to require the parolee to "only associate with persons of good reputation." Rules of this type gave the parole officer great discretionary power. Offenders knew that their parole could be revoked for a technical violation at almost any time—a situation not conducive to reform and respect for the law. The parolee's attitude was often, "If I'm going to get busted for a technical violation, I might as well do something *really* wrong." Today, however, the rules of parole are much more reasonable and realistic.

STATEMENT OF PAROLE AGREEMENT

The members of the parole board agree that you have earned the opportunity of parole and eventual release from your present conviction. The board is therefore ordering a parole release in your case.

Parole status has a twofold meaning: first, it is a trust status in which the parole board accepts your word that you will do your best to abide by the conditions of parole set down in your case; second, by state law, the Adult Parole Authority has the legal duty to enforce the conditions of parole even to the extent of arrest and return to the institution.

The following conditions of parole apply to your parole release:

1. Upon release from the institution, report as instructed to your parole officer (or any other person designated), and thereafter report as often as directed.

2. Secure written permission of the Adult Parole Authority before leaving the [said] state.

3. Obey all municipal ordinances and state and federal laws, and at all times conduct yourself as a responsible, law-abiding citizen.

4. Never purchase, own, possess, use, or have under your control a deadly weapon or firearm.

5. Follow all instructions given by your parole officer or other officials of the Adult Parole Authority.

6. If you have any problems with the conditions or instructions of your parole, you may request a meeting with your parole officer's supervisor. The request should state your reasons for the conference, and it should be in writing if possible.

7. Special conditions.

I have read, or have had read to me, the foregoing conditions of my parole. I fully understand them and I agree to observe and abide by them.

Witness   *Parole Candidate*
                 Date

Enhancing parole prediction: Actuarial tables Parole boards are engaged in a type of activity that most people associate with tea leaves and crystal balls—namely, predicting the future. The decision to release or not to release an inmate involves an appraisal of an individual's likely future behavior, lawful or criminal. In study after study, the main criteria affecting this prediction have been the seriousness of the crime for which the offender was convicted and the perceived prospects for successful parole.

To increase the objectivity of prediction—and consequently its reliability and validity—parole boards use statistical tables to augment the subjective aspect of their decision making. If a potential parolee is known to act in a certain way (e.g., he or she has dropped out of school), a parole board can make some rather accurate estimates about other behavior of that person (e.g., he or she may have been sent to a state training school). To put it another way, if a young man is in a juvenile correctional facility, a parole board can generally make some fairly accurate assumptions about his background—such as the likelihood that he has a spotty educational record. These assumptions are not guesses in the usual sense, however; they are derived from actuarial tables. Just as life insurance companies determine premiums using actuarial tables based on life expectancies, so also can actuarial tables be developed based on the probability of institutional incarceration for various groups.

The actuarial tables assume that people are alike in certain respects. In insurance, it is assumed that most people will reach a particular age; in parole, it is assumed that some percentage of dropouts will eventually run afoul of the law. But there are many cases in which these assumptions are wrong. Some insurees die shortly after they sign a policy, and some dropouts do well. Nevertheless, insurance companies rely on the actuarial approach. Actuaries forecast efficiently with regard to groups; association—what goes with what—is their interest. Predictions of individual behavior using actuarial tables assume that factors affecting individuals are less influential than factors that cause behavior to conform to the pattern exhibited by most individuals in a particular group.

Clinical prediction, on the other hand, is based on an intensive and exhaustive study of forces and factors that combine to shape the uniqueness of the individual. In this approach, no two people are alike, and no two individuals are anything more than similar in terms of significant characteristics. Thus, to make an individual prediction, the predictor must have a deep understanding of who the individual is and how he or she is likely to react in a given situation.

One of the best-known actuarial tables is the Salient Factor Scale, which was developed in 1973 and 1974 by the Federal Parole Commission, and whose use was mandated by the Federal Parole Commission and Reorganization Act of 1976. This scale relates time served to the severity of the crime and the level of parole risk. Data were obtained from ratings made by parole commissioners. Base-sentence ranges, shown in **table 15.2,** were established for seven categories of offenses by computing the mean time served for these crimes.

No one is suggesting, however, that prediction tables should take the place of parole boards. For one thing, it is unlikely that parole boards will

TABLE 15.2 Federal parole guidelines

Offense severity (Some crimes eliminated or summarized)	Salient factor score (Parole prognosis)			
	Very good	Good	Fair	Poor
LOW: possession of a small amount of marijuana; simple theft under $1,000	6–10 months	8–12 months	10–14 months	12–18 months
LOW/MODERATE: income tax evasion less than $10,000; immigration law violations; embezzlement, fraud, forgery under $1,000	8–12 months	12–16 months	16–20 months	20–28 months
MODERATE: bribery; possession of 50 pounds or less of marijuana, with intent to sell; illegal firearms; income tax evasion, $10,000 to $50,000; nonviolent property offenses, $1,000 to $19,999; auto theft, not for resale	12–16 months	16–20 months	20–24 months	24–32 months
HIGH: counterfeiting; marijuana possession with intent to sell, 50 to 1,999 pounds; auto theft, for resale; nonviolent property offenses, $20,000 to $100,000	16–20 months	20–26 months	26–34 months	34–44 months
VERY HIGH: robbery; breaking and entering bank or post office; extortion; marijuana possession with intent to sell over 2,000 pounds; hard drugs possession with intent to sell, not more than $100,000; nonviolent property offenses over $100,000 but not exceeding $500,000	26–36 months	36–48 months	48–60 months	60–72 months
GREATEST I: explosive detonation; multiple robbery; aggravated felony (weapon fired—no serious injury); hard drugs, over $100,000; forcible rape	40–55 months	55–70 months	70–85 months	85–110 months
GREATEST II: aircraft hijacking; espionage; kidnapping; homicide	Greater than above. No specific ranges because of limited number and extreme variation in cases.			

Adapted from Kevin Krajick, "Parole: Discretion Is Out, Guidelines Are In," *Corrections Magazine* 4(1978):46.

relinquish their authority to any instrument, however recommended it may be based on scientific research. A more realistic alternative is Glaser's (1964) suggestion that actuarial tables be used to complement the subjective aspects of parole deliberations and to provide a valuable check on bias or prejudice.

Innovations in parole In 1965, the state of Ohio introduced a program of *shock probation*, or *shock parole*, that allowed the courts to impose a brief sentence of incarceration, followed by probation. The rationale for the program was to impress offenders with the seriousness of their crimes (thus, the prison sentence), but to release them for community supervision before they became "prisonized." (As Reid (1981) points out, "shock parole" is actually the better term: probation is technically an *alternative* to confinement; parole is a conditional release following a period of incarceration.)

Encouraged by its experience, Ohio passed a shock parole statute in 1974 that permitted shock parole for many prisoners after a six-month prison sentence. Eligibility criteria included the following:

1. The offense for which sentence was imposed must not be aggravated murder or murder.
2. The prisoner must not be a second offender.
3. The prisoner must not be dangerous.
4. The prisoner must not appear to need future confinement as part of his or her correction or rehabilitation.
5. The prisoner must give evidence that he or she is not likely to commit another offense.

The number of inmates released on shock parole in Ohio reached a high of 691 in 1974. That number has since declined because of an adverse Ohio Supreme Court decision, negative publicity, and the adoption of newer and more stringent guidelines for parole eligibility. Ironically, as shock parole was eclipsed in Ohio, several other states began to look at it as a possible way to reduce prison overcrowding.

Another approach to conditional release involves a three-way contract between the inmate, the parole board, and correctional authorities. This approach, designated as contract parole or Mutual Agreement Programming (MAP), lays out, in a legally binding contract, a series of specific activities that the inmate agrees to undertake for self-improvement. The parole board, in turn, agrees to a fixed parole date contingent upon the inmate's successful completion of the program. It is the responsibility of correctional authorities—the third party in the contract—to provide needed services and resources to inmates and to monitor their progress.

As Reid has noted, the contract parole arrangement "is aimed not only at giving the inmate more participation in the decision with regard to his or her future, but also at providing a mechanism by which parole boards will have to be more definite and more articulate about their decision making and give more thought to the reasons for their decisions" (1981, p. 340). The contract arrangement also promotes long-range planning by both the

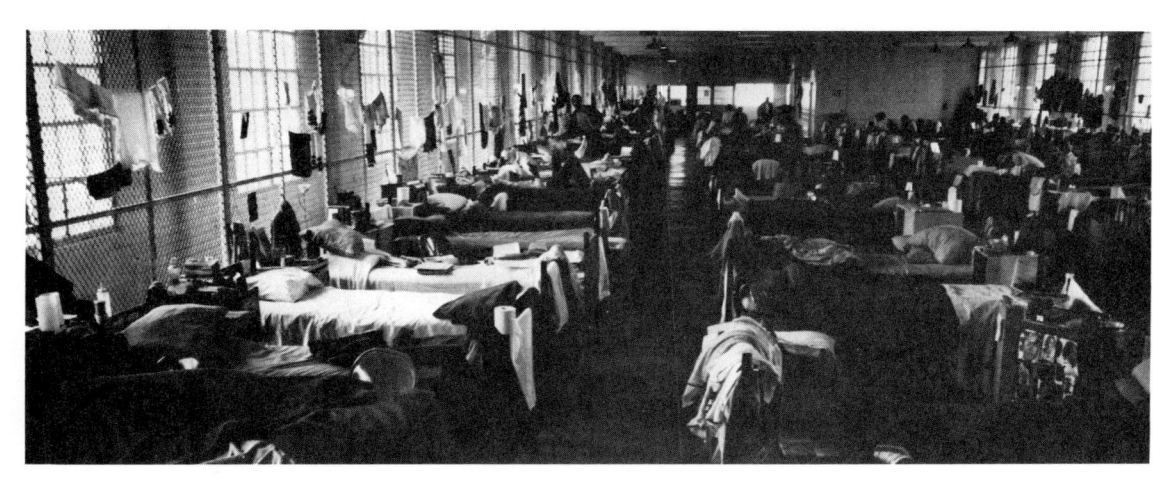

Overcrowding at Maryland House of Corrections. Courtesy Bill Powers/Corrections Magazine.

inmate and the institution. However, a MAP program is difficult to implement and "requires persistence and determination on the part of administrators" (Keve 1981, p. 317). Many institutions simply lack the training and counseling services necessary to permit the inmate to fulfill MAP objectives.

An even more serious flaw of contract parole is that the various parties in the contract are not equals. Because prisoners are fully aware that their involvement in a MAP program is a crucial factor in determining how long they will stay in prison, they can scarcely be considered free agents in the negotiation (Morris 1974). But despite its drawbacks, contract parole is a worthwhile and progressive pursuit.

An intriguing experiment in parole is currently underway in California. Described below, this system was first tried in 1980 after the state's decision to adopt determinate sentencing. Parole officials, concerned that determinate sentencing would all but eliminate parole, maintained that the new model would allow researchers to determine whether or not parole supervision has a demonstrable effect on recidivism. The model is based on a point system for assessing risks and assigning levels of supervision.

SEPARATING THE COP FROM THE COUNSELOR
S. Gettinger Corrections Magazine

Janice M.'s crime was a ten.

"On 3-23-76 the body of the victim was discovered in the orange grove," the presentence report read. "Janice M., along with three others, had been responsible for the torture, beating, stabbing, and strangulation which led to the death of the victim. . . . Janice had been the one who injected the victim with battery acid."

On a form titled "risk assessment," the parole agent wrote "actual torture murder," and then marked down the numeral "10." Leafing through the thick file that the prison sent him when Janice was paroled, he noted that she had several previous convictions for drug offenses and prostitution. He gave her an eight, on a scale of ten, for her past criminal behavior. Her habits of drug and alcohol abuse earned another ten. Janice had previously failed on probation, so that was worth eight points. He multiplied each score by a fraction that represented its importance and added up the figures. Overall, on a scale of ten, Janice came out with a risk score of 8.90.

Janice's high score means that she is a potential danger to the community and warrants very close surveillance by a California state parole agent. The point system is part of a "new model" for parole supervision adopted by the California Division of Parole and Community Services in January 1980. The point system is used to determine whether a parolee is a "control" case, a "service" case—meaning that social services are more important than surveillance—or a minimum-supervision case. Parole agents are also divided up into the three categories: minimum-supervision agents, "control" agents, who act as the personal police of parolees, and "service" agents, who arrange for social services. Agents' activities are spelled out in detail and carefully monitored by supervisors; agents complain that most of their discretion has been taken away. . . .

This system is a significant change in the way parole is administered in California. The "new model" has several features which make it different from the way that parole has traditionally operated in California and in most other states:

- ☐ Numerical assessments of risks and needs. Other states have adopted point systems
- ☐ Specific direction by supervisors. They tell a parole agent exactly what actions to take on each case, and how many hours to determine whether an inmate should be released on parole. But California, where release depends only on the length

of the determinate sentence, uses it to determine the type of parole supervision.
- Different styles of supervision. Any parolee with a risk score of 7.5 or above is considered a "control" case. . . .
- Minimum supervision. Any case that scores below 3.75 on both risks and needs is put into a separate caseload, with few reports required and services provided only upon request.
- Specialization of parole agents by styles of superivision. "Control" agents and "service" agents are forbidden to handle problems outside of their specialties.
- Specific direction by supervisors. They tell a parole agent exactly what actions to take on each case, and how many hours per month they are to devote to it.

Before the system was instituted, administrators predicted that 40 percent of all cases would fall into the control category, 38 percent into service emphasis, and 22 percent would merit minimum supervision. . . . Late last year, 84 percent of the 14,000 parolees in California were classified as control cases; eight percent were service cases and eight percent minimum supervision. The assignment of the state's 367 parole agents reflects approximately a six-to-one ratio of control to service.

Reproduced from S. Gettinger, "Separating the Cop from the Counselor," *Corrections Magazine* (1981): 34–35. Copyright 1981 by Corrections Magazine and Criminal Justice Publications, Inc., 19 W. 34th St., New York, N.Y. 10001.

The effectiveness of parole "No one who works in the field of parole," Keve observes, "doubts the fact that good work on the part of concerned parole officers has been of real effect in helping some or many ex-prisoners become established successfully on return to the community. At the same time, however, the well-entrenched faith in the necessity of parole supervision is not supported by objective research" (1981, p. 313). Evaluating the success or failure of parole supervision involves many of the same difficulties encountered in gauging the effectiveness of probation. Because success and failure are extremely difficult to measure, it is risky to compare the results of various studies.

Keve cites a 1971–72 Minnesota project that compares two groups of paroled youthful offenders (involving both boys and girls). One group received routine parole supervision; the other was given attention only upon request. After ten months, the revocation rates of the two groups were compared. There was no discernible difference between unsupervised and supervised girls, but supervised boys had a significantly *higher* rate of parole violation than unsupervised boys. Says Keve: "It is uncertain what this proves. It easily may be that supervised boys have their paroles revoked more often simply because they are more likely to be caught, whereas the unsupervised boys more easily get by without being caught" (1981, p. 313). Such findings emphasize the danger of using recidivism as a success-failure criterion for parole. Recidivism is often interpreted to mean failure (i.e., the offender has slipped back into his old ways), when, in fact, it often means that the offender committed some act that constituted a technical probation or parole violation (e.g., taking a 100-mile drive to see his mother in Jacksonville when he was not supposed to leave Tampa, or spending the night with a former girlfriend who is on parole for a drug offense). So, in fact, recidivism does not necessarily mean that the offender went out and committed another crime.

In a later study, Sacks and Logan (1979) took advantage of the release of 167 incarcerated felons whose sentences were set aside by a Connecticut court. Prisoners whose discharge meant outright release without supervision were compared with a control group of 57 prisoners who were given routine parole supervision. After one year, the groups were compared on the basis of new arrests and convictions. As the researchers noted, "37% of the control group (parolees) failed while 63% of the experimental group (dischargees) failed" (Sacks and Logan 1979, p. 97). They interpreted these results to indicate that parole had "definite, but modest, effects" on recidivism (ibid., p. 97).

The beleaguered status of parole Parole has been attacked by a variety of groups and individuals, including the American Friends Service Committee and U.S. Bureau of Prisons Director Norman Carlson. A typical attack is the indictment delivered by the Citizens Inquiry on Parole and Criminal Justice, Inc.: "Parole is a tragic failure. Conspiring with other elements of the criminal justice system—unnecessary pre-trial detention, over-long sentences, oppressive conditions—it renders American treatment of those who break society's rules irrational and arbitrary" (1975, p. 38).

A bill was introduced in Congress in 1977 to establish a Federal Commission on Sentencing. The objective of the proposal was to reduce sentencing disparity by providing standard sentences for various categories of criminal offenses. The sentences would reflect the importance of such factors as the seriousness of the crime, the degree of public concern, and mitigating circumstances. As Keve observes, "Although the act says nothing about parole, it is the general assumption that it is one firm step in the direction of eventual elimination of parole in the federal system" (1981, p. 305).

Other forms of conditional release

Work release The pioneering reform efforts of Crofton in Ireland in the nineteenth century provided prisoners with a chance to work within the community prior to release. This idea has been revived in recent years, and work release has become an important part of institutional programs. Under work release, offenders are allowed to work at jobs in the community and still receive the benefit of programs and services at the institution.

The first legislation of work release was a 1913 Wisconsin statute that allowed misdemeanants to work at their jobs while they served short sentences in jail. Then in 1957, North Carolina applied the principles of the Wisconsin statute to felony offenders under limited conditions; Michigan and Maryland soon followed suit with similar acts. In 1965, Congress passed the Federal Prisoner Rehabilitation Act, which provided for work release, furloughs, and community treatment centers for federal prisoners. Many states shortly took similar action.

Work release is not really an alternative to incarceration. Rather, it provides a chance for offenders to test their work skills, to control their own behavior in the community, and to spend the major part of the day away from the institution. Because the inmate is required to return to the institution, work release is actually only a *partial* alternative to incarceration.

The benefit of work release is more than allowing inmates to be outside the prison walls for part of each day. If an inmate has a family, his or her earnings can be used to keep the family off welfare or to augment public assistance. Income might also be used to reimburse victims or to acquire a modest savings account. One of the major advantages of work release, however, is that private citizens can observe offenders working in the community without creating problems for themselves or others. Association with fellow workers who enjoy stable lives in freedom may also give offenders support and guidance that they can not gain inside prison walls. In the American tradition, the ability to produce a day's work is highly valued, and an inmate's return to normal work may instill a needed feeling of self-worth.

Study release Study release is a recent innovation in corrections. Before 1960, only Connecticut had an operational study release program. As of 1974, however, forty-one states had programs of some kind, most of them open to both male and female participants (Smith, McKee, and Milan 1974). The range of educational services offered by such programs is extremely broad, ranging from vocational training and basic adult skills to college education.

Variables involved in the screening of offenders for study release are comparable to those used for work release: severity of offense, time served, custody grade, educational needs, and attitudes of the offender. Because education is so important in our achievement-oriented society, programs that seek to increase the marketability of offenders are plausible alternatives to imprisonment. We are not in a position, however, to make broad statements about the value of such programs, because we are still waiting for reliable information on study release outcomes.

Furloughs Furloughs are another form of partial incarceration. Work release, study release, and furloughs extend the limits of confinement by allowing unsupervised absences from prison. Furloughs and home visits have been used informally for many years. The death of a family member or some other crisis situation have been the most common reasons for furloughs. States have passed legislation to make furloughs a legal tool of

A resident of Milwaukee's Baker House, a pre-release center, goes to work. Courtesy Tony O'Brien/Corrections Magazine.

corrections, so their use has been expanded. Most furloughs are granted for home visits during holidays. They are also used just prior to release to ease the transition from confinement to freedom. It is probable that furloughs will be granted more and more frequently as correctional administrators gain experience in their use.

Graduated release An offender who serves a long sentence in an institutional setting may suffer culture shock when he or she is suddenly returned to the community. Just as astronauts must reenter the atmosphere in a series of steps, so too the offender needs to reenter society gradually. Thus, *graduated release programs* have been developed to ease the culture shock experienced by institutionalized offenders. Any preparation for release is better than none, but preparation that includes periods of nonincarceration is even more effective.

The periods immediately before and after the release of an offender are especially critical to the social readjustment of the offenders. Most ex-offenders know that they will have serious problems trying to reestablish a life for themselves outside the institution. Their fears and apprehensions build as they approach the time for release. In fact, some inmates even commit minor infractions of prison rules to postpone their release. These deliberate offenses allow them to remain in the total dependency of the institution. In recognition of this phenomenon, many correctional administrators have established prerelease and postrelease programs to assist offenders through these critical periods. Topics covered in such programs include how to get a driver's license, how to open a savings account, how to use credit, how to fill out an employment application, and how to adjust to sex and family.

The Sam Houston Institute of Contemporary Corrections provides some pointers for prerelease and graduated release programs (Frank 1973, p.p. 228–29):

1. Prerelease preparation should begin as early as possible in the sentence and inmates should know in advance the purpose and intention of the program.
2. Reliance must be placed on a sound program and not upon the use of special privileges as an enticement to participation.
3. The program should be organized with realistic goals in mind and should be part of the total treatment process.
4. The counseling program should deal with the immediate problems of adjustment, rather than with underlying personality problems.
5. Participants should be carefully selected on an individual basis, rather than according to predetermined arbitrary standards.
6. Employee-employer relationships, rather than custodian-inmate relationships, should exist between staff and inmates.
7. Every effort should be made to enlist the support and participation of the community, and family contact should be encouraged.
8. Whenever possible, work release should be included.

9   The center itself should be minimum security and should encourage personal responsibility. If prerelease programs are to be part of the treatment process, there should be some provision for determining their effectiveness.

Graduated release and prerelease programs are not either-or alternatives to incarceration, but they do recognize the destructive and dependency-producing effects of imprisonment.

Halfway houses Although halfway houses were originally conceived as residences for homeless offenders released from prison, they have also been used for other purposes. Small residences that provide shelter have been managed by prison aid societies for over a century. And in recent years, halfway houses have been viewed as possible nuclei for community-based networks of residential treatment centers. There is also a move to use halfway houses as prerelease guidance centers.

In 1961, the Federal Bureau of Prisons established prerelease guidance centers in several metropolitan areas. Offenders are sent to one of these centers several months before they become eligible for parole. Center personnel are selected based on their treatment orientation and their aptitude for counseling. While at a center, the offender is allowed to work and attend school in the community without supervision, and he or she may participate in a number of programs at the center. This approach has been copied

Baker House, a pre-release center in Milwaukee. Opposition to new halfway houses in Wisconsin and many other states has intensified in recent years. Courtesy Tony O'Brien/Corrections Magazine.

by many states, and it appears to be worthwhile with adequate staff and supervision.

The PORT program The Probated Offenders Rehabilitation and Training (PORT) program in Rochester, Minnesota, was developed in 1979 to fill the gap between probation and institutionalization. PORT is a live-in, community-based treatment program for young adult and juvenile offenders who defy conventional correctional practices. Located on the grounds of the Rochester State Hospital, PORT offers a combination of group therapy and behavior modification. Some twelve to fifteen counselors of both sexes, most college students, reside in the building and help provide a healthy culture for program participants. Offenders work up a scale from one (minimal freedom) to five (maximum freedom) by demonstrating their ability to handle responsibility in school and work situations. Backsliding is recognized as a normal occurrence, and appropriate measures are taken to deal with it. Because of PORT's success, the Minnesota Department of Corrections has used it as a model for several other halfway houses in the state.

Diversion

Diversion refers to organized efforts to use alternatives to the criminal process. To qualify as diversion, efforts must be made *following* a violation of the law and *before* adjudication. This definition may include some traditional conceptions of *prevention*. For instance, the exercise of discretion at some point in the criminal justice process may result in the *informal* diversion of an offender. Only about 30 percent of reported property offenses in the United States result in arrest, and only about one third of those arrests result in conviction. These statistics indicate that informal preconviction diversion is used extensively.

Police agencies practice informal diversion by using their extensive powers of discretion at the time of arrest. Police have been reluctant to formalize their discretion practices because they fear the public will regard the practice as a weakness, or believe they are assuming responsibilities that are rightly those of prosecutors and the courts. As a result, most formalized programs are aimed at the youthful offender in an effort to prevent the start of a crime career. Another example of diversion at the police level is the family crisis intervention approach. By identifying conflict situations early on, police officers trained to invervene in family disturbances can prevent the escalation of violence. If they are unable to resolve the conflict on the scene, they may refer the antagonists to a community agency. This kind of training is now a standard part of professional development in many law enforcement agencies.

The judicial system is also engaged in diverting offenders. Diversion efforts of the prosecutor typically involve the exercise of discretion to "nol pros" (i.e., nolle prosequi)—the suspension of formal prosecution against a suspect when the prosecutor feels that a judicial proceeding would not serve the best interests of the community or the offender. The courts get involved with diversion when they use civil commitment for individuals who might benefit from hospital treatment. However, the constitutionality of civil commitment procedures is currently being questioned, and their continued use is in doubt. A more common and reasonable use of diversion by the courts is the pretrial intervention program. These programs use both paid workers and community volunteers to provide counseling, employment services, and education to defendants who are eligible based on such factors as sex, age, residence, employment status, present charge, pretrial release status, and prior record.

Diversion programs all have the same goal—provide a reasonable alternative to incarceration in large, punitively oriented prisons. Most programs now in effect are informal responses to ambiguous legislation. Thus, the value of such programs is difficult, if not impossible, to estimate. For the programs to succeed, the goals, methods, and procedures of diversion must be articulated and integrated into the rest of the criminal justice system. And procedures for operating and evaluating diversion programs must be developed.

Diverson programs are most effective when they are integrated into a community-based correctional system with alternative levels of supervision and custody. Converting informal programs into formalized, accountable programs must be done without creating rigidity and inflexibility. If controls over community-based programs are too restrictive, the programs will become "institutions without walls." Diversion should be seen as the threshold of the community corrections system and designed to remove as many offenders as possible from the criminal process *before* conviction and criminalization occur.

Alcohol and drug abuse programs

Detoxification centers In *Robinson* v. *California* (370 U.S. 660 [1962]), the U.S. Supreme Court held that a California statute making it a criminal offense to be addicted to a narcotic drug was unconstitutional because it amounted to cruel and unusual punishment. The decision was based on a view of addiction as an illness rather than a crime. The argument of cruel and unusual punishment was also applied in the lower court cases of *Driver* v. *Hinnant* (356 F.2d 761 [1966]) and *Easter* v. *District of Columbia* (361 F.2d 50 [1966]). In the latter case, chronic alcoholism was allowed as a defense to a charge of public intoxication.

In *Powell* v. *Texas* (392 U.S. 514 [1968]), the U.S. Supreme Court upheld the conviction of a chronic alcoholic charged with public intoxication. However, the vote in the case was 5:4, and the opinions indicate that the court might decide differently in a future case involving the same constitutional questions. At any rate, the trend had been set by these cases and by the findings and recommendations of several commissions, including the President's Commission on Law Enforcement and Administration of Justice (1967).

The recognition of alcoholism as a disease rather than a crime was furthered in 1973 by the drafting of the Uniform Alcoholism and Intoxication Treatment Act by the National Conference of Commissioners on Uniform State Laws. Guided by this model, several states passed laws to decriminalize public intoxication and to remove its control from the criminal justice system. As in the case of Florida's Myers Act (also known as the Comprehensive Alcoholism Prevention, Control, and Treatment Act), these laws treat alcoholism as a disease rather than as a crime and seek to provide treatment for the alcoholic.

The rationale behind these laws was put into action in 1966 when the St. Louis (Missouri) Police Department opened the nation's first *civil detoxification center*. A federal demonstration grant provided the financing, and a standing order from the chief of police codified the new procedure. An arrested drunk is now offered the choice between criminal processing and "voluntary" detoxification (Nimmer 1971). If a qualified offender chooses detoxification (a person who requires hospitalization for a physical disease or someone charged with a serious crime does not qualify), he or she is transported to the detoxification center for a seven-day stay. A summons charging the "patient" with public drunkeness and setting a court date is left with the center's staff. If the person completes the seven-day program, the summons is torn up on his or her release. If the person leaves the center against medical advice, the criminal process is resumed and the patient-offender is prosecuted for drunkenness.

The St. Louis program continues to operate under these guidelines. It offers emergency medical care of the highest quality, but it reaches only a fraction of those who could benefit from it. In addition, it provides no effective aftercare for the patient-offender following detoxification. This program has succeeded in conserving court time and jail space—but that is about all. No convincing evidence has been produced to show that the

Public drunkenness is seen increasinsgly as a problem for civil detoxification rather than arrest. Courtesy Harry Wilkes/Stock, Boston.

program has intervened successfully in the degenerative, repetitive life cycles of most of its patients.

DWI offenses Public drunkenness is primarily a public nuisance; offenders are rarely violent and their prosecution is often a matter of aesthetic, rather than criminal, concern. Drunk driving, on the other hand, is a serious offense. The gravity of the problem is not conveyed by the number of arrests for "driving while under the influence" (DWI)—although such offenses reached a record high nationwide of 947,100 in 1975. Of greater concern is the fact that more than 50 percent of the nation's traffic fatalities in a given year (25,000 to 30,000) occur in accidents that directly or indirectly involve alcohol consumption. Although the official designation of "driving while under the influence" does not distinguish between alcohol and narcotics, alcohol consumption accounts for the overwhelming majority of DWI arrests.

To cope with the highway carnage caused by the drunk driver, the U.S. Department of Transportation, through the National Highway Safety Administration, initiated the Alcohol Safety Action Project (ASAP) in 1966. ASAP is a series of twenty-one countermeasures that involve law enforcement agencies, courts, schools, and the media in an effort to enlist support for various programs. Included in ASAP is DWI Counterattack, an eight-hour course for drunk drivers enrolled by the court. The course teaches about the effects of alcohol on the body and attempts to change attitudes about drinking while driving. In some jurisdictions, people arrested for DWI offenses are given the option to have adjudication withheld on the condition that they attend a DWI Counterattack course.

Addiction treatment The National Advisory Commission on Criminal Justice Standards and Goals (1973) suggests a multimodality approach to drug treatment. The commission recommends crisis intervention and drug emergency centers, facilities and personnel for methadone maintenance, facilities and personnel for narcotics antagonist programs; therapeutic community programs staffed entirely or largely by ex-addicts; closed and open residential treatment facilities, and halfway houses staffed primarily by residents.

Crisis intervention and emergency treatment programs Crisis intervention and emergency treatment programs supply addicts with emergency medical aid and psychological services—such as hot-line telephones and counseling.

Methadone maintenance Addicts treated by methadone maintenance receive a daily oral dose of methadone, usually in a controlled clinical setting (Nelkin 1973). Addicts receive increasing amounts of methadone until they reach a dose regarded as sufficient to provide a cross-tolerance that will block the euphoric effects of heroin. However, because methadone does not dull depression or anxiety (as heroin does), this treatment is only successful if addicts are highly motivated to give up heroin.

Residents of Synonon, a residential treatment center for drug addicts. Courtesy Brooks/Cole Publishing Co., Monterey, CA.

The commission considers methadone maintenance to be a more satisfactory method of treatment than the heroin maintenance system used in Great Britain. As Nelkin points out, "Unlike heroin, methadone is absorbed effectively through the gastrointestinal tract and is effective for a full 24 house. It is, therefore, administered orally only once a day" (1973, p. 38). Also, the addict does not require increasingly larger doses of methadone to remain comfortable, and the symptoms of methadone withdrawal are less intense than the symptoms of heroin withdrawal. The possibility of complete withdrawal from methadone remains uncertain, however. One study claims that methadone withdrawal is harmless, with little danger of severe physical reaction; but many programs have had only limited success withdrawing patients that were stabilized on methadone.

Methadone maintenance has been criticized because it offers only a medical solution to a complex social, political, and psychological problem. It has also been argued that, because methadone does not produce euphoria, addicts will seek other drugs. Another problem is the illegal use of methadone: if a stabilized addict is allowed to take home a small supply, the drug may fall into the hands of addicts not participating in the maintenance program.

Narcotic antagonist treatment programs Narcotic antagonist treatment programs use chemotherapy to block the effects of heroin and other narcotics. The goal is to create a pharmacological state, whereby the effect of any narcotic is nullified. The ultimate aim is to stop all drug use.

Therapeutic communities In the drug-free environment of therapeutic communities, the drug user is viewed as an underdeveloped, immature personality. Residents are expected to remain in therapeutic communities for extended periods of time, ranging from eighteen months to two years or more. These communities have been criticized on the grounds that only a small number of their residents are successfully rehabilitated.

Residential treatment facilities The commission recommends that residential treatment facilities include both closed and open centers and halfway houses. Closed facilities provide a therapeutic environment in which an addict can live free of drug use—with the help of constraints such as locked doors. Open centers have the same basic services as closed centers, but they lack physical (and other) restraints to keep residents inside. Halfway houses provide lodging and support services for residents making the transition from an institutional setting to the open community. These houses are also available to persons already in the community who require temporary support.

Community correctional centers

The essential element in successful community-based corrections is the coordination of activities and services for *all* offenders. Presently, most programs function as separate entities under separate branches of government. However, there are a number of community-based facilities that approach an integrated community correctional center. Such centers are generally open institutions located in the community and using community resources to provide services. The centers can be used for a variety of purposes, including detention, treatment, holding, and prerelease. One type of facility that can be developed into an integrated center is the jail.

A community correctional center derived from an existing jail would provide residential care to four major categories of inmates: persons awaiting trial, persons serving sentences, persons leaving major institutions, and short-term returnees. These inmates would use the center only after the court has taken advantage of all diversionary and alternative procedures—such as release on personal recognizance, release under supervision, and use of summons and warrants by the police. In the treatment of pretrial inmates, it must be remembered that these individuals have not been found guilty of a crime. Thus, no phase in their treatment should imply guilt. In the 1970 jail census, 52 percent of the jail population had not been convicted but was awaiting arraignment or trial. This indicates the magnitude of the problem in providing services and programs to this group. Nonconvicted detainees should be separated from convicted offenders and from persons who are mentally or physically ill. And various types of security and treatment should be provided.

The community correctional center can also benefit the sentenced offender. Jails traditionally confine misdemeanants, and felons are sentenced to state prisons. However, there is reason to believe that it might be effective to treat nondangerous felons the way misdemeanants are treated. But this theory is probably too advanced for most jurisdictions, and it is probable that most community correctional centers will continue to handle only minor offenders and misdemeanants. Nevertheless, some jurisdictions have tried more imaginative methods of handling the convicted offender—methods such as work release, study release, and weekend sentencing. Jurisdictions with small halfway houses might consider using these facilities for some categories of jailed offenders.

The community correctional center permits programs that are found in many contemporary halfway-*out* and halfway-*in* houses. Offenders preparing for release from state institutions may be transferred to community centers, where they can be gradually reintegrated into the mainstream. Released ex-offenders might also use the centers to obtain help and guidance instead of reverting to criminal behavior. This two-way function is in line with attempts to reduce involuntary returns to control. The model is used widely in the mental health field, where outpatient service and temporary voluntary recommitment have helped some offenders to avoid major problems and to receive more effective treatment.

The community correctional center is a reasonable alternative to the traditional jail and it is an important move toward the integration of all correctional services within a state or region. For these centers to be effective, they must include accurate observation of the individual, intensive staff-client interaction, opportunities for reality confrontation and reality testing, discussions, some element of choice, positive leisure-time options, optimal living and constructive learning situations, and community and group interaction.

Summary

The answer to correctional problems is not to close down all the prisons; this approach does not take all factors into account. When we speak of alternatives to incarceration, we refer to a carefully selected group of convicted or accused offenders. The primary goal of the correctional system is to protect the public. All programs must be designed with that goal in mind, or they will be doomed to early failure and public rejection.

It must not be forgotten that crime and violence cause public fear, concern, and overreaction. Overselling community-based programs as a panacea for *all* offenders leads the public to think that those who *will* benefit from such programs will be thrown together with those who *will not*. Newspaper headlines seldom point out that most recidivists come from institutions, and the public usually favors sterner policies for *all* offenders. If community programs are oversold, public reaction might well result in all offenders being locked up, regardless of the cost. If this happens, public fear might cause a shift backward toward a hard-line attitude about corrections. A proper balance between small, humane, and program-oriented maximum security institutions and community-based programs must be maintained for the foreseeable future. Until we develop effective programs for offenders who are so drug-dependent, violent, or disadvantaged that they can not be helped, we must have some method to keep society safe. The remaining offenders, however, should be given more opportunities for participation in community-based programs.

The criminal justice system needs as many alternatives to incarceration as possible for the offender who presents little, if any, danger to the community. Other offenders may have to remain in maximum security institutions until new and effective ways of treating them are found. Institutions can be made more humane, however, with an orientation toward treatment and with closer ties to the community. Community members should be encouraged to come into institutions, where their presence will provide models of behavior for inmates and will help establish ties with offenders who must remain incarcerated. The prison, in a modified form, still has a valuable place in the correctional system for that 15 to 20 percent of convicted offenders who require this level of control. For the great majority of convicted and diverted offenders, however, partial or total alternatives to incarceration are more reasonable.

As mentioned earlier, proponents of community-based corrections often exaggerate their results. Many claims are being carefully examined and have not yet been proven valid; most programs examined seem to be about as effective as institutional programs. And if community-based programs are no more effective than institutional programs, is it worth the cost and effort to use a community-based system? Or is it more realistic to continue using the institution? From a financial standpoint, the answer to the first question would probably be yes. In a Des Moines, Iowa, project, it was found that residential corrections were approximately four times *cheaper* than on-going institutional programs (Smykla, 1981). The cost differential is even more pronounced for community-based programs that do not require a residential facility.

When the savings are clear and the protection afforded the public is equal to or better than that provided by institutions, the shift from institutional to community corrections can be made. It has been clearly shown that community-based treatment is more humane and that it relieves the offender of the burden of institutionalization. It has also been demonstrated that offenders placed in fortresslike prisons are subject to physical danger, a loss of ties to the community, and reduced self-esteem. A system that avoids these problems, that is cheaper, more—or at least equally—effective, and keeps the offender in the community is hard to fault. For these reasons, the movement toward community corrections has gained great support in the past decade.

issue paper

COMMUNITY CORRECTIONS—IN ANYONE'S COMMUNITY BUT OURS!

Putting the "community" in community corrections has been opposed wherever it has been tried. As Krajick observes:

> People do not want criminals on their block almost anywhere in America. Community resistance to the opening of halfway house facilities has emerged as a central issue in community corrections; it has forced more slowdowns and compromises in the development of residential community corrections programs than any other factor (1980, p. 15).

Although community resistance is not unique to corrections—residential settings for the mentally ill, mentally retarded, and even the elderly have faced antagonism from civic groups—it is likely to be the most vehement. People may object to the presence of a residential center for old people on the grounds that it will depress property values, but their opposition to a halfway house is based on *fear*. They expect to be robbed, raped, burglarized, or murdered by the residents.

It does little good for a correctional administrator to point out that convicts on work release are usually carefully screened to eliminate violent offenders. As the superintendent of a prerelease center in New Jersey states, "You're never more than one step from an incident that could close you down." Unfortunately, crimes have been committed by inmates participating in community corrections:

1. In Pascagoula, Mississippi, an inmate escaped from a work release center in 1977 and raped the daughter of a state senator. Officials had to close the center for a few months until the heat from the crime died down.

2. In Tarpon Springs, Florida, an inmate left a work release center one night in 1977 and broke into a nearby house, where he raped and murdered an elderly woman. Nearby residents, mostly retired people, threatened to burn down the center. It stayed open, but admission standards were tightened.

3. In April 1977, residents of three different New York City work release centers committed a rape, a murder, and an armed robbery. As a result, legislature was quickly passed forbidding the department of corrections from sending anyone except property offenders with short records to these centers. There are very few such offenders in New York State prisons, so the number of New York inmates on work release has declined. Available spaces at the work release centers have remained unfilled because of a lack of eligible prisoners.

Faced with vigorous neighborhood opposition, correctional administrators have tried the "midnight cowboy" approach of slipping into a community without contacting anyone—in the hope that the facility will go unnoticed, or, at least, will not attract antagonism. Needless to say, this approach has not been successful. "If you don't involve the neighbors," says David Fogel, former head of the Minnesota Department of Corrections, "they're going to wake up one morning and see who came to breakfast—two murderers, two rapists, and six armed robbers" (Krajick 1980).

NOT ON MY BLOCK
K. Krajick Corrections Magazine

First they called Ray Messegee at home and threatened to cut him up with chain saws. Then the residents of the small town of Elbe, Washington, changed their minds. They decided they would hang him instead. Messegee, an administrator with the Washington Department of Corrections, has the job of trying to convince residents of towns like Elbe that they should host work release centers for convicted criminals. He received the calls soon after he proposed a center eight miles from Elbe. A few weeks later, after Messegee made his first pitch for the work release center, a gang of drunken loggers roared into a public meeting at the Elbe firehouse where Messegee was speaking. Outside, they had already threatened to tar and feather him, or perhaps to shoot him. Several loggers broke through a line of police officers inside the firehouse and one grabbed Messegee, screaming that he was going to "string him up" for bringing criminals into the town. Outside, rifle shots went off. Police and local officials calmed down the mob and no one was hurt. But Messegee got the idea: The people of Elbe did not want a work release center in their community. And they did not get one.

Reproduced from K. Krajick, "'Not on my block': Local Opposition Impedes the Search for Alternatives," *Corrections Magazine* 6 (1980):15. Copyright 1980 by Corrections Magazine and Criminal Justice Publications, Inc., 19 W. 34th St., New York, N.Y. 1001.

In Carbondale, Illinois, a two-story frame house selected as the site for a work release center was burned to the ground two weeks before its scheduled opening. Fire officials classified the blaze as arson, but there were no arrests. Nonviolent tactics were equally effective in closing a center in Chicago. When a work release center was opened in an inner city neighborhood over the objections of community residents, inspectors began showing up from nearly every city department to find violations in fire safety, building codes, sanitation, and other things covered by city ordinances. Corrections officials finally succumbed to the harassment and closed the center down.

In many cases, community resistance has driven correctional authorities to locate "community" facilities in business, commercial, or industrial areas, thus defeating the original purpose of the program. Usually, facilities end up in run-down, economically depressed, and blighted parts of the city—such as in an abandoned warehouse, a delapidated hotel that went out of business, or a former railroad station.

Corrections authorities have sought assistance from the National Training Institute for Community Residential Treatment Programs. The institute, under the direction of Rob Moran, is part of the International Halfway House Association. It offers forty-hour seminars for correctional administrators at various locations throughout the country. Sponsored by the National Institute of Corrections, these seminars devote eight hours to methods of dealing with community opposition. According to Krajick:

> Students are taught how to identify the formal and informal power bases in a community and how to contact them about the planned program. Much of the Institute's training prepares students to face a zoning board. "You have to know exactly what your answers will be to every conceivable question," says Moran. The seminar includes a mock zoning hearing.
>
> If the center is approved, advises Moran, the next step is to establish a community advisory board to serve as a channel for information about the center and to give the neighbors a sense that they have a degree of influence over its operation. And, says Moran, "you have to show the community that you have something to offer them—

some kind of tangible benefit to your being there. It can't just be take, take, take." To this end, many centers encourage inmates to cut grass or shovel snow for elderly or incapacitated neighbors, and to work in volunteer social service programs. Many centers strive to keep their buildings and yards as clean and well-decorated as possible so that the neighbors cannot complain about their appearance (1980, pp. 18–19).

Another approach that has had some success is contracting with private social service organizations to find sites, sponsor community programs, and operate centers. The YMCA and Salvation Army are especially popular as "front" organizations, because they enjoy a wholesome reputation. The U.S. Bureau of Prisons has been very active in this area. The federal prison system, which contracts with four hundred private and local agencies, has about three thousand inmates in halfway houses around the country.

At a time when policymakers are calling upon community corrections programs to provide alternatives to overcrowded prisons, it is distressing to find that the community approach has been all but abandoned in many jurisdictions—mostly because of community opposition. The importance and magnitude of the problem suggest that drastic measures will be required to improve the situation. We have had a variety of presidential commissions and task forces in the past to deal with various aspects of the crime problem; perhaps it is time to ask for yet another.

Discussion and review

1. What is meant by the contention that probation is a combination of treatment and punishment? Can such a combination be expected to work?
2. How does probation differ from a suspended sentence? What is "probation without adjudication"?
3. Discuss the process of revocation of probation. What are some of the issues raised by revocation?
4. How can we measure success or failure in probation? What alternatives are there to using recidivism as the primary variable?
5. What are some of the major problems in parole selection?
6. Discuss the pros and cons in the use of actuarial tables in parole selection. What is the Salient Factor Scale?
7. What are some of the advantages of contract parole?
8. How does California attempt to "separate the cop from the counselor" in its parole operations?
9. What are some arguments for abolishing parole? Do you think we are better off with or without a parole system?
10. Outline the advantages and disadvantages of community-based corrections. Is there any realistic way to overcome community resistance to correctional facilities in residential areas?

Glossary

Contract parole (Mutual Agreement Programming) System in which the parole board, correctional department, and inmate agree to a three-way contract in which the prisoner assumes responsibility for his or her own rehabilitation program, with the goal of obtaining parole release on a specific date.

Diversion Removal of offenders from the criminal justice system by channeling them into alternative programs; also describes the process of sentencing offenders to a community-based correctional program rather than to prison.

Furlough Temporary leave of absence given to an inmate housed in an institution; usually consists of a brief visit to the home or the community.

Halfway house A community correctional facility that provides a residence for convicted offenders who do not require the secure custody of a prison; also a transitional setting for prisoners being released from a correctional institution.

Parole Supervision of an offender in the community before expiration of his or her sentence. If parole conditions are violated, parole may be revoked and the offender may be returned to the institution for the remainder of the sentence.

Probation A form of sentencing that allows the offender to remain free in the community under supervision and subject to conditions set by the court; violation of these conditions may lead to revocation.

Shock parole (Probation) System in which an offender is imprisoned for a brief period of time (to acquaint him or her with the rigors of incarceration), after which he or she is released under supervision.

Work release Temporary release from prison to work in the community. Persons on work release may reside at a facility within the community or they may commute from the prison to their work site.

References

Allen, H. E., Carlson, E. W., and Parks, E. C. *Critical Issues in Adult Probation.* Washington, D.C.: U.S. Government Printing Office, 1979.

Barnes, H. E., and Teeters, N. K. *New Horizons in Criminology.* Englewood Cliffs, N.J.: Prentice-Hall, 1959.

Carter, R. M., and Wilkins, L. T. *Probation, Parole, and Community Corrections.* New York: Wiley, 1976.

Citizens Inquiry on Parole and Criminal Justice, Inc. *Prison Without Walls: Report on New York Parole.* New York: Praeger, 1975.

DiCerbo, E. C. "When Should Probation Be Revoked?" *Federal Probation* 30 (1966): 11–17.

Epstein, R., et al. *The Legal Aspects of Contract Parole.* College Park, Maryland: The American Correctional Association, 1976.

Frank, B., ed. *Contemporary Corrections.* Reston, Va.: Reston, 1973.

Glaser, D. *The Effectiveness of a Prison and Parole System.* Indianapolis, Ind.: Bobbs-Merrill, 1964.

Griswold, H. J., Misenheimer, M., Powers, A., and Tromanheiser, E. *An Eye For an Eye.* New York: Holt, Rinehart and Winston, 1970.

Keve, P. W. *Corrections.* New York: Wiley, 1981.

Krajick, K. "Probation: The Original Community Program." *Corrections Magazine* 6 (1980): 7–13.

Morris, N. *The Future of Imprisonment.* Chicago: University of Chicago Press, 1974.

Murchek, P. "Probation Without Adjudication." Paper delivered at the 18th annual Southern Conference on Corrections, Tallahassee, Florida, 25-27 February 1973.

National Advisory Commission on Criminal Justice Standards and Goals. *Corrections.* Washington, D.C.: U.S. Government Printing Office, 1973.

National Council on Crime and Delinquency, Research Center West. "National Probation Reports Feasibility Study on *NPR National Aggregate Probation Data Inquiry.*" *Probation in the U.S.: 1979.* San Francisco: National Council on Crime and Delinquency, 1981.

Nelkin, D. *Methadone Maintenance: A Technological Fix.* New York: George Braziller, 1973.

Nimmer, D. *Two Million Unnecessary Arrests.* Chicago: American Bar Association, 1971.

Porter, E. M. "Criteria for Parole Selection." *Proceedings of the American Correctional Association.* New York: American Correctional Association, 1958.

President's Commission on Law Enforcement and Administration of Justice. *Task Force Report: Corrections.* Washington, D.C.: U.S. Government Printing Office, 1967.

Reid, S. T. *The Correctional System: An Introduction.* New York: Holt, Rinehart and Winston, 1981.

Sacks, H. R., and Logan, C. H. *Does Parole Make a Difference?* Storrs, Conn.: School of Law Press, University of Connecticut, 1979.

Smith, R. M., McKee, J. M., and Milan, M. A. "Study-Release Policies of American Correctional Agencies: A Survey." *Journal of Criminal Justice*[2] (1974): 357–63.

Smykla, J.O. *Community-Based Corrections: Principles and Practices.* New York: Macmillan, 1981.

Cases

Driver v. *Hinnant* 356 F.2d 761 (4th Cir. 1966).
Easter v. *District of Columbia* 361 F.2d 50 (D.C. Cir. 1966).
Powell v. *Texas* 392 U.S. 514, 88 S.Ct. 2145, 20 L.Ed.2d 1254 (1968).
Robinson v. *California* 370 U.S. 660, 82 S.Ct. 1417 (1962).

16
juvenile justice

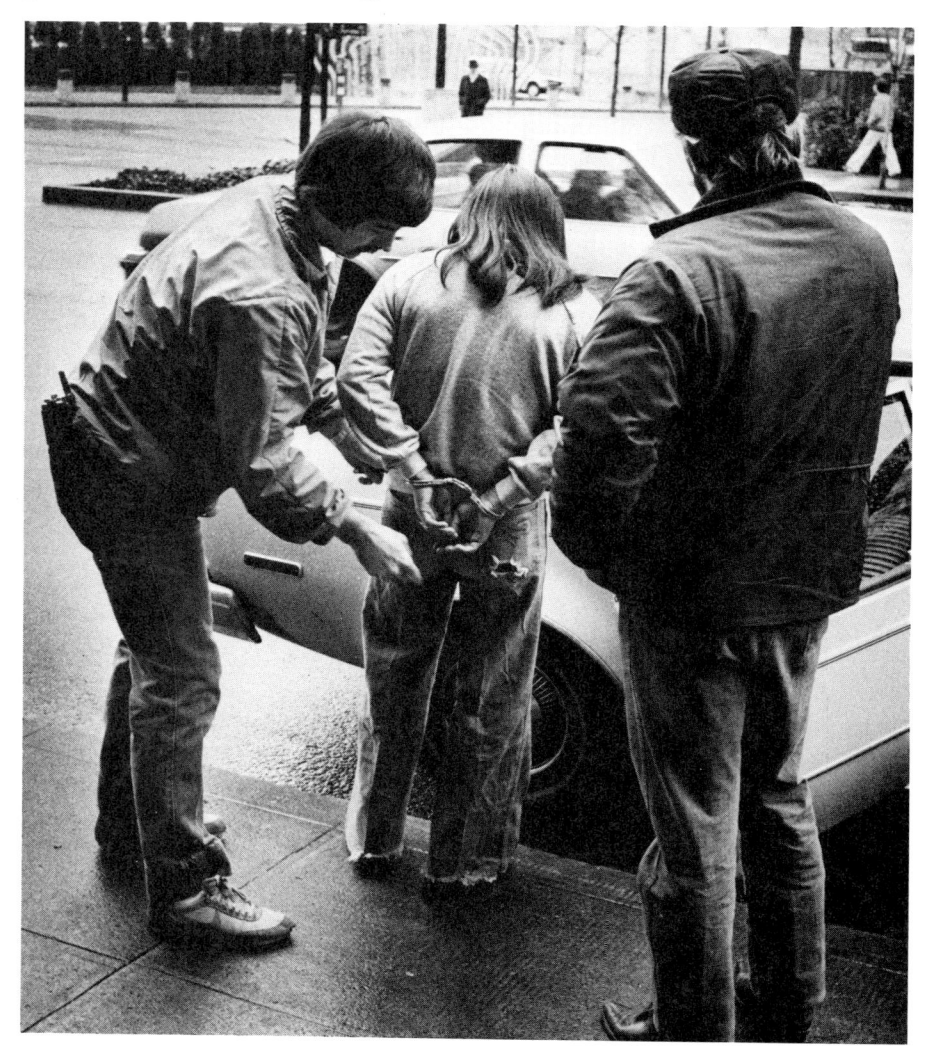

The creation of delinquency
Development of the juvenile court
The first courts: 1899 to 1967
Where we are today
Language of the courts
Types of juveniles handled by the system
Police contact and intake
Postadjudication alternatives
Correctional programs
Community-based programs
    Residential programs
    Nonresidential programs
Training schools
    Contemporary institutions
    Training schools of the future
Prevention and diversion
Prevention
    Community reorganization
    Education
    Employment
    Recreation
Diversion
    The police
    Intake and the courts
    Programs outside the juvenile justice system
    Youth service bureaus
    Runaway programs
Community supervision
Juvenile probation
Juvenile aftercare
The quality of supervision
Revocation
Evaluating the programs
Violent juvenile offenders
Violence in the schools
Intervention
Lock 'em up—give up—try harder
Summary
Issue paper: Waiver and certification—trying juveniles in adult court

SINCE the 1970s, the general public in the United States has believed that juvenile crime is out of control, that juveniles are responsible for most serious crimes committed (especially crimes of violence), and that juvenile offenses are rising at a spectacular rate each year. Official crime statistics indicate that this belief may be justified with regard to *adult* crime, but that it is not supported by figures for *juvenile* crime (*Uniform Crime Reports* 1982). Between 1977 and 1981, violent crimes committed by persons under the age of eighteen increased 3.9 percent, but property crimes committed by juveniles *decreased* 11.3 percent during the same period. Offense rates for adults rose in both categories.

But these figures are not grounds for complacency. Juveniles may not be committing crimes as frequently as the public believes, but they are still responsible for a substantial number of violent crimes and serious property offenses. In 1981, 20 percent of all crimes cleared by arrest were committed by persons under eighteen; 623,018 crimes were committed by youngsters fifteen years old or younger in the United States (**table 16.1**). According to the *Uniform Crime Reports* (1982), juveniles accounted for 29 percent of all robberies, 43 percent of all burglaries, and 40 percent of all motor vehicle thefts committed in 1981.

The juvenile offender is generally handled in a system distinct from the rest of the criminal justice system. Until recently, the courts that dealt with juvenile cases had few of the features generally associated with a judicial tribunal. The orientation of the courts was toward treatment; there was relatively little concern for determining guilt or innocence of the juvenile through traditional court procedures. Under a guiding philosophy called *parens patriae*, judges were expected to act as "kind and loving parents" and to do whatever they could to direct juvenile offenders toward socially acceptable conduct. The approach was designed to spare the youngster the punishment and stigma of criminality.

Some critics point out that, although the original objectives of this approach were laudable in theory, they simply could not be achieved in practice. Thus, the juvenile court was doomed to failure because it assumed responsibilities that far exceeded its resources: it tried to take the place of a failed educational system, a broken home, or the collapse of informal social control formerly carried out by the neighborhood.

Other critics are concerned with the inability of the juvenile justice system to deal with juveniles who commit serious felony offenses such as murder, rape, robbery, assault, and arson. Juvenile court authorities like Judge Seymour Gelber of Dade County, Florida, maintain that the juvenile court is no longer relevant to today's juvenile criminals, especially those charged with crimes against the person. When one encounters a hulking fifteen-year-old in juvenile detention who is charged with forcible rape and homicide and learns that this is the "child" named in the juvenile court petition—the juvenile court equivalent of indictment—it is difficult to believe that this is the kind of client the founders of the juvenile justice system had in mind. And it does not help much that the terms *delinquent* and *criminal* are widely used as though they were synonymous.

TABLE 16.1 Total index crime arrests in 1981 of persons under the age of twenty-five

Offense charged	Total arrests, all ages	Number of persons arrested				Percent of total arrests			
		Under 15	Under 18	Under 21	Under 25	Under 15	Under 18	Under 21	Under 25
Total	10,293,575	623,018	2,035,748	3,775,581	5,629,422	6.1	19.8	36.7	54.7
Murder and nonnegligent manslaughter	20,432	205	1,858	4,880	8,829	1.0	9.1	23.9	43.2
Forcible rape	30,050	1,193	4,449	9,254	15,593	4.0	14.8	30.8	51.9
Robbery	147,396	10,250	42,214	74,983	104,807	7.0	28.6	50.9	71.1
Aggravated assault	266,948	10,458	37,332	74,875	125,352	3.9	14.0	28.0	47.0
Total violent crimes	464,826	22,106	85,853	163,992	254,581	4.8	18.5	35.3	54.8
Burglary	489,533	71,782	208,650	312,089	387,077	14.7	42.6	63.8	79.1
Larceny-theft	1,197,845	172,064	417,346	620,134	790,649	14.4	34.8	51.8	66.0
Motor vehicle theft	122,188	11,913	49,449	74,087	93,195	9.7	40.5	60.6	76.3
Arson	19362	5,014	8,210	10,658	13,044	25.9	42.4	55.0	67.4
Total property crime	1,828,928	260,773	683,655	1,016,968	1,283,965	14.3	37.4	55.6	70.2
Crime index total	2,293,754	282,879	769,508	1,180,960	1,538,546	12.3	33.5	51.5	67.1

Data from U.S. Department of Justice, *Uniform Crime Reports 1981* (Washington, D.C.: U.S. Government Printing Office, 1982), p. 177, by permission of the U.S. Department of Justice.

THE FAILED SYSTEM

The juvenile justice system . . . evolved over the past several decades on the theory that there is no such thing as a bad boy, or at least none beyond salvage. However, horrendous his crime, he is still fit for rehabilitation, given time and patience. If he is underage, he is usually not photographed and rarely fingerprinted. Records of his crimes are kept confidential and then destroyed after he becomes a legal adult. He is thus reborn with a *tabula rasa*—no evidence whatsoever of his misconduct. James Higgins, a juvenile judge in New Haven, reflects the attitude of many apologists for the system. "We treat delinquency," he says, "as a civil inquiry into the doings of a child. The court does not consider the child a criminal—irresponsible, perhaps, but not a criminal."

When a cherubic lad of nine was brought into a Washington, D.C. court for crippling an old woman by pushing her down a flight of stairs, the judge told the prosecutor: "I'm sorry, but nothing you can say will convince me that child is guilty." Complains Robert M. Ross, a former assistant corporation counsel in Washington: "Some judges and prosecutors have told me they thought a third to a half of all juvenile cases could be solved simply by sitting the kid down and giving him a stern lecture." That attitude might have served well in the halcyon days of Huck Finn and Penrod, when pranks were the principal business before the courts. Says Judge Seymour Gelber of Dade County, Florida: "The juvenile courts weren't conceived for the brutal act. They were created with the image of Middle America."

Aside from the shaky assumptions on which it rests, the juvenile court is notoriously inefficient. . . . Cases are backed up in the overburdened, understaffed system. Complainants and witnesses, who are nervous to begin with and sometimes threatened by the offenders, become exasperated with waiting and walk out. Case dismissed.

Even if the case proceeds, the deck is stacked in favor of the defendant. A juvenile may not be able to read or write but he can recite his *Miranda* rights without pausing for breath. When he is arrested, his main effort—and his laywer's—is to get the case thrown out on some technicality, and he often succeeds. In a San Francisco police squad room, the cops toss darts at an unusual board. Its rings are labeled: *Investigate further, Admonish, Cite,* and the bullseye is *Complaint withdrawn.* Police Lieut. George Rosko sums up the whole juvenile process: "It fosters the kid's belief that he can beat the system. He goes through the court, comes back to the neighborhood, and he's a hero."

From "The Youth Crime Plague," *Time,* 11 July 1977, pp. 25–26. Copyright 1977 Time Inc. All rights reserved. Reprinted by permission from TIME.

Fortunately, the juvenile courts now appear to be moving in a new direction (for reasons we explore later in this chapter). An increased emphasis on due process safeguards for the accused juvenile is helping to shape the juvenile court into something resembling a "junior criminal court." At the same time, in response to public demands for community protection, growing numbers of juveniles are being placed under the jurisdiction of the adult criminal justice system; many groups believe that the juvenile justice system can no longer handle serious youthful offenders. In the issue paper at the end of this chapter, we examine some of the problems raised by the certification or *transfer* of juveniles to the jurisdiction of adult criminal courts.

The creation of delinquency

Delinquency is a relatively new concept. Throughout the Middle Ages, and even as late as the seventeenth century, youths engaged in behavior that today would probably result in their adjudication as delinquent—and their parents would probably be charged with contributing to the delinquency of minors. Many children, as soon as they could talk, used obscene language, drank without restriction in taverns and at home, had sexual experiences freely or under duress, rarely attended school and, when they did, carried arms and fought duels (Empey 1976). Today, however, most people feel that this kind of behavior should be curbed among juveniles.

This change in attitude toward youthful behavior resulted from a change in the conception of childhood and children. In the late sixteenth and early seventeenth centuries, it was widely believed that children require distinctive preparation to become productive members of the community. This view influenced the development of schools, whose function was to assist parents in providing both intellectual and moral training. If children were to attend school, the period of childhood had to be extended, a circumstance that justified restricting children's behavior on the grounds that they were too immature or too naive to engage in certain behaviors. Initially, this conception of childhood influenced mostly the middle class: lower class and minority children were not affected until the nineteenth or early twentieth century.

During the early 1800s, institutions for children called "houses of refuge" were established to combat the negative influences of inadequate families and disorganized communities. Designed to serve as family substitutes, these facilities supplied the discipline, affection, and training that parents were not able, predisposed, or available to provide. At the New York House of Refuge,

> ... the first bells rang at sunrise to wake the youngsters, the second came fifteen minutes later to signal the guards to unlock the individual cells. The inmates stepped into the hallways and then, according to the manager's description, "marched in order to the washroom ... from the washroom they are paraded in open air (the weather permitting), where they are arranged in ranks, and undergo a close and critical inspection as to cleanliness and dress." Inmates next went in formation to chapel for prayer ... and afterwards spent one hour in school. At seven o'clock the bells announced breakfast and then, a half hour later, the time to begin work. The boys spent until noon in the shops, usually making brass nails or cane seats, while the girls washed, cooked, and made and mended the clothes. "At twelve o'clock," officials reported, "a bell rings to call all from work, and one hour is allowed for washing ... and dinner. ... At one o'clock a signal is given for recommencing work, which continues to five o'clock in the afternoon, when the bell rings for the termination of the labor day." There followed thirty minutes to wash and eat, two and a half hours of evening classes and, finally to end the day, evening prayers. "The children," concluded the Refuge account, "ranged in order, and are marched to the Sleeping Halls where each takes possession of a separate compartment, and the cells are locked, and silence is enforced for the night" (New York House of Refuge, *Seventh Annual Report*, pp. 253–55, as cited by Rothman 1971, pp. 225-226).

Although these child-saving institutions were thought by reformers to hold great promise for changing the behavior of wayward youth, they became—in reality—places to house the youthful misfits of society. In light of the discipline, regimen, and living conditions that characterized these institutions, it is not surprising that they did little to change the conduct of their charges. (Punishment included increased work loads, loss of play periods, a diet of bread and water, solitary confinement, wearing a ball and chain, and whippings.) By 1850, these institutions were not producing children who would become upstanding members of the community, but instead were turning out children who—at best—thought, marched, and otherwise behaved like robots.

But other conditions overshadowed these negative results, making the need for child-saving facilities even more critical. The latter part of the nineteenth century brought rapid urban growth, an influx of immigrants, and a marked increase in social instability (Empey 1978). Immigrants who arrived in the United States were generally poor and lived in deteriorated areas with high rates of crime and delinquency. Their patterns of behavior—sexual, marital, and linguistic—viewed as deviant, thus providing a rationale for treating them as inferior and as threats to the social order. Further, the theories of Charles Darwin, as applied to social life, provided justification for regarding immigrants as *biologically* inferior.

Out of these views on the immigrant community emerged two major themes that had important implications for the continued institutionalization of children. One focused on the "disruptive" conditions of life in industrial urban slums; the second, heavily influenced by Darwin's ideas, attributed crime to biological factors. If crime could be ascribed to social conditions such as poverty and family instability, then these factors could possibly be changed—or at least their more adverse influences could be mitigated—by subjecting affected persons to countervailing influences. On the other hand, however, despite the contention by some authorities that crime is rooted in biological factors, human behavior was still considered to be susceptible to environmental influence. Nevertheless, these two themes underscored the need for institutions designed to counter adverse biological and social influences.

During this same era, groups of middle-class women became preoccupied with the so-called child-saving movement. Appalled by the depraved conditions of life in urban slums, these women sought to establish institutions to reverse negative influences and give youngsters a chance to become conventional members of society. At this point, an interesting paradox existed: While it was recognized that the houses of refuge had failed to meet their objectives as "superparents," they were still seen as the only substitute for a natural home providing the education, discipline, and benign environment needed to counteract adverse biological and social factors. This issue was resolved by blaming the failure of these institutions on the methods they employed, rather than on the objectives themselves. This view required that new institutions be built.

The new facilities thus established were called industrial schools and reformatories. Industrial schools, which replaced the houses of refuge, were organized along the cottage or family system. Reformatories, originally intended to replace prisons, came to be used as institutions for youthful offenders convicted of crimes (their philosophy and programs were consistent with the views of the day on how youths should be handled).

Both the reformatory and the industrial school failed miserably. Although their objectives were sound, the methods employed were, in most cases, no better than those employed by the houses of refuge. Discipline was repressive and ranged from benevolent despotism to tyrannical cruelty (Teeters and Reinemann 1950). Floggings were common, but were among the less cruel punishments inflicted on youngsters. The regimen was rigid: mass formations and military drills were emphasized. The main program of reform involved long hours of tedious work. At industrial schools, the principal work was farm labor, which was of doubtful value to youngsters who returned to the city. In essence, these facilities differed from houses of refuge only in name and location.

The failure of these institutions after a century of experimentation with various juvenile facilities may be surprising, but a valuable lesson was learned; our experiences in the nineteenth century demonstrated the futility of trying to use institutions as a method of social control in periods of rapid social and ideological change. These early facilities provided only a temporary means of incapacitating dangerous offenders; they were not up to the task of socializing or redirecting youthful criminals. As Empey (1976) observes, even if there had been reformatories on every street corner, it is doubtful that they would have been able to do much to moderate the effects of industrialization, immigration, and urbanization, or to have served as surrogate parents and produced the same kind of person as would a nuclear family in a small rural community. Almost a century has passed since we first tried to devise urban institutions to provide justice and opportunity and to offset the problems faced by children in a pluralistic society. Unfortunately, time seems to have done little to improve our ability to deal with the situation, and we are far from encouraged about the future.

Despite the ineffectiveness of nineteenth-century methods of dealing with children, it must be noted that childhood had been recognized by the close of the century as a status distinct from adulthood—one that afforded its occupants exemptions from certain kinds of behavior expected of adults. Children were acknowledged as a distinct group that required not only different correctional facilities, but also regulations and laws to protect them against exploitation by our economic system. The recognition of these needs helped bring about the establishment of the juvenile court. (See **table 16.2** for a summary of developments in juvenile justice from 1646 to the present. **Table 16.3** lists various stages in the creation of the juvenile court.)

Development of the juvenile court

The first juvenile court was created in Chicago, Illinois, in 1899. In many respects, this court represented the dawn of a new era for our legal system. Previously, our court processes had the objectives of retribution and deterrence, and they gave little attention to individual differences. By the turn of the century, however, the teachings and research in the new area of social science began to impact on the legal system. It was recognized that differences existed between offenders, regardless of whether or not they

TABLE 16.2 Juvenile justice developments: 1646 to present

System (Period)	Major developments	Influences	Child-State relationship	Parent-State relationship	Parent-Child relationship
Puritan (1646–1824)	Massachusetts Stubborn Child Law (1646).	Christian view of child as evil; economically marginal agrarian society.	Law provides symbolic standard of maturity; support for family as economic unit.	Parents considered responsible for and capable of controlling child.	Child considered both property and spiritual responsibility of parents.
Refuge (1824–1899)	Institutionalization of deviants, New York House of Refuge established (1824) for delinquent and dependent children.	Enlightenment; immigration and industrialization.	Child seen as helpless, in need of state intervention.	Parents supplanted as state assumes responsibility for correcting deviant socialization.	Family considered to be a major cause of juvenile deviancy.
Juvenile court (1899–1960)	Establishment of separate legal system for juveniles—Illinois Juvenile Court Act (1899).	Reformism and rehabilitative ideology; increased immigration, urbanization, large-scale industrialization.	Juvenile court institutionalizes legal irresponsibility of child.	Parens Patriae doctrine gives legal foundation for state intervention in family.	Further abrogation of parents' rights and responsibilities.
Juvenile rights (1960–present)	Increased "legalization" of juvenile law—Gault decision (1966). Juvenile Justice and Delinquency Prevention Act (1974) calls for deinstitutionalization of status offender.	Criticism of juvenile justice system on humane grounds; civil rights movements by disadvantaged groups	Movement to define and protect rights as well as provide services to children.	Reassertion of responsibility of parents and community for welfare and behavior of children.	Attention given to children's claims against parents. Earlier emancipation of children.

Adapted from U.S. Department of Justice, Reports of the National Juvenile Assessment Centers, *A Preliminary National Assessment of the Status Offender and the Juvenile Justice System* (Washington, D.C.: U.S. Government Printing Office, 1980), p. 29, by permission of the U.S. Department of Justice.

had committed the same offense. This recognition implied that differences in physical and mental conditions, as well as in environmental influences, should be taken into account in judicial decisions. The result was the birth of "individualized justice."

To put the concept of individualized justice into operation, the courts had to examine a wide variety of psychological and social factors that had nothing to do with guilt or innocence in a strict legal sense. Consideration was given to the economic, social, cultural, and emotional factors that shape the individual and to data regarding the offender's education, career, family, employment record, and community environment. The purpose of this diagnosis was to provide information that could be used to determine the type of treatment needed by the offender.

TABLE 16.3 Antecedents of the juvenile court

1825	New York House of Refuge was opened, followed by houses in Boston (1826), Philadelphia (1828), and New Orleans (1845).
1831	Illinois passed a law that allowed penalties for certain offenses committed by minors to differ from the penalties imposed on adults.
1841	John Augustus inaugurated probation and became the nation's first probation officer.
1854	State industrial school for girls opened in Lancaster, Massachusetts (first cottage-type institution).
1858	State industrial school for boys in Lancaster, Ohio, adopted a cottage-type system.
1863	Children's Aid Society founded in Boston. Members of the organization attended police and superior court hearings, supervised youngsters selected for probation, and did the investigation on which probation selection was based.
1869	Law enacted in Massachusetts to direct State Board of Charities to send agents to court hearings that involved children. The agents made recommendations to the court that frequently involved probation and the placement of youngsters with suitable families.
1870	Separate hearings for juveniles were required in Suffolk County, Massachusetts. New York followed by requiring separate trials, dockets, and records for children; Rhode Island made similar provisions in 1891.
1899	In April, Illinois adopted legislation creating the first juvenile court in Cook County (Chicago). In May, Colorado established a juvenile court.

The first courts: 1899 to 1967

The establishment (by statute) of the first juvenile court in Illinois in 1899 marked the beginning of an era of "social jurisprudence" (Faust and Brantingham 1979). Although the juvenile court was a bona fide court, its procedures were dramatically different from adult court proceedings. The court's major objective was to help the wayward child become a productive member of the community. The determination of guilt or innocence, using standard rules of evidence, was not of primary importance. Instead, the purpose of the court hearing was to determine "What is he, how has he become what he is, and what had best be done in his interest and in the interest of the state to save him from a downward career" (ibid., p. 112). In other words, court procedures were to be more diagnostic than legal in nature, giving major consideration to the information obtained on the youngster's environment, heredity, as well as his physical and mental condition (Mack 1979).

The aim of the Illinois juvenile court was prevention and rehabilitation, not punishment. And youngsters who violated the law were called juvenile delinquents, not criminals; this term implied that the juveniles were wayward children in need of assistance from the court, their new "superparent." The juvenile court judges were to assume the "parental" role in an atmosphere less threatening than that of the adult criminal court—reviewing the behavior of youngsters, disciplining them when appropriate, and devising a course of action to prevent further delinquent behavior. To aid in these tasks, the court hired psychologists, psychiatrists, and social workers to prepare comprehensive reports on youngster's backgrounds and psychological characteristics. The goals and methods of the juvenile court remained essentially unchanged until 1967.

Where we are today

Given the basic commitment to rehabilitation rather than punishment, juvenile courts developed along the lines of social casework. Hearings were conducted in an informal atmosphere, and testimony and background data were introduced without regard to rules of evidence. In addition, the juvenile was denied many of the rights guaranteed by due process—including representation by counsel, confrontation with one's accuser, cross-examination, and the right to invoke the privilege against self-incrimination.

In *Kent* v. *United States* (383 U.S. 541, 546 [1966]), Justice Abe Fortas of the U.S. Supreme Court expressed concern that the guiding philosophy of the juvenile court—parens patriae—had not been realized. Youngsters were getting the worst of both worlds: they were denied the rights accorded adults, and they did not receive the care and treatment promised under the parens patriae doctrine.

The *Kent* decision raised many issues and paved the way for the Supreme Court to come to grips with these problems in the *Gault* decision (*In re Gault*, 387 U.S. 1 [1967]). Gerald Gault, a fifteen-year-old, was sentenced to confinement for the "remainder of his minority" (six years) for an offense that carried a maximum *adult* penalty of only two months. During hearings, Gault was deprived of most of the procedural rights afforded his adult counterparts. His appeal was heard by the U.S. Supreme Court on the following issues: right to notice of the charge, right to counsel, right to confrontation and cross-examination of witnesses, privilege against self-incrimination, right to a transcript of the proceedings, and right to an appellate review.

As a result of the *Kent*, *Gault*, and subsequent decisions (e.g., *In re Winship* [397 U.S. 358 (1970)]), the juvenile court process now has two distinct phases: an *adjudication phase*, which accords juveniles the same due process rights as adults, with the exception of a jury trial; and a *disposition phase* in which, following a determination of guilt, a treatment or rehabilitation plan is drawn up.

Language of the courts

The terms used in criminal courts have been changed to apply to juvenile justice. For example, "petition" replaces "complaint," "summons" replaces "warrant," "finding of involvement" replaces "conviction," and "disposition" replaces "sentencing." The words "child," "youth," and "youngster" are used synonymously to denote a person of juvenile court age. Juvenile court laws define a child as any person under a specified age no matter how mature or sophisticated he or she may seem. Juvenile jurisdictions in at least two thirds of the states define persons under eighteen as children; the other states also include youngsters between the ages of eighteen and twenty-one. The most significant terms used in the juvenile system are defined in **table 16.4.**

Types of juveniles handled by the system

As noted earlier, youngsters who break laws are not the only concern of juvenile authorities. Some children need the protection of the state just to fulfill the most basic needs of life. Such youngsters—referred to as *dependent children*—often come to the attention of the juvenile or family court because their parents have died and they can not receive adequate support from other family members. In other cases, children have to be taken away from parents or relatives for their own protection and welfare. For example, children may be subjected to sexual or physical abuse—the typical circumstances of the battered child. These *neglected children* (as they are referred to by the juvenile court) usually become the concern of authorities as a result of reports from neighbors, friends, or relatives. Even when they are severely abused, children tend to remain loyal to their parents; thus, neglect is seldom reported by the children themselves.

Delinquency itself takes two different patterns. The first type of delinquency includes those offenses that would be considered crimes if they were committed by adults. Burglary, larceny, and motor vehicle theft are examples of property crimes that fall into this category. The second category is *status offenses*—violations of statutes that apply exclusively to juveniles. Legislation for status offenses is often worded ambiguously. Phelps cites an example from section 601 of the California Welfare and Institutions Code:

> Any person under the age of 18 years who persistently or habitually refuses to obey the reasonable and proper orders or directions of his parents, guardian, custodian, or school authorities, or who is beyond the control of such person, or any person who is a habitual truant from school within the meaning of any law of this state, or who from any cause is in danger of leading an idle, dissolute, lewd, or immoral life, is within the jurisdiction of the juvenile court which may adjudge such person to be a ward of the court (1976, p. 37).

How does a youngster prove that he or she is not leading "an idle, dissolute, lewd, or immoral life"?

Juvenile justice authorities are sharply divided on the issue of who should have jurisdiction over status offenses. Those who wish to leave jurisdiction with the juvenile court argue that today's status offender is tomorrow's adult criminal, and that further acts of delinquency can not be prevented unless such juveniles are discovered. Their opponents maintain that "the processing of juveniles in the formal authoritarian agencies is likely to reinforce the pattern of delinquency which the system proposes to eradicate" (Phelps 1976, p. 38). These critics emphasize that the social services usually required to deal effectively with the problems of the status offender can be made available without formal adjudication.

TABLE 16.4 The language of juvenile and adult courts

Juvenile court term	Adult court term
Adjudication: decision by the judge that a child has committed delinquent acts.	Conviction of guilt
Adjudicatory hearing: a hearing to determine whether the allegations of a petition are supported by the evidence beyond a reasonable doubt.	Trial
Adjustment: the settling of a matter so that parties agree without official intervention by the court.	Plea bargaining
Aftercare: the supervision given to a child for a limited period of time after he or she is released from training school but while he or she is still under the control of the juvenile court.	Parole
Commitment: a decision by the judge to send a child to training school.	Sentence to imprisonment
Delinquent act: an act that if committed by an adult would be called a crime. The term does not include such ambiguities and noncrimes as "being ungovernable," "truancy," "incorrigibility," and "disobedience."	Crime
Deliquent child: a child who is found to have committed an act that would be considered a crime if committed by an adult.	Criminal
Detention: temporary care of an allegedly delinquent child who requires secure custody in physically restricting facilities pending court disposition or execution of a court order.	Holding in jail
Dispositional hearing: a hearing held subsequent to the adjudicatory hearing to determine what order of disposition should be made for a child adjudicated as delinquent.	Sentencing hearing
Hearing: the presentation of evidence to the juvenile court judge, his or her consideration of it, and his or her decision on disposition of the case.	Trial
Juvenile court: the court that has jurisdiction over children who are alleged to be or found to be delinquent. Juvenile delinquency procedures should not be used for neglected children or for those who need supervision.	Court of record
Petition: an application for a court order or some other judicial action. Hence, a "delinquency petition" is an application for the court to act in a matter involving a juvenile apprehended for a delinquent act.	Accusation or indictment
Probation: the supervision of a delinquent child after the court hearing but without commitment to training school.	Probation (with the same meaning as the juvenile court term)
Residential child care facility: a dwelling (other than a detention or shelter care facility) that is licensed to provide living accommodations, care, treatment, and maintenance for children and youth. Such facilities include foster homes, group homes, and halfway houses.	Halfway house
Shelter: temporary care of a child in physically unrestricting facilities pending court disposition or execution of a court order for placement. Shelter care is used for dependent and neglected children and minors in need of supervision. Separate shelter care facilities are also used for children apprehended for delinquency who need temporary shelter but not secure detention.	Jail
Take into custody: the act of the police in securing the physical custody of a child engaged in delinquency. The term is used to avoid the stigma of the word "arrest."	Arrest

Police contact and intake

As noted in **figure 16.1,** the police officer is usually the first representative of societal authority and the criminal justice system to come in contact with a youthful offender. According to the President's Commission on Law Enforcement and the Administration of Justice, "Contacts with police are the gateway into the system of delinquency and criminal justice," (1967, p. 420). Over a million youngsters have contact with the police each year, one third of whom appear in juvenile court.

Police contact with juveniles may result from juvenile involvement in serious offenses, disturbances, or status offenses. A substantial number of contacts occur just because juveniles are out and about—which brings them to the attention of officers on patrol. Because juveniles often move in groups, they seem more suspicious and more difficult to control. And because they tend to congregate at shopping plazas, street corners, fast-food operations, and the like, they may be the object of complaints requiring police attention.

Police have a variety of alternatives available to them in making dispositions in juvenile cases:

1. *Warn and Release.* In the case of a minor offense, a police officer may simply warn a youth not to engage in the same type of behavior again. The youth may be further advised that future violations will result in official action.

2. *Release and Report.* The juvenile may be released, but an official report will be prepared detailing the incident.

3. *Release to Parents.* A juvenile may be placed in the custody of his or her parents with just a warning or an official report. The Task Force on Juvenile Justice Delinquency Prevention (1976) recommends that the primary criterion for release to parents should be whether the juvenile is a threat to public safety. Another important consideration is the parents' ability to control and discipline their child (Kobetz and Bosarge 1973). This type of disposition is not suitable when the parent or guardian is indifferent to the youngster's criminal behavior or is unable to provide the concern and supervision the youngster needs to stay out of further difficulty.

4. *Agency Referral.* Depending on departmental policies, the availability of appropriate programs, and police awareness of community resources, juveniles may be referred to community-based social service agencies or welfare agencies. Police are in an ideal position to divert youths from the juvenile justice system to community agencies, where they can receive the help they need without the stigma associated with processing by the juvenile court. Typical police referrals are to youth service bureaus, special school programs, boy clubs, the YMCA, community mental health agencies, and drug programs.

5. *Juvenile Court Referral.* Depending upon the jurisdiction, a police officer can use several methods to bring a juvenile offender to the atten-

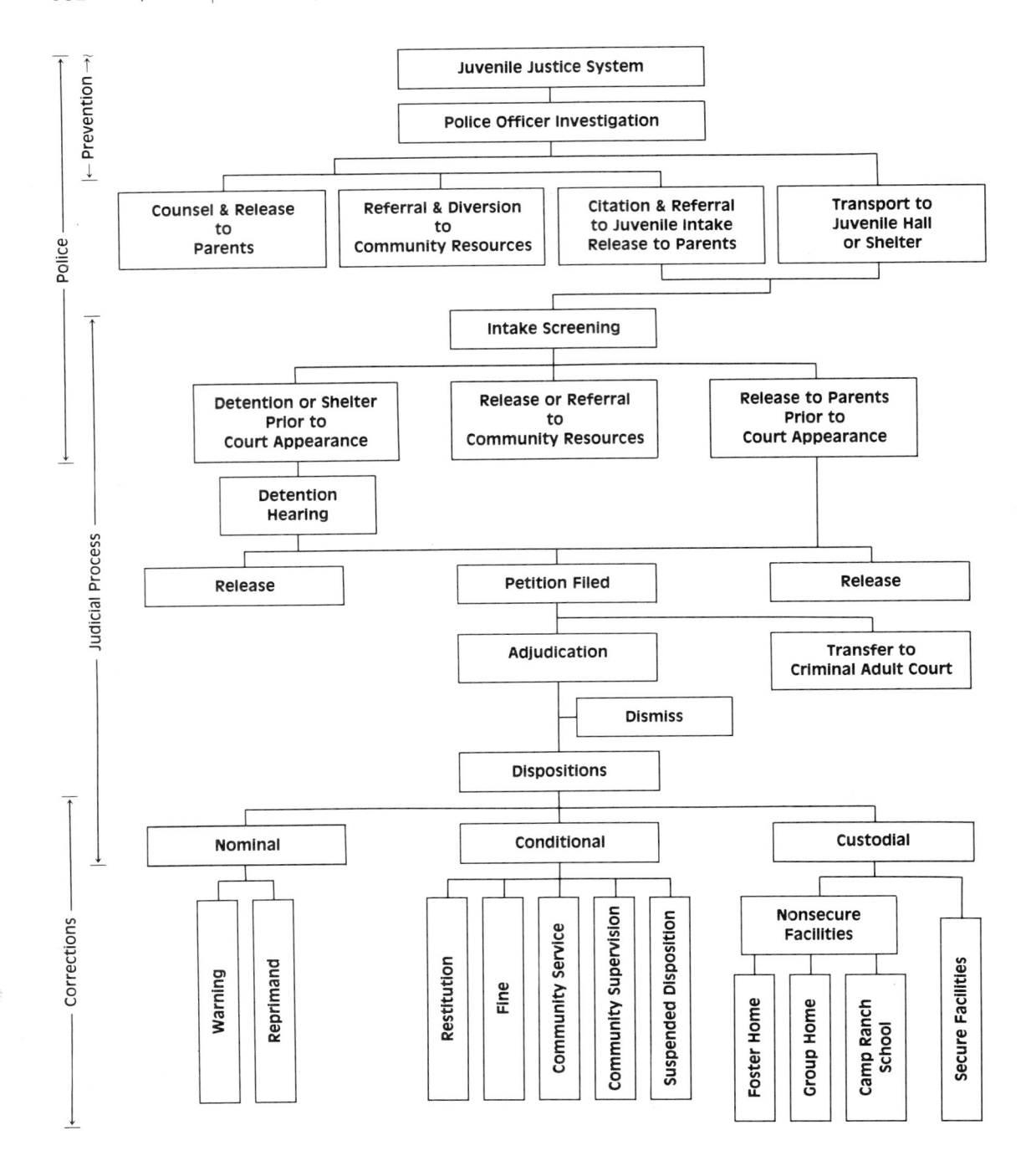

FIGURE 16.1 Procedures of the criminal justice system. Reprinted from the National Advisory Committee on Criminal Justice Standards and Goals, Task Force on Juvenile Justice and Delinquency Prevention, Report of the Task Force on Juvenile Justice and Delinquency Prevention (Washington, D.C.: U.S. Government Printing Office, 1976), p. 9, by permission of the U.S. Department of Justice.

tion of the juvenile court. Rather than taking a youngster into custody, for example, an officer can issue a citation or make a formal report to juvenile intake or the juvenile court and release the youngster to the custody of parents or guardians. The National Advisory Committee on Criminal Justice Standards and Goals (1976) recommends that police departments make maximum use of state statutes that permit police agencies to issue written citations and summons in lieu of taking the juvenile into custody. This recommendation is consistent with the committee's philosophy of using the least coercive alternative available to preserve public order, safety, and individual liberties. The police may also take a youngster into custody and deliver him or her to juvenile intake or detention.

Juveniles diverted from the system by the police are referred to the juvenile court intake unit, which is frequently staffed by probation officers. The primary purpose of intake is to determine if youngsters accused of criminal acts or status offenses should be diverted from the juvenile court. Intake officers consider a variety of factors in making this decision. First, they must decide if the juvenile falls within the jurisdiction of the court by virtue of his or her age, the place where the offense took place, and the nature of the offense itself. For example, a juvenile can be beyond a court's jurisdiction if he or she is above juvenile court age, has committed the offense in another jurisdiction, or is involved in behavior considered deviant but not prohibited by law.

In many jurisdictions, intake workers must also ascertain the legal sufficiency of the referred offense and determine if there is sufficient evidence to support the allegations of delinquent conduct. Following this, a decision is made whether or not to refer the case to the juvenile court. In making this decision, intake workers consider the seriousness and time of day of the alleged offense; the type of neighborhood where the youth lives; and the youth's age, attitude toward authority, involvement in religious activities, prior court and police contacts, home environment, school record, reaction to sanctions previously imposed, and present interests and activities. In recent years, the intake function has taken on increasing importance because of the dual emphasis on diverting as many youths as possible, while at the same time protecting the community.

After an assessment of the legal and social factors associated with the case, the intake worker must decide on an appropriate disposition: outright dismissal, informal adjustment, informal probation, consent decrees, or filing of a petition. Complaints are dismissed if the intake worker determines that the alleged violation is not within the jurisdiction of the juvenile court. Informal adjustment involves a decision to close the case after the youngster is warned or on the provision that the youngster meet certain conditions (such as restitution, private treatment, involvement in a diversion program, or an agreement by the parents to improve supervision).

Informal probation generally involves a period of informal supervision during which the youngster is required to fulfill certain requirements such as attending school or obeying his or her parents. To insure the equity and protection of the juvenile's rights, the National Advisory Committee on

Criminal Justice Standards and Goals (1976) recommends that four procedural safeguards be followed: (1) that the facts of the case against the juvenile be undisputed; (2) that all parties, including the juvenile, agree to the informal probation disposition; (3) that a reasonable time limit—three to six months—be placed on the informal probation; and (4) that no petition should be filed following the agreement of all parties involved to the conditions of the probation.

A consent decree is a midpoint between informal supervision and a formal disposition. It involves a formal order for treatment or supervision to be provided by the court staff or another agency. The decree requires the approval of the judge and the consent of the child and his or her parents. The advantage of this disposition is not only that it eases the case load of the court, but also that it protects the community while enabling the juvenile to avoid the stigma of formal adjudication. To protect the rights of the juvenile, the advisory committee recommends that decrees not be issued unless there is sufficient evidence that the juvenile committed the alleged offense; that they be limited to a period of six months, or at the most a year; and that they do not require the juvenile to be removed from the family. In this way, staff members can provide juveniles with supervision or services without requiring them to go through formal adjudication.

Postadjudication alternatives

In deciding on a disposition for adjudicated juveniles, judges can exercise considerable discretion and are limited only by available resources and statutory requirements. The options open to them include probation, warning the youngster, placing the youngster in the custody of his or her parents, levying a fine, ordering restitution, assigning work, placing the youngster in a foster home, group home, or halfway house, or—as a final resort—committing the youngster to a training school.

Correctional programs

The 1975 Detention and Correctional Facility Census reports that, as of 30 June 1975, there were 53,108 juveniles in public and private long-term correctional facilities—training schools, ranches, forestry camps or farms, halfway houses, and group homes (U.S. Department of Justice (1979). The average age of these juveniles was fifteen, and more than three quarters of them were male. In addition, over 50 percent of the youngsters in public institutions were being held for felonies, 21 percent for misdemeanors, 6 percent for drug offenses, and 15 percent for status offenses. Approximately 64 percent of the males, but only 25 percent of the females, were confined for felony offenses; 43 percent of the females and only 10 percent of the males were detained for status offenses.

The National Assessment of Juvenile Corrections constructed the following profile of the average youngster in our correctional institutions in 1975:

He was likely to be male, non-white, about sixteen years old, and from the lower socioeconomic class. He had probably been committed for a property crime (although a female probably would have been committed for a status offense), and was no stranger to the police or juvenile court. He had probably been on probation or even in an institution at least once previously. He is no angel—he readily admits to drinking, using drugs, and skipping school; but neither is he a hardened criminal—he had probably not frequently engaged in serious criminal behavior such as robbery or breaking and entering. The girls in the sample were far less frequently as seriously delinquent, but still had considerable contact with the juvenile justice system (Vinter 1976, p. 51).

Despite the heavy emphasis on placing juveniles in community correctional programs, the 1975 census on juvenile facilities reports that over 50 percent of the youths detained were in training schools, while just under 20 percent were in group homes and halfway houses (U.S. Department of Justice, 1979).

Community-based programs

Community-based programs for juveniles developed on two premises: (1) that traditional institutional programs are ineffective, at best, and, at worst, actually reinforce delinquency, and (2) that alternative environments are needed to help youths who do not require institutionalization in order to protect the community (President's Commission on Law Enforcement and Administration of Justice 1967; National Advisory Committee on Criminal Justice Standards and Goals 1973). These programs take place in both residential and nonresidential facilities. Residential programs include foster homes, group homes, and halfway houses; nonresidential programs range from those that provide sporadic supervision (e.g., probation and aftercare) to those that supervise youngsters for all or part of the day.

Residential programs Foster homes board neglected, dependent, and delinquent youngsters. Foster parents are paid by the state to provide supervision within the home. Delinquent and status offenders are placed in foster homes when it is believed that unsuitable circumstances in the parental home may have contributed to the problem behavior. Misbehavior by juveniles is sometimes a result of parent-child conflicts, child abuse, the inability or unwillingness of parents to provide appropriate support and supervision, and parental problems—alcoholism, mental illness, or criminal behavior. Foster parents can provide the juvenile with the supervision and support lacking in the real family and can do so in a more sustained manner than a probation officer. Also, this type of placement removes the juvenile from the neighborhood and companions with whom he or she previously engaged in deviant behavior. At an average cost of $2,500 per year per juvenile, the foster home is the least expensive alternative to institutionalization.

Group homes, group residences, and group foster homes are all terms used to describe programs that provide residential care for groups of four to twelve youngsters. The residences may be owned or rented by the state, a private agency, or the house parents. Typically, they are operated by a husband and wife assisted by one or more staff members. The objective is to provide a family environment for youngsters who can not adjust to a one-to-one relationship with foster parents, but who can benefit from and adjust to a family environment in the company of their peers.

Halfway houses are small facilities that serve as few as five residents but typically have populations of between ten and twenty-five. Standing somewhere between the community and training schools, these facilities serve youngsters released from an institution as part of a reintegration program, as well as those who come directly from the juvenile court. One of the advantages of these programs is that they provide an alternative placement for youngsters who require more supervision than they can receive in nonresidential programs, yet do not require the level of supervision and security provided by training schools.

Nonresidential programs Day treatment programs provide supervision for juveniles for all or part of the day, but they do not require that a youngster live at the facility housing the program. Juveniles in these programs require more supervision than can be provided through probation or aftercare, yet they are judged to be capable of living at home during their involvement. Thus, these youngsters are forced to confront the problems that contribute to their delinquency: school problems, adverse community influences, family difficulties, and work problems. Counseling and group sessions focus on problems that the youngsters encounter in their daily lives. Also, because youths usually live near the program facility, staff members can work closely with the parents to achieve successful home adjustment. Day treatment programs usually cost less than halfway houses because they use community resources and services and they do not provide housing, meals, and clothing for their clients.

Another nonresidential approach to changing delinquent behavior is known as "wilderness therapy." Programs that use this approach include Outward Bound, Homeward Bound, and VisionQuest. Using the lure of adventure and strenuous physical challenge, these programs give urban delinquents an opportunity to develop a sense of their own potential. At the same time, the youths strengthen their commitment to society. By confronting their fears and overcoming difficult tasks, these youngsters develop self-reliance, prove their self-worth, and define their personhood. Outward Bound, which serves as a model for many other adventure programs, has a three-week course divided into four parts: "basic skills training; a long expedition; the solo, a three-day period of solitude; and the final testing events," (Hold and Wilpers 1975, p. 155). In basic skills training, youths learn how to travel and survive in a wilderness environment. Programs are conducted in the mountains, in the forests of national parks, on the sea, in canoe country, and in the desert.

Training schools

In spite of efforts to place adjudicated delinquents in community-based correctional programs, the training school still handles most delinquent youths. On an average day in 1975, there were 189 state training schools in operation, with a total population of 27,500—compared with 195 halfway houses and group homes with just over 2,000 residents (U.S. Dept. of Justice, 1979). Training schools report populations ranging from 5 to 9 residents to more than 500; the median capacity in 1975 was 139 residents, down from 184 in 1971. Over three fourths of the training school population was male, with an average stay of 7.6 months; more than half of the male population was being held for felony offenses. The average cost of holding a juvenile in training school in 1975 was $10,910—a figure that has probably risen substantially in recent years.

Contemporary institutions Today's training schools are self-contained, relatively large, confinement facilities for youngsters removed from the community. The programs vary according to the extent to which they emphasize their dual goals of custody and rehabilitation. Compared with adult institutions, these facilities most closely resemble minimum security institutions. Most are located in rural areas, so security is provided primarily by their isolation. Some of the institutions—those located near pop-

Juvenile correctional institutions have been separate from adult prisons since the early nineteenth century, but many provide little more than custodial care. Courtesy Charles Harbutt/Magnum.

ulated areas—have fences or security patrols on their perimeters; few have guard towers. Many resemble small colleges or boarding schools in design.

The cottage concept is the predominant housing model for most contemporary schools. Residents live in cottages that house up to sixty youths (although many house fewer than twenty). Cottage staff are frequently called house parents, and married couples are sometimes recruited for these positions—with the goal of providing a homelike atmosphere.

Education, both academic and vocational, is the principal type of program offered at training schools. Academic programs fit three categories of students: those who will return to a conventional school; those who will go to work; and those who want to earn a high school equivalency diploma before going to work. Many youngsters require extensive remedial help because of previous school failures. Youths performing at a level far below their age require nontraditional school programs that emphasize basic skills and use interesting learning materials. (Computer-based instruction is sometimes used to provide immediate feedback to youngsters who have difficulty deferring gratification.

The education curriculum may include survival skills, budgeting, contracts, sex education, nutrition, and drug education. The quality of the curriculum depends on such factors as funding, staffing, and state standards. In general, however, educational programs at training schools are far more effective than casework and counseling at other institutions, because the teaching role is better understood and there is a well-established training program for teachers).

Training schools of the future A decline in the juvenile population, the removal of status offenders from training schools, and the emphasis on community-based alternatives to institutionalization will undoubtedly contribute to a future reduction in the training school population. Countering this trend will be the concern over protecting the public from the dangerous or violent juvenile offender. Thus, we can expect a policy that refers status offenders and youths engaged in less serious delinquent acts to community-based treatment programs, while potentially dangerous youths will be committed to training schools. As a result, training schools of tomorrow will probably house a higher percentage of older, minority, and serious offenders than ever before (Wilson 1978).

Prevention and diversion

As Ward (1978) suggests, the concept of delinquency prevention has probably been with us as long as we have sought to differentiate juveniles from adult offenders. *Prevention* refers to any attempt to forestall anticipated delinquent behavior. *Diversion*, on the other hand, deals with delinquent behavior that has already occurred; thus, it falls within the province of control. Diversion had antecedents within the child-saving movement. Recall that separate institutions for juveniles and the juvenile court itself were originally developed to divert youth from the harsh and punitive orientation of the adult criminal justice system.

Prevention

Prevention encompasses programs ranging from those intended to reduce criminal opportunities to those directed at ameliorating adverse conditions presumed to cause (or contribute to) delinquency. Most programs focus on community reorganization, education, employment, and recreation.

Community reorganization Community reorganization programs—also known as area projects, inclusive neighborhood programs, and social action programs—assume that delinquent behavior results from social and cultural conditions, rather than from individual disturbances, pathologies, or inadequacies (Stratton and Terry 1968). Moreover, because delinquency rates and cultural and social conditions vary from community to community, the type of program developed depends to a great extent on the nature and composition of the particular community or neighborhood.

The Chicago Area Projects, which have been operating since 1934, are among the most well-known community reorganization programs. Another prominent program is Mobilization of Youth, started in 1962 and based on the delinquency and opportunity thesis of Cloward and Ohlin (1960). Following the pattern of the Chicago Area Projects, this program emphasizes the involvement of local residents in delinquency prevention. It includes more than thirty separate action programs in the areas of work, education, services to individuals and families, and group and community organization.

Education Prevention programs can also focus on general public education and the education of at-risk youths. Public education might include programs on drug and alcohol abuse or parent effectiveness training. Programs for youth often involve school activities.

Theories and research on delinquency suggest that delinquent behavior is partly a result of negative school experiences (Schafer and Polk 1967). School occupies a strategic place in the lives of youths, because it provides the skills and values needed to structure legitimate alternatives. Thus, school has the potential to offset or neutralize some of the pressures toward delinquency created by adverse family or community conditions. On the other hand, an unsatisfactory school experience can push a youth toward delinquency. Programs such as Head Start and Higher Horizons, as well as less academically oriented career education programs, are designed to strengthen the positive aspects of a school experience.

Employment Unemployment and underemployment are also thought to be major contributors to delinquency (Fleisher 1966; Cloward and Ohlin 1960; and Singell 1965). A job serves to integrate the individual into the dominant structure of society by providing a legitimate way to achieve success, by giving the individual a stake in legitimate social order, and by serving as a check on behavior. Unemployed youths have little at stake if they disobey the laws; thus, they may turn their efforts toward achieving success by illegitimate means. In contrast, employed youth may decide that they would lose more as a result of being apprehended for delinquent behavior than they would gain by the perpetration of such acts.

Comprehensive employment programs seek to expand the number of employment opportunities, to create job training and manpower development opportunities, and to break down the barriers that unjustly exclude persons from productive employment (National Advisory Committee on Criminal Justice Standards and Goals 1976). A number of these programs offer juveniles on-the-job training in industry; others, like the National Youth Corps, provide both academic and business education.

Recreation The idea that recreation can prevent delinquency is reflected in the proverb "The Devil makes mischief for idle hands." This simplistic view was the rationale for the hundreds of playgrounds built in our major cities in the early 1900s, and it was also used to some extent to justify settlement houses in lower income areas. Some delinquency is probably related to the misuse of leisure time, but recreational activities alone can not prevent delinquency. Following a survey of available research on recreation, Beck and Beck concluded that "these studies neither demonstrated in any conclusive fashion that recreation prevented delinquency, nor were they able to demonstrate conclusively that recreation was without value in delinquency prevention" (1967, p. 334).

Recognizing the limitations of conventional approaches to using recreational programs in delinquency prevention, youth organizations such as the Boy Scouts and Girl Scouts developed special programs to deal with these shortcomings. Other organizations developed detached worker programs for youngsters involved in gang delinquency. Developed in response to research showing that gang members do not participate in traditional recreation programs, detached worker programs send workers into the community to seek out work with gangs "on their own turf."

Diversion

The idea of diversion, as already noted, dates back to the beginning of the juvenile justice system. The recent emphasis on diversion can be credited to the President's Commission on Law Enforcement and Administration of Justice (1967), which recommends the increased use of alternatives to the juvenile justice system.

The following discussion on diversion focuses on the police, the courts, and probation departments. However, many diversion programs are *administered* by schools, juvenile welfare boards, and other community agencies, or by special organizations established for that purpose. Many school, employment, and recreation programs are also used by communities to divert youth from the juvenile justice system. These programs are discussed in chapter 18.

The police As the law enforcement agents of our social system, the police must often make discretionary judgements as to how a juvenile should be handled. In fact, police discretion accounts for as much as 90 percent of all diversion. Patrol officers have always had to make decisions as to whether to ignore an incident, to handle a juvenile informally, or to take him or her into custody for further processing. Prompting by the availability of funds and frustration with existing community programs, some police departments have established and operated diversion programs. Some departments operate youth service bureaus, even though such programs were originally intended to be independent of the juvenile justice system.

Intake and the courts Intake workers—who are usually probation officers, juvenile court personnel, or state youth service counselors—are in a strategic position to reduce the penetration of juveniles further into the juvenile justice system. "Penetration" is a term used to characterize a youngster's contacts with the formal agencies of the system. Intake workers can warn and release juveniles, refer them to outside programs, place them on informal probation, or file a petition with the juvenile court. Pressures on juvenile court intake units have led them to develop their own diversion programs to minimize penetration.

Programs outside the juvenile justice system Diversion programs that operate outside the juvenile justice system are in the best position to fulfill the goals of diversion. That is, they can provide a juvenile with assistance without the stigma of involvement in programs associated with official agencies of social control. These programs are sponsored by a variety of community organizations, including departments of children's services, welfare departments, mental health departments, religious organizations, and nonprofit organizations established to provide services to children and young people.

Youth service bureaus Youth service bureaus are a hallmark of the diversion movement. Although the first such bureau was started in Chicago in 1958 and others were established in the mid-sixties, the real growth in these programs resulted from a recommendation by the President's Commission on Law Enforcement and Administration of Justice (1967) for the establishment of neighborhood agencies to provide services to youths.

Bureaus obtain their referrals from schools, the police, juvenile courts, parents, neighbors, and young people and their friends. They assist youngsters and their families in identifying problems that underlie delinquent behavior, and act to ensure that youngsters get the services they need. By accepting only voluntary referrals and by making referrals only to programs agreed to by the youngster and his or her parents, the bureaus attempt to avoid stigmatizing their clients.

Realizing that they would be of little value without outside resources, youth service bureaus work with citizens to develop needed services that are not available. Bureaus contract for services, encourage existing agencies to expand their programs or develop special services, and develop programs of their own to fill voids in available services.

To prevent further difficulties on the part of their clients and other juveniles, bureaus also attempt to deal with some of the conditions within the community that contribute to the problems of youngsters. An effort is made to change attitudes and practices that discriminate against problem youth and exacerbate their antisocial behavior. The bureaus have the responsibility to educate, consult, demonstrate, and—when necessary—resort to political pressure to insure that resources and institutions are responsive to the needs of their clients.

Runaway programs Most cities have developed runaway programs independent of the juvenile justice system. These programs view runaways not as criminals, but as youths who have difficulties at home or who have no permanent residence. The programs typically provide shelter and counseling, with the goal of providing the runaway with refuge and an opportunity to reflect on his or her problems and consider solutions. Programs vary according to the time limits of the program and whether or not youngsters are required to contact their parents and to obtain parental permission to remain in a program.

Most runaway programs offer only short-term care—from a few days to a couple of weeks. Some programs, however, have long-term residential facilities and outreach workers who frequent areas where runaways congregate. Others help youths obtain jobs or get back into school once they return home. A youth's participation is voluntary; hence, the extent to which a youngster benefits depends largely on whether he or she takes advantage of the services offered. Some youngsters merely use runaway centers as "crash pads"; for others, the centers provide an opportunity to resolve problems with their parents, to obtain placement in a foster home or a long-term residential program, or to develop a workable plan for independent living.

Community supervision

Community supervision of juveniles includes probation and aftercare services. Probation is viewed as a desirable disposition for youths who need some supervision but do not require the level of control supplied by nonresidential day treatment programs or residential community-based programs. Aftercare, in the form of supervision and services, is frequently required for juveniles released from training schools or community-based facilities.

Juvenile probation

Juvenile probation actually preceded the first juvenile court. Probation is a legal status, imposed by the juvenile court, that permits a youth to remain in the community under the guidance and supervision of a probation officer. It typically involves "(a) a judicial finding that the behavior of the child has been such as to bring him within the purview of the court; (b) the imposition of conditions on his continued freedom; and (c) the provision of means for helping him to meet these conditions and for determining the degree to which he meets them" (National Council on Crime and Delinquency 1967, p. 231).

Probation involves much more than merely giving a youngster another chance; it is also intended to enable the youngster to adjust to the free community. From a variety of standpoints, probation represents the most desirable formal alternative to the juvenile court. While on probation, juveniles are able to: (1) live at home and maintain family ties; (2) remain in school or retain their jobs; (3) maintain their involvement in community activities; and (4) avoid the stigma of being removed from their home and placed in a residential program. The alternative also costs less than placing youth in residential programs.

Probation is the most frequent disposition used by the juvenile court. In 1976, there were 362,201 juveniles on probation, compared with only 34,255 youths in long-term facilities (training schools, ranches, forestry camps, farms, halfway houses and group homes) in 1975 (Flanagan, Hindelang, and Gottfredson 1980).

Juvenile aftercare

Aftercare is the juvenile equivalent of parole. It involves "the release of a child from an institution at the time when he can best benefit from release and from life in the community under the supervision of a counselor" (President's Commission on Law Enforcement and Administration of Justice 1967, p. 149). The term "aftercare" was proposed in an effort to dissociate juvenile programs from the legalistic language and concepts of adult parole.

Historically, juvenile aftercare in the United States can be traced to the system of indenture employed by houses of refuge in the early nineteenth century. The superintendents of these facilities were authorized to bind as apprentices youngsters they believed were reformed. Total control of the children was invested in their guardians, who could supervise boys until the age of twenty-one, girls until the age of eighteen. Within these limits, the employer made the decision as to when a youth had earned the right to be discharged. Females were usually indentured as domestics, and males were placed on farms, on ships, in stores, or in factories.

The problem with indenture was that there was initially no follow-up to determine how youths were being treated. Thus, the youngsters depended upon the goodwill of their employers, who could treat them either as slaves, employees, or foster children. States did not assume responsibility for supervising the youngsters until the middle of the nineteenth century, when New York appointed an agent to supervise indentured children and guard them against abuse. Despite this early development, however, aftercare did not become an integral part of the juvenile rehabilitation system until the 1950s (National Council on Crime and Delinquency 1967). Even today, aftercare in most states is considered to be the least developed aspect of corrections and is viewed by many observers as being less effective than adult parole.

According to a recent national study, there were 53,347 juveniles involved in aftercare programs in 1976 (Vinter 1976). The purpose of aftercare is to aid the juvenile in the transition from the restricted institution to the relatively free environment of the community. Implicit is the belief that the youth's institutional experience represents only the first phase of the treatment process, the second phase being completed in the community under the guidance and supervision of aftercare workers. Planning for aftercare should be an essential part of all institutional programs and should begin immediately after a youth is committed to the institution (National Council on Crime and Delinquency 1967). A wide range of placement options is required because of differences in age, experience, community conditions, and medical and psychological problems.

Consideration must also be given to the impact of institutionalization on youth. Some youngsters become more sophisticated and antisocial as a result of their training school experience; others become dependent and timid. There are also vast differences in the community settings to which these youngsters return. Most juveniles return to their old communities and are therefore exposed to the same conditions (e.g., peer influences) that originally contributed to their delinquency. And many youngsters must overcome the stigma of confinement in a juvenile institution. Thus, each youngster has specific needs that require the use of all available resources both within and outside the institution.

The advantages of good aftercare more than justify the required investment of time and money. First, aftercare provides a transitional period in which youths can adjust to the community with the assistance and support of a parole officer. The parole officer can help youngsters and their families to cope with problems that may have contributed to prior delinquency, to readjust to school, or to secure employment. A good aftercare program can also minimize a youth's length of stay at an institution: authorities are likely to expand the number of early releases if they know that released youths will be supervised by aftercare workers. Another advantage is that it costs less to keep a youth on parole than to retain him or her in a juvenile training school. Based on a national survey, the National Council on Crime and Delinquency (1967) estimates that aftercare costs less than one tenth as much as institutional care. And although the council suggests that this cost difference reflects, to a large extent, the inadequacy of aftercare programs, these programs would still be vastly cheaper than institutional care even if their funding was increased substantially. Many of the inadequacies exist simply because aftercare workers are assigned case loads of two hundred or more adolescents. (Optimum case loads for community supervision are discussed in the next section.) Given the adverse effects of institutionalization, as well as the potential benefits of good aftercare, it appears that increased funding of aftercare programs would be a wise investment.

The quality of supervision

Youths on probation are under the jurisdiction of the juvenile court; as a rule, youths on aftercare are under the jurisdiction of an agency or a state system. Youths on probation are more likely to have less serious and less extensive records than youths involved in aftercare; and youths on aftercare have to readjust to the community after their period of institutionalization. In spite of these differences, however, probation and aftercare are based on many of the same principles and considerations and they have similar requirements.

First, there is a need for the development of a comprehensive services plan based on the youth's needs and the availability of community programs and resources. This plan should be developed by the aftercare or probation worker in conjunction with the youth, his or her significant others (e.g., parents), and representatives of programs in which the youth will participate. It is recognized that certain constraints have to be placed on a youth's freedom while under supervision, but these constraints should not interfere with the juvenile's regular employment, schooling, or other activities needed for normal development and growth (National Advisory Committee on Criminal Justice Standards and Goals 1976). If juveniles are not subjected to unreasonable restrictions, it is more likely that they will not violate the conditions of their supervision.

The major elements of effective supervision are surveillance, service, and counseling. Thus, the probation or aftercare worker must perform both police and counseling functions. Counseling requires trust between counselor and client, but the police function—the duty to ferret out client violations—makes the establishment of trust difficult or impossible. In surveillance, the worker is required to maintain contact with the youngster, his or her parents, school, and other persons directly concerned with the youth's adjustment to community life. It is the worker's responsibility to determine not only the extent to which the youth is meeting his or her commitments, but also how well the family, school, and others are conforming to their responsibility as agreed upon in the comprehensive plan.

In performing the service function, the worker must assess the extent to which the problems confronting the youth and his or her family may be ameliorated by available community resources—including community mental health centers, state employment agencies, health departments, vocational training programs, drug and alcohol abuse programs, and recreational programs. Based on that assessment, the worker must then develop a plan to use these services effectively for each child and family.

The counseling function is the most important and demanding of the aftercare or probation worker's responsibilities. For counseling to be effective, the worker must establish a relationship with a youth based on mutual confidence, trust, and understanding. In the course of individual or group sessions, the youngster, his or her family, and other persons directly involved must be helped to confront and comprehend the personal or environmental problems that contribute to delinquency.

The extent to which a worker can provide a juvenile with effective supervision depends largely on the size of the worker's case load. The National Advisory Committee on Criminal Justice Standards and Goals (1976) argues that community supervision workers should carry no more than twenty-five active cases at any time. This figure was derived from various projects and studies that demonstrate conclusively that a worker with twenty-five cases spends only an hour and a half each month in face-to-face contact with each youth. While this may be enough for some juveniles, it is marginal for most, and woefully inadequate for a few. Thus, a case load management system should be developed based on the recognition that not all juveniles require the same level of supervision and not all respond to the same approach.

Revocation

As noted in chapter 15, probation revocations are generally handled by the juvenile court; the aftercare agency typically has the authority to revoke aftercare. Although juveniles are not *legally* entitled to a hearing prior to aftercare revocation, many jurisdictions do voluntarily provide due process hearings to avoid subsequent legal action. As a rule, a youth's parole or probation should be revoked only if he or she engages in behavior that would have brought them to the attention of the juvenile court were they not already under supervision (National Advisory Committee on Criminal Justice Standards and Goals 1976). However, there are some cases in which the conditions of probation or aftercare are so critical to the integrity of supervision that any violation necessitates a hearing.

Evaluating the programs

The success of probation aftercare is difficult to assess, because authorities do not agree as to how success should be defined. Research indicates that some programs are effective within certain limitations (Scarpitti and Stephenson 1968). Some studies show that more intense supervision relates to program success, but other studies refute this conclusion.

Violent juvenile offenders

Adults often observe that kids can "get away with murder." Actually, this is sometimes literally true. Few violent juveniles are ever institutionalized. Trojanowicz refers to a study by the Office of Juvenile Services in New York which indicated that less than 5 percent of over five thousand juveniles arrested in New York City for violent crimes (murder, kidnapping, forcible rape, assault, and arson) from July 1973 to June 1974 were sent to an institution (1978). Andrew Vogt, executive director of Colorado District Attorneys Association, says that, "in effect, we have created a privileged class in society" ("The Youth Crime Plague," *Time*, 11 July 1977, p. 19).

Most juvenile violence is random, casual, and purposeless—not for profit or even vengeance, but strictly for kicks. The victims are the elderly and the young, the handicapped and the helpless; the perpetrators are indifferent to the people they have slashed, shot, and beaten into insensibility. Remorse is so rare that a fifteen-year-old boy in New York who murdered a high school girl so he could steal her bicycle received a sentence of only eighteen months in an unlocked rehabilitation center because the judge was impressed by the boy's "repentance." ("Fifteen-year-old draws Probation for Murder," *Tampa Tribune* 1978).

PROFILES IN JUVENILE VIOLENCE

Chicago. Johnny, 16, who had a long record of arrests for disorderly conduct, simple battery and aggravated assault, lured a motorist into an alley. He drew a .22 cal. pistol and shot the driver six times, killing him. Johnny was arrested yet again, but he was released because witnesses failed to show up in court. Today he is free.

New Orleans. Steven, 17, was first arrested for burglary when he was eleven and diagnosed as psychotic. But he kept escaping from the state hospital and was seized for 22 different crimes, including theft and attempted murder. Just four days after he was charged with robbery and attempted murder, he was arrested for raping and murdering a young nurse.

Wilmington. Eric, 16, who had escaped conviction for a previous mugging charge, pleaded guilty to knocking down an 86-year-old woman and stealing her purse. Three months later, the woman is still hospitalized and is not expected to walk again. Eric was released into the custody of his father. Since then, he has been charged with three burglaries. Says Detective James Strawbridge: "He's going to kill somebody some day, and he's still out there."

Houston. Lawrence was 15 when he was charged with murdering two brothers in his neighborhood: Kenneth Elliott, 11, and Ronald Elliott, 12. Lawrence tied up Kenneth, castrated him and stabbed him twice in the heart. Then he cut off the boy's head, which he left about 50 feet from the body. He also admitted killing Ronald, whose body was never found, in similar fashion. Like all other offenders in juvenile facilities in Texas, Lawrence was released from prison when he turned 18.

From "The Youth Crime Plague." *Time,* 11 July 1977, p. 18. Copyright 1977 Time Inc. All rights reserved. Reprinted by permission from TIME.

Juvenile gangs have undergone a revival in recent years in our nation's largest cities. Today, urban gangs are responsible for roughly one quarter of all juvenile crimes committed each year. Gone are the knives, clubs, bicycle chains, and homemade "zip" guns used as weapons in yesterday's "rumbles." The gang wars of today (fought over the possession of "turf") feature sophisticated weaponry—AR-15s, M-16s, grenades, and plastic explosives—that would do credit to a military assault troop.

In addition to being better armed, today's gangs, or "clicks," have a tighter, more cohesive, and more durable structure. At the top is the "prez," who gains his or her position by being the most ruthless and violent member of the gang—and who remains on top only as long as he or she meets every challenge of authority. Under the "prez" is the "veep," who collects dues, supervises the recruitment and initiation of new members, and manages internal affairs. The "war counselor" serves as general: he or she plans "gang hits" and "rip-offs" and commands "gestapo squads" composed of "enforcers." Weapons are the responsibility of the "armorer," who maintains them and stashes them in a safe place.

Miller (1976) reports that there may be as many as twenty-seven hundred gangs in the nation's six largest cities: New York, Los Angeles,

Chicago, Detroit, Philadelphia, and San Francisco; the membership in these gangs may be as high as 81,500. According to Trojanowicz,

> In some cities, gangs have gotten out of control to the point where regular activities in the community are disrupted. Armed bands of young gang members board buses and physically force passengers to give up wallets and other personal items. Gang members are getting so bold that not only do they show total disregard for their fellow man, but they have no fear of police or any formal consequence for their actions (1978, p. 402).

In Detroit, Michigan, gang violence prompted the governer to order state police to patrol the city's highways and freeways.

Violence in the schools

Schools have always had discipline problems, but it is only recently that they have taken on some of the properties of maximum security prisons. The U.S. Senate Subcommittee on Juvenile Delinquency (chaired by Senator Birch Bayh) reports that in 747 school districts across the country (out of a total of 16,600), there are annually over seventy thousand assaults on teachers, more than a hundred student murders, and $500 million in property losses from vandalism—a figure equal to the cost of the entire supply of textbooks for all schools in the country.

Disturbing as these figures are, they only begin to indicate the gravity of the situation in many school districts. In some cases, the educational process is threatened with extinction. Approximately two hundred thousand pupils are truants on an average school day in New York City; and in

Katos Wunchcus, a teenage gang in New York City. Reproduced from M.J. Goldstein, B.L. Baker, and K.R. Jamison, Abnormal Psychology, Boston: Little, Brown, 1980,m p. 446, by permission of the authors and publishers.

some areas, the only way schools can get through the motions of providing educational services is to have armed guards patrolling the corridors. Teachers in these schools develop symptoms of "battle fatigue" and joke bitterly about asking for "combat pay."

Intervention

The decision to use (or not use) correctional treatment or intervention assumes greater urgency when the juveniles involved have committed violent crimes rather than deliquent acts not involving persons). Dale Mann (1976), a Rand Corporation consultant to the National Institute for Juvenile Justice and Delinquency Prevention, has conducted an extensive study of correctional intervention programs with violent juvenile offenders. Two questions were addressed in the study: (1) What interventions are used with serious juvenile offenders? (2) How well do these interventions work? "Serious" juvenile offenders were defined as those who had been adjuged delinquent (i.e., convicted of nonnegligent homicide, armed robbery, forcible rape, aggravated assault, or arson).

The first problem Mann encountered was in trying to determine the number of juvenile offenders in custody who could be classified as serious offenders. Based on the *Uniform Crime Reports of the United States* (1975), seventy-three thousand juveniles were arrested in 1974 for violent crimes. One might reasonably expect that a substantial number of these juveniles were dealt with by placement in a reasonably secure institution. If such was the case, these offenders would have added to the pouplation already incarcerated. But such was *not* the case. By the time Mann tracked the seventy-three thousand offenders through the various stages of the juvenile justice system and subtracted those who had been "processed out," he found that only *six thousand* of the offenders were undergoing some type of treatment in an institutional or extrainstitutional setting; and the total institutional population of juvenile offenders in the country was only forty thousand.

Mann's findings reinforce the view that juveniles can get away with almost anything, including murder. And it supports the contention that serious juvenile offenders usually continue to commit crimes of violence—despite repeated arrests and juvenile court appearances—until they are old enough to be handled in an adult criminal court. Mann insists that the serious juvenile offenders identified in his study are more important than their number indicates:

> Because of the crimes they have committed, they are regarded as dangerous. Because they are young, they are thought to deserve opportunities to change themselves or to be rehabilitated. The two perceptions merge into one aspiration for successful treatment when it is recognized that a successful intervention also *reduces the danger* posed to society by this group (1976, pp. 10–11).

Intervention with violent juvenile offenders takes place within settings that range from secure correctional facilities to community-based facilities. Mann identifies the following modes of intervention which can be used;

1. *Intervention Based on Clinical Psychology and Psychiatry.* This type of intervention relies on psychotherapy, transactional analysis, Gestalt therapy, and other types of therapy on a group or individual basis.
2. *Intervention Based on Sociology and Social Work.* This type of intervention emphasizes the restructuring of the social environment and the positive use of the peer group (e.g., an approach called Guided Group Interaction).
3. *Intervention Based on Schooling.* According to Mann, "the use of schooling as a behavior-changing treatment for offenders is based on two facts: (1) the vast majority of juvenile offenders experienced failure in school, and (2) social and vocational advancement for such juveniles is blocked without academic training" (ibid. pp. 12–13).
4. *Intervention Based on Vocational Education.* This type of intervention stresses the acquisition of job skills to gain access to legitimate opportunities for reinforcing the "stake in conformity."

Mann also identifies what might be called a "no-intended-treatment" situation that involves "doing time" in an institution without exposure to any kind of treatment or intervention. Just because treatment programs are not provided, however, there is no reason to assume that institutionalization *by itself* will not have some effect on the subsequent behavior of the offender. Unfortunately, Mann's study did not address this issue.

In summarizing his findings, Mann stresses two considerations that are not specific to the evaluation of intervention techniques with violent juvenile offenders, but that are endemic to the whole enterprise of assessing behavior-change approaches. First, Mann notes that treatment outcomes in most programs are defined in terms of behavior within the institution—not with reference to the characteristics of the offense for which the offender was adjudicated (convicted). Thus, behavior change that is accomplished within the institutional or program setting may not carry over into the postrelease period. Second, the absence of agreement on just what *are* the salient behavioral characteristics of the serious juvenile offender makes it nearly impossible to locate and evaluate programs that concentrate exclusively on changing the behavior of these offenders.

In response to the general question What works?, Mann's survey reports that each of the four intervention modes described herein attained limited success in the treatment of serious juvenile offenders: "While these positive effects were not as well documented, as dramatic, or as long-lasting as might be wished, each of the four treatment modalities could legitimately claim to have changed some behavior on the part of some juvenile offenders" (ibid., p. viii). Among the characteristics of successful programs, Mann lists such factors as client choice (i.e., discretion about whether or not to enter a program), involvement in and commitment to the program, availability of a wide range of techniques to the program or institutional staff, the readiness of the staff to profit from their own failures and a variety of standard features associated with successful practice in learning situations—clear goals and tasks, behavior models, early and frequent successes, rewards for appropriate behavior, and credible training relevant to the demands of the real world.

Lock'em up—give up—try harder

In Dale Mann's (1976) view, serious juvenile offenders can be dealt with in one of three ways (1976):

1. By making a vigorous attempt to implement the punish-deter-incapacitate policy, the basis of the "lock'em up and throw away the key" approach.
2. By giving up and doing nothing, which means that the problem will be deferred until the juvenile is no longer a juvenile but a problem for the adult criminal justice authorities.
3. By making more use of available approaches toward correctional intervention (while recognizing the absence of a panacea, a universally effective approach to treatment). This "try harder" alternative requires that improvements be made elsewhere in the juvenile justice system and that efforts be pursued to develop new and more effective intervention strategies.

Mann believes that his findings strongly support the third alternative. He sides with the Indian guru, maintaining that it is better to light a single candle than to curse the darkness.

Most of the violent juveniles in the programs that Mann studied are in the category of "life-style violent juveniles" (as characterized by Vachss and Bakal [1979]). These juveniles are born and reared in a subculture of violence, are socialized into patterns of exploitative aggression, and are prone to chronic violence. A much smaller number of youths who come to the attention of the juvenile court exhibit a propensity for occasional outbreaks of impulsive violence related to severe personality disturbances, including psychosis. The latter juveniles are really a problem for the mental health system rather than the criminal justice system, but the provisions for their care and treatment are even sketchier than the provisions for the life-style violent juvenile.

Vachss and Bakal present detailed proposal for a secure treatment unit that realistically combines custody and treatment within a single facility. The unit would feature a multifaceted program intended to resocialize the life-style violent juvenile into more acceptable, prosocial behavior. Treatment would be carried out within a secure context specifically designed to eliminate or drastically reduce the adverse effects of confinement. Although the proposal does not detail the programs that would be used, the concept of the secure treatment unit represents a quantum leap in correctional planning for the serious juvenile offender. The critics of the concept undoubtedly object to the cost of the needed facilities, but Vachss and Bakal point out that the cost of continuing with present approaches and facilities if even more prohibitive. Further, human cost is impossible to measure in dollars and cents.

Summary

The juvenile justice system evolved as an attempt to deal constructively with the problems of dependent, neglected, and delinquent youngsters within an informal, nonadversarial setting. The first juvenile courts operated as a blend of the social casework agency and the criminal court. However, the procedural informality of these courts often resulted in the denial to juveniles of rights guaranteed to adults under the Constitution. Thus, in a series of important decisions in the 1960s, the U.S. Supreme Court eventually extended due process and equal protection rights to juveniles.

The police and the courts make a strong effort to divert as many youths as possible from the juvenile justice system. Once a juvenile is adjudicated delinquent, a variety of postadjudication alternatives are available to the court in the form of residential and nonresidential programs. As many delinquents as possible are handled in community-based correctional programs, but the training school continues to house most adjudicated delinquents. Release from training school may allow a youngster to remain in the community under aftercare supervision, a status that roughly corresponds to parole for adult offenders.

Large U.S. cities are experiencing a resurgence of gang violence. Juveniles who participate in gang activity often belong to the category of "life-style violent juveniles"—youth born and reared in a subculture that reinforces exploitative aggression. Thus far, the juvenile justice system has been unable to deal effectively with these offenders. Many juveniles who commit violent crimes are shuttled in and out of the system until they become the responsibility of the adult criminal courts.

issue paper

WAIVER AND CERTIFICATION—TRYING JUVENILES IN ADULT COURT

Prior to the advent of the child-saving movement (in the early 1800s) and the emergence of the juvenile court (in 1899), youngsters who committed crimes were tried by the criminal courts—and they often received sentences that were not appreciably lighter than those meted out to adult offenders. Now, after three quarters of a century of the parens patriae doctrine and the manifest inability of the juvenile justice system to deal effectively with violent juvenile offenders and persistent property offenders, there appears to be a growing conviction that the system has failed to live up to its promises and aspirations. State legislators are recommending that juvenile statutes be rewritten to permit a firmer approach toward the serious juvenile offender. National commissions have gone even further, proposing that all individual rehabilitation programs be replaced with offense-based, determinate sentencing and that all delinquency jurisdiction be transferred to the criminal courts.

Of course, some of this interest and activity is purely rhetorical—the inevitable response of politicians to public concern and indignation and demands that they "crack down" on juvenile crime. In fact, there is nothing new about the use of certification or judicial waiver to transfer delinquent youths to adult court. As Rubin (1979) points out, all but a very few states have long allowed such procedures; recent developments have only broadened the latitude of provisions for discretionary transfer.

How do youths fare in adult courts? Contrary to the general belief that youths are treated more harshly in adult courts than in juvenile courts, adult courts do not sentence most youths to confinement; this conclusion is based on a recently completed three-year study (Hamparian et al. 1982). Hamparian and his colleagues report that just over half of the youths in their study that were judicially waived were given sentences that did not involve incarceration (i.e., they were fined or put on probation). And the research did not substantiate the belief that the main reason for waiving juveniles to adult court is to see that they receive stiffer sentences.

Only 32 percent of juvenile waivers to adult court were done because of crimes against the person—again countering the view that only youths who commit violent offenses are sent to adult courts. Property crimes accounted for 45 percent of the waivers, and the remaining 23 percent were for public order offenses and other minor offenses (such as being drunk in public). The typical youth referred to adult court was seventeen, male, and white.

In states such as Minnesota, recent changes in the laws governing juveniles have been aimed at persistent property offenders. Thus, the current Minnesota law exceeds the guidelines laid down in 1979 by the American Bar Association's Commission on Juvenile Justice Standards. The commission recommends that youths fifteen years of age or older be certified for adult court only if they are charged with murder or some other crime of violence, if they have a record of serious violent offenses, or if there is clear and convincing evidence that they can not be handled by a juvenile correctional institution.

"THEY TOLD ME TEENAGERS DON'T MAKE IT HERE."
E. Kiersch Corrections Magazine

Baby-faced, golden-haired Andrew C. looks up at a gun turret, high above the granite wall, and says, "The kids here have a name for this place. We call it Greystone College." Surrounded by miles of barbed wire, fortress-like grey stone walls, and menacing-looking guards, Andrew likes to sound tough and cynical. But he is only 17, and he has had numerous problems adjusting to Minnesota's maximum security prison at St. Cloud. Older inmates have tried to rape him; he has been taken off a laundry detail for fighting. In the first 11 months of his five-year sentence for burglary, he has been sent to segregation eight times.

If Andrew had been convicted before August 1980, he would have been sent to the tree-lined, almost pastoral juvenile facility at Red Wing. There, near the banks of the Mississippi River, Andrew would have lived in a white cottage, would have attended a modern, well-equipped vocational shop or school, and would have had ample opportunities for sports activities, or just plain lolling on the grass. Andrew would also have slept easier at night. No one would be talking about hanging himself, or demanding various favors in return for "protection," or making homosexual advances.

But under Minnesota's revised juvenile justice statutes, effective in August, 1980, chronic offenders like Andrew are being sent to state prisons and county jails. The new law has made it much easier to "certify" juvenile offenders as adults. As of October 1, there were twenty-nine 16 and 17-year-olds at St. Cloud, and an unknown number in county jails and workhouses. (Juvenile offenders certified as adults can be sent to any state prison, including Stillwater and the new maximum-security prison at Oak Park, but so far all have been sent to St. Cloud, which has always held younger adult offenders.)

Even "tough teenagers like Andrew find adult prison traumatic. "A year ago I wanted to be certified," said the lank 17-year-old, nervously touching his smooth, boyish face. "I had heard stories about this place, but they didn't bother me. I was sick of the counseling and the Mickey Mouse games they play at Red Wing. I just wanted to do my time and get it over with. But I've seen young kids get messed up here. It doesn't matter how tough you are or how many guards you're willing to fight. The noise at night, the crying, the guys you have to pal around with, that's what gets to you." His voice cracking, he concluded, "I wish I had listened to those people at Red Wing. They told me teenagers didn't make it here."

Reproduced from E. Kiersh, "Minnesota Cracks Down on Chronic Juvenile Offenders," *Corrections Magazine* 7 (1981): pp. 21–22. Copyright 1981 by Corrections Magazine and Criminal Justice Publications, Inc., 19 W. 34th St., New York, N.Y. 10001.

As Kiersh (1981) observes, it is no accident that the Minnesota law comes down hard on chronic property offenders. He quotes the principal author of the bill, a University of Minnesota law professor who was formerly a prosecutor: "I went into court and couldn't get kids with 30 or 40 burglaries certified." Further, "when juveniles turn up in criminal court for the first time, they're treated as instant virgins. Judges don't look at their previous offenses and treat them as leniently as first offenders." But the new law is intended as a first step toward integrating juvenile and adult records, thus building a record of offenses against juveniles in adult court.

Civil libertarians have not joined in any chorus of protest condemning the new juvenile laws. Why not? For one thing, these laws confer on juvenile offenders the due process rights they have often been denied in juvenile courts. They also exclude the admission at trial of psychiatric reports, school records, and other kinds of "soft" evidence that are practically standard in juvenile court proceedings. Another benefit of adult criminal court is that the defendant has the right to plea bargain.

But the new laws do have opponents. Says David Gilman, former head of the American Bar Association's (ABA) project on juvenile justice standards:

> The ABA standards echo the idea of proportionality, or the most severe punishment for most severe criminals. If someone burgles, you don't treat him like some who raped. When you talk about doing away with the juvenile court you're really talking about going after the low-level property offender. But what are you going to do with them? Castrate them, brand them? I can buy the fact that rehabilitation often doesn't work. But what are we going to do? Is society just safe for the short time a kid is locked up? But what about when he gets out? What's going to happen with those 14, 15, and 16 year olds when they get out? And what's going to happen to us? (Kiersh 1981, p. 28).

If the number of juveniles who end up in state prison as a result of waiver and certification procedures continues to increase, Gilman's questions are eventually going to get answered.

Discussion and review

1. What were the principal objectives of the child-saving movement? How influential was this movement in the development of the juvenile court?
2. Discuss the concept of "individualized justice" and the role it played in the emergence of the juvenile court in the United States.
3. Discuss the implications of the *Gault* case for the juvenile justice system.
4. In addition to delinquents, what other types of youngsters are handled by the juvenile courts?
5. How do status offenses differ from crimes?
6. What alternative dispositions are available to the police and the intake worker in handling juvenile cases?
7. Describe the postadjudication alternatives available to the court in the disposition of juvenile cases.
8. Identify and discuss the advantages and disadvantages of community-based residential and nonresidential programs for juveniles.
9. Describe the goals and methods of youth services bureaus.
10. What are the essential elements in effective community supervision of delinquent youngsters?
11. What are the implications of Mann's finding that only a small percent of serious juvenile offenders arrested each year for violent crimes participate in treatment programs?
12. Describe the modes of intervention outlined by Mann for dealing with the serious juvenile offender. How do Vachss and Bakal propose to deal with the life-style violent juvenile?
13. What are some of the major issues raised by new legislation calling for the transfer or waiver of juveniles to the jurisdiction of adult courts? Are there any advantages for the juvenile in such action?

Glossary

Delinquent A juvenile who violates the criminal law or commits a status offense.

Dependent children Juveniles placed under the jurisdiction of a juvenile or family court because of a court finding that the care provided by the parent, guardian, or custodian falls short of the standard of proper care.

Diversion The removal of an offender from the criminal justice system by channeling him or her into a social casework, mental health, or other type of agency. The term has also been used to describe the handling of juveniles in a system separate from the adult criminal justice system and the sentencing of offenders to community-based correctional facilities rather than to prison.

Juvenile A person subject to the jurisdiction of the juvenile court based on an age limit imposed by statute. Jurisdiction is based on the age of the juvenile at the time the misconduct occurred; thus, a person twenty years of age would be tried in juvenile court for a crime committed when he or she was seventeen.

Neglected children Children subjected to sexual or physical abuse by parents or other family members.

Parens patriae Historical doctrine holding that the state is the ultimate parent of the child. The doctrine provided the rationale for the jurisdiction of the juvenile court as a substitute parent to guide, train, care for, and maintain custody of juveniles.

Status offense The violation of a statute that applies only to juveniles and that has no counterpart in the adult criminal code (e.g., truancy, running away from home, "incorrigibility").

Transfer Decision by a juvenile court to waive jurisdiction over an alleged delinquent and allow him or her to be prosecuted as an adult in criminal court. At a transfer hearing, probable cause must be shown to support the charge that the juvenile committed the offense.

References

Beck, B. M., and Beck, D. B. "Recreation and Delinquency." In *Task Force Report: Juvenile Delinquency and Youth Crime* by the President's Commission on Law Enforcement and Administration of Justice. Washington, D.C.: U.S. Government Printing Office, 1967.

Cloward, R. A., and Ohlin, L. E. *Delinquency and Opportunity: A Theory of Delinquent Gangs.* Glencoe, Ill.: Free Press, 1960.

Empey, L. T. "The Social Construction of Childhood, Delinquency, and Social Reform." In *The Juvenile Justice System,* edited by M.W. Klein. Los Angeles, Calif.: Sage, 1976.

Empey, L. T. *American Delinquency: Its Meaning and Construction.* Homewood, Ill.: Dorsey, 1978.

Faust, F. L., and Brantingham, P. J., eds. *Juvenile Justice Philosophy: Readings, Cases, and Comments.* St. Paul, Minn.: West, 1979.

"Fifteen-year-old Draws Probation for Murder." *Tampa Tribune,* 9 May 1978, p. 8A.

Flanagan, T. J., Hindelang, M. J., and Gottfredson, M. R. *Sourcebook on Criminal Justice Statistics.* Washington, D.C.: U.S. Government Printing Office, 1980.

Fleisher, B. M. *The Economics of Delinquency.* Chicago: Quadrangle, 1966.

Hamparian, D. M.; Estep, L. K.; Muntean, S. M.; Priestino, R. R.; Swisher, R. G.; Wallace, P. L.; and White, J. L. *Youth in Adult Courts: Between Two Worlds.* Washington, D.C.: U.S. Department of Justice, Office of Juvenile Justice and Delinquency Prevention, 1982.

Kiersh, E. "Minnesota Cracks Down on Chronic Juvenile Offenders." *Corrections Magazine* 7 (1981): 21.

Kobetz, R. W., and Bosarge, B. B. *Juvenile Justice Administration.* Gaithersburg, Md.: International Association of Chiefs of Police, 1973.

Mack, J. C. "The Juvenile Court. In *Juvenile Justice Philosophy: Readings, Cases, and Comments,* edited by F. L. Faust and P. J. Brantingham. St. Paul, Minn.: West, 1979.

Mann, D. *Intervening with Convicted Serious Juvenile Offenders.* Washington, D.C.: U.S. Government Printing Office, 1976.

Miller, W. B. *Violence by Youth Gangs and Youth Groups as a Crime Problem in Major American Cities.* Washington, D.C.: U.S. Government Printing Office, 1976.

National Advisory Committee on Criminal Justice Standards and Goals. *Report of the Task Force on Juvenile Justice and Delinquency Prevention.* Washington, D.C.: U.S. Government Printing Office, 1976.

National Council on Crime and Delinquency. "Corrections in the United States." *Crime and Delinquency* 13 (1967): 1–281.

Nold, J., and Wilpers, M. "Wilderness Training as an Alternative to Incarceration." In *A Nation Without Prisons,* edited by C. R. Dodge, Lexington, Mass.: Lexington, 1975.

Phelps, T. R. *Juvenile Delinquency: A Contemporary View.* Pacific Palisades, Calif.: Goodyear, 1976.

President's Commission on Law Enforcement and Administration of Justice. *Task Force Report: Corrections.* Washington, D.C.: U.S. Government Printing Office, 1967.

Rothman, D. *The Discovery of the Asylum.* Boston: Little, Brown, 1971.

Rubin, H. T. "Retain the Juvenile Court? Legislative Developments, Reform Directions, and the Call for Abolition." *Crime and Delinquency* 25 (1979): 281–98.

Scarpitti, F. R., and Stephenson, R. M. "A Study of Probation Effectiveness." *Journal of Criminal Law, Criminology, and Police Science* 54 (1968): 361–69.

Schafer, W. E., and Polk, K. "Delinquency in the Schools." In *Task Force Report: Juvenile Delinquency and Youth Crime*, by the President's Commission on Law Enforcement and Administration of Justice. Washington, D.C.: U.S. Government Printing Office, 1967.

Singell, L. "Economic Opportunity and Juvenile Delinquency: A Case Study of the Detroit Labor Market." Ph.D. dissertation, Wayne State University, 1965.

Stratton, J. R., and Terry, R. M. *Prevention of Delinquency: Problems and Programs*. New York: Macmillan, 1968.

Tetters, N. K., and Reinemann, J. O. *The Challenge of Delinquency*. Englewood Cliffs, N.J.: Prentice-Hall, 1950.

Trojanowicz, R. C. *Juvenile Delinquency: Concepts and Control*. Englewood Cliffs, N.J.: Prentice-Hall, 1978.

U.S. Department of Justice. Uniform Crime Reports in the United States. Washington, D.C.: U.S. Government Printing Office, 1975.

———. *Children in Custody: A Report on the Juvenile Detention and Correctional Facility Census of 1975*. Washington, D.C.: U.S. Government Printing Office, 1979.

———. *Uniform Crime Reports in the United States*. Washington, D.C.: U.S. Government Printing Office, 1982.

Vachss, A. H., and Bakal, Y. *The Life-Style Violent Juvenile: The Secure Treatment Approach*. Lexington, Mass.: Lexington Books, 1979.

Vinter, R. D. *Time Out: A National Study of Juvenile Correctional Programs*. National Assessment of Juvenile Corrections. Ann Arbor: University of Michigan Press, 1976.

Ward, F. W. "Prevention and Diversion in the United States." In *The Changing Faces of Juvenile Justice*, edited by V. L. Stewart. New York: New York University Press, 1978.

Wilson, R. "The Long-Term Trend is Down: Diversion into Community Programs Has Continued—Despite Public Reaction to Youth Crime." *Corrections Magazine* 2 (1978): 3–11.

"The Youth Crime Plague." *Time*, 11 July 1977, pp. 18–19.

Cases

In re Gault 387 U.S. 1, 87, S.Ct. 1428, 18 L.Ed.2d 527 (1967).
Kent v. U.S. 383 U.S. 541, 546; 86 S.Ct. 1045, 1049-50; 16 L.Ed.2d 84 (1966).
In re Winship 397 U.S. 358, 90 S.Ct. 1068, 25 L.Ed.2d 368 (1970).

17
the victims of crime

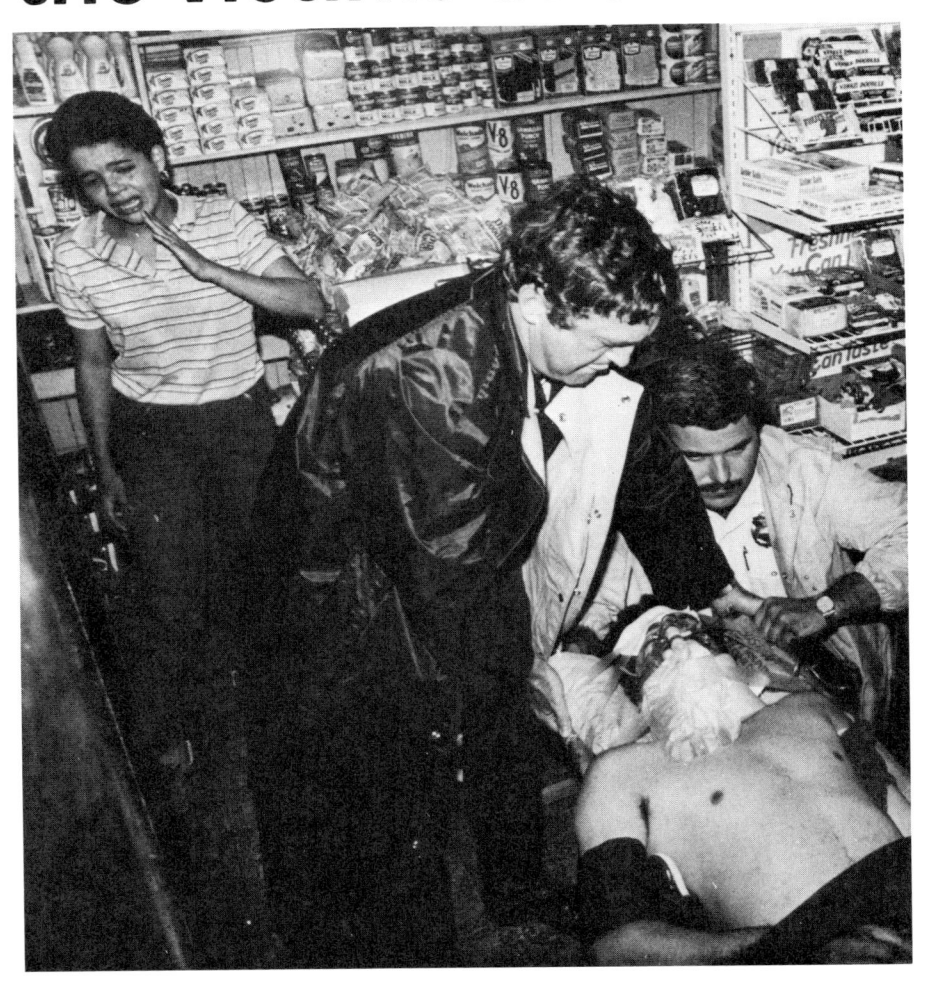

The victim in historical perspective
Talion law
Early forms of compensation
The criminal-victim relationship
Victim precipitation of crime
Victimization studies
Compensation and restitution
Delivery of victim services
Good Samaritans and bystanders
Summary
Issue paper: A larger slice of the law—Crime victims fighting back

Crime victims can hardly be blamed for feeling that the American system of criminal justice has totally neglected them in an exaggerated concern for the rights of offenders. Not only do victims suffer financial losses, but also they are often forced to pay for the treatment of their injuries. In contrast, the criminal receives free medical attention. Public funds pay for the prosecution, and if the criminal has no money, public funds also pay for the defense.

Further, victims may be threatened with reprisal by defendants who are freed on bail or on their own recognizance. They can be intimidated by domineering defense attorneys and forced to take days off from work to appear as witnesses in hearings which are postponed again and again. Rarely are they notified of court dates, and no one bothers to keep them posted about the results of plea bargaining. Months may pass before they are able to recover stolen property being held as evidence.

A recent report of the President's Task Force on Victims of Crime (1982) outlines a series of proposals that, if implemented, might begin to redress these long-standing inequities. Recommendations range from training persons who deal with crime victims to be more courteous and sensitive, to modifying the Exclusionary Rule and abolishing parole. The task force also supports state and federal legislation to require that victim impact statements be presented to the court before sentencing, that victims and witnesses be protected from intimidation, and that victims of sexual assault not be compelled to pay for physical examinations or for medical kits used to collect evidence.

Another recommendation is that federal funding be provided for victim *compensation:* "It is simply unfair that victims should have to liquidate their assets, mortgage their homes or sacrifice their health or education or that of their children while the offender escapes responsibility for the financial hardship he has imposed" (p. 79). Thirty-six states now have at least token funds for victims, but almost all such funds are inadequately financed; some contain so little money that state officials try to keep them a secret.

The task force also feels that hospitals should be required to give emergency treatment to crime victims without regard to their ability to pay; payment should be collected from state compensation funds. Further, judges should order offenders to make *restitution* to victims whenever possible, even when the offender is sent to prison, and should then make sure the payments are actually made. Judges should also give as much weight to the interests of the victims as to the interests of the defendants when ruling on continuances. There should also be more referral and counseling services for victims, involving not only social agencies but also the mental health community and ministry. Prosecutors should be sure that victims are informed about the progress of the case, and victims should get police protection if they are being harassed.

The task force also makes several highly controversial proposals: that bail be denied to persons judged to be clearly dangerous; that parole be abolished (because it undercuts the courts and is unfair to victims, and because parole boards lack accountability); and that the Exclusionary Rule regarding evidence be abolished. The task force has concluded that the

Exclusionary Rule "does not work, severely compromises the truth-finding process, imposes an intolerable burden on the system and prevents the court from doing justice" [p. 28]). Finally, the task force proposes an amendment to the Constitution that would add the following statement to the Sixth Amendment: "Likewise, the victim in every criminal prosecution shall have the right to be present and to be heard at all critical stages of judicial proceedings" (p. 114).

Serious objections have been raised to several of the task force's recommendations that go beyond cosmetic changes in how victims are treated. But it will take more than courtesy and sensitivity to correct the criminal justice system's excessive concern for offenders and its lack of fairness for the victims that society has failed to protect. Congress made a start with its Omnibus Victims Protection Act of 1982, but the act was just that—a start. As the task force makes clear, much more must be done before our system of justice can claim to be just to those who should be its primary concern: "To be a victim at the hands of the criminal is an unforgettable nightmare. But to then become a victim at the hands of the criminal justice system is an unforgivable travesty. It makes the criminal and the criminal justice system partners in crime" (p. 9). Model programs have been developed to deliver victim services (Dussich 1975), but such programs require funding to become fully operational.

Increasing concern for the crime victim within the criminal justice system and the agencies of local, state, and federal governments has been paralleled by a revival of the criminologist's interest in the victim. Although criminologists have contributed to what (as Edelhertz and Geis [1974] point out) has been "gracelessly dubbed" over a period of more than two centuries as the field of *victimology—the systematic study of criminal-victim relationships—the crime victim has never occupied a position of prominence in the field of criminology. Recently, however, attention has been directed toward various groups within society that are especially prone to victimization by criminal offenders—the elderly, children, and the poor.*

THE PERFECT VICTIM

Mike Maryn of Passaic, New Jersey, has been called the perfect mugging victim. Maryn, age 56, is 5 feet 9 inches tall, weighs 150 pounds, and walks with a cane. He has been mugged 83 times by young boys, teenagers, men and even several women.

Maryn has been hospitalized over twenty times because of the muggings. He has been stabbed, shot at twice, and hit over the head with a pipe. His ear was partly cut off; his nose was broken; his ribs were kicked in; his teeth were knocked out; and his skull was fractured.

Passaic's perfect victim has lost more than $2,000 in cash and several bags of groceries. He is now broke, unemployed, and on welfare. The police say that Mike Maryn is easily open to attack because of his nonthreatening appearance, and because he is often on the streets at night. Police also have noted that Maryn drinks a little and has a "cocky attitude" which might contribute to his victimization.

At one point the Passaic police offered to give Maryn a walkie-talkie so that he could call for help. But he turned them down. "It would only be taken from me," he said.

"Crime and Its Victims," *Bill of Rights in Action* 12 (1978): p. 15.

Another player in the crime problem who has been insufficiently researched is the bystander. The *Good Samaritan* who intervenes to prevent a potential victim from harm by a criminal predator and the bystander who watches passively as someone is assaulted mark two extremes of participant-observer behavior that pose interesting and significant problems for society and the criminologist. The notorious case of Catherine Genovese, who was murdered outside her New York apartment while neighbors listened to her screams but did not help her, focused national attention on bystander behavior during violent crimes.

The victim in historical perspective

Redress of injury was once the responsibility of the victims themselves, their immediate families, or others bound to them by blood or tribal loyalties. Thus, the beginnings of social control are apparent in the transition from the individual quest for retaliation to the identification of injuries sustained by the victim with the interests of the victim's family or social group. This idea of familial or blood relationships is central to the concept of the "blood feud." Consanguinity implied a responsibility on the part of the individual's relatives to act on his or her behalf in seeking compensation or vengeance for injuries sustained as the result of a criminal act.

With the increase in population and the growth of the organs of social control, however, it became necessary for the rest of society to set limits on the blood feud. An obvious problem with the private vendetta was the lack of effective means to bring a particular dispute to conclusion. Once started, vendettas tended to become perpetual: each injury spawned a search for vengeance in the form of a counterinjury, and an endless cycle of retaliation and counterretaliation was thus inflicted on society. By transferring this concept from the individual to the nation, and from one society to the international scene, it is possible to see in the vendetta a similarity to the modern arms race and the need for imposing stringent limitations upon weapons and armaments.

Talion law

Talion law *(lex talionis)*, discussed in Chapter 2, represented an early effort by society to constrain the widening circle of damage caused by the blood feud. Central to this law was the concept of "equivalent retaliation." An individual who had suffered injury or loss of property was entitled to a fair and just recompense—one that did not exceed the original injury or loss. Thus, talion law was an effort toward social defense (i.e., toward the imposition of curbs upon parties to the vendetta to protect and maintain the social organization of the tribe or clan).

Early forms of compensation

Additional efforts to mitigate the depredations of the blood feud resulted in the idea of compensation—the payment of damages to placate the victim and to satisfy, at least partially, the desire for vengeance. But compensation has not always been equal to the damage: Fry (1951) notes that the Law of Moses required fourfold restitution for stolen sheep and fivefold restitution for cattle; and Schafer (1968) observes that the 18th century B.C. Code of Hammurabi—which was notorious for its deterrent cruelty—sometimes demanded as much as thirty times the value of the damage caused. Says Schafer, "The criminal's obligation to pay was enforced not in the interest of the victim, but rather for the purpose of increasing the severity of the criminal's punishment" (p. 12).

In time, a tariff system was introduced that set appropriate levels of recompense in relation to the type and extent of injuries inflicted upon the victim. But the system generally did not apply to rape or murder, which were seen as too serious to be compensated for, except in terms of in-kind retaliation. On occasion, however, even homicide was atoned for by a fine in livestock large enough to humiliate the offender and thus appease the desire for revenge.

In one form or another, the system of compensation has prevailed in many cultures of the world. In the Germanic tribes, most injuries were punished by fines called *faida*, meaning "the feud commuted for money." In the development of Anglo-Saxon law, the *bot* (a money payment used to atone for criminal action) came into use, although some classes of particularly serious offenses had no bot—that is, they were "botless" or "bootless." The amount of restitution to be provided in the form of bot was determined by the nature of the crime and the age, sex, or rank of the injured party. Rank was established by a system of *wergilds*, which outlined a hierarchy among the injured parties: a free-born man was worth more than a slave, a man was worth more than a woman, and an adult was worth more than a child. Out of these distinctions developed a complicated system of regulations that constituted the earliest codified law of the Anglo-Saxons.

With the establishment of the king as a strong central authority, the conception of crime changed, as did the methods used to deal with lawbreakers. A crime was defined as an offense against the king's peace and was consequently dealt with by public authority. The dominant way of handling offenders shifted away from compensation and restitution to various methods of corporal punishment and, more recently, to incarceration.

Decline in concern for the victim and for compensation or restitution seems to have been widespread in Western civilization. But this trend was opposed by various individuals and by international prison congresses from the middle of the nineteenth century until well into the twentieth century. Schafer (1977) points out that at the International Prison Congress held in Stockholm, Sweden, in 1878, Sir George Arney, Chief Justice of New Zealand, proposed a return to the ancient practice of requiring an offender to make reparation to the victim. And participants in the International Penal Association Congress at Christiania, Sweden, in 1895, agreed that modern law does not sufficiently consider the reparation due to injured parties; that, in the case of petty offenses, time should be given for indemnification; and that prisoners' earnings in prison might be used for reparation (Schafer, 1977, p. 18).

Four years later (in 1899), the problem of victim compensation was extensively discussed at the International Prison Congress in Paris. One of the principal questions on the agenda was, Is the victim of a delict sufficiently armed by modern law to enable him to obtain indemnity from the person who has injured him? Despite this early interest among criminologists, however, the victim's case at the turn of the century was still not advanced with much success.

By the middle of the twentieth century, interest in the idea of compensation to crime victims had been renewed. This phenomenon, which may be seen as part of a more general concern for civil rights and the rights of minorities, has led to a renewed emphasis by criminologists on the victim's role in the criminal-victim relationship.

The criminal-victim relationship

Hans von Hentig published *The Criminal and His Victim: Studies in the Sociobiology of Crime* in 1948. Hentig advanced the notion that victims themselves often contribute significantly to their own victimization. He suggested that the relationship between the perpetrators and victims of some crimes may be more complex than is recognized by our criminal laws.

Hentig saw the relationship between criminal and victim as one of mutuality. To speak of mutuality is to raise questions about the distinctness of such categories as "victims" and "criminals." As Hentig points out, although the "mechanical outcome of a criminal action may be profit to one party, harm to another, the psychological interaction between the criminal and victim, carefully observed, will not submit to this kindergarten label" (p. 384).

Victim precipitation of crime

As already noted, some people—by virtue of age, sex, infirmity, or similar factors—can be considered potentially more vulnerable to various crimes than are people who do not possess such characteristics. The concept of *victim precipitation*, however, goes considerably beyond victim proneness by postulating that certain personality or behavioral characteristics or certain aspects of relationships may contribute directly to victimization. That is, according to victim precipitation, the blame for various criminal acts is *shared* by the criminal offender and the victim.

In his classic study of murder, criminologist Marvin Wolfgang (1958) introduced the concept of victim-precipitated homicide. According to this concept, certain actions of homicide victims (such as brandishing a weapon or striking the first blow) help to bring about the victim's own death. One out of four of the victims in Wolfgang's study met this criterion. Wolfgang maintains that, in at least some cases, two potential offenders come together in a potential homicide situation, and it is pure chance that one becomes a victim, and the other a perpetrator.

It is widely believed that some rape victims are responsible, either consciously or by default, for their own vitimization—that by word, provocative behavior, dress, or manner, the victim gives the offender the impression that she (or he) is available for sexual liaison. Amir defines victim-precipitated rape this way:

> The term "victim precipitation" describes those rape situations in which the victim actually, or so it was deemed, agreed to sexual relations but retracted before the actual act or did not react strongly enough when the suggestion was made by the offender(s). The term applies also to cases in risky situations marred with sexuality, especially when she uses what could be interpreted as indecency in language and gestures, or constitutes what could be taken as an invitation to sexual relations (1971, p. 266).

According to Amir, 19 percent of the 646 rapes he studied in Philadelphia were victim precipitated; but a study conducted by the National Commission on the Causes and Prevention of Violence (1970) showed that less than 5 percent of rapes that occurred in seventeen U.S. cities could be categorized as victim precipitated.

The issue of victim precipitation in both homicide and forcible rape is complex, delicate, and highly controversial. The law is far from clear on the relative culpability of the victim in many cases. The principle of causation in criminal law is often expressed as *sine qua non* ("without which not"), meaning that the harm would not have resulted but for the act of the defendant. But what about the act of the *victim*?

It is easy to imagine a situation in which a woman's acceptance of overtures toward intimacy may result in encouraging the man to make overtures which she is unready or unwilling to accept. Her "message" may be completely misinterpreted by the other party. Whatever she intended, it is very unlikely that she was encouraging the man to proceed to the extremity of sexual assault. Nevertheless, a sequence of events of this kind might help explain—not justify, but explain—how a rape transpired. And although most circumstances do not excuse an offender's behavior, they may influence the disposition of the case by supporting a reduced charge or a reduced sentence—or the complete withholding of prosecution.

Victimization studies

The official counting of crimes is susceptible to many errors. A major reason for inaccuracy in official crime statistics is that people are reluctant, for a variety of reasons, to report that they have been victimized. Fortunately, victimization studies provide supplemental crime data. Victimization surveys and investigations ask people to indicate the frequency and types of crimes that have been perpetrated against them. In addition to gathering information on selected crimes of violence and theft, these surveys also collect data on the characteristics of victims and the circumstances surrounding criminal acts—including victim-offender relationships, characteristics of offenders, victim self-protection, extent of victim injuries, time and place of occurrence, economic consequences to victims, use of weapons, whether or not the police were called, and reasons advanced for *not* calling the police.

The first nationwide victimization studies were conducted for the President's Commission on Law Enforcement and Administration of Justice. The best known of these studies—a broad-based, well-designed survey conducted by the National Opinion Research Center in 1966—involved interviews in ten thousand households throughout the continental United States. Based on this survey, researchers estimated that the rate of victimization for index crimes was more than twice the rate reported in the FBI's Uniform Crime Reports.

Another series of victimization studies was carried out in twenty-six American cities between 1972 and 1974 (U.S. Department of Justice 1974, 1975a, 1975b). Decker (1977) combined the data from these studies and compared them with FBI crime data for the same years. As shown in **table 17.1,** he found that victims reported almost three times as many index offenses as were recorded in the Uniform Crime Reports. In addition, the uniform crime reports showed a substantial increase in the rate of crime victimization, but the victimization studies did not reflect any significant increase in the number of victims.

Between 1973 and 1976, the FBI's Uniform Crime Reports registered approximately a 30 percent increase in index offenses, including a 12 percent rise in violent crimes and a 23 percent rise in property offenses. For this same period, victimization surveys reported an increase of only 1 percent in crimes of violence and 5.5 percent in property crimes (U.S. Department of Justice 1980, 1981). The figures from these two sources are not totally comparable, of course, but they do suggest that victimization studies may be a more accurate indicator of increases in crime, because they are not subject to the same reporting and recording problems that affect the FBI's Uniform Crime Reports.

TABLE 17.1 Difference of means test for official and survey estimates of crime

	Mean rate (Per 100,000) VIC	UCR	t Value	Degrees of freedom	Significance
Rape	137	50	8.05	25	*
Robbery	1621	582	9.98	25	*
Aggravated assault	766	360	5.28	25	*
Larceny	9581	2737	8.92	25	*
Burglary	6187	2065	13.64	25	*
Motor vehicle theft	1073	1186	−1.68	25	0.10
Violent crime rate	2525	993	9.94	25	*
Property crime rate	16954	5875	10.94	25	*
Overall crime rate	19478	6868	11.11	25	*

*Significant beyond 0.0005.

Reproduced from S. H. Decker, "Official Crime Rates and Victim Surveys: An Empirical Comparison," *Journal of Criminal Justice* (5) 1977: 51, by permission of the author and publisher.

In general, victimization surveys confirm that groups disproportionately involved in the perpetration of crimes—the young, males, the poor, and the black—are also the groups most likely to be victimized (both by crimes against the person and crimes against property). In addition, residents of the central city—our urban ghettos—are much more vulnerable to crime victimization than people who live in nonmetropolitan areas or suburbs. Among commercial victims, retail stores suffer the highest rates of burglary and robbery.

Personal crimes of violence predominantly involve members of the same race. In approximately two thirds of such crimes, victims and perpetrators are strangers to one another. However, rape and robbery more frequently involve strangers than does assault; and both white and black males are more likely than white and black females to be victims of crimes of violence perpetrated by strangers.

The value of information obtained from victimization studies depends on the accuracy and reliability of the survey techniques. A key issue is the adequacy of the sample on which the results are based. Other factors include the fallibility of memory of the crime victims and the truthfulness—or lack of it—that characterizes survey responses.

Early victimization studies (those conducted for the President's Commission on Law Enforcement and Administration of Justice in 1966) were criticized because approximately one quarter of the people who were approached refused to be interviewed, thus introducing an immediate bias in the sample. The National Opinion Research Center's study was challenged because only one available adult in each household was questioned—a method that produced an overrepresentation of women and older persons (the people most likely to be at home during the day). These problems were overcome in later surveys in which everyone over the age of twelve in a household was interviewed; these surveys obtained nearly 100 percent participation of eligible persons and eliminated the excessive reliance on the responses of a single individual in a household.

Victims do not always remember crimes that were perpetrated against them during a given time period. And in some cases, they may not even be aware that they *were* victims (e.g., in such offenses as fraud, embezzlement, or buying stolen property). It is also possible that victimization figures are inflated by respondents who give false reports to justify illegal tax deductions or spurious insurance claims. Unfortunately, there is no easy way to gauge the extent of such overreporting.

Compensation and restitution

Although the terms "compensation" and "restitution" are often used interchangeably, they refer to quite different procedures and points of view. The rationale of compensation is that the state is obligated to bear the responsibility for failing to protect the victim from a criminal act. According to this view, victim compensation is a societal obligation analogous to unemployment compensation, public assistance, or aid to the disabled (Schafer 1977). By requiring the payment of a sum of money, compensation laws seek to redress damage done to the victim. In states without such laws, the only recourse available to the victim is to file a civil suit for damages. Such suits are rarely effective, however, because most criminal offenders are poor, unemployed or underemployed, and possess few tangible assets.

VICTIM NEGLECT

Let us consider a hypothetical case. You are assaulted by an individual whom you discover prowling in your garage, and you suffer moderate injuries which require medical attention, at today's exorbitant prices. Because the would-be felon did not have the opportunity to misappropriate any of your property, and because your injuries were of the "moderate" variety, the charge is reduced to trespassing, a misdemeanor, and the defendant is subjected only to a fine. What portion of the fine is given to you, the innocent victim, to assuage your feelings and to mitigate your medical expenses? Nothing, of course.

Change the scenario and make the offense a felony assault, from which you receive serious injuries. The defendant is convicted and sent to prison. There his medical, educational, vocational, and maintenance needs are fully serviced, at no cost to him. His teeth are fixed, his health is mended, his educational level is improved, he is provided with work skills, and he receives "all the trimmings" on such solemn occasions as Christmas. Supposing you, the victim, are poor—and it is the poor who are the primary victims of crime—and you have no medical insurance, a large family, and a limited income. You cannot even provide "all the trimmings" for your family at the proper holidays.

If you are the victim of a felony assault under such circumstances, you can be potentially destroyed financially or reduced to the demeaning existence that is the lot of the welfare recipient. Nor will sophisticated, scholarly theories about rehabilitation assuage your personal agony. The average victim of crime has a more pragmatic view of justice. . . .

Reproduced from L. P. Carney, *Corrections and the Community* (Englewood Cliffs, N J.: Prentice-Hall, 1977), pp. 103–4.

The first victim compensation legislation was introduced in New York and California in 1965. Today, nearly a third of the states and the federal government have enacted such legislation, and it is probable that the remaining states will do so in the near future. As Kratcoski and Walker observe, "Victim compensation has gained in popularity as a counterbalance to prevailing trends in criminal justice, particularly judicial decisions on offender civil rights, which seemingly have afforded more protection to offenders than to victims" (1978, p. 358).

Most victim compensation programs authorize payment only when the victim has suffered personal injury, not just a loss of property. Moreover, they usually require that victims suffer some *minimum* level of damage or injury before they become eligible for benefits, and they set a maximum ceiling on the amount of compensation the victim can receive. Claims are screened and payments are awarded by a state-appointed board of commissioners responsible for administering the program.

Experience with victim compensation programs has revealed a number of problems inherent in compensation statutes and their effective implementation. Among the major problems are fraudulent claims and attempts at multiple recovery; questionable awards that violate the statute itself or the criteria for eligibility; inflated bills for medical expenses submitted by physicians, hospitals, and pharmacies; and the failure of programs to award compensation of any amount to victims who submit applications. According to Brooks (1975), there is a tendency in nearly all jurisdictions for applicants to be discouraged by bureaucratic red tape and long delays.

Restitution sometimes involves partial or complete payments voluntarily offered by adult criminal offenders—particularly for white-collar crimes—to allay prosecution or to mitigate the sentence. More commonly, however, it involves offender-restitution-to-the-victim schemes that consider both punishment and offender rehabilitation. Such schemes have been adopted experimentally in the United States in recent years, primarily by juvenile courts.

Restitution by adult offenders, either as a condition of probation or voluntarily offered, has been largely limited to cases of fraud, embezzlement, forgery, and other white-collar offenses. As MacNamara and Sullivan observe, "On more than one occasion such offers of restitution and their acceptance come perilously close to the compounding of felonies" (1974, p. 224). These authors also note that court-ordered restitution directed by juvenile court judges against juvenile offenders or their parents has often been less concerned with restoring the victim than with teaching the offender a lesson. In cases involving vandalism against schools, churches, and public property, there is usually little relationship between the amount of restitution—usually paid in services rather than in money—and the actual extent of damage.

A noteworthy attempt at offender repayment to the crime victim is being made at the Minnesota Restitution Center, a community-based correctional program operated by the Minnesota Department of Corrections (1976). The program is offered to selected property offenders sentenced to the Minnesota State Prison, the State Reformatory for Men, and the Minnesota Institution for Women. Participating offenders make restitution to the victim or victims of their crimes. Eligibility for the program is established in a thorough screening designed to eliminate offenders that have a history of drug dependency, severe psychiatric problems, or assaultive offenses, and intelligent individuals who have adequate social skills but have chosen to live outside the law and have not demonstrated any consistent attempt at lawful employment. Once selected for the program, an offender works out a restitution plan with the victim. He or she then becomes a resident of Restitution House until full restitution is made. During this period, the offender must pay for room and board and contribute to the support of his or her own family.

Delivery of victim services

In response to a growing public concern for the plight of victims of criminal offenses, a variety of programs have been developed in recent years to provide victim services. Such programs address both immediate and long-term goals, and services range from crisis intervention by police officers in

A Minnesota inmate signing a restitution contract. Courtesy Bill Powers/Corrections Magzaine.

the emergency treatment of victims to the mobilization of community support for crime prevention activities. An interesting proposal by Dussich (1972) is to establish a community ombudsman to assist crime victims by intervening in the crisis and directing the victim to community resources. Victim service programs can be seen as a formalization of community support and action formerly supplied by neighborhood residents.

Dussich (1975) has also thoroughly analyzed various victim service models and their efficacy. In these analyses, Dussich focused on the objectives or functions—categorized as *primary* or *secondary*—of each model. The primary function of each model, he discovered, is to deliver a broad range of services to crime victims on behalf of the respective agencies that host the programs. These services include:

1. Assuming immediate responsibility for the victim at the scene of the crime
2. Referring or transporting the victim to emergency medical or social service facilities
3. Providing the victim with a companion for a period immediately following the crime
4. Addressing the victim's family situation
5. Protecting the victim from unnecessary exploitation by the media, the police, and the courts
6. Thorough follow-up and assurance of adequate delivery of public assistance services
7. Assisting victims with their responsibilities to the court as key witnesses
8. Counseling victims to prevent revictimization
9. Using information from victim contacts to plan community crime prevention activities

10 Developing public awareness programs to refine the goals of victim services

11 Coordinating victim volunteer programs to supplement existing manpower needs

12 Assisting the families of victims with aftermath arrangements (e.g., insurance, funerals, compensations)

13 Conducting victimization surveys to pinpoint high victimization areas

14 Providing the victim with information about the progress of the case and his or her role and responsibilities in the legal process

Secondary functions of victim service include encouraging victims to report crimes to the police and gathering information from victims to assist in police crime prevention (functions specific to the *police model*), and, in the case of the *district attorney model*, notifying victim-witnesses about court appearances and helping them adjust their schedules to the court's schedule. Additional secondary functions—such as maintaining a hot line for crime victims in need of immediate help or providing victims with a community services directory of key resources—are appropriate to all models.

Dussich notes that victim service programs may be located administratively within a police agency, the office of the public prosecutor, a hospital, or various other agencies (including the office of the county manager, a religious mission, a private agency, or a volunteer agency). "The phenomenon of manifest self-interest occurs in all models. The host agency, in large part, determines *what* the priorities are, and *how* they will be carried out" (1975, p. 7). Thus, a program within a police agency offers the advantage of quick referral; yet many victims shy away from anything associated with the police and are likely to refuse services from this source. Similarly, programs within the office of the public prosecutor gain from identification with the prestige and authority of the judicial process; on the other hand, however, the tendency of the prosecution to stress the victim's role as a *witness*, rather than as a *victim*, and the lack of proximity to referral services are distinct disadvantages.

The religious mission is a ready-made, caring agency that is already staffed and funded and offers the advantages of the dedication of its personnel and its acceptance within the community. In general, private agencies are more flexible than publicly funded programs in the delivery of services. Unfortunately, however, such agencies are apt to suffer from difficulties in gaining access to the processes of the criminal justice system. "Referrals to these programs . . . are made reluctantly and subsequent referrals made by the program to other community resources are given low priority" (Dussich 1975, p. 9). Volunteer programs also suffer the disadvantage of being outside the formal criminal justice system—despite community support and a high level of motivation and enthusiasm among volunteer participants. Like private agencies, volunteer agencies are extremely restricted in their ability to make lasting changes within the system.

The value of any program, Dussich observes, is measured by its ability to deliver services to its clients. He identifies the two most relevant functions of a victim services program as victim restoration and crime reduction. The three critical factors in victim restoration are physical recuperation from assault, emotional readjustment from trauma, and improvement of living conditions altered by the victimization. In terms of crime reduction, target areas include increased crime reporting, increased offender conviction, increased offender responsibility, and crime prevention. Dussich remarks that the specialized handling of these services is developing into a new profession called "victim advocacy." The main mission of the victim advocate is to "address the plight of victims locally and generate new techniques, strategies, and systems for humanizing the way victims are dealt with by the criminal justice system" (1975, p. 1).

Dussich's belief that the role of victim advocate must be legitimized and institutionalized is perhaps best exemplified by his proposal to establish victim ombudsmen in the community. It is abundantly clear from Dussich's review of victim service models that the variety of services required by victims can not be encompassed by any single public or private agency. Thus, we will probably witness a period of experimentation, of trial and error, in which victim service models and programs will be judged in terms of their results. In any event, we will probably end up with a number of programs in various host agencies within the public and private sectors, supported by both private and federal funding.

Good Samaritans and bystanders

An event that occurred in New York City in 1964 raised disturbing questions about the social climate of the large city and the response of urban Americans to citizens who fall victim to crime. In the early morning hours of 13 March 1964, a young woman named Catherine Genovese was stabbed to death outside her apartment in a middle-class neighborhood of Queens. Thirty-eight of her neighbors witnessed at least part of the attack, but none of them went to her aid or even called the police until after she was dead. *New York Times* editor Abe Rosenthal, author of the book *Thirty-Eight Witnesses*, observes that most of the witnesses were "neither defiant or terribly embarrassed nor particularly ashamed. The underlying attitude or explanation seemed to be fear of involvement of any kind" (1964, pp. 78–79). Witnesses defended their inaction with such statements as, "I was tired," "We thought it was a lover's quarrel," "I didn't want my husband to get involved," and "I don't know."

The publicity surrounding the Genovese case provoked speculation—lay and professional—on the motives of the thirty-eight neighbors and the significance of the entire episode. The obvious question—Why didn't someone help?—was asked repeatedly. And researchers Milgram and Hollander (1970) asked the more significant question, Why *should* anyone have helped? Why should anyone have taken the trouble to go to the aid of the victim or even to call the police?

There are no easy answers to these questions. However, it is believed that a number of social conditions that characterize urban industrial life set up barriers to bystander action. Because most interaction in modern society takes place on an impersonal level, a positive response to another person's plight requires an expression of care and concern that is atypical of the way people respond in most situations (Shaskolsky 1970). In addition, the middle class is not socialized to deal with or use violence, even when it is called for or justified by the circumstances. Within a highly specialized society such as ours, extraordinary situations are assumed to be the concern of specialists—in this case, the police. Often, however, people fail even to summon the police, a failure that has been attributed to the reluctance of bystanders to intervene in situations in which they have no personal mandate and which may cause them embarrassment, resentment, and possible physical danger. In addition, people may take refuge in the belief that the police have already been summoned or in the feeling that the police would be unable to do anything anyway (McCall 1975).

NON CITIZEN ACTION
Cheryl McCall PEOPLE Weekly

The day was sunny, and hundreds of people strolled the Brooklyn neighborhood. Suddenly a man walked out of a doorway carrying an apparently unconscious woman. He went to a car at the curb, opened the trunk and stuffed her inside as if she were a laundry bag. He slammed the trunk and drove off.

The incident was unusual even by the sometimes bizarre standanrds of behavior in New York City. Yet among several witnesses who paused to watch, not one stepped forward to question the man. No one wrote down the car's license number. No one called the police.

An isolated case, an atypical reaction? Not at all, says Harold Takooshian, an assistant professor of psychology at Fordham University, and he has films to prove it. The "trunk abduction" scene was carefully staged by student volunteers and repeated 20 times over several weeks while a hidden movie camera photographed it. The lack of public response proved depressingly consistent.

For more than two years Takooshian has conducted a study of citizen apathy in New York and 19 other U.S. and Canadian cities. He already has ample evidence to suggest that urban Good Samaritans are in critically short supply.

In a series of experiments in New York City, Takooshian sent out his volunteers—some of them obviously too young to be car owners—to jimmy open 310 locked cars and to walk off with fur coats, cameras, TV sets and CB radios planted inside by the researchers. Every effort was made to make the little dramas appear suspicious. Yet of some 3,500 witnesses, only nine showed interest enough to inquire, "Is this your car?" Five of those who intervened were policemen. Another who responded with more than ordinary vigor was a visitor from Cleveland: At first he actually helped the researcher break into the car, then realized something was wrong. At that point, Takooshian says, "He took off after our man and was trying to kill him with his bare hands. We had to rush over to pull him off."

Takooshian used men and women of differing ages and races as the "thieves." They dressed in various styles and worked both rich and poor neighborhoods. "The rate of intervention was very low," the professor reports. "We found that the appearance of the suspect, the appearance of the car or the time of day and neighborhood did not matter."

Outside New York City, says research associate Herzel Bodinger, results tended to be better, but nothing to cheer about. Phoenix scored highest in the number of public-spirited citizens with a 25 percent "intervention rate." San Francisco, Fort Lauderdale, Los Angeles and Chicago all had 20 percent. At the opposite end, Boston, Baltimore, Buffalo, Toledo, Miami and Ottawa came up zero. "Cities where the police have a reputation for law and order,"

Filmed by a hidden camera, a psychology student tempts citizen interaction by prying a car lock and taking a fur coat. New Yorkers stared but refused to react in this and thirty other similarly staged thefts. Courtesy Michael Abramson/Gamma-Liaison.

Takooshian says, "had high intervention rates. Citizens tend to get involved." But he cautions, "We don't know yet if there is a correlation."

A native New Yorker with a Ph.D. in social psychology, Takooshian, a 30-year-old bachelor, has had considerable personal experience with crime—as a victim. He has been mugged, his Manhattan apartment burglarized, and he has lost four motorcycles to thieves. He is particularly incensed that his 92-year-old grandmother has been robbed a dozen times in broad daylight in the south Bronx. No arrests resulted from any of the crimes.

On the chance that some citizens refuse to intervene out of fear for their own safety, the researchers introduced a new twist: A uniformed policeman, armed with gun, nightstick and handcuffs, was stationed 50 feet away. "Not a single witness said a word to him," reports Takooshian, "but five people warned the thief to look out for the cop." After one test researchers interviewed a sidewalk vendor who snarled, "I saw it, but I don't give a bleep. Take the whole block; it's not mine."

Takooshian acknowledges that there was heated argument among his students at Fordham this spring over a highly publicized case in which a Manhattan photographer, Paul Keating, was killed when he tried to stop two muggers from attacking a teenager. "People believe the streets belong to the criminal and the object is to stay alive," Takooshian despairs. "Some reacted as if Keating's death was his own fault. It burns me up when they say he shouldn't have intervened." Police often counsel against getting involved in a fight, but Takooshian says, "Nobody should just walk by if he sees a crime in progress." If direct intervention is dangerous, he suggests, gather with other bystanders at a safe distance and yell at the offender in an attempt to frighten him away. At the very least, phone the police.

"One sociologist has called Americans a nation of willing victims," Takooshian says. "If people became more involved, I'm sure street crimes would decrease." The reason, he adds, is embarrassingly basic: "Criminals don't want to be caught."

Republished from Cheryl McCall, PEOPLE Weekly July 28, © 1980, Time Inc.

Latané and Darley (1970) have studied the circumstances under which bystanders *do* take action to aid a victim. They indicate that the intervention process involves a sequence of five decisions: the bystander (1) notices that something is happening; (2) interprets the event as an emergency; (3) assumes some degree of personal responsibility for helping; (4) decides the appropriate form of assistance to be given; and (5) implements the intervention. McCall maintains that the most critical factor in bystander response is the assumption of personal responsibility. Research indicates that this action is *inversely* related to the number of persons present in a given situation (Latané and Darley 1970). That is, the more persons that witness a situation, the less likely it is that any one of them will act to help the victim. Latané and Darley suggest four reasons why this occurs (1970, p. 125):

1 Other bystanders inhibit the potential helper by serving as an audience to his or her actions.
2 Other bystanders guide behavior; if they are inactive, the potential helper will also be inactive.
3 The interactive effect of the two proccesses of guidance and inhibition will be much greater than either alone; if each bystander sees other bystanders momentarily frozen by audience inhibition, each may be misled into thinking that the situation must not be serious.
4 The presence of other people dilutes the responsibility and urge to act felt by any single bystander (this is referred to as diffusion of blame or responsibility).

Conklin points out that the American system of law does not generally require a witness to an emergency to help the victim if the predicament is not caused by the witness. In fact, says Conklin, "Anglo-American law warns witnesses that they face certain risks if they try to help a victim and fail; sometimes they may be sued for harming the victim as a result of errors they commit during their rescue attempt. Our legal system thus discourages bystander aid to victims" (1975, p. 217).

In nations such as France and Germany, however, affirmative action by witnesses is *required* by the law under certain conditions. But American law not only fails to require such assistance, it also provides relatively little opportunity for a witness to collect for injuries suffered during a rescue attempt. Thus, there are no incentives to help a victim. Rather, in its failure to absolve the well-intentioned rescuer from a civil suit by a victim or a victim's dependents, the law actually *discourages* altruistic behavior by a prospective helper. Fear of legal repercussions may inhibit willingness to help even in situations that do not involve a threat of physical injury.

One of the major obstacles to the passage of Good Samaritan legislation is that there is no organized effort to support such laws. In addition, the public does not completely understand that, despite their status as specialists, the police require a great deal of public cooperation to function effectively. In addition, police officers, physicians, and firefighters tend to be critical of citizens for amateurish attempts to render aid in emergencies.

Despite these obstacles, however, Conklin feels that Good Samaritan legislation is needed:

> Knowing the people are not legally obligated to help victims or to intervene in a crime may make potential offenders more likely to commit a crime. This will reinforce public fears and make Good Samaritan laws even more difficult to pass. Still, the absence of such laws is not the major reason that people do not respond to victims in distress, although such laws might occasionally influence behavior. The presence of a law, even if unenforced and lacking strong impact on behavior, might create confidence that *others* would help. This could increase social solidarity and make people more willing to walk the streets at night because of the feeling that they could depend on others to help in an emergency. This view might be inaccurate, but it still could be self-fulfilling if it leads people to spend more time on the street, since potential criminals might be less willing to commit crimes in the sight of others. For such an effect to occur, a potential offender would have to feel that there was some chance of being interfered with or reported to the police by witnesses (pp. 222–23).

Until or unless the behavior of people in public places is supported by such legislation, this observation by Alan Barth will probably hold true:

> Let us bear in mind . . . that the original Good Samaritan extolled by St. Luke was fortunate in not arriving on the scene until after the thieves had set upon the traveler, robbed him, and beaten him half to death. The Samaritan cared for him and showed him great kindness, but he did not put himself in peril by doing so. Perhaps this is about as much as can be reasonably asked by the ordinary mortal man (1966 p. 163).

Summary

Victims of crime and their relationships with criminals were briefly explored in this chapter. Beginning with an historical sketch of the ways in which various societies in the past have dealt with the victim of crime, the pioneering work of Hentig and Mendelsohn in the development of victim typologies was discussed and some consideration was given to the issue of victim compensation and restitution. Models for the delivery of victim services were also examined briefly. Victimization surveys and their significance for the assessment of crime were treated in some detail, and the chapter concluded with several observations on the bystander who remains a passive witness to someone else's victimization.

issue paper

A LARGER SLICE OF JUSTICE—CRIME VICTIMS FIGHTING BACK

In January 1983, a federal judge in New York upheld a jury award of $30,000 to the parents of Bonnie Joan Garland, a twenty-year-old Yale University student who was bludgeoned to death by her boyfriend, Richard Herrin, when she told him she was breaking off their relationship. Herrin was found guilty of manslaughter and sentenced to eight to twenty-five years. Outraged by the sentence, Ms. Garland's parents filed a $3.3 million suit against Herrin in 1979, seeking damages for wrongful death. The resulting judgment against Herrin in 1983 held that he had recklessly caused the Garlands severe emotional distress. Says Bonnie's mother, "Now a criminal can't say, 'I have no responsibility for the damage I've done you.'" (Brach, 1983, p. 40).

In Denver, a young woman named Stacey Johnson was approached late at night in a suburban parking lot by a man who asked her to help him get his truck started. After driving around in a fruitless search for jumper cables, the two returned to the lot, where without warning, the man stabbed Ms. Johnson seven times, putting her in the hospital for a month. Her assailant, a twenty-eight-year-old named Gary Tucker, was eventually sentenced to eight years for attempted murder. Ms. Johnson filed a civil suit against him for $6 million in damages. Jurors decided that this was not sufficient recompense for the injuries inflicted, and they raised the sum to $8 million. "I wanted to punish him," said Ms. Johnson, "I wanted to strike back" (ibid.).

In St. Louis the police finally apprehended two men accused of burglarizing a physician's office five times in a single year. The men pled guilty to a lesser charge, were fined $50 apiece, and were placed on two years' probation. The irate physician filed a suit for $200,000 in punitive damages. His attorney said that the suit was intended to "put the word out on the street that potential burglars are taking risks not only with the authorities but also with the people being victimized" (Rottenberg 1980, p. 22).

These people—the grief-stricken parents of a murdered girl, the assault victim, and the physician—are among the growing number of crime victims turning

Joan and Paul Garland, parents of Bonnie Garland, were awarded $30,000 by a federal jury for emotional distress they suffered when their daughter was beaten to death. Courtesy Wide World Photos.

Richard Herrin, left, convicted murderer of Bonnie Garland. Courtesy N.Y. Daily News.

to the civil courts when the criminal courts fail to provide satisfaction. Regardless of financial awards for damages, such action relieves these victims of feelings of helplessness and frustration that occur when the criminal justice system seems more concerned with the rights of criminals than with the rights of the victims. As an attorney in Wyoming says, "Such cases are as close to basic historical justice as man has ever known" (Beach 1983, p. 40).

The satisfaction of suing a criminal like Herrin may be purely symbolic, however. As F. Lee Bailey has observed, violent crimes are not ordinarily committed by the wealthy. Nevertheless, there are exceptions, and government is making it easier for victims to lay hold of their assailants' assets. Several states have passed "Son of Sam" laws (named for David Berkowitz, the multiple "lover's lane" slayer) that require criminals to put into state-controlled escrow funds any profits made from books or recounts of their crimes. These funds are used to satisfy claims from victims or their survivors. The widow of a man stabbed to death by Jack Henry Abbott, protégé of Norman Mailer and author of *In the Belly of the Beast* (1981), has already sued for damages under New York's "Son of Sam" law.

When the criminal has no money, some victims gain tangible satisfaction by suing a "third party" whose carelessness or negligence was responsible for the crime. For example, in 1979, a widow sued the state of Washington after her husband was slain by a prison inmate participating in a "Take a Lifer to Dinner" program. The court held that the warden and the state were negligent in allowing a man with a record of forty felonies and seventeen escape attempts to leave the prison grounds. The widow collected $186,000 (Rottenberg 1980). And a couple in California sued the California Youth Authority after their son was assaulted by a youth who had been released from jail without receiving the psychiatric treatment ordered as a condition of his release. The case was settled out of court for more than $200,000.

All such cases are not directed against government agencies, however. A Denver secretary who was sexually assaulted in her apartment was awarded a total of $350,000 from her assailant and the building developer. Her attacker was an employee who obtained a master key as a result of the developer's carelessness. In July 1976, singer Connie Francis, who was the victim of a rape in a motel in West-

Connie Francis and her husband, Joseph Garzilli, outside federal court in Brooklyn, N.Y., during the civil trial involving her lawsuit against Howard Johnson Motor Lodges. Courtesy Wide World Photos.

bury, New York, was awarded $2.5 million by a Brooklyn federal court jury. Her lawsuit against Howard Johnson's charged that the motel chain had been negligent in failing to provide adequate door locks and other security measures.

Despite the skepticism of F. Lee Bailey, attorney Frank Carrington, an official of the Crime Victims Legal Advocacy Institute and a member of the Presidential Task Force on Victims of Crime, believes that civil litigation can be effective as a new weapon for crime victims. Carrington goes even further in suggesting that victim advocate groups should seek state funds to finance such lawsuits, just as defendants receive free legal counsel. Says Carrington:

> The idea of state assistance in filing victims' rights lawsuits is certainly novel. Moreover, it would appear to stand up under analysis. We have seen the growth of any number of state-funded human rights and civil rights boards and commissions charged with the laudable task of enforcing the civil rights of our citizens. Why, then, should not the government get into the business of enforcing the rights of victims of crime? (1981, p. 311).

Why not, indeed? As Carrington himself observes, the victims of crime in the United States are long overdue for their day in civil court.

Discussion and review

1. How did early societies attempt to provide compensation or restitution to the victims of crime?
2. Discuss von Hentig's contributions to victimology. How did he view the criminal-victim relationship?
3. Why is the concept of victim precipitation so controversial? In your judgment, is the concept adequately supported by the evidence?
4. What are victimization surveys and why are they important?
5. Summarize the major findings of victimization studies. What are some of the principal limitations of these findings?
6. Distinguish between compensation and restitution. What kinds of problems have been encountered at the state level in the operation of compensation programs?
7. Discuss the Minnesota Restitution Center's approach to victim restitution. Is this an adequate and effective model for establishing similar centers elsewhere in the country?
8. What are the main functions of a victim services delivery system? Can these services be handled better by a single, unified system or by a diversity of programs?
9. What are some of the issues raised by the bystander responses in the murder of Catherine Genovese.
10. What is your position (pro or con) on Good Samaritan legislation? Defend your stand.
11. Discuss the role of the civil courts in providing redress for crime victims. As Frank Carrington suggests, should the state help fund civil lawsuits?

Glossary

Compensation Action taken by the state to restore some or all of the losses sustained by a crime victim.

Composition The sum of money paid by the aggressor to the victim (or to the victim's family if the victim dies) as satisfaction for wrong or personal injury.

Good Samaritan doctrine The concept that a person who sees another person in imminent and serious peril through the negligence of another can not be charged with contributory negligence (as a matter of law) in risking his or her own life or serious injury in attempting to effect a rescue (provided the attempt is not recklessly or rashly made).

Ombudsman An official or semi-official office to which people may come with grievances against the government. The ombudsman stands between citizen and government and represents the citizen.

Restitution The repayment by a criminal, in money or services, of losses suffered by the victim or society as a result of the criminal's offense.

Victim precipitation The direct, immediate, and positive contribution of a victim to the occurrence of the crime. The term is used primarily to refer to crimes against the person (homicide, rape, and assault).

Victimology A growing body of fact and theory that reflects the systematic study of crime victims, their relationship with criminals, and programs intended for assistance and reparation.

References

Abbott, J. H. *In the Belly of the Beast: Letters from Prison.* New York: Random House, 1981.
Amir, M. *Patterns in Forcible Rape.* Chicago: University of Chicago Press, 1971.
Barth, A. "The Vanishing Samaritan." In *The Good Samaritan and the Law*, edited by J. M. Ratcliffe. New York: Doubleday, 1966.
Beach, B. H. "Getting Status and Getting Even." *Time*, 7 February 1983, p. 40.
Brooks, J. "How Well Are Criminal Injury Compensation Programs Performing?" *Crime and Delinquency* 21 (1975):50–56.
Carrington, F. "Victim Rights Litigation—A Wave of the Future?" In *Perspectives on Crime Victims*, edited by B. Galaway and J. Hudson. St. Louis, Mo.: C. V. Mosby, 1981.
Conklin, J. E. *The Impact of Crime.* New York: Macmillan, 1975.
Decker, S. H. "Official Crime Rates and Victim Surveys: An Empirical Comparison." *Journal of Criminal Justice* 5 (1977):47–54.
Dussich, J. P. J. "The Victim Ombudsman." *Governor's Council on Criminal Justice.* Tallahassee, Fla.: State of Florida, 1972.
Dussich, J. P. J. "Victim Service Models and Their Efficacy." A paper presented to the International Advanced Study Institute on Victimology and the Needs of Contemporary Society. Bellagio, Italy, July 1-12, 1975.
Edelhertz, H., and Geis, G. *Public Compensation to Victims of Crime.* New York: Praeger, 1974.
Fry, M. *The Arms of the Law.* London: Gollancz, 1951.
Hentig, H. von. *The Criminal and his Victim: Studies in the Sociobiology of Crime.* New Haven, Conn.: Yale University Press, 1948.
Kratcoski, P. C., and Walker, D. B. *Criminal Justice in America.* Glenview, Ill.: Scott Foresman, 1978.
LaFave, W. R., and Scott, A. W. *Criminal Law.* St. Paul, Minn.: West, 1972.
Latané, B., and Darley, J. *The Unresponsive Bystander: Why Doesn't He Help?* New York: Appleton-Century-Crofts, 1970.
McCall, G. J. *Observing the Law: Application of Field Methods to the Study of the Criminal Justice System.* Rockville, Md.: National Institute of Mental Health, 1975.
MacNamara, D. E. J., and Sullivan, J. J. "Composition, Restitution, Compensation: Making the Victim Whole." In *Victimology*, edited by I. Drapkin and E. C. Viano. Lexington, Mass.: Lexington Books, 1974.
Milgram, S., and Hollander, P. "The Murder They Heard." In *Violence: Causes and Solutions*, edited by R. Hartogs and E. Artzt. New York: Dell, 1970.
Minnesota Department of Corrections. *The Minnesota Restitution Center.* Minneapolis, Minn.: State of Minnesota, 1976.
National Commission on the Causes and Prevention of Violence. *Crimes of Violence.* Washington, D.C.: U.S. Government Printing Office, 1970.
President's Task Force on Victims of Crime. *Final Report, December 1982.* Washington, D.C.: U.S. Government Printing Office, 1982.
Rosenthal, A. M. *Thirty-Eight Witnesses.* New York: McGraw-Hill, 1964.
Rottenberg, D. "Crime Victims Fighting Back." *Parade*, 16 March 1980, pp. 21–23.
Schafer, S. *The Victim and His Criminal.* New York: Random House, 1968.
Schafer, S. *Victimology: The Victim and His Criminal.* Reston, Va.: Reston, 1977.
Shaskolsky, L. "The Innocent Bystander and Crime." *Federal Probation* 34 (1970):44–48.
U.S. Department of Justice, Law Enforcement Assistance Administration, National Criminal Justice Information and Statistics Service. *Crimes and Victims: A Report of the Dayton-San Jose Pilot Surveys of Victimization.* Washington, D.C.: U.S. Government Printing Office, 1974.
———. *Criminal Victimization Surveys in the Nation's Five Largest Cities.* Washington, D.C.: U.S. Government Printing Office, 1975a.
———. *Criminal Victimization Surveys in Thirteen American Cities.* Washington, D.C.: U.S. Government Printing Office, 1975b.
———. *Criminal Victimization in the United States, 1975.* Washington, D.C.: U.S. Government Printing Office, 1977.
———. *Criminal Victimization in the United States, 1978.* Washington, D.C.: U.S. Government Printing Office, 1980.
———. *Criminal Victimization of California Residents.* Washington, D.C.: U.S. Government Printing Office, 1981.
Wolfgang, M. E. *Patterns of Criminal Homicide.* Philadelphia: University of Pennsylvania Press, 1958.

18
crime control and prevention

Historical overview

Citizen responsibility in crime prevention
Getting involved
A sense of community

Attacking the infrastructure
Education
Employment
Recreation
Counseling and treatment

Neighborhood action
Block clubs
Neighborhood watches
Citizen patrols
    Building patrols
    Neighborhood patrols
    Social service patrols
    Community protection patrols
Environmental design

Crime reporting projects
WhistleStop
Radio watches
Crime Stoppers
Educational programs

Court volunteers

Correctional volunteers

Summary

Issue paper: The Guardian Angels—Good Samaritans or vigilantes?

ALL societies impose sanctions to protect lawful members of society from individuals or groups that engage in deviant behavior. The sanctions imposed and the means employed to control or prevent such behavior are as diverse and complex as human nature itself. In this chapter, we look at some of the recent developments in crime control and prevention and examine the recommendations of several highly respected national commissions. We also examine some of the social factors that lead to crime—such as unemployment, poor education, and lack of recreational opportunities. Further, we discuss what action citizens can take to reduce the crime that emanates from these factors. Lastly, we examine how citizens can work with the police, courts, and corrections to make each component of the criminal justice system more efficient, more effective, and more responsive to the needs of society.

Historical overview

Great Britain is the world leader in modern crime prevention. Impetus was provided early on by Oliver Cromwell, Thomas deVeil, Henry Fielding, and Sir Robert Peel. Fielding, better known as a novelist and political satirist, is credited with initiating the first crime prevention measures in the mid-1700s. He had two goals: to stamp out existing crime and to prevent future outbreaks of crime (Duncan 1980).[1]

Fielding's emphasis on crime prevention was revolutionary among criminologists of the day. He felt that three steps were needed to ensure achievement of his goals: (1) development of a strong police force; (2) organization of an active group of citizens (a body of citizen householders); and (3) initiation of action to remove some of the causes of crime and the conditions in which it flourishes.

Although developed in the eighteenth century, these steps remain basic to crime prevention and still serve as a model for many contemporary crime prevention programs. When Henry Fielding died in 1754, his half-brother, John Fielding, took over his work. This statement is attributed to John Fielding: "... it is much better to prevent even one man from being a rogue than apprehending and bringing forty to justice" (Texas Crime Prevention Institute 1978 p. 3).

But Fielding's emphasis on crime prevention did not last. Law enforcement officials soon found their time taken up by investigation, apprehension, and prosecution of criminals. Thus, efforts to prevent crime decreased until the 1950s, when Great Britain launched a national crime prevention campaign. By 1963, the Home Office Crime Prevention Training Center had been established in Stafford, England. The center offered formal training in crime prevention to all British police. The principles taught there have become an integral part of the British police function today.

Modern prevention concepts were formally developed in the United States in the early 1960s. Although crime prevention had been the primary focus of private security firms for more than a hundred years, early attempts by law enforcement officials were sporadic. In 1968, John C. Klotter of the University of Louisville (Kentucky) School of Police Administration began studying the British concept of crime prevention and its potential for the American criminal justice system. Klotter's efforts led to the establishment in 1971 of the *National Crime Prevention Institute* (NCPI), sponsored jointly by the Law Enforcement Assistance Administration (LEAA) of the Department of Justice, the Kentucky Crime Commission, and the University of Louisville. Nearly five thousand criminal justice personnel have been trained in the principles and practices of crime prevention at NCPI.[2]

The field has grown significantly since 1971, and several other crime prevention training centers have been established (the Texas Crime Prevention Institute is a prime example). Hundreds of law enforcement agencies, community organizations, and private groups have undertaken crime prevention programs, and new programs are being developed in communities every day. Sponsorship of these programs by the LEAA, state and local governments, and private sources has increased the acceptance of crime prevention practices.

In 1978, LEAA established the *National Center for Community Crime Prevention* within the Institute of Criminal Justice Studies at Southwest Texas University in San Marcos, Texas. The center was established to teach crime prevention skills to citizens representing community-based organizations across the United States. It is committed to dispelling the notion that crime control is the sole responsibility of the criminal justice system.

Citizen responsibility in crime prevention

Citizen involvement in crime prevention is not only desirable, but also necessary (National Advisory Commission on Criminal Justice Standards and Goals 1974).[3] The President's Commission on Law Enforcement and Administration of Justice (1967) emphasizes that direct citizen action is needed to improve law enforcement and that crime prevention should become the business of every American and every American institution. Police and other specialists alone can not control crime: they need all the help the community can give them.

A task force of the National Commission on the Causes and Prevention of Violence notes that

> government programs for the control of crime are unlikely to succeed all alone. Informed private citizens, playing a variety of roles, can make a decisive difference in the prevention, detection and prosecution of crime, the fair administration of justice, and the restoration of offenders to the community (1969, p. 278).

But these and other pleas for citizen action are heeded by few. Most citizens agree that crime prevention is everybody's business, but, as indicated in the previouis chapter, few accept crime prevention as their *own* duty.

The idea that crime prevention is the duty of each citizen is not new. In the early days of law enforcement—well over a thousand years ago—the peace-keeping system encouraged the concept of mutual responsibility.

Individuals were responsible not only for their own actions, but also for the actions of their neighbors. Citizens who observed a crime were obligated to rouse their neighbors and pursue the criminal. Thus, for the most part, peace was kept not by officials but by the entire community.

With specialization in law enforcement, citizens began to delegate their personal responsibilities to paid officials. Law enforcement became a mutifaceted specialty, as citizens relinquished more and more of their crime prevention activities. But such specialization has its drawbacks: in the absence of citizen assistance, neither manpower, nor improved technology, nor money can enable law enforcement to shoulder the monumental burden of combating crime in America.

The need today is for a more balanced allocation of law enforcement duties among specialists and citizenry—for citizens to reassume many of their former responsibilities.

> Community leadership appears all too willing to delegate (or default) its responsibility for dealing with anti-social behavior. Eventually that responsibility is assumed by large, public agencies. . . . [The extremely expensive services of these agencies] never seem to catch up with the need. They come too late to be "preventive" in the most desirable sense of the word. Moreover, the policies are controlled from political and administrative centers far removed from the "grass roots". . . . where delinquency and crime originate through obscure and complex processes."

And in its report *State-Local Relations in the Criminal Justice System*, the Advisory Commission on Intergovernmental Relations notes that

> the distance between city hall or county courthouse and neighborhoods is often considerable. As a result, the delivery of services may be slow, communication channels may be cumbersome, and policy-makers may be unaware of the real needs of neighborhood areas. Moreover, highly centralized decision-making may deter citizens from participating in crime prevention efforts (1971, p. 269).

Many crime prevention authorities believe that the responsibility for planning and implementing some anticrime programs should be placed at the lowest level consistent with sound decision making—that is, in the neighborhood with the individual citizen. Some also advocate that neighborhoods receive financial and technical assistance from the government to spur grass-roots citizen involvement. And in response to recommendations for government decentralization issued by the Advisory Commission on Intergovernmental Relations, the National Advisory Commission on Civil Disorders, and the National Commission on Urban Problems, many people now advocate neighborhood citizen councils that would exercise substantial control over the delivery of neighborhood services, including those related to crime prevention.

Getting involved

The typical citizen response to the crime problem is to demand greater action by the police, the courts, correctional institutions, and other government agencies. Citizens seldom ask what they can do themselves. And when the public finally does decide to act, its activities often are short-lived, sporadic outbursts in response to particularly heinous crimes or crimes that occur too close to home. Fortunately, such limited and frequently counterproductive actions are yielding to more informed citizen involvement in crime prevention.[5]

Before citizens take action, however, they should be aware of the many approaches possible for any given problem. For example, an individual who wants to prevent illicit gambling in the community might inform neighbors that the proceeds from such activities help finance the importation of hard drugs by organized crime. The same goal might also be pursued through a block or neighborhood crime prevention organization. In one case, members of a neighborhood association followed numbers runners to determine the neighborhood gambling network. This information was then turned over to local police.

Further members of churches, social clubs, fraternal groups, or civic associations can exert pressure on their officers and other organization members to discontinue limited and informal—but nonetheless illegal—gambling that occurs on the premises. Slot machines, sports pools, and punchboards may provide enjoyment for a club's membership, but they may also supply funds to criminal elements. Finally, as an employer or employee, a citizen can be alert for signs of inplant gambling. As recommended by the Committee for Economic Development, "Individually, businessmen can clean their own houses. Organized gambling need not be tolerated on business premises . . ." (1972, p. 62).

Concerned citizens can also combat crime through regional or national crime prevention organizations, trade associations, educational institutions, political parties, unions, charities, foundations, and professional societies. For example, the executive vice president of the American Institute of Certified Public Accountants once issued this call to action:

> There are already cases on record where publicly traded companies have become dominated by hoodlums. CPA's should be watchful of changes in ownership and management of their clients.
>
> If they find a once solid company taken over or influenced by unsavory elements, they may have to make a difficult decision. They may decide to withdraw from the engagement or may feel obligated to remain on the scene to protect innocent investors and creditors.
>
> Auditors are expected to have absolute integrity. Any evidence of organized crime coming their way should trigger prompt and drastic action to discharge their professional responsibilities. It should also bring forth cooperation with authorities to discharge their civic duties (Savoie 1969).

No one is asking any organization to make extraordinary sacrifices on behalf of crime prevention. What is suggested is that decisions relating to daily operations be reviewed in terms of their crime prevention impact: Are crimes that come to the attention of the organization reported to the police? Are community crime prevention efforts considered for the organization's charitable donations? Is time off for jury duty or court testimony granted grudgingly? Are management controls so loose that they invite crime?

Even if crime prevention is not the main purpose of an organization, crime prevention opportunities probably still exist. Such opportunities need not focus directly on specific crimes. Tenant patrols may help prevent burglaries in apartment buildings, and cargo security councils formed and supported by local transportation companies may reduce the incidence of cargo theft. But so also will programs aimed at increasing the employability of the jobless, furthering the education of the dropout, supplying adequate medical treatment to the alcoholic and the drug addict, and providing recreational and other constructive activities for youth.

Almost any organization can support and engage in the latter crime prevention activities—which, in the long run, are far more effective than tenant patrols or cargo security councils. Studies reveal that more than 80 percent of prison inmates are high school dropouts, and that the majority of inmates in correctional facilities are functional illiterates (Chamber of Commerce of the United States 1970, p. 62). And research indicates a high correlation between unemployment (or lack of salable job skills) and crime; in some penal institutions, as many as 40 percent of the inmates have no previous sustained work experience. There is also a high correlation between drug addiction and robbery.

Collective efforts by citizens may be directed at strengthening the crime prevention activities of government agencies (e.g., courts, corrections, and law enforcement agencies), or at bolstering anticrime measures undertaken within the private sector. For instance, a block crime prevention asssociation may focus on self-help measures to increase the safety of persons and property over and above the protection afforded by local police. Other citizen groups, such as local chambers of commerce, might sponsor surveys of police effectiveness, propose more effective ways to select judges, or promote community-based correctional facilities.

Citizens may participate in the crime prevention efforts of government agencies by attending community relations meetings conducted by the local police department, by volunteering for probation and programs administered by the city court, by serving as parole volunteers under the supervision of a state parole commission, or by volunteering to help social or rehabilitative agency improve the delivery of its services. Voluntary service by citizens *within* government agencies is also possible. Citizen volunteers may act under the close supervision of an agency, or they may be involved in an advisory capacity—their role being to react to plans and decisions of the agency. Finally, citizens may share planning and decision-making powers with the agency.

Many organizations play important crime prevention roles as a result of initiative taken by their members. Organized efforts to reduce crime do not *replace* individual action: they result *from* it. And organizations do not relieve citizens of their crime prevention duty; rather, they offer citizens excellent reasons and opportunities for exercising that duty.

A sense of community

Important as it is, individual action in crime prevention is not enough. Our society is built upon the premise that people are responsible both for themselves and for the general welfare of others. Exclusive reliance on self-oriented or family-oriented approach to crime prevention can only isolate individuals and families from one another. If that happens, the crime prevention effectiveness of a community as a whole becomes considerably less than the sum of its parts. Indeed, with citizens looking out for themselves only, there is no community and no strength in numbers—only a fragmentation that will embolden criminal elements. Burglars, for example, are encouraged if they know that they do not have to contend with the eyes and ears of an entire neighborhood, but only with the immediate obstacles in an apartment or house intended for entry.

A self-centered approach to crime prevention also causes individuals to transform their residences into fortresses. This action, in turn, increases social isolation and the inability of the block or neighborhood to present a united front against crime. Thus, without a sense of community, the crime prevention potential of mutual aid and mutual responsibility remains unfulfilled.

Attacking the infrastructure

As mentioned earlier, citizens can prevent crime by focusing on the social factors that lead to crime: poor education, unemployment, a lack of recreation, and a lack of adequate counseling and treatment. These factors are the infrastructure, or foundation, of crime.

Education

Many citizens are involved in encouraging school dropouts to complete their education. For example, the "Keep a Child in School" program in Charleston, West Virginia, works with students on a one-to-one basis and makes sure that they have adequate clothing and supplies. Tutors are provided for students who fall behind in their work or need special help.

Other groups offer alternative educational opportunities, such as street academies or vocational programs. New York City's Harlem Prep is one of the best-known and most successful street academies in the country. It is supported by contributions from foundations and industry, and its purpose is to prepare high school dropouts for college. The Philadelphia Urban Coalition runs a vocational program for inner-city high school youths who have poor reading skills and are planning to drop out. The school system and the business community cooperate to give youths the training they need for specific jobs in specific industries. In some areas, citizens are instrumental in familiarizing students with the law and how it affects them. A sixteen-page booklet, "You and the Law" is produced by Kiwanis International and distributed to teenagers to help them understand the concept of freedom under the law.

Many parents donate their time to schools on a daily basis, preparing instructional materials and helping teachers in the classroom. Citizen action has also contributed to the establishment of community schools and neighborhood councils that advise school administrators. Individuals also assist schools in counseling youths on drug use, pregnancy, family breakdown, employment, and various forms of antisocial behavior. Citizens can also get involved by establishing scholarship funds.

Employment

Many business people are working to place disadvantaged youths in summer jobs and in part-time jobs during the school year. The National Alliance of Businessmen's JOBS program has placed almost a million youths in jobs in private business and industry. At the urging of the Urban Coalition and other citizen organizations, some companies are filling a certain percent of new jobs with the hard-core unemployed, and they are setting up new eligibility standards in this regard. In Riverside, California, a group of employers founded the Job Opportunities Council to recruit the hard-core unemployed.

Some citizen groups promote "hire first, train later" programs, in which applicants undergo a two-week orientation program prior to placement with an employer; the employer then provides on-the-job training and other support. But job training and counseling may also come through the citizen organization. Project Bread—a nationwide jobs training program—started in Salem, Massachusetts, as one individual's idea to teach ex-addicts how to earn a living as cooks. Other groups are active in disseminating job information to people who live in areas of high unemployment.

Recreation

Some citizen organizations finance or operate summer camps for disadvantaged youth, and organize sports activities and tournaments. "Send a Kid to Camp" programs sponsored by many local newspapers solicit funds to provide young people with new experiences and recreational opportunities. And some individuals, acting in a "big brother" capacity, regularly take youths to sporting, entertainment, and cultural events.

Some groups finance youth centers or spearhead drives for better parks and other municipal recreational facilities. Current interest in ecology has spurred citizens to develop nature trails in the city and to take teenagers for hikes or camping trips in nearby rural areas. To reach urban youth, the National Audubon Society has established nature demonstration centers at wildlife sanctuaries; three of these centers are located on the outskirts of large cities.

A special program in Washington, D.C., teaches inner-city children about the ecology within the city and encourages them to discover nature trails within their own communities. A top priority for many citizens is to develop additional forms of organized recreation—such as talent shows, arts and crafts classes, and special interest programs that focus on car repair, aviation, weather, motorcycle safety, music, and dancing.

In some cities, citizens have established neighborhood councils that hire gang members to build small parks. Others have organized adventure clubs that feature mountaineering and trips to wilderness areas. One citizen group in an effort to channel youthful energy into constructive pursuits, has authored a booklet on volunteer opportunities for teenagers.

Counseling and treatment

Citizens can counsel and advise youths and adults within a variety of organizational frameworks. For example, counseling might occur in the context of a hot line established to help persons with drug-related problems. There are now over three hundred hot lines in the country for various types of problems. Counseling might also occur at a local YMCA, which refers persons with serious problems to community agencies that supply medical and mental health services, drug abuse rehabilitation, contraceptive counseling, juvenile aid, and legal and psychological services. The Listening Post in Bethesda, Maryland, is a telephone hot line and center for young people who need advice and help. Volunteers at the center create a warm, accepting environment and provide constructive alternatives for troubled youth.

Citizens also volunteer at counseling centers that work to develop better and more secure relationships between children and their parents. Others volunteer at clinics or treatment centers to assist professionals who treat drug or alcohol problems. The Cincinnati (Ohio) Free Clinic, which offers detoxification and medical services to drug-involved individuals, has on staff about four hundred professional and nonprofessional volunteers. In addition to medical aid, these volunteers offer telephone counseling and crisis intervention services.

Educational campaigns against drug abuse are often supported and conducted by citizen groups. At Auburn University in Auburn, Alabama, twenty-two pharmacy students developed a drug abuse program for Alabama high schools. Traveling in teams of two or three, the students show films, lecture, and distribute literature about drug use. In some companies, businesspeople and union officials have embarked on a joint program of education, referral, and follow-up for persons with alcohol problems.

In some cities, citizen groups provide the bulk of financial support for treatment centers. One group supplies over two thirds of the operating funds for a facility offering residential care for addicts and heavy drug users—the Memphis House in Memphis, Tennessee. This facility also offers at-home teaching and helps residents find jobs and housing before they return to the community.

Neighborhood action

As you have seen, the three components of the criminal justice system—the police, the courts, and corrections—are supplemented and strengthened by a wide range of citizen activities. In the rest of this chapter, we examine some of the more important of these activities in detail. This particular section focuses on neighborhood action.

Block clubs

Block clubs may well be the best starting point for organized citizen response to crime. At the block level, citizens can see what is going on in their neighborhoods and can recognize suspicious people or behavior. Citizens also have a vested interest at the block level (e.g., property values, neighborhood safety). And the organizer's task is simplified at the block level, because it is easier to bring together a limited number of people in a specific geographic area than to arrange a community-wide effort (Minnesota Crime Prevention Center 1978, p. 3).

Block security programs improve citizen awareness and concern about public safety by assigning street surveillance or assistance responsibilities to block mothers, block parents, or other individuals (Yin 1976, p. 121). Early contact with the police is important when these programs are implemented.

Neighborhood watches

Neighborhood watches are typical in citizen crime prevention activity. Such programs attempt to improve the reporting of crimes or suspicious activity in the neighborhood. Neighborhood residents are urged to be sensitive to any signs of criminal activity and are often given special telephone numbers to call in case of emergency (ibid.).

Information about neighborhood watches has been widely disseminated by the National Neighborhood Watch Program, which was established in 1972 under a grant to the National Sheriffs' Association from the Law Enforcement Assistance Administration. The program concludes that

Roadside sign at DeKalb County, Georgia, border announces block parent crime prevention program. Courtesy DeKalb County (Georgia) Police Department.

Block parent assists neighborhood children. Courtesy DeKalb County (Georgia) Police Department.

after 4 years of continued growth and refinement, the National Neighborhood Watch Program is a highly effective, nationally based effort reaching millions of citizens. It is efficiently administered by the National Sheriffs' Association and promoted by a balanced, sound program of news media and special audience coverage. The program has gained and maintained major momentum which is currently reflected by the enthusiasm of program participants and by a level of demand, for new or resupply materials, which exceeds supply (Midwest Research Institute 1977, p. 4).

A recent inmate-interview project involving admitted burglars revealed that a neighborhood watch program is the most effective deterrent against burglary. The majority of burglars interviewed said that merely being noticed by a neighbor was enough to deter them. All indicated that they would leave an area if challenged by a neighbor (Palmer 1978, pp. 7–8).

The positive impact of neighborhood watches seems to relate to the number of participants and the degree of personal interaction. Large groups with low involvement have little success in reducing crime or improving the sense of security. In contrast, smaller, more intensive programs can have a positive impact, resulting in improved crime reporting and an eventual reduction in crime and the *fear* of crime (National Institute of Law Enforcement and Criminal Justice 1978, p. 6).

Citizen patrols

Disturbed by crime in their neighborhoods, some citizens have initiated *citizen patrols* to protect neighborhood residents. In some cases, the residents themselves patrol; other neighborhoods hire security guards to do it. Some vehicle patrols cover neighborhood sections and maintain contact through citizen-band radios. Others concentrate on specific buildings or housing areas. More than two hundred resident patrols in sixteen urban areas were identified by the National Evaluation Program in a 1977 report on citizen patrol projects (Yin 1977, p. 111). The National Evaluation Program report is an executive summary of a more extensive report published by the Rand Corporation. The Rand study defines residential patrols as groups that (1) have specific patrol or surveillance routines; (2) have the principal purpose of preventing criminal acts; (3) are controlled by a citizens' organization or a public housing authority; and (4) are directed primarily at residential—rather than commercial—areas (ibid., p. 1).

The Rand study's main contribution to the knowledge of residential patrols was more descriptive than evaluative. For example, research in representative cities involving more than a hundred patrols led to the following conclusions (ibid., pp. 29–31):

1 Contemporary patrols emphasize residential crime prevention. This emphasis is in contrast to the riot-pacification functions highlighted in most literature from the early 1960s.

2. It is estimated that more than eight hundred resident patrols are currently active in urban areas in the United States—in neighborhoods of varied income and racial composition.

3. Contemporary patrols vary widely in cost, but most operate on a small budget on a voluntary basis.

4. Patrols may be divided into four types: building patrols, neighborhood patrols, social service patrols, and community protection patrols.

5. Contemporary resident patrols are susceptible to occasional vigilantism, but not as frequently as the mass media suggests.

6. Building patrols in public housing differ from other building patrols in that the crime problem in public housing may be partially attributable to the residents themselves.

7. Several factors influence a patrol's ability to operate and achieve its goals: personnel, organizational affiliation, and bureaucratization.

Building patrols The main objective of *building* (or tenant) *patrols* is to protect specific buildings and the adjacent grounds (Yin 1976, pp. 55–56). Buildings protected may vary from high-income, high-rise dwellings, to low-income housing for the elderly, to detached houses with private access. Building patrols are distinctive in four ways: (1) they operate in areas with minimal local police activity; (2) they are usually supervised by an official organization that in some way represents the tenants of the buildings being protected; (3) the principal duties of the patrol are to prevent crime and to keep unwanted strangers out of buildings or the immediate area; and (4) patrol members, except in public housing projects, are usually paid guards.

Neighborhood patrols *Neighborhood patrols*, in contrast to building patrols, usually have a poorly defined area of surveillance (ibid., p. 61). The area may cover several blocks, may not have strict boundaries, and may not be patrolled as intensively as buildings. Few neighborhood patrols operate twenty-four hours a day, and because they mainly cover streets and other public areas rather than buildings, they frequently coordinate their activities with the local police. Finally, because it is difficult for neighborhood patrols to distinguish between area residents and strangers, such patrols can only focus on observed behaviors that appear undesirable or suspicious. In contrast, building patrols can screen strangers and deny them access to the premises.

Neighborhood patrols are used in areas of all income levels and ethnic compositions. They may be conducted on foot or in cars, and they may cover certain areas related to activities such as children walking to and from school. When a patrol observes a suspicious incident, it usually reports the observation by radio to a base station or to the police.

Social service patrols *Social service patrols* are building or neighborhood patrols that perform social service functions (ibid., p. 69). The main reason for distinguishing social service patrols is that they tend to have functions other than crime prevention that transcend the immediate objectives of other types of patrols. The social service patrol may be organized around a variety of community responsibilites, of which patrolling is only one. For instance, a patrol might be involved in escorting senior citizens or in providing employment opportunities for youths. There may be a purposeful attempt to recruit youths suspected of causing some of the neighborhood's crime problems to serve as patrol members.

Community protection patrols *Community protection patrols* serve as either building, neighborhood, or social service patrols, but they also monitor police activities (ibid., p. 74). The monitoring is carried out because of a fear of police harassment based on previous incidents or on a generally antagonistic relationship with the police. The emergence of community protection groups is associated with the civil rights movement and the urban riots of the 1960s. In particular, several black patrols were formed in the South—often in connection with urban disorders—to protect black residents from the white community.

Environmental design

A widely recognized crime prevention program in the North Asylum Hill area of Hartford, Connecticut, combines many of the neighborhood security activities discussed herein with a redesign of the neighborhood's traffic patterns. The goal was to decrease burglaries, robberies, and purse snatchings. Streets were closed and traffic was rerouted to diminish through-traffic, to enhance the area's residential character, and to increase residents' use of public space. This well-researched and successful application of the theories of crime prevention through environmental design underscores the importance of neighborhood cohesion in crime control (U.S. Department of Justice, Law Enforcement Assistance Administration, Nation-

Badge identifies volunteers who accompany elderly persons on errands. Courtesy Wilmington, Delaware, Police Department.

al Institute of Law Enforcement and Criminal Justice 1979, pp. 1–2). The following "Tale of Two Projects" (Newman 1978, pp. 39–48) illustrates the importance of environmental design in crime prevention.

A TALE OF TWO PROJECTS

Brownsville and Van Dyke are strikingly different in physical design, while housing comparatively identical populations in size and social characteristics. The high-rise towers at Van Dyke are almost totally devoid of defensible space qualities, while the buildings at Brownsville are comparatively well-endowed with such qualities. It should be mentioned, even before beginning the comparison, that Brownsville, the better of the two projects, is still far away from answering all defensible space design directives.

Review of the objective data on the physical characteristics of the two projects reveals many striking parallels. The projects are almost identical in size, each housing approximately 6,000 persons, and are designed at exactly the same density: 288 persons per acre. Major differences arise in the composition of buildings and the percentage of ground-level space they occupy. Brownsville buildings cover 23 percent of the available land, whereas Van Dyke buildings cover only 16.6 percent of the total land area—including nine, three-story buildings which occupy a large percentage of space but house only 24 percent of the total project population. In addition, the two projects differ in design in that Brownsville is comprised of low, walk-up and elevator buildings, three to six stories, while the latter is comprised of a mix of three-story buildings and fourteen-story high-rise slabs (87 percent of the apartment units at Van Dyke are located in the high-rise slabs). The two projects are located across the street from one another and share the same Housing Authority police and New York City police services.

Differences in physical design of the Brownsville and Van Dyke projects are apparent even to the casual observer. Van Dyke Houses has the appearance of a large, monolithic project. The most dominant buildings are the thirteen, fourteen-story slabs. In less evidence are the nine, three-story structures. Each of the buildings at Van Dyke sits independently on the site, with large open spaces separating it from its neighbors. At the center of the project is a single, large open area, used for a Parks Department playground and for automobile parking. By means of its design, this large open area has been distinctly separated from and is unrelated to the surrounding buildings.

None of the buildings at Van Dyke may be entered directly from the public street. Entrance requires that tenants leave the public street and walk onto project paths that wind into internal project areas, blind to street surveillance. The only areas of the project grounds which relate somewhat to buildings are the small seating areas in the channel of space between the double row of buildings. The functional entrance to the high-rise buildings is a small door shared by 112 to 136 families. This door is located directly off the project paths, with no gradation or distinction indicated by the design of the grounds in front of the building lobby.

Two low-speed elevators carry families to their living floors in each of the high-rise buildings. Elevators are placed directly opposite the building entrances, as mandated by the Housing Authority, to improve surveillance from the outside. Full benefit is not derived from this arrangement, however, since entrances face the interior of the project rather than the street.

The housing floors of the high-rise buildings are each occupied by eight families. The elevator stops in the middle of the corridor, and the apartment units are reached by walking left or right down a dead-end corridor with apartments positioned on both sides (a double-loaded corridor).

In contrast, Brownsville Houses presents the appearance of being a smaller project, due to the disposition of units in smaller and more diverse clusters of buildings. It might

The fourteen and three-story Van Dyke Houses (left side of street) and the smaller building clusters of the Brownsville Houses (right side). Although tenant populations are identical, crime and vandalism rates are 40 to 150 percent higher in Van Dyke Houses. Courtesy Oscar Newman, Institute of Planning and Housing, New York University, New York, N.Y.

be said that the buildings and the way in which they were placed on the site has been used to divide the project into smaller, more manageable zones. The ground areas have been humanized through their relationship with the individual residential buildings. Activities that take place in small project spaces adjoining buildings have become the business of the neighboring residents, who assume a leading role in monitoring them.

All residents and police who have been interviewed at Brownsville perceive the project as smaller and more stable than Van Dyke. All intruders, including police and interviewers, feel more cautious about invading the privacy of residents at Brownsville. By contrast, their attitude toward the invasion of the interior corridors at Van Dyke is callous and indifferent.

This emphasis on space division carries over into the design of the buildings interiors of Brownsville Houses. Individual buildings are three- and six-story structures with six families sharing a floor. The floor is further divided, by an unlocked swinging door, into two vestibules shared by three families each. In the six-story buildings there is an elevator which stops at odd floors, requiring residents of upper stories to walk up or down one flight, using an open stairwell around which apartment doors are clustered. Vertical communication among families is assured by this relationship of elevators to apartments, and also by the presence of open stairwells connecting the floors.

At the ground level, the building lobby leads up a short flight of stairs to several apartments that maintain surveillance over activity in this small entryway. On all floors, tenants have been found to maintain auditory surveillance over activity taking place in the halls by the device of keeping their doors slightly ajar. These features of the building have allowed occupants to extend their territorial prerogatives into building corridors, hallways, and stairs. Those mothers of young children at Brownsville who allow their children the freedom to play on landings and up and down the stairwells monitor their play from within the apartment. A mere interruption in the din of children at play was found to bring mothers to their doors as surely as a loud scream.

By contrast, most young chidren at Van Dyke are not allowed to play in the corridors outside their apartments. The halls of Van Dyke and other high-rise buildings are designed solely for their corridor function and are inhospitable to the fantasy-play of children. In addition, too many families utilize a typical high-rise hall for a mother to comfortably leave her child there unsupervised. For the same reason, mothers are reluctant to leave their door ajar for surveillance—too many people, including strangers and guests of neighbors, wander through the Van Dyke halls unchecked and unquestioned. Finally, to give children real freedom in the use of the building would require their using the elevator or fire stairs to gain access to other floors. But both these areas are frightening and would take the children out of the surveillance zone of the mother and other tenants. The elevator cab is sealed by a heavy metal door that cannot be opened manually. The fire stairwells are designed to seal floors in the event of a fire. A by-produce of their fireproofing is that noises within the stairwells cannot be heard in the corridors outside. Criminals often force their victims into these areas because the soundproofing feature and low frequency of use make the detection of a crime in progress almost impossible.

The sense of propriety which is apparent in the way tenants of Brownsville Houses use their halls to monitor and maintain surveillance over children and strangers appears to have carried over to the grounds adjacent to building entrances. Because of the unique construction of the buildings, there are areas on the ground level just outside the front door of the building where parents can allow their children to play, while maintaining contact with them through their kitchen windows. Interviews have revealed that the range of spaces into which young children are permitted to roam is greater in Brownsville than in Van Dyke.

Finally, where entries to Van Dyke high-rise buildings serve 130 families, Brownsville buildings are entered through different doors, each serving a small number of families (nine to thirteen). The ground area adjacent to these entries has been developed for use by adults, and for play by young children. Parents feel confident about allowing their children to play in these clearly circumscribed zones. Frequently, these entry areas are located just off the public street, and serve to set off the building from the street itself by acting as an intervening buffer area. The placement of entrances just off the street avoids the dangers created at Van Dyke: forcing tenants to walk along blind interior project paths to get to their buildings.

[**Table 18.1** and **table 18.2** reveal] that the tenants of Brownsville and Van Dyke are rated similarly on overall indexes of socio-economic status, family stability, and ethnic, racial, and family composition. It is also clear that these rough similarities are consistent from year to year. Comparison of demographic data over the period 1962 to 1969 reveals few exceptions to this overall pattern of identity between the projects.

It was a widely held belief that many so-called "problem families," displaced by the Model Cities renewal programs, were among recent move-ins to Van Dyke. Many people drew an immediate correlation between the higher crime rate at Van Dyke and this change in population. Information was therefore obtained on a representative sample of families who have moved into the two projects over the past three years. Sample data on one of every five move-ins reveal no striking differences in the social characteristics of residents in both projects.

The total number of move-ins in the past three years in any case constituted fewer than 5 percent of the project population in both Van Dyke and Brownsville. To blame problems of the Van Dyke project on a small number of "bad seeds" is clearly gratuitous. However, to insure that these mean figures were not misleading, frequency distributions

TABLE 18.1 Tenant statistics

Characteristic	Van Dyke	Brownsville
Total population	6,420	5,390
Average family size	4.0	4.0
Number of minors	3618 (57.5%)	3,047 (57.8%)
Percent families black	79.1%	85.0%
Percent families white	5.6%	2.6%
Percent families Puerto Rican	15.3%	12.4%
Average gross income	$4,997	$5,056
Percent on welfare	28.8%	29.7%
Percent broken families	29.5%	31.7%
Average number of years in project	8.5	9.0
Percent of families with two wage earners	12.2%	11.0
Number of children in grades 1–6	839	904

Source: New York City Housing Authority Records, 1968.

TABLE 18.2 A comparison of physical design and population density

Physical measure	Van Dyke	Brownsville
Total size	22.35 acres	19.16 acres
Number of buildings	23	27
Building height	13–14 story 9–3 story	6-story with some 3-story wings
Coverage	16.6	23.0
Floor area ratio	1.49	1.39
Average number of rooms per apartment	4.62	4.69
Density	288 persons/acre	287 persons/acre
Year completed	1955 (one building added in 1964)	1947

Source: New York City Housing Authority Project Physical Design Statistics.

were plotted for each variable which permitted such treatment. For example, the frequency of each family size varying from one to fifteen was plotted separately for Brownsville and Van Dyke and reveals no apparent reason to doubt the representativeness of these summary statistics . . . .

Crime and vandalism are major problems at both Van Dyke and Brownsville Houses. The problem has become serious over the past ten years, with the decline of the old Brooklyn community and the failure to create renewal opportunities. The area surrounding both projects is severely blighted; store owners conduct business in plexiglass booths to protect themselves from addicts. The local library requires two armed guards on duty at all times. The local hospital claims it records fifteen teen-age deaths per month due to overdoses of drugs.

[**Table 18.3**] presents data on major categories of crime for both projects as collected by housing police. Data are presented on specific crimes, including robbery, possession of drugs, and loitering. A comparison of 1969 crime incident rates (see [table 18.3]) and maintenance rates (see [**table 18.4**]) for the two projects was quite revealing. In summary, Van Dyke Homes was found to have 50 percent more total crime incidents, with over three and one-half times as many robberies (384 percent), and 64 percent more felonies, misdemeanors, and offenses than Brownsville. Another measure

TABLE 18.3 Comparison of crime incidents

Crime incidents	Van Dyke	Brownsville
Total incidents	1,189	790
Total felonies, misdemeanors, and offenses	432	264
Number of robberies	92	24
Number of malicious mischief	52	28

Source: New York City Housing Authority Police Records, 1969.

TABLE 18.4 Comparison of maintenance

Maintenance	Van Dyke (constructed 1955)	Brownsville (constructed 1947)
Number of maintenance jobs of any sort (work tickets) through 4/70	3,301	2,376
Number of maintenance jobs, excluding glass repair	2,643	1,651
Number of nonglass jobs per unit	1.47	1.16
Number of full-time maintenance staff	9	7
Number of elevator breakdowns per month	280	110

Source: New York City Housing Authority Project Managers' bookkeeping records.

of security can be understood from examination of the rate of decline of facilities. Even though Brownsville Houses is an older project, beginning to suffer from natural decay, Van Dyke annually required a total of 39 percent more maintenance work. It is interesting to note that the average outlay of time and funds for upkeep of Van Dyke is significantly higher than that of Brownsville. Not only is there less need of repair at Brownsville, but tenants themselves play a greater role in seeing to the cleanliness of buildings either through insistence on the upkeep of janitorial services or by individual effort.

One of the most striking differences between the two projects concerns elevator breakdowns. The far greater number of breakdowns at Van Dyke is primarily a function of more intensive use. However, more breakdowns are due to vandalism at Van Dyke than at Brownsville. This form of vandalism is especially diagnostic, showing that adolescents who tamper with Van Dyke elevators do not have a sense of identity with the people they inconvenience.

As a measure of tenant satisfaction, Brownsville Houses, with smaller room sizes in similarly designated apartment units, has a lower rate of move-outs than Van Dyke Houses. To avoid historical accident and subsequently limited conclusion, results were tabulated annually over an eight-year period, including sampling of move-ins to the two projects. These data have provided additional confirmation of the differences in crime and vandalism between the projects that cannot be assigned to differences in their tenant populations.

It is unwarranted to conclude that this data provide final and definitive proof of the influence of physical design variables on crime and vandalism. It is equally misleading to assume, as management officials initially did, that the differences can be explained away by variations in tenant characteristics in the two projects. The project manager assumed that Van Dyke Houses had a larger number of broken families and that these families had a larger number of children than those at Brownsville. The statistics do not bear out this assumption, but the image described by the manager and other public officials suggests the extent of the problem and may in turn contribute to it.

There are some elementary differences in the physical construct of the projects which may contribute to the disparity of image held by officials. Police officers revealed that they found Van Dyke Houses far more difficult to patrol. To monitor activity in the enclosed fire stairs requires that a patrolman take the elevator to the upper floor and then walk down to the ground level, alternating at each floor between the two independent fire-stair columns.

Police express pessimism about their value at Van Dyke Houses. About Brownsville they are much more optimistic and, in subtle ways, respond to complaints with more vigor and concern. All these factors produce a significant positive effect in Brownsville. At Van Dyke the negative factors of anonymity, police pessimism, pessimism about police, and tenant feelings of ambiguity about strangers (caused by large numbers of families sharing one entrance) conspire to progressively erode any residual faith in the effectiveness of community or official response to crime.

In summary, it seems unmistakable that physical design plays a very significant role in crime rate. It should also be kept in mind that the defensible space qualities inherent in the Brownsville design are there, for the most part, by accident. From a critical, defensible space viewpoint, Brownsville is far from perfect. The comparison of the crime and vandalism rates in the two projects was made using gross crime data on both projects. Twenty-three percent of the apartments at Van Dyke consist of three-story walk-up buildings serving a small number of families. It is likely that comparative data on crime rates in the low buildings versus the towers at Van Dyke would reveal significant differences. This would make the comparison of crime rates between Van Dyke and Brownsville even more startling.

Crime reporting projects

Many civic organizations, in cooperation with law enforcement agencies, sponsor area-wide campaigns to encourage the public to report crimes or information about suspected crimes. Some citizen crime reporting projects operate independently, whereas others are integral components of comprehensive community programs. Some typical crime reporting projects are described in the following paragraphs.

WhistleStop

WhistleStop is a community signal system that facilitates the reporting of in-progress crimes by victims and witnesses. Citizens are urged to carry whistles and to use them if they are victimized, if they observe a crime, or if they hear another whistle. Persons who hear the whistles are supposed to telephone the police and then "sound the alarm" in an effort to disrupt the crime (Gibbs 1977, pp. 89–90).

Radio watches

Participants in *radio watches* must have access to two-way, citizen-band, or ham radios in personal, company, or taxi vehicles. They are urged to report suspicious activities through dispatchers or directly to police departments that monitor emergency frequencies (Bickman 1977). Recent estimates indicate that more than forty-six citizen-band radio patrols are in operation in Chicago (Biggs 1977, pp. 91–92). The Civilian Radio Taxi Patrol in New York City was started in spring of 1973 as the result of cab drivers' concern about street crime and the lack of public cooperation with the police. Cab owners formed an association and obtained training and support from local police. These volunteer patrols have been a significant factor in preventing crime on the streets (Washnis 1976, pp. 78–79).

Crime Stoppers

Crime Stoppers programs provide special telephone lines to facilitate anonymous reporting of suspicious or criminal activity. Some of the programs offer monetary rewards for information leading to convictions, with the amount of the reward often determined by citizen committees. The Albuquerque (New Mexico) Crime Stoppers, established in 1976, is funded by public contributions and controlled by an eighteen-member civilian board of directors. The project issues select case reports to newspapers and sixty-second public service announcements to radio stations. A local television station films a two-minute reenactment of the "crime of the week." The Albuquerque project is just one of many similar programs across the country.

Educational programs

A variety of educational approaches can be used to encourage witnesses to report crimes. For example, presentations can be made before civic and service groups, schools, parent-teachers associations, church organizations, and other community groups. Another approach involves membership projects, which are similar to group presentations except that they usually demand greater involvement because of membership requirements. A third approach is home presentation.

Court volunteers

According to some estimates, most of the volunteers within the criminal justice system are found within the court component. Some one hundred thousand volunteers are estimated to be affiliated with well over a thousand courts. Most are volunteers in probation, but volunteers are involved in all of these capacities: advisory council member, arts and crafts teacher, home skills teacher, recreation leader, coordinator or administrator of programs, employment counselor, foster parent (group or individual), group guidance counselor, information officer, support services worker, neighborhood worker, office worker (clerical, secretarial), volunteer for one-to-one assignment to probationers, professional skills volunteer, public relations worker, community education counselor, record keeper, religious guidance counselor, tutor, and educational aide.

One of the first court volunteer programs began in Royal Oak, Michigan, with eight volunteers. This program, Volunteers in Probation, is now a nationwide organization associated with the National Council on Crime and Delinquency. Studies at Royal Oak indicate that volunteers and professionals working together can provide intensive probation services that can not be supplied in any other way. When probationers from Royal Oak were compared with probationers from nonvolunteer courts, it was found that those from Royal Oak were not only less hostile, but also that their recidivism rates were drastically lower (15 percent for Royal Oak probationers, 50 percent for the other group).

Court watching is an activity in which citizens monitor the performance of judges and prosecutors, the reasons for delays and continuances, the presence of bail bond solicitors, and the consistency of sentences for comparable offenses. As a result of their court watching experience, a group of women in Montgomery County, Maryland, published a detailed report on juvenile court and care procedures.

Many citizens concerned about extensive pretrial detention have launched studies and reforms to minimize its use (consistent with public safety). The Washington (D.C.) Pretrial Justice Program shares these concerns and has conducted three studies on the pretrial period. The program helps persons who have been detained in jail by reporting and attempting to resolve cases of error and delay and by securing admission of some defendants into community programs.

Other citizen groups have implemented innovative projects to divert defendants from the criminal justice system at a point between arrest and trial—thereby reducing case loads. And improved communication between lawyer and client is the objective of other citizen efforts. Businesspeople have volunteered their time to study how court systems can effect speedier justice without adding to the court staff. The judicial process in New York City has been accelerated due to the work of the Economic Development Council, a coalition of 130 businesspeople. The council found that court backlogs could be reduced by applying businesslike methods to court procedures, a plan that did not require additional public funds.

In a court-administered program, volunteers counsel delinquent youths and their parents in an attempt to strengthen family ties. Court volunteers in Kalamazoo, Michigan, spend several hours a month with their court-assigned families. In addition to listening sympathetically to the families' problems, the volunteers help them find medical and other aid and provide transportation. Citizen organizations also finance court studies and propose improved methods for selecting judges. Under a court referral program in Alameda County, California, community agencies receive over a hundred misdemeanants each month who have agreed to contribute several hours of their time to a nonprofit agency in lieu of fine or imprisonment.

Finally, family courts employ liaison referral workers—that is, volunteers who explain the court process to apprehensive parents, gather information about the family to assist the judge, and help families obtain aid from appropriate community agencies. In some jurisdictions, courts use volunteers to assist the families of delinquents to meet immediate needs and to resolve pressing problems.

Correctional volunteers

The corrections component of the criminal justice system is receiving increased attention from both professionals and citizens. Citizen effort in corrections may pertain to prisoners, to ex-prisoners, or to persons in transition to or from prison.

Qualified citizens volunteer medical and legal aid to inmates and conduct inspections and surveys of jails, prisons, and juvenile institutions. The Osborne Society has found these surveys useful in encouraging reform and reorganization of state institutions. The society is a national, nonprofit organizaion that helps juvenile and adult correctional institutions prepare offenders for useful and successful lives in society. Members of other citizen organizations work with prisoners on a one-to-one basis, offering services such as tutoring and recreational activities. Amicus, Inc., in Minneapolis, Minnesota, matches volunteers with inmates upon request. The volunteer, acting as a friend, visits an inmate at least once a month and writes letters regularly while the inmate is in prison.

Through a program of study and discussion, volunteers can also help inmates prepare for release from the institution. The volunteers act as counselors and listeners, and as intermediaries between inmates and their families. Some citizen programs attempt to improve the self-confidence of inmates, who frequently are convinced that they are losers who can not change their lives. This is the purpose of Project Self-Respect, which uses over two hundred volunteers at the Shelby County (Tennessee) Penal Farm. The volunteers help inmates improve their attitudes toward themselves and others so they will be better equipped to function in the community.

Friends Outside, based in Los Altos, California, is a community organization that works to meet the immediate needs of inmates and their families by providing friendship, support, recreation, transportation, food, furniture, and clothing. Other organizations provide education and job training to offenders, and still others press for needed correctional legislation and try to educate the public about the problems of offenders and correctional institutions.

Recall that many convicted persons are in halfway houses or on parole—rather than in prison. Here again, citizens can help. Homes for runaways and other children in trouble frequently are funded or staffed by citizens. These residences may be group homes housing fifteen to twenty youths, or they may be foster homes. Group homes usually have regular counseling sessions, study periods, housekeeping chores, and recreational opportunities. In other residential programs, offenders work or attend school in the community while they progress through stages of increasing responsibility prior to release. A group home in Little Rock, Arkansas, offers an alternative to incarceration for delinquent and predelinquent girls. And the Women's Prison Association and Home in New York City houses women making the transition from institutional supervision to community life.

Upon release, ex-offenders frequently need services that can be supplied by concerned citizens. One organization publishes a guide to services for ex-offenders. Many citizens actively help ex-offenders find jobs and obtain welfare, medical and legal aid, and adequate clothing and housing. Ex-offenders with alcohol or drug problems are referred to appropriate community agencies. Some business associations—including many Jaycee chapters—have job training programs for ex-inmates.

Summary

The idea of crime prevention started in England in the mid-1700s. Three objectives set forth by Henry Fielding laid the foundation for our current concepts of crime prevention: development of a strong police force; organization of active citizen groups; and initiation of action to remove some of the causes of crime and the conditions in which it flourishes.

Modern crime prevention concepts were not formally adopted in the United States until the 1960s, when the National Crime Prevention Institute was founded with joint funding from the U.S. Department of Justice, the Law Enforcement Assistance Administration, the Kentucky Crime Commission, and the University of Louisville (Kentucky). Since that time, other crime prevention centers have been established, and many police departments now have units created specifically to address the issues of crime prevention and to set up liaisons with citizen groups.

Citizen involvement in crime prevention is not only desirable, but also necessary. Citizen efforts should be aimed at the infrastructure of crime—toward problems such as unemployment, poor education, and lack of recreation activities.

Citizens can take many actions to supplement and strengthen the various components of the criminal justice system. For example, they can institute neighborhood security activities, citizen patrols, and crime reporting programs. They can work with the courts as volunteers in probation, as court watchers (monitoring the performances of judges and prosecutors), as volunteers in intervention programs to divert defendants from the criminal justice system at a point between arrest and trial (thus reducing case loads), and as volunteer counselors for delinquent youth and their parents. In corrections, citizens can volunteer medical and legal aid to inmates; inspect and survey jails, prisons, and juvenile institutions; counsel and listen to inmates and serve as intermediaries between them and their families; and provide job training programs for inmates (through business associations).

issue paper

THE GUARDIAN ANGELS—GOOD SAMARITANS OR VIGILANTES?

Citizens and the police have many opportunities to cooperate in crime prevention. However, if citizens lack confidence in prevention programs, or if they have lost faith in the ability of the police to protect them, they may act *on their own* to protect themselves, their families, and their property. Whether other citizens and the police view such groups as realists looking out for their own welfare or as vigilantes may depend upon the group's membership and the extent of its activities. Since 1979, no other group has so dramatically captured the attention and imagination of citizens, the police, and the media as New York City's Guardian Angels.

Who are they?

The Guardian Angels were founded in 1979 by a twenty-five-year-old high school dropout, Curtis Sliwa, out of a growing concern about crime in his neighborhood and a belief that the police were unable or unwilling to do anything about it. He originally formed a small group called the Magnificent 13. Today, the Guardian Angels number nearly a thousand and have chapters in such cities as Pittsburgh, New Orleans, Los Angeles, Newark, and Boston (Edelman 1981).[6]

Most of the Angels come from the poorer sections of the city. Almost 65 percent are Hispanic, 20 percent are black, and 5 percent are Oriental. Two dozen are female. Sliwa says that his mission and the mission of the Angels—beyond the immediate issue of crime and fear—is to provide "role models for the young ones committing the atrocious crimes, young guys hanging out, smoking dope, and drinking wine. Even the hardest of the hard will try to do something good if only given the opportunity."

Sliwa is articulate. He can shift his speech from gutteral slang laced with street expletives, which he uses often when talking to the Angels, to well-reasoned answers and anecdotes polished during interviews with the press.

How do they operate?

The Guardian Angels board a subway en masse in the rear car before advancing through the train. They check for trouble in each car and scan each platform by craning their necks out of the doors when the train pulls into a station. They are continually checking on each other's safety using whistles and shouts. They are always moving, shuttling from car to car and train to train along a designated route that often transports them halfway across the city in a four-hour tour. They will unceremoniously kick graffiti scribblers off the trains after confiscating their magic markers and spray paint. Angels are not allowed to carry weapons, and they are frisked by a team leader before going out on patrol.

The Guardian Angels have been described as a cross between a special-forces military squad and a street gang. In groups of ten or more, they patrol the New York City subways day and night looking for "bad guys." Some of them wear martial-arts uniforms or jungle fatigues with spit-shined combat boots and red berets (often embossed with studs, pins, patches, racoon tails, and long strings of colored beads).

Reaction of the criminal justice system

Many people in New York City's criminal justice system speak with high regard of Sliwa and his Angels. For example, Robert Keating, the city Coordinator for Criminal Justice, says, "He's a tough kid; someone the Angels respect. Most of the kids come from such bad areas that Curtis might be the first real leader they've encountered. He's also their conduit to something outside the ghetto."

"To call them vigilantes is nonsense," says Mario Merola, the Bronx district attorney. "The municipal and state governments have not met their obligation to provide the kind of security that's needed on the subway. It's true they're not trained, but the mere presence of a uniform is the kind of deterrence we're looking for."

In contrast, however, leaders of the New York City Transit Police Patrolman's Association say that the Angels are publicity mongers whose role comes dangerously close to vigilantism. They also question the exploits of the angels, who claim to have stopped more than a hundred crimes—including an assault on a transit police officer. The association president, William McKechnie, while not denegrating the motives of most Angels, believes that what they represent is dangerous: "They act far beyond the scope of the ordinary citizen. They don't have training in when to use and not to use force. What happens if they are injured or if they injure a commuter in their over-zealous pursuit?"

Curtis Sliwa (left), founder of the Guardian Angels. Courtesy Bernard Edelman.

Citizen reactions

According to one free-lance writer in New York, most people in the city, especially subway riders, are enchanted with the Angels. One Manhattan resident wrote to the *New York City Post* and said, "The Guardian Angels are very much appreciated by commuters who must take the subway every day. I'd like to thank them for making me feel safe for a change." Another citizen, writing to the *Sunday News Magazine,* said, "I am truly impressed with their courage and initiative. If the judicial system and the police can't stop crime, maybe the Angels can."

Nonaffiliation with police departments

Thus far, the Angels have rejected any formal affiliation with the New York City Transit Police Department. Sliwa once rejected a department request that he submit to the city the names, addresses, and phone numbers of his members. "It is something the police can use to harrass us," he said.

In October 1981, Chief Meehan of the Transit Police Department offered a program to the Angels that would recognize them as auxiliary police officers. The police would provide Angels with identification cards and develop a training program on subway safety, laws governing citizen arrests, lawful use of force, and communication techniques and procedures. Sliwa rejected the proposal, insisting that the Angels remain independent.

The national network

Today, the Angels claim to have twenty-two hundred members, with eighteen hundred more in training in cities across the country. In the process of expansion, the Angels hope to shed their image as a squad of reformed ghetto toughs. In the Midwest and West, many volunteers are middle-class whites. Says Sliwa, "In Los Angeles I was astounded to see blond-haired, blue-eyed boys drive up in cars with surfboards, park, and go on patrol."

The Angels' effort to forge a national network has had mixed success. In New Orleans, Angels nabbed a knife-wielding robber with a record of fifty-seven previous arrests and a pickpocket who turned out to be a murder suspect wanted by police. But in other cities, their impact has not been so evident. A police spokesman in Pasadena, assessing the Angel patrol at the Tournament of Roses Parade, summed up the verdict of many observers: "No runs, no hits, no errors." In Boston, the Angels predicted that there would be 250 volunteers on patrol by the end of 1983; there are only 60 so far. "They attracted a lot of attention," says Paul DiNatale of the Massachusetts Bay Transit Authority, "and now the question is, Where are they?"

A bigger problem than numbers, however, may be the quality of the protection offered. *Chicago Sun-Times* reporter Michael Codtes, who went undercover and became a Guardian Angel recruit, drew a disturbing picture of his three-month training period. He charges that recruits were poorly trained in citizens' legal rights, that two violence-prone youths were graduated simply to bolster the size of the chapter, and that the group was wracked by a power struggle between co-leaders dubbed by the rank and file as "Mr. Ego" and "Mr. Mouth."

Sliwa calls reports of problems "exaggerated," but some Angels are less reluctant to acknowledge troubles. Admits Rahni Fiduccia of Chicago: "Most applicants think the Guardian Angels are a glorified Bruce Lee squad and they just want to go out there and smash heads." Says Boston chapter leader Susan Piver: "The idea never should have been to blitz Boston. We are limited by manpower and we are limited by funds." Growing pains are inevitable, but if the Guardian Angels fall short on their promises, they will undermine their own effectiveness. Says Piver, "We've got to build from the ground up, and that takes time" ("Guardian Angels Growing Pain," *Time*, 18 February 1982, p. 21).

Conclusion

The Guardian Angels were certainly not the first group of citizens—nor will they be the last—to mobilize outside the formal structure of the criminal justice system for self-protection or the protection of others. The formation of similar groups will depend directly on the public's perception of the ability of the formal structure of the criminal justice system to protect citizens and their property and to dispense justice even handedly and swiftly.

Discussion and review

1. What were the three steps identified by Henry Fielding for stamping out existing crime and preventing future outbreaks of crime?
2. What role did citizens play in crime prevention before the specialization of law enforcement?
3. What dangers are associated with self-centered approaches to crime prevention?
4. What are some of the major features of crime prevention programs directed at education, employment, and recreational opportunities?
5. What are some of the major features of block clubs, neighborhood watches, citizen patrols, building patrols, neighborhood patrols, social service patrols, and community protection patrols?
6. How can environmental design affect the incidence of crime?
7. Describe some typical crime reporting projects.
8. How can citizen volunteers get involved in correctional activities?
9. Why were the Guardian Angels formed?
10. How would you describe the Guardian Angels—as Good Samaritans or as vigilantes?

Glossary

Block club A group of persons who live in the same general vicinity and work together to improve citizen crime awareness and to educate citizens about public safety.

Building patrol A citizen patrol whose major objective is to protect specific buildings and adjacent grounds.

Citizen patrol Citizens who patrol their neighborhoods in vehicles and maintain contact with each other through citizen-band radios; may concentrate on specific buildings in housing areas.

Community protection patrol A citizen patrol that monitors the police—in addition to serving as a building patrol, a neighborhood patrol or a social service patrol. The monitoring is done because of fear of harassment by the police based on previous incidents or on a generally antagonistic relationship with the police.

National Center for Community Crime Prevention A center established to teach crime prevention skills to citizens representing community-based organizations across the United States; part of the Institute of Criminal Justice Studies at Southwest Texas University in San Marcos.

National Crime Prevention Institute One of the best known and highly regarded crime prevention training programs for law enforcement officers; located at the University of Louisville, Louisville, Kentucky.

Neighborhood patrol A citizen patrol that usually has a poorly defined area of surveillance. Patrols may be conducted in cars or on foot and may cover specific areas related to such activities as children walking to and from school.

Neighborhood watch A program aimed at improving citizen reporting of crimes or suspicious events and people in their neighborhoods.

Radio watch A program that involves the use of two-way citizen-band or ham radios in personal, company, or taxi vehicles. Participants are urged to report suspicious activities through dispatchers or directly to police departments that monitor emergency frequencies.

Social service patrol A citizen patrol that performs a variety of community functions—from senior citizen escort services to private protection for older citizens.

WhistleStop A community signal system that facilitates the reporting of in-progress crimes by victims and witnesses.

References

Advisory Commission on Intergovernmental Relations. *State-Local Relations in the Criminal Justice System*. Washington, D.C. U.S. Government Printing Office, 1971.

Bickman, L. *Citizen Crime Reporting Projects*. Washington, D.C.: U.S. Government Printing Office, 1977.

Chamber of Commerce of the United States. *Marshalling Citizen Power Against Crime*. Washington, D.C.: Chamber of Commerce of the United States, 1970.

Committee for Economic Development. *Reducing Crime and Assuring Justice*. New York: Committee for Economic Development, 1972.

Duncan, J. T. *Citizen Crime Prevention Tactics: A Literature Review and Selected Bibliography*. Washington, D.C.: U.S. Government Printing Office, April 1980.

Edelman, B. "Does New York Need the Guardian Angels?" *Police Magazine*, May 1981, pp. 51–56.

Gibbs, L. A. *Fourth Paper in the Balance: Citizen Efforts to Address Criminal Justice Problems in Cook County, Illinois*. Chicago, Ill.: Chicago Law Enforcement Study Group, 1977.

"Guardian Angels Growing Pain." *Time*, 18 February 1982, p. 21.

Midwest Research Institute. *Evaluation of the National Sheriffs' Association National Research Watch Program*. Kansas City, Mo.: Midwest Research Institute, 1977.

Minnesota Crime Prevention Center. *Block Club Organizing for Crime Prevention*. Minneapolis, Minn.: Minnesota Crime Prevention Center, 1978.

National Advisory Commission on Criminal Justice Standards and Goals. *A Call for Citizen Action: Crime Prevention and the Citizen*. Washington, D.C.: U.S. Government Printing Office, 1974.

National Advisory Commission on Criminal Justice Standards and Goals. *A National Strategy to Reduce Crime*. Washington, D.C.: U.S. Government Printing Office, 1973.

National Commission on the Causes and Prevention of Violence. *Staff Report: Law and Order Reconsidered*. Washington, D.C.: U.S. Government Printing Office, 1969.

National Institute of Law Enforcement and Criminal Justice. "Community Security Research and Development." Mimeographed. Washington, D.C.: U.S. Government Printing Office, 1978.

Newman, O. *Defensible Space*. New York: Collier, 1978.

Palmer, P. W. *Burglar Prevention: Inmate Interview Project*. Lakewood, Colo.: Lakewood Department of Public Safety, 1978.

The President's Commission on Law Enforcement and the Administration of Justice. *The Challenge of Crime in a Free Society*. Washington, D.C.: U.S. Government Printing Office, 1967.

Savoie, L. M. "What Issues Will Challenge CPA's in the 1970's?" Paper read at the 1969 convention of the Ohio Society of CPAs.

Texas Crime Prevention Institute. "History and Principles." In *Principles and Practices of Crime Prevention: An Introduction*. San Marcos, Tex.: Southwest Texas University, 1978.

U.S. Department of Justice, Law Enforcement Assistance Administration, National Institute of Law Enforcement and Criminal Justice. *Research Bulletin*. Washington, D.C.: U.S. Government Printing Office, June 1979.

Washnis, G. J. *Citizen Involvement in Crime Prevention*. Lexington, Mass.: D. C. Heath, 1976.

Yin, R. K. *Patrolling the Neighborhood Beat: Residents and Residential Security*. Santa Monica, Calif.: Rand, 1976.

Yin, R. K. *Citizen Patrol Projects*. Washington, D.C.: U.S. Government Printing Office, 1977.

Notes

1. This discussion of the historical overview of crime prevention activities, along with the accompanying references, was adapted from J. T. Duncan, *Citizen Crime Prevention Tactics: A Literature Review and Selected Bibliography* (Washington, D.C.: U.S. Government Printing Office, 1980), pp. 2, 3, 21–25.

2. Students in the NCPI course are exposed to such topics as environmental criminology; crime risk management; intrusion detection devices; crime and the older person; armed robbery prevention; rape prevention; lighting for crime prevention; crime analysis; locks and hardware; and community planning for crime prevention.

3. This discussion of crime prevention and citizen action, along with the accompanying references, was adapted from the National Advisory Commission on Criminal Justice Standards and Goals, *A Call for Citizen Action: Crime Prevention and the Citizen* (Washington, D.C.: U.S. Government Printing Office, 1974), pp. 1–10.

4. Statement by E. K. Nelson, quoted in Kenneth Polk, *Non-Metropolitan Delinquency: An Active Program* (Washington, D.C.: U.S. Department of Health, Education, and Welfare, 1969), p. 11.

5. For more information on the role of citizens in crime prevention programs, see National Advisory Commission on Criminal Justice Standards and Goals, A National Strategy to Reduce Crime. (Washington, D.C.: U.S. Government Printing Office, 1973).

6. This discussion of the Guardian Angels was adapted, with permission, from B. Edelman, "Does New York Need the Guardian Angels?" *Police Magazine*, May 1981, pp. 51–56.

index

Abortion, 56, 68
Abramowitz, Stephen I., 119, 143
Accidents, automobile, see Traffic bureau
Accommodation, role of, 19-20
Actus reus, 53, 71
Adams, S., 342
Addiction, see Drug addiction
Adjudication phase, 498
Adler, Alfred, 124
Administrative law, 51
Adversary system, 25, 62, 65, 227-30, 243-44, 250, 308
Affirmative action (in police departments), 202-10, 223
Aftercare, juvenile, 513-16
Aggravated assault, 82-84, 103, 109, 174
Agreement, 53
Aikman, A., 364
Alcatraz, 399-401
Alcoholism:
    care in prison of, 370
    detoxification centers, 475-77
    police, 212-14
Alcohol Safety Action Project (ASAP), 477
Alexander, A., 94
Allen, H. E., 340, 460
Alpert, L., 294
American Bar Association, 350-51, 353, 525
American Law Institute, 68, 349
American Psychiatric Association (APA), 326-27
Americans for Effective Law Enforcement (AELE), 60-62
American Society of Crime Laboratory Directors, 180
Amir, M., 537
Amnesty, 454
Anomie, 135, 145
Antisocial behavior, inhibition of, 123
Appeal(s), 25, 38, 259, 287-88, 323, 351-53
Appellate court, 282, 283, 284, 286, 287-88, 302
Argersinger v. *Hamlin*, 238
Arney, Sir George, 535
Arraignment process, 257, 259, 260-61, 276
Array (veniremen), 313, 329
Arrest(s), 21, 256, 258, 276
    by patrol officer, 158-59

Arrest(s)—cont'd
    by police investigator, 172
    rewards for, 197-98
Arson, 94-97, 104, 109
Aryan Brotherhood, 432, 449
Assault:
    aggravated, 82-84, 103, 109, 174
    psychological impact of, 8
Assigned counsel system, 238-39, 241-43, 244-45, 250
Atavism, 117-18, 145
Auburn (New York) system, 396-97, 420
Augustus, John, 456, 457
Automobiles, see Drunk driving; Motor vehicle theft; Traffic bureau
Autonomic nervous system (ANS), 122-23
Aversive conditioning, 145
    of deviant sexual behavior, 132-34

Bail, 262-65, 276, 383
    jumper, 274-75
Bailey, F. Lee, 550
Bailiff, 297, 302
Bakal, Y., 338, 521
Baker, N., 24-25
Ballew v. *Georgia*, 317
Banks, L., 288
Bar associations, 231, 250, 292, 293
Bard, M., 8, 38
Bargaining:
    plea, 23, 38, 236-37, 250
    sentence, 268
Barker, J. C., 133
Barnes, H. E., 23-24, 456
Barth, Alan, 548
Bases, N. C., 267
Batchelor, I. R. C., 120
Bayley, C. T., 344-45
Beats (police), 161-62
Beck, B. M., 510
Beck, D. B., 510
Bedau, H. A., 68
Behavior modification, 132-34, 141
Bell, B., 122
Belli, Melvin, 48
Bentham, Jeremy, 334-35
Berkowitz, Leonard, 106
Betts v. *Brady*, 238
Bicycle theft, 91-92
Bill of particulars, 262

585

Bill of Rights, 57 (*See also specific amendments*, e.g. First; Fourth; Sixth; etc.)
Biological factors, 117-24, 143
Biosocial theory, 122-23
Biotechnology, 142-44
Bird, Rose, 295
Bittaker, Lawrence, 357
Black gangs (in prison), 430-31
Black is beautiful, 426, 427
Black Muslims, 427-30
Black Panther Party, 430
Black separatism, 426, 427-30, 449
Bloch, P., 177, 258, 261
Block clubs, citizen, 564, 582
Blood feud, 534
Booked (to be), 256
Booster box/skirts/bloomers, 93, 109
Bounty hunters, 274-75
Brain disease, 143
Brain-wave studies, 121
Brantingham, P. J., 497
Brill, S., 301
Brooks, Charlie, J., 357
Brooks, J., 541
Brookwater, James T., 446
Brown v. *Mississippi*, 62
Bruce, Lenny, 16
Buck, George A., 173, 174
Buckhout, Robert, 315, 317, 356
Building patrols, citizen, 566, 582
Burglary, 8, 88-90, 103, 109, 174
Burke, R. J., 296
Burnout, 437, 449
Business crimes, *see* White-collar crimes
Butner (North Carolina) correctional facility, 405, 408-11
Bystanders, 534, 544-48

Cannon, Noel, 301
Capital punishment, 355-58
Carp, R., 294
Carrington, Frank, 551
Cartwright, Samuel A., 142
Case disposition factors, 269-71
Case law, 51
Case loads, 170-71, 236, 240-41, 250, 352
  juveniles, 515-16
Causation principle, 55-56
Certification (of juveniles to adult court), 523-24
Certiorari, 284, 302
Challenges for cause, 313, 329
Challenge of Crime in a Free Society, The, 30
Chamelin, N. C., 298
Chambliss, W. J., 44
Chandler, Raymond, 22-23
Change of venue, 262, 329
Charging the jury, 320-21
Charge (the), bargain concerning, 267, 268, 269
Chicago Area Projects, 509
Chicago police, 97-99
Chicano gangs, 431-32
Chop shops, 91, 92, 109

Chorover, S. L., 142, 143
Churchill, Winston, 69
CIA, 13
Circumstantial evidence, 308, 329
Citizen patrols, 565-67, 582
Citizen responsibility (in crime prevention), 557-61
Civil injury, 52
Civil law, 49
Civil libertarians, 60
Civil rights activism, 12
Civil rights:
  Fourteenth Amendment and, 57-58
  police and demonstrations for, 201
Civil War, 57
Class, social, 117, 136, 137
Clearance rates, 79, 81, 82, 84, 86, 88, 103-4, 109
Clearing the books, 99, 109
Cleaver, Eldridge, 428-30
Cleveland, Ohio, 99
Clinical perspective, 124
Closing arguments, 320
Cloward, R. A., 136
Coffey, A., 18, 19, 51
Cohen, A. K., 137, 434
Colgrove v. *Battin*, 317
Collateral attack, 351-52, 359
Combination facilities, 365, 390
Common Cause, 12
Common law, 49, 52, 71, 229
Common-law rule (on use of deadly force), 217, 223
Commonwealth v. *Welansky*, 54
Community-based programs:
  corrections in, 28-29
  for juveniles, 505-8, 511-12
Community correctional centers, 479-80, 482-84
Community protection patrols, 567, 582
Community relations (*See also* Neighborhood justice centers):
  offender-, 454
  police-, 160-61
Community reorganization programs, 509
Community (sense of), crime prevention and, 560-61
Compensation (for victims), 532, 534-36, 539-41, 552
Competency:
  of evidence, 309, 329
  mental, 325-28
Complaint (the), issuance of, 256, 257, 258, 276
Compromise, 20
Computer revolution, crime(s) since, 32-35
Concurrence (of *actus reus* and *mens rea*), 54-55
Concurrent charges, bargain for, 268
Concurrent sentence, 345
Conditional release, 461-80
Confessions (in criminal trial), 311
Confidential communication, 310
Confinement, *see* Jail(s); Prison(s); Sentencing

Conformity, *see* Deviance
Con games, 11
Coniff, R., 33, 144
Conklin, J. E., 4, 5, 547, 548
Con man, electronic, 33-35
Conrad, J. P., 439, 443
Consecutive sentence, 345
Consensual crimes, 15-16, 36, 68-70
Consent decree, 504
Conspiracy, criminal, 53
Constitution, 57-66 (*See also specific Amendments, e.g.* First; Fourth; Sixth; *etc.*)
Consumer advocacy, 11
Containment theory, 138-39, 141
Contingency management program, 132, 145
Contraband, 373-74, 390, 442
Contract parole, 467-68, 485
Control beat, 162
Conventional crimes, 10
Convictions, prosecutors', 23-24, 267
Cooper, Irving Ben, 301
Cooperation, interagency, 18
Correctional institutions, 16, 26-29, 392-421 (*see also* Jail(s); Prison(s))
  historical perspectives, 394-97
  for youth, 415-16, 421, 504-5
Correctional issues, 340-43
Correctional volunteers, 576-77
Counsel, right to, 58-59, 63-66, 237-38
Counseling:
  crime prevention and, 563
  of juveniles, 515
Counts (of prisoners), 373, 390
Court administrator, the, 298
Court clerk, the, 298
Court reporter, the, 298
Courts, 16, 25-26, 280-304
  administrative personnel, 297-98
  appellate, 282, 283, 284, 286, 287-88, 302
  defined, 282-83
  federal system of, 283-86
  of first instance, 284, 302
  of first resort, 246-49
  of general jurisdiction, 283, 286, 288, 302
  inferior (lower), 283, 286, 288-89, 303
  intermediate appellate, 283, 285, 286, 287-88, 302
  of last resort, 283, 286-87, 302
  of limited jurisdiction, 283, 286
  of original jurisdiction, 282, 283, 288
  police testimony in, 159
  of record, 282-83
  relationship of jails to, 382-83
  state and local, 286-89
  superior (higher), 283
  trial, 282, 286, 288
Court volunteers, 574-76
Cressey, D. R., 56, 115, 272, 293-94, 433
Crime concealment, arson for, 95
Crime data/statistics, 2, 5, 10, 97-100, 109, 490-91, 538

Crime data/statistics—cont'd
  clearance rates, 79, 81, 82, 84, 86, 88, 103-4, 109
  property crimes, 88, 89, 90-92, 94, 490
  violent crimes, 76, 81, 82, 84, 86, 87, 490, 519
Crime Index, FBI's, 10, 77, 103, 109, 491, 538-39
Crime laboratories, 178-83
Crime reporting projects/programs, 573-74
  FBI's Uniform, 76-78, 103, 109, 491, 538-39
Crime(s) (*See also specific kinds, e.g.* Juvenile; Murder; Property; Rape; Violent; White-collar; *etc.*):
  defining, classifying, 9-16, 42, 51-52
  due process versus control of, 29-31, 57-59, 66
  economic impact of, 4-7
  elements of, 24, 38
  factors used in analysis of, 173-74
  high-tech, 32-35
  historical perspectives on, 3-4, 47-51, 114
  nature, distribution, of, 74-110
  psychological and social impact of, 7-9, 86, 100-102
  trends, 78-97
Crime Stoppers programs, 574
Criminal behavior, *see* Criminality
Criminal homicide, 76, 79-82, 109 (*See also* Manslaughter; Murder)
Criminalistics, 32, 178-79, 190
Criminality, 112-47
  bail as encouraging, 264
  biological factors, 117-24
  control of, 142-44
  economic factors, 11-13, 36, 115-17, 140
  psychological factors, 124-34, 141
  sociological theories, 134-37
  sociopsychological theories, 137-39
Criminal Justice Act (1964), 238, 242
Criminal justice system, 16-31, 36
  role of jail in, 380-84, 385
Criminal law, 49-51, 53-57, 66
Criminology, radical, 115, 116-17, 146
Criminal procedure, 53, 57-66
Criminal trial, 256, 306-31
Crisis intervention, 477
Critical stage/point (right to counsel), 65, 66
Critical stereotype (police detective bureau), 169
Cromwell, Oliver, 69
Cross-examination, 318-19, 329
Crouch, B. M., 444, 445
Cutlery control (in jails), 377-78, 390

Dangerousness (of offenders), 399
Danto, Bruce L., 215-16, 386
Darley, J., 547
Davis, A. J., 418
Dead bang cases, 270
Deadly force, police use of, 217-22, 223

Deathbed statements, 311
Death penalty, 355-58
de Beaumont, G., 364
Decker, S. H., 538
Decriminalization:
 consensual crimes, 68-70
 deviant behavior, 46-47
Defendant, 229, 250
Defense:
 case for the, 319-20
 the insanity, 325-28
Defense attorneys, 236-43, 244, 250
Definite sentence, 343-44, 345
Degree of the offense, 321
Delinquency, *see* Juvenile crime/delinquency
Delinquent (defined), 490, 526
Delinquent subculture, 137
Demonical possession, 114
Deming, R., 317
De novo, 288
Dependent children, 499, 526
Detective bureau, police, 150, 167-83, 184
Determinate sentence, 344
Deterrence, 30, 335, 336-37, 355-56, 359, 394-97
de Tocqueville, A., 364
Deviance, 42-43, 45-47, 69-70, 135, 139 (*See also* Sex offenders; Values)
Diabetics, care in jail of, 370-71
Differential association theory, 138, 141
Dinitz, S., 437, 438, 443
Directed verdict, 319, 329
Direct evidence, 308, 329
Direct examination, 318, 329
Disciples (gang), 430, 433, 434, 436, 449
Discovery, the, 259
Discretion, role of, 19, 20, 69
 judicial sentencing, 334
 police, 20-21, 233
 prosecutor, 23-24, 232-36, 250
Discrimination (*See also* Class, social; Minorities; Racism):
 reverse, 208-10, 224
Dishlacoff, L., 214
Dismissal, 25-26, 261, 319
Disposition (consensual criminals), 69
Disposition phase (in juvenile court), 498
District attorney, 231, 250 (*See also* Prosecutor)
District Court, U.S., 285-86
Diversion:
 of delinquents, 508, 510-12, 526
 of offenders, 474-75, 485
Dropped charges, bargain for, 268
Drug addiction:
 prisoners', 372, 378-79, 390
 treatment approaches, 477-79
Drug use, 5, 15, 16, 56, 69
Drunk driving, 477
Due process:
 crime control versus, 29-31
 juvenile's right to, 498, 524
 revolution (the), 57-59, 66
 right to appeal aspect of, 323
Dunn, M. M., 394

Dunn, R. S., 394
Durant, W., 47, 48, 49
Durkheim, Emile, 135
Dussich, J. P. J., 542-44
Dusky v. *United States*, 325
DWI (driving while under the influence), 477

East, Jon, 447
Economic crimes, 11-13, 36, 115-17, 140
Economic impact (of crime), 4-7
Economic power, 44
Edelhertz, H., 8-9, 11
Education (*See also* Schools):
 crime prevention and, 561-62, 574
 in delinquency prevention, 509
 of police (collegiate), 196-202
Eighth Amendment, 352, 355
Eisenberg, T., 212
Eldefonso, E., 18, 19, 51
Electroencephalograph (EEG), 121, 145
Electronic data processing (EDP), 32
Elkins v. *United States*, 59
Ellison, K., 8, 38
Ellison, Katherine W., 315, 317, 356
El-Rukns (gang), 430, 434, 436-37, 449
Empey, L. T., 495
Employment:
 crime prevention and, 562
 for delinquency prevention, 509-10
En banc decision, 285, 303
Enforcement, *see* Law enforcement; Traffic bureau
Environmental design, crime prevention through, 567-73
Epilepsy, 120-21, 146
Episodic dyscontrol syndrome, 143
Equal employment opportunities, 202-10
Equality, ideal of, 56-57, 66
Equal protection, Fourteenth Amendment and, 57-59
Equity Funding swindle, 34-35
Erikson, Erik, 124
Errors, 25, 60-62
Ervin, Frank, 142, 143
Ervin, Sam, 265, 267
Escobedo v. *Illinois*, 59, 62, 63
Ethnic relations, police approach to, 201
Ethnic succession (immigrants), 13, 36
Evidence:
 crime laboratory's role in, 178-83
 model statute, 61
 police (technician) collection of, 170, 180
 rules of, 308-11
Exclusionary Rule, 59-62, 532-33
Expert witnesses, 310-11, 329
Express waiver (of jury trial), 312
Extortion, arson used for, 95

Fag (inmate), 425, 450
F.A.L.N., 187-89
Family, the, 42
 conflict, 201
Farr, R., 33

Faust, F. L., 497
FBI, 10, 13, 14
    Crime Laboratory, 180, 181-83
    Uniform Crime Reports, 76-78, 103, 109, 491, 538-39
Fear, 7, 13
Feldman, D., 128-29
Felonies, 10, 51-52, 56, 109, 192, 217, 276
    bail for, 263
    initiating prosecution in cases of, 258-61
Fielding, Henry, 556
Fielding, John, 556
Field interrogation files, 173, 190
Field training officer (police), 151, 190
Fifth Amendment, 62-63, 261, 352
File maintenance, police detective bureaus, 172-75
Fines, as punishment, 48
Fingerprint records, 183
First Amendment, 341
Flat-time sentence, 343-44, 462
Florida Penal Code, 50-51
Folkways, 43
Follow-up investigation, police detectives', 171, 172, 190
Forcible rape, 8, 81, 84-87, 103, 109, 174, 418-19
Forensic science, 178, 190
Forer, Lois G., 296-97
Forfeiture (of bail), 263
Forgery, 174
Forst, B., 177
Fortas, Abe, 65, 498
Fosdick, Raymond, 169
Foster homes, 505
Fourteenth Amendment, 57-59, 352, 355, 463
Fourth Amendment, 59-62, 352
Fraiman, Arnold G., 301
Frank, B., 472
Frank, J., 308
Frankel, M. E., 350
Frankfurter, Felix, 59
Franzen, Gail, 435
Freud, Sigmund, 124, 126-27, 335
Frisks (of prisoners), 374-76, 390
Fruit of the poisonous tree doctrine, 59
Fry, M., 535
Fugue, 146
Fuller, L. L., 230
Furloughs, 471-72, 485
Furman v. *Georgia*, 355
Future (high-tech) crime, 32-35

Gallows, 394, 420
Galvanic skin response (GSR), 122, 146
Gambling, 5, 15, 16, 56, 68, 69, 559
Gangs:
    juvenile, 517-18
    racial, in prison, 430-37, 439-42
Garland, Joan and Paul, 439
Gault (Gerald), *In re*, 341, 498
Gaylin, W., 348
Geis, G., 70, 258, 261
Gelber, Seymour, 490

Genetic factors, 118-19, 122-24, 140, 142-44, 494
Genovese, Catherine, 534, 544
Gibbons, D. C., 343
Gideon, Clarence Earl, 64-66
Gideon v. *Wainwright*, 58, 65, 238, 351-52
Gilman, David, 525
Glaser, D., 342, 466
Glasser, William, 125
Good-faith mistakes/exceptions, 60-62
Good Samaritans, 534, 544-48, 552
Gorillas (inmate), 425, 449
Government (the state):
    authority of, 49, 257, 318-19
    crimes by, against, 13-15
    expenditures, 5-7
Graduated release programs, 472-73
Grand jury, the, 261, 276
Great Law of Pennsylvania, 394, 420
Greenberg, B., 177
Griswold, H. J., 463
Group homes (for juveniles), 506
Grünhut, M., 336-37
Guardian Angels, the, 578-81
Guards (prison), 437-39, 444-48
Guilt, finding of, 230
Guilty mind, 54
Guilty pleas, 239, 241, 258, 260-61, 268-69 (*See also* Plea bargaining)
Gun control, 105-8

Habeas corpus, 352, 359
Hacks (guards), 426, 449
Halfway houses, 29, 473-74, 485
    for juveniles, 506
Hall, J., 53
Halleck, S. L., 125-26
Hallucinations (of the mentally ill), 371-72, 390
Hammurabi, 47, 49, 535
Hamparian, D. M., 523
Harm, principle of, 53, 55
Harris, Kaye, 29
Hartinger, W., 18, 19
Harvey, Kenneth, 15
Health, police officers', 210-17
Hearnes, W. E., 293
Hearsay, 311, 330
Hedonistic calculus, 334-35
Hentig, Hans von, 536
Heroism, arson and, 96-97
High-tech crime, 32-35
Hinckley, John W., Jr., 326, 327
Historical perspectives, 3-4, 47-51, 114
    correctional institutions, 394-97
    crime control and prevention, 556-57
    juvenile delinquency, 492-95, 496, 497
    police detective bureau, 168-69
    punishment, 47, 114, 334
    victims, 534-36
Hollander, P., 544
Homosexual behavior, consenting, 68, 69
Homosexual rape, in correctional institutions, 418-19
Homosexuals, in police work, 206-8
Hooton, Ernest, 144

Horney, Karen, 124
Houses of refuge, 493-94, 513
Hughes, James, 246, 249
Humanity, crimes against, 52
Hung jury, 322
Hurtado v. *California*, 57-58
Huxley, Aldous, 133
Hyperactivity, 119-20

Illinois Ten Percent Deposit Plan, 265
Impeachment of witness, 319, 330
Incapacitation (restraint), 337-38, 359
Incident report, police, 170
Incorporation views, 58
Indecent exposure, 50-51
Indenture, juvenile, 513
Indeterminate sentence, 344, 345, 347, 359-60
Indictment, an, 259, 260, 276
Indigents, defense of, 237-43, 250, 263
Industrial schools, 494-95
Inferior courts, 283, 286, 288-89, 303
Information, an, 259, 260, 276
Ingram, G. L., 405, 408, 409, 411
Innocence:
    bail and presumption of, 262
    directed verdict of, 319
    plea bargaining and, 269
In re Gault, 341, 498
Insanity defense, 325-28
Insurance, arson to defraud, 95
Intangibles, criminal law dealing with, 55
Interest groups, 45
Intermediate appellate courts, 285, 286, 287-88
Internal sickness model, 125-26
International Association of Chiefs of Police (IACP), 76
Intervention techniques, 343, 519
Intimidation, arson used for, 95
Investigation:
    police detective, 150, 167-83
    Rand study of, 176-78, 184, 565-66
Iran, 47-48
Irwin, J., 433
Ivkovich, Vladimir, 91

Jacobs, J. B., 434
Jaffe, Sidney, 274-75
Jailhouse lawyers, 63-66
Jail(s), 362-91 (*See also* Prison(s)):
    American system of, 364-69
    bail or, 262
    care of special prisoners in, 369-73
    populations, 368-69, 384-85
    purpose of, 365-68
    security techniques and procedures, 373-80, 385
    types of, 365
James, J. A., 120
Janis, I. L., 297
Jealousy, arson motivated by, 95
Job enrichment, 199, 224
Job stress:
    judiciary, 294-97
    police, 153, 210-12, 223, 224

Johnson, E. H., 263
Johnson, Lyndon B., 52
Johnson v. *Louisiana*, 322
Johnson v. *Zerbst*, 237, 238
Joy riding, 94
Judge(s)/judiciary, 289-97
    defined, 282
    job stress factor, 294-97
    judging the, 300-1
    occupational socialization of, 293-94
    selection of, 290-93
Jurisdiction, court's, 282-83
Jury, the, 312-17
    charging, 320-21
    deliberations, 321-22
    grand, 261, 276
    hung, 322
    scientific selection, 314-16
    size, 316-17
Jury trial, 308
Just desserts, law of, 335
Justice, administration of, 16-31, 36
Justices, Supreme Court, 283-84
Juvenile courts, 299, 495-99
    diversion from, 508, 510-12, 526
Juvenile crime/delinquency, 489-528
    cost of, 6-7
    defined, 498-99, 526
    factors in, 115, 119-20, 121, 136, 494
    labeling of, 139
    language of, 498-99, 500
    statistics, 490, 491
    violent, 516-22

Kansas City Patrol Experiment, 161-63, 199
Kaplan, J., 20-21, 308
Kassoff, Edwin, 301
Kaufman, I. R., 326
Keeley, Patricia, 357-58
Kelling, George L., 161, 162
Kennedy, John F., 14
Kennedy, Robert F., 265
Kent v. *United States*, 498
Kerper, H. B., 59, 282, 309, 311
Keve, P. W., 468, 469, 470
Key control (in jails), 376-77, 390
Kidnapping, 34-35, 50
Kiersh, E., 524
King, Martin Luther, 13
Kirk, Paul L., 179
Klotter, John C., 556-57
Kneedler, H. L., 347, 348
Kors, Alan C., 114
Krajick, K., 454, 482, 483-84
Kratcoski, P. C., 350, 353, 540
Kroes, W. H., 212
Kukla, R. J., 105

Labeling perspective, the, 47, 139, 141
LaFave, W. L., 233
Laite, William, 418
Lake Butler (Florida) Reception and Medical Center, 414
Lane, Mike, 435

Language, juvenile and adult courts', 498-99, 500
La Nuestra Familia, 431-32, 449
Larceny-theft, 87, 90-94, 103, 109, 174
Last resort, courts of, 283, 286-87
Latané, B., 547
Latent investigation, police detectives', 171, 172, 190
Latin Kings (gang), 430, 433, 434, 449
Law (the):
    classification of crime and, 9-16, 42, 51-52
    common, 49, 52, 71
    courts as interpreters of, 25-26, 280-304
    criminal, 49-51, 53-57, 66
    norms, values, deviance, and, 29-31, 42-47, 69-70, 139
    rule of, 66
    talion, 47-48, 71, 534
Law enforcement:
    of consensual crime, 68-69
    policies, police, and, 20-22
Lazarus, A., 134
Leading questions, 319, 330
Learning theory, 130-34, 141
Legal aid system, 237-39, 250
Legality principle, 53
Legal malpractice, 241, 250
Legal sufficiency, 24
LeGrande, J. L., 318
Lehtinen, M., 270
Lejins, Peter P., 201
Leo, John, 100
Levinson, H., 295
Levy, Ruth, 21
Lewis, Anthony, 295
Lewis, D. L., 95-96
Lewis, P. W., 58
Light cases, 270
Likert, Rensis, 199
Lillyquist, M. J., 132
Limbic brain disease, 143
Linear process model, 18-19
Lipton, D., 342
Little, Joan, 316
Lobaugh, Ralph, 461-62
Lockwood, D., 419
Logan, C. H., 469-70
Lombroso, Cesare, 117-18
Lustig v. United States, 59
Lykken, D. T., 122

Macauley, Thomas B., 229
Mackey v. Procunier, 341
MacNamara, D. E. J., 541
Maddox, Lester, 28
Magistrate, the, 257-58, 282
Magistrates courts, U.S., 286
Magnuson, E., 81, 87
Makielski, Stanley J., 45
Mala in se, 71
Mala prohibita, 71
Malcom X, 427, 429-30, 449
Malicious mischief, fires caused by, 95
Malpractice, legal, 241, 250

Mandatory sentence, 344
Manhattan Bail Project, 264-65
Mann, Dale, 519-20, 521
Mann, L., 297
Manslaughter, nonnegligent, 79-82, 103
Mapp v. Ohio, 58, 59
Marijuana use, 16, 56
Marion (Illinois) Federal Correctional Center, 401-3
Mark, Vernon, 142, 143
Marquart, J. W., 444, 445
Martinson, R., 342, 437
Marxist approach, 115, 116
Masters, John, 131
Materiality, evidence's, 309, 330
Mather, L. M., 269-73
Mattick, H. W., 364
Maxi-maxi prisons, 399-411, 420
Maximum security prisons, 397-99, 420
Maximum sentence, 348-49
May, E., 446
McCaghy, C. H., 117
McCall, G. J., 547
McCann, Robert E., 200
McCarthy, J. J., 248
McCleery, R., 434
McConnell, J., 134
McDonald, W. F., 267
McFadden, Robert D., 187
McGee, R. A., 347
McGillis, Daniel, 247-48
McGrath, J., 106
McGregor, Douglas, 199
McKechnie, William, 579
Media image, police detective bureau, 168
Mediation, in neighborhood justice centers, 246
Medium security correctional centers, 411-12, 420
Mednick, S. A., 121, 122
Mempa v. Rhay, 66
Mens rea, 53, 54, 71
Mental health program, prison, 410-11
Mental illness model, 125-26, 201, 325-28, 371-72, 390
Merchant (inmate), 425, 449
Merlis, S., 121
Merola, Mario, 579
Merrill, Judge, 341
Merton, Robert K., 135-36
Messinger, S. L., 442
Methadone maintenance, 477-78
Mexican Mafia, 431-32, 450
Milgram, S., 544
Military courts, 299
Military dictatorship, 69-70
Miller, Walter B., 137, 434, 517
Minimum security correctional centers, 413, 420
Minimum sentence, 344, 347
Minnesota Correctional Facility, 403-5
Minnesota Restitution Center, 541
Minorities, police recruitment of, 202-4, 223
Miranda, Ernesto, 62-63, 64
Miranda v. Arizona, 59, 62-63, 169

Index

Misdemeanor(s), 10, 51-52, 256-58, 263, 276
Mistakes, 25, 60-62
Mistrial, 322
Mitford, Jessica, 134
M'Naghten Rule, 325-26
Mollenhoff, Clark, 300
Montagu, James J., 124
Moolman, V., 94
Moran, Rob, 483
Mores, 43 (*See also* Norms; Values)
Morris, Norval, 28, 275, 408-9, 437
Moses, Law of, 535
Moslem style, 47-48
Motions:
    in felony cases, 259, 261-62
    in jury trials, 319
Motor vehicle theft, 91, 94, 104, 109, 174
Murchek, P., 456-57
Murder, 79-82, 103, 106-7, 121, 174
    death penalty for, 356-58
Murphy, J. J., 275
Murphy, Patrick, 97
Mutual Agreement Programming (MAP), 467-68, 485

Nader's Raiders, 11
Narcotic antagonist programs, 478
Narcotics, *see* Drug addiction; Drug use
Nassi, Alberta J., 119, 143, 340
National Advisory Commission on Criminal Justice Standards and Goals:
    criminal justice system structure, 17-18
    crime laboratories, 181
    drug treatment, 477
    gun control, 107-8
    juvenile justice, 502, 503-4, 515
    plea bargaining, 268, 271-72
    police agencies' functions, 22
    probation, 461
    review process (appeals), 352, 353
National Center for Community Crime Prevention, 557, 582
National Crime Prevention Institute, 557, 582
National Retail Merchants Association, 92
National Rifle Association (NRA), 105
National Sheriffs' Association (NSA), 77
Nature, crimes against, 50, 52
Nazi crimes, 52
Neglected children, 499, 526
Negotiation, plea, 256, 267-75
Neighborhood action (crime control and prevention), 563-73
Neighborhood justice centers, 192, 246-49
Neighborhood patrols, 566, 582
Neighborhood watches, 564-65, 582
Nelkin, D., 478
Nettler, G., 134-35
Neubauer, D., 291, 294
Newman, D. J., 268
New Mexico State Penitentiary, 405, 406-8
Niederhoffer, A., 446

Night Prosecutor Program, 246
Nixon, Richard M., 14
No bill finding, 261
Nolle prosequi (nol pross), 258, 277
Nolo contendere, 260, 277
Nonresidential programs, juvenile, 506
Normality, crime's, 135
Normlessness, deviant's, 135
Norms, 42-43 (*See also* Values)
Nutrition factor, 119-20

Oak Park Heights (Minnesota) Correctional Facility, 403-5
Offbrands, 431
Offenders, repeat, *see* Recidivism
Offender score, 350, 351
Offense score, 350, 351
Office of Juvenile Justice and Delinquency Protection (OJJDP), 6-7
Ohlin, L. E., 136
Ombudsman, 542, 552
Omnibus Crime Control and Safe Streets Act (1968), 6, 196
Omnibus Victims Protection Act (1982), 533
On the record, 282
Opening statements, 317-20
Opinion (as evidence), 310
Ordeal, trial by, 48-49
Organized crime, 13, 15, 36
Original jurisdiction, 282, 283
Orthomolecular psychiatry, 119, 120, 146
Orwell, George, 133
Outward Bound, 506
Overfiled reasonable doubt cases, 270

Packer, H., 337
Packer, Herbert L., 29, 30, 70
Palmer, John, 246, 249
Parens patriae, 341, 360, 490, 498, 527
Parole, 28, 454, 458, 462-70, 485
    abolishing, 532
    conditions, 464
    effectiveness, 469-70
    innovations, 466-68
    prediction guidelines, 465-66
    selection, 462-64
Participative management, 199, 224
Passion, crimes of, 356
Patrick, J., 440
Patrol bureau (police), 150-63, 183-84
    activities, 155-59, 170
    evaluating, 197-200
    Kansas City experiment, 161-63, 199
    role in preliminary investigations, 177
    teamwork, 159-61
Pauling, Linus, 119
Paulsen, Norman, 435
Peddlar (inmate), 425, 449
Peer groups, 42
Penal code:
    Model, 68, 218-19, 349
    reforms, 348-49
Penal sanction, requirement of, 57
Penitentiaries, 395
Penn, William, 394

Pennsylvania system, 396, 397, 420
Penology, 26
People of the state, 257 (*See also* Government)
Peoples, K. D., 58
Peremptory challenges, 313, 330
Perkins, R. M., 42
Person, crimes against the (*See also* Murder; Rape):
  victim-offender relationship in, 192
Personal crimes, 11
Personality, search for a criminal, 130, 145 (*See also* Psychological factors)
Peters, Edward, 114
Petersilia, J., 337
Peterson, I., 35
Phelps, T. R., 499
Physical injury, 55
Physique, character and, 117-18
PICO (Pilot Intensive Counseling Organization), 342
Pillories, 394, 420
Piver, Susan, 581
Plea bargaining, 23, 38, 236-37, 250
Plea negotiation, 256, 267-75
Pluralistic society, 70
Police, the, 16, 20-23, 148-92
  arrests by, 158-59, 172, 197-98
  attendance at public gatherings, 157-58
  benevolent and community services, 158
  crime data manipulation by, 97-100
  evaluation of, 76, 197
  health, 210-18
  juveniles; contact with, 501-4, 510-11
  management goals, 199-200
  misconduct, 60
  noncrime calls for service, 156-57
  patrol bureau, 150-63
  preliminary investigations by, 158
  professionalization of, 196-202, 222
  relationship of jails to, 381-82
  team work, 159-61
Political factors, in prisons, 339
Political crimes, 13-15, 36, 96
Politicality, criminal law's, 56
Pollack, H., 308
Popper, R., 353
Pornography, 16, 56
PORT (Probated Offenders Rehabilitation and Training) program, 474
Porter, E. M., 462-63
Postconviction remedies, 353 (*See also* Appeal(s))
Poverty, 116-17, 140
Powell v. *Alabama*, 237
Powell v. *Texas*, 475
Power:
  discretionary, *see* Discretion
  money and, 44
Prediction:
  biotechnology, control, and, 142-44
  EEG used for, 121
  guidelines for parole, 465-66

Prediction:—cont'd
  punishment and, 337
Preliminary hearing, 258-60, 261, 277
Preliminary investigation, 170, 177, 190
Prerelease centers, 29
Prescriptions (social), 43
Presentence investigation, 259, 457-58
Presser, S., 105
Pressure groups, 45
Presumptive sentencing, 344-45
Pretrial detention facilities, 365, 390
Pretrial motions, 261-62, 277
Pretrial procedures, 254-78
Prevention, crime, 556-84 (*See also* Deterrence)
  citizen responsibilitiy, 557-61
  juvenile, 501, 503, 508-10
  police role, 22-23, 161-63
  punishment and, 394-97
Preventive detention, issue of, 265, 267
Prima facie, 261
Principled deviance, 14
Prior jeopardy, 261
Prison(s), 26-28, 365, 392-421 (*See also* Jail(s)):
  adverse results of confinement in, 338
  alternatives to, 28-29, 452-86
  black movement in, 426-30
  conditional, graduated release from, 461-80
  inmate social system before 1960, 424-26
  guards in, 437-49, 444-48
  maxi-maxi, 399-411, 420
  maximum security, 397-99, 420
  medium security, 411-12, 420
  minimum security, 413, 420
  punitive orientation, 26
  racial gangs in, 430-37, 439-42
  restoring control to, 439-42
  social, political, racial forces in, 422-51
  system, 338-43
  for women, 415
Privacy of mind, 341
Private wrong, 52
Privileged communication, 310
Proactive beat, 162, 190
Probable cause, 258
Probation, 19, 28, 454-61, 485
  conditions of, 458
  juvenile, 500, 512-13, 514-15
  revocation of, 458-59
  shock, 466-67, 485
  success rates in, 459-61
Probation officer, 459
Productivity, police, 198-99
Professional criminals (burglars), 90
Professionalization, police, 154, 190, 196-202, 222
Profit, from arson, 95
Prohibition, 56
Property crimes, 5, 7-8, 10, 79, 88-97, 104 (*See also* Arson; Burglary; Larceny-theft; Motor vehicle theft; Robbery):
  by juveniles, 490, 523, 524

Proscriptions (social), 43
Prosecution:
  initiating (misdemeanors), 256-58
  initiating (felonies), 258-61
  waiver of, 83, 109
Prosecutors, 16, 23-25, 177, 230-36, 244, 250
Prostitution, 5, 15, 16, 68, 69, 70
Psychiatric afflictions:
  arson and, 95-96
  EEG, delinquency, and, 121
Psychiatry, 124-26, 140-41, 326-27
Psychoanalysis, 124-25, 126-30
Psychological factors, 124-34, 141
Psychological impact, crime's, 7-9, 86, 100-102
Psychosexual development (Freud), 127-28
Public defender system, 238-41, 244, 250
Public-order offenses, 15, 36-37, 68, 263
Public wrong, 52
Puerto Rico, 187-89
Punishment, 26, 30, 31, 52
  historical perspectives on, 47, 114, 334
  in normative structure, 42-43
  to prevent crime, 394-97 (See also Deterrence)
  probation as, 455
  rehabilitation and, 338-43, 345
  self-, 129
  sentencing, 334-38
  stipulation in criminal law, 56, 57
Pyromaniacs, 95-96

Quality of life, assault on, 8-9
Quinney, R., 44, 116
Quota system, police traffic-law enforcement, 166-67, 191

Racism, 117, 142, 201, 355
  in prisons, 339, 418-19, 426-37, 449-50
Radical criminology, 115, 116-17, 146
Radio watches, 573-74, 582-83
Rand, Ayn, 133
Rand Corporation, 176-78, 184, 565-66
Rank, Otto, 124
Rape, forcible, 8, 81, 84-87, 103, 109, 174, 537
  homosexual, in correctional institutions, 418-19
Rapo (inmate), 426
Rat (inmate), 425, 450
Reactive beat, 162, 191
Reagan, Ronald, 108, 326, 327
Real cons (real men), 426
Real evidence, 308
Reality principle, 129
Reasonable doubt cases, 270-71
Rebuttal (in jury trial), 320, 330
Reception and classification centers, 413-15, 421
Recidivism, 19, 37, 336, 342
  parole's effects on, 469-70
  probation, 460
Reckless, Walter C., 138, 141
Record, Court of, 282-83

Record keeping, court clerk's, 298
Recreation:
  crime prevention and, 562-63
  for delinquency prevention, 510
Recross-examination, 319
Redd, Marvin, 435
Redirect examination, 319
Reduction (crime), team policing for, 199
Reduction in charge, 267
Reduction in sentence, 268
Reed, Alvin, 436
Reformatories, youth, 415-16, 494-95
Reforms:
  bail, 264-65
  penal code, 348-49
  plea negotiation, 271-73
  sentencing, 348-51
Regression, psychological, 125
Rehabilitation, 3, 28, 31, 334, 360
  disillusionment with, 337, 342, 437
  in jails, 373, 384, 385
  in prisons, 404-5, 408-9
  punishment and, 338-43, 345
Reid, S. T., 344, 461-62, 466, 467
Reinforcement, psychological, 132
Reiser, M., 212
Release (from prison), balancing sentencing rates and, 345-46
Release on (own) recognizance (ROR), 256-57, 264, 265, 266, 277, 383
Relevance (of evidence), 309
Remarque, Erich Maria, 131
Reparation, 535
Repression, psychological, 125, 127-28
Res gestae, 311
Residential treatment facilities/programs, 479
  for juveniles, 505-6
Responsibility:
  citizen (in crime prevention), 557-61
  criminal, 54, 325-26
Restitution (to crime victims), 532, 541, 552
Retaliation, 47-48, 71, 434-35
Retribution, 30, 335, 344, 360
Revenge, 47-48, 95, 344, 535
Reverse discrimination, 208-10, 224
Review process (appeals), 352-53
Revocation:
  juvenile parole or probation, 516
  probation, 458-59
Rewards:
  in normative structure, 42-43
  punishment and, 334-35
Rhodes, Robert, 140
Right guys (inmate), 426, 450
Robbery, 8, 46, 87-88, 103, 109, 174
Roberts, M. D., 212
Robin, G. D., 51-52, 296, 315
Robinson, B., 430-31
Robinson v. California, 475
Rodin, E., 121
Rodriguez, Fernando Zamora, 63, 64
Roebuck, J., 13-14
Rosenhan, David, 126
Rosenthal, Abe, 544

Rosett, A., 272, 293-94
Rossi, P. E., 2
Roth, M., 125
Row, Charles, 436
Rubin, Ted, 259
Rules, 53, 57-66 (*See also* Law, the):
　of evidence, 308-11
Runaway programs, 512

Sabotage, arson used for, 95
Sacks, H. R., 469-70
Samenow, Stanton, 130
Sanctuary, Right of, 455
Santobello v. *New York*, 268
Satchell, Michael, 401
Saturday night special, 105, 109
Savoie, L. M., 559
Scacco, A. M., 418, 419
Schafer, S., 535
Schizophrenia:
　arson and, 96
　in family, 121
Schmidt, A. K., 399, 401
Schools, 42 (*See also* Education):
　training, 507-8
　violence in, 518-19
Schuman, H., 105
Schur, E. M., 45-46, 68
Schweitzer, Louis, 264
Schwitzgebel, R., 134
Screening process:
　police incident reports, 170-71
　suspects, 24-25
Screws (guards), 426-449
Search and seizure (issue), 58-62
Secondary crime, 69
Security:
　medium facility, 412
　jail, 373-80, 385
　maxi-maxi prison, 399-411
　maximum prison, 397-99
Selective traffic enforcement, 165-66, 190
Self-improvement, prison inmates', 408-9
Self-incrimination, 62-63
Senna, J., 345, 350
Sentenced facilities (jail), 365, 390
Sentences:
　bargain concerning, 268
　death, 355-58
　definite, 343-44, 345
　in felony offenses, 259
　flat-time, 343-44, 462
　indeterminate, 344, 345, 347, 359-60
　mandatory, 344
　maximum, 348-49
　minimum, 344, 347
　suspended, 455-56
Sentencing, 332-61
　alternatives, 26, 27-29, 452-86
　bail, jail, and, 263
　balancing release rates and, 345-46
　councils and institutes, 350-51
　disparities, 346-48
　guidelines, 349-50, 351
　gun control violation, 107
　pressure on judges about, 295-96

Sentencing—cont'd
　punishment, 334-38
　reforms, 348-51
　stage, 322-23, 354
　structures, 343-45, 346
Seriousness, case's, 270, 271
Sex offenders, 369, 372-73, 390, 419
　aversive conditioning of, 132-34
Sexual crimes, 50-51, 52 (*See also* Rape)
Shakedown (of prisoners), 373-74, 390
Sheriff's departments (traffic enforcement
　　policies), 167
Shireman, C. H., 342-43
Shock parole (Probation), 466-67, 485
Shoplifting, 92-94
Shorthand doctrine, 57
Short time (between arrest and court ap-
　　pearance), 257-58
Schubert, G., 289-90
Sick-outs, 437, 450
Siegel, L., 345, 350
Sierra Club, 12
Silber, D. E., 343
Silberman, C. E., 4
Silver-platter doctrine, 59
Silverstein, L., 240, 243
Simonsen, C. E., 340
Sixth Amendment, 63-66, 237, 352, 533
Skin-conductance studies, 122
Skinner, B. F., 335
Skolnick, J., 150-51
Skolnick, J. H., 446
Slater, E., 125
Sliwa, Curtis, 578-79, 580
Smith, A., 308
Smith, G. W., 270
Smith, T., 350
Social behavior, continuum of, 43
Social class factor, 117, 136, 137
Social conflict, police and, 202
Social impact, crime's, 7-9, 100-102
Socialization, 42-43
　of prison guards, 444-48
Social sanctions, 43, 68
Social-service function, police's, 22-23
Social service patrols (citizen), 566-67,
　　583
Society, pluralistic, 70
Sociological theories, 134-37, 141
Sociopsychological theories, 137-39, 141
Solvability factors, in police detective bu-
　　reaus, 171
Soul (quality of), 427, 450
Special prisoners, 369, 390
Specificity requirement, criminal law's,
　　56
Speech, criminal acts of, 53-54
Spite, arson motivated by, 95
Square John (inmate), 426
Squealer (inmate), 425, 450
Stake in conformity, 70
Standing mute, 260-61
Stare decisis, 51, 71, 290, 303
State (the), *see* Government
States (the):
　AELE model, statutes, 61-62

States (the):—cont'd
  courts, 286-88
  Supreme Court and, 57-59
Statistics, see Crime data/statistics
Status offenses, 499, 527
Statutory law, 50-51
Stephens, Gene, 143
Stewart, Potter, 59
Sting operation, 175
Stocks, 394, 421
Stratton, J. G., 295
Street wisdom, 198, 224
Stress:
  judicial work, 294-97
  police work, 153, 210-12, 223, 224
Strict-liability offenses, 54
Structural approach, to criminality, 135-36
Study release, 471
Subcultural approach, to criminality, 136-37
Substantive criminal law, 53-57, 66
Sugar factor (in behavior), 119-20
Suicide, 135
  jail prisoners, 373, 386-89
  police, 214-16
Suinn, R. M., 131
Sullivan, J. J., 541
Summary jurisdiction, magistrate's, 258
Summations, 320
Superior courts, 283
Supervision, of juveniles, 514-16
Supreme Court, 283-85
  due process, 57-59
  jury size, 317
  plea negotiation, 268
  right to counsel, 58-59, 63-66, 237-38
  search and seizure, 58-62
  self-incrimination, 62-63
Surrebuttal, 320
Sutherland, Edwin H., 11, 56, 115, 138, 141
Swanson, Charles, 58, 365
Sweet, William, 142
Sykes, G. M., 442
Syndicated (organized) crime, 13, 15, 36
System, myth of criminal justice, 17-18
Systems analysis, 18

Talion law, 47-48, 71, 534
Tappan, P., 53
Tax violation, 46
Taylor, Robert W., 185
Team policing, 159-61, 184, 191, 199
Teeters, N. K., 23, 456
Territo, L., 58, 368
Terrorism, 15, 96, 185-89
Testimony (evidence), 308
Theft, see Burglary; Robbery
Therapeutic communities, 478
Thomas, W. H., 264, 265, 275
Thornton, W. E., 120
Thrasher, F. M., 434
Token economies, 132, 146
Tool control (in jail), 376, 390

Tort, 52
Traffic bureau, police, 150, 159, 163-67, 184, 191
Toughs (inmate), 425, 450
Training schools, 507-8
Transfer, of juvenile to adult court, 523, 527
Transnational activity, 186
Treatment:
  ability to provide effective, 340, 342-43
  crime prevention and facilities for, 563
  labeling, harm, and, 139, 141
  police role in, 22
  rehabilitation as, 338-43
  right to, 340-41
  right to refuse, 341-42
  of violent juvenile offenders, 521
Trial:
  court, 282, 286, 288
  criminal, 256, 306-31
  by ordeal, 48-49
Trojanowicz, R. C., 516, 518
True bill (of indictment), 261
Trust, abuses of, 11
Turner, W. J., 121

Ulman, J., 287
Unanimous verdict, 322
Unconscious (the), criminality and, 128-30
Uniform Crime Reporting Program (UCR), 76-78, 103, 109, 491, 538-39
Uniformity, ideal of, 56-57
United States Constitution, see Constitution; Government; Supreme Court
United States v. *Williams*, 60
Utilitarianism, 30

Vachss, A. H., 338, 521
Values, 29-31, 43-45
Vandalism, fires caused by, 95
Van Den Haag, A., 437
Van Gogh, Vincent, 121
Vanity, arson and, 96-97
Variation, normative, 43
Vengeance (revenge), 47-48, 95, 344, 535
Veniremen (array), 313, 329
Vera Institute of Justice, 177, 264, 265
Verdict:
  criminal trial, 311, 322, 330
  directed, 319, 329
  unanimous, 322
Vice, suppression of, 69
Vice Lords (gang), 430, 433, 434, 450
Victimization studies, 537-39
Victimless crimes, 15, 37 (See also Consensual crimes)
Victimology, 533, 552
Victims (of crime), 531-53
  compensation for, 532-36
  delivery of services to, 541-43
  impact on, 4-9, 86, 100-102
  precipitation (of crime) by, 536-37, 552
  rape, 84-86, 537
  uncooperative, 82

Vietnam war, 13, 52
Violent crimes, 7-8, 76, 79-88, 103-4, 201
    (*See also* Assault; Manslaughter; Murder; Rape; Robbery)
    juvenile, 490, 516-22
Visitation control, jail, 379-80
Vogt, Andrew, 516
Voir dire, 313, 330
Volunteers:
    correctional, 576-77
    court, 574-76
Von Hirsh, A., 437

Wainwright, Louis, 346
Waiver:
    express, of jury trial, 312
    juvenile, to adult court, 523-25
    of prosecution, 83, 109
Walker, D. B., 350, 353, 540
War crimes, 52
Ward, D. A., 399, 401
Ward, F. W., 508
Wardens (prison), 438-39
Warrants (for arrest), 256, 263, 277
Warren, Earl, 58, 265
Watergate, 12, 13, 14
Weakling (weak sister), 425, 450
Weapons effect, the, 106-7, 109
Weeber, S. C., 13-14
Weeks v. *United States*, 59
Weidman, D., 177
Wheeler, R., 294

Whisenand, P. M., 154-55
WhistleStop, 573, 583
White Citizen Council, 432, 450
White-collar crime, 5, 8-9, 10, 11-13, 37
White gangs, 432
Wicker, Thomas, 301
Wilderness therapy, 506
Williams, J. S., 106
Williams, R. M., 43
Williams, Theatrice, 446
Williams v. *Florida*, 316-17
Wilson, James Q., 342, 437
Wolf (inmate), 425, 450
Wolfenden Report, 68
Wolfgang, Marvin E., 337, 536
Wolf v. *Colorado*, 59
Women:
    correctional institutions for, 415
    in police work, 204-6, 223
Wood, F. W., 405
Working-class jobs, 200, 224
Workplace crimes, 10
Work release, 29, 470-71, 485
Wright, J. D., 2
Writ of certiorari, 286-87

XYY syndrome, 119, 142, 146

Yarnell, H. H., 95-96
Yochelson, Samuel, 130
Youth corrections centers, 415-16, 421
Youth service bureaus, 511-12